NETWORKING IN THE INTERNET AGE

ALAN DENNIS
Indiana University

JOHN WILEY & SONS, INC.

ACQUISITIONS EDITOR	Beth Lang Golub
ASSISTANT EDITOR	Cynthia Snyder
EDITORIAL ASSISTANT	Lorraina Raccuia
MARKETING MANAGER	Gitti Lindner
SENIOR PRODUCTION EDITOR	Norine M. Pigliucci
SENIOR DESIGNER	Harry Nolan
PHOTO EDITOR	Sara Wight
PRODUCTION MANAGEMENT SERVICES	Hermitage Publishing Services
COVER PHOTOGRAPH	Steven Hunt/The Image Bank

This book was set in Times Roman by Hermitage Publishing Services and printed and bound by Donnelley Crawfordsville. The cover was printed by Phoenix Color Corporation.

This book is printed on acid-free paper. ∞

ISBN: 0-471-20189-8

Printed in the United States of America

10 9 8 7 6 5 4 3 2 1

To Eileen and Alec

ABOUT THE AUTHOR

Alan Dennis is a Professor of Information Systems in the Kelley School of Business at Indiana University, and holds the John T. Chambers Chair in Internet Systems. The Chambers Chair was established to honor John Chambers, president and chief executive officer of Cisco Systems Inc., the worldwide leader in networking technologies for the Internet.

Prior to joining Indiana University, Professor Dennis spent nine years at The University of Georgia, where he won Richard B. Russell Award for Excellence in Undergraduate Teaching. Professor Dennis has a bachelor's degree in computer science from Acadia University in Nova Scotia, Canada and an MBA from Queen's University in Ontario, Canada. His Ph.D. in management information systems is from the University of Arizona. Prior to entering the Arizona doctoral program, he spent three years on the faculty of the Queen's School of Business.

Professor Dennis has extensive experience in the development and application of groupware and Internet technologies, and developed a Web-based groupware package called Consensus @nyWARE,™ now owned by SoftBicycle Corporation. He has won seven awards for theoretical and applied research, and has published more than 80 business and research articles, including those in *Management Science, MIS Quarterly, Information Systems Research, Academy of Management Journal, Organizational Behavior and Human Decision Making, Journal of Applied Psychology, Communications of the ACM,* and *IEEE Transactions on Systems, Man, and Cybernetics.* His first book, co-authored with his wife Eileen, was *Getting Started with Microcomputers,* published in 1986.

Professor Dennis is also an author (along with Barbara Wixom of the University of Virginia) of *Systems Analysis and Design: An Applied Approach, Systems Analysis and Design: An Object-oriented Approach with UML* (with Barbara Wixom of the University of Virginia and David Tegarden of Virginia Tech), and *Business Data Communications and Networking* (with Jerry FitzGerald), all available from Wiley. Dennis is the co-chair of the Internet Technologies Track of the Hawaii International Conference on System Sciences. He has served as a consultant to BellSouth, Boeing, IBM, Hughes Missile Systems, the U.S. Department of Defense, and the Australian Army.

PREFACE

Over the past years, many fundamental changes have occurred in data communications and networking that will shape the future for decades to come. Networking applications such as the Internet and World Wide Web have exploded into the business world. High speed modems providing megabit data rates over regular telephone lines are becoming common. New local area network (LAN) and backbone technologies providing gigabit speeds are now available, with wireless technologies becoming widely accepted. Metropolitan area network (MAN) and wide area network (WAN) technologies providing terabit and petabit speeds are on the horizon. The integration of voice and data communication is moving forward rapidly.

The Internet and the technologies it uses (e.g., TCP/IP) have become a unifying force in networking. The Internet is *the* standard for the design and interconnection of networks today; it is the glue that holds quite literally millions of networks together. At the same time as we have seen the rise of the Internet, we have also seen Ethernet become the dominant technology in LANs and backbones. The simplicity and elegance of Ethernet, coupled with its widespread adoption, has driven most competing technologies from the marketplace. As the Internet has become *the* standard for designing and interconnecting networks, Ethernet has become *the* standard for network hardware for most businesses, universities, and even homes. Wireless Ethernet now offers even greater potential, as does the movement of Ethernet into MANs and WANs.

Perhaps the most important change over the past decade has been the recognition of the strategic importance of networking in both the public and private sector. Today, almost all computers are networked. As we move into the 21st century, we now realize that the importance of the network has surpassed the importance of the computer.

Purpose of This Book

The goal of this book is to provide a fundamental understanding of how networks operate in the Internet age.

- It provides a solid conceptual and practical understanding of how current network technologies operate (including those not yet in widespread commercial production); it deliberately omits several older legacy technologies (e.g., token ring, SNA).
- It provides frameworks to analyze the benefits and limitations of these technologies to help managers choose among them, and—most importantly—to analyze the benefits and limitations of future technologies not yet developed.

- It provides some insight in to the design, management, and security aspects of these networks.

This book has two intended audiences. First and foremost, it is a university textbook. Each chapter introduces, describes, and then summarizes fundamental concepts and applications. Management focus boxes highlight key issues and describe how networks are actually being used today. Technical focus boxes highlight key technical issues and provide additional detail. Minicases at the end of each chapter provide the opportunity to apply these technical and management concepts. Moreover, the text is accompanied by a detailed *Instructor's Manual,* that provides additional background information, teaching tips, and sources of material for student exercises, assignments, and exams. Finally, our Web page (at www.wiley.com/college/dennis) will continue to update the book.

Second, this book is intended for the professional who works in data communications and networking. The book has many detailed descriptions of the technical aspects of communications, along with illustrations where appropriate. Moreover, managerial, technical, and sales personnel can use this book to gain a better understanding of fundamental concepts and trade-offs not presented in technical books or product summaries.

Overview of the Book

The book begins with a summary of the history of networks and then turns to the fundamental network model that forms the foundation for much of networking: the OSI model. The OSI model is the primary organizing model for virtually all of networking today, and is used as the organizing theme for this book.

Chapter 2 starts at the top of the OSI model by examining the application layers. This chapter explains application architectures (e.g., client server) and how the Web, e-mail, and other Internet applications work.

Chapter 3 moves to the next set of layers in the OSI model, the Internetworking layers (Transport and Network). This chapter explains what these layers do, with a focus on TCP/IP. At the end of this chapter, you should have a solid understanding of how the Internet works.

The next chapters (3-8) examine the hardware layers (data link and physical) for each basic type of network: local area networks, backbone networks, metropolitan and wide area networks, the Internet, and wireless local area networks. Each chapter focuses on the dominant technologies used in these types of networks, and presents a framework for analyzing their performance that can be used to understand the benefits and limitations of today's technologies, as well as future technologies that have not yet been developed.

The final chapters (9-11) examine management aspects of networking, including network design, network security, and network management.

Supplements

The text is accompanied by several supplements for instructors:

- An Instructor's Manual prepared by Tim Kelly of Robert Morris University, provides additional background information, teaching tips, war stories, answers to the end of chapter questions, and sources of material for student exercises and assignments.

- A Test Bank, prepared by Mary Burns of the University of South Florida, Sarasota, provides approximately 80 test questions for each chapter in multiple choice, true/false, and short answer formats. A computerized version of the test bank will also be available.

- PowerPoint slides, created by Gene Mesher of California State University, Sacramento, provide full color lecture notes that highlight key concepts and figures from the text.

- Web Resources, created by Michael Much of Hennepin Technical College, provide instructors and students with weblinks to resources that can help to reinforce and build upon the major concepts in each chapter. See www.wiley.com/college/dennis.

Acknowledgments

My thanks to the many people who contributed to the preparation of this book. I am indebted to the staff at John Wiley & Sons for their support, including: Beth Lang Golub, Information Systems editor; Cynthia Snyder, assistant editor; Lorraina Raccuia, editorial assistant; Norine Pigliucci, senior production editor; Harry Nolan, senior designer; and Gitti Lindner, marketing manager.

I would also like to thank the reviewers for their assistance, often under short deadlines:

John Griffin, Weber State University
Brian Janz, University of Memphis
William Hartman, Nova Southeastern University
Gene Mesher, California State University, Sacramento
Ron Pike, California State University, Chico

And finally, thanks to my friends at Cisco for their advice and support:

John Chambers
John Morgridge
Craig Smythe
Mike Snively
Scott Sprinkle

Alan Dennis
Bloomington, Indiana
http://www.kelley.indiana.edu/ardennis

PHOTO CREDIT LIST

Chapter 2

Page 57: Adrian Weinbrecht/Stone.

Chapter 4

Page 109: Courtesy of International Business Machines Corporation. Page 122: Courtesy South Hills Datacomm. Page 123: Courtesy Alan Dennis. Page 126: Courtesy South HIlls Datacomm.

Chapter 5

Page 149: Courtesy Alan Dennis.

Chapter 8

Page 247: Courtesy Alan Dennis

SUMMARY TABLE OF CONTENTS

CONTENTS

CHAPTER 1

INTRODUCTION TO DATA COMMUNICATIONS

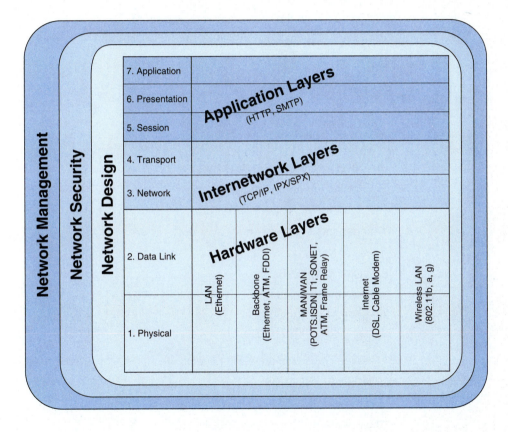

THIS CHAPTER introduces the basic concepts of data communications. It begins by describing why it is important to study data communications and how the invention of the telephone, the computer, and the Internet have transformed the way we communicate. Next, the basic types and components of a data communications network are discussed.

The importance of a network model based on layers and the importance of network standards are examined. The chapter concludes with an overview of three key trends in the future of networking.

OBJECTIVES

- Be aware of the history of communications, information systems, and the Internet
- Be aware of the applications of data communications networks
- Be familiar with the major components of and types of networks
- Understand the role of network layers
- Be familiar with the role of network standards
- Be aware of three key trends in communications and networking

CHAPTER OUTLINE

INTRODUCTION

   A Brief History of Communications in North America

   A Brief History of Information Systems

   A Brief History of the Internet

DATA COMMUNICATIONS NETWORKS

   Components of a Network

   Types of Networks

NETWORK MODELS

   Application Layers

   Internetwork Layers

   Hardware Layers

   Message Transmission Using Layers

NETWORK STANDARDS

   The Importance of Standards

   The Standards-Making Process

   Common Standards

FUTURE TRENDS

   Pervasive Networking

   The Integration of Voice, Video, and Data

   New Information Services

SUMMARY

INTRODUCTION

Over the past few years, it has become clear that world has changed forever. We are now in the information age — the second Industrial Revolution, according to John Chambers, CEO of Cisco, one of the world's leading data communications and networking technology companies. The first Industrial Revolution revolutionized the way people worked by introducing machines and new organizational forms. New companies and industries emerged and old ones died off.

The second Industrial Revolution is revolutionizing the way people work though networking and data communications. The value of a high-speed data communications network is that it brings people together in way never before possible. In the 1800s it took several weeks for a message to reach North America by ship from England. By the 1900s it could be transmitted within the hour. Today, it can be transmitted in seconds. Collapsing the *information lag* to Internet speeds means that people can communicate and access information anywhere in the world regardless of their physical location. In fact, today's problem is that we cannot handle the quantities of information we receive.

Data communications and networking is a truly global area of study, both because the technology enables global communication, and because new technologies and applications often emerge from a variety of countries and spread rapidly around the world. The World Wide Web, for example, was born in a Swiss research lab, was nurtured through its first years primarily by European universities, and exploded into mainstream popular culture due to a development at an American research lab.

One of the problems in studying a global phenomenon lies in explaining the different political and regulatory issues that have evolved and currently exist in different parts of the world. Rather than attempt to explain the different paths taken by different countries, we have chosen simplicity instead. While we retain a global focus on technology and its busi-

MANAGEMENT FOCUS *1 - 1*

CAREER OPPORTUNITIES

It's a great time to be in information technology. The technology-fueled new economy has dramatically increased the demand for skilled IT professionals. The U.S. Bureau of Labor Statistics estimates that there are currently 80,000 IT jobs that are unfilled. IT salaries have responded, and have risen rapidly. Annual starting salaries for our undergraduates at Indiana University range from $40,000 to $50,000. While all areas of IT have shown rapid growth, the fastest salary growth has been for those with skills in Internet development, networking, and telecommunications. People with a few years of experience in these areas can make $65,000 to $80,000—not counting bonuses.

The demand for networking expertise is growing for two reasons. First, the Internet and communication dereg-

ulation has significantly changed how businesses operate and has spawned thousands of small startup companies. Second, there has been a host of new hardware and software innovations that have significantly changed the way networking is done.

These trends and the shortage of qualified network experts has also led to the rise in certification. Most large vendors of network technologies such as Microsoft, Cisco, and Novell provide certification processes (usually a series of courses and formal exams) so that individuals can document their knowledge. Certified network professionals often earn $10,000 to $20,000 more than similarly skilled uncertified professionals—provided they continue to learn and maintain their certification as new technologies emerge.

ness implications, we focus exclusively on North America in describing the political and regulatory issues surrounding communications and networking. We do, however, take care to discuss technological or business issues where fundamental differences exist between North America and the rest of the world.

A Brief History of Communications in North America

Today we take data communications for granted, but it was pioneers like Alexander Graham Bell who developed the basic electrical and electronic systems that ultimately evolved into voice and data communications networks. In 1874, Bell developed the concept for the telephone at his father's home in Brantford, Ontario, Canada, but it would take him and his assistant, Tom Watson, another two years of work in Boston to develop the first telephone capable of transmitting understandable conversation in 1876. Later that year, Bell made the first long distance call (about 10 miles) from Paris, Ontario, to his father in Brantford.

When the telephone arrived, it was greeted by both skepticism and adoration, but within five years it was clear to all that the world had changed. To meet the demand, Bell started a company in the United States while his father started a company in Canada. In 1879, the first private manual telephone switchboard (private branch exchange or PBX) was installed. By 1880, the first pay telephone was in use, and the telephone became a way of life because anyone could call from public telephones.

In 1892, the Canadian government began regulating telephone rates. By 1910, the Interstate Commerce Commission (ICC) had the authority to regulate interstate telephone businesses in the United States. In 1934, this was transferred to the Federal Communications Commission (FCC).

The first transcontinental telephone service and the first transatlantic voice connections were both established in 1915. The telephone system grew so rapidly that by the early 1920s there were serious concerns that even with the introduction of dial telephones (which eliminated the need for operators to make simple calls) there would not be enough trained operators to work the manual switchboards. Experts predicted that by 1980, every single woman in North America would have to work as a telephone operator if growth in telephone usage continued at the current rate (at the time, all telephone operators were women).

The first commercial microwave link for long distance telephone transmission was established in Canada in 1948. In 1951, the first direct long distance dialing without an operator began. The first international satellite telephone call was sent over the *Telstar* satellite in 1962. By 1965, there was widespread use of commercial international telephone service via satellite. Fax services were introduced in 1962. Touch-tone telephones were first marketed in 1963. Picturefone service, which allows users to see as well as talk with one another, began operating in 1969.

Until 1968, Bell Telephone/AT&T controlled the U.S. telephone system. No telephones or computer equipment other than those made by Bell Telephone could be connected to the phone system, and only AT&T could provide telephone services. In 1968, after a series of lawsuits, the Carterfone court decision allowed non-Bell equipment to be connected to the Bell System network. This important milestone permitted independent telephone and modem manufacturers to connect their equipment to the U.S. telephone networks for the first time.

Another key decision in 1970 permitted MCI to provide limited long distance service in the United States in competition with AT&T. Throughout the 1970s, there were many arguments and court cases over the monopolistic position that AT&T held over U.S. communication services. On January 1, 1984, AT&T was divided in two parts under a consent decree devised by a federal judge. The first part, AT&T, provided long distance telephone services in competition with other *interexchange carriers (IXCs)* such as MCI and Sprint. The second part, a series of seven *regional Bell operating companies (RBOCs)* or *local exchange carriers (LECs),* provided local telephone services to homes and businesses. AT&T was prohibited from providing local telephone services and the RBOCs were prohibited from providing long distance services. Intense competition began in the long distance market as MCI, Sprint, and a host of other companies began to offer services and dramatically cut prices under the watchful eye of the FCC. Competition was prohibited in the local telephone market so the RBOCs remained a regulated monopoly under the control of a multitude of state laws. The Canadian long distance market was opened to competition in 1992.

During 1983 and 1984 traditional radio telephone calls were supplanted by the newer cellular telephone networks. In the 1990s, cellular telephones became commonplace and pocket sized. Demand grew so much that in some cities (e.g., New York and Atlanta) it became difficult to get a dial tone at certain times of the day.

In February 1996, the U.S. Congress enacted the Telecommunications Competition and Deregulation Act of 1996. The Act replaced all current laws, FCC regulations, and the 1984 consent decree and subsequent court rulings under which AT&T was broken up. It also overruled all existing state laws and prohibited states from introducing new laws. Practically overnight, the local telephone industry in the United States went from a highly regulated and legally restricted monopoly to open competition.

Local service in the United States is now open for competition. The *common carriers* (RBOCs, IXCs, cable TV companies, and other LECs) are permitted to build their own local telephone facilities and offer services to customers. To increase competition, the RBOCs must sell their telephone services to their competitors at wholesale prices, who can then resell them to consumers at retail prices. Most analysts expected the big IXCs (e.g., AT&T) to quickly charge into the local telephone market, but they have been slow to move. Meanwhile, the RBOCs have been aggressively fighting court battles to keep competitors out of their local telephone markets and attempting to merge with each other and with the IXCs, prompting many complaints from Congress and the FCC. At best, the RBOCs can only hope to delay competition, not prevent it, because it is clear that Congress and the FCC want competition.

There has been active competition in the long distance telephone market for many years, but RBOCs have been prohibited from providing long distance services. The Telecommunications Act now permits the RBOCs to provide long distance outside the regions in which they provide local telephone services. However, they are prohibited from providing long distance services inside their region until at least one viable competitor exists for local telephone services. Several local telephone companies have moved aggressively into the long distance market, but have focused exclusively on out-of-region long distance by buying long distance services from AT&T and other IXCs and reselling them. To date, few RBOCs have moved into the in-region long distance market because few face real local competition.

Virtually all RBOCs, LECs, and IXCs have aggressively entered the Internet market. Today, there are more than 5,000 Internet service providers (ISPs) who provide dial-in access to the Internet to millions of small business and home users. Most of these are small companies that lease telecommunications circuits from the RBOCs, LECs, and IXCs and use them to provide Internet access to their customers. As the RBOCs, LECs, and IXCs move into the Internet market and provide the same services directly to consumers, the smaller ISPs are facing heavy competition.

A Brief History of Information Systems

The natural evolution of information systems in business, government and home use has forced the widespread use of data communications networks to interconnect various computer systems. However, data communications have not always been considered important.

In the 1950s, computer systems used batch processing, and users carried their punched cards to the computer for processing. By the 1960s, data communications across telephone lines became more common. Users could type their own batches of data for processing using online terminals. Data communications involved the transmission of messages from these terminals to a large central mainframe computer and back to the user.

During the 1970s, online real-time systems were developed that moved the users from batch processing to single transaction-oriented processing. Database management systems replaced the older file systems and integrated systems were developed where the entry of an online transaction in one business system (e.g., order entry) might automatically trigger transactions in other business systems (e.g., accounting, purchasing). Computers entered the mainstream of business and data communications networks became a necessity.

The 1980s witnessed the microcomputer revolution. At first, microcomputers were isolated from the major information systems applications, serving the needs of individual users (e.g., spreadsheets). As more people began to rely on microcomputers for essential applications, the need for networks to exchange data among microcomputers and between microcomputers and central mainframe computers became clear. By the early 1990s, more than 60 percent of all microcomputers in American corporations were networked—connected to other computers.

Today, the microcomputer has evolved from a small, low-power computer into a very powerful easy-to-use system, with a large amount of low-cost software. Today's microcomputers have more raw computing power than a mainframe of the 1980s. Perhaps more surprisingly, corporations today have far more total computing power sitting on desktops in the form of the microcomputers than they have in their large central mainframe computers.

As we move into the new century, the most important aspect of computers is *networking*. The Internet is everywhere, and virtually all corporate computers are networked. Most corporations are rapidly building distributed systems in which information systems applications are divided among a network of computers. This form of computing, called client–server computing, will dramatically change the way information systems professionals and users interact with computers. The office of the future that interconnects microcomputers, mainframe computers, fax machines, copiers, teleconferencing equipment, and other equipment will put tremendous demands on data communications networks.

These networks already have had a dramatic impact on the way business is conducted. Networking played a key role—among many other factors—in the growth of Wal-Mart into one of the largest forces in the North American retail industry and in the process

MANAGEMENT FOCUS *1-2*

NETWORKS IN THE GULF WAR

The lack of a good network can also cost more than money. During Operation Desert Shield/Desert Storm, the U.S. Army, Navy, and Air Force lacked one integrated logistics communications network. Each service had its own series of networks, making communication and cooperation difficult. But communication among the systems was essential. Each day a Navy jet would fly into Saudi Arabia to exchange diskettes full of logistics information with the Army—an expensive form of "wireless" networking.

This lack of an integrated network also created problems transmitting information from the United States into the Gulf. More than 60 percent of the containers of sup-plies arrived without documentation. They had to be unloaded to see what was in them and then reloaded for shipment to combat units.

The logistics information systems and communication networks experienced such problems that some Air Force units were unable to quickly order and receive critical spare parts needed to keep planes flying. Officers were telephoning the U.S.-based suppliers of these parts and instructing them to send the parts via Federal Express.

Fortunately, the war did not start until the United States and its allies were prepared. Had Iraq attacked, things might have turned out differently.

---

has transformed the retailing industry. Wal-Mart has 34 mainframes, 5,000 network file servers, 18,000 microcomputers, 90,000 handheld inventory computers, and 100,000 net-worked cash registers. (As an aside, it is interesting to note that every single microcomputer built by IBM in the United States during the third quarter of 1997 was purchased by Wal-Mart.) At the other end of the spectrum, the lack of a sophisticated data communications network was one of the key factors in the bankruptcy of Macy's in the early 1990s.

In retail sales, it is critical to manage inventory. Macy's had a traditional 1970s inventory system. At the start of the season, buyers would order products in large lots to get volume discounts. Some products would be very popular and sell out quickly. When the sales clerks did a weekly inventory and noticed the shortage, they would order more. If the items were not available in the warehouse (and very popular products were often not available), it would take six to eight weeks to restock them. Customers would buy from other stores, and Macy's would lose the sales. Other products, also bought in large quantities, would be unpopular and have to be sold at deep discounts.

In contrast, Wal-Mart negotiates volume discounts with suppliers based on total purchases, but does not specify particular products. Buyers place initial orders in small quantities. Each time a product is sold, the sale is recorded and every day or two the complete list of purchases is transferred over the network (often via satellite) to the head office, a distribution center, or the supplier. Replacements for the products sold are shipped almost immediately and typically arrive within days. The result is that Wal-Mart seldom has a major problem with overstocking an unwanted product or running out of a popular product (unless, of course, the supplier is unable to produce it fast enough).

A Brief History of the Internet

The *Internet* is one of the most important developments in the history of both information systems and communication systems because it is both an information system and a communication system. The Internet was started by the U.S. Department of Defense in 1969 as a network of four computers called ARPANET. Its goal was to link a set of comptuers operated by several universities doing military research. The original network grew as more computers and more computer *networks* were linked to it. By 1974, there were 62 computers attached. In 1983, the Internet split into two parts, one dedicated solely to military installations (called Milnet) and one dedicated to university research centers (called the Internet) that had just under 1,000 host computers or servers.

In 1985, the Canadian government completed its leg of BITNET to link all Canadian universities from coast to coast and provided connections into the American Internet (BITNET was a competing network to the Internet developed by the City University of New York and Yale University). In 1986, the U.S. National Science Foundation created NSFNET to connect leading U.S. universities. By the end of 1987, there were 10,000 servers on the Internet and 1,000 on BITNET.

Performance began to slow down due to increased network traffic, so in 1987 the National Science Foundation decided to improve performance by building a new high-speed backbone network for NSFNET. It leased high-speed circuits from several IXCs and in 1988 connected 13 regional Internet networks containing 170 LANs and 56,000 servers. The Canadian National Research Council followed in 1989 and replaced BITNET with a high-speed network called CA*net that used the same communication language as the Internet. By the end of 1989 there were almost 200,000 servers on the combined U.S. and Canadian Internet.

Similar initiatives were undertaken by most other countries around the world, so that by the early 1990s, most of the individual country networks were linked together into one worldwide network of networks. Each of these individual country networks was distinct (each had its own name, access rules, and fee structures), but all networks used the same standards as the U.S. Internet network so they could easily exchange messages with each other. Gradually, the distinctions among the networks in each of the countries began to disappear, and the U.S. name, the Internet, began to be used to mean the entire worldwide network of networks connected to the U.S. Internet. By the end of 1992, there were more than 1 million servers on the Internet.

Originally, commercial traffic was forbidden on the Internet (and the other individual country networks) because the key portions of these networks were funded by the various national governments and research organizations. In the early 1990s, commercial networks began connecting into NSFNET, CA*net, and the other government-run networks in each country. New commercial online services began offering access to anyone willing to pay, and a connection into the worldwide Internet became an important marketing issue. The growth in the commercial portion of the Internet was so rapid that it quickly overshadowed university and research use. In 1994, with more than 4 million servers on the Internet (most of which were commercial), the U.S. and Canadian governments stopped funding their few remaining circuits and turned them over to commercial firms. Most other national governments soon followed. The Internet was now commercial.

The Internet has continued to grow at a dramatic pace. No one knows exactly how large the Internet is, but estimates suggest there are 40 million servers and 400 million people on the Internet, both of which are growing rapidly (see cyberatlas.internet.com). In the mid-1990s, most Internet users were young (under 35 years old) and male, but as the Internet matures, its typical user becomes closer to the underlying average in the population as a whole (i.e., older and more evenly split between men and women). In fact, the fastest-growing segment of Internet users are retirees.

TECHNICAL FOCUS *1-1*

INTERNET DOMAIN NAMES

Internet address names are strictly controlled; otherwise, someone could add a computer to the Internet that had the same address as another computer. Each address name has two parts, the computer name and its domain. The general format of an Internet address is therefore *computer. domain.* Some computer names have several parts separated by periods, so some addresses have the format *computer.computer.computer.domain.* For example, the main university Web server at Indiana University is called www. indiana.edu, while the Web server for the Kelley School of Business at IU is www.kelley.indiana.edu.

Since the Internet began in the United States, the American address board was the first to assign domain names to indicate types of organization. Some common U.S. domain names are:

EDU	for an educational institution, usually a university
COM	for a commercial business
GOV	for a government department or agency
MIL	for a military unit
ORG	for a nonprofit organization

As networks in other countries were connected to the Internet, they were assigned their own domain names. Some international domain names are:

CA	for Canada
AU	for Australia
UK	for the United Kingdom
DE	for Germany

Several new top-level domains were introduced in 2000 that focus on specific types of businesses, such as

AERO	for aerospace companies
MUSEUM	for museums
NAME	for individuals
PRO	for professionals such as accountants and lawyers

Many international domains structure their addresses in much the same way as the U.S. does. For example, Australia uses *EDU* to indicate academic institutions, so an address such as *xyz.edu.au* would indicate an Australian university.

DATA COMMUNICATIONS NETWORKS

Data communications is the movement of digital information (usually computer data, but increasingly other forms of digital data such as voice and video) from one point to another by means of electrical or optical transmission systems. Data communications networks facilitate more efficient use of computers and improve the day-to-day control of a business by providing faster information flow. They also provide message transfer services to allow computer users to talk to one another via electronic mail, chat, and video streaming.

Components of a Network

There are three basic hardware components for a data communications network: a server or host computer (e.g., microcomputer, mainframe), a client (e.g., microcomputer, terminal), and a circuit (e.g., cable, modem) over which messages flow. Both the server and client also need special-purpose network software that enables them to communicate.

The *server* (or *host computer*) stores data or software that can be accessed by the clients. In client–server computing, several servers may work together over the network with a client computer to support the business application.

The *client* is the input/output device at the user's end of a communication circuit. It typically provides users with access to the network and the data and software on the server.

The *circuit* is the pathway through which the messages travel. It is typically a copper wire, although fiber optic cable and wireless transmission are becoming more common. There are many devices in the circuit that perform special functions such as hubs, switches, routers, and gateways.

Strictly speaking, a network does not need a server. Some networks are designed to connect a set of similar computers that share their data and software with each other. Such networks are called *peer-to-peer* networks because the computers function as equals, rather than relying on a central server or host computer to store the needed data and software. Computers run network software that enables them to function both as a client and as a server. Authorized users can connect to any computer that permits access and use their hard drive(s) and printer as though they were physically attached to their own computers. Peer-to-peer networks often are slower than dedicated server networks because if you access a computer that is also being used by its owner, it slows down both the owner and the network. In general, peer-to-peer networks have less capability, support a more limited number of computers, provide less sophisticated software, and can prove more difficult to manage than dedicated server networks. However, they are cheaper both in hardware and software, so they are most appropriate for small networks. The Internet also enables peer-to-peer computing in which individual users can share files with each other without using a server.

Figure 1-1 shows a small network that has four microcomputers (clients) connected by a *hub* and *cables* (circuit). In this network, messages move through the hub to and from the

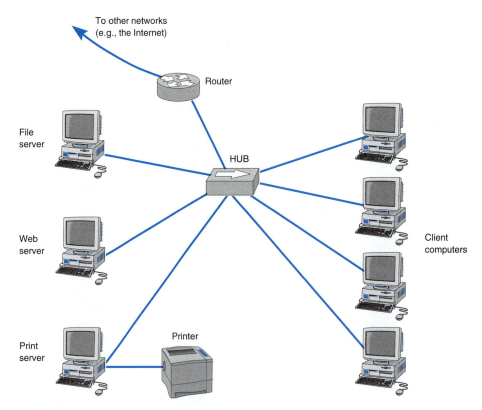

FIGURE 1-1 Example of a local area network (LAN).

computers. All computers share the same circuit and must take turns sending messages. The *router* is a special device that connects two or more networks. The router enables computers on this network to communicate with computers on other networks (e.g., the Internet).

This network has three servers. While one server can perform many functions, networks are often designed so that a separate computer is used to provide different services. The *file server* stores data and software that can be used by computers on the network. The *print server,* which is connected to a printer, manages all printing requests from the clients on the network. The *Web server* stores documents and graphics that can be accessed from any Web browser such as Internet Explorer. The Web server can respond to requests from computers on this network or any computer on the Internet. Servers are usually microcomputers (often more powerful than the other microcomputers on the network), but may be minicomputers or mainframes.

Types of Networks

There are many different ways to categorize networks. One of the most common ways is to look at the geographic scope of the network. Figure 1-2 illustrates four types of networks: local area networks, backbone networks, metropolitan area networks, and wide area networks. The distinctions between these are becoming blurry. Some network technologies now used in local area networks were originally developed for wide area networks, while some local area network technologies have influenced the development of metropolitan area network products. Any rigid classification of technologies is certain to have exceptions.

A *local area network (LAN)* is a group of microcomputers or other workstation devices located in the same general area. A LAN covers a clearly defined small area, such one floor or work area, a single building, or a group of buildings. The upper-left diagram in Figure 1-2 shows a small LAN located in the records building at McClellan Air Force Base in Sacramento before it was closed. LANs support moderately high-speed data transmission, commonly operating at 10 to 100 million bits per second (10–100 Mbps). LANs are discussed in Chapter 4.

Most LANs are connected to a *backbone network,* a larger, central network connecting several LANs, other backbones, metropolitan area networks, and wide area networks. Backbone networks typically span up to several miles and provide very-high-speed data transmission, commonly to 100 to 1000 Mbps. The second diagram in Figure 1-2 shows a backbone network that connects the LANs located in several buildings at McClellan AFB. backbones are discussed in Chapter 5.

A *metropolitan area network (MAN)* connects LANs and backbones located in different areas to each other and to wide area networks. MANs typically span from 3 to 30 miles. The third diagram in Figure 1-2 shows a MAN connecting the backbone networks at several former military and government complexes in Sacramento. Some organizations develop their own MANs using similar technologies as backbones. These networks provide moderately fast transmission rates, but can prove costly to install and operate over long distances. Unless an organization has a continuing need to transfer large amounts of data, this type of MAN is usually too expensive. More commonly, organizations use public data networks provided by common carriers (e.g., the telephone company) as their MANs. With these MANs, data transmission rates typically range from 64,000 bits per second (64 Kbps) to 100 Mbps, although newer technologies promise data rates of over 10 billion bits per second (10 Gbps). MANs are discussed in Chapter 6.

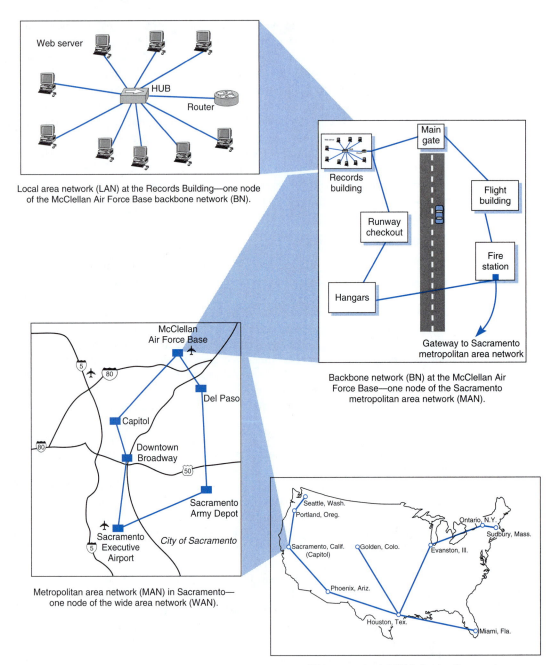

Local area network (LAN) at the Records Building—one node of the McClellan Air Force Base backbone network (BN).

Backbone network (BN) at the McClellan Air Force Base—one node of the Sacramento metropolitan area network (MAN).

Metropolitan area network (MAN) in Sacramento— one node of the wide area network (WAN).

Wide area network (WAN) showing Sacramento connected to nine other cities throughout the U.S.

FIGURE 1-2 The hierarchical relationship of a local area network (LAN) to a backbone network (BN) to a metropolitan area network (MAN) to a wide area network (WAN).

Wide area networks (WANs) connect backbones and MANs (see Figure 1-2). Most organizations do not build their own WANs by laying cable, building microwave towers, or sending up satellites (unless they have unusually heavy data transmission needs or highly specialized requirements, such as the Department of Defense). Instead, most organizations lease circuits from interexchange carriers (e.g., AT&T, MCI, Sprint), and use those to transmit their data. WAN circuits provided by interexchange carriers come in all types and sizes, but typically span hundreds or thousands of miles and provide data transmission rates from 56 Kbps to 10 Gbps. WANs are also discussed in Chapter 6.

Two other common terms are *intranet* and *extranet.* An intranet is a LAN that uses the same technologies as the Internet (e.g., Web servers, Java, HTML) but is open only to those inside the organization. For example, some pages on a Web server may be open to the public and accessible by anyone on the Internet, but other pages may be on the intranet and therefore hidden from those who connect to the Web server from the Internet at large. Sometimes the intranet is provided by a completely separate Web server hidden from the Internet. The intranet for the Information Systems Department at Indiana University, for example, provides information on faculty expense budgets, class scheduling for future semesters (e.g., room, instructor), and discussion forums.

An extranet is similar to an intranet in that it too uses the same technologies as the Internet, but instead is provided to invited users outside the organization who access it over the Internet. It can provide access to information services, inventories, and other internal organizational databases that are provided only to customers, suppliers, or those who have paid for access. Typically users are given passwords to gain access, but more sophisticated technologies such as smart cards or special software may also be required. Many universities provide extranets for Web-based courses so that only those students enrolled in the course can access course materials and discussions.

NETWORK MODELS

There are many ways to describe and analyze data communications networks. All networks provide the same basic functions to transfer a message from sender to receiver, but each network can use different network hardware and software to provide these functions. All of these hardware and software products must work together to successfully transfer a message.

One way to accomplish this is to break the entire set of communications functions into a series of layers, each of which can be defined separately. In this way, vendors can develop software and hardware to provide the functions of each layer separately. The software or hardware can work in any manner and can be easily updated and improved, as long as the interface between that layer and the ones around it remains unchanged. Each piece of hardware and software can then work together in the overall network.

There are many different ways in which the layers in a network can be designed. The two most important network models are the OSI model and the Internet model. The *Open Systems Interconnection Reference Model* (usually called the *OSI Model* for short) helped change the face of network computing. Before the OSI model, most commercial networks used by businesses were built using proprietary nonstandardized technologies developed by one vendor (remember that the Internet was in use at the time, but it was not widespread

Groups of Layers	OSI Model	Early Internet Model
Application Layers	7. Application Layer	4. Application Layer
	6. Presentation Layer	
	5. Session Layer	
Internetwork Layers	4. Transport Layer	3. Transport Layer
	3. Network Model	2. Network Model
Hardware Layers	2. Data Link Layer	1. Hardware Layer
	1. Physical Layer	

FIGURE 1-3 Network models. OSI = Open Systems Interconnection Reference model.

and certainly was not commercial). During the late 1970s, the International Organization for Standardization (ISO) created the Open Systems Interconnection (OSI) subcommittee whose task was to develop a framework of standards for computer-to-computer communications. In 1984, this effort produced the 7-layer OSI Model.

The OSI model is the most talked about and most referred to network model. If you choose a career in networking, the OSI model will be on the network certification exams offered by Microsoft, Cisco, Novell, and other vendors of network hardware and software. However, you will probably never use a network based on the OSI model. Simply put, the OSI model never caught on commercially in North America, although some European networks use it, and some network components developed for use in the United States arguably use parts of it.

Most people today integrate the OSI model and the 4-layer model used by the original Internet developers (see Figure 1-3) into a hybrid that includes the best of both, which is what we do in this book. Although each of the seven layers in the OSI model is separate and distinct, the layers are often so closely coupled in practice that decisions in one layer impose certain requirements on other layers around them. This integrated model groups the traditional seven layers of the OSI model into three related groups of layers found in the Internet model (see Figure 1-3).

Application Layers

The *application layers* are the user's connection to the network. They include the application software used on the network and other software used to connect the application to the network. The application layers have three closely related layers: application, presentation, and session.

Layer 7: Application Layer The *application layer* is the user's access to the network. Its primary purpose is to provide a set of application programs and utilities that create and send messages on the network, and respond to messages that are received over the network. For example, a Web browser such as Internet Explorer enables you to create and send requests for Web pages and to process pages it receives in response to those requests. Other network-specific applications at this layer include network monitoring and network management.

Layer 6: Presentation Layer   The *presentation layer* formats the data for presentation to the user. Its job is to accommodate different interfaces on different computers so the application program need not worry about them. It is concerned with displaying, formatting, and editing user inputs and outputs. For example, the presentation layer might perform encryption and decryption of data (e.g., Secure Sockets Layer [SSL]), data compression, and translation between different data formats. Any function (except those in layers 1 to 5 below it) that is requested sufficiently often to warrant finding a general solution is placed in the presentation layer. Many networks do not have software installed at the presentation layer, so it is not used.

Layer 5: Session Layer   The *session layer* is responsible for initiating, maintaining, and terminating each logical session between end users. It arranges for all the desired and required services between session participants, such as logging on to circuit equipment and performing security checks. Session termination provides an orderly way to end the session, as well as a means to abort a session prematurely. The session layer also handles session accounting so the correct party receives the bill. This is done when you log in to a secure network that requires a password.

Internetwork Layers

The job of the *internetwork layers* is to connect the applications to the network and to determine the best route through the network from the message sender to the receiver. The internetwork layers have two closely related layers: transport and network.

Layer 4: Transport Layer   The *transport layer* deals with end-to-end issues, such as procedures for entering and departing from the network. It establishes, maintains, and terminates logical connections for the transfer of data between the original sender and the final destination of the message. The transport layer performs four functions. First, it is responsible for linking the application layer software to the network and establishing end-to-end connections between the sender and receiver when such connections are needed. Second, it provides tools so that addresses used at the application layer (e.g., www.indiana.edu) can be translated into the numeric addresses used at the lower layers (e.g., 129.79.78.8). Third, it is responsible for breaking long messages it receives into several smaller messages to make them easier to transmit (if needed). Fourth, it ensures that all the smaller messages have been received, eliminates duplicate messages, and performs flow control to ensure that no computer is overwhelmed by the number of messages it receives.

Layer 3: Network Layer   The *network layer* performs routing. It determines the next computer the message should be sent to in order to follow the best route through the network. It can also find the hardware layer address for that computer if needed.

Hardware Layers

The job of the *hardware layers* is to move a message from one computer or device to another computer or device, without error, once the internetwork layers have determined the best route. The hardware layers have two closely related layers: physical and data link.

Layer 2: Data Link Layer

The *data link layer* manages the physical transmission circuit in layer 1. The data link layer performs three functions. First, it controls the physical layer by deciding when to transmit messages over the media. Second, because layer 1 accepts and transmits only a raw stream of bits without understanding their meaning or structure, the data link layer must create and recognize message boundaries; that is, mark where a message starts and where it ends. Third, it can detect and eliminate any errors that occur during transmission. It also provides the connection between the hardware layers and the internetwork layers above it.

Layer 1: Physical Layer

The *physical layer* is concerned with transmitting data bits (zeros or ones) over a communication circuit. This layer defines the rules by which ones and zeros are transmitted, such as voltages of electricity, number of bits sent per second, and the physical format of the cables and connectors used. The physical layer includes all the *hardware* devices (e.g., computers, modems, and hubs) and physical *media* (e.g., cables and satellites).

Message Transmission Using Layers

Each computer in the network has software that operates at each of the layers and performs the functions required by those layers (or hardware in the case of the physical layer). Each layer in the network uses a formal language or *protocol* that is simply a set of rules that define what the layer will do and provides a clearly defined set of messages that software at that layer needs to understand. For example, the protocol used at the application layer for Web applications is HTTP (which is described in more detail in Chapter 2). In general, all messages sent in a network pass through all 7 layers, but sometimes the presentation and session layers are not used because there is no data encryption or passwords needed. Figure 1-4 shows how we can design networks using layers. At the application layers, we can pick and choose a variety of different application layer protocols. For example, suppose we wanted to use the Web. We would need to install software on our computer that would understand the protocol used on the Web, which is Hypertext Transport Protocol (HTTP). Internet Explorer and Netscape Communicator both speak HTTP. Whenever we click on a Web site, the software creates an HTTP message that is sent to the Web server requesting the page we want. If we want to use e-mail, we need to have a software package such as Outlook or Eudora that can understand the protocols used by e-mail, such as Simple Mail Transfer Protocol (SMTP). Whenever we send an e-mail message, the software will create an SMTP message and send it to the person to whom we have addressed the message. We can add new applications to our client computers or to our servers simply by adding software that understands the application protocol that we wish to use.

At the internetwork layer, we again have a choice of protocols. The most common protocols are Transport Control Protocol/Internet Protocol (TCP/IP) that are the protocols

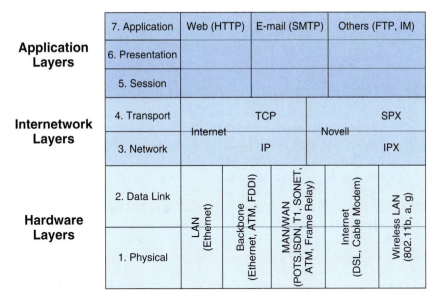

	7. Application	Web (HTTP)	E-mail (SMTP)	Others (FTP, IM)		
Application Layers	6. Presentation					
	5. Session					
Internetwork Layers	4. Transport	Internet — TCP		Novell — SPX		
	3. Network	IP		IPX		
Hardware Layers	2. Data Link	LAN (Ethernet)	Backbone (Ethernet, ATM, FDDI)	MAN/WAN (POTS,ISDN, T1, SONET, ATM, Frame Relay)	Internet (DSL, Cable Modem)	Wireless LAN (802.11b, a, g)
	1. Physical					

FIGURE 1-4   How the layers fit together in practice.

required by the Internet. Any computer connected to the Internet must understand TCP/IP. In fact, it is the use of TCP/IP that makes the Internet, the Internet; anyone on the Internet can use any application protocols they want and choose any hardware layer protocols they want, but all must use TCP/IP, because it is the Internetwork layers that enable computers to find other computers, and route messages to them. Another common set of protocols is SPX/IPX, which is often used in LANs that have Novell servers. As with the application layer protocols, many computers have software for both TCP/IP and SPX/IPX installed, so they can communicate with computers on the Internet and with Novell servers.

At the hardware layers, we again have a wide array of protocols that can be used. LANs tend to use one type of protocols (e.g., Ethernet), while MANs and WANs use different protocols better suited to longer distances. In this case, because the hardware layers provide the physical connection between computers, most computers have just one protocol installed because they have just one physical network connection.[1] In general, computers can only communicate with other computers that use the same protocol. So, if my computer uses Ethernet, it can only communicate with other computers that use Ethernet. Fortunately, there are many devices (e.g., routers) than can translate between different hardware layer protocols. When we connect an Ethernet LAN to a backbone network or to a MAN or WAN we just need to make sure that we buy a device that will convert from Ethernet on the LAN side to whatever the backbone, MAN, or WAN uses on the other side. This also means that we do not care what hardware layer protocols are in use by other computers on the Internet. As long as we use the same application layer protocols (e.g., HTTP, SMTP) and the same internetwork layer protocols (i.e., TCP/IP), then we can communicate.

[1] There are exceptions, of course. My laptop has three physical connections and thus three protocols: a traditional Ethernet connection for our LAN, a wireless Ethernet card, and a modem for dial-up when I travel.

To start with a simple example, Figure 1-5 shows how a message requesting a Web page would be sent on the Internet. In this example, we assume no encryption and no passwords, so we have bypassed layers 5 and 6.

First, the user first creates a message at the application layer using a Web browser by clicking on a link (e.g., *get the home page at www.somebody.com*). The browser translates the user's message (the click on the Web link) into the HTTP protocol. The rules of HTTP define a specific format—called an HTTP request *message*—that all Web browsers must use when they request a Web page. For now, you can think of the HTTP request as an envelope or *packet* into which the user's message *(get the Web page)* is placed. In the same way that an envelope placed in the mail needs certain information written in certain places (e.g., return address, destination address), so does the HTTP request. The Web browser fills in the necessary information in the HTTP request, drops the user's request inside the packet, and then passes the HTTP request (containing the Web page request) to the transport layer (bypassing the presentation and session layers).

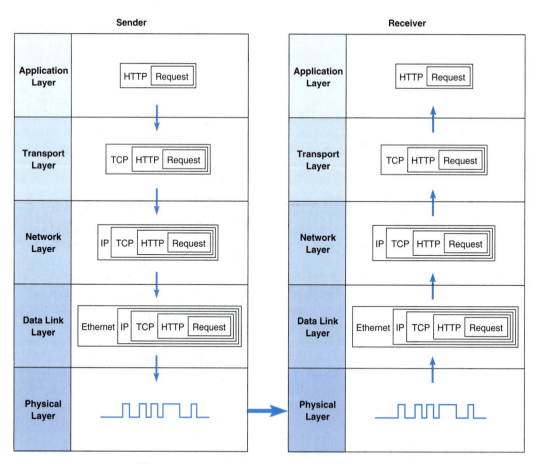

FIGURE 1-5 Message transmission using layers. IP = Internet Protocol; HTTP = Hypertext Transfer Protocol; TCP = Transmission Control Protocol.

The transport layer on the Internet uses a protocol called TCP, and it too has its own rules and its own packets. TCP is responsible for breaking large messages into a set of smaller packets for transmission and for opening a connection to the server for the transfer of this set of packets. In this case, the message is so short that it doesn't need to be broken into smaller parts. If the application layer does not know the numeric Internet address for the Web server, then the transport layer can help the application layer translate the text address (i.e., www.somebody.com) into its numeric address. For simplicity, we will assume that the application layer knows the numeric Internet address. So in this case, the transport layer places the HTTP request message inside a TCP *segment* (which is again much like envelope or a packet) and fills in the information needed by the TCP segment and passes the TCP segment (which contains with the HTTP request, which in turn contains the user's message) to the network layer.

The network layer on the Internet uses a protocol called IP, which has its own rules and packets. IP selects the next stop on the message's route through the network. It places the TCP packet inside an IP *packet* (and fills in the IP information) and passes the IP packet (which contains the TCP segment, which in turn contains the HTTP message, which in turn contains the message) to the data link layer.

If you are connecting to the Internet using LAN, your data link layer probably uses a protocol called Ethernet, which also has its own rules and packets. The data link layer formats the message with start and stop markers, places the IP packet inside an Ethernet *frame* (fills in the information in the frame), and instructs the physical hardware to transmit the Ethernet frame (which contains the IP packet, which contains the TCP segment, which contains the HTTP request, which contains the message).

The physical layer in this case is network cable connecting your computer to the rest of the network. The computer will take the Ethernet frame (complete with the IP packet, the TCP segment, the HTTP request, and the message) and send it as a series of electrical pulses through your cable to the server.

When the server gets the message, this process is performed in reverse. The physical hardware translates the electrical pulses into computer data and passes the message to the data link layer. The data link layer uses the start and stop markers in the Ethernet frame to identify the frame. If a message is received without error, the data link layer will then strip off the Ethernet frame and pass the IP packet (which contains the TCP segment, the HTTP request, and the message) to the network layer. The network layer checks the IP address and, if it is destined for this computer, strips off the IP packet and passes the TCP segment (which contains the HTTP request and the message) to the transport layer. The transport layer processes the message, strips off the TCP segment, and passes the HTTP request to the application layer for processing. The application layer (i.e., the Web server) reads the HTTP request and the message it contains (the request for the Web page) and processes it by generating an HTTP response containing the Web page you requested. Then the process starts again as the page is sent back to you.

There are three important points in this example. First, there are many different software packages and many different packets that operate at different layers to successfully transfer a message. Networking is in some ways similar to the Russian dolls that fit neatly inside each other. The major advantage of using different software and protocols means that it is easy to develop new software, because all one has to do is write software for one level at a time. The developers of Web applications, for example, do not need to write software to perform error checking or routing because those are performed by the data link and network layers. Developers can simply assume those functions are performed and just focus on the application layer. Likewise, it is simple to change the software at any level (or add new application protocols), as long as the interface between that layer and the ones around it remains unchanged.

Second, it is important to note that for communication to be successful, each layer in one computer must be able to communicate with its matching layer in the other computer. For example, the physical layer connecting the client and server must use the same type of electrical signals to enable each to understand the other (or there must be a device to translate between them). Ensuring that the software used at the different layers is the same is accomplished by *standards*. A standard defines a set of rules, called *protocols,* that explain exactly how hardware and software that conform to the standard is required to operate. Any hardware and software that conforms to a standard can communicate with any other hardware and software that conforms to the same standard. Without standards, it would be virtually impossible for computers to communicate.

Third, the major disadvantage of using a layered network model is that it is somewhat inefficient. There are several layers each with their own software and packet formats—a packet is the generic term for an HTTP request, TCP segment, IP packet, or an Ethernet frame.[2] Sending a message involves many software programs (often one for each protocol) and many different types of packets. The packets add to the total amount of data that must be sent (thus slowing down transmission), and the different software packages increase the processing power needed in the computers. Because the protocols are used at different layers and are stacked on top of each other (take another look at Figure 1-4), the set of software to understand the different protocols is often called a *protocol stack.*

NETWORK STANDARDS

The Importance of Standards

Standards are necessary in almost every business and public service entity. The primary reason for standards is to ensure that hardware and software produced by different vendors can work together. Without networking standards, it would be difficult—if not impossible—to develop networks that easily share information. Standards also mean that customers are not locked into one vendor. They can buy hardware and software from any vendor whose equipment meets the standard. In this way, standards help to promote more competition and hold down prices. The use of standards makes it much easier to develop software and hardware that link different networks because software and hardware can be developed one layer at a time.

The Standards-Making Process

There are two types of standards: *formal* and *de facto.* A formal standard is developed by an official industry or government body. For example, there are formal standards for appli-

---

[2] You could just say an HTTP packet, a TCP packet, or an Ethernet packet and everyone would understand you, but each layer has its preferred term for the packet concept.

cations such as Web browsers (e.g., HTML), for network layer software (e.g., IP), data link layer software (e.g., Ethernet IEEE 802.3), and for physical hardware (e.g., V.90 modems). Formal standards typically take several years to develop, during which time technology changes, making them less useful. The race between Netscape and Microsoft in Web browsers is a good example. Just as a new standard for HTML is developed, Netscape and Microsoft add new features to their browsers that do not conform to the standard, starting a new round of the standards process.

De facto standards are those that emerge in the marketplace and are supported by several vendors, but have no official standing. For example, Microsoft Windows is a product of one company and has not been formally recognized by any standards organization, yet it is a de facto standard. In the communications industry, de facto standards often become formal standards once they have been widely accepted.

The formal *standardization process* has three stages: specification, identification of choices, and acceptance. The *specification* stage consists of developing a nomenclature and identifying the problems to be addressed. In the *identification of choices* stage, those working on the standard identify the various solutions and choose the optimum solution from among the alternatives. *Acceptance,* which is the most difficult stage, consists of defining the solution and getting recognized industry leaders to agree on a single, uniform solution. As with many other organizational processes that have the potential to influence the sales of hardware and software, standards-making processes are not immune to corporate politics and the influence of national governments.

International Organization for Standardization (ISO)   One of the most important standards-making bodies is the *International Organization for Standardization (ISO),*[3] which makes technical recommendations about data communications interfaces (see www.iso.ch). ISO is based in Geneva, Switzerland. The membership is composed of the national standards organizations of each ISO member country. In turn, ISO is a member of the International Telecommunications Union (ITU), whose task is to make technical recommendations about telephone, telegraph, and data communications interfaces on a worldwide basis. ISO and ITU usually cooperate on issues of telecommunications standards, but they are mutually independent standards-making bodies, and they are not required to agree on the same standards.

International   Telecommunications   Union—Telecommunications Group (ITU-T)   The Telecommunications Group (ITU-T) is the technical standards-setting organization of the United Nations International Telecommunications Union (ITU), which is also based in Geneva (see www.itu.int). ITU is composed of representatives from about 200 member countries. Membership was originally focused on just the public telephone companies in each country, but a major reorganization in 1993 changed this, and ITU now encourages members from public and private sector organizations who operate computer or communications networks (e.g., RBOCs) or build software and equipment for them (e.g., AT&T).

---

[3] You're probably wondering why the abbreviation is *ISO,* not *IOS.* Well *ISO* is a word (not an acronym) derived from the Greek *isos,* meaning "equal." The idea is that with standards all are equal.

MANAGEMENT FOCUS 1-3

HOW NETWORK PROTOCOLS BECOME STANDARDS

There are many standards organizations around the world, but perhaps the best known is the Internet Engineering Task Force (IETF). IETF sets the standards that govern how much of the Internet operates.

IETF, like all standards organizations, tries to seek consensus among those involved before issuing a standard. Usually, a standard begins as a protocol (i.e., a language or set of rules for operating) developed by a vendor (e.g., HTML). When a protocol is proposed for standardization, IETF forms a working group of technical experts to study it. The working group examines the protocol to identify potential problems and possible extensions and improvements, and then issues a report to IETF.

If the report is favorable, the IETF issues a request for comment (RFC) that describes the proposed standard and solicits comments from the entire world. Most large software companies likely to be affected by the proposed standard prepare detailed responses. Many "regular" Internet users also send their comments to the IETF.

The IETF reviews the comments and possibly issues a new and improved RFC, which again is posted for more comments. Once no additional changes have been identified, it becomes a *proposed standard.*

Usually several vendors adopt the proposed standard and develop products based on it. Once at least two vendors have developed software based on it, and it has proven successful in operation, the proposed standard is changed to a draft standard. This is usually the final specification, although some protocols have been elevated to Internet standards, which usually signifies a mature standard not likely to change.

The process does not focus solely on technical issues; almost 90 percent of IETF's participants work for manufacturers and vendors, so market forces and politics often complicate matters. One former IETF chair who worked for a hardware manufacturer has been accused of trying to delay the standards process until his company had a product ready, although he and other IETF members deny this. Likewise, former IETF directors have complained that members try to standardize every product their firms produce, leading to a proliferation of standards, only a few of which are truly useful.

SOURCE: "How Networking Protocols Become Standards," *PC Week,* March 17, 1997; "Growing Pains," *Network World,* April 14, 1997.

American National Standards Institute (ANSI)   The *American National Standards Institute* is the coordinating organization for the U.S. national system of standards, both technology and nontechnology (see www.ansi.org). ANSI has about 1,000 members, both public and private organizations, in the United States. ANSI is a standardization organization, not a standards-making body, in that it accepts standards developed by other organizations and publishes them as U.S. standards. Its role is to coordinate the development of voluntary national standards and to interact with ISO in order to develop national standards that comply with ISO's international recommendations. ANSI is a voting participant in ISO and ITU-T.

Internet Engineering Task Force (IETF)   IETF sets the standards that govern how much of the Internet will operate (see www.ietf.org). The IETF is unique in that it doesn't really have official memberships. Quite literally anyone is welcome to join its mailing lists, attend its meetings, and comment on developing standards. The role of IETF and the other Internet organizations is discussed in more detail in Chapter 7, also see Management Focus 1-3 on how network protocols become standards.

Institute of Electrical and Electronics Engineers (IEEE)   The *Institute of Electrical and Electronics Engineers* is a professional society in the United States whose Standards Association (IEEE-SA) develops standards (see standards.ieee.org). The IEEE-SA is probably most known for its standards for local area networks. Other countries have their own similar groups; for example, the British counterpart of IEEE is the Institution of Electrical Engineers (IEE).

Common Standards

There are many different standards used in networking today. Each standard usually covers one layer in a network. Figure 1-6 outlines some of the most commonly used standards. At this point, these models are probably just a maze of strange names and acronyms, but by the end of the book, you will have a good understanding of each of these. Figure 1-5 provides a brief road map for some of the important communication technologies we will discuss in this book.

For now, there is one important message you should understand from Figure 1-6: For a network to operate, many different standards must be used simultaneously. The sender of a message must use one standard at the application layer, another one at the transport layer, another one at the network layer, another one at the data link layer, and another one at the physical layer. Each layer and standard are different, but all must work together in order to send and receive messages.

The sender and receiver of a message must use the same standards or, more likely, there are devices between the two that translate from one standard into another. Because different networks often use software and hardware designed for different standards, there is usually a lot of translation between different standards.

Layer	Common Standards
7. Application layer	HTTP, HTML (Web) MPEG, H.323 (audio/video) IMAP, POP (e-mail)
4. Transport layer	TCP (Internet) SPX (Novell LANs)
3. Network layer	IP (Internet) IPX (Novell LANs)
2. Data link layer	Ethernet (LAN) PPP (dial-up via modem)
1. Physical layer	RS-232C cable (LAN) Category 5 cable (LAN) V.92 (56-Kbps modem)

FIGURE 1-6   Some common data communications standards.

FUTURE TRENDS

Between now and the year 2010, data communications will grow faster and become more important than computer processing itself. Both go hand in hand, but we have moved from the computer era to the communications era. There are three major trends driving the future of communications and networking. All are interrelated, and it is difficult to consider one without the others.

Pervasive Networking

Pervasive networking means that communications networks will be everywhere; virtually any device will be able to communicate with any other device in the world. This is true in many ways today, but the what is important is the staggering rate at which we will be able to transmit data. Figure 1-7 illustrates the dramatic changes in the amount of data we can transfer. For example, in 1980, the capacity of a traditional telephone-based network (e.g., one that would allow you to dial up another computer from your home) was about 300 bits per second (bps). In relative terms, you could consider this like a pipe that would enable you to transfer one speck of dust every second. By the 1990s, we were routinely transmitting data at 9,600 bps, or about a grain of sand every second. By 2000, we were able to transmit either a pea (modem at 56 Kbps) or a ping pong ball (DSL at 1.5 Mbps [1.5 million bits per second]) every second over that same telephone line. In the very near future, we will have the ability to transmit 40 Mbps using wireless technologies—or in relative terms, about one basketball per second. A new laser-based wireless technology promises data rates of 10 Gbps (10 gigabits per second—10 billion bits per second) in the not-so-distant future—the relative equivalent of a one-car garage per second.

From 1980 to 2000, LAN and backbone technologies increased capacity from about 128 Kbps (a sugar cube per second) to 10 Mbps (a baseball) or 100 Mbps (a beach ball) (see Figure 1-7). In only a few years, backbones routinely will be running at 10 Gbps or the relative equivalent of a one-car garage per second.

The changes in WAN and Internet circuits have been even more dramatic (see Figure 1-7). From a typical size of 56 Kbps in 1980 to the 622 Mbps of a high-speed circuit in 2000, most experts now predict a high-speed WAN or Internet circuit will be able to carry 25 Tbps (25 terabits or 25 trillion bits per second) in a few years—the relative equivalent of a skyscraper 50 stories tall and 50 stories wide. Our sources at IBM Research suggest that this may be conservative; they predict a capacity of 1 Pbps (1 petabit or 1 quadrillion bits per second [a million billion]), which is the equivalent of a skyscraper 300 stories tall and wide (Figure 1-7). To put this in a different perspective, in January 2002, the total size of the Internet was estimated to be 850 petabits (i.e., adding together every file on every computer in the world that was connected to the Internet). In other words, just *one* 1 Pbps circuit could download the entire contents of today's Internet in less than 15 minutes. Of course, no computer in the world today could store that much information—or even just one second of the data transfer.

The term *broadband communication* has often been used to refer to these new high-speed communication circuits. *Broadband* is a technical term that refers to a specific type of data transmission that is used by one these circuits (i.e., DSL). However, its true technical meaning has become overwhelmed by its use in the popular press to refer to high-speed circuits in general. Therefore, we too will use "broadband" to refer to circuits with data speeds of 1 Mbps or higher.

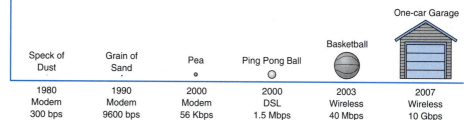

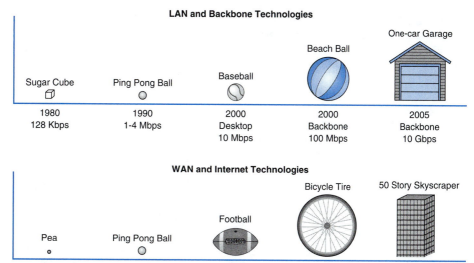

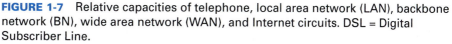

FIGURE 1-7   Relative capacities of telephone, local area network (LAN), backbone network (BN), wide area network (WAN), and Internet circuits. DSL = Digital Subscriber Line.

The initial costs of the technologies used for these broadband circuits will be very high, but competition will gradually drive them down. The challenge for businesses will be how to use them. When we have the capacity to transmit virtually all the data we want over a high-speed, low-cost circuit, how will we change the way businesses operate? Economists have long talked about the globalization of world economies. Data communications has made it a reality.

The Integration of Voice, Video, and Data

A second key trend is the integration of voice, video, and data communications, sometimes called *convergence*. In the past, the telecommunications systems used to transmit video signals (e.g., cable TV), voice signals (e.g., telephone calls), and data (e.g., computer data

TECHNICAL FOCUS *1-2*

A CITYWIDE CONVERGENCE PROJECT

The City of Oceanside, California had two separate networks, one for data and one for voice (i.e., telephone calls) for its three main office buildings and 33 smaller offices. They now have one integrated voice and data network connecting all locations.

The integrated network is broken into three logical groups for security and redundancy, so if one part of the network fails, network traffic can roll over onto one of the two remaining groups. Each of the three network groups has a network server that is connected to the users' computers via a LAN designed to support both data and voice traffic (using ATM, see Chapter 8). Each user's phone either plugs into his or her computer or into a wall jack that runs to a 24-telephone line phone hub that is connected into the LAN. The user's computer (or the phone hub) converts the voice phone call into computer data that travels

through the LAN and out on a backbone network to other city offices or to the phone company where it is processed in the same manner as a traditional phone call. The network also enables video from over 140 video cameras in the police station's holding cells, parking lots, beaches, busy intersections, and so on to be easily shared.

City employees are given inexpensive traditional phones or can use headsets and screenphones on their computer. The only real change was having to get used to accessing PBX-style phone features, such as conference calling and call transfers, through their computers. And interestingly enough, the cost of the single integrated network was less than the two separate traditional networks.

SOURCE: "A Citywide Convergence Project," *Network Magazine,* February 18, 2000.

---

or e-mail) were completely separate. One network was used for data, one for voice, and one for cable TV.

This is rapidly changing. The integration of voice and data is largely complete in wide area networks. The interexchange carriers such as Sprint provide telecommunications services that support data and voice transmission over the same circuits, even intermixing voice and data on the same physical cable. One Sprint service, for example, combines voice and data into one network—one that treats local calls and long distance calls the same.

The integration of voice and data has been much slower in local area networks and local telephone services. Some companies have successfully integrated both on the same network, but some still lay two separate cable networks into offices, one for voice and one for computer access.

The integration of video into computer networks has been much slower, partly due to past legal restrictions, and partly due to the immense communications needs of video. However, this integration is now moving quickly due to inexpensive video technologies. CNN, in conjunction with Intel, now offers its CNN and *Headline News* broadcasts digitally. Subscribers to this service receive the regular TV broadcasts in a format that can be transmitted over local area networks. This way users can receive the same audio and video TV images in a window on their computer.

New Information Services

A third key trend is the provision of new information services on these rapidly expanding networks. In the same way that the construction of the U.S. interstate highway system spawned new businesses, so will the construction of worldwide integrated

MANAGEMENT FOCUS *1-4*

KEEPING UP WITH TECHNOLOGY

The data communications and networking area changes rapidly. Significant new technologies are introduced and new concepts are developed almost every year. It is therefore important for network managers to keep up with these changes.

There are at least three useful ways to keep up with change. First and foremost for users of this book is the Web site for this book, which contains updates to the book, additional sections, teaching materials, and links to useful Web sites: www.wiley.com/college/dennis.

Second, there are literally hundreds of thousands of Web sites with data communications- and networking-related information. Search engines can help you find them.

Third, there are many useful magazines that discuss computer technology in general and networking technology in particular. These include *Network Computing, Data Communications, InfoWorld, InfoWeek,* and *CIO Magazine.*

---

communications networks. The *Web* has changed the nature of computing so that now anyone with a computer can be his or her own publisher. One can find information on virtually anything on the Web. The problem becomes one of assessing the accuracy and value of information. In the future, we can expect information services to appear that help ensure the quality of the information they contain. Never before in the history of the human race has so much knowledge and information been available to ordinary citizens. The challenge we face as individuals and organizations is assimilating this information and using it effectively.

Today, many companies are beginning to use *application service providers (ASPs)* rather than developing their own computer systems. An ASP develops a specific system (e.g., an airline reservation system, a payroll system), and companies purchase the service without ever installing the system on their own computers. They simply use the service, the same way you might use a Web hosting service to publish your own Web pages, rather than attempting to purchase and operate your own Web server. Some experts are predicting that by 2010, ASPs will have evolved into *information utilities.* An information utility is a company that provides a wide range of standardized information services, the same way that electric utilities today provide electricity or telephone utilities provide telephone service. Companies would simply purchase most of their information services (e.g., e-mail, Web, accounting, payroll, logistics) from these information utilities, rather than attempting to develop their systems and operate their own servers.

SUMMARY

Introduction   The information society, where information and intelligence are the key drivers of personal, business, and national success, has arrived. Data communications is the principal enabler of rapid information exchange and will become more important than the use of computers themselves in the future. Successful users of data communications, such as Wal-Mart, can gain a significant competitive advantage in the marketplace.

Network Definitions   A local area network (LAN) is a group of microcomputers or terminals located in the same general area. A backbone network is a large central network that connects almost everything on a single company site. A metropolitan area network (MAN) encompasses a city or county area. A wide area network (WAN) spans cities, states, or national boundaries.

Network Model   Communications networks are often broken into a series of layers, each of which can be defined separately, to enable vendors to develop software and hardware that can work together in the overall network. In this book, we use a seven-layer model, organized into three groups of layers. The application layers group includes the application layer (layer 7: the application software used by the network user), the presentation layer (layer 6: network software such as encryption and compression), and the session layer (layer 5: session logon and logoff). The internetwork layers include the transport layer (layer 4, which takes the message generated by the application layer and, if necessary, breaks it into several smaller messages) and the network layer (layer 3, which addresses the message(s) and determines their route through the network). The hardware layers include the data link layer (layer 2, which formats the message to indicate where it starts and ends, decides when to transmit it over the physical media, and detects and corrects any errors that occur in transmission) and the physical layer (layer 1, which is the physical connection between the sender and receiver, including the hardware devices, e.g., computers, terminals, and modems, and physical media, e.g., cables, and satellites).

Standards   Standards ensure that hardware and software produced by different vendors can work together. A formal standard is developed by an official industry or government body. De facto standards are those that emerge in the marketplace and are supported by several vendors, but have no official standing. Many different standards and standards-making organizations exist.

Future Trends   Pervasive networking will change how and where we work and with whom we do business. As the capacity of networks increases dramatically, new ways of doing business will emerge. The integration of voice, video, and data onto the same networks will greatly simplify networks and enable anyone to access any media at any point. The rise in these pervasive, integrated networks will mean a significant increase in the availability of information and new information services such as ASPs and information utilities.

KEY TERMS

American National Standards Institute (ANSI)
application layer
application layers
application service provider (ASP)
AT&T
backbone network
bps
broadband communications
circuit
client
common carrier
convergence
data link layer
extranet

Federal Communications Commission (FCC)
file server
Gbps
host computer
hardware layers
information utility
Institute of Electrical and Electronics Engineers (IEEE)
interexchange carrier (IXC)
International Telecommunications Union—Telecommunications Group (ITU-T)
Internet Engineering Task Force (IETF)

Internet model
Internet service providers (ISPs)
internetwork layers
intranet
Kbps
layers
local area network (LAN)
local exchange carrier (LEC)
Mbps
metropolitan area network (MAN)
monopoly
network layer
Open Systems Interconnection Reference Model (OSI Model)

Pbps
peer-to-peer network
physical layer
presentation layer
print server
protocol
protocol stack
regional Bell operating company (RBOC)
server
session layer
standards
Tbps
transport layer
Web server
wide area network (WAN)

QUESTIONS

1. How can data communications networks affect businesses?

2. Discuss three important applications of data communications networks in business and personal use.

3. Define *information lag* and discuss its importance.

4. Describe the progression of communications systems from the 1800s to the present.

5. Describe the progression of information systems from the 1950s to the present.

6. Describe the progression of the Internet from the 1960s to the present.

7. How do LANs differ from MANs, WANs, and backbones?

8. What is a circuit?

9. What is a client?

10. What is a host or server?

11. Why are network layers important?

12. Describe the seven layers in the OSI network model and what they do.

13. Why do we often consider the OSI layers as being grouped in a certain way?

14. Explain how a message is transmitted from one computer to another using layers.

15. Describe the three stages of standardization.

16. How are Internet standards developed?

17. Describe two important data communications standards-making bodies. How do they differ?

18. What is the purpose of a data communications standard?

19. What are three of the largest interexchange carriers (IXCs) in North America?

20. Name two RBOCs. Which one(s) provide services in your area?

21. Discuss three trends in communications and networking.

22. Why has the Internet model replaced the OSI model?

23. In the 1980s, there were many more protocols in common use at the data link, network, and transport layers than there are today. Why do you think the number of commonly used protocols at these layers has declined? Do you think this trend will continue? What are the implications for those who design and operate networks?

24. The number of standardized protocols in use at the application layer has significantly increased from the 1980s to today. Why? Do you think this trend will continue? What are the implications for those who design and operate networks?

EXERCISES

1-1. Investigate the long distance carriers (IXCs) and local exchange carriers (LECs) in your area. What services do they provide and what pricing plans do they have for residential users?

1-2. Discuss the issue of communications monopolies and open competition with an economics instructor and relate his or her comments to your data communications class.

1-3. Find a college or university offering a specialized degree in telecommunications or data communications and describe their program.

1-4. Describe a recent data communications development you have read about in a newspaper or magazine and how it may affect businesses.

1-5. Investigate the networks in your school or organization. Describe the important LANs and backbone networks in use (but do not describe the specific clients, servers, or devices on them).

1-6. Use the Web to search the IETF Web site (www. ietf.org). Describe one standard that is in the request for comment stage.

1-7. Discuss how the revolution/evolution of communications and networking is likely to affect how you will work and live in the future.

MINI-CASES

I. Big E. Bank

Nancy Smith is the director of Network Infrastructure for Big E. Bank (BEB). BEB has just purchased Ohio Bank (OB), a small regional bank that has 30 branches spread over Ohio. OB has a WAN connecting the five cities in which it has branches to OB's main headquarters in Columbus. It has a series of MANs in those cities, which in turn connect to the LANs in each of the branches. The OB network is adequate, but uses very different data link, network, and transport protocols than those used by BEB's network. Nancy's task is to connect OB's network with BEB's network. She has several alternatives. Alternative A is to leave the two networks separate but install a few devices in OB's headquarters to translate between the set of protocols used in the BEB network and those in the OB network so that messages can flow between the two networks. Alternative B is to replace all the WAN, MAN, and LAN network components in OB's entire network so that OB uses the same protocols as BEB and the two can freely communicate. Alternative C is to replace the devices in the OB WAN (and possibly the MANs) so that each city (or each branch, if the MANs are replaced as well) can communicate with the BEB network, but the LANs in individual branches remain unchanged. In this case, the device connecting the MAN (or the branch) will translate between the OB protocols and the BEB protocols. Your job is to develop a short list of pros and cons for each alternative and make a recommendation.

II. Global Consultants

John Adams is the Chief Information Officer (CIO) of Global Consultants (GC), a very large consulting firm with offices in more than 100 countries around the world. GC is about to purchase a set of several Internet-based financial software packages that will be installed in all of their offices. There are no standards at the application layer for financial software, but several software companies that sell financial software (call them Group A) use one de facto standard to enable their software to work with others' software. However, another group of financial software companies (call them Group B) use a different de facto standard. While both groups have software packages that GC could use, GC would really prefer to buy one package from Group A for one type of financial analysis and one package from Group B for a different type of financial analysis. The problem, of course, is that then the two packages cannot communicate and GC's staff would end up having to type the same data into both packages. The alternative is to buy two packages from the same group—so that data could be easily shared—but that would mean having to settle for second best for one of the packages. While there have been some reports in the press about the two groups of companies working together to develop one common standard that will enable all software to work together, there is no firm agreement yet. What advice would you give Mr. Adams?

III. Better Networks, Take 1

Your friend Bill, who has a small computer networking company, has developed a new approach to networking (called Simple Networking [SN]) that does not use the seven layers of the OSI model. It replaces layers 2 through 6 with one layer. It will work with existing layer-7 application software that uses standard Internet protocols and with standard layer-1 hardware such as Ethernet LANs, but it will run only on Windows computers. It runs much faster than current software because it is one package instead of several different ones that must interact. However, it cannot run over the Internet, so companies using SN must install special computers to connect their networks to the Internet that translate between the SN protocols used inside of the company and Internet protocols used on the Internet. What advice would you give Bill? Do you think the idea makes sense?

IV. Better Networks, Take 2

Read Minicase III. Suppose your friend is actually Bill Gates, and the company developing SN is Microsoft. What advice would you give Bill? Do you think the idea makes sense?

CHAPTER 2

APPLICATION LAYERS

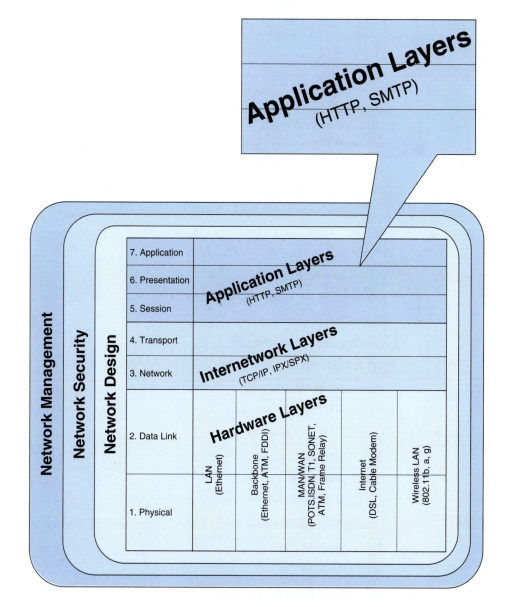

THE **APPLICATION** layers (application, presentation, and session) are the software that enables the user to perform useful work. The software at the application layer is the reason for having the network because it is this software that provides the business value. This chapter examines the three fundamental types of application architectures used at the application layer (host-based, client-based, client–server). It then looks at the Internet and the primary software application packages it enables: the Web, e-mail, Telnet, FTP, and instant messaging.

OBJECTIVES

- Understand host-based, client-based, and client–server application architectures
- Understand how the Web works
- Understand how e-mail works
- Be aware of how FTP, Telnet, and instant messaging work

CHAPTER OUTLINE

INTRODUCTION

APPLICATION ARCHITECTURES

   Host-Based Architectures

   Client-Based Architectures

   Client–Server Architectures

   Best Practice Architectures

WORLD WIDE WEB

   How the Web Works

   Inside an HTTP Request

   Inside an HTTP Response

ELECTRONIC MAIL

   How E-Mail Works

   Inside an SMTP Packet

   Listserv Discussion Groups

   Attachments in MIME

OTHER APPLICATIONS

   File Transfer Protocol (FTP)

INTRODUCTION

Network applications are the software packages that run in the application layer. You should be quite familiar with many types of network software, because it is these application packages that you use when you use the network. In many respects, the only reason for having a network is to enable these applications.

In this chapter, we will first discuss three basic architectures for network applications and how each of those architectures affects the design of networks. Since you probably have a good understanding of applications such as the Web and word processing we will use those as examples of different application architectures. We will then examine several common applications used on the Internet (e.g., Web, e-mail) and use those to explain how application software interacts with the networks. By the end of this chapter, you should have much better understanding of the application layer in the network model and what exactly we meant when we used the term *packet* in Chapter 1.

While the software at the session and presentation layers sometimes plays a role in networks, this chapter focuses on the software at the application layer. Software at the presentation layer (e.g., secure sockets layer [SSL]) for encryption is discussed in Chapter 10 with other network security hardware and software.

APPLICATION ARCHITECTURES

In Chapter 1, we discussed how the three basic components of a network (client computer, server computer, and circuit) work together. In this section, we will get a bit more specific about how the client computer and the server computer can work together to provide application software to the users. An *application architecture* is the way in which the functions of the application layer software are spread among the clients and servers in the network.

The work done by any application program can be divided into four general functions. The first is *data storage.* Most application programs require data to be stored and retrieved, whether it is a small file such as a memo produced by a word processor, or a large database such as an organization's accounting records. The second function is *data access logic,* the processing required to access data, which often means database queries in SQL. The third function is the *application logic* (sometimes also called business logic), which is the actual work performed by the application. The fourth function is the *presentation logic,* the presentation of information to the user and the acceptance of the user's commands. These four functions, *data storage, data access logic, application logic,* and *presentation logic,* are the basic building blocks of any application.

TECHNICAL FOCUS *2-1*

CLIENTS AND SERVERS

There are many different types of clients and servers that can be part of a network, and the distinctions between them have become a bit more complex over time. Generally speaking, there are four types of computers that are commonly used as servers:

- A *mainframe* is a very large general-purpose computer (usually costing millions of dollars) that is capable of performing *very* many simultaneous functions, supporting *very* many simultaneous users, and storing *huge* amounts of data.

- A *minicomputer* is a large general-purpose computer (usually costing hundreds of thousands of dollars) that is capable of performing many simultaneous functions, supporting many simultaneous users, and storing large amounts of data. Minicomputers are sometimes used as database servers in client–server networks.

- A *microcomputer* is the type of computer you use. Microcomputers used as servers can range from a small microcomputer, similar to a desktop one you might use, to one costing $50,000 or more.

- A *cluster* is a group of computers (often microcomputers or workstations) linked together so that they act as one computer. Requests arrive at the cluster (e.g., Web requests) and are distributed among the computers so that no one computer is overloaded. Each computer is separate, so that if one fails, the cluster simply bypasses it. Clusters are more complex than single servers because work must be quickly coordinated and shared among the individual computers. Clusters are very scalable because one can always add one more computer to the cluster.

There are five types of clients:

- A *microcomputer* is the most common type of client today.

- A *terminal* is a device with a monitor and keyboard, but no CPU. *Dumb terminals,* so named because they do not participate in the processing of the data they display and have the bare minimum required to operate as input and output devices (a TV screen and a keyboard). In most cases when a character is typed on a dumb terminal, it transmits the character through the circuit to the server for processing. Every keystroke is processed by the server, even simple activities such as the up arrow. *Intelligent terminals* were developed to reduce the processing demands on the server and have some small internal memory and a built-in, programmable microprocessor chip. Many simple functions such as moving the cursor or displaying words in different colors are done by the terminal, thus saving processing time on the server.

- A *workstation* is a more powerful microcomputer designed for use in technical applications such as mathematical modeling, computer-assisted design (CAD), and intensive programming. As microcomputers become more powerful, the difference between a microcomputer and a workstation is blurring.

- A *network computer* is designed primarily to communicate using Internet-based standards (e.g., HTTP, Java) but has no hard disk. It has only limited functionality.

- A *transaction terminal* is designed to support specific business transactions, such as the automated teller machines (ATM) used by banks. Other examples of transaction terminals are point-of-sale terminals in a supermarket.

There are many ways in which these four functions can be allocated between the client computers and the servers in a network. There are three fundamental application architectures in use today. In *host-based architectures,* the server (or host computer) performs virtually all of the work. In *client-based architectures,* the client computers perform most of the work. In *client–server architectures,* the work is shared between the servers and clients. The client–server architecture is becoming the dominant application architecture.

Host-Based Architectures

The very first data communications networks developed in the 1960s were host-based, with the server (usually a large mainframe computer) performing all four functions. The clients (usually terminals) enabled users to send and receive messages to and from the host computer. The clients merely captured keystrokes and sent them to the server for processing, and accepted instructions from the server on what to display. See Figure 2-1.

This very simple architecture often works very well. Application software is developed and stored on the one server along with all data. If you've ever used a terminal (or a microcomputer with the Telnet software), you've used a host-based application. There is one point of control, because all messages flow through the one central server. In theory, there are economies of scale, because all computer resources are centralized (but more on cost later).

There are two fundamental problems with host-based networks. First, the server must process all messages. As the demands for more and more network applications grow, many servers become overloaded and unable to quickly process all the users' demands. Prioritizing users' access becomes difficult. Response time becomes slower, and network managers are required to spend increasingly more money to upgrade the server. Unfortunately, upgrades to the mainframes that usually are the servers in this architecture are "lumpy." That is, upgrades come in large increments and are expensive (e.g., $500,000); it is difficult to upgrade "a little."

Client-Based Architectures

In the late 1980s, there was an explosion in the use of microcomputers and microcomputer-based local area networks. Today, more than 90 percent of most organizations' total computer processing power now resides on microcomputer-based LANs, not in centralized mainframe computers. Part of this expansion was fueled by a number of low-cost, highly popular applications such as word processors, spreadsheets, and presentation graphics programs. It was also fueled in part by managers' frustrations with application software on host mainframe computers. Most mainframe software is not as easy to use as microcomputer software, is far more expensive, and can take years to develop. In the late 1980s, many large organizations had application development backlogs of two to three years; that is, getting any new mainframe application program written would take years. New York

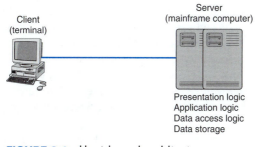

Client
(terminal)

Server
(mainframe computer)

Presentation logic
Application logic
Data access logic
Data storage

FIGURE 2-1 Host-based architecture.

Client
(microcomputer)

Server
(microcomputer)

Presentation logic
Application logic
Data access logic

Data storage

FIGURE 2-2 Client-based architecture.

City, for example, had a six-year backlog. In contrast, managers could buy microcomputer packages or develop microcomputer-based applications in a few months.

With client-based architectures, the clients are microcomputers on a local area network, and the server is usually another microcomputer on the same network. The application software on the client computers is responsible for the presentation logic, the application logic, and the data access logic; the server simply stores the data. See Figure 2-2.

This simple architecture often works very well. If you've ever used a word processor and stored your document file on a server (or written a program in Visual Basic or C that runs on your computer but stores data on a server), you've used a client-based architecture.

The fundamental problem in client-based networks is that all data on the server must travel to the client for processing. For example, suppose the user wishes to display a list of all employees with company life insurance. All the data in the database (or all the indices) must travel from the server where the database is stored over the network circuit to the client, which then examines each record to see if it matches the data requested by the user. This can overload the network circuits, because far more data is transmitted from the server to the client than the client actually needs.

Client–Server Architectures

The most common architecture for the Internet is the client–server architecture. Client–server architectures attempt to balance the processing between the client and the server by having both do some of the logic. In these networks, the client is responsible for the presentation logic while the server is responsible for the data access logic and data storage. The application logic may reside either on the client, or on the server, or be split between both.

Figure 2-3 shows the simplest case with the presentation logic and application logic on the client and the data access logic and data storage on the server. In this case, the client software accepts user requests and performs the application logic that produces database requests that are transmitted to the server. The server software accepts the database requests, performs the data access logic, and transmits the results to the client. The client software accepts the results and presents them to the user. When you use a Web browser to get pages from a Web server, you've used a client–server architecture. Likewise if you've ever written a program that uses SQL to talk to a database on a server, you've used a client–server architecture.

For example, if the user requests a list of all employees with company life insurance, the client would accept the request, format it so that it could be understood by the server,

FIGURE 2-3   Two-tier client–server architecture.

and transmit it to the server. On receiving the request, the server searches the database for all requested records and then transmits only the matching records to the client, which would then present them to the user. The same would be true for database updates; the client accepts the request and sends it to the server. The server processes the update and responds (either accepting the update or explaining why not) to the client, which displays it to the user.

One of the strengths of client–server networks is that they enable software and hardware from different vendors to be used together. But this is also one of their disadvantages because it can be difficult to get software from different vendors to work together. One solution to this problem is *middleware* software that sits between the application software on the client and the application software on the server. Middleware does two things. First, it provides a standard way of communicating that can translate between software from different vendors. Many middleware tools began as translation utilities that enabled messages sent from a specific client tool to be translated into a form understood by a specific server tool.

TECHNICAL FOCUS *2-2*

A MONSTER CLIENT–SERVER ARCHITECTURE

Every spring, Monster.com, one of the largest job sites in the United States, with an average of more than 3 million visitors per month, experiences a large increase in traffic. Aaron Braham, vice president of operations, attributes the spike to college students who increase their job search activities as they approach graduation.

Monster.com has 150 Web servers and 30 database servers in its main site in Indianapolis and plans to move that to 400 over the next year by gradually growing the main site, and adding a new site with servers in Maynard, Massachusetts just in time for the spring rush. The main Web site has a set of load-balancing devices that forward Web requests to the different servers depending on how busy they are.

Braham says the major challenge is that 90 percent of the traffic is not simple requests for Web pages, but rather search requests (e.g., what network jobs are available in New Mexico) which require more processing and access to the database servers. Monster.com has more than 350,000 job postings and more than 3 million resumes on file, spread across its database servers. Several copies of each posting and resume are kept on several database servers to improve access speed and provide redundancy in case a server crashes, so just keeping the database servers in sync so that they contain correct data is a challenge.

SOURCE: "Resume Influx Tests Mettle of Job Sites' Scalability," *Internetweek,* May 29, 2000.

The second function of middleware is to manage the message transfer from clients to servers (and vice versa) so that clients need not know the specific server that contains the application's data. The application software on the client sends all messages to the middleware, which forwards them to the correct server. The application software on the client is therefore protected from any changes in the physical network. If the network layout changes (e.g., a new server is added), only the middleware must be updated.

There are literally dozens of standards for middleware, each of which is supported by different vendors, and each of which provides different functions. Two of the most important standards are Distributed Computing Environment (DCE) and Common Object Request Broker Architecture (CORBA). Both of these standards cover virtually all aspects of the client–server architecture, but are quite different. Any client or server software that conforms to one of these standards can communicate with any other software that conforms to the same standard. Another important standard is Open Database Connectivity (ODBC), which provides a standard for data access logic.

Two-Tier, Three-Tier, and n-Tier Architectures   There are many ways in which the application logic can be partitioned between the client and the server. The example in Figure 2-3 is one of the most common. In this case, the server is responsible for the data, and the client, the application and presentation. This is called a *two-tier* architecture, because it uses only two sets of computers: one set of clients and one set of servers.

A *three-tier architecture* uses three sets of computers as shown in Figure 2-4. In this case, the software on the client computer is responsible for presentation logic, an application server(s) is responsible for the application logic, and a separate database server(s) is responsible for the data access logic and data storage.

An *n-tier architecture* uses more than three sets of computers. In this case, the client is responsible for presentation, a database server(s) is responsible for the data access logic and data storage, and the application logic is spread across two or more different sets of servers. Figure 2-5 shows an example of an *n*-tier architecture of a groupware product called TCBWorks, developed at the University of Georgia. TCBWorks has four major components. The first is the Web browser on the client computer that a user uses to access the system and enter commands (presentation logic). The second component is a Web server that responds to the user's requests, either by providing HTML pages and graphics (application logic), or by sending the request to the third component, a set of 28 C programs that perform various functions such as adding comments or voting (application

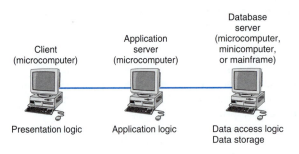

FIGURE 2-4   Three-tier client–server architecture.

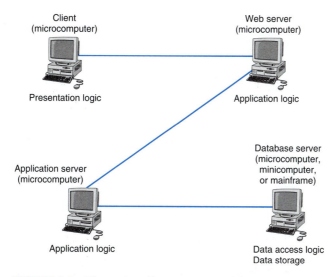

FIGURE 2-5   The *n*-tier client–server architecture.

logic). The fourth component is a database server that stores all the data (data access logic and data storage). Each of these four components is separate, making it easy to spread the different components on different servers, and to partition the application logic on two different servers.

The primary advantage of an *n*-tier client–server architecture compared to a two-tier architecture (or a three-tier to a two-tier) is that it separates out the processing that occurs to better balance the load on the different servers; it is more "scalable." In Figure 2-5, we have three separate servers which provide more power than if we had used a two-tier architecture with only one server. If we discover that the application server is too heavily loaded, we can simply replace it with a more powerful server, or even put in two application servers. Conversely, if we discover the database server is underused, we could put data from another application on it.

There are two primary disadvantages to an *n*-tier architecture compared to a two-tier architecture (or a three-tier to a two-tier). First, it puts a greater load on the network. If you compare Figures 2-3, 2-4, and 2-5, you will see that the *n*-tier model requires more communication among the servers; it generates more network traffic so you need a higher-capacity network. Second, it is much more difficult to program and test software in *n*-tier architectures than two-tier architectures because more devices have to communicate to complete a user's transaction.

Thin Clients versus Thick Clients   Another way of classifying client–server architectures is by examining how much of the application logic is placed on the client computer. A *thin client* approach places little or no application logic on the client (e.g., Figure 2-5), while a *thick client* approach places all or almost all of the application logic on the client (e.g., Figure 2-3). There is no direct relationship between thin and thick clients and two-, three- and *n*-tier architectures. For example, Figure 2-6 shows a typical Web

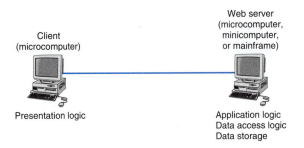

Client
(microcomputer)

Web server
(microcomputer,
minicomputer,
or mainframe)

Presentation logic

Application logic
Data access logic
Data storage

FIGURE 2-6   The typical two-tier thin-client architecture of the Web.

architecture: a two-tier architecture with a thin-client. One of the biggest forces favoring thin clients is the Web.

Thin clients are much easier to manage. If an application changes, only the server with the application logic needs to be updated. With a thick client, the software on all of the clients would need to be updated. Conceptually, this is a simple task; one simply copies the new files to the hundreds of affected client computers. In practice, it can be a very difficult task.

Thin client architectures are the wave of the future. More and more application systems are being written to use a Web browser as the client software, with Java applets (containing some of the application logic) downloaded as needed. This application architecture is sometimes called the *distributed computing model.*

Best Practice Architectures

Each of the preceding architectures has certain costs and benefits, so how do you choose the "best practice" architecture? In many cases, the architecture is simply a given; the organization has a certain architecture and one simply has to use it. In other cases, the organization is acquiring new equipment and writing new software, and has the opportunity to develop a new architecture, at least in some part of the organization. Figure 2-7 summarizes three major sets of factors in understanding a best practice.

Cost of Infrastructure   One of the strongest driving forces of client–server architectures is cost of infrastructure (the hardware, software, and networks that will support the application system). Simply put, personal computers are more than 1,000 times cheaper

	Host-Based	**Client-Based**	**Client–Server**
Cost of infrastructure	High	Medium	Low
Cost of development	Low	Medium	Medium
Scalability	Low	Medium	High

FIGURE 2-7   Factors involved in choosing architectures.

than mainframes for the same amount of computing power. The microcomputers on our desks today have more processing power, memory, and hard disk space than a mainframe of the early 1990s and the cost of the microcomputers is a fraction of the cost of the mainframe. Therefore, the cost of client–server architectures is low compared to server-based architectures that rely on mainframes. Client–server architectures also tend to be cheaper than client-based architectures because they place less of a load on networks and thus require less network capacity.

Cost of Development   The cost of developing systems is an important factor when considering the financial benefits of client–server architectures. Developing application software for client-based architectures is usually the cheapest, because there are many GUI development tools for simple standalone computers that communicate with database servers (e.g., Visual Basic, Access). Developing application software for client–server architectures used to be very complex and expensive, but as new tools have been developed (e.g., Microsoft's .Net suite of tools) costs have steadily dropped. The cost differential may change as more companies gain experience with client–server applications; new client–server products are developed and refined, and client–server standards mature. However, given the inherent complexity of client–server software and the need to coordinate the interactions of software on different computers there is likely to remain a cost difference compared to host-based architectures.

Likewise, merely updating the network with a new version of client–server software is complicated. In a host-based network, there is one place in which application software is stored; to update the software, you simply replace it there. With client–server networks, you must update all clients and all servers. For example, suppose you want to add a new server and move some existing applications from the old server to the new one. All application software on all thick clients that send messages to the application on the old server must now be changed to send to the new server. While this is not conceptually difficult, it can be an administrative nightmare.

Scalability   *Scalability* refers to the ability to increase or decrease the capacity of the computing infrastructure in response to changing capacity needs. The most scalable architecture is client–server computing, because servers can be added to (or removed from) the architecture when processing needs change. For example, in a four-tier client-server architecture, one might have 10 Web servers, 4 application servers, and 3 database servers. If the application servers begin to get overloaded, it is simple to add another 2 or 3 application servers.

Also the types of hardware that are used in client–server (e.g., minicomputers) typically can be upgraded at a pace that most closely matches the growth of the application. In contrast, host-based architectures rely primarily on mainframe hardware that needs to be scaled up in large, expensive increments, and client-based architectures have ceilings above which the application cannot grow because increases in use and data can result in increased network traffic to the extent that performance is unacceptable.

Summary   A review of Figure 2-7 should indicate the current recommended best practice application architecture. For most projects a client–server architecture, usually a three-tier thin or thick client–server architecture, is recommended.

WORLD WIDE WEB

The Web was first conceived in 1989 by Tim Berners-Lee at the European Laboratory for Particle Physics (CERN) in Geneva. His original idea was to develop a database of information on physics research, but he found it difficult to fit the information into a traditional database. Instead, he decided to use a *hypertext* network of information. With hypertext, any document can contain a link to any other document.

CERN's first Web browser was written in 1990, but it was 1991 before it was available on the Internet for other organizations to use. By the end of 1992, several browsers had been written for UNIX computers by CERN and several other European and American universities, and there were about 30 Web servers in the entire world. In 1993, Marc Andreessen, a student at the University of Illinois, led a team of students that wrote Mosaic, the first graphical Web browser, as part of a project for the university's National Center for Supercomputing Applications (NCSA). By the end of 1993, the Mosaic browser was available for UNIX, Windows, and Macintosh computers, and there were about 200 Web servers in the world. In 1994, Andreessen and some colleagues left NCSA to form Netscape, and half a dozen other startup companies introduced commercial Web browsers. Within a year, it had become clear that the Web has changed the face of computing forever. NCSA stopped development of the Mosaic browser in 1996, as Netscape and Microsoft began to invest millions to improve their browsers.

How the Web Works

The Web is a good example of a two-tier client–server architecture (see Figure 2-8). Each client computer needs an application layer software package called a *Web browser*. There are many different browsers, such as Netscape Navigator and Microsoft Internet Explorer. Each server on the network that will act as a Web server needs an application layer software package called a *Web server*. There are many different Web servers, such as those produced by Netscape, Microsoft, and Apache.

To get a page from the Web, the user must type in the Internet *uniform resource locator (URL)* for the page he or she wants (e.g., www.yahoo.com), or click on a link that provides the URL. The URL specifies the Internet address of the *Web server* and the directory and name of the specific page wanted. If no directory and page is specified, the Web server will provide whatever page has been defined as its home page. If no server name is specified, the Web browser will presume the address is on the same server and directory as the page containing the URL.

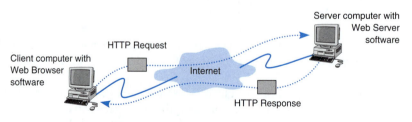

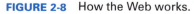

FIGURE 2-8   How the Web works.

For the requests from the Web browser to be understood by the Web server, they must use the same standard *protocol* or language. If there was no standard and each Web browser used a different protocol to request pages, then it would be impossible for a Netscape Web browser to communicate with a Microsoft Web server, for example.

The standard protocol for communication between a Web browser and a Web server is *Hypertext Transfer Protocol (HTTP).*[1] In order to get a page from a Web server, the Web browser issues a special packet called an *HTTP request* that contains the URL and other information about the Web page requested (see Figure 2-8). Once the server receives the HTTP request, it processes it, and sends back an *HTTP response,* which will be the requested page, or an error message (see Figure 2-8).

This request–response dialogue occurs for every file transferred between the client and the server. For example, suppose the client requests a Web page that has two graphic images. Graphics are stored in separate files from the Web page itself using a different file format than the HTML used for the Web page (in jpeg, for example). In this case, there would be three request–response pairs. First, the browser would issue a request for the Web page, and the server would send the response. Then, the browser would begin displaying the Web page and notice the two graphic files. The browser would then send a request for the first graphic and a request for the second graphic, and the server would reply with two separate HTTP responses, one for each request.

Inside an HTTP Request

The HTTP request and HTTP response are examples of the packets we introduced in Chapter 1 that are produced by the application layer and sent down to the transport, network, data link, and physical layers for transmission through the network. The HTTP response and HTTP request are simple text files that take the information provided by the application (e.g., the URL to get) and format it in a structured way so that the receiver of the message can clearly understand it.

An HTTP request from a Web browser to a Web server has three parts. Only the first part is required; the other two are optional.

- The *request line,* which starts with a command (e.g., GET), provides the URL and ends with the HTTP version number that the browser understands. The version number ensures that the Web server does not attempt to use a more advanced or newer version of the HTTP standard that the browser does not understand.

- The *request header,* which contains a variety of optional information such as the Web browser being used (e.g., Internet Explorer) and the date.

- The *request body,* which contains information sent to the server, such as information that the user has typed into a form.

Figure 2-9 shows an example of an HTTP request for a page on our Web server, formatted using version 1.1 of the HTTP standard. This request has only the request line and the request header, because no request body is needed for this request. This request

[1] The formal specification for HTTP version 1.1 is provided in RFC 2616 on the IETF's Web site. The URL is www.ietf.org/rfc/rfc2616.txt.

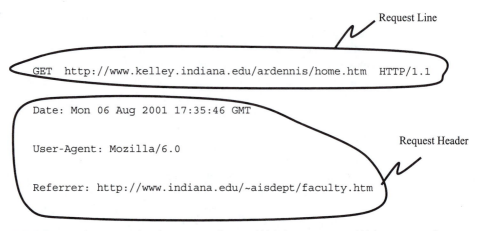

Request Line

GET http://www.kelley.indiana.edu/ardennis/home.htm   HTTP/1.1

Date: Mon 06 Aug 2001 17:35:46 GMT

User-Agent: Mozilla/6.0

Request Header

Referrer: http://www.indiana.edu/~aisdept/faculty.htm

FIGURE 2-9   An example of a request from a Web browser to a Web server using the HTTP (Hypertext Transfer Protocol) standard.

includes the date and time of the request (expressed in Greenwich Mean Time [GMT], the time zone that runs through London, England) and name of the browser used ("Mozilla" is the code-name for Netscape Navigator). The "referrer" field means that the user obtained the URL for this Web page by clicking on a link on another page, which in this case is a list of faculty at Indiana University (i.e., www.indiana.edu/~aisdept/faculty.htm). If the referrer field is blank, then it means the user typed the URL himself or herself.

Inside an HTTP Response

The format of an HTTP response from the server to the browser is very similar to the HTTP request. It too has three parts, but only the last part is required; the first two are optional. If the server cannot provide the request body, then it must provide the response status.

- The *response status,* which contains the HTTP version number the server has used, a status code (e.g., *200* means "okay"; *404* means not found), and reason phrase (a text description of the status code).
- The *response header,* which contains a variety of optional information such as the Web server being used (e.g., Apache), the date, and the exact URL of the page in the response.
- The *response body,* which is the Web page itself.

Figure 2-10 shows an example of a response from our Web server to the request in Figure 2-9. This example has all three parts. The response status reports "okay," which means the requested URL was found and is included in the response body. The response header provides the date, the type of Web server software used, the actual URL included in the response body, and the type of file. In most cases, the actual URL and the requested URL are the same, but not always. For example, if you request a URL but do not specify a

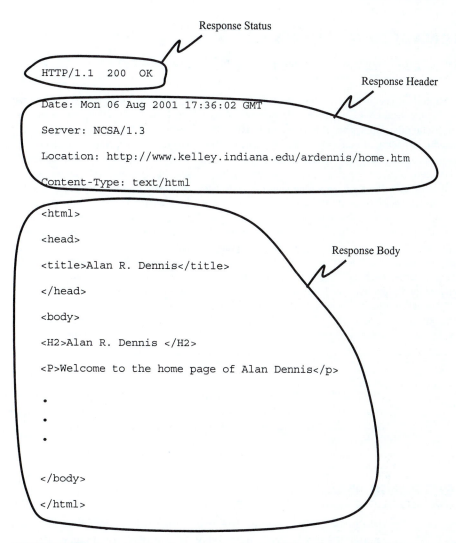

Response Status

HTTP/1.1 200 OK

Response Header

Date: Mon 06 Aug 2001 17:36:02 GMT

Server: NCSA/1.3

Location: http://www.kelley.indiana.edu/ardennis/home.htm

Content-Type: text/html

<html>

<head>

<title>Alan R. Dennis</title>

</head>

<body>

<H2>Alan R. Dennis </H2>

<P>Welcome to the home page of Alan Dennis</p>

•

•

•

</body>

</html>

Response Body

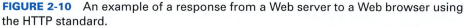

FIGURE 2-10 An example of a response from a Web server to a Web browser using the HTTP standard.

file name (e.g., www.indiana.edu), you will receive whatever file is defined as the home page for this server, so the actual URL will be different from the requested URL (e.g., www.indiana.edu/home.htm).

The response body in this example shows a Web page in *Hypertext Markup Language (HTML)*. The response body can be in any format, such as text, Microsoft Word, Adobe PDF, or a host of other formats, but the most commonly used format is HTML. HTML was developed by CERN at the same time as the first Web browser and has evolved rapidly ever since. HTML is covered by standards produced by the IETF, but Microsoft and Netscape keep adding new additions to the HTML standard with every release of their browsers, so the HTML standard keeps changing.

MANAGEMENT FOCUS *2-1*

FREE SPEECH REIGNS ON THE INTERNET ... OR DOES IT?

In a landmark decision in 1997, the U.S. Supreme Court ruled that the sections of the 1996 Telecommunications Act restricting the publication of indecent material on the Web and the sending of indecent e-mail were unconstitutional. This means that anyone can do anything on the Internet, right?

Well, not really. The court decision affects only Internet servers located in the United States. Each country in the world has different laws that govern what may and may not be placed on servers in that country. For example, British law restricts the publication of pornography, whether on paper or on Internet servers.

Many countries such as Singapore, Saudi Arabia, and China prohibit the publication of certain political information. Since much of this "subversive" information is published outside of their countries, they actively restrict access to servers in other countries.

Other countries are very concerned about their individual cultures. In 1997, a French court convicted Georgia Institute of Technology of violating French language law. Georgia Tech operates a small campus in France that offers summer programs for American students. The information on the campus Web server was primarily in English because classes are conducted in English. This violated the law requiring French to be the predominant language on all Internet servers in France.

The most likely source of problems for North Americans lies in copyright law. Free speech does not give permission to copy from others. It is against the law to copy and republish on the Web any copyrighted material or any material produced by someone else without explicit permission. So don't copy graphics from someone else's Web site, or post your favorite cartoon on your Web site, unless you want to face a lawsuit.

HTML is fairly easy to learn, so you can develop your own Web page. There are many Web sites with good tutorials on HTML; Yahoo! lists more than a dozen. The easiest way to develop a page is to start with a page developed by someone else or to use an HTML editor.

ELECTRONIC MAIL

Electronic mail (or *e-mail*) was one of the earliest applications on the Internet and is still among the most heavily used today. With e-mail, users create and send messages to one user, several users, or all users on a *distribution list.* Most e-mail software enables users to send text messages and attach files from word processors, spreadsheets, graphics programs, and so on. Many e-mail packages also permit you to filter or organize messages by priority. For example, all messages from a particular user (e.g., your boss) could be given top priority, so they always appear at the top of your list of messages.

E-mail has several major advantages over regular mail. First, it is fast: Delivery of an e-mail message typically takes seconds or minutes, depending on the distance to the receiver. Even messages sent to other countries usually take only a few minutes or hours to deliver, compared to days for regular mail or courier services. E-mail users often call regular paper mail *snail mail* because it moves so slowly by comparison.

A second major benefit is cost. E-mail is cheaper because it costs virtually nothing to transmit the message over the network, compared to the cost of a stamp or a courier charge. E-mail is also cheaper in terms of the time invested in preparing the message. The expectations and culture of sending and receiving e-mail is different from that of sending regular letters. Regular business letters and interoffice memos are expected to be error free and formatted according to certain standards. A recent analysis of office processes estimated that it costs between $3 to $10 to prepare and send a paper letter, including printing and supply costs, clerical time, and proofreading time. In contrast, most e-mail users accept less well-formatted messages, and slight typographical errors are often overlooked so less time is spent on perfecting the appearance of the message.

E-mail can substitute for the telephone, thus allowing you to avoid *telephone tag* (the process of repeatedly exchanging voice mail messages because neither you nor the person you are trying to call is in when the other calls). A study of telephone tag in large organizations found that it took an average of three calls and messages before the parties actually got to speak to each other. E-mail can often communicate enough of a message so that the entire "conversation" will take less time than a phone call. It is particularly effective for multinational organizations, which have people working in different time zones around the world.

Several standards have been developed to ensure compatibility between different e-mail software packages. Any software package that conforms to a certain standard can send messages that are formatted using its rules. Any other package that understands that particular standard can then relay the message to its correct destination; however, if an e-mail package receives a mail message in a different format, it may be unable to process it correctly. Many e-mail packages send using one standard, but can understand messages sent in several different standards. Three commonly used standards are SMTP, X.400, and CMC. In this book, we will discuss only SMTP, but CMC and X.400 both work essentially the same way. SMTP, X.400, and CMC are different (in the same way that English differs from French or Spanish), but several software packages are available that translate between them, so that companies that use one standard (e.g., CMC) can translate messages they receive that use a different standard (e.g., SMTP) into their usual standard as they first enter the company and then treat them as "normal" e-mail messages after that.

How E-Mail Works

The *Simple Mail Transfer Protocol (SMTP)* is the most commonly used e-mail standard simply because it is the e-mail standard used on the Internet.[2] E-mail is in many ways similar to how the Web works, but is a bit more complex. SMTP e-mail is usually implemented as a two-tier client–server application, but not always. We will first explain how the normal two-tier architecture works and then quickly contrast that with two alternate architectures.

Two-Tier E-Mail Architecture   With a two-tier client–server architecture, each client computer runs an application layer software package called a *user agent,* which is usually more commonly called an "e-mail client" (see Figure 2-11). There are many common e-mail client software packages, such as Eudora, Outlook, and Netscape Messenger. The user creates the e-mail message using one of these e-mail clients, which formats the message into an SMTP packet that includes information such as the sender's address and the destination address.

---

[2] The formal specification for SMTP is provided in RFC 822 on the IETF's Web site. The URL is www.ietf.org/rfc/rfc0866.txt.

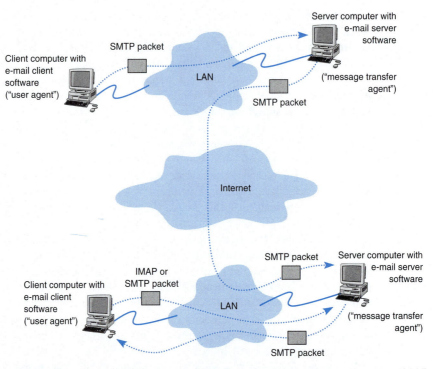

FIGURE 2-11 How SMTP (Simple Mail Transfer Protocol) e-mail works. IMAP = Internet Message Access Protocol; LAN = local area network.

The user agent then sends the SMTP packet to a mail server that runs a special application layer software package called a *message transfer agent,* which is more commonly called "mail server software" (see Figure 2-11).

This e-mail server reads the SMTP packet to find the destination address and then sends the packet on its way through the network—often over the Internet—from mail server to mail server until it reaches the mail server specified in the destination address (see Figure 2-11). The mail transfer agent on the destination server then stores the message in the receiver's mailbox on that server. The message sits in the mailbox assigned to the user who is to receive the message until he or she checks for new mail.

The SMTP standard covers message transmission between mail servers (i.e., mail server to mail server) and between the originating e-mail client and its mail server. A different standard is used to communicate between the receiver's e-mail client and his or her mail server. Two commonly used standards for e-mail client to mail server communication are *Post Office Protocol (POP)* and *Internet Message Access Protocol (IMAP).* While there are several important technical differences between POP and IMAP, the most noticeable difference is that before a user can read a mail message with a POP (version 3) e-mail client, the e-mail message must be copied to the client computer's hard disk and deleted from the mail server. With IMAP, e-mail messages can remain stored on the mail server after they are read. IMAP therefore offers considerable benefits to users who read their e-mail from many different computers (e.g., home, office, computer labs) because they no longer need to worry about having old e-mail messages scattered across several client computers; all e-mail is stored on the server until it is deleted.

In our example in Figure 2-11, when the receiver next accesses his or her e-mail, the e-mail client on his or her computer contacts the mail server by sending an IMAP or POP packet that asks for the contents of the user's mailbox. Figure 2-11 shows this as an IMAP packet, but it could just as easily be a POP packet. When the mail server receives the IMAP or POP request, it sends the original SMTP packet created by the message sender to the client computer, which the user reads with the e-mail client. Therefore, any e-mail client using POP or IMAP must also understand SMTP to create messages and to read messages it receives. Both POP and IMAP provide a host of functions that enable the user to manage his or her e-mail, such as creating mail folders, deleting mail, creating address books, and so on. If the user sends a POP or IMAP request for one of these functions, the mail server will perform the function and send back a POP or IMAP response packet that is much like the status line in an HTTP response packet.

Host-Based E-Mail Architectures

When SMTP was first developed, host-based architectures were the rule, so SMTP was first designed to run on mainframe computers. If you use a text-based version of Linux or UNIX, chances are you are using a host-based architecture for your e-mail.

With this architecture, the client computer in Figure 2-11 would be replaced by a terminal that would send all of the user's keystrokes to the server for processing. The server would then send characters back to the terminal to display. All software would reside on the server. This software would take the user's keystrokes, create the SMTP packet, and then send it on its way to the next mail server.

Likewise, the receiver would use a terminal that would send keystrokes to the server and receive letters back to display. The server itself would be responsible for understanding the user's commands to read a mail message and sending the appropriate characters to the user's terminal so he or she could read the e-mail message. If you were wondering why the SMTP standard does not include the delivery of the message to the receiver's client computer, you should now understand. Because no software existed on the receiver's terminal, the SMTP standard did not include any specification about how the receiver's mail server software should display messages. Communication between the mail server and the receiver's terminal was left to the e-mail software package running on the server. Because each package and each terminal was different, no standards were developed to cover communication between the terminal and the server. The POP and IMAP protocols only emerged in the Internet era when the use of microcomputers became common.

Three-Tier Client–Server Architecture

The three-tier client–server e-mail architecture uses a Web server and Web browser to provide access to your e-mail. With this architecture, you do not need an e-mail is client on your client computer. Instead, you use you Web browser. This type of e-mail is sometimes called "Web-based e-mail" and is provided by a variety of companies such as Hotmail.

You use your browser to connect to a page on a Web server that lets you write the e-mail message by filling in a form. When you click the send button, your Web browser sends the form information to the Web server inside an HTTP request (see Figure 2-12). The Web server runs a program (written in C or Perl, for example) that takes the information

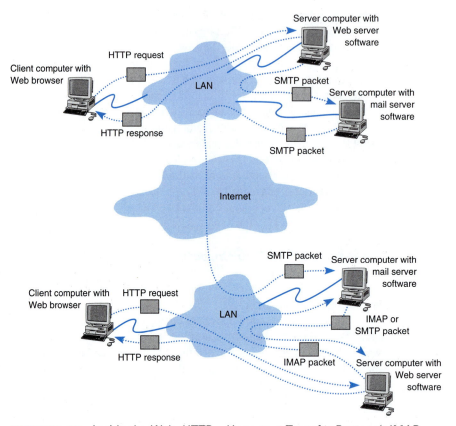

FIGURE 2-12   Inside the Web. HTTP = Hypertext Transfer Protocol; IMAP = Internet Message Access Protocol; LAN = local area network; SMTP = Simple Mail Transfer Protocol.

from the HTTP request and builds an SMTP packet that contains the e-mail message (and while not important to our example, it also sends an HTTP response back to the client). The Web server then sends the SMTP packet to the mail server, which processes the SMTP packet as though it came from a client computer. The SMTP packet flows through the network in the same manner as before. When it arrives at the destination mail server, it is placed in the receiver's mailbox.

When the receiver wants to check his or her mail, he or she uses a Web browser to send an HTTP request to a Web server (see Figure 2-12). A program on the Web server (in C or Perl, for example) processes the request and sends the appropriate IMAP (or POP) request to the mail server. The mail server responds with an IMAP (or POP) packet, which a program on the Web server converts into an HTTP response and sends to the client. The client then displays the e-mail message in the Web browser.

A simple comparison of Figures 2-11 and 2-12 will quickly show that the three-tier approach using a Web browser is much more complicated than the normal two-tier approach. So why do it? Well, it is simpler to just have a Web browser on the client computer, rather than requiring the user to install a special e-mail client on his or her computer and then set up the special e-mail client to connect to the correct mail server using either POP or IMAP. It is simpler for the user to just type the URL of the Web server providing the mail services into his or her browser and begin using mail.

It is also important to note that the sender and receiver do not have to use the same architecture for their e-mail. The sender could use a two-tier client–server architecture and the receiver a host-based or three-tier client–server architecture. Because all communication is standardized using SMTP between the different mail servers, how the users interact with their mail servers is unimportant. Each organization can use a different approach. This is one of the key impacts of standards.

In fact, there is nothing to prevent one organization from using all three architectures simultaneously. At Indiana University, we usually access our e-mail through an e-mail client (e.g., Outlook), but we can also access it over the Web because many of us travel internationally and find it easier to borrow a Web browser with Internet access than to borrow a computer with an Outlook e-mail client and set it up to use the Indiana mail server.

Inside an SMTP Packet

SMTP defines how message transfer agents operate and how they format messages sent to other message transfer agents. An SMTP packet has two parts:

- The *header,* which lists source and destination e-mail addresses, possibly in text form (e.g., "Pat Smith") as well as the address itself (e.g., psmith@somewhere.com), date, subject, and so on.
- The *body,* which is the word DATA, followed by the message itself.

Figure 2-13 shows a simple e-mail message formatted using SMTP. The header of an SMTP message has a series of fields that provide specific information such as the sender's e-mail address, the receiver's address, date, and so on. The information in quotes on the *to* and *from* lines is ignored by SMTP; only the information in the angle brackets is used as e-mail addresses. The *message ID* field is used to provide a unique identification code so that

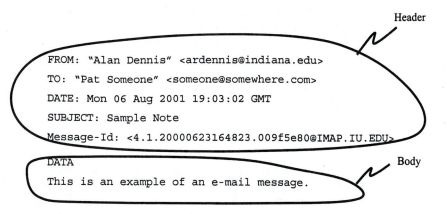

Header

```
FROM: "Alan Dennis" <ardennis@indiana.edu>
TO: "Pat Someone" <someone@somewhere.com>
DATE: Mon 06 Aug 2001 19:03:02 GMT
SUBJECT: Sample Note
Message-Id: <4.1.20000623164823.009f5e80@IMAP.IU.EDU>
DATA
    This is an example of an e-mail message.
```

Body

FIGURE 2-13 An example of an e-mail message using the SMTP (Simple Mail Transfer Protocol) standard.

TECHNICAL FOCUS *2-3*

SMTP TRANSMISSION

SMTP is an older protocol and is rather complicated to transmit; if we were going to design it again, we would likely find a simpler transmission method. Conceptually, we think of an SMTP packet as one packet. However, SMTP mail transfer agents transmit each element within the SMTP packet as a separate packet and wait for the receiver to respond with an "OK" before sending the next element.

For example, in Figure 2-13, the sending mail transfer agent would send the *from* address, and wait for an OK from the receiver. Then it would send the *to* address and wait for an OK, then the date, and so on, with the last item being the entire message sent as one element.

the message can be tracked. The message body contains the actual text of the message itself.

Listserv Discussion Groups

A Listserver (or *Listserv*) group is a simply a mailing list of users who have joined together to discuss some topic. Listserv groups are formed around just about every topic imaginable, including cooking, skydiving, politics, education, and British comedy. Some are short lived while others continue indefinitely. Some permit any member to post messages, others permit only certain members to post messages. Most businesses have Listservs organized around job functions, so that it is easy to reach everyone in a particular department.

There are two parts to every Listserv. The first part, the *Listserv processor,* processes commands such as requests to subscribe, unsubscribe, or to provide more information about the Listserv. The second part is the *Listserv mailer.* Any message sent to the Listserv mailer is re-sent to everyone on the mailing list. To use a Listserv, you need to know the addresses of both the processor and the mailer.

To subscribe to a Listserv, you send an e-mail message to the Listserv processor, which adds your name to the list (see Technical Focus 2-4 for the message format). It is important that you send this message to the processor, not the mailer, otherwise your subscription message will be sent to everyone on the mailing list, which might be embarrassing.

For example, suppose you want to join a Listserv on widgets that has a processor address of listerv@abc.com, and the mailer address is widget-1@abc.com. To subscribe, you send an e-mail message to listerv@abc.com containing the text: *subscribe widget-l your name.* To send a message to everyone on this Listserv, you would e-mail your message to widget-l@abc.com.

Attachments in MIME

As the name suggests, SMTP is a simple standard that permits only the transfer of text messages. It was developed in the early days of computing, when no one had even thought about using e-mail to transfer nontext files such as graphics or word processing documents. Several standards for nontext files have been developed that can operate together with SMTP, such as *Multipurpose Internet Mail Extension (MIME),* uuencode, and binhex.

TECHNICAL FOCUS *2-4*

LISTSERV COMMANDS

There are many different commands that can be sent to the listserv processor to perform a variety of functions. These commands are included as lines of text in the e-mail message sent to the processor. Each command must be placed on a separate line. Some useful commands include:

- SUBSCRIBE Listserv-mailer-name your-name: Subscribes you to a mailing list (e.g., *subscribe maps-l robin jones*).
- UNSUBSCRIBE Listserv-mailer-name your-name: Unsubscribes you from the mailing list (e.g., *unsubscribe maps-l robin jones*).

- HELP: Requests the Listserv to e-mail you a list of its commands.
- LIST: Requests the Listserv to e-mail you a list of all Listserv groups that are available on this Listserv processor.
- LIST DETAILED: Requests the Listserv to e-mail you a detailed description of all Listserv groups that are available on this Listserv processor and are public.

Each of the standards is different, but all work in the same general way. The MIME software, which exists as part of the e-mail client, takes the nontext file such as a Power-Point graphic file, and translates each byte in the file into a special code that looks like regular text. This encoded section of "text" is then labeled with a series of special fields understood by SMTP as identifying a MIME-encoded attachment and specifying information about the attachment (e.g., name of file, type of file). When the receiver's e-mail client receives the SMTP message with the MIME attachment, it recognizes the MIME "text" and uses its MIME software (that is part of the e-mail client) to translate the file from MIME "text" back into its original format.

OTHER APPLICATIONS

There are literally thousands of applications that run on the Internet and on local area networks. Most application software that we develop today, whether for sale or for private internal use, runs on a network. We could spend years talking about different network applications and still only cover a small number.

Fortunately, most network application software works in much the same way as the Web or e-mail. In this section, we will briefly discuss only three commonly used applications: FTP, Telnet, and instant messaging.

File Transfer Protocol (FTP)

File Transfer Protocol (FTP) enables you to send and receive files over the Internet. FTP works much like HTTP. FTP requires an application layer program on the client computer and an FTP server application program on a server. There are many software packages that use the FTP standard, such as WS-FTP. The user uses his or her client to send FTP requests to the FTP server. The FTP server processes these requests and sends back FTP packets containing the requested file.[3]

There are two types of FTP sites: closed and anonymous. A closed site requires users to have permission before they can connect and gain access to the files. Access is granted by providing an account name with a password. For example, a network manager or web-master would write a Web page using software on his or her client computer and then use FTP to send it to a specific account on the Web server.

The most common type is an *anonymous FTP* site, which permits any Internet user to login using the account name of *anonymous*. When using anonymous FTP, you will still be asked for a password. It is customary to enter your Internet e-mail address as the pass-word (e.g., smith@allstate.edu).

Many files and documents available via FTP have been compressed to reduce the amount of disk space they require. Since there are many types of data compression pro-grams, it is possible that a file you want has been compressed by a program you lack, so you won't be able to access the file until you find the decompression program it uses. That's one of the "advantages" of the decentralized, no-rules structure of the Internet.

Telnet

Telnet enables users on one computer to login to other computers on the Internet. Telnet requires an application layer program on the client computer and an application layer pro-gram on the server or host computer. There are many programs that conform to the Telnet standard, such as EWAN. Once Telnet makes the connection from the client to the server, you can login to the server or host computer in the same way as you would if you dialed in with a modem; you must know the account name and password of an authorized user. Tel-net can be faster or slower than a modem depending on the amount of traffic on the Inter-net. In any event, Telnet enables you to connect to a remote computer without incurring long distance telephone charges.

Because Telnet was designed in the very early days of the Internet, it assumes your client is a dumb terminal. Therefore, when you use Telnet you are using a host-based archi-tecture. All keystrokes you type in the Telnet client are transferred one by one to the server computer for processing. The server processes those commands—including simple key-strokes such as up-arrow or down-arrow—and transfers the results back to the client com-puter, which displays the letters and moves the cursor as directed by the server.[4]

Telnet can be useful because it enables you to access your server or host computer without sitting at its keyboard. Most network managers use Telnet to work on servers, rather than physically sitting in front of them and using their keyboards. Telnet also poses a great security threat, because it means that anyone on the Internet can attempt to login to your account and use it as they wish. One commonly used security precaution is to prohibit remote logins via Telnet unless a user specifically asks for his or her account to be author-ized for it, or to permit remote logins only from a specific set of Internet addresses. For

---

[3] The formal specification for FTP is provided in RFC 2640 on IETF's Web site. The URL is www.ietf.org/rfc/rfc2640.txt.

[4] The formal specification for Telnet is provided in RFC 2355 and RFC 854 on IETF's Web site. The URLs are www.ietf.org/rfc/rfc2355.txt and www.ietf.org/rfc/rfc0854.txt.

TECHNICAL FOCUS *2-5*

OTHER TYPES OF SERVICES AND SERVERS

There are quite literally thousands of different types of application layer services that are provided to network users. Some of the more common ones in LANs include:

File servers allow many users to share the same set of files on a common, shared disk drive. The hard disk volume can be of any size, limited only by the size of the disk storage itself. Files on the shared disk drive can be made freely available to all network users, shared only among authorized users, or restricted to only one user. Each file server has a *network operating system (NOS)* such as NT that enables users to access its files as though they were local drives on the users' computers.

Print servers handle print requests on the LAN. By offloading the management of printing from the main LAN file server or database server, print servers help reduce the load on them and increase network efficiency in much the same way that front end processors improve the efficiency of mainframe computers. Print servers have traditionally been separate computers, but many vendors now sell "black boxes" that perform all the functions of a print server at much less than the cost of a standalone computer.

Remote access servers (RASs) enable users to dial into and out of the LAN by telephone. A RAS lets users dial into the LAN and perform all the same functions as though they were physically connected to the LAN itself. RASs are best for applications that move only small amounts of

information and do not require high speed beyond the limited capabilities of regular telephone lines. LANs typically provide data transmission rates of 10 to 100 Mbps, while telephone lines typically provide only 56 Kbps.

A *storage area network (SAN)* is a LAN devoted solely to data storage. When the amount of data to be stored exceeds the practical limits of servers, the SAN plays a critical role. The SAN has a set of high-speed storage devices and servers that are networked together using a very-high-speed network (often using a technology called *fibre channel* that runs over a series of multigigabit point-to-point fiber optic circuits). Servers are connected into the normal LAN and to the SAN, which is usually reserved only for servers. When data is needed, clients send the request to a server on the LAN, which obtains the information from the devices on the SAN and then returns it to the client.

The devices on the SAN may be a large set of database servers or a set of network-attached disk arrays. In other cases, the devices may be *network-attached storage (NAS)* devices. A NAS is not a general-purpose computer like a server that runs a server operating system (e.g., NT, Linux), but instead is specially designed to just respond to requests for files and data. A NAS has a small processor and a large amount of disk storage and is designed solely to respond to data requests. A NAS can also be attached to LANs, where it functions as a fast database server.

---

example, the Web server for this book will only accept Telnet logins from computers located in the same building. Chapter 10 discusses network security.

Instant Messaging

One of the fastest-growing Internet applications is *instant messaging (IM)*. With IM, you can exchange real-time typed messages or chat with your friends. Some IM software also enables you to verbally talk with your friends in the same way as you might use the telephone or to use cameras to exchange real-time video in the same way you might use a videoconferencing system. Several types of IM currently exist, including ICQ and AOL instant messenger.

IM works in much the same way as the Web. The client computer needs an IM client software package that communicates with an IM server software package that runs on a server. When the user connects to the Internet, the IM client software package sends an IM request packet to the IM server, informing it that the user is now online. The IM client software package continues to communicate with the IM server to monitor what other users

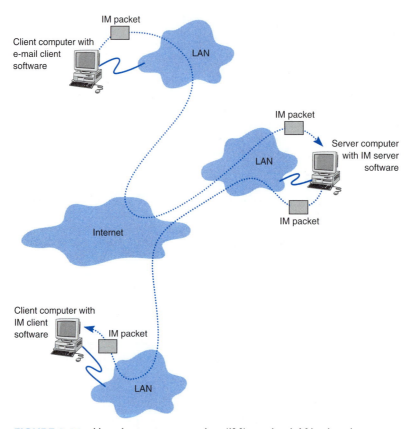

FIGURE 2-14 How instant messaging (IM) works. LAN = local area network.

have connected to the IM server. When one of your friends connects to the IM server, the IM server sends an IM packet to your client computer so that you now know that your friend is connected to the Internet. The server also sends a packet to your friend's client computer so that he or she knows that you are on the Internet.

With the click of a button, you can both begin chatting. When you type text, your IM client creates an IM packet that is sent to the IM server (see Figure 2-14). The server then retransmits the packet to your friend. Several people may be part of the same chat session, in which case, the server sends a copy of the packet to all of the client computers. IM also provides a way for different servers to communicate with each other. IM also enables peer-to-peer messaging so that the messages can avoid the server and move directly between the two client computers.

Videoconferencing

Videoconferencing provides real-time transmission of video and audio signals to enable people in two or more locations to have a meeting. In some cases, videoconferences are held in special-purpose meeting rooms with one or more cameras and several video display monitors

FIGURE 2-15   Desktop videoconferencing.

to capture and display the video signals. Special audio microphones and speakers are used to capture and play audio signals. The audio and video signals are combined into one signal that is transmitted though a metropolitan or wide area network to people at the other location. Most of this type of videoconferencing involves two teams in two separate meeting rooms, but some systems can support conferences of up to eight separate meeting rooms.

The fastest-growing form of videoconferencing is *desktop videoconferencing.* Small cameras installed on top of each computer permit meetings to take place from individual offices (see Figure 2-15). Special application software (e.g., CUSeeMe, Net Meeting) is installed on the client computer and transmits the images across a network to application software on a videoconferencing server. The server then sends the signals to the other client computers that want to participate in the videoconference. In some cases, the clients can communicate with each other without using the server. The cost of desktop videoconferencing ranges from less than $100 per computer for inexpensive systems to more than $4,000 for high-quality systems. Some systems have integrated conferencing software with desktop videoconferencing, enabling participants to communicate verbally and, by using applications such as white boards, to attend the same "meeting" while they are sitting at the computers in their offices.

The key benefits of videoconferencing are the time and cost savings that can result. By using videoconferencing, meeting participants no longer need to spend time and money in travel. Videoconferencing was slow to take hold in many organizations because of its high initial installation costs (between $20,000 and $100,000 per meeting room). Today, however, most large organizations with offices in different parts of the country or the world use it, and there is a growing demand for desktop systems. Desktop systems now outsell room-based systems three to one, but the growth has been slower than expected.

The transmission of video requires a lot of network capacity. Most videoconferencing uses data compression to reduce the amount of data transmitted. Surprisingly, the most common complaint is not the quality of the video image, but the quality of the voice transmissions. Special care needs to be taken in the design and placement of microphones and speakers to ensure quality sound and minimal feedback.

Most videoconferencing systems were originally developed by vendors using different formats, so many products were incompatible. The best solution was to ensure that all hardware and software used within an organization was supplied by the same vendor, and to hope that any other organizations with whom you wanted to communicate used the same equipment. Today, three standards are in common use: H.320, H.323, and MPEG-2 (also called ISO 13818-2). Each of these standards was developed by a different organization and is supported by different products. They are not compatible, although some application software packages understand more than one standard. H.320 is designed for room-to-room videoconferencing over high-speed telephone lines. H.323 is a family of standards designed for desktop videoconferencing and simple audioconferencing over the Internet. MPEG-2 is designed for faster connections such as a LAN or specially designed, privately operated WAN.

Webcasting is a special type of one-directional videoconferencing in which content is sent from the server to the user. The developer creates content that is downloaded as needed by the users and played by a plug-in to a Web browser. At present, there are no standards for Webcast technologies, but the products by RealNetworks.Com are the de facto standards.

SUMMARY

Application Architectures There are three fundamental application architectures. In host-based networks, the server performs virtually all of the work. In client-based networks, the client computer does most of the work; the server is used only for data storage. In client–server networks, the work is shared between the servers and clients. The client performs all presentation logic, the server handles all data storage and data access logic, and one or both perform the application logic. Client–server networks can be cheaper to install and often better balance the network loads, but are far more complex and costly to develop and manage.

World Wide Web One of the fastest-growing Internet applications is the Web, which was first developed in 1989. The Web enables the display of rich graphical images, pictures, full motion video, and sound. The Web is the most common way for businesses to establish a presence on the Internet. The Web has two application software packages, a Web browser on the client and a Web server on the server. Web browsers and servers communicate with each other using a standard called HTTP. Most Web pages are written in HTML, but many also use other formats. The Web contains information on just about every topic under the sun, but finding it and making sure the information is reliable are major problems.

Electronic Mail With e-mail, users create and send messages using an application layer software package on client computers called user agents. The user agent sends the mail to a server running an application layer software package called a mail transfer agent, which then forwards the message through a series of mail transfer agents to the mail transfer agent on the receiver's server. E-mail is faster and cheaper than regular mail, and can substitute for telephone conversations in some cases. Several standards have been developed to ensure compatibility between different user agents and mail transfer agents. SMTP, POP, and IMAP are used on the Internet. X.400 and CMC are other commonly used standards.

KEY TERMS

anonymous FTP
application architecture
application logic
CA*net
client–server architecture
cluster
Common Messaging
   Calls (CMC)
data access logic
data storage
desktop video-
   conferencing
distributed computing
distribution list
domain
dumb terminal
e-mail
thick client
file server
File Transfer Protocol
   (FTP)
H.320
H.323

host-based architecture
HTTP request
HTTP response
Hypertext Markup
   Language (HTML)
Hypertext Transfer
   Protocol (HTTP)
instant messaging (IM)
intelligent terminal
Internet
Internet Mail Access
   Protocol (IMAP)
Listserv
mainframe
message transfer agent
metasearch engine
microcomputer
minicomputer
MPEG-1
MPEG-2
Multipurpose Internet
   Mail Extension
   (MIME)

Netscape
network attached storage
   (NAS)
network computer
NSFNET
n-tier architecture
Post Office Protocol
   (POP)
presentation logic
print server
protocol
remote access server
   (RAS)
request body
request header
request line
response body
response header
response status
search engine
server-based architecture
Simple Mail Transfer
   Protocol (SMTP)

snail mail
spider
storage area network
   (SAN)
Telnet
telephone tag
terminal
thick client
thin client
three-tier architecture
transaction terminal
two-tier architecture
uniform resource locator
   (URL)
user agent
videoconferencing
World Wide Web
Web browser
Web server
workstation
X.400

QUESTIONS

1. What are the different types of application architectures?

2. Describe the four basic functions of an application software package.

3. What are the advantages and disadvantages of host-based networks versus client–server networks?

4. What is middleware and what does it do?

5. Suppose your organization was contemplating switching from a host-based architecture to client–server. What problems would you foresee?

6. Which is less expensive: host-based networks or client–server networks? Explain.

7. Compare and contrast two-tiered, three-tiered, and n-tiered client–server architectures. What are the technical differences and what advantages and disadvantages does each offer?

8. How does a thin client differ from a thick client?

9. What is a network computer?

10. What do each of the following tools enable you to do: the Web, e-mail, FTP, Telnet?

11. For what is HTTP used? What are its major parts?

12. For what is HTML used?

13. Describe how a Web browser and Web server work together to send a Web page to a user.

14. How is e-mail useful?

15. Describe how mail user agents and message transfer agents work together to transfer mail messages.

16. What roles do SMTP, POP, and IMAP play in sending and receiving e-mail on the Internet?

17. What are the major parts of an e-mail message?

18. What is X.400 and CMC?

19. What is FTP and why is it useful?

20. What is Telnet and why is it useful?

21. What is a Listserv and how could you use it to get information?

22. Explain how instant messaging works.

23. Compare and contrast the application architecture for videoconferencing with the architecture for e-mail.

24. Which of the three application architectures for e-mail (two-tier client-server, Web-based, and host-based) is "best"? Explain.

25. Some experts argue that thin-client client–server architectures are really host-based architectures in disguise and suffer from the same old problems. Do you agree? Explain.

26. You can use a Web browser to access an FTP server simply by putting ftp:// in front of the URL (e.g., ftp://xyz.abc.com). If that server has FTP server software installed, then the FTP server will respond instead of the Web server. What is your browser doing differently to access the FTP server? (*Hint:* This question is more difficult than it seems, because we haven't explained how the server knows to pass certain types of packets to the right software, i.e., HTTP requests to the Web server software and SMTP packets to the e-mail software). At this point, don't worry about it. Linking the network to the application layer is the job of the transport layer, which is explained in Chapter 3.

27. Will the Internet become an essential business tool like the telephone or will it go the way of the dinosaurs? Discuss.

EXERCISES

2-1. Investigate the use of the three major architectures by a local organization (e.g., your university). Which architecture(s) is used most often and what do they see their organization doing in the future? Why?

2-2. What are the costs of client–server versus host-based architectures? Search the Web for at least two different studies and be sure to report your sources. What are the likely reasons for the differences between the two?

2-3. Investigate the costs of dumb terminals, intelligent terminals, network computers, minimally equipped microcomputers, and top-of-the-line microcomputers. Many equipment manufacturers and resellers are on the Web, so it's a good place to start looking.

2-4. What application architecture does your university use for e-mail? Explain.

MINI-CASES

I. Deals-R-Us Brokers (Part 1)

Fred Jones, a distant relative of yours and president of Deals-R-Us Brokers (DRUB), has come to you for advice. DRUB is small brokerage house that enables its clients to buy and sell stocks over the Internet, as well as place traditional orders by phone or fax. DRUB has just decided to offer a set of stock analysis tools that will help its clients more easily pick winning stocks, or so Fred tells you. Fred's information systems department has presented him with two alternatives for developing the new tools. The first alternative will have a special tool developed in C++ that clients will download onto their computers to run. The tool will communicate with the DRUB server to select data to analyze. The second alternative will have the C++ program running on the server; the client will use his or her Web browser to interact with the software on the server.

    a. Classify the two alternatives in terms of what type of application architecture they use.

    b. Outline the pros and cons of the two alternatives and make a recommendation to Fred about which is better.

II. Deals-R-Us Brokers (Part 2)

Fred Jones, a distant relative of yours and president of Deals-R-Us Brokers (DRUB), has come to you for advice. DRUB is small brokerage house that enables its clients to buy and sell stocks over the Internet, as well as place traditional orders by phone or fax. DRUB has just decided to put in a new e-mail package. One vendor is offering an SMTP-based two-tier client–server architecture. The second vendor is offering a Web-based e-mail architecture. Fred doesn't understand either one, but thinks the Web-based one should be better because, in his words, "the Web is the future."

    a. *Briefly* explain to Fred, in layman's terms, the differences between the two.
    b. Outline the pros and cons of the two alternatives and make a recommendation to Fred about which is better.

III. Tools N' Technologies

Janet McNeal is the chief software architect for Tools N' Technologies (TNT), a small software development firm that specializes in software tools for the hotel and motel industry. TNT has developed several traditional Visual Basic programs and some newer tools that run over the Web just by using a browser. She has been disappointed with the quality of the software TNT can develop because many of the things one can do in a traditional program can't be done on the Web. For example, it is simple to click on an item and drag and drop it in a new location in Windows or on an Apple, but this is impossible on the Web. Newer tools and approaches such as Java and Microsoft's .Net offer the potential to change this.

    a. Classify application architecture of software built using Java on the client.
    b. Outline the pros and cons of Java-based client software.

CHAPTER 3

INTERNETWORK LAYERS

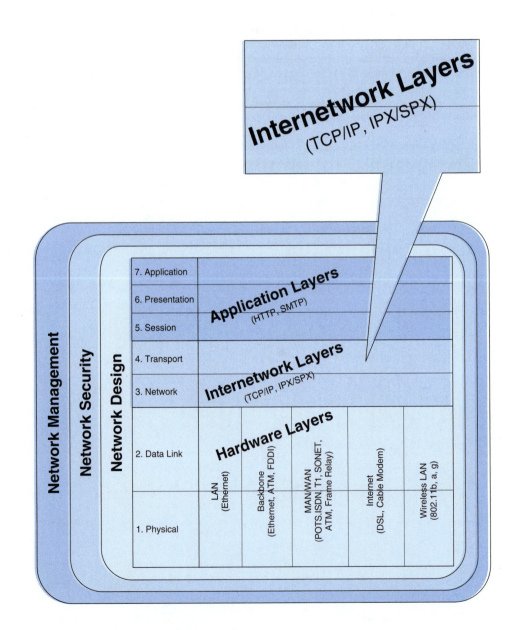

THE INTERNETWORK layers connect the application software in the application layers with the hardware layers that actually move messages from one computer to another. The two internetwork layers (the network layer and transport layer) together are responsible for moving messages from end to end in a network. The transport layer (layer 4) performs four functions: establishing end-to-end connections (including linking the application layer to the network), addressing (finding the address of the ultimate destination computer), segmenting (breaking long messages into smaller packets for transmission) and reliable delivery (ensuring all messages that are transmitted are received). The network layer (layer 3) performs two functions: routing (determining the next computer to which the message should be sent to reach the final destination) and addressing (finding the address of that next computer). There are several standard transport and network layer protocols that specify how packets are to be organized, in the same way that there are standards for application layer packets. In this chapter, we look at four major protocols: TCP/IP, IPX/SPX, X.25, and SNA. TCP/IP, the protocol used on the Internet is the most important, so this chapter takes a detailed look at how it works.

OBJECTIVES

- Be aware of four transport/network layer protocols
- Be familiar with segmenting and linking to the application layer
- Be familiar with reliable delivery
- Be familiar with addressing
- Be familiar with routing
- Understand how TCP/IP works

CHAPTER OUTLINE

INTRODUCTION

INTERNETWORK PROTOCOLS

    Transmission Control Protocol/Internet Protocol (TCP/IP)

    Internetwork Packet Exchange/Sequenced Packet Exchange (IPX/SPX)

    X.25

    Systems Network Architecture (SNA)

TRANSPORT LAYER FUNCTIONS

    Linking to the Application Layer

    Segmenting

    Reliable Delivery

INTRODUCTION

The internetwork layers (layer 4, transport layer, and layer 3, network layer) connect the application software in the application layers with the hardware layers that actually move messages from one computer to another. There are several different protocols that can be used in the internetwork layers, in the same way there are several different application layer protocols. TCP/IP is the most commonly used set of protocols and is well on its way to eliminating the other protocols. Therefore, this chapter focuses almost exclusively on TCP/IP.

The transport layer, layer 4 and the layer closest to the application layers, links the application software in the application layer with the network and is responsible for the end-to-end delivery of the message. The transport layer accepts outgoing messages from the application layer (e.g., HTTP, SMTP, and so on as described in Chapter 2) and segments and addresses them for transmission. The network layer (layer 3) takes the messages from the transport layer and routes them through the network by selecting the best path from computer to computer through the network (and also does addressing when needed). The network layer relies on the hardware layers to actually move the messages from computer to computer. In most cases, when the hardware layers detect an error in a message, they discard the message; that is, they throw it away and make no attempt to fix the error. The transport layer is therefore responsible for making sure that all messages that are sent are actually received at the destination. This is called providing a *reliable delivery service.* As we saw in Chapter 1, each layer in the network has its own set of protocols that are used to hold the data generated by higher layers, much like a set of Russian dolls; see Figure 3-1.

The network and transport layers also accept incoming messages from the hardware layers and organize them into coherent messages that are passed to the application layer. For example, a large e-mail message might require several data link layer packets to transmit.

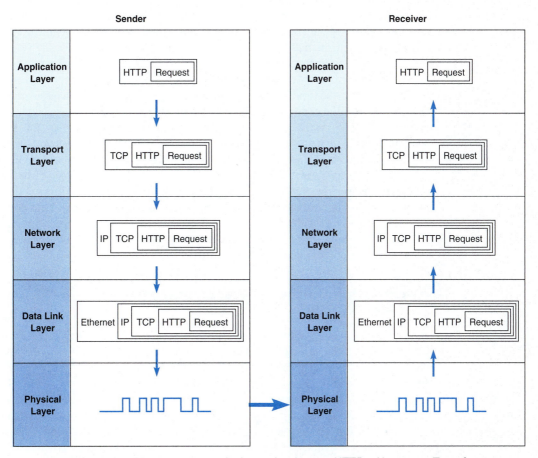

FIGURE 3-1   Message transmission using layers. HTTP = Hypertext Transfer Protocol; IP = Internet Protocol; TCP = Transmission Control Protocol.

The transport layer at the sender would break the message into several smaller packets and give them to the network layer to route, which in turns gives them to the data link layer to transmit. The network layer at the receiver would receive the individual packets from the data link layer, process them, and pass them to the transport layer, which would reassemble them into the one e-mail message before giving it to the application layer.

In this chapter, we provide a brief look at four sets of transport and network layer protocols, before turning our attention to how TCP/IP works.

INTERNETWORK PROTOCOLS

There are many different transport/network layer protocols. Each protocol performs essentially the same functions, but each is incompatible with others unless there is software to translate between them. Many vendors have software with *multiprotocol stacks,* which means that the software supports several different transport/network protocols. The software recognizes which protocol an incoming message uses and automatically uses that protocol to process the message.

Some transport/network layer protocols (e.g., TCP/IP, IPX/SPX) are compatible with a variety of different hardware layer protocols (e.g., Ethernet, frame relay) and can be used interchangeably in the same network. In other cases, network layer protocols are tightly coupled with data link layer protocols and applications and cannot easily be used with other protocols (e.g., X.25, SNA). These differences reflect the philosophy of the protocol's developers. SNA, for example, was originally developed as a complete networking architecture, designed to provide an end-to-end solution for IBM customers using entirely IBM or IBM-compatible hardware and software. TCP/IP, in contrast, was designed to be used by a variety of organizations, each of which might be using very different hardware and software, and therefore had to combine easily with many different types of data link layer protocols.

This section provides an overview of the four major network protocols: TCP/IP, IPX/SPX, X.25, and SNA. TCP/IP is the dominant protocol and many organizations are trying to eliminate all protocols except TCP/IP.

Transmission Control Protocol/Internet Protocol (TCP/IP)

The *Transmission Control Protocol/Internet Protocol (TCP/IP)* was developed for the U.S. Department of Defense's Advanced Research Project Agency NETwork (ARPANET) by Vinton Cerf and Bob Kahn in 1974. TCP/IP is the transport/network layer protocol used on the Internet. It is also the world's most popular network layer protocol, used by almost 70 percent of all backbone, metropolitan, and wide area networks. In 1998, TCP/IP moved past IPX/SPX as the most common protocol used on LANs.

TCP/IP allows reasonably efficient and error-free transmission. Because it performs error checking, it can send large files across sometimes unreliable networks with great assurance that the data will arrive uncorrupted. TCP/IP is compatible with a variety of data link protocols, which is one reason for its popularity.

As the name implies, TCP/IP has two parts. TCP is the transport layer protocol that links the application layer to the network layer. It performs segmenting: breaking the messages it receives from the application layers into smaller segments (or packets, if you prefer to call them that), numbering them, ensuring each segment is reliably delivered, and putting them back together into one message at the destination. IP is the network layer protocol and performs addressing and routing. IP software is used at each of the intervening computers through which the message passes; it is IP that routes the message to the final destination. The TCP software only needs to be active at the sender and the receiver, because TCP is involved only when data comes from or goes to the application layers.

A typical TCP segment has a 192-*bit* header (24 bytes) This header is composed of many different fields that provide information about the packet. The source and destination ports are used to link the application to the network, while the ACK and checksum are used to ensure reliable delivery. We will discuss these fields in more detail later in the chapter (see Figure 3-2).

IP is the network layer protocol. Two forms of IP are currently in use. The older form is IP version 4 (IPv4), which usually has a 160-*bit* header (20 bytes) although the actual

Source port	Destination port	Sequence number	ACK number	Header length	Unused	Flags	Flow control	Checksum	Urgent pointer	Options	User data
16 bits	16 bits	32 bits	32 bits	4 bits	6 bits	6 bits	16 bits	16 bits	16 bits	32 bits	Varies

FIGURE 3-2   Transmission Control Protocol (TCP) packet. ACK = acknowledgment; CRC = cyclical redundancy check.

Version number	Header length	Type of service	Total length	Indentifiers	Flags	Packet offset	Hop limit	Protocol	Checksum	Source address	Destination address	Options	User data
4 bits	4 bits	8 bits	16 bits	16 bits	3 bits	13 bits	8 bits	8 bits	16 bits	32 bits	32 bits	0–320 bits	Varies

FIGURE 3-3   Internet Protocol (IP) packet (version 4). CRC = cyclical redundancy check.

Version number	Priority	Flow name	Total length	Next header	Hop limit	Source address	Destination address	User data
4 bits	4 bits	24 bits	16 bits	8 bits	8 bits	128 bits	128 bits	Varies

FIGURE 3-4   Internet Protocol (IP) packet (version 6).

length depends on the length of the seldom used options field (see Figure 3-3). This header contains source and destination addresses, packet length, and packet number. IPv4 is being replaced by IPv6, which has a 320-*bit* header (40 bytes) (see Figure 3-4). The primary reason for the increase in size is an increase in the address from 32 bits to 128 bits. Simply put, the dramatic growth in the usage of the Internet meant that unless the addressing format was changed, we would have run out of addresses by the turn of the century. IPv6's simpler packet structure makes it easier to perform routing and supports a variety of new approaches to addressing and routing. The changes included in IPv6 also suggested ways to improve TCP, so a new version of TCP is currently under development.

The size of the message field depends on the data link layer protocol used. TCP/IP is commonly combined with Ethernet. Ethernet usually has a maximum frame size of about 1,500 bytes, so the maximum size of a TCP message field is slightly smaller because the both the TCP segment and the IP packet add additional overhead bytes.

Internetwork Packet Exchange/Sequenced Packet Exchange (IPX/SPX)

Internetwork Packet Exchange/Sequenced Packet Exchange (IPX/SPX) is based on a routing protocol developed by Xerox in the 1970s. IPX/SPX is primarily used by Novell Netware. Novell has replaced IPX/SPX with TCP/IP as its default protocol, but some organizations still use IPX/SPX.

As the name implies, IPX/SPX has two parts. IPX/SPX is similar to TCP/IP in concept, but different in structure. SPX is the transport layer protocol and performs the same segmenting functions of TCP: breaking the application message into smaller segments, numbering them, ensuring each segment is reliably delivered, and putting them in the proper order at the destination. IPX is the network layer protocol and performs the same routing and addressing functions as IP.

X.25

X.25 is a standard developed by ITU-T for use in wide area networks. It is a mature, global standard used by many international organizations. It is seldom used in North America, except by organizations with WANs that have extensive non-North-American sections. X.25 also has two parts. X.3 is the transport layer protocol and performs the segmenting functions of TCP. Packet layer protocol (PLP) is the network layer protocol and performs the routing and addressing functions similar to IP. PLP is typically combined with LAP-B at the data link layer. ITU-T recommends that packets contain 128 bytes of application data, but can support packets containing up to 1,024 bytes.

Systems Network Architecture (SNA)

Systems Network Architecture (SNA) is an approach to networking developed by IBM in 1974. SNA is used only on IBM and compatible mainframes. The major problem with SNA is that it uses proprietary nonstandard protocols, which makes it difficult to integrate SNA networks with other networks that use industry standard protocols. Routing messages between SNA networks and other networks, and even between IBM SNA networks and IBM LANs (which use industry standard protocols), requires special equipment. Most experts expect that SNA will disappear in time, either because current SNA users will switch to other products that use TCP/IP, or because IBM will replace SNA protocols with TCP/IP.

TRANSPORT LAYER FUNCTIONS

The transport layer links the application software in the application layer with the network and is responsible for the end-to-end delivery of the message. One of the first issues facing the application layer is to find the numeric network address of the destination computer. Different protocols use different methods to find this address. Depending on the protocol—and which expert you ask—finding the destination address can be classified as a transport layer function, a network layer function, or a data link layer function, or is a responsibility of the application layer with help from the operating system. In this book, we classify it as a transport layer function, but in all honesty, understanding how it works is more important than memorizing how we classify it. The next section will discuss addressing at the network layer and transport layer together. In this section, we focus on the three unique functions performed by the transport layer: linking the application layer to the network, segmenting, and providing reliable delivery.

Linking to the Application Layer

Most computers have many application layer software packages running at the same time. Users often have Web browsers, e-mail programs, word processors, and so on in use at the same time on their client computers. Likewise, many servers act as Web servers, mail servers, FTP servers, and so on. When the transport layer receives an incoming message, the transport layer must decide to which application program it should be delivered. It makes no sense to send a Web page request to e-mail server software.

With TCP/IP, each application layer software package has a unique *port address.* Any message sent to a computer must tell TCP (the transport layer software) the application layer port address that is to receive the message. Therefore, when an application layer program generates an outgoing message, it tells the TCP software its own port address (i.e., the *source port address*) and the port address at the destination computer (i.e., the *destination port address*). These two port addresses are placed in the first two fields in the TCP segment (see Figure 3-2).

Port addresses can be any 16-bit (two byte) number. So how does a client computer sending a Web request to a Web server know what port address to use for the Web server? Simple: On the Internet, all port addresses for popular services such as the Web, e-mail, FTP, and so on have been standardized. Anyone using a Web server should set up the Web server with a port address of 80. Web browsers therefore automatically generate a port address of 80 for any Web page you click on. FTP servers use port 21, Telnet 23, SMTP 25, and so on. Network managers are free to use whatever port addresses they want, but if they use a nonstandard port number, then the application layer software on the client must specify the correct port number.[1]

Segmenting

Some messages or blocks of application data are small enough that they can be transmitted in one frame at the data link layer. However, in other cases, the data in one application message (e.g., a large graphics file) is too large to be sent in one data link layer frame and must be broken into several parts. As far as the application layer is concerned, the message should be transmitted and received as one large block of data. However, the hardware layers can only transmit messages of certain lengths. It is therefore up to the sender's transport layer to break the data into several smaller segments that can be sent by the data link layer across the circuit. At the other end, the receiver's transport layer must receive all these separate segments and recombine them into one large message for the application layer.

Segmenting means to take one outgoing message from the application layers and break it into a set of smaller segments for transmission through the network. It also means to take the incoming set of smaller segments from the network layer and reassemble them into one message for the application layer. Depending on what the application layer software chooses, the incoming segments can either be delivered one at a time or held until all segments have arrived and the message is compete. Web browsers, for example, usually request delivery of segments as they arrive, which is why your screen gradually builds a piece at a time. Most e-mail software, on the other hand, usually requests that messages be delivered only after all segments have arrived and TCP has organized them into one intact message, which is why you usually don't see email messages building screen by screen.

---

[1] One way to make a Web server private would be to use a different port number (e.g., 8080). Any Web browser wanting to access this Web server would then have to explicitly include the port number in the URL. For example: www.abc.com:8080.

Packet Sizes One of the challenges at the transport layer is deciding how big to make the packets (or segments, packets, and frames, to be more precise), because packet size affects the efficiency of network transmission and how much data can be transmitted through a given network circuit. Each communication protocol has both information bytes and overhead bytes. *Information* bytes are those used to convey the user's meaning (e.g., the URL of the Web page you request). *Overhead* bytes are the control bytes used for purposes such as identifying packet numbers, error control, and marking the start and end of characters and packets. TCP, for example, has 20 bytes of overhead in each packet, while IPv6 has 40 bytes.

Transmission efficiency is defined as the total number of information bytes (i.e., bytes in the message sent by the user) divided by the total bytes in transmission (i.e., information bytes plus overhead bytes). Each of the packets we use in transmitting a message increases the number of overhead bytes. Suppose, for example, you want to access the Web page for Indiana University and you use your Web browser to enter the URL (www.indiana.edu). The total number of information bytes is 15, one for each character in the URL (see Figure 3-5). The URL is surrounded by an HTTP request that varies in length depending on the optional information the browser supplies (let's assume it is 100 bytes, all of which are considered overhead). The HTTP request is in turn surrounded by a TCP segment (which we know has 24 bytes of overhead from Figure 3-2) and an IPv6 segment (40 bytes of overhead). We know that these packets in turn will be surrounded by a frame at the data link layer. For the moment, let's assume this is an Ethernet frame, which we will see in Chapter 4 has a length of 33 bytes. This gives a transmission efficiency of 15/212 or about 7 percent (see Figure 3-5).

This is not very efficient. This means that of every 100 bytes transmitted, about 7 of them are used to transport the user's message and about 93 are wasted on overhead. Or, if you have a modem running at 56 Kbps, your Web browser is really only getting 7 percent of that (4 Kbps), with the rest wasted in overhead.[2] Simply put, the Internet is not designed

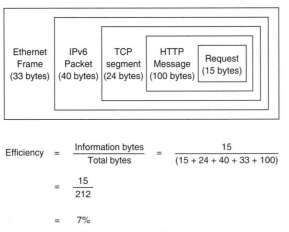

$$\text{Efficiency} = \frac{\text{Information bytes}}{\text{Total bytes}} = \frac{15}{(15 + 24 + 40 + 33 + 100)}$$

$$= \frac{15}{212}$$

$$= 7\%$$

FIGURE 3-5 Transmission efficiency calculations.

[2] As you will see in later chapters, we seldom use Ethernet as the data link layer protocol for modems, but the protocol we do use (PPP) is not much more efficient.

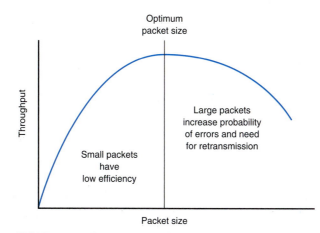

FIGURE 3-6 Packet size effects on throughput.

to transfer very short messages such as HTTP requests. Instead, it is designed to transfer longer messages such as HTML and graphics files.

We can improve efficiency by increasing the size of the packets we send. Suppose, for example, we have a 100 K file that we want to transmit in response to a HTTP request. We could transmit it in one packet. In this case, we weuld have 100,000 bytes of information and 100,212 total bytes including the overhead, giving an efficiency of about 99.8 percent.

However, there is a problem in using really large packets. Although efficiency is better, any time a packet is received containing an error, the entire packet must be retransmitted. Thus, if an entire file were sent as one large packet (e.g., 100 K), and 1 bit was received in error, the entire 100 K packet would have to be sent again. Clearly this is a waste of capacity. Furthermore, the probability that a packet contains an error increases with the size of the packet; larger packets are more likely to contain errors than smaller ones, simply due to the laws of probability.

Thus in designing a protocol, there is a trade-off between large and small packets. Small packets are less efficient, but are less likely to contain errors and cost less (in terms of circuit capacity) to retransmit if there is an error. See Figure 3-6.

Throughput is the total number of information bits received per second, after taking into account the overhead bits and the need to retransmit packets containing errors. Generally speaking, small packets provide better throughput for circuits with more errors, while larger packets provide better throughput in less error-prone networks. Fortunately, in most real networks, the curve shown in Figure 3-6 is very flat on top, meaning that there is a range of packet sizes that provides almost optimum performance. Packet sizes vary greatly among different networks, but most packet sizes tend to be from 2,000 to 9,000 bytes.

When the transport layer software is set up, it is told the maximum segment size (called *maximum transport unit* or MTU). If the MTU is not specified, TCP uses the default size of 536, which was selected back in the early days of the Internet when networks were more error prone than they are today. In any case, the TCP software running on the sender has no idea what size is best for the destination. Therefore, the transport layer at the sender usually negotiates with the transport layer at the receiver to settle on the best segment size to use. This negotiation is done by establishing a *TCP connection* between the sender and receiver.

Connection-Oriented Routing *Connection-oriented routing* sets up a *TCP connection* (also called a *virtual circuit*) between the sender and receiver. A virtual circuit is one that *appears* to the application software to use a direct cable between the two computers, even though it actually does not. In this case, the transport layer software sends a special packet (called a SYN) to the receiver's TCP/IP software requesting that a connection be established. The receiver either accepts or rejects the connection and together they settle on the segment sizes the connection will use.

Once the connection is established, the packets flow between the sender and receiver following the same route through the network (routing is discussed in a later section in this chapter). All packets in the same message arrive at the destination in the same order in which they were sent, so putting the packets back together again in the right order is simple.

When the transmission is complete, the sender sends a special packet (called a FIN) to close the connection. Once the sender and receiver agree, the circuit is closed and all record of it is deleted.

Connectionless Routing *Connectionless routing* is an alternative type of routing in which each packet is treated separately and makes its own way through the network. Unlike connection-oriented routing, no connection is established. The sender simply sends the packet(s) as separate unrelated entities, and it is possible that different packets will take different routes through the network depending on the type of routing used and the amount of traffic. Because packets following different routes may travel at different speeds, they may arrive out of sequence at their destination. The sender's transport layer therefore puts a sequence number on each packet (or segment, to be more precise), in addition to information about the message stream to which the packet belongs. The network layer must reassemble them in the correct order before passing the message to the application layer.

TCP/IP can operate either as connection-oriented or connectionless. When connection-oriented routing is desired, both TCP and IP are used. TCP establishes the virtual circuit with the destination and informs IP to route all messages along this virtual circuit. When connectionless routing is desired, the TCP segment is replaced with a User Datagram Protocol (UDP) segment. The UDP segment has less overhead than the TCP segment (only 8 bytes of overhead) because it contains only the source port, destination port, message length, and error control.

Connectionless routing is most commonly used when the application data or message can fit into one single segment. One might expect, for example, that because HTTP requests are often very short, that they might use UDP connectionless routing rather than TCP connection-oriented routing. However, HTTP always uses TCP. All of the application layer software we have discussed so far uses TCP (HTTP, SMTP, FTP, Telnet). UDP is most commonly used for control messages such as addressing (DHCP, discussed later in this chapter), routing control messages (RIP, discussed later in this chapter), and network management (SNMP, discussed in Chapter 9).

Quality of Service *Quality of service (QoS)* routing is a special type of connection-oriented routing in which different connections are assigned different priorities. For example, videoconferencing requires fast delivery of packets to ensure that the images and voices appear smooth and continuous; they are very time dependent, because delays in routing will seriously affect the quality of the service provided. E-mail packets, on the other hand, have no such requirements. While everyone would like to receive e-mail as fast as possible, a 10-second delay in transmitting an e-mail message will not have the same consequences as a 10-second delay in a videoconferencing packet.

With QoS routing, different *classes of service* are defined, each with different priorities. For example, a packet of a videoconferencing image would likely get higher priority than an SMTP packet with an e-mail message and thus be routed first. When the transport layer software attempts to establish a connection (i.e., a virtual circuit), it specifies the class of service that connection requires. Each path through the network is designed to support a different number and mix of service classes. When a connection is established, the network ensures that no connections are established that exceed the maximum number of circuits of that class on a given circuit.

QoS routing is common in certain types of networks (e.g., ATM, as discussed in Chapter 5). The Internet provides several QoS protocols that can work in a TCP/IP environment. Resource Reservation Protocol (RSVP) and Real-Time Streaming Protocol (RTSP) both permit application layer software to request connections that have certain minimum data transfer capabilities. As one might expect, RTSP is geared toward audio/video streaming applications, while RSVP is more general purpose.

RSVP and RTSP are used to create a connection (or virtual circuit) and request a certain minimum guaranteed data rate. Once the connection has been established, they use Real-Time Transport Protocol (RTP) to send packets across the connection. RTP contains information about the sending application, a packet sequence number, and a time stamp so that the data in the RTP packet can be synchronized with other RTP packets by the application layer software if needed.

With a name like Real-Time *Transport* Protocol, one would expect RTP to replace TCP and UDP at the transport layer. It does not. Instead, RTP is combined with UDP (if you read the previous paragraph carefully, you noticed that RTP does not provide source and destination port addresses). This means that each real-time packet is first created using RTP and then surrounded by a UDP packet, before being handed to the IP software at the network layer.

Reliable Delivery

One of the functions of the transport layer is ensuring that there is a reliable delivery of messages from the sender to the receiver; that is, ensuring that all the packets that the application layers have given to the transport layer to send have been received successfully at the final destination. As we discussed earlier, the hardware layers are responsible for detecting errors and making sure that no packets containing errors are delivered. In most cases, they simply discard packets that contain errors. It is therefore the responsibility of the transport layer to provide reliable delivery services.

In most cases, when an error occurs, it is detected by the hardware layers and the packets or frames containing the errors are thrown away and never reach the transport layer at the destination. In the early days of the Internet, not all hardware layers provided good error detection, so the ability to detect errors was built into TCP. Most error detection procedures work by having the sender perform a mathematical calculation on the outgoing message and including the result in a special field in the packet attached to the message. The receiver performs the same mathematical calculations on the message it receives and matches its results against the error detection data that were transmitted with the message. If the two match, the message is assumed to be correct. If they don't match, then an error has occurred.

Checksum Error Detection. TCP uses a *checksum* as its error detection system. The entire TCP segment is broken into 16-bit parts and the parts are added together using ones-complement arithmetic. The checksum is then the ones-complement of this sum, which is included in the checksum field of the TCP segment. Since we do not know the value of the checksum field before we do the calculations, it is presumed to be all zeros for the calculations. When TCP receives an incoming segment, it performs the same arithmetic (using all zeros for the checksum field rather than its true value) and then compares the checksum it calculated to the checksum in the checksum field. If the two are the same, then no errors are assumed to have occurred. If they are different, then an error has occurred and the incoming packet is discarded just as should have happened at the hardware layers.

Any time errors occur, segments are lost. TCP must therefore have a way to keep track of what segments have been successfully received at the destination and what segments have been thrown away due to errors. TCP does this by requiring the receiver to *acknowledge* all messages it receives.

Stop-and-Wait Error Correction. With a simple *stop-and-wait* acknowledgment system, the sender sends one segment and then stops and waits for the receiver send an acknowledgment (called an *ACK*) before sending the next segment. Once the receiver, receives the segment – assuming that the segment was not discarded due to errors – the receiver sends an ACK back to the sender, indicating that it received the segment without errors. Because it takes a few milliseconds for the segment to travel from the sender to the receiver and for the ACK to travel back to the sender (or perhaps longer if the sender and receiver are far apart), it may take several seconds for an entire message to be sent.

Figure 3-7 shows how a stop-and-wait acknowledgment system would send three segments and receive three acknowledgments. Each segment is numbered (using the

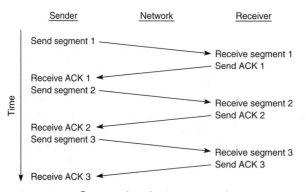

FIGURE 3-7 Stop-and-wait error control.

sequence number field in the TCP segment) so that the receiver can make sure that the segments are assembled in the proper order and to make sure that no segments have been lost. When TCP sends an ACK, the ACK includes the sequence number so that the sender is completely sure of what data has been successfully sent.

Sometimes, an error will occur. If this happens, either at the hardware layer in any of the computers or devices between the sender and receiver or at the receiver itself, the segment with the error will be discarded. Therefore, it will not be acknowledged. The sender will continue to wait until it receives an ACK that will never come, because the receiver has not received the segment. TCP therefore waits for the ACK only for a set number of milliseconds after each transmission before it assumes the message was lost or discarded. After the sender waits for this length of time, and no ACK has been received, a *timeout* occurs, and TCP retransmits the segment.

Selecting the best length of time to wait before a timeout can be challenging. Setting it too long, means that the sender is wasting time waiting. Setting it too short means that the sender wastes transmission capacity in the network by sending duplicate messages (the sender can identify duplicate messages from TCP sequence number). Every time TCP opens a new connection, it begins calculating the average and standard deviation for the time it takes between sending a segment and when the ACK is received. Every time it sends a segment and receives an ACK, the average roundtrip time and standard deviation for that connection is updated. The timeout is usually set at between 2 and 4 standard deviations longer than the average roundtrip time.

Sliding Window Error Correction.
The simple stop-and-wait acknowledgment system can take a long time to send a message because the sender stops and waits for an ACK after each segment before sending the next. Modern TCP therefore uses a technique called *sliding window,* in which the sender does not wait for an ACK after sending each segment; instead it just sends the next segment. See Figure 3-8. In this case several segments are sent before any acknowledgments are received. By comparing Figure 3-7 to Figure 3-8, you can see that sliding window takes less time to send segments than does stop-and-wait.

All segments are numbered so that the receiver can put the segments in the correct order. If an error occurs and a segment is discarded, the receiver detects this by seeing that

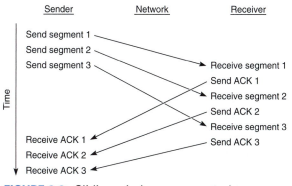

FIGURE 3-8 Sliding window error control.

a segment with an expected sequence number has not been received. When this happens, the receiver stops sending ACKs (even for those segments successfully received) and waits for the lost segment to be transmitted again. The sender continues to send segments, but eventually will timeout on the lost segment and retransmit it. Once the receiver receives the missing segment, it sends an ACK for this segment as well as all segments it has received with higher sequence numbers. Depending upon the transmission time required, the sender may have timed out on other segments and have started to retransmit those unnecessarily; once the ACKs are received it will resume sending where it left off prior to the timeout.

One issue in using sliding window is deciding how many segments should be sent before an ACK is received. That is, how many unacknowledged segments should be in transit at one time before the sender stops and waits for an ACK. If too many segments are sent too quickly, then it is possible that the receiving computer could be overwhelmed. For example, if a client computer was uploading a file to a server and sent too many segments too quickly, the server might run out of memory before writing the file to disk.

Flow control means ensuring that the computer sending the message is not transmitting too quickly for the receiver. When a TCP connection is first opened, the sender and receiver agree on the maximum number of unacknowledged TCP segments than can be in transit. The sender sends segments as quickly as it can, but once it reaches this maximum number, it stops transmitting segments until it receives an ACK. When it receives an ACK for a segment, it can send another segment. By using ACKs in this way, the receiver can control the rate at which it receives information. With sliding window, the receiver does not send an ACK until it is ready to receive more segments.

This ability to control the flow of information and the visual imagery it triggered was how sliding window got its name. Visualize the sender having a set of segments to send in memory stacked in order from first to last. Now imagine, a "window" that moves through the stack from first to last. As a segment is sent, the window expands to cover it, meaning that the sender is waiting for an ACK for the segment. Suppose we have a window size of 8 segments (see Figure 3-9a) which means we can send at most eight segments before we have to stop and wait for an ACK. Once we receive an ACK, the window moves forward dropping the first sent segment out of the window, indicating that it has been sent and received successfully (see Figure 3-9b).

a) Eight segments have been sent and are awaiting acknowledgment

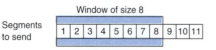

b) An acknowledgment of segment 1 is received, so segment 9 is
   transmitted and the window slides

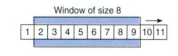

FIGURE 3-9 Sliding window.

ADDRESSING

Before you can send a message, you must know the destination address. It is extremely important to understand that each computer has several addresses, each used by a different layer. One address is used by the data link layer, another by the network layer, and still another by the application layer.

When the users work with application software, they typically use the application layer address. For example, in Chapter 2, we discussed application software that used Internet addresses (e.g., www.indiana.edu). This is an *application layer address* (or a *server name*). When a user types an Internet address into a Web browser, it must first be translated into a network layer address. See Figure 3-10.

The network layer software uses a *network layer address.* The network layer protocol used on the Internet is IP, so this Web address (www.indiana.edu) is translated into an IP address that is 4 bytes long when using IPv4 (e.g., 129.79.127.4); see Figure 3-10. This process is similar to using a phone book to go from someone's name to his or her phone number.[3]

The network layer then determines the best route through the network to the final destination. Based on this routing, the network layer identifies the *data link layer address* of the next computer to which the message should be sent. If the data link layer is running Ethernet, then the network layer IP address would be translated into an Ethernet address. Chapter 4 shows that Ethernet addresses are 6 bytes in length, so a possible address might be 00-0F-00-8114-00 (Ethernet addresses are usually expressed in hexadecimal); see Figure 3-10.

Assigning Addresses

In general, the data link layer address is permanently encoded hardware and can never be changed. Hardware manufacturers have an agreement that assigns each manufacturer a unique set of permitted addresses, so even if you buy hardware from different companies, they will never have the same address. Whenever you install a network card into a computer, it immediately has its own data link layer address that uniquely distinguishes it from every other computer in the world.

Network layer addresses are generally assigned by software. Network layer software packages often have a configuration file that specifies the network layer address for that

Address	Example Software	Example Address
Application layer	Web browser	www.kelley.indiana.edu
Network layer	Internet protocol	129.79.127.4
Data link layer	Ethernet	00-0C-00-F5-03-5A

FIGURE 3-10   Types of addresses.

---

[3] If you ever want to find out the IP address of any computer, simply enter the command *ping* followed by the application layer name of the computer at the DOS prompt (e.g., ping www.indiana.edu).

computer. Network managers can assign any network layer addresses they want. It is important to ensure that every computer on the same network has a unique network layer address, so every network has a standards group that defines what network layer addresses can be used by each organization.

Application layer addresses (or server names) are also assigned by a software configuration file. Virtually all servers have an application layer address, but most client computers do not. This is because it is important for users to easily access servers and the information they contain, but there is usually little need for someone to access someone else's client computer. As with network layer addresses, network managers can assign any application layer address they want, but a network standards group must approve application layer addresses to ensure that no two computers have the same application layer address. Network layer addresses and application layer addresses go hand in hand, so the same standards group usually assigns both (e.g., www.indiana.edu at the application layer means 129.79.78.4 at the network layer). It is possible to have several application layer addresses for the same computer. For example, one of the Web servers in the Kelley School of Business at Indiana University is called both www.kelley.indiana.edu and pacioli.kelley.indiana.edu.

Internet Addresses   No one is permitted to connect a computer to the Internet unless they use approved network and application layer addresses. *ICANN (Internet Corporation for Assigned Names and Numbers)* is responsible for managing the assignment of network layer addresses (i.e., IP addresses) and application layer addresses (e.g., www.indiana.edu). ICANN sets the rules by which new *domain names* (e.g., .com, .org, .ca, .uk) are created and IP address numbers assigned to users. ICANN also directly manages a set of Internet domains (e.g., .com, .org, .net) and authorizes private companies to become *domain name registrars* for those domains. Once authorized, a registrar can approve requests for application layer addresses and assign IP numbers for those requests. This means that individuals and organizations wishing to register an Internet name can use any authorized registrar for the domain they choose, and different registrars are permitted to charge different fees for their registration services. Many registrars are authorized to issue names and addresses in the ICANN-managed domains, as well as domains in other countries (e.g., .ca, .uk, .au).

Several application layer addresses and network layer addresses can be assigned at the same time. IP addresses are often assigned in groups, so that one organization receives a set of numerically similar addresses for use on its computers. For example, Indiana University has been assigned the set of application layer addresses that end in .indiana.edu and .iu.edu and the set of IP addresses in the 129.79.x.x range (i.e., all IP addresses that start with the numbers 129.79).

One of the problems with the current address system is that the Internet is quickly running out of addresses. While the 4-byte address of IPv4 provides more than 1 billion possible addresses, the fact that they are assigned in sets significantly limits the number of usable addresses. For example, the address range owned by Indiana University includes about 65,000 addresses, but we will probably not use all of them.

The IP address shortage was one of the reasons behind the development of IPv6 discussed previously. IPv6 has 16-byte addresses, meaning there are in theory about 3.2×10^{38} possible addresses—more than we can dream about. Once IPv6 is in wide use, the current Internet address system will be replaced by a new system based on 16-byte addresses. Most experts expect that all the current 4-byte addresses will simply be assigned an arbitrary 12-byte prefix (e.g., all zeros) so that the holders of the current addresses can continue to use them.

Subnets Each organization must assign the IP addresses it has received to specific computers on its networks. In general, IP addresses are assigned so that all computers on the same local area network have similar addresses. For example, suppose an organization has just received a set of addresses starting with 128.192.x.x. It is customary to assign all the computers in the same LAN numbers that start with the same first three digits, so the Business School LAN might be assigned 128.192.56.x, which means all the computers in that LAN would have IP numbers starting with those numbers (e.g., 128.192.56.4, 128,192.56.5, and so on); see Figure 3.11. The Computer Science LAN might be assigned 128.192.55.x, and likewise, all the other LANs at the university and the backbone network that connects them would have a different set of numbers. Each of these LANs is called a TCP/IP *subnet* because they are logically grouped together by IP number.

While it is customary to use the first 3 bytes of the IP address to indicate different subnets, it is not required. Any portion of the IP address can be designated as a subnet by using a *subnet mask*. Every computer in a TCP/IP network is given a subnet mask to enable it to determine which computers are on the same subnet (i.e., LAN) as it is, and which computers are outside of its subnet. Knowing whether a computer is on your subnet or not is very important for message routing, as we shall see later in this chapter.

For example, a network could be configured so that the first 2 bytes indicated a subnet (e.g., 128.184.x.x), so all computers would be given a subnet mask giving the first 2 bytes as the subnet indicator. This would mean that a computer with an IP address of 128.184.22.33 would be on the same subnet as 128.184.78.90.

IP addresses are binary numbers, so partial bytes can also be used as subnets. For example, we could create a subnet that has an IP address from 128.184.55.1 to 128.184.55.127, and another subnet with addresses from 128.184.55.128 to 128.184.55.254.

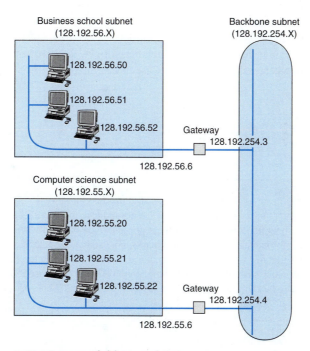

FIGURE 3-11 Address subnets.

Dynamic Addressing   To this point, we have said that a computer knows its network layer address from a configuration file that is installed when the computer is first attached to the network. However, this leads to a major network management problem. Any time a computer is moved or its network is assigned a new address, the software on each individual computer must be updated. This is not difficult, but is very time consuming because someone must go from office to office editing files on each individual computer.

The easiest way around this is *dynamic addressing*. With this approach, a server is designated to supply a network layer address to a computer each time the computer connects to the network. This is commonly done for client computers, but is usually not done for servers.

The most common standard for dynamic addressing is *Dynamic Host Control Protocol (DHCP)*. Instead of providing a network layer address in a configuration file, the software on the client is configured so that it contacts a DHCP server to obtain an address. In this case, when the computer is turned on and connects to the network, it first issues a broadcast DHCP message that is directed to any DHCP server that can "hear" the message. This message asks the server to assign the requesting computer a unique network layer address. The server runs a corresponding DHCP software package that responds to these requests and sends a message back to the client giving it its network layer address (and its subnet mask).

The DHCP server can be configured to assign the same network layer address to the computer each time it requests an address (based on its data link layer address), or it can *lease* the address to the computer by picking the "next available" network layer address from a list of authorized addresses. Addresses can be leased for as long as the computer is connected to the network or for a specified time limit (e.g., two hours). When the lease expires, the client computer must contact the DHCP server to get a new address. Address leasing is commonly used by Internet service providers (ISPs) for dial-up users. ISPs have many more authorized users than they have authorized network layer addresses because not all users can login at the same time. When users login, they are assigned a temporary TCP/IP address that is reassigned to the next user when the previous one hangs up.

TECHNICAL FOCUS *3-1*

SUBNET MASKS

Subnet masks tell computers what part of an IP address is to be used to determine whether a destination is in the same subnet or in a different subnet. A subnet mask is a 4-byte binary number that has the same format as an IP address. A 1 in the subnet mask indicates that that position is part of the subnet address. A 0 indicates that it is not.

A subnet mask of 255.255.255.0 means that the first 3 bytes indicate the subnet; all computers with the same first 3 bytes in their IP addresses are on the same subnet. This is because 255 expressed in binary is 11111111.

In contrast, a subnet mask of 255.255.0.0 indicates that the first 2 bytes indicate the same subnet.

Things get more complicated when we use partial-byte subnet masks. For example, 255.255.255.128 means the first 3 bytes and the next bit indicate the same subnet, because 128 in binary is 10000000. Likewise 255.255.254.000 would indicate the first 2 bytes and 7 bits, because 254 in binary is 11111110.

Dynamic addressing greatly simplifies network management in non-dial-up networks too. With dynamic addressing, address changes need to be done only to the DHCP server, not each individual computer. The next time each computer connects to the network or whenever the address lease expires, it automatically gets the new address.

Address Resolution

In order to send a message, the sender must be able to translate the application layer address (or server name) of the destination into a network layer address and in turn translate that into a data link layer address. This process is called *address resolution*. There are many different approaches to address resolution that range from completely decentralized (each computer is responsible for knowing all addresses) to completely centralized (there is one computer that knows all addresses). TCP/IP uses two different approaches, one for resolving application layer addresses into IP addresses and a different one for resolving IP addresses into data link layer addresses.

Server Name Resolution   Server name resolution is the translation of application layer addresses into network layer addresses (e.g., translating an Internet address such as www.yahoo.com into an IP address such as 204.71.200.74). This is done using the *Domain Name Service (DNS)*. Throughout the Internet there are a series of computers called *name servers* that provide DNS services. These name servers run special address databases that store thousands of Internet addresses and their corresponding IP addresses. These name servers are in effect the "directory assistance" computers for the Internet. Any time a computer does not know the IP number for a computer, it sends a message to the name server requesting the IP number. There are about a dozen high-level name servers that provide IP addresses for most of the Internet, with thousands of others that provide IP addresses for specific domains.

Whenever you register an Internet application layer address, you must inform the registrar of the IP address of the name server that will provide DNS information for all addresses in that name range. For example, because Indiana University owns the .indiana.edu name, it can create any name it wants that ends in these two words (e.g., www.indiana.edu, www.kelley.indiana.edu, abc.indiana.edu). When it registers, it must provide the IP address of the DNS server that it will use to provide the IP addresses for all the computers within this domain name range (i.e., everything ending in .indiana.edu). Every organization that has many servers also has its own DNS server, but smaller organizations that have only one or two servers often use a DNS server provided by their Internet service provider. DNS servers are maintained by network managers, who update their address information as the network changes. Name servers can also exchange information about new and changed addresses among themselves (replication).

When a computer needs to translate an application layer address into an IP address, it sends a special DNS request to its DNS server.[4] This message asks the DNS server to send to the requesting computer the IP address that matches the Internet application layer address provided. If the DNS server has a matching name in its database, it sends back a special DNS response message with the correct IP address. If that DNS server does not

---

[4] DNS requests and responses are usually short, so they use UDP as their transport layer protocol. That is, the DNS request is passed to the transport layer, which surrounds it in a UDP packet before handing it to the network layer.

have that Internet address in its database, it will send the same request to another DNS server elsewhere on the Internet.[5]

For example, if someone at the University of Toronto asked for a Web page on our server (www.kelley.indiana.edu) at Indiana University, the software on their client computer will send a DNS request to the University of Toronto DNS server; see Figure 3-12. This DNS server probably does not know the IP address of our server, so it will forward the

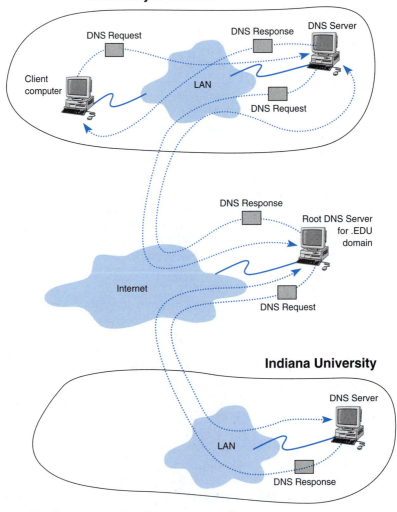

FIGURE 3-12 How the DNS system works.

[5] This is called recursive DNS resolution and is the most common approach used on the Internet. DNS servers can also use iterative DNS resolution, whereby the client is told that the DNS server does not know the desired address but is given the IP address of another DNS server that can be used to find the address. Because recursive is more common, that is what we describe.

MANAGEMENT FOCUS *3-1*

OPERATOR ERROR MAKES NET GO NUTS

At 2:30 A.M. on July 17, 1997, the Internet was thrown into chaos. A computer operator at Network Solutions Inc., the company that maintained the master DNS server for the Internet, ignored alarms on the computer, which then sent incorrect DNS information for the *.com* and *.net* domains to the 10 primary Internet DNS servers around the world.

The problem was corrected by 6:30 A.M., but it took several more hours before the corrected information was replicated around the world to other, lower-level, DNS servers. By then several million requests for Web pages and e-mail messages sent to the *.com* and *.net* domains were returned as undeliverable because of the bad DNS information.

SOURCE: *Atlanta Journal-Constitution,* July 18, 1997.

---

request to the DNS root server that it knows stores addresses for the *.EDU* domain. The .EDU root server probably does not know our server's IP address either, but it knows that the DNS server on our campus can supply the address. So it forwards the request to the Indiana University DNS server, which responds to the .EDU server with a DNS response containing the requested IP address. The .EDU server in turn sends it to the DNS server at the University of Toronto, which in turn sends it to the computer that requested the address.

This is why it sometimes takes a long time to access certain sites. Most DNS servers know the names and IP addresses only for the computers in their part of the network. Some store frequently used addresses (e.g., www.yahoo.com). If you try to access a computer that is far away, it may take a while before your computer receives a response from a DNS server that knows the IP address.

Once your application layer software receives an IP address, it is stored in a server address table. This way, if you ever need to access the same computer again, your computer does not need to contact a DNS server. Most server address tables are routinely deleted whenever you exit the application program.

Data Link Layer Address Resolution In order to actually send a message, the network layer software must know the data link layer address of the computer to send the message to. The final destination may be far away (e.g., sending from Toronto to Indiana). In this case, the network layer would *route* the message by selecting a path through the network that would ultimately lead to the destination (routing is discussed in the next section). The first step would be to send the message to a computer in its subnet that is the first step on this route.

To send a message to a computer in its subnet, a computer must know the correct data link layer address. In this case, the TCP/IP software sends a *broadcast message* to all computers in its subnet. A broadcast message, as the name suggests, is received and processed by all computers in the same LAN (which is usually designed to match the IP subnet). The message is a specially formatted request using *Address Resolution Protocol (ARP)* that says, "Whoever is IP address xxx.xxx.xxx.xxx, please send me your data link layer address." The software in the computer with that IP address then sends an ARP response with its data link layer address. The sender transmits its message using that data link layer address. The sender also stores the data link layer address in its address table for future use.[6] Because all computers in a subnet must be able to hear these broadcast messages, the subnet is sometimes called a *broadcast domain*.

ROUTING

In many networks, there are many possible routes or paths a message can take to get from one computer to another. For example, in Figure 3-13, a message sent from computer A to computer F could travel first to computer B and then to computer C to get to computer F— or it could go first to computer D and then to computer E to get to computer F.

Routing is the process of determining the route or path through the network that a message will travel from the sending computer to the receiving computer. Every computer that performs routing has a *routing table* developed by the network manager that specifies how messages will travel through the network. In its simplest form, the routing table is a two-column table. The first column lists every computer in the network, while the second column lists the computer to which this computer should send messages if they are destined for the computer in the first column. Figure 3-14 shows a routing table that might be used by computer B in Figure 3-13.[7]

Obviously, the Internet is more complicated than the simple network in Figure 3-13; it has millions of computers attached. How can we possibly route messages on the Internet? Well, it turns out that most parts of the Internet are connected only to a few other parts of the Internet. That is, any one part of the Internet, such as your university, probably has only two or three connections into the Internet. When messages arrive at the computer that

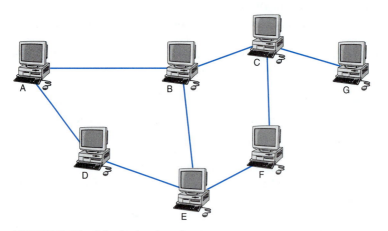

FIGURE 3-13   A typical network.

[6] It would be pretty reasonable at this point to guess that because ARP requests and responses are small, they use UDP in the same way that DNS requests and responses do. But they don't. Instead ARP packets replace both the TCP/UDP and IP and are placed directly into the data link layer protocol with no transport or network layer packets.

[7] If you ever want to find out the route through the Internet from your computer to any other computer on the Internet, simply enter the command *tracert* followed by the application layer name of the computer at the DOS prompt (e.g., tracert www.indiana.edu).

Destination	Route
A	A
C	C
D	A
E	E
F	E
G	C

FIGURE 3-14   Routing table.

connects your university to the Internet, that computer must choose over which circuit to send the message. Imagine, for example, that computer B in Figure 3-13 is the computer that connects your university to the Internet, and that the other computers in this figure are different parts of the Internet. Some parts of the Internet are best reached by one circuit (e.g., the part represented by computer A) while others are best reached via the other circuit (e.g., the part represented by computer E). In this case, the computer is told that messages sent to IP addresses in a certain range (e.g., 127.x.x.x) should go on one circuit, while messages to addresses in a different range (e.g., 12.x.x.x) should go on a different circuit. In some cases, computers can be reached equally well on either circuit (e.g., computer D), in which case the network manager may arbitrarily choose one circuit or configure the software to choose either circuit as it likes.

Imagine yourself as a packet that needs to travel over the Internet from the University of Texas to the University of Alberta (e.g., an HTTP request). As you leave the University of Texas on the Internet, you reach a fork in the path. A sign says Texas one way, all other destinations straight ahead (see Figure 3-15). While this sign does not explicitly tell you how to get to the University of Alberta, it is clear; you continue on straight ahead. As you reach the next fork in the path there is another sign. Once again, your destination is not listed, but nonetheless, the direction you need to take is clear. The next sign includes your destination in a range of destinations (Canada), so you turn down that path. The next sign again contains your destination in a range of destinations (Alberta), so you take that path and at last you see a sign to your destination. This is one way in which the Internet works.

Because routing is an important function, we often use special-purpose devices called *routers* to build and maintain the routing tables and perform routing. We will explain more about routers in Chapter 5.

Types of Routing

There are three fundamental approaches to routing: centralized, static, and dynamic routing. As you will see in the TCP/IP example section later in this chapter, the Internet uses all three approaches.

Centralized Routing   With centralized routing, all routing decisions are made by one central computer or router. Centralized routing typically is commonly used in host-based networks (see Chapter 2), and in this case, routing decisions are rather simple. All

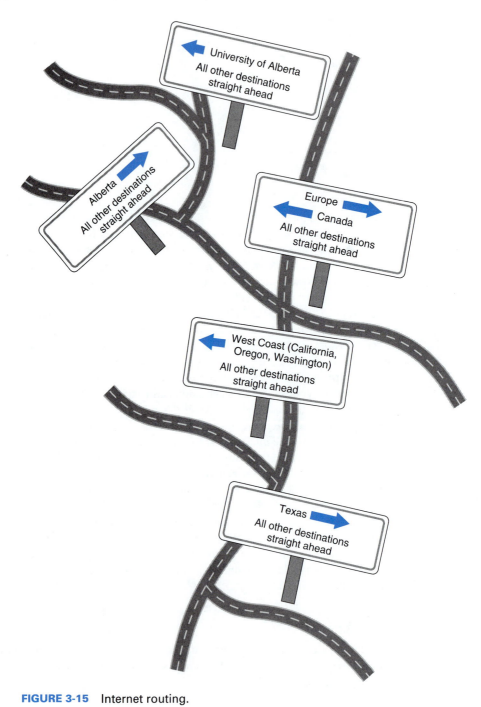

FIGURE 3-15 Internet routing.

computers are connected to the central computer or router, so any message that needs to be routed is simply sent to the central computer or router, which in turn retransmits the message on the appropriate circuit to the destination.

Static Routing   With decentralized routing, all computers or routers in the network make their own routing decisions following a formal routing protocol. In MANs and WANs, the routing table for each computer is developed by its individual network manager (although network managers share information). In local area networks or backbone networks, the routing tables used by all computers on the network are usually developed by one individual or a committee. Most decentralized routing protocols are self-adjusting, meaning that they can automatically adapt to changes in the network configuration (e.g., adding and deleting computers and circuits).

With *static routing,* routing decisions are made in a decentralized manner by individual computers or routers. The routing table is developed by the network manager and changes only when computers are added to or removed from the network. For example, if the computer recognizes that a circuit is broken or unusable, the computer will update the routing table to indicate the failed circuit. If an alternate route is available, it will be used for all subsequent messages. Otherwise, messages will be stored until the circuit is repaired. When new computers are added to the network, they announce their presence to the other computers, which automatically add them into their routing tables. Static routing is commonly used in networks that have few routing options that seldom change.

Dynamic Routing   With *dynamic routing* (or *adaptive routing*), routing decisions are made in a decentralized manner by individual computers or routers. It is used when there are multiple routes through a network and it is important to select the best route. Dynamic routing attempts to improve network performance by routing messages over the fastest possible route, away from busy circuits and busy computers. An initial routing table is developed by the network manager, but is continuously updated by the computers themselves to reflect changing network conditions.

With *distance vector* dynamic routing, computers or routers count the number of *hops* along a route. A hop is one circuit, so that a route from one computer to another that passes through only one other computer (e.g., from A to C through B in Figure 3-13) would be two hops, while a route that passes through three computers (e.g., A to C via D, E, and F in Figure 3-13) would be four hops. With this approach, computers periodically (usually every 1–2 minutes) exchange information on the hop count and sometimes the relative speed of the circuits in the route with their neighbors.

With *link state* dynamic routing, computers or routers track the number of hops in the route, the speed of the circuits in each route, and how busy each route is. In other words, rather than just knowing a route's distance, link state routing tries to determine the how fast each possible route is. Each computer or router periodically (usually every 15–30 minutes) exchanges this information with other computers or routers in the network, so that each computer or router has the most accurate information possible. Link state protocols are preferred to distance vector protocols in large networks because they more quickly spread reliable routing information throughout the entire network when major changes occur in the network. They are said to *converge* more quickly.

There are two drawbacks with dynamic routing. First, it requires more processing by each computer or router in the network than centralized routing or static routing. Computing resources are devoted to adjusting routing tables rather than sending messages, which can slow down the network. Second, the transmission of routing information "wastes" network capacity. Some dynamic routing protocols transmit status information every minute, which can significantly reduce performance.

Routing Protocols

A routing protocol is a protocol that is used to exchange information among computers to enable them to build and maintain their routing tables. You can think of a routing protocol as the language that is used to build the signs in Figure 3-15. When new paths are added or paths are broken and cannot be used, messages are sent among computers using the routing protocol.

It can be useful to know all possible routes to a given destination. However, as a network gets quite large, knowing all possible routes becomes impractical; there are simply too many possible routes. Even at some modest number of computers, dynamic routing protocols become impractical because of the amount of network traffic they generate. For this reason, networks are often subdivided into autonomous systems of networks.

An *autonomous system* is simply a network operated by one organization, such as IBM or Indiana University or an organization that runs one part of the Internet. Remember that we said the Internet was simply a network of networks. Each part of the Internet is run by a separate organization such as AT&T, Sprint, and so on. Each part of the Internet or each large organizational network connected to the Internet can be a separate autonomous system.

The computers within each autonomous system know about the other computers in that system and usually exchange routing information because the number of computers is kept manageable. If an autonomous system grows too large, it can simply be split into smaller parts. The routing protocols used inside an autonomous system are called *interior routing protocols*.

Protocols used between autonomous sytems are called *exterior routing protocols*. While interior routing protocols are usually designed to provide detailed routing information about all or most computers inside the autonomous systems, exterior protocols are designed to be more careful in the information they provide. Usually, exterior protocols provide information only about the preferred or the best routes, rather than all prossible routes.

There are many different protocols that are used to exchange routing information. Five are commonly used onthe Internet: BGP, ICMP, RIP, OSPF, and EIGRP.

1. *Border Gateway Protocol (BGP)* is a dynamic exterior routing protocol used on the Internet to exchange routing information between autonomous sytems (i.e., large sections of the Internet). While BGP is the preferred routing protocol between Internet sections, it is seldom used inside companies because it is large and complex and is often hard to administer.

2. *Internet Control Message Protocol (ICMP)* is the simplest and most basic interior routing protocol on the Internet. ICMP is simply an error-reporting protocol that

enables computers to report routing errors to message senders. ICMP also has a very limited ability to update routing tables.[8]

3. *Routing Information Protocol (RIP)* is a dynamic distance vector interior routing protocol that is commonly used in smaller networks, such as those operated by one organization. The network manager uses RIP to develop the routing table. When new computers are added, RIP simply counts the number of computers in the possible routes to the destination and selects the route with the least number. Computers using RIP send broadcast messages every minute or so (the timing is set by the network manager) announcing their routing status to all other computers. RIP is used by both TCP/IP and IPX/SPX.

4. *Open Shortest Path First (OSPF)* is another dynamic link state interior routing protocol that is commonly used on the Internet. It uses the number of computers in a route as well as network traffic and error rates to select the best route. OSPF is more efficient than RIP because it normally doesn't use broadcast messages. Instead it selectively sends status update messages directly to selected computers or routers. OSPF is the preferred interior routing protocol used by TCP/IP.

TECHNICAL FOCUS *3-2*

ROUTING ON THE INTERNET

The Internet is a network of autonomous system networks. Each autonomous system operates its own interior routing protocol while using BGP as the exterior routing protocol to exchange information with the other autonomous systems in the Internet. While there are a number of interior routing protocols, OSPF is the current preferred protocol and most organizations that run the autonomous system forming large parts of the Internet use OSPF.

Figure 3-16 shows how a small part of the Internet might operate. In this example, there are six autonomous systems (e.g., Sprint, AT&T), three of which are shown in more detail. Each autonomous system has a *border router* that connects it to the adjacent autonomous systems and exchanges route information via BGP. In this example, autonomous system A is connected to autonomous system B, which in turn is connected to autnomous system C. A is also connected to C via a route through systems D and E. If someone in A wants to send a message to someone in C, the message should be routed through B because it is the fastest route. The autonomous systems must share route information via BGP so that the border routers in each system know what routes are preferred. In this case, B would inform A that there is a route through it to C (and a route to E), and D would inform A that it has a route to E, but D would not inform A that there is a route though it to C. The border router in A would then have to decide which route to use to reach E.

Each autonomous system can use a different interior routing protocol. In this example, A and C use OSPF and B uses RIP. RIP is simpler, so that every minute or so all routers broadcast route information to their neighbors. B is a rather simple network with only a few devices and routes, so RIP is probably a reasonable choice. A and C are more complex and use OSPF. Most organizations that use OSPF create a special router called a *designated router* to manage the routing information. Every 15 minutes or so, each router sends its routing information to the designated router, which then broadcasts the revised routing table information to all other routers. If a designated router was not used, then every router would have to broadcast its routing information to all other routers, which would result in a very large number of messages. In the case of autonomous system C, which has 7 routers, this would required 42 separate messages (7 routers each sending to 6 others). By using a designated router, we now have only 12 separate messages (the 6 other routers sending to the designated router, and the designated router sending the complete set of revised information back to the other 6).

---

[8] ICMP is the protocol used by the ping command.

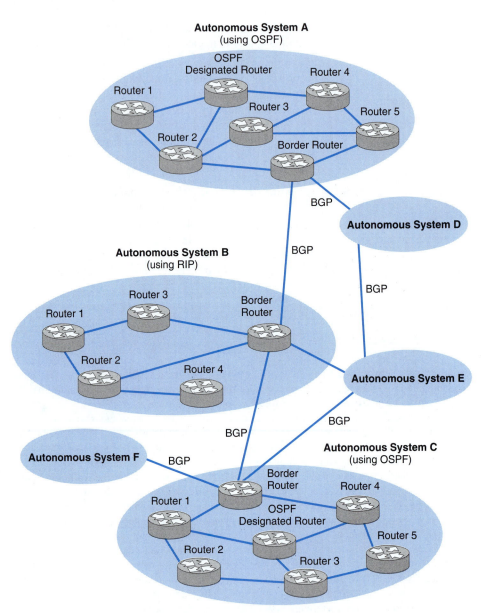

FIGURE 3-16   Routing on the Internet with Border Gateway Protocol (BGP), Open Shortest Path First (OSPF), and Routing Information Protocol (RIP).

5. *Enhanced Interior Gateway Routing Protocol (EIGRP)* is a dynamic link state interior routing protocol developed by Cisco and is commonly inside organizations. EIGRP records information about a route's transmission capacity, delay, reliability, and load. EIGRP is unique in that computers or routers store their own routing table as well as the routing tables for all of their neighbors, so they have a more accurate understanding of the network.

Multicasting

The most common type of message in a network is the usual transmission between two computers. One computer sends a message to another computer (e.g., a client requesting a Web page). This is called a *unicast message.* Earlier in the chapter, we introduced the concept of a *broadcast message* that is sent to all computers on a specific LAN or subnet. A third type of message, called a *multicast message,* is used to send the same message to a group of computers.

Consider a videoconferencing situation in which four people want to participate in the same conference. Each computer could send the same voice and video data from its camera to the computers of each of the other three participants using unicasts. In this case, each computer would send three identical messages, each addressed to the three different computers. This would work, but would require a lot of network capacity. Alternately, each computer could send one broadcast message. This would reduce network traffic (since each computer would send only one message), but every computer on the network would process it, distracting them from other tasks. Broadcast messages usually are transmitted only within the same LAN or subnet, so this would not work if one of the computers was outside the subnet.

The solution is multicast messaging. Computers wishing to participate in a multicast send a message to the sending computer or some other computer performing routing along the way using a special type of packet called *Internet Group Management Protocol (IGMP).* Each multicast group is assigned a special IP address to identify the group. Any computer performing routing knows to route all multicast messages with this IP address onto the subnet that contains the requesting computer. The routing computer sets the data link layer address on multicast messages to a matching multicast data link layer address. Each requesting computer must inform its data link layer software to process incoming messages with this multicast data link layer address. When the multicast session ends (e.g., the videoconference is over), the client computer sends another IGMP message to the organizing computer or the computer performing routing to remove it from the multicast group.

MANAGEMENT FOCUS *3-2*

TOY STORY

You don't have to be a math major to figure out it's more efficient to send one file once to 200 locations than to send the 200 copies of the same file, one at a time, to each of those locations. But that's what Toys Я Us did for 10 years before multicasting.

Toys Я Us used to send software updates to its 865 stores over its VSAT satellite network one file at a time using unicast messages. This took so much network capac-

ity, that it could be done only at night when the stores were closed. It also took so much time, that not all stores could be updated on the same night. Transferring a 1 megabyte file to 250 stores took just over six hours.

With IP multicasting, transferring the same 1 megabyte file now takes less than four minutes.

SOURCE: *PC Week,* October 21, 1996.

TCP/IP EXAMPLE

So far we have discussed the functions of the transport and network layers: linking to the application layer, segmenting, providing reliable delivery addressing, and routing. In this section, we tie all of these concepts together to take a closer look at how these functions actually work using TCP/IP.

When a computer is installed on a TCP/IP network (or dials into a TCP/IP network), it must be given four pieces of addressing and routing information before it can operate. This information can be provided by a configuration file, or via a DHCP server. The information is:

1. Its IP address.
2. A subnet mask, so it can determine what addresses are part of its subnet.
3. The IP address of a DNS server, so it can translate application layer addresses into IP addresses.
4. The IP address of a gateway (more commonly called a router) leading outside of its subnet, so it can route messages addressed to computers outside of its subnet (this presumes the computer is using static routing and there is only one connection from it to the outside world through which all messages must flow).

These four pieces of information are the minimum required. A server would also need to know its application layer address.

In this section we use a simple network to illustrate how TCP/IP works (see Figure 3-18). For simplicity, we will assume that all networks use Ethernet as the data link layer (which is discussed in the next chapter) and will only focus on Web requests at the application layer. This figure shows an organization that has four LANs connected by a backbone network. The backbone network also has a connection to the Internet. Each computer has two or three addresses. Each client computer has an IP address and an Ethernet address. Each server has an IP address, an Ethernet address, and an application layer address.

TECHNICAL FOCUS *3-3*

FINDING YOUR COMPUTER'S TCP/IP SETTINGS

If your computer can access the Internet, it must use TCP/IP. You can find out your TCP/IP settings by using a Windows utility called winipcfg (pronounced *win-i-pee-con-fig*). Click on the *Start* button and then select *Run*. Type *winipcfg* in the window and click *OK*.

Click on the *More Info>>* button, and you should see a screen like that shown in Figure 3-17. If you have an Ethernet card but it is not shown in the "adapter" information in the center of the screen, use the drop-down list to select it.

This screen shows the basic TCP/IP information and Ethernet information, such as the Ethernet adapter address (e.g., 00-B0-D0-F7-B8-F4), the IP address (e.g., 192.168.1.104), the subnet mask (e.g., 255.255.255.0), and the default gateway (e.g., 192.168.1.1). The DNS server address is shown near the top of the screen (e.g., 24.12.70.15). You can also see that this computer uses dynamic addressing by the DHCP server address (e.g., 192.168.1.1). The buttons at the bottom of the screen enable you to release the dynamic address and renew it.

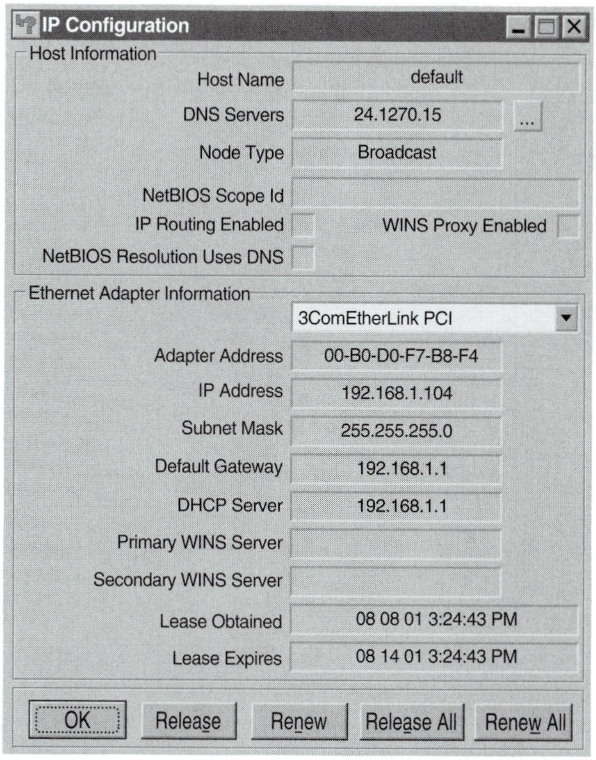

FIGURE 3-17 TCP/IP configuration information.

Each building is configured as a separate subnet. For example, Building A has the 128.192.98.x subnet, while Building B has the 128.192.95.x subnet. The backbone is its own subnet 128.192.254.x. Each building is connected to the backbone via a TCP/IP gateway (or router) that has two IP addresses and two data link layer addresses, one for the connection into the building and one for the connection onto the backbone. The organization has several Web servers spread throughout the four buildings. The DNS server and the gateway onto the Internet are located directly on the backbone itself.

In the following sections we will describe how messages are sent through the network. For the sake of simplicity, we will initially ignore the need to establish and close TCP connections. Once you understand the basic concepts, we will then add these in to complete the example.

Known Addresses, Same Subnet

Let's start with the simplest case. Suppose that a user on a client computer in Building A (128.192.98.130) requests a Web page from the Web server in the same building (www1.anyorg.com). We will assume that this computer knows the network layer and data link layer addresses of the Web server (e.g., it has previously requested pages from this server, and the addresses are in its address tables). Since the application layer software knows the IP address of the server, it uses its IP address, not its application layer address.

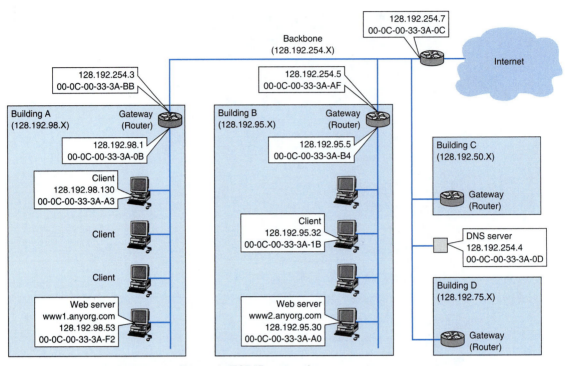

FIGURE 3-18   Example TCP/IP network.

In this case, the application layer software (i.e., Web browser) passes an HTTP request containing the user request message to the transport layer software requesting a page from 128.192.98.53. The transport layer software (TCP) would take the HTTP request, add a TCP segment, and then hand the one segment to the network layer software (IP). The network layer software will compare the destination address (128.192.98.53) to the subnet mask (255.255.255.0) and discover that this computer is on its own subnet. The network layer software will then search its data link layer address table and find the matching data link layer address (00-0C-00-33-3A-F2). The network layer would then attach an IP packet and pass it to the data link layer, along with the destination Ethernet address. The data link layer would surround the packet with an Ethernet frame and transmit it over the physical layer to the Web server.[9]

The data link layer on the Web server would receive the bits from the physical layer, interpret the Ethernet frame, and pass the IP packet (containing the TCP segment and HTTP request) to its network layer software. The network layer software (IP) would then process the IP packet, see that it was destined to this computer, and pass the TCP segment to the transport layer software (TCP). This software would process the TCP segment, see that there was only one segment, and pass the HTTP request to the Web server software.

The Web server software would find the page requested, attach an HTTP response, and pass it to its transport layer software. The transport layer software (TCP) would break

---

[9] We will discuss how Ethernet transmits messages from one computer to another in the next chapter.

the Web page into several smaller segments, usually each less than 1,500 bytes in length, and attach a TCP segment (with a segment number to indicate the order) to each. Each would then go to the network layer software, get an IP packet attached that specified the IP address of the requesting client (128.192.98.130), and be given to the data link layer with the client's Ethernet address (00-0C-00-33-3A-A3) for transmission. The data link layer on the server would transmit the frames over the physical layer in the order in which the network layer passed them to it.

The client's data link layer software would receive the frames from the physical layer and pass each to the network layer. The network layer software (IP) would check to see that the packets were destined for this computer and pass them to the transport layer software. The transport layer software (TCP) would assemble the separate segments in order back into one Web page and pass each in turn to the Web browser to display on the screen.

Known Addresses, Different Subnet

Suppose this time that the same client computer wanted to get a Web page from a Web server located somewhere in Building B (say www2.anyorg.com). Again assume that all addresses are known and are in the address tables of all computers. In this case, the application layer software would pass an HTTP request to the transport layer software (TCP) with the Internet address of the destination www2.anyorg.com: 128.192.95.30. The transport layer software (TCP) would make sure that the request fit in one segment and hand it to the network layer. The network layer software (IP) would then use its subnet mask and would recognize that the Web server is located outside of its subnet. Any messages going outside the subnet must be sent to the gateway (128.192.98.1), whose job it is to process the message and send the message on its way into the outside network. The network layer software would check its address table and find the Ethernet address for the gateway. It would therefore set the data link layer address to the gateway's Ethernet address on this subnet (00-0C-00-33-3A-0B) and pass it to the data link layer and then physical layer for transmission.

The gateway's physical layer would receive the message and its data link layer would pass the message to the network layer software (IP). The network layer software would read the IP address to determine the final destination. The gateway would recognize that this address (128.192.95.30) needed to be sent to the 128.192.95.x subnet. It knows the gateway for this subnet is 128.192.254.5. It would pass the packet back to its data link layer, giving the Ethernet address of this gateway (00-0C-00-33-3A-AF).

This gateway would receive the message and read the IP address to determine the final destination. The gateway would recognize that this address (128.192.95.30) was inside its 128.192.95.x subnet and search its data link layer address table for this computer. It would then pass the packet the data link layer along with the Ethernet address of (00-0C-00-33-3A-A0) for transmission.

The www2.anyorg.com Web server would receive the message and process it. This would result in a series of TCP/IP packets addressed to requesting client (128.192.98.130). These would make their way through the network in reverse order. The Web server would recognize that this IP address is outside its subnet and send the message to the 128.192.95.5 gateway using its Ethernet address (00-0C-00-33-3A-B4). This gateway would then send the message to the gateway for the 128.192.98.x subnet (128.192.254.3) using its Ethernet address (00-0C-00-33-3A-BB). This gateway would in turn send the message back to the client (128.192.98.130) using its Ethernet address (00-0C-00-33-3A-A3).

This process would work in the same way for Web servers located outside the organization on the Internet. In this case, the message would go from the client to the 128.192.98.1 gateway, which would send it to the Internet gateway (128.192.254.7), which would send it to its Internet connection. The message would be routed through the Internet from gateway to gateway until it reached its destination. Then the process would work in reverse to return the requested page.

Unknown Addresses

Let's return to the simplest case (requesting a Web page from a Web server on the same subnet), only this time we will assume that the client computer does not know the network layer or data link layer address of the Web server. For simplicity, we will assume that the client knows the data link layer address of its subnet gateway, but after you read through this example, you will realize that obtaining the data link layer address of the subnet gateway is straightforward (it is done the same way as the client obtains the data link layer address of the Web server).

Suppose the client computer in Building A (128.192.98.130) wants to retrieve a Web page from the www1.anyorg.com Web server, but does not knows its address. The Web browser realizes that it does not know the IP address after searching its IP address table and not finding a matching entry. Therefore, it issues a DNS request to the name server (128.192.254.4). The DNS request is passed to the transport layer (TCP), which attaches a TCP segment (or a UDP packet, depending upon the configuration) and hands the message to the network layer.

Using its subnet mask, the network layer (IP) will recognize that the name server is outside of its subnet. It will attach an IP packet and set the data link layer address to its gateway's address. The gateway would process the message and recognize that the 128.192.254.4 IP address is on the backbone. It would transmit the packet using the name server's Ethernet address. The name server would process the DNS request and send the matching IP address back to the client via the 128.198.98.x subnet gateway.

The IP address for the desired computers makes its way back to the application layer software, which stores it in its IP table. It then issues the HTTP request using the IP address for the Web server (128.192.98.53) and passes it to the transport layer, which in turn passes it to the network layer. The network layer uses its subnet mask and recognizes that this computer is on its subnet. However, it does not know the Web server's Ethernet address. Therefore, it broadcasts an ARP request to all computers on its subnet, requesting that the computer whose IP address is 128.192.98.53 respond with its Ethernet address.

This request would be processed by all computers on the subnet, but only the Web server would respond with an ARP packet giving its Ethernet address. The network layer software on the client would store this address in its data link layer address table and send the original Web request to the Web server using its Ethernet address.

This process works the same for a Web server outside the subnet, whether in the same organization or anywhere in the Internet. If the Web server is far away (e.g., Australia), it will likely involve searching more than one name server, but the process is the same.

TCP Connections

Whenever a computer transmits data from itself to another computer, it must choose whether to use a connection-oriented service via TCP or a connectionless service via UDP. Most application layer software such as Web browsers (HTTP), e-mail (SMTP), FTP, and Telnet use connection-oriented services. This means that before the first packet is sent, the transport layer first sends an SYN packet to establish a connection. Once the connection is established, then the data packets begin to flow. Once the data is finished, the connection is closed with a FIN packet.

In the examples above, this means that the first packet sent is really a SYN packet, followed by a response from the receiver accepting the connection, and then the packets as described above. There is nothing magical about the SYN and FIN packets; they are addressed and routed in the same manner as any other TCP packets. But they do add to the complexity and length of the example, so we have omitted them.

A special word is needed about HTTP requests. When HTTP was first developed, Web browsers opened a separate TCP connection for each HTTP request. That is, when they requested a page, they would open a connection, and send the single packet requesting the Web page. The Web server would accept the connection, send as many packets as needed to transmit the requested page, and the close the connection. If the page included graphic images, the Web browser would open and close a separate connection for each request. This requirement to open and close connections for each request was time consuming and wasn't really necessary. With the newest version of HTTP, Web browsers open one connection when they first issue an HTTP request and leave that connection open for all subsequent HTTP requests to the same server.

TCP/IP and Network Layers

In closing this chapter, we want to return to the layers in the network model and take a closer look at how messages flow through the layers. Figure 3-19 shows how the message from the client computer in Building A would flow through the network layers in the different computers and devices on its way to the server in Building B. Once again, we have omitted the session and presentation layers for simplicity.

The message starts at the application layer of the client computer (lower left), which generates an HTTP packet. This is passed to the client computer's TCP software, which surrounds the HTTP packet with a TCP segment. The IP software then surrounds this with an IP packet. The Ethernet software surrounds this with an Ethernet frame, and then the frame is transmitted by the physical layer to the gateway for Building A.

The physical layer in the gateway processes the Ethernet frame and removes it, before passing the IP packet to the IP software in the gateway. The gateway routes the packet and sees that the next hop is to the gateway in Building B. The IP packet is then passed down to the Ethernet software, which creates a new Ethernet frame, and the physical layer transmits the frame to the gateway in Building B.

The gateway in Building B repeats this same process. The physical layer receives the frame, passes it to the Ethernet software, which removes the Ethernet frame and passes the IP packet to the IP software. The IP software routes the IP packet and passes the IP packet

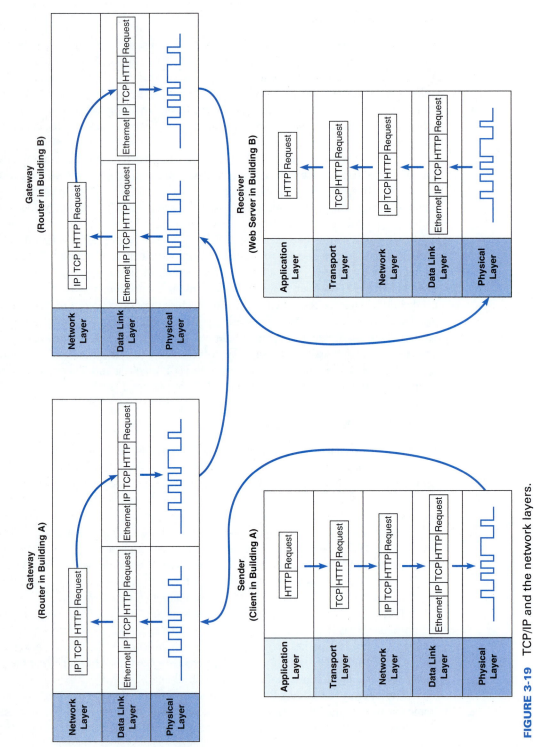

FIGURE 3-19 TCP/IP and the network layers.

back to the Ethernet software, which creates a new Ethernet frame and gives the frame to the physical layer for transmission to the server.

The physical layer in the server receives the frame, passes it to the Ethernet software, which removes the Ethernet frame and passes the IP packet to the IP software. The IP software recognizes that the server is the final destination and removes the IP packet before passing the TCP segment to the TCP software. The TCP software performs error checking and (assuming no errors) creates an ACK to be sent to the client computer, before removing the TCP segment and passing the HTTP message to the application layer. If there were an error, the TCP software would simply throw the segment away and wait for the client to retransmit the segment.

There are two important things to remember from this example. First, at all gateways along the way, the packet moves through the hardware layers (physical and data link) and up to the network layer (IP), which then routes the IP packet and sends it back down to the hardware layers to be transmitted on the next hop. While the network layer (IP) is involved at all computers and devices along the way, the transport layer is involved only at the sending computer (to create the TCP packet) and at the final destination (to receive the packet and send an ACK). Thus TCP is used at both ends of the transmission, but not along the way.

Second, at each hop (at each computer or device along the way), the Ethernet frame is removed and a new one created. However, the IP packet and the packets above it (TCP segments and HTTP messages) never change. They are created and removed only by the original message sender and the final destination.

SUMMARY

Transport and Network Layer Protocols   Many different standard transport and network protocols exist to perform addressing (finding destination addresses), routing (finding the best route through the network), and segmenting (breaking large messages into smaller segments for transmission and reassembling them at the destination). All provide formal definitions for how addressing and routing are to be executed and specify packet structures to transfer this information between computers. TCP/IP, IPX/SPX, X.25, and SNA are the four most commonly used network layer protocols. TCP/IP is the most common.

Transport Layer   The transport layer (TCP) uses the source and destination port address to link the application layer software to the network. TCP is also responsible for segmenting—breaker large messages into smaller segments for transmission and reassembling them at the receiver's end. When connection-oriented routing is needed, TCP establishes a connection or virtual circuit from the sender to the receiver. When connectionless routing is needed, TCP is replaced with UDP. Quality of service provides the ability to prioritize packets so that real-time voice packets are transmitted more quickly than simple e-mail messages. TCP is responsible for providing reliable delivery services, which means ensuring that segments actually do arrive at the destination. This is done by including a checksum for detecting errors in the TCP segment and by having the receiver acknowledge all messages it receives. If the sender fails to get receive an acknowledgment it sends the segment again.

Addressing   Computers can have three different addresses: application layer address, network layer address, and data link layer address. Data link layer addresses are usually part of the hardware, while network layer and application layer addresses are set by software. Network layer and application layer addresses for the Internet are assigned by Internet registrars. Addresses within one organization are usually assigned so that computers in the same LAN or subnet have the similar addresses, usually with the first 3 bytes the same. Subnet masks are used to indicate whether the first 2 or 3 bytes (or partial bytes) indicate the same subnet. Some networks assign network layer addresses in a configuration file on the client computer, while others use dynamic addressing in which a DHCP server assigns addresses when a computer first joins the network.

Address Resolution   Address resolution is the process of translating an application layer address into a network layer address, or translating a network layer address into a data link layer address. On the Internet, network layer resolution is done by sending a special message to a DNS server (also called a name server) that asks for the IP address (e.g., 128.192.98.5) for a given Internet address (e.g., www.cba.uga.edu). If a DNS server does not have an entry for the requested Internet address, it will forward the request to another DNS server that it thinks is likely to have the address, which will either respond, or forward it to another DNS server, and so on until the address is found or it becomes clear that the address is unknown. Resolving data link layer addresses is done by sending an ARP request in a broadcast message to all computers on the same subnet that asks the computer with the requested IP address to respond with its data link layer address.

Routing   Routing is the process of selecting the route or path through the network that a message will travel from the sending computer to the receiving computer. With centralized routing, one computer performs all the routing decisions. With static routing, the routing table is developed by the network manager and remains unchanged until the network manager updates it. With dynamic routing, the goal is to improve network performance by routing messages over the fastest possible route; an initial routing table is developed by the network manager, but is continuously updated to reflect changing network conditions, such as message traffic. BGP, RIP, ICMP, OSPF, and EIGRP are examples of dynamic routing protocols.

TCP/IP Example   In TCP/IP, it is important to remember that the TCP and IP packets are created by the sending computer and never change until the message reaches its final destination. The IP packet contains the original source and ultimate destination address for the packet. The sending computer also creates a data link layer frame (e.g., Ethernet) for each message. This frame contains the data link layer address of the current computer sending the frame and the data link layer address of the next computer in the route through the network. The data link layer frame is removed and replaced with a new frame at each computer at which the message stops as it works its way through the network. Thus the source and destination data link layer addresses change at each step along the route, whereas the IP source and destination addresses never change.

KEY TERMS

acknowledgment (ACK)
address resolution
Address Resolution
  Protocol (ARP)
addressing
application layer address
autonomous systems
Border Gateway
  Protocol (BGP)
border router
broadcast
broadcast domain
checksum
connectionless routing

connection-oriented
  routing
data link layer address
designated router
distance vector routing
domain name
domain name registrar
Domain Name Service
  (DNS)
dynamic addressing
Dynamic Host
  Control Protocol
  (DHCP)
dynamic routing

Enhanced Interior
  Gateway Routing
  Protocol (EIGRP)
exterior routing protocol
flow control
hop
interior routing protocol
Internet address classes
Internet Control
  Message Protocol
  (ICMP)
Internet Corporation for
  Assigned Names and
  Numbers (ICANN)

Internet Group
  Management
  Protocol (IGMP)
Internetwork Packet
  Exchange/
  Sequenced Packet
  Exchange
  (IPX/SPX)
link state routing
multicast
name server
network layer address
Open Shortest Path First
  (OSPF)

Packet Layer Protocol (PLP)
segmenting
path control
Quality of Service (QoS)
router
routing

Routing Information Protocol (RIP)
routing table
sliding window
static routing
stop-and-wait
subnet
subnet mask

System Network Architecture (SNA)
throughout
timeout
Transmission Control Protocol/Internet Protocol (TCP/IP)
unicast

User Datagram Protocol (UDP)
virtual circuit
X.25
X.3

QUESTIONS

1. What does the transport layer do?
2. What does the network layer do?
3. What are the parts of TCP/IP and what do they do? Who is the primary user of TCP/IP?
4. What are the parts of IPX/SPX and what do they do? Who is the primary user of IPX/SPX?
5. What are the parts of X.25 and what do they do? Who is the primary user of X.25?
6. What are the parts of SNA and what do they do? Who is the primary user of SNA?
7. Compare and contrast the three types of addresses used in a network.
8. How is TCP different from UDP?
9. How does TCP establish a connection?
10. What is a subnet and why do networks need them?
11. What is a subnet mask?
12. How does dynamic addressing work?
13. What benefits and problems does dynamic addressing provide?
14. What is address resolution?
15. How does TCP/IP perform address resolution for network layer addresses?
16. How does TCP/IP perform address resolution for data link layer addresses?
17. What is routing?
18. How does decentralized routing differ from centralized routing?
19. What are the differences between connectionless and connection-oriented routing?
20. What is a virtual circuit?
21. What is quality-of-service routing and why is it useful?
22. Compare and contrast unicast, broadcast, and multicast messages.
23. Explain how multicasting works
24. How does TCP provide reliable delivery services?
25. Explain how the checksum field in the TCP segment is used.
26. How does stop-and-wait error correction differ from sliding window?
27. What is flow control and why is it important?
28. Explain how the client computer in Figure 3-15 (128.192.98.130) would obtain the data link layer address of its subnet gateway.
29. Why does HTTP use TCP and DNS use UDP?
30. How does static routing differ from dynamic routing? When would you use static routing? When would you use dynamic routing?
31. What type of routing does a TCP/IP client use? What type of routing does a TCP/IP gateway use? Explain.
32. Why would a network manager want to have only TCP/IP as their transport/network layer protocols?
33. What is the transmission efficiency of a 10-byte Web request sent using HTTP, TCP/IP, and Ethernet? Assume the HTTP request has 100 bytes of overhead in addition to the 10-byte URL and the Ethernet frame has 33 bytes of overhead.
34. What is the transmission efficiency of a 1,000-byte file sent in response to a Web request HTTP, TCP/IP, and Ethernet? Assume the HTTP request has 100 bytes of overhead in addition to the 10-byte URL and the Ethernet frame has 33 bytes of overhead.
35. What is the transmission efficiency of a 5,000-byte file sent in response to a Web request HTTP, TCP/IP, and Ethernet? Assume the HTTP request has 100 bytes of overhead in addition to the 10-byte URL and the Ethernet frame has 33 bytes of overhead.

EXERCISES

3-1 What network layer protocol(s) are used your organization's backbone network? Why?

3-2 Would you recommend dynamic addressing for your organization? Why?

3-3 Look at your network layer software (either on a LAN or dial-in) and see what options are set—but don't change them! You can do this by using the RUN command to run winipcfg. How do these match the fundamental addressing and routing concepts discussed in this chapter?

3-4 Suppose a client computer (128.192.95.32) in Building B in Figure 3-18 requests a large Web page on the server in Building A (www1.anyorg.com). Assume that the client computer has just been turned on and does not know any addresses other than those in its configuration tables. Assume that all gateways and Web servers know all network layer and data link layer addresses.

a. Explain what messages would be sent and how they would flow through the network to deliver the Web page request to the server.

b. Explain what messages would be sent and how they would flow through the network as the Web server sent the requested page to the client.

c. Describe, but do not explain in detail, what would happen if the Web page contained several graphic images (e.g., GIF or JPEG files).

MINI-CASES

I. Fred's Donuts

Fred's Donuts is large regional bakery company that supplies baked goods (e.g., donuts, bread, pastries) to cafeterias, grocery stores, and convenience stores in three states. They have five separate bakeries and office complexes spread over the region and want to connect the five locations. Unfortunately, the network infrastructure at the five locations has grown up separately and thus there are three different network/transport layer protocols in use (TCP/IP, SPX/IPX, and SNA). How can they connect the locations that use different protocols together? (*Hint:* This was briefly discussed in Chapter 1). Should they continue to use the three different protocols or move to one protocol (and if so, which one)? Explain.

II. Central University

Suppose you are the network manager for Central University, a medium-size university with 13,000 students. The University has 10 separate colleges (e.g., business, arts, journalism), three of which are relatively large (300 faculty and staff, 2,000 students, and three buildings) and seven of which are relatively small (200 faculty and staff, 1,000 students, and one building). In addition, there are another 2,000 staff members that work in various administration departments (e.g., library, maintenance, finance) spread over another 10 buildings. There are four residence halls that house a total of 2000 students. Suppose the university has the 128.100.xxx.xxx address range on the Internet. How would you assign the IP addresses to the various subnets? How would you control the process by which IP addresses are assigned to individual computers? You will have to make some assumptions to answer both questions, so be sure to state your assumptions.

III. Web Creations

Belinda Tan runs a 15-person Web development firm called Web Creations that builds and runs Web sites for a variety of small companies. The business has been growing quite rapidly and Belinda expects to hire another 5 people this year and probably 5 to 7 more next year. She will probably have to move to new office space next year too, because the current offices can hold only about 20 people. Each staff member has a desktop computer, in addition to the 5 Web and database servers used by Web Creations. Belinda also expects to buy several more servers and replace the existing ones with bigger ones. At present, Web Creations is using static addressing, but Belinda is wondering if she should consider dynamic addressing. Outline the pros and cons of static and dynamic addressing and make a recommendation.

IV. Worldwide Charity

Worldwide Charity is a charitable organization whose mission is to improve education in developing countries. In each country, they have a small headquarters and usually 5 to 10 offices in outlying towns. Staff communicate with each other via e-mail on older computers donated to the organization. Because Internet service is not reliable in many of the towns in these countries, the staff usually phone headquarters and use a very simple Linux e-mail system that uses a server-based network architecture. They also upload and download files. What range of packet sizes is likely to be used?

HARDWARE LAYERS:
LOCAL AREA NETWORKS

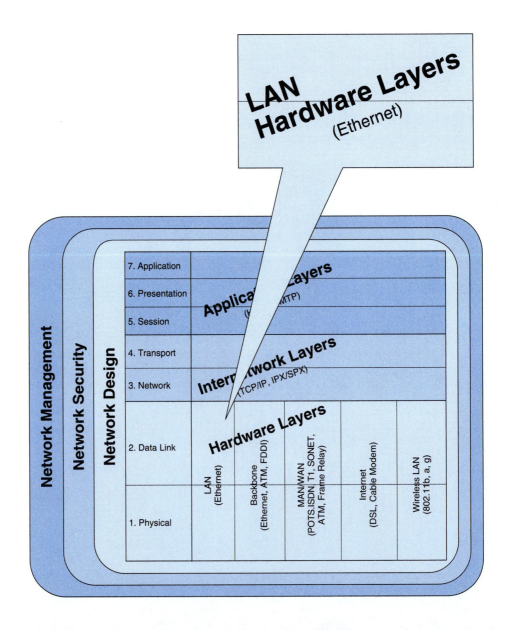

THIS CHAPTER examines how the hardware layers (physical and data link layers) in a local area network (LAN) work together to move a message from one computer or device to another. We describe the major hardware and software components of a LAN and explain how data is transmitted through the physical circuits. We also examine the two most commonly used LAN technologies (traditional Ethernet and switched Ethernet) and present a best practice recommendation for LAN design.

OBJECTIVES

- Understand the major components of LANs
- Understand shared Ethernet and switched Ethernet topologies
- Understand Ethernet media access control
- Understand Ethernet error control
- Be familiar with Ethernet message delineation
- Be familiar with how data is transmitted through physical circuits
- Understand the best practice recommendations for LAN design

CHAPTER OUTLINE

INTRODUCTION

TOPOLOGY

   Shared Ethernet

   Switched Ethernet

MEDIA ACCESS CONTROL

ERROR CONTROL

   Error Detection

   Error Correction

MESSAGE DELINEATION

   Codes

   Frame Layout

   Frame Size

DATA TRANSMISSION IN THE PHYSICAL LAYER

   10Base-T

   Fast Ethernet

INTRODUCTION

There used to be many different types of *local area network (LAN)* technologies, such as token ring and Arcnet, but gradually the world has changed so that one technology—Ethernet—dominates. Almost 95 percent of all LANs installed today use some form of *Ethernet*. Ethernet was originally developed by DEC, Xerox, and Intel but has since become a standard formalized by the Institute of Electrical and Electronics Engineers (IEEE) as IEEE 802.3.[1] In this chapter, we discuss only Ethernet LANs.

The hardware layers are composed of two layers: layer 2, data link layer, and layer 1, physical layer. Together, these two layers are responsible for moving messages from one computer to the next computer in the route decided by the internetwork layers above them. The physical layer is responsible for moving the bits given to it by the data link layer over the physical cables from the sender to the receiver. The data link layer links the hardware layers to the internetwork layers and performs three basic functions: It marks the start and end of message (message delineation); it controls when to transmit; and it can perform error control.

Ethernet has a fairly sophisticated error control system, more sophisticated in fact than that of TCP. Ethernet can both detect errors and correct them. However, because errors are rare in modern LANs, error correction is optional. Most organizations simply use the default settings, which causes Ethernet to detect errors but not correct them; when an error is discovered, the frame with the error is discarded the same way as TCP discards segments when it discovers an error.

These three functions are spread between two different parts of the data link layer, called the *logical link control (LLC)* sublayer and the *media access control (MAC)* sublayer. The LLC is usually implemented in software, while most of the MAC functions have been transferred into hardware to make them faster. By separating the data link layer functions into these two parts, it makes it easier to split the implementation to improve performance. It also makes it easier to reuse the LLC software in other technologies, as we will see in wireless LANs later in the book. The LLC sublayer is responsible for linking the hardware layers to the internetwork layers and performs most of the error control function, while the MAC sublayer performs media access control, message delineation, and some of the error control function.

---

[1] The IEEE 802.3 version of Ethernet is slightly different from the original version, but the differences are relatively minor. The formal specification for Ethernet is provided in the 802.3 standard on the IEEE standards Web site at grouper.ieee.org/groups/802/3.

There are several different types of Ethernet that can run at different data speeds. Although each of these versions of Ethernet works in the same basic manner, there are differences at the physical layer in the type of cables that are used and the way in which data are transmitted through the cables. 10Base-T is the version that runs at 10 Mbps (10 million bits per second) over twisted-pair cables. The 10 in the name indicates the speed, the Base in the middle indicates that digital transmission is being used, and the T at the end indicates the type of cable (we will discuss the types of cables and how digital transmission works later in this chapter). 100Base-T (sometimes called *fast Ethernet*) runs at 100 Mbps over twisted-pair cables, while 100Base-F runs at 100 Mbps over fiber-optic cables. Newer versions of Ethernet run at 1 Gbps, 10 Gbps, or 40 Gbps, usually over fiber-optic cables. Names for these newer versions, called *gigabit Ethernet,* have not settled down in the marketplace; the 1 Gbps version is often called 1000Base-T, 1000Base-F, or 1 GbE. The other versions are called 10 GbE and 40 GbE.

In this chapter, we first present the two basic topologies of Ethernet LANs—the ways in which the network can be built. Then we focus on the three functions of the data link layer: media access control, error control, and message delineation. Next we examine the physical layer: the different cables that are used by the different types of Ethernet and how data are actually transmitted through them. We close with our recommendations for the best practice LAN design.

TOPOLOGY

Topology is the basic geometric layout of the network—the way in which the computers on the network are interconnected. It is important to distinguish between a logical topology and a physical topology. A *logical topology* is how the network works conceptually, much like a logical DFD or logical ERD in systems analysis and design or database design. A *physical topology* is how the network is physically installed, much like a physical DFD or physical ERD. The logical topology reflects how the network works on the inside, from the point of view of the bits flowing through it, while the physical topology reflects how the network is built from the outside from the perspective of the people using it.

Ethernet has two different logical topologies (*shared Ethernet* and *switched Ethernet*), but both have the same physical topology. Shared Ethernet is the original topology, while switched Ethernet is the newer topology. As you might expect, the newer switched Ethernet gives better performance—and is more expensive.

Shared Ethernet

In addition to the computers, there are three principal components of a shared Ethernet LAN that together form its topology: the network interface cards, the cables, and the hub (see Figure 4-1).

Network Interface Cards   The *network interface card (NIC)* is used to connect the computer to the network cable and is one part of the physical layer connection among the computers in the network. Many computers come with a NIC built in, but sometimes a separate NIC must be installed. Some laptops, for example, have a special port that enables network cards to be installed without physically opening them (i.e., PCMCIA).

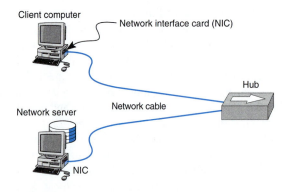
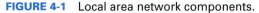

FIGURE 4-1 Local area network components.

Cables Each computer must be physically connected by network cable to the other computers in the network. Each of the different speeds of Ethernet requires a different type of cable. Most LANs are built with *twisted-pair cable* or *fiber-optic cable,* as we will discuss in detail later in this chapter.

Data can flow through cables in one of three different modes (see Figure 4-2). *Simplex* is one-way transmission, such as that in radio or TV transmission. *Half-duplex* is two-way transmission, but you can transmit in only one direction at a time. A half-duplex communication link is similar to a walkie-talkie link; only one computer can transmit at a time, so the computers must take turns transmitting. With *full-duplex* transmission, you can transmit in both directions simultaneously, with no waiting. Half-duplex is the most common in shared Ethernet LANs.

Hubs A *hub* serves two functions. First, a hub provides an easy way to connect network cables. A hub can be thought of as a junction box, permitting new computers to be connected to the network as easily as plugging a power cord into an electrical socket (see Figure 4-3). Each connection point where a cable can be plugged in is called a *port.* Hubs are

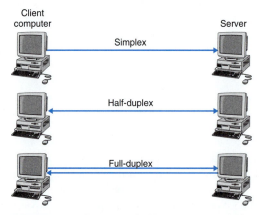

FIGURE 4-2 Simplex, half-duplex, and full-duplex transmissions.

FIGURE 4-3 Network hub.

commonly available in 4-, 8-, 16-, and 24-port sizes, meaning that they provide anywhere from 4 to 24 ports into which network cables can be plugged. When no cables are plugged in, transmissions bypass the unused port. When a cable is plugged into a port, the transmission travels down the cable as though it was directly connected to the cables attached to the hub. Some hubs and switches also enable different types of cables to be connected and perform the necessary conversions (e.g., twisted pair to fiber optic).

The second major function is to act as a repeater. As electrical or light signals travel through a cable, they gradually become weaker and weaker, in the same way that someone's voice gradually becomes weaker and weaker the farther you walk away from him or her. This gradual weakening of the data signal as it travels through the cable is called *attenuation*. All LAN cables are rated for the maximum distance they can be used (typically 100 meters for twisted pair, and 200–500 meters or even several kilometers for fiber optic cable). Any shared Ethernet LAN that spans more than these distances—and most do—must use a hub to regenerate the signal.

Hubs are simple devices that operate at the physical layer. They simply move electricity or light with no understanding of the data that the electrical or light signal contains. They are junction boxes; nothing more. Any time a signal enters a hub on any cable, the hub retransmits the signal on *all* other cables attached to the hub. This means that only one signal can arrive at the hub at one time. If two signals reach the hub at the same time, the hub will attempt to retransmit both signals to all attached cables, resulting in a collision and messages that cannot be understood. Thus computers attached to a hub must share the circuit that runs through the hub and take turns using it. Computers attached to the same hub must be careful not to attempt to transmit at the same time. The type of circuit created by a hub is called a *multipoint circuit* or a *shared circuit.*

Logical Topology   Shared Ethernet's logical topology—how it operates on the inside—is a *bus topology.* All computers are connected to one multipoint half-duplex circuit running the length of the network that is called the bus. The top part of Figure 4-4 shows Ethernet's logical topology. All messages from any computer flow onto the shared central cable (or bus) and through it to all computers on the LAN. Every computer on the bus receives *all* messages sent on the bus, even those intended for other computers. Before processing an incoming message, the Ethernet software on each computer checks the data link layer address and processes only those addressed to itself.

Physical Topology   The bottom part of Figure 4-4 shows the physical topology of a shared Ethernet LAN. From the outside, an Ethernet LAN *appears* to be a *star topology* in which all cables connect to the central hub.

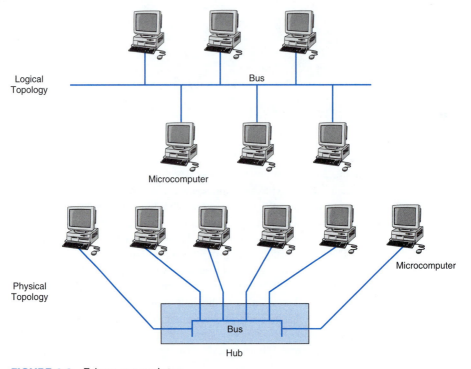

FIGURE 4-4 Ethernet topology.

Many Ethernet LANs span sufficient distance to require several hubs. In this case, the hubs are connected via cable in the same manner as any other connection in the network (see Figure 4-5).

Switched Ethernet

Switched Ethernet has the same NICs and cables as shared Ethernet, but a switch replaces the hub. This type of switch is often called a *workgroup switch* (because it is designed to support a small set of computers in one LAN) or a *layer-2 switch* (because it uses the layer-2 data link layer address, (i.e., the Ethernet address), to decide where to send the message). Shared Ethernet and switched Ethernet are identical, except for the difference between hubs and switches.

Switches A switch performs the same two functions as a hub (acting as a junction box and a repeater) but differs from a hub in one very important way. A hub provides a shared multipoint circuit while a switch provides a set of separate *point-to-point circuits*. Each circuit connected to a switch is *not* shared with any other devices; only the switch and the attached computer use it. In most cases, the switch and the computer must still take turns using the point-to-point circuit because it is usually a *half-duplex* circuit so only the computer or the switch can transmit at one time. Occasionally, companies build switched Ethernet LANs using full-duplex circuits, but this is more expensive than using half-duplex circuits.

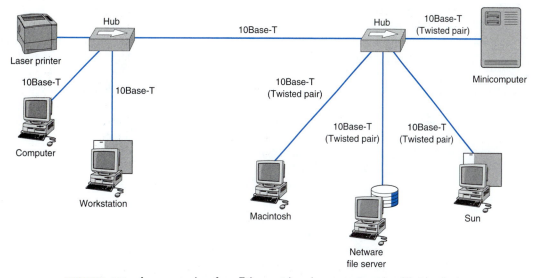

FIGURE 4-5   An example of an Ethernet local area network with two hubs.

Switches have chips on board that enable them to understand the Ethernet frames that pass through them. They can understand the Ethernet data link layer frames and read the information they contain. All Ethernet frames contain a destination address that specifies the destination computer for the frame. When a switch receives a frame it looks at the address on the frame and retransmits the frame only on the circuit on which it needs to go, not to all circuits as a hub would.

So how does a switch know which circuit is connected to what computer and where to send messages? The switch uses a *forwarding table* that is very similar to the routing tables discussed in Chapter 3. The table lists the Ethernet address of the computer connected to each port on the switch. When the switch receives a frame it compares the destination address on the frame to the addresses in its forwarding table to find the port number on which it needs to transmit the frame.

When switches are first turned on, their forwarding tables are empty; they do not know what Ethernet address is attached to what port. Switches *learn* addresses to build the forwarding table. When a switch receives a frame, it reads the frame's source address (the address of the computer that sent the frame) and compares this address to its forwarding table. If the address is not in the forwarding table, the switch adds it along with the port on which the message was received.

If a switch receives a frame with a destination address that is not in the forwarding table, the switch must still send the frame to the correct destination. In this case, it will retransmit the frame to all ports, except the one on which the frame was received. So, for the first few minutes until the forwarding table is built, the switch acts like a hub. But as its forwarding table becomes more complete, it begins to act more and more like a switch. In a busy network, it takes only a few minutes for the switch to learn most addresses and match them to port numbers.

Topology   The physical topology of switched Ethernet is the same as that of shared Ethernet: a star. What differs is the logical topology: Switched Ethernet's logical topology is a set of separate point-to-point circuits—a star—not the shared bus of shared Ethernet. See Figure 4-6.

In traditional shared Ethernet, all devices share the same multipoint circuit and must take turns using it. When a message is sent from one computer to another, it enters the hub, and the hub retransmits it to *all* the computers attached to the hub. Each computer looks at the Ethernet address on incoming frames and if the address on the frame does not match its address, it discards the frame. This process ensures that no two computers transmit at the same time, because they are always listening and do not transmit when they are receiving a message, even if the message is not addressed to them. If the hub did not send the message to all computers, a computer could begin transmitting at the same time as another computer and never be aware of it.

When a switch receives a frame from a computer it looks at the address on the frame and retransmits the frame only on the circuit connected to that computer, not to all circuits as a hub would. For example, in Figure 4-7, if Computer A sends a frame to the switch destined for Computer C, the switch retransmits it only on the circuit connected to Computer C. In contrast, with shared Ethernet, the frame would be sent to B, C, and the server.

Switches use a *store-and-forward* approach to managing LAN traffic. Unlike a hub, in which all attached cables form one shared circuit and so the hub can process only one frame at a time (forcing all attached computers to wait until the one frame is transmitted and it is someone else's turn), a switch is built so that it can simultaneously send or receive

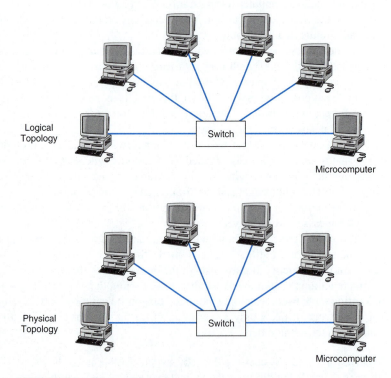

FIGURE 4-6 Ethernet topology.

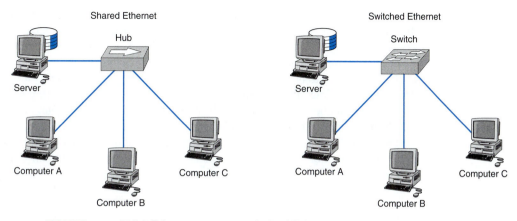

FIGURE 4-7   802.3 Ethernet versus switched Ethernet.

frames on *all* the attached circuits. In Figure 4-7, Computer A could be sending a frame to the server at the same time as Computer B sends one to Computer C.

It is possible that two computers may attempt to transmit a frame to the same computer at the same time. For example both A and B send a frame to C. In this case, the switch chooses which frame to transmit first (usually, the first frame it receives is sent first), and temporarily stores all other frames for that circuit in its internal memory. When the frame is finished being transmitted and the circuit is again free, the switch then retransmits (or forwards) the temporarily stored frames.

MEDIA ACCESS CONTROL

When computers share one communication circuit as they do in shared Ethernet or on half-duplex cables, media access control is important. If two computers on the same circuit transmit at the same time, their transmissions will become garbled. Such "collisions" must be prevented, or if they do occur, there must be a way to recover from them. This is called *media access control.*

Ethernet uses a *contention*-based media access control technique called *Carrier Sense Multiple Access with Collision Detection (CSMA/CD)*. CSMA/CD is very simple in concept: Listen until you are sure the circuit is free and then transmit. Computers listen for a short period of time to make sure no other devices are transmitting (9.6 microseconds) and then transmit their data. If another computer is transmitting, they wait until that computer stops and then transmit. As an analogy, suppose you are talking with a small group of four or five friends. As the discussion progresses, each person tries to "grab the floor" when the previous speaker finishes. Usually, the other members of the group yield to the first person who jumps in right after the previous speaker.

Ethernet's CSMA/CD protocol can be termed "ordered chaos." As long as no other computer attempts to transmit at the same time, everything is fine. However, it is possible that two computers located some distance from one another can both listen to the circuit, find it empty, and begin to transmit simultaneously. This simultaneous transmission is called a *collision*. The two messages collide and destroy each other.

The solution to this is to listen while transmitting, called *collision detection (CD)*. If the NIC detects any signal other than its own, it presumes that a collision has occurred and sends a jamming signal. All computers stop transmitting and wait for the circuit to become free before trying to retransmit. The problem is that the computers that caused the collision could attempt to retransmit at the same time. To prevent this, each computer waits a random amount of time after the colliding message disappears before attempting to retransmit. Chances are both computers will choose a different random amount of time and one will begin to transmit before the other, thus preventing a second collision. However, if another collision occurs, the computers again wait a random amount of time before trying again. This does not eliminate collisions completely, but it reduces them to manageable proportions.

ERROR CONTROL

Network errors are a fact of life in data communications networks. Depending on the type of circuit, they may occur every few hours, minutes, or seconds because of noise on the lines. No network can eliminate all errors, but most errors can be prevented, detected, and corrected by proper design. Normally, errors appear in bursts (so that many bits are changed at one time) followed by a long period of error-free transmission bits at a time. The most common source of noise is impulse noise—occasional bursts of random electricity, sometimes due to machinery or lightning. There are many techniques to prevent errors, but the most common is to use shielded cable. Error control in networks has two separate but related functions: error detection and error correction.

TECHNICAL FOCUS *4-1*

SOURCES OF ERROR

There are many different factors that can cause errors in data communications. The most common are:

- *Line outages* are catastrophic failures of communication circuits for brief periods and may be caused by construction workers accidentally cutting a cable, faulty equipment, storms, loss of power, and any other failure that causes a short circuit.

- *Impulse noise* (sometimes called a *spike*) is the most common source of errors. Impulse noise is heard as a click or a crackling noise and can last as long as 1/100 of a second. Some of the sources of impulse noise are voltage changes in adjacent lines, lightning flashes during thunderstorms, fluorescent lights, heavy machinery, and poor connections in circuits. Shielding can often reduce impulse noise.

- *Crosstalk* occurs when one circuit picks up signals in another. It occurs between pairs of wires that are carrying separate signals, and in wireless links in which one antenna picks up a minute reflection from another antenna. Crosstalk between lines increases with increased communication distance, increased proximity of the two wires, increased signal strength, and higher-frequency signals. Wet or damp weather can also increase crosstalk. Crosstalk is usually due to the improper installation of cables and can be fixed by repairing the faulty connections.

- *Echoes* are caused by poor connections that cause the signal to reflect back to the transmitting equipment and can be fixed by repairing the faulty connections.

Error Detection

As we discussed in Chapter 3, most error detection procedures work by sending extra error detection data with each message. These error detection data are added to each message by the sender based on some mathematical calculations performed on the message. The receiver performs the same mathematical calculations on the message it receives and matches its results against the error detection data that were transmitted with the message. If the two match, the message is assumed to be correct. If they don't match, an error has occurred.

In general, the larger the amount of error detection data sent, the greater the ability to detect an error. However, as the amount of error detection data is increased, the throughput of useful data is reduced, because more of the available capacity is used to transmit these error detection data and less is used to transmit the actual message itself. Therefore, the efficiency of data throughput varies inversely as the desired amount of error detection is increased.

Ethernet uses an error detection scheme called *cyclical redundancy check (CRC)*. With CRC, a message is treated as one long binary number, P. Before transmission, the data link layer (or hardware device) divides P by a fixed binary number, G, resulting in a whole number, Q, and a remainder, R/G. So, $P/G = Q + R/G$. For example, if $P = 58$ and $G = 8$, then $Q = 7$ and $R = 2$. G is chosen so that the remainder R will be either 8 bits, 16 bits, 24 bits, or 32 bits.[2]

The remainder, R, is appended to the message as the error-checking characters before transmission. The receiving hardware divides the received message by the same G, which generates an R. The receiving hardware checks to ascertain whether the received R agrees with the locally generated R. If it does not, the message is assumed to be in error.

There are many different types of CRC, depending on the length of the fixed binary number used to divide by and the resulting size of the remainder. The most commonly used CRC codes are CRC-16 (a 16-bit version), CRC-CCITT (another 16-bit version using a different value for G), and CRC-32 (a 32-bit version).

The CRC approach will always detect short errors that are less than or equal to the number of bits it uses. For example, CRC-16 is guaranteed to detect errors if 16 or fewer bits are affected. If the error is longer than the CRC, then CRC is not perfect but is close to it. CRC-16 will detect about 99.998 percent of all errors longer than 16 bits, while CRC-32 will detect about 99.99999998 percent of all errors longer than 32 bits. Ethernet uses CRC-32.

Error Correction

As we noted at the start of the chapter, error correction in Ethernet is optional. The default setting – that is, the setting used unless it is explicitly changed by the network manager – is to use error detection *without* error correction. If an error is detected, the frame containing the error is simply discarded. This means that some higher level protocol such as TCP must ensure reliable delivery or there is a chance that data will be lost.

When error correction is turned on, Ethernet uses a technique called *stop-and-wait ARQ* (ARQ is an abbreviation of Automatic Repeat reQuest), which is similar to the error control technique used by TCP.

---

[2] CRC is actually more complicated than this because it uses polynominal division, not "normal" division as illustrated here. Ross Williams provides an excellent tutorial on CRC at www.ross.net/crc/crcpaper.html.

With stop-and-wait ARQ, the sender stops and waits for a response from the receiver after each data frame. After receiving a frame, the receiver sends either an *acknowledgment (ACK)* if the frame was received without error, or a *negative acknowledgment (NAK)* if the message contained an error. If it is an ACK, the sender continues with the next message. If it is a NAK, the sender resends the previous message. Stop-and-wait ARQ is, by definition, a half-duplex transmission technique (see Figure 4-8).

Things become a bit more complicated when we consider that messages and ACKs and NAKs can get lost. Suppose, for example, that the sender sends a message and it is lost (due to error or a collision). The sender will continue to wait until it receives an ACK or a NAK that will never come, because the receiver has not received the message. To prevent this, Ethernet waits a set number of milliseconds before it *times out*, assumes the message was lost, and retransmits the message. However, this too poses a problem, because if the message was received and it was just the ACK that was lost (not the message), the receiver now gets a duplicate message. The solution for this is for the receiver to retain a copy of the last message received so that duplicate messages can be recognized.

Stop-and-wait ARQ is also useful in providing *flow control*. Flow control means ensuring that the computer sending the message is not transmitting too quickly for the receiver. For example, if a client computer was sending information too quickly for a server to store a file being uploaded, the server might run out of memory to store the file. By using ACKs and NAKs the receiver can control the rate at which it receives information. With stop-and-wait ARQ, the receiver does not send an ACK until it is ready to receive more frames.

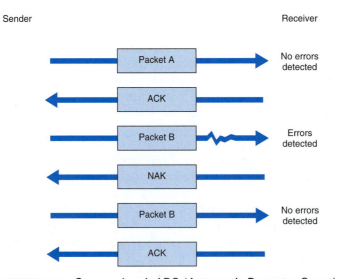

FIGURE 4-8 Stop-and-wait ARQ (Automatic Repeat reQuest). ACK = acknowledgment; NAK = negative acknowledgment.

MANAGEMENT FOCUS *4 - 1*

FINDING THE SOURCE OF IMPULSE NOISE

Several years ago, the campus radio station at The University of Georgia received FCC approval to broadcast using a stronger signal. Immediately after they started broadcasting, the campus backbone network became unusable due to impulse noise. It took two days to link the impulse noise to the radio station, and when the radio station returned to its usual broadcast signal the problem disappeared.

However, this was only the first step in the problem. The radio station wanted to broadcast at full strength and there was no good reason why the stronger broadcast should affect the backbone in this way. After two weeks of effort, the problem was discovered. A short section of the backbone ran above ground between two buildings. It turns out that the specific brand of outdoor cable we used was particularly tasty to squirrels. They had eaten the outer insulating coating off of the cable, making it act like an antennae to receive the radio signals. The cable was replaced with a steel-coated armored cable so the squirrels could not eat the insulation. Things worked fine when the radio station returned to its stronger signal.

MESSAGE DELINEATION

Message delineation (also called *framing*) means to mark the start and end of messages. The physical layer is responsible for transmitting messages as a series of electrical or light pulses, but has no understanding of the message. It is up to the data link layer to format the message so that the stream of bits transferred by the physical layer can be understood.

Codes

For data to be understood by both the sender and receiver, both must agree on a standard system for representing the letters, numbers, and symbols that make up the messages. A *coding scheme* (often called a *code* for short) is the language that computers use to represent data. All coding schemes have a set of *characters* that are symbols that have a common, constant meaning. A character might be the letter *A* or *b,* or it might be a number such as 1 or 2. Characters also may be special symbols such as ? or &. Characters in data communications, as in computer systems, are represented by groups of *bits* that are binary zeros (0) and ones (1). The groups of bits representing the set of characters that are the "alphabet" of any given system are called a coding scheme. A *byte* is a group of consecutive bits that is treated as a unit or character. One byte normally is composed of 8 bits and usually represents one character, but some coding schemes use 5,6,7,8, or 9 bits to represent a character.

The most commonly used coding scheme is *United States of America Standard Code for Information Interchange (USASCII),* more commonly called *ASCII* (pronounced *ass-key*). There are several types of ASCII, including a 7-bit coding scheme that has 128 valid character combinations, and an 8-bit one that has 256 combinations. The number of combinations can be determined by taking the number 2 and raising it to the power equal to the number of bits in the code. In this case $2^7 = 128$ characters or $2^8 = 256$ characters. Ethernet usually uses 8-bit ASCII.

Frame Layout

Ethernet's data link layer uses a frame format in the same way that the network layer has IP packets to enable the sender and receiver to communicate. There are at present five different versions of Ethernet, each with different frame layouts and sizes. Figure 4-9 shows the frame layout for the IEEE 802.3ac standard, which is the newest version and is likely to become the most commonly used version. There are four distinct parts to the Ethernet frame: preamble, MAC header, LLC data, and MAC trailer.

Preamble   The purpose of the *preamble* is to mark the start of the Ethernet frame. The receiver is constantly monitoring the physical circuit for possible incoming data. When the receiver recognizes the bit patterns of the 8-byte preamble, it understands that the Ethernet frame is about to follow and begins to process the incoming data. The preamble has two parts. The first is a set of 7 sync bytes that have alternating 1s and 0s (i.e., 10101010). The second is a 1-byte start-of-frame delimiter (10101011). When the receiver recognizes the start-of-frame delimiter, it knows that the MAC header immediately follows.

MAC Header   The purpose of the *MAC header* is to provide the addresses and to indicate where the frame ends. The first field in the MAC header is the 6-byte *destination address,* which specifies the Ethernet address of the receiver. The next is the 6-byte *source address* field, which specifies the Ethernet address of sender. An Ethernet frame can vary in length depending on the length of the message it contains, so the 2-byte *length* field indicates the length in 8-bit bytes of the message portion of the frame; this length field is required because without it, the receiver would have no way of knowing when the message ended.

The *VLAN tag* field is an optional 4-byte address field used by virtual LANs (VLANs), which are discussed in Chapter 5. The Ethernet frame uses this field only when VLANs are in use; otherwise the field is omitted, and the length field immediately follows the source address field. When the VLAN tag field is in use, the first 2 bytes are set to the number 24,832 (hexadecimal 81-00), which is obviously an impossible frame length. When Ethernet sees this frame length, it knows that the VLAN tag field is in use. When the frame length is some other value, it assumes that VLAN tags are not in use and that the length field immediately follows the source address field.

Preamble	MAC Header	LLC Protocol Data Unit	MAC Trailer

Sync Bytes	Start of Frame	Destination Address	Source Address	VLAN Tag	Length	DSAP	SSAP	Control	Data	FCS
7 bytes	1 byte	6 bytes	6 bytes	4 bytes	2 bytes	1 byte	1 byte	1-2 bytes	43-1497 bytes	4 bytes

FIGURE 4-9   Ethernet 802.3ac frame layout.

LLC Protocol Data Unit   The LLC *Protocol Data Unit (PDU)* is created by the LLC sublayer (while the other parts of the Ethernet frame are created by the MAC sublayer). The LLC PDC contains the packet data from the internetwork layers (i.e., the IP packet that contains the TCP segment that contains the application layer message) and is used to link the hardware layers to the internetwork layers. The 1-byte *Destination Service Access Point (DSAP)* specifies the internetwork layer software that is to receive the network layer packet, while the 1-byte *Source Service Access Point (SSAP)* specifies the internetwork layer software that generated the network layer packet. The DSAP and SSAP serve essentially the same function as the port field in the TCP segment. IP software, for example, is assigned a DSAP and SSAP of 10111011 (AA in hexadecimal), while IPX software is assigned a DSAP and SSAP of 11100000 (E0 in hexadecimal). When the LLC software receives an incoming frame with a DSAP of AA, it knows that it contains an IP packet and will pass it to the IP software.

The control field is used to hold the frame sequence numbers and ACKs and NAKs used for error control, as well as to enable the data link layers of communicating computers to exchange other control information. The last 2 bits in the first byte are used to indicate the type of control information being passed and whether the control field is 1 or 2 bytes (e.g., if the last 2 bits of the control field are 11, then the control field is 1 byte in length). In most cases, the control field is 1-byte long.

The data field contains the message passed to the data link layer by the network layer software and is often an IP packet (which contains a TCP segment, which contains an HTTP, SMTP, or similar request with the user's message). The maximum length of the data field is 1,497 bytes and the minimum is 43 bytes. The minimum is not usually an issue, because messages often include a 24-byte TCP segment and a 40-byte IP packet, but if the data is shorter than 43 bytes, it is padded with null characters. As we discussed in the previous chapter, larger packets are more efficient and provide greater throughput, with the ideal packet size for most networks being somewhere between 2,000 and 8,000 bytes. A newer version of Ethernet is currently in the standards process that is the same as 802.11ac, but will permit *jumbo frames* that increase the maximum size of the data field to 9,000 bytes.

MAC Trailer   The purpose of the MAC trailer is to support error control. The MAC trailer has just one field, the 4-byte *Frame Check Sequence (FCS)*. As mentioned above, Ethernet uses CRC-32.

Frame Size

The size of an Ethernet frame depends on which version of Ethernet is being used (i.e.,802.3ac as shown in Figure 4-9 or one of the other versions), whether VLAN tagging is in use, and the length of the control field. Assuming that 802.3ac is being used, that VLAN tagging is in use, and that the control field is only 1 byte, then the Ethernet frame has a total of 33 bytes of overhead, in addition to the overhead added by the higher-layer packets such as IP and TCP.

As you read other books or surf the Web, you may find that some sources say Ethernet frames are 20 or 26 bytes in length. These are not incorrect; they are just using different

MANAGEMENT FOCUS *4-2*

GIGABIT ETHERNET MAPS THE HUMAN GENOME

In the fall of 2000, an initial working draft of the human genome (the basic genetic makeup of the human body) was published. Gigabit Ethernet played a key role.

Incyte Genomics, a major player in the project, had been using 100Base-T but found its networks crumbling under the need to move an average of 70 terabits of data a day over its networks among its 1,300 high-power servers. It replaced more than 500 of its most heavily used circuits with 1000Base-T. Many of those circuits use time division multiplexing to combine several physical 1000Base-T circuits into 4 to 6 Gbps logical circuits.

SOURCE: "Genome Project Meets Gigabit Ethernet," *Network World,* September 18, 2000.

versions of Ethernet.[3] And for historical reasons, some authors do not include the 8-byte preamble and/or the 3- to 4-byte LLC PDU in their overhead length calculations.

DATA TRANSMISSION IN THE PHYSICAL LAYER

There are two fundamentally different types of data that can flow through the physical circuit: *digital* and *analog.* Computers produce digital data that are binary, either on or off, zero or one. In contrast, telephones produce analog data whose electrical signals are shaped like the sound waves they transfer; they can take on any value in a wide range of possibilities, not just 0 or 1.

Data can be transmitted through a circuit in the same form it is produced. Most computers, for example, transmit their data through digital circuits, while analog voice data can be transmitted through telephone networks in analog form. Data also can be converted from one form into the other for transmission over network circuits. For example, digital computer data can be transmitted over an analog telephone circuit by using a modem that converts the digital computer data into analog telephone data. LANs use digital transmission because the computers attached to them produce digital data.

There are also two basic ways in which data can be transmitted through a physical cable. *Serial mode* transmission means that a stream of data is sent over a cable sequentially in a bit-by-bit fashion as shown in Figure 4-10a. In this case, only one physical wire inside the cable is used and all data must be transmitted over that one wire. The transmitting device sends 1 bit, then a second bit, and so on, until all the bits in the character are transmitted. With *parallel mode,* there are many separate physical wires inside the cable and all bits of each character are transmitted at the same time on the separate wires. If the transmission uses an 8-bit coding scheme then there must be eight physical wires inside the cable so that all 8 bits of the character are transferred simultaneously. Figure 4-10b

---

[3] Fast Ethernet and gigabit Ethernet include two extra 1-byte fields. One replaces one of the preamble bytes at the start of the packet. The other is placed at the end of the packet and is treated as a normal idle byte because it is placed in the interframe gap (the 9.6-millisecond time period in which CSMA/CD waits before transmitting). For these reasons, most authors ignore them—and we will too!

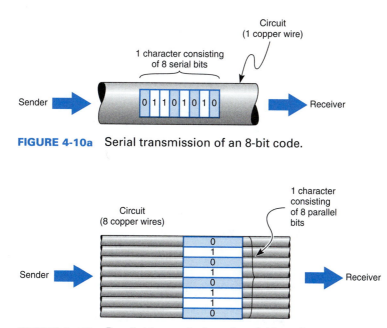

FIGURE 4-10a   Serial transmission of an 8-bit code.

FIGURE 4-10b   Parallel transmission of an 8-bit code.

shows how all 8 bits of one character could travel down a parallel communication circuit. The circuit is physically made up of eight separate wires, wrapped in one outer coating. Each physical wire is used to send 1 bit of the 8-bit character. However, as far as the user is concerned (and the network for that matter), there is only one circuit; each of the wires inside the cable bundle is simply connected to a different part of the plug that connects the computer to the bundle of wire.

In this section, we examine how Ethernet LANs transmit data over the physical cables that connect them. We begin with 10Base-T and then move to fast Ethernet, and then gigabit Ethernet.

10Base-T

The earliest forms of 10 Mbps Ethernet ran over coaxial cable, a special type of copper cable that today is more expensive and harder to work with than twisted-pair cable. Because it is seldom used today (except in cable TV networks), we do not discuss it here.

Twisted-Pair Cable   The most commonly used type of cable in Ethernet LANs is *twisted-pair cable,* insulated pairs of copper wires that are packed close together (see Figure 4-11). The paired wires are twisted to minimize the electromagnetic interference and crosstalk between wires. Twisted-pair wire comes in a variety of standard configurations that provide different transmission speeds and costs. *Category 3* cables (usually called cat 3) have two pairs of wires (four wires total), while *category 5* cables (usually called cat 5) have four sets of pairs (eight wires total) as shown in Figure 4-11. Twisted-pair cable can be purchased either as normal *unshielded twisted pair (UTP)* or as *shielded twisted pair (STP),* which has additional shielding to reduce interference that may cause errors in trans-

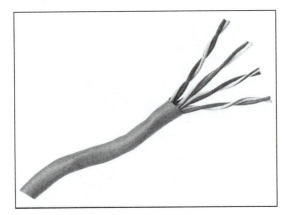

FIGURE 4-11 Twisted-pair wire.

mission. The maximum length of cat 3/5 cable for 10Base-T is 100 meters from the computer to the hub or switch.

In order to successfully send and receive messages, both the sender and receiver have to agree on which wire in the bundle will be used for what purpose, and what electrical voltages will be used. Because there are several wires in cat 3 or cat 5 cables, it would be reasonable to assume that parallel transmission is used—but it isn't; 10-Base-T uses a rather unintuitive approach to transmission. 10Base-T uses serial transmission over cat 3 cables (two pairs of two wires). One pair of two wires is used to transmit from the computer to the hub (or switch), while the other pair of two wires is used to receive data from the hub (or switch). Both wires in each pair transmit the same signal but with opposite polarity; the transmit+ wire uses positive charges while the transmit– uses negative charges. This redundancy helps reduce error and also reduces interference between the wires in the pair. Thus, 10Base-T is capable of full-duplex transmission at the hardware level, but it usually is implemented only as half-duplex.

Today, 10Base-T is most often wired with cat 5 cable, which has four pairs of wire in each cable. Yet, only two pairs are used so that cat 3 can still be used if desired. Figure 4-12 shows the way in which cat 5 cables are wired. The cable is wired into an *RJ-45 connector*,[4] which is an 8-pin connector used to plug into NICs, hubs, and switches. Pins 1 and 2 are the wires used to transmit from the computer's NIC, while pins 3 and 6 are used to receive transmissions at the computer's NIC. The pins on the hub or switch are reversed; that is, pins 1 and 2 deliver the computer's NIC's transmissions, so they are the receive pins at the hub or switch, while 3 and 6 are the transmit pins at the hub or switch.[5]

[4] To be very precise, it is not an RJ-45 connector, but rather a version of the RJ-45 designed for network use. The RJ-45 is designed for telephone use, which tolerates higher interference. Just about everyone calls it an RJ-45 connector, but if you ever buy a *real* RJ-45 connector designed for telephone use and try to build a LAN cable yourself to save a few dollars, it won't work.

[5] Any time you want to directly connect two computer NICs or two hubs/switches, you must use a *crossover cable* that connects pins 1 and 2 at one end to pins 3 and 6 at the other (and vice versa).

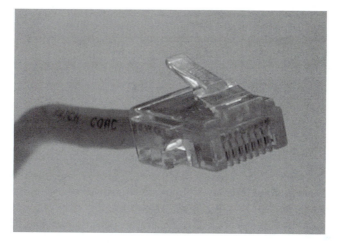

Pin Number	Color (EIA/TIA 568B standard)	Name
1	White with orange stripe	Transmit +
2	Orange with white stripe or solid orange	Transmit −
3	White with green stripe	Receive +
4	Blue with white stripe or solid blue	Not used
5	White with blue stripe	Not used
6	Green with white stripe or solid green	Receive −
7	White with brown stripe or solid brown	Not used
8	Brown with white stripe or solid brown	Not used

FIGURE 4-12   Pins used by 10Base-T and 100Base-T at the computer end.

Data Transmission   In order to successfully send and receive messages, both the sender and receiver have to agree how bits will be transmitted over the specific wires in the cable. They must understand both how fast the data will be sent and what electrical voltages will be used to represent a binary 1 and a binary 0. 10Base-T transmits at a rate of 10 Mbps or 10 million bits per second. This means that the computers divide each second into 10 million time periods in which they can send data. Each time period (100 *nanoseconds,* i.e., 100 billionths of a second) contains 1 bit, either a binary 1 or a binary 0. Thus each wire in the cat 3 or cat 5 cable must be cable of carrying a signal that changes 10 million times per second; we call this a *signaling rate* of 10 million hertz or 10 MHz.

One of the challenges in transmitting this fast is making sure that the clock at the receiver is synchronized with the clock at the sender so they can both understand when one of these 100-nanosecond time periods starts and stops. If the clocks are not synchronized then the sender could be trying to read what it thinks is the end of the fourth bit while the sender is sending the start of the fifth bit. This is done by using *Manchester encoding.*

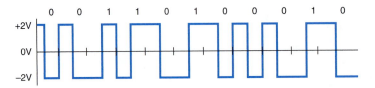

FIGURE 4-13 Manchester encoding.

Manchester encoding is a special type of signaling in which the signal is changed from high voltage (2 volts) to low voltage (0 volts) or vice versa in the middle of the signal. A change from low to high is used to represent a 1, while the opposite (a change from high to low) is used to represent a 0. See Figure 4-13. Thus, in the exact middle of each time period, the signal voltage changes. This "heartbeat" synchronizes the clocks.

Fast Ethernet

Fast Ethernet is the version of Ethernet that runs at 100 Mbps. There are two flavors in common use: *100Base-Tx* (almost always called *100Base-T*), which runs at 100 Mbps over cat 5 twisted-pair cable, and *100Base-F,* which runs at 100 Mbps over fiber-optic cable.[6]

100Base-T   100Base-T transmits data over cat 5 cables using serial transmission. It uses exactly the same wiring and connector pin configurations as 10Base-T, so the wiring for the two types of LANs is identical (see Figure 4-12). The maximum length of cat 5 cable for 100Base-T is 100 meters from the computer to the hub or switch.

100Base-T does not use Manchester encoding. 100Base-T uses *4B5B coding,* in which the data are sent in groups of 5 bits, the first four of which are data, and the last one is used for clock-synchronizing purposes and to minimize interference. The fifth bit is chosen to ensure than no more than 4 out of the 5 bits have the same value. Because of the high speed at which the data are being transmitted, a long series of all 1s or all 0s would result in a long transmission of positive or negative voltage, which has a greater chance of causing interference to other wires than an alternating positive and negative pattern of voltages. Also, without regular changes in signal as is done in Manchester encoding, it becomes increasingly difficult to ensure that the clocks on the sender and receiver are synchronized. Adding this extra fifth bit every 4 bits of data ensures that no long single-level transmissions are sent and ensures a transition for clock synchronizing.

In order to achieve a data rate of 100 Mbps when using 4B5B, the sender and receiver have to operate at 125 MHz, because only 4 out of every 5 bits transmitted contain data. 100Base-T uses a technique called *Multi-Level Transmission—3 Level* (MLT-3) to transmit the 4B5B codes through the cable. With MLT-3, three levels of voltage are defined, +1 volts, 0 volts, and −1 volts. MLT-3 is based on changes in voltages as is Manchester encoding, but in a different way. To send a binary 0, MLT-3 simply maintains the same voltage as used in the previous time slot. To transmit a binary 1, the voltage is changed to an adjacent level (e.g., from –1 to 0 or 0 to +1).

Because 100Base-T is wired in exactly the same manner as 10Base-T, most 100Base-T NICs, hubs, and switches are *autosensing,* which means that when a NIC is first powered on, it exchanges messages with the hub or switch to see whether to use 10Base-T or 100Base-T. If the NIC, hub, or switch detects a 100Base-T device on the other end, it uses 100Base-T; if it detects a 10Base-T device, it uses 10Base-T. As with 10Base-T, 100Base-T is physically wired for full-duplex, but is most often installed using half-duplex.

100Base-F   100Base-F uses *fiber-optic cable.* Instead of carrying signals in the traditional electrical form, this fiber-optic cable uses high-speed streams of light pulses from lasers or LEDs (light emitting diodes) that carry information inside hair-thin strands of glass optical fibers. Figure 4-14 shows a fiber-optic cable and depicts the strand or optical core, the cladding (the outer covering over the fiber core), and how light rays travel in optical fibers.

The first fiber-optic systems were step index *multimode fiber (MMF),* meaning that the light could reflect inside the cable at many different angles. MMF cables experience excessive signal weakening (attenuation) and dispersion (spreading of the signal so that different parts of the signal arrive at different times at the destination). For these reasons, MMF is often limited to about 550 meters. Graded index MMF attempts to reduce this problem by changing the refractive properties of the glass fiber so that as the light approaches the outer edge of the fiber, it speeds up, which compensates for the slightly longer distance it must travel compared to light in the center of the fiber. Therefore, the light in the center is more likely to arrive at the same time as the light that has traveled at the edges of the fiber. This increases the effective distance to just under 1,000 meters.

Single-mode fiber (SMF) cables transmit a single direct beam of light through a cable that ensures the light only reflects in one pattern, in part because the core diameter is smaller. This smaller diameter core allows the fiber to send a more concentrated light beam resulting in faster data transmission speeds and longer distances, often up to 100 kilometers. However, because the light source must be perfectly aligned with the cable, SMF cables use lasers (rather than the LEDs used in multimode systems) and therefore require more expensive NICs and switches.

Fiber-optic cable is thinner and lighter than unshielded twisted pair, weighing less than 10 pounds per 1,000 feet and requiring far less space when cabled throughout a building. Fiber optic comes in several grades; three of the most commonly used in LANs are 62.5/125 MMF, 50/125 MMF, and 10/125 SMF. The first number refers to the width of the fiber strand that transmits the light (e.g., 62.5 micrometers), while the second refers to the size of the cladding around the fiber (e.g., 125 micrometers).

However, fiber-optic cables are more expensive than twisted-pair cables. They are also not as flexible as twisted-pair cables, because the glass can be broken if bent too sharply. Generally speaking, when companies choose to use fiber cables rather than twisted-pair cables, it is because they need to run the cables farther than they can run twisted-pair cables.

100Base-F transmits data over multimode fiber-optic cables using serial transmission. It uses a pair of 61.5/125 MMF, usually joined together as one cable. One strand of fiber is used by the computer's NIC to transmit while the other is used by the NIC to

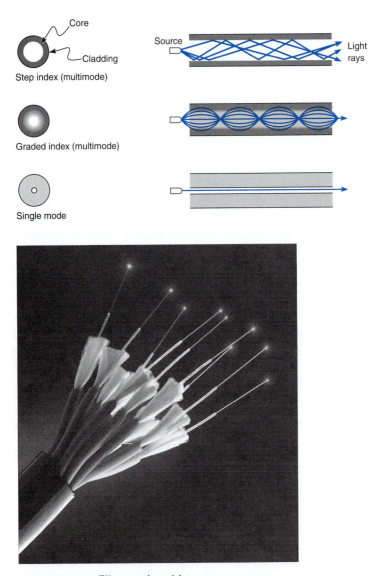

Core

Cladding

Step index (multimode)

Source

Light rays

Graded index (multimode)

Single mode

FIGURE 4-14 Fiber-optic cable.

receive from the hub or switch. So, it too is wired for full-duplex, but is often configured to use half-duplex. While 100Base-F can be used in shared Ethernet topologies, it is almost always used in switched topologies. The maximum length of MMF for 100Base-F is usually 412 meters from the computer to the hub or switch (one version of 100Base-F can run 20 kilometers using SMF).

100Base-F transmits data through the fiber strands by varying the brightness of the light. A binary 0 is transmitted as a dim light, while a binary 1 is transmitted as a brighter light. This technique is called *non-return-to-zero (NRZ)* because the light is never turned

TECHNICAL FOCUS *4-2*

COMMONLY USED NETWORK CABLE STANDARDS

There are many standard types of twisted-pair cable and fiber-optic cable. Categories 2–4 of UTP are seldom used today.

Name	Type	Data Rate (Mbps)	Often Used By	Cost[1] ($/foot)
Category 1[2]	UTP	1	Modem	.04
Category 2	STP	4	4 Mbps token ring[3]	.35
Category 3	UTP	10	10Base-T Ethernet	.05
Category 4	STP	16	16 Mbps token ring[3]	.60
Category 5	UTP	100	100Base-T Ethernet	.07
Category 5	STP	100	100Base-T Ethernet	.16
Category 5e[4]	UTP	125	1,000Base-T Ethernet	.13
Category 6[5]	UTP	200	1,000Base-T Ethernet	.18
Category 7[5]	STP	600	1,000Base-T Ethernet	.30
62.5/125	MMF	1000	1 Gbe	.45
50/125	SMF	1000	1 Gbe	.75

Notes

1. These are approximate costs for cables. They change, but will give you a sense of the relative differences in costs among the different options.

2. Category 1 is standard telephone-voice-grade twisted pair, but can also be used to support low-speed analog data transmission.

3. Token ring is an old LAN technology seldom used today.

4. Cat 5e is an improved version of cat 5 that has better insulation and a center plastic pipe inside the cable to keep the individual wires in place and reduce noise from crosstalk, so that it is better suited to 1000Base-T.

5. The standards for cat 6 and cat 7 have not been finalized.

---

off (i.e., it never returns to zero light in the same way that the MLT-3 of 100Base-T does on occasion return to zero volts).

Gigabit Ethernet

Gigabit Ethernet is a family of techniques that run at 1 billion bits per second and higher. The family includes 1-Gbps and 10-Gbps data rates, with faster versions on the horizon.

1 GbE—Gigabit Ethernet   One type of gigabit Ethernet (commonly called 1 GbE) is simply Ethernet that runs at 1000 Mbps or 1 Gbps. Like fast Ethernet, 1 GbE can run over twisted-pair cables or fiber-optic cables.[7] While gigabit Ethernet can be used in shared topologies, it is almost always used in switched topologies.

The version of 1 GbE that runs over twisted-pair cables is called *1000Base-T.* 1000Base-T runs over one cat 5 cable by using parallel transmission. That is, it uses each of the four pairs of wires in the cat 5 cable as a separate half-duplex circuit with a transmit

[7] There is also a version called 1000Base-CX that runs over a special type of copper cable for distances of 25 meters or less, but this is seldom used.

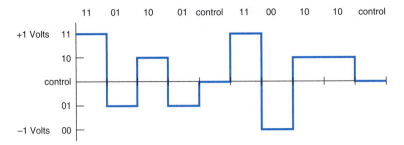

FIGURE 4-15 Pulse Amplitude Modulation–5 encoding.

and receive wire pair. We now have four parallel circuits running through the one cable, so in each clock tick we can send four signals at a time through the cable. As you will recall, fast Ethernet used a 4B5B coding scheme in which the set of 5 bits (4 data, 1 overhead) were transmitted at 125 MHz (i.e., 125 million times per second) giving a speed of 100 Mbps; 125 MHz is the fastest data rate at which the wires in cat 5 can reliably transmit for any reasonable distance. However, 125 MHz times 4 bits per signal equals only 500 Mbps. In order to get 1,000 Mbps, we have to do something more creative.

Until now, we talked about transmitting 1 bit in each time interval by using a higher voltage and a lower voltage (e.g., see Manchester encoding in Figure 4-13). Gigabit Ethernet uses the same 125 MHz clock speed as fast Ethernet, but sends 2 bits in each time interval using *pulse amplitude modulation–5* (PAM–5). With PAM–5, five different voltage levels are defined, ranging from +1 volts to –1 volts (see Figure 4-15). Four of these voltage levels are used to send data. One voltage is defined to be the 2-bit pattern 00, another is defined to be 01, another 10, and another 11. The fifth voltage level is used for the fifth control bit. So, in each time period, the sender sends one electrical pulse at one of the five defined voltage levels, which represent a certain pattern of 2 bits, rather than just 1 bit as with Manchester encoding. Two bits per time interval times 125 time intervals per second times four separate circuit pairs in each cat 5 cable equals 1,000 Mbps.

Because we are now sending 2 bits per signal using five different voltage levels rather than just two voltage levels as with Manchester encoding or 4B5B, the signal is now more susceptible to noise or interference. This is because it is more difficult for the NIC to distinguish among differences in five voltage levels rather than in two voltage levels because the differences between levels are smaller. It takes a much smaller amount of noise to trick the NIC into thinking a signal sent at one voltage level is actually at a different level. For this reason, most organizations use cat 5e cable for 100Base-T; cat 5e is a version of cat 5 cable specially modified to reduce errors when used in 1000Base-T installations. Cat 6 cable has also been proposed, which has a capacity of 250 MHz. The maximum length of cat 5/5e/6 cable for 1000Base-T is 100 meters from the computer to the hub or switch.

There are two versions of fiber-optic gigabit Ethernet: *1000Base-SX* uses MMF, while *1000Base-LX* uses either MMF or SMF, depending on the distance you need to run the cable. 1000Base-LX using SMF can run up to 5 kilometers, but using MMF it is 220

MANAGEMENT FOCUS *4-3*

MANAGING NETWORK CABLING

In the "old days," cable was installed wherever it was simple to install it. Today, wiring is much more formal. You must consider a number of items when installing cables or when performing cable maintenance:

- Perform a physical inventory of any existing cabling systems and document those findings in the network cable plan.

- Properly maintain the network cable plan. Always update cable documentation immediately on installing or removing a cable or hub. Insist that any cabling contractor provide "as-built" plans that document where the cabling was actually placed, in case of minor differences from the construction plan.

- Establish a long-term plan for the evolution of the current cabling system to whatever cabling system will be in place in the future.

- Obtain a copy of the local city fire codes and follow them. For example, cables used in airways without conduit need to be plenum certified (i.e., covered with a fire retardant jacket).

- Conceal all cables as much as possible to protect them from damage and for security reasons.

- Properly number and mark both ends of all cable installations as you install them. If a contractor installs cabling, always make a complete inspection to ensure that all cables are labeled.

---

meters or 550 meters depending on the grade of MMF. Both fiber versions use *8B10B encoding* to transmit their data. As you might guess, 8B10B is an enhanced version of the 4B5B used in fast Ethernet. The data is sent in 10-bit groups (8 data, two overhead) at a signaling rate of 1.25 GHz, which gives 1 Gbps of data. Dim light is used to send binary 0s, while brighter light is used to send binary 1s. 8B10B is used because fiber optics suffer from the same problems as electrical circuits when there are long transmissions of either a constant bright light or constant dim light. The 2 overhead bits are chosen to prevent long transmissions of bright or dim light.

10 GbE—Gigabit Ethernet and Beyond

Work is currently underway for *10 GbE,* which will run at 10 Gbps over MMF for short distances and over SMF for longer distances.[8] 10 GbE is switched full-duplex, meaning that it runs in switched Ethernet topologies in which only two computers are connected to the circuit and the circuit can be used by both devices to transmit simultaneously. There are two versions of 10 GbE, the basic one targeted at LAN operations, and one designed to make it easy to interconnect 10 GbE LANs and backbones into current high-speed WANs.

The LAN version of 10 GbE uses parallel transmission through four separate MMF or SMF fibers in each cable. Within each fiber, it uses the same 8B10B coding scheme as 1 GbE (8 data bits plus 2 overhead bits) but increases the clock speed to 3.125 GHz to give 2.5 Gbps in each individual fiber. Four fibers times 2.5 Gbps give a total of 10 Gbps.

The WAN version of 10 GbE uses *64B66B coding* (64 bits of data plus 2 bits of overhead) transmitted at 10.26 GHz through one fiber, giving a data rate of 9.95 Gbps.

Of course, 10 GbE will not be the end point. Faster and faster versions of Ethernet will continue to be developed. Several researchers have proposed 40 GbE, so it is likely to be the next version of gigabit Ethernet.

---

[8] For the latest on 10 GbE, see www.10gea.org.

THE BEST PRACTICE LAN DESIGN

The past few years have seen major changes in LAN technologies (e.g., gigabit Ethernet, switched Ethernet). As technologies have changed, so too has our understanding of the best practice design for LANs.[9]

Effective Data Rates

The *effective data rate* of the hardware layers is the maximum practical speed in bits that the hardware layers can be expected to provide. The effective data rate depends on four basic factors. The first factor is the nominal data rate provided by the physical layer; that is, the data rate specified by the hardware (e.g., 10Base-T provides a nominal rate of 10 Mbps). The second is the error rate, because this determines the how many retransmissions must occur. The third is the efficiency of the data link layer protocols used. As discussed in the previous chapter, efficiency is the percentage of a transmission that contains user data, and is dependent on the number over overhead bytes in the transmission. The final factor is the efficiency of the media access control protocol; that is, how well the media access control protocol can use the nominal data rate.

Data Link Protocol Efficiency
Shared Ethernet and switched Ethernet share the same data rates, the same types of cables that can be assumed to have the same error rates and the same data link protocol with the same efficiency. The efficiency of the Ethernet data link protocols (excluding higher-level protocols such as TCP/IP) is fairly good. For every 1,500-byte frame transmitted, there are 33 bytes of overhead on the frame itself. Thus assuming we have no errors requiring a frame to be retransmitted, we have an efficiency of about 98 percent if we send 1,500-byte frames (1467/1500 = 97.8%). If we use jumbo frames (9,000 bytes), then the efficiency is about 99.6 percent. Conversely, if we transmit mostly small frames (e.g., 150-byte Web requests), then data link protocol efficiency is only about 82 percent (150/183). (Remember that these calculations do not include the overhead imposed by higher-level packets such as TCP/IP.)

Average efficiency depends on typical pattern of frame sizes and thus differs from LAN to LAN, depending on the users and what applications they use. To estimate an average efficiency, we must make some assumptions about the nature of traffic in a "typical" LAN, thus any estimate we derive could differ from the actual efficiency of a specific LAN, if the pattern of traffic in the LAN was different from our assumptions. Generally speaking, the pattern of traffic in most LANs for Web or e-mail applications is a small HTTP or SMTP request sent from the client to a server, followed by a long series of large packets from the server to the client providing a Web page or e-mail message. Thus, most traffic is large packets. If we assume that each short packet is followed by 20 large packets (e.g., each Web request produces a set of files totaling 30–50 K in response), then our average efficiency is about 97 percent. Thus we will use 97 percent as a reasonable estimate of Ethernet's data link layer protocol efficiency for typical LAN traffic. It is also important to

---

[9] We thank our friends at Cisco Systems Inc., the market leader in LAN and backbone networking, for helping us think about this.

note that this assumes that virtually no errors occur, which is a reasonable assumption for most LAN environments today.

Media Access Control Protocol Efficiency   Shared Ethernet and switched Ethernet differ in the media access control protocol. It is generally accepted that Ethernet's CSMA/CD media access control protocol works very well in low-traffic networks. As traffic increases and network utilization increases, collisions become more common. Several mathematical models, simulations, and real experiments with shared and switched Ethernet running at different data rates using different assumptions about the number of computers on the network and the types of traffic they generate (e.g., large packets versus short packets) have been done. Ethernet performance varies based on the assumptions one uses, but a general pattern does emerge.

As shown in Figure 4-16, the response time delays experienced by users are low when there is little traffic (lower delays are better). Response time delays increase slowly as traffic increases to about 50 percent of the nominal data rate. Once the 50 percent capacity mark is reached, response time delays increase much more quickly as traffic increases, until about 80 percent of capacity is reached. Past 80 percent, delays increase exponentially as traffic increases.

In other words, Ethernet LANs work very well and their users experience few response time delays as long as the total amount of traffic in the LAN remains under 50 percent of the nominal data capacity. As traffic increases to between 50 percent and 80 percent of capacity, users experience noticeable delays but can still use the network. Once capacity hits 80 percent, the delays make the network effectively unusable.

This means, for example, that a shared hub-based LAN using 10Base-T is really only capable of providing a total network capacity of just under 5 Mbps (97% efficiency × 50% capacity × 10 Mbps = 4.85 Mbps). This capacity is shared by all computers on the LAN. So in order to estimate the effective data of shared Ethernet, we must make some assumptions about the number of computers that will be active—that is, *simultaneously* be sending and receiving data over the network. The key word here is *simultaneously;* a typical shared

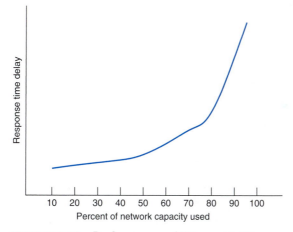

FIGURE 4-16   Performance of Ethernet LANs.

Technology	Effective Data Rate per User		
	Low Traffic	**Moderate Traffic**	**High Traffic**
Shared 10Base-T	2.5 Mbps	1 Mbps	500 Kbps
Shared 100Base-T	37.5 Mbps	15 Mbps	7.5 Mbps
Switched 10Base-T	9 Mbps	9 Mbps	9 Mbps
Switched 100Base-T	90 Mbps	90 Mbps	90 Mbps
Full Duplex 1 GbE	1.8 Gbps	1.8 Gbps	1.8 Gbps
Full Duplex 10 GbE	18 Gbps	18 Gbps	18 Gbps

Assumptions:
1. **Most frames are 1500 bytes or larger**
2. **No transmission errors occur**
3. **Low traffic means 2 active users, moderate traffic means 5 active users, high traffic means 10 active users**

FIGURE 4-17 Effective data rate estimates for Ethernet.

Ethernet LAN today has about 20 computers, and except for computer labs, most computers are not simultaneously sending and receiving data. Even when users are actively using the computer, they are seldom constantly sending and receiving data; most users pause to read the Web pages or e-mail messages they retrieve.

In a low-traffic network, we might expect only one or two of the attached users to simultaneously attempt to send or receive data over the network. With two users, the total capacity is divided among both users. So if we had two active computers in a low-traffic 10Base-T shared Ethernet environment, this would mean that on average, each computer could realistically use about 2.5 Mbps. In a moderate-traffic LAN, we might have five active users, meaning each computer could realistically use about 1 Mbps on average. In a high-traffic environment with 10 active computers on one 10Base-T hub, this would mean that, on average, each computer could realistically use about 500 Kbps on average. See Figure 4-17.

Tests have shown that shared 100Base-T can run close to 80 percent of capacity with very few delays. On a high-traffic LAN with 10 active computers using shared 100Base-T, this would mean that each computer could realistically use about 7.5 Mbps on average (97% efficiency × 80% capacity × 100 Mbps = 7.8 Mbps). See Figure 4-17.

Switched Ethernet dramatically improves network performance because each computer has its own dedicated circuit, rather than the one common shared multipoint circuit in shared Ethernet. Because there are only two devices on each half-duplex point-to-point circuit (e.g., the switch and a computer), the probability of a collision is lower. Most experts believe we can effectively use up to about 95 percent of the switched Ethernet capacity before performance becomes a problem. In 10Base-T switched LAN, each computer circuit would have an effective capacity of about 9 Mbps (97% efficiency × 95% capacity × 10 Mbps = 9.2 Mbps). In a 100Base-T switched LAN, each computer would have about 92 Mbps (95% efficiency × 95% capacity × 100 Mbps = 92 Mbps). Because each computer has its own circuit connecting it to the switch, it is unaffected by the amount of traffic generated by the other computers on the switch—assuming, of course, that not all computers are trying to send a message to the same computer or device attached to the switch, which is sometimes the case.

Gigabit Ethernet is most often implemented in full-duplex switched environments, which means it provides 1 Gbps in both directions simultaneously. It provides a data rate of about 900 Mbps, but one could argue that since this is full-duplex and available in both directions simultaneously, a better relative number might be 1.8 Gbps per computer. Ten GbE is similar so it provides about 18 Gbps per computer.

Figure 4-17 provides a summary of the effective data rates. These rates provide a general guide, because, as we noted above, one must make certain assumptions about the typical frame sizes, error rates, reasonable response time expectations of users, number of active users, and so on. It is also important to note that these numbers do not include the effects of higher-layer packets (e.g., TCP/IP) in the calculations—they focus only on the hardware layers.

Costs

When new technologies are first introduced, they are expensive. As time passes, their prices drop as new technologies appear that outperform them. Today, shared 10Base-T Ethernet equipment is very cheap and shared 100Base-T is relatively inexpensive, because both are quite old in design. Switched Ethernet, both 10Base-T and 100Base-T, are also relatively inexpensive. 1 GbE and 10 GbE are both quite expensive.

Recommendations

Given these trade-offs in costs and effective data rates, there are several best practice recommendations (see Figure 4-18). Switched 10Base-T is less susceptible to response time delays as traffic increases, so it is more robust as traffic increases. While some network managers intentionally design for low-traffic networks, the best practice is to design for the worst case—because network traffic always increases—unless there are some unusual characteristics in the environment or the size of the network is limited. Thus for most networks, switched 10Base-T provides the best trade-off between cost and performance. As the cost of technology continues to drop, pure 10Base-T devices are starting to disappear.

Most networks	Switched 10Base-T Ethernet over Category 5 cables
Very small networks (e.g., home networks)	Traditional shared 10Base-T Ethernet over Category 5 or Category 3 cables
Networks with high demands (e.g., multimedia networks)	Switched 100Base-T Ethernet over Category 5 cables or full duplex 1 GbE over MMF

FIGURE 4-18 Best practice LAN recommendations.

The difference in manufacturing cost between 10Base-T and 100Base-T devices is small, so some vendors are discontinuing 10Base-T only devices and selling 10/100 autosensing devices that run at 10 Mbps or 100 Mbps at almost the same cost as 10Base-T devices.

Most network managers install category 5 or 5e cables (rated to 100 Mbps) even though category 3 cables are sufficient for 10Base-T because the additional cost for cat 5/5e is very small and this provides room for upgrades to 100Base-T or 1000Base-T.

For very small networks, such as home networks connecting only a handful of computers, traditional shared 10Base-T over cat 5/5e cable should prove sufficient because of their low traffic demands. For networks with very high traffic needs switched 100Base-T or 1 GbE over MMF is recommended, although as the price of gigabit Ethernet drops, it will be become the recommended best practice.

In most LANs, the majority of the network traffic is to and from the server, or to and from the connection from the LAN to the backbone network (i.e., the gateway or router). In most LANs, this circuit is the network bottleneck. Each computer is transmitting at 10 Mbps, but if the circuit to the server is also 10 Mbps, there is often a traffic jam. The solution to this is to use a 10/100 switch that provides 10 Mbps circuits to the client computers, but a 100-Mbps circuit to the server or backbone. While traffic jams will still occur, the higher speed on the bottleneck circuit will mean they will clear up much more quickly.

SUMMARY

Topology   With shared Ethernet, the LAN is designed with a shared bus logical topology and a star physical topology. All computers are connected to a hub (essentially a junction box and repeater) via unshielded twisted-pair (UTP) or shielded twisted-pair (STP) cable. Hubs retransmit all signals they receive on any cable to all other cables, so computers must take their turns transmitting so that the cables are shared. With switched Ethernet, the switch replaces the hub and controls the flow of messages so messages go only to the one computer to which they are addressed. Thus the switch forms a set of point-to-point circuits that are used only by the switch and the one computer on each cable, so the cables are no longer shared by many computers.

Media Access Control   Ethernet uses CSMA/CD to control when computers can transmit. Computers listen for a short period of time to make sure no other devices are transmitting (9.6 microseconds) and then transmit their data. If another computer is transmitting, they wait until that computer stops and then transmit. A collision occurs when two or more computers attempt to transmit at the same time. When a collision occurs, both computers stop transmitting and wait a random amount of time before attempting to retransmit.

Error Control   Error detection is done by attaching error detection data based on the CRC-32. With CRC, a message is treated as one long binary number. The sender divides this number by a preset number and attaches the remainder (a 32-bit number) to the message. The receiver divides the message it receives by the same number and matches the remainder it gets against the error detection data that was transmitted with the message. If the two match, the message is assumed to be correct. Ethernet is usually configured to discard messages containing errors, so that higher-level protocols (e.g., TCP) must ensure reliable delivery services. However, when error correction is turned on and an error is detected, the receiver sends a NAK to the sender requesting that the message be transmitted.

Message Delineation   Message delineation means to mark the start and end of messages. There are several standard versions of Ethernet. The one we believe will become the most popular marks the start of the message by sending a 7-byte set of synchronization bits followed by a 1-byte start-of-frame delimiter. Whenever the receiver sees this specific bit pattern, it knows that an Ethernet frame is starting. The Ethernet frame has a length field, so that the receiver can determine exactly where the frame ends.

Data Transmission   The physical layer is responsible for moving the bits given to it by the data link layer through the physical media. Although each version of Ethernet has the same data link layer software, each version has different types of physical cables and uses different approaches to transmit data through them. 10Base-T uses cat 3 or cat 5 twisted-pair cables with Manchester encoding. 100Base-T uses 4B5B coding over cat 5 cables, while 100Base-F uses bright/dim light over 61.2/125 MMF fiber cables. 1000Base-T uses PAM-5 coding over cat 5 or 5e cables. 1000Base-SX and 1000Base-LX use 8B10B coding over MMF or SMF. The LAN version of 1 GbE uses 8B10B coding over MMF or SMF, while the WAN-compatible version uses 64B66B encoding over MMF or SMF.

Best Practice LAN Design   The best practice LAN design depends on cost and the effective data rate of the LAN hardware layers, which in turn depend on the nominal data rate provided by the physical layer, the error rate, the efficiency of the data link layer protocol, and the efficiency of the media access control protocol. Given the trade-offs in costs and effective data rates, the best LAN design for most networks is switched 10Base-T with category 5/5e cables. For very small networks, such as home networks connecting only a handful of computers, traditional shared 10Base-T over cat 5/5e cable may prove sufficient because of their low traffic demands. For networks with very high traffic needs switched 100Base-T is recommended, although as the price of gigabit Ethernet drops, it will be become the recommended best practice.

KEY TERMS

analog data
ASCII
attenuation
autosensing
bottleneck
bus topology
cable plan
cabling
character
code
coding scheme
collision
collision detection (CD)
contention
Carrier Sense Multiple
    Access with Collision
    Detection
    (CSMA/CD)
category 3 cable
    (cat 3)
category 5 cable
    (cat 5)
crossover cable
cyclical redundancy
    check (CRC)

Destination Service
    Access Point
    (DSAP)
digital data
effective data rate
Ethernet
fast Ethernet
fiber-optic cable
flow control
forwarding table
Frame Check Sequence
    (FCS)
framing
full-duplex
gigabit Ethernet
half-duplex
hub
IEEE 802.3
jumbo frames
layer-2 switch
logical link
    control (LLC)
    sublayer
logical topology
MAC header

MAC trailer
maximum transport unit
    (MTU)
media access control
    (MAC) sublayer
message delineation
Multi-Level
    Transmission–
    3 Level (MLT-3)
multimode fiber
    (MMF)
multipoint circuit
nanosecond
network interface card
    (NIC)
network operating
    system (NOS)
network profile
non-return-to-zero
    (NRZ)
overlay network
PCMCIA slot
peer-to-peer networks
physical topology
port

preamble
Protocol Data Unit
    (PDU)
Pulse Amplitude
    Modulation–
    5 (PAM-5)
RJ-45 connector
shared circuit
shared Ethernet
shielded twisted pair
    (STP)
signaling rate
single-mode fiber
    (SMF)
Source Service Access
    Point (SSAP)
star topology
stop-and-wait ARQ
store-and-forward
switch
switched Ethernet
timeout
topology
transceiver
twisted-pair cable

United States of America	user profile	10Base-5	1000Base-SX
Standard Code for	workgroup switch	10Base-T	1 GbE
Information Inter-	4B5B coding	100Base-F	10 GbE
change (USASCII)	8B10B coding	100Base-T	40 GbE
unshielded twisted pair	64B66B coding	100Base-Tx	
(UTP)	10Base-2	1000Base-LX	

QUESTIONS

1. Define *local area network*.

2. What does the data link layer do? What does the physical layer do?

3. What is a NIC? What is a hub? What is a switch?

4. What is a topology?

5. How does the logical topology differ from the physical topology?

6. How does a shared Ethernet topology differ from a switched Ethernet topology?

7. What are the primary advantages and disadvantages of switched Ethernet?

8. Compare and contrast category 5 UTP, category 5e UTP, and category 5 STP.

9. How does fiber-optic cable differ from STP?

10. What are the different types of fiber-optic cable?

11. In what ways is a hub similar to a switch? How do they differ?

12. How does a multipoint circuit differ from a point-to-point circuit?

13. How do half-duplex circuits differ from full-duplex circuits?

14. How do layer-2 switches know where to send the frames they receive? Describe how switches gather and use this knowledge.

15. What distinguishes serial transmission from parallel transmission?

16. Briefly describe how CSMA/CD works.

17. Describe how Ethernet detects errors.

18. Explain how errors are corrected.

19. Explain the terms *10Base-2, 10Base-T, 100Base-T, 1000Base-T, 10GbE, 10/100 Ethernet.*

20. How does Ethernet mark the start and end of messages?

21. What is a coding scheme?

22. What are the parts of an Ethernet frame?

23. Why should CSMA/CD networks be built so that no more than 50 percent of their capacity is dedicated to actual network traffic?

24. How does analog transmission differ from digital transmission?

25. How does MMF differ from SMF?

26. How does 10Base-T transmit data through the physical circuit?

27. How does 100Base-T transmit data through the physical circuit?

28. How does 100Base-F transmit data through the physical circuit?

29. How does 1000Base-T transmit data through the physical circuit?

30. How does 1000Base-F transmit data through the physical circuit?

31. How does 10 GbE transmit data through the physical circuit?

32. What are the best practice recommendations for LANs?

33. What are the two factors that are important in making recommendations for LAN design?

34. It is said that hooking some computers together with a cable does not make a network. Why?

35. Are NAKs really needed or can Ethernet function without them? If they are not needed, why do we use them?

36. Many businesses are now contemplating replacing their cat 5 cable with MMF or SMF. What advice would you give them?

37. During the 1990s, there was intense competition between two technologies (10-Mbps Ethernet and 16-Mbps token ring) for the LAN market. Ethernet was promoted by a consortium of vendors while token ring was primarily an IBM product, even though it was standardized. Ethernet won, and no one talks about token ring anymore. Outline a number of reasons why Ethernet might have won. (*Hint:* The reasons were both technical and business.)

EXERCISES

4-1. Survey the LANs used in your organization. Are they Ethernet, switched Ethernet, or some other standard? Why?

4-2. Document one LAN (or LAN segment) in detail. What devices are attached, what cabling is used, and what is the topology? What does the cable plan look like?

4-3. You have been hired by a small company to install a simple LAN for their 18 Windows computers. Develop a simple LAN and determine the total cost (i.e., select the cables, hubs/switches, and NICs and price them).

4-4. Draw how a series of four separate messages would be *successfully* sent from one computer to another if the first message was transferred without error, the second was initially transmitted with an error, the third was initially lost, and the ACK for the fourth was initially lost.

MINI-CASES

I. Designing a New Ethernet

One important issue in designing Ethernet lies in making sure that if a computer transmits a frame, any other computer that attempts to transmit at the same time will be able to hear the incoming frame before it stops transmitting, or else a collision might go unnoticed. For example, assume that we are on Earth and send an Ethernet frame over a very long piece of cat 5 wire to the Moon. If a computer on the Moon starts transmitting at the same time as we do on Earth and finishes transmitting before our frame arrives at the Moon, there will be a collision but neither of us will detect it; the frames will be garbled, but no one will know why. So, in designing Ethernet, we must make sure that the length of cable in the LAN is shorter than the length of the shortest possible message that can be sent. Otherwise, a collision could go undetected.

   a. Let's assume that the smallest possible message is 64 bytes (including the 33-byte overhead). If we use 10Base-T, how long (in meters) is a 64-byte message? While electricity in the cable travels a bit slower than the speed of light, once you include delays in the electrical equipment in transmitting and receiving the signal, the effective speed is only about 40 million meters per second. (*Hint:* First calculate the number of seconds it would take to transmit the message then calculate the number of meters the signal would travel in that time, and you have the total length of the message).

   b. If we use 10 GbE, how long (in meters) is a 64-byte message?

   c. The answer in part b is the maximum distance any single cable could run from a switch to one computer in a switched Ethernet LAN. How would you overcome the problem implied by this?

II. Pat's Petunias

You have been called in as a network consultant by your cousin Pat, who operates a successful mail-order flower business. She is moving to a new office and wants to install a network for her telephone operators who take phone calls and enter orders into the system. The number of operators working varies depending on the time of day and day of the week. On slow shifts there are usually only 10 operators, while at peak times there are 50. She has bids from different companies to install (a) a traditional shared Ethernet 10Base-T network, (b) a switched Ethernet 10Base-T network, (c) a switched Ethernet 100Base-T network, or (d) a switched 100Base-F network. What would you recommend?

III. Eureka!

Eureka! is a telephone and Internet-based concierge service that specializes in obtaining things that are hard to find (e.g., Superbowl tickets, first-edition books from the 1500s, Fabergé eggs). It currently employs staff who work 24 hours per day (over three shifts), with usually 5 to 7 staff working at any given time. Staff answer the phone and respond to requests entered on the Eureka! Web site. Much of their work is spent on the phone and on computers searching on the Internet. They have just leased a new office and are about to wire it. They have bids from different companies to install (a) a traditional shared Ethernet 10Base-T network, (b) a switched Ethernet 10Base-T network, (c) a switched Ethernet 100Base-T network, or (d) a switched 100Base-F network. What would you recommend?

CHAPTER 5

HARDWARE LAYERS: BACKBONE NETWORKS

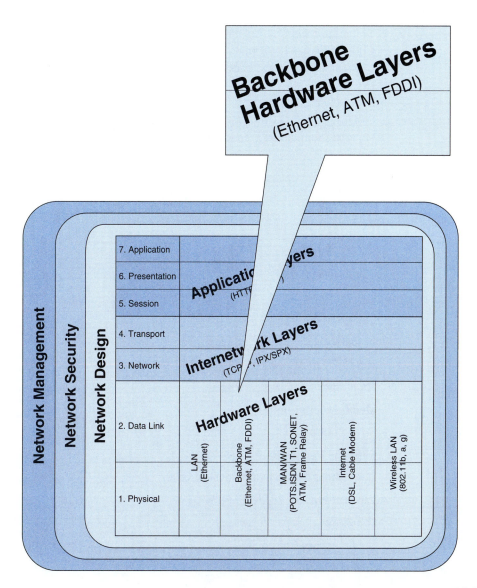

THIS CHAPTER examines backbone networks that are used to link LANs together and to connect LANs to MANs and WANs. We begin with the various types of devices used in backbone networks and discuss several backbone architectures. We then turn to two technologies designed primarily for use in the backbone (ATM and FDDI). The chapter ends with a discussion of the best practice design for backbone networks.

OBJECTIVES

- Understand hierarchical backbones and the devices they use
- Understand flat backbones and the devices they use
- Understand collapsed backbones and the devices they use
- Understand VLANs and the devices they use
- Be familiar with FDDI
- Be familiar with ATM
- Understand the best practice recommendations for backbone design

CHAPTER OUTLINE

INTRODUCTION

BACKBONE ARCHITECTURES

Hierarchical Backbone

Flat Backbone

Collapsed Backbone

Virtual LAN

FIBER DISTRIBUTED DATA INTERFACE

Topology

Media Access Control

Error Control

Message Delineation

Data Transmission in the Physical Layer

ASYNCHRONOUS TRANSFER MODE

Topology

Media Access Control

Error Control

INTRODUCTION

A *backbone network* is a network that connects many networks. Backbone networks typically use high-speed circuits to interconnect a series of LANs and provide connections to other backbones, MANs, WANs, and the Internet. A backbone that connects many backbones spanning several buildings at a single location is often called a *campus network*. A backbone network also may called be an *enterprise network* if it connects all networks within a company, regardless of whether it crosses state, national, or international boundaries.

Many of the same high-speed technologies used in LANs are often used in backbone networks (e.g., 100Base-T, 1000Base-T). However, two technologies originally developed for use in MANs and WANs have also been refined for use in backbones: FDDI and ATM. Both originally offered much higher speeds than Ethernet, but the performance of gigabit Ethernet now outshines both FDDI and ATM. Many organizations continue to use FDDI and ATM, but over the past year, the sales of both have dropped sharply. We will discuss FDDI and ATM in this chapter, but because their use may be declining, we will do so in somewhat less detail. Several experts believe that gigabit Ethernet will eliminate FDDI and ATM in the backbone by 2005.

Backbones offer more flexibility in design than do LANs, and the design of backbones often affects performance almost as much the specific technologies they use. Network designers often think about three distinct technology layers[1] when they design backbone networks (see Figure 5-1). The layer closest to the users is the *access layer,* the technology used in the LANs attached to the backbone network as described in the previous chapter (e.g., 100Base-T, switched 10Base-T). While the access layer is not part of the backbone network, the technologies used in the LANs (or access layer) can have major impacts on the design of the backbone.

The *distribution layer* is the part of the backbone that connects the LANs together. This is the part of the backbone that often contains the "TCP/IP gateways" described in

---

[1] Try not to confuse the layers in the network model (application layer, transport layer, and so on) with the layers of backbone technology we are describing here. They are different. We would have preferred to use a different word than "layer" to describe these, but unfortunately that is the term used in the industry.

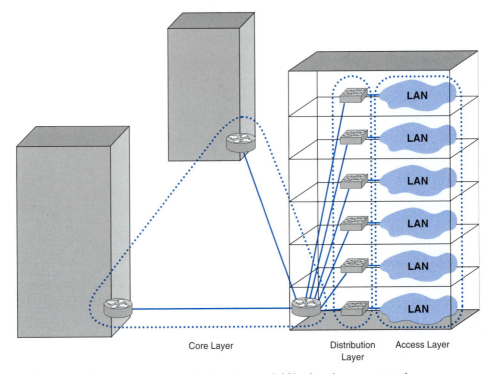

FIGURE 5-1 Backbone network design layers. LAN = local area network.

Chapter 3. It usually runs throughout one building. Large buildings usually have several distribution layer backbones.

The *core layer* is the part of the backbone that connects the different backbone networks together, often from building to building. The core layer is the campus network or the enterprise network. Some small organizations are not large enough to have a core layer; their backbone spans only the distribution layer. Other organizations are large enough that they have a core network at several locations that are in turn connected by WANs.

The architecture of the backbone—the fundamental way in which it is designed—has a critical impact on overall network performance, almost as much of an impact as the network technology selected for use in the backbone. In the sections that follow, we first describe the four basic backbone architectures and how they operate and then examine two technologies that can be used in the backbone, before closing with our best practice recommendations. We assume that you are comfortable with the material on TCP/IP in Chapter 3; if you are not, you may want to go back and review the last section of that chapter titled *"TCP/IP Example"* before you continue reading.

BACKBONE ARCHITECTURES

The *backbone architecture* refers to the way in which the backbone interconnects the networks attached to it and how it manages the way in which packets from one network move through the backbone to other networks. While there are an almost infinite number of ways in which network designers can build backbones, there are really only four fundamental architectures that can be combined in different ways: hierarchical backbone, flat backbone, collapsed backbone, and virtual LAN. These four architectures are mixed and matched to build sets of backbones. We examine each in turn.

Hierarchical Backbone

Hierarchical backbones move packets along the backbone based on their network layer address (i.e., layer-3 address). A hierarchical backbone is the basic backbone architecture that we used to illustrate how TCP/IP worked in Chapter 3. It is arguably the oldest form of backbone architecture and until the mid-1990s was the best practice design.

Technical Design Figure 5-2 illustrates a hierarchical backbone used at the distribution layer. There are a series of LANs (access layer) each connected by a TCP/IP gateway (usually a router) to a single shared media backbone network. Each of the LANs is a separate TCP/IP subnet. Message traffic stays within each subnet unless it specifically needs to leave the subnet to travel elsewhere on the network, in which case the network layer address (e.g., IP) is used to move the packet.

The TCP/IP gateways can be either routers, routing switches, or gateways. *Routers* operate at the network layer and move packets based on their network layer address (i.e., IP or IPX). As we saw in Chapter 3, routers maintain routing tables that provide the information about the best paths from the router to destination by exchanging information in

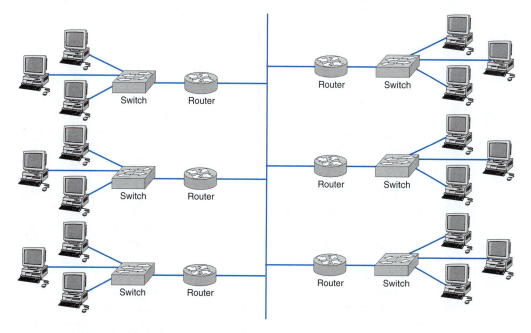

FIGURE 5-2 Hierarchical backbone architecture.

routing protocols such as RIP. Computers in the LAN (access layer) must address their messages to the router, which then strips off the data link layer frame and processes the network layer packet. Routers forward only those messages that need to go to other networks, based on their network layer address. Because routers operate at the network layer, they connect two or more network segments that use the *same or different* data link protocols, but the *same* network protocol.

Some routers are single-protocol routers in that they can process only one type of network layer packet (i.e., just IP or just IPX). Many routers today are multiprotocol routers in that they can process several different types of network layer packets (i.e., both IP and IPX), because many networks use different network layer protocols.

Routing switches (also called *layer-3 switches*) work in exactly the same manner as routers, but they operate much faster because the routing is done by hardware, not software. Many routing switches offer *wire speed* routing, which means they can process incoming packets at the same speed as the hardware layers they serve, thus introducing virtually no delay in moving packets from one network to another. In contrast, most routers introduce a small but noticeable delay in moving packets from one network to another.

Gateways operate at both the network and transport layer and use network layer addresses in processing messages just like routers or routing switches. Gateways connect two or more networks that use *different* network and transport layer protocols. Gateways translate one set of network and transport layer protocols into another (e.g., TCP/IP in to IPX/SPX or SNA). They also often translate data link layer protocols, and open sessions between application programs, thus overcoming both hardware and software incompatibilities. More complex gateways even take care of such tasks as code conversion (e.g., converting from ASCII into EBCDIC, a code sometimes used by IBM mainframes). One of the most common uses of gateways is to enable LANs that use TCP/IP and Ethernet to communicate with IBM mainframes that use SNA.

Operating Characteristics   With a hierarchical backbone, each LAN is usually a separate entity, relatively isolated from the rest of the network. The primary advantage of the hierarchical backbone is that it clearly segments each part of the network connected to the backbone. Each segment or subnet (usually a LAN or another backbone) has its own subnet addresses that can be managed by a different network manager. Each segment of the backbone also can use different data link layer technologies because the router, routing switch, or gateway can translate between data link layer protocols.

Flat Backbone

Flat backbones move packets along the backbone based on their data link layer address (i.e., layer-2 address). They were developed in the mid-1980s to reduce costs, because at the time routers were very expensive. They are still sometimes used today.

Technical Design   Figure 5-3 illustrates a distribution layer flat backbone with a bus topology. This figure shows the same series of LANs as in Figure 5-2, but now the LANs are connected by bridges or layer-2 switches (rather than routers, routing switches, or gateways) to the single shared media backbone network. As you can see, a flat backbone looks very similar to a hierarchical backbone. With a flat backbone, however, the entire network

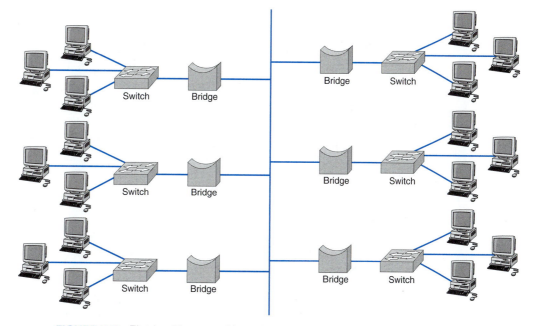

FIGURE 5-3   Flat backbone architecture.

(backbone and all connected network segments) is on the *same subnet.* All LANs are part of the same overall network and all must have the same data link layer protocol. This is in sharp contrast to the hierarchical backbone in which the LANs were separate and could use different technologies.

   Bridges are very similar to the layer-2 switches discussed in Chapter 4 used in switched LANs. They operate at the data link layer (or layer-2) and connect two or more network segments that use the *same* data link layer protocols and addresses. They use the data link layer address to forward frames between LANs and, like layer-2 switches, they learn addresses by reading the source and destination addresses. However, they are much slower than layer-2 switches, and as the cost of layer-2 switches has dropped, bridges have become obsolete, although they are still in use in older networks.

   Both bridges and layer-2 switches are *transparent* to the network in that the devices attached to the segments they serve do not know that they are there. To move messages through a bridge or a layer-2 switch, the sender sets the address in the Ethernet frame to the address of the destination computer (e.g., the router that serves as the TCP/IP gateway for the subnet), and the frame moves unchanged through the bridges and layer-2 switches to the destination. Neither the sender nor receiver are aware of the bridges and layer-2 switches through which the message passed because they do not change the message and play no role in the addressing of the message (compare this with the routers or routing switches in the hierarchical backbone that change the data link layer frames and to which frames must be specifically addressed).

Operating Characteristics   Flat backbones have several distinct advantages and disadvantages compared with routed backbones. First, layer-2 switches are much less expensive than routers or routing switches. Second, they are usually simpler to install because the network manager does not need to worry about building many different subnets and assigning a whole variety of different subnet masks and addresses in each part of the network. However, since the backbone and all attached networks are considered part of the same subnet, it is more difficult to permit different individuals to manage different parts of the network (e.g., LANs); a change in one part of the network has the potential to significantly affect all other parts. Also, it is possible to run out of IP addresses if the entire network has many computers.

The single most important problem is network speed. Layer-2 switching is faster than routing, so one might expect the flat backbone to be faster. For small networks, this is true. For large networks, it is not; large flat backbones are slower than large hierarchical backbones. Because flat backbones and all networks connected to them are part of the same subnet, broadcast messages (e.g., address requests) must be permitted to travel everywhere in the flat backbone. This means, for example, that a computer in one LAN attempting to find the data link layer address of a server in the same LAN will issue a broadcast message that will travel to every computer on every LAN attached to the backbone. In contrast, on a hierarchical backbone such messages would never leave the LAN in which they originated.

There are many different types of broadcast messages other than address requests (e.g., a printer reporting it is out of paper; a server about to be shut down). These broadcast messages quickly use up network capacity in a large flat network. The result is slower response times for the user. In a small network, the problems are not as great, because there are fewer computers to issue such broadcast messages.

Collapsed Backbone

Collapsed backbones are probably the most common type of backbone network used in the distribution layer (i.e., within a building); most new networks today use collapsed backbones. They also are making their way into the core layer as the campus backbone, but routed backbones are also common.

Technical Design Collapsed backbone networks use a star topology with one device, usually a switch, at its center. Figure 5-4 shows a collapsed backbone connecting the same series of LANs. Here, the backbone circuit and set of routers or bridges is replaced by one switch and a set of circuits to each LAN. The collapsed backbone has more cable, but fewer devices. There is no backbone cable. The "backbone" exists only in the switch, which is why this is called a collapsed backbone.

Operating Characteristics Collapsed backbones can operate at either layer-2 with layer-2 switches or at layer 3 with routing switches. Those at layer 2 operate in many ways like flat backbones, while those at layer 3 operate like hierarchical backbones. Figure 5-4 shows a layer-3 collapsed backbone because a routing switch is used.

There are two major advantages to collapsed backbones compared to their hierarchical or flat cousins. First, performance is improved. With hierarchical or flat backbones, the backbone circuit was shared among many LANs (six LANs, in the case of Figure 5-2); each had to take turns sending messages. With the collapsed backbone, each connection

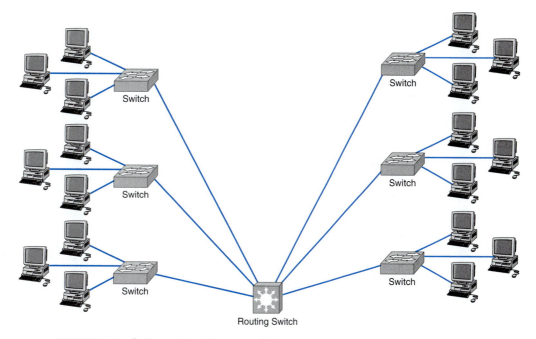

FIGURE 5-4   Collapsed backbone architecture.

into the switch is a separate point-to-point circuit. The switch enables simultaneous access, so that several LANs can send messages to other LANs at the same time. Throughput is increased significantly, often by 200 percent to 600 percent, depending on the number of attached LANs and the traffic pattern.

Second, there are far fewer networking devices in the network. In Figure 5-4, one switch replaces six routers. This reduces costs and greatly simplifies network management. The key backbone device is in one physical location, and all traffic must flow through the switch. If something goes wrong or if new cabling is needed, it can all be done at the switch.

Collapsed backbones can be built using a layer-2 switch or a routing switch as the backbone device. Those using layer-2 switches function in the same way as flat backbones and thus have the same two drawbacks: Because data link layer addresses are used to move packets, there is more broadcast traffic flowing through the network and it is harder to isolate and separately manage the individually attached LANs. Collapsed backbones built using routing switches function in the same way as hierarchical backbones, so they do not have these drawbacks.

Collapsed backbones also have two relatively minor disadvantages, regardless of whether they use layer-2 switches or routing switches. First, they use more cable, and the cable must be run longer distances, which sometimes means that fiber-optic cables must be used. Second, if the central switch fails, so does the entire backbone network. However, if the reliability of the switch is the same as the reliability of the routers in Figure 5-2, then there is less chance of a failure (because there are fewer devices to fail). For most organizations, these disadvantages are outweighed by benefits offered by collapsed backbones.

Rack-Mounted Collapsed Backbone Most organizations now use collapsed backbones in which all network devices for one part of the building are physically located in the same room, often in a *rack* of equipment. This form of collapsed backbone is graphically shown in Figure 5-5. This has the advantage of placing all network equipment in one place for easy maintenance and upgrade, but does require more cable. In most cases, the cost of the cable itself is only a small part of the overall cost to install the network, so the cost is greatly outweighed by the simplicity of maintenance and the flexibility it provides for future upgrades.

The room containing the rack of equipment is sometimes called the *main distribution facility (MDF)* or central distribution facility (CDF). See Figure 5-6. The cables from all computers and devices in the area served by the MDF (often hundreds of cables) are run into the MDF room. Once in the run they are connected into the various devices. The devices in the rack are connected among themselves using very short *patch cables*.

With rack-mounted equipment, it becomes simple to move computers from one LAN to another. In the traditional hierarchical backbone design shown in Figure 5-2, for example, all the computers in the same general physical location are connected to the same switch and thus all receive the same capacity. If some of the computers in the upper-right corner of Figure 5-2 need switched 100Base-T, then all computers must get switched 100Base-T. It is very difficult to provide different capacities to computers in the same physical area without providing two different devices.

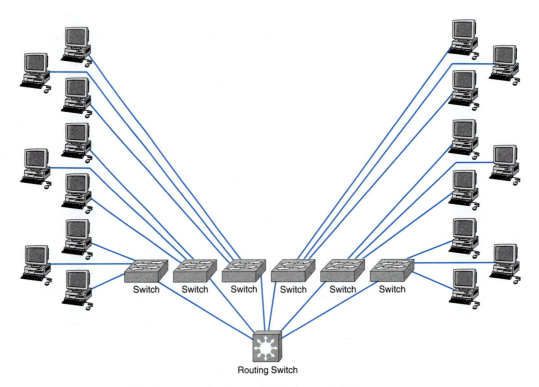

FIGURE 5-5 Rack-mounted collapsed backbone architecture.

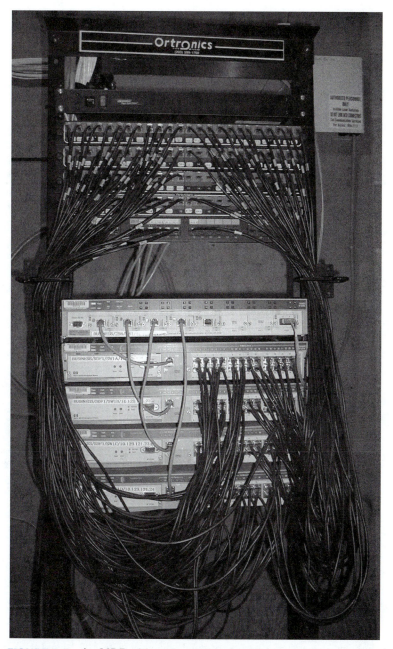

FIGURE 5-6 An MDF with rack-mounted equipment. A layer-2 chassis switch with six 100Base-T modules (center of photo) connects to four 24-port 10Base-T switches. The chassis switch is connected to the campus backbone using 100Base-F over fiber optic cable. The cables from each room are wired into the rear of the patch panel (shown at the top of the photo), with the ports on the front of the patch panel labeled to show which room is which. Patch cables connect the patch panel ports to the ports on the switches.

With an MDF, all cables run into the MDF. If computers on one switch need a different capacity than other computers in the same physical area, it is straightforward to unplug the cables of several high-demand computers from low-capacity switches and plug them into one or more high-capacity switches. This means that network capacity is no longer tied to the physical location of the computers; computers in the same physical area can be connected into very different network segments based on their needs.

Chassis-Based Collapsed Backbone Sometimes a *chassis switch* is used instead of a rack. A chassis switch enables users to plug *modules* directly into the switch. Each module is a certain type of network device. One module might be a 16-port 10Base-T hub, another might be a router, while another might be an 4-port 100Base-T switch, and so on. The switch is designed to hold a certain number of modules and has a certain internal capacity, so that all the modules can be active at one time. For example, a switch with five 10Base-T hubs, two 10Base-T switches (with 8 ports each), a 100Base-T switch (with 4 ports), and a 100Base-T router would have to have an internal switching capacity of at least 710 Mbps (5×10Mbps $+ 2 \times 8 \times 10$Mbps $+ 4 \times 100$ Mbps $+ 100$ Mbps $= 710$ Mbps).

There are two key advantages of chassis switches. The first is flexibility. It is simple to add new modules with additional ports as the LAN grows, and to upgrade the switch to use new technologies. For example, if you want to add gigabit Ethernet or ATM (discussed below) you simply lay the cable and insert the appropriate module into the switch. The second advantage of the chassis-based collapsed backbone is speed. With a rack-mounted collapsed backbone, cables are used to connect the individual devices together. Suppose, for example, we have five layer-2 100Base-T switches each with 24 ports that are connected to one routing switch via cat 5e cables. The maximum amount of data that each layer-2 switch can send to the routing switch is 100 Mbps, yet each switch has 24 ports running at 100Mbps. If two or more computers start transmitting at once, the switch can process the traffic, but now the cable to the routing switch becomes a bottleneck. Chassis-based collapsed backbones do not have this problem. Because the modules plug directly into the chassis switch, the switch provides the capacity needed by the module (which is in this case is 24×100 Mbps $= 2.4$ Gbps).

Virtual LAN

For many years, the design of local area networks remained relatively constant. However, in recent years, the introduction of high-speed switches has begun to change the way we think about local area networks. Switches offer the opportunity to design radically new types of LANs. Most large organizations today have traditional LANs, but many are considering the *virtual LAN (VLAN),* a new type of LAN/backbone architecture made possible by intelligent, high-speed switches. VLANs are standardized as IEEE 802.1q and IEEE 802.1p.

VLANs are networks in which computers are assigned to LAN segments (i.e., TCP/IP subnets or broadcast domains) by software, rather than by hardware. In the section above, we described how in rack-mounted collapsed backbone networks, a computer could be moved from one switch to another by unplugging its cable and plugging it into a different switch. VLANs provide the same capability via software so that the network manager does not have to unplug and replug physical cables to move computers from one segment

MANAGEMENT FOCUS *5-1*

CENTRAL PARKING COLLAPSES

Central Parking, based in Nashville, operates 4,500 parking lots and 100 offices in 42 states and 13 countries. Its rapid growth had brought its headquarters backbone network to its knees; network outages occurred daily as the network routinely hit its maximum capacity.

The new network uses one layer-3 switch as a collapsed backbone for its core layer (see Figure 5-7). This switch manages traffic for 42 IP subnets, through a series of 48-gigabit Ethernet circuits (most of which are fiber optic, but a few use cat 6), and 48 10/100 Ethernet circuits over cat 6 cable. Central Parking's 20 main servers are connected directly to the switch as a server farm.

Two other layer-2 switches act as the distribution layer and access layer for almost 200 desktop PCs using 10/100 Ethernet over cat 6. These switches are connected to the core switch via multiple gigabit over fiber circuits, so that the circuits between the switches do not become bottlenecks.

Several routers provide distribution layer backbones to Central's offices around the world through a series of WANs and the Internet.

SOURCE: "Central Parking Puts the Brakes on Network Downtime," *Network Magazine,* November 2000.

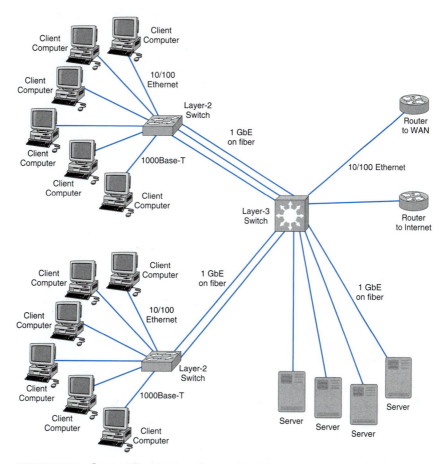

FIGURE 5-7 Central Parking's collapsed backbone.

to another. There are two basic approaches to designing VLANs: single-switch VLANs and multiswitch VLANs.

Single-Switch VLAN A *single-switch VLAN* means that the VLAN operates only inside one switch. The computers on the VLAN are connected into the one switch and assigned by software into different VLANs (see Figure 5-8). The network manager uses special software to assign the dozens or even hundreds of computers attached to the switch to different VLAN segments. The VLAN segments function in the same way as physical LAN segments; the computers in the same VLAN act as though they are connected to the same physical switch or hub. For example, broadcast messages sent by computers in a VLAN segment are sent only to the computers on the same VLAN. VLANs can be designed so that they act as though computers are connected via hubs (i.e., several computers share a given capacity and must take turns using it) or via workgroup switches (i.e., all computers in the VLAN can transmit simultaneously). While switched circuits are preferred to the shared circuits of hubs, buying VLAN switches with the capacity to provide a complete set of switched circuits for hundreds of computers is more expensive than those that permit shared circuits.

We should also note that it is possible to have just one computer in a given VLAN. In this case, that computer has a dedicated connection and does not need to share the network capacity with any other computer. This is commonly done for servers.

There are four ways in which computers attached to VLAN switches can be assigned to the specific virtual LANs inside them. The first approach, used by *port-based VLANs* (also called *layer-1 VLANs*), uses the physical layer port number on the front of the VLAN switch

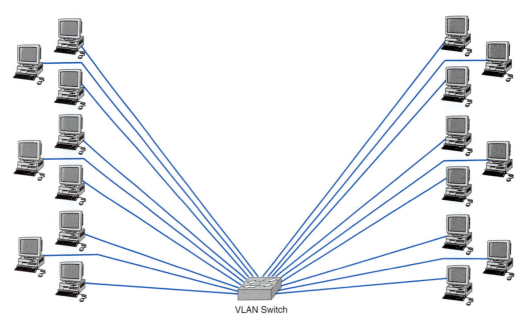

VLAN Switch

FIGURE 5-8 Single-switch VLAN architecture.

to assign computers to VLAN segments. Each computer is physically cabled into a specific port on the VLAN switch. The network manager uses special software provided by the switch manufacturer to instruct the switch which ports are assigned to which VLAN. This means that the network manager must know which computer is connected to which port.

The second approach, used by *MAC-based VLANs* (also called *layer-2 VLANs*), uses the data link layer address to form the VLANs. The network manager uses special software to instruct the switch as to which incoming data link layer addresses are assigned to which VLAN segment. The advantage of a layer-2 VLAN is that it is simpler to manage when computers are moved. If a computer is moved in a layer-1 VLAN, then the network manager must reconfigure the switch to keep that computer in the same VLAN because the computer has moved from one port to another. With a layer-2 VLAN, no reconfiguration is needed. Although the computer may have moved from one port to another, it is the permanently assigned data link layer address that is used to determine which VLAN the computer is on.

The third approach, used by *IP-based VLANs* (also called *layer-3 VLANs*), uses the network layer address to form the VLANs. As before, the network administrator uses special software to instruct the switch as to which network layer addresses are assigned to which VLAN. Layer-3 VLANs reduce the time spent reconfiguring the network when computers move in the same way as layer-2 VLANs. Layer-3 VLANs tend to be a bit slower at processing each message than layer-2 VLANs because processing layer-3 protocols is slightly slower than processing layer-2 protocols.

The fourth approach, used by *application-based VLANs* (also called *policy-based VLANs* or *layer-4 VLANs*), uses the type of application indicated by the port number in the TCP segment in combination with the IP address to form the VLAN groups. As before, the network administrator uses special software to instruct the switch as to which types of packets from which addresses are assigned to which VLAN. This process is very complex because the network manager must decide on a variety of different factors in forming the VLANs. The advantage is a very precise allocation of network capacity. Now VLANs can be formed to allocate a certain amount of network capacity for Web browsing to certain individuals, so much to Web browsing for others, so much to transaction processing, and so on. In this way, the network manager can restrict the amount of network capacity used by potentially less productive applications (e.g., Web surfing) and thus provide much better allocation of resources.

Multiswitch VLAN A *multiswitch VLAN* works the same way as a single-switch VLAN, except that now several switches are used to build the VLANs (see Figure 5-9). In this case, the switches must be able to send frames among themselves in a way that identifies the VLAN to which the frame belongs.

As discussed in Chapter 4, the latest version of the IEEE 802.3 Ethernet frame now includes a tag field used to carry the VLAN information. In this case, when a frame needs to go from one VLAN switch to another VLAN switch, the first switch revises the incoming Ethernet frame to insert the VLAN tag information into the frame. The VLAN tag information is used to move the frame from switch to switch within the VLAN network. When the frame arrives at the final destination switch, the Ethernet frame is usually revised again to remove the VLAN tag information so the Ethernet frame is identical to the one that entered the VLAN before being sent to the destination computer.

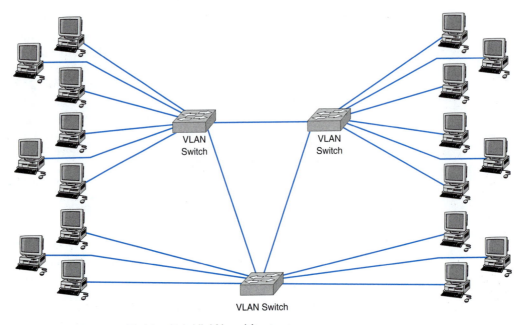

FIGURE 5-9 Multiswitch VLAN architecture.

Operating Characteristics VLANs offer two advantages compared to the other three network architectures. The first advantage lies in their ability to very precisely manage the flow of traffic on the LAN and backbone. VLANs make it much simpler to manage the broadcast traffic that has the potential to seriously reduce performance, and to more precisely allocate resources to different types of traffic. The bottom line is that VLANs offer faster performance than the other three backbone architectures. The second advantage is the ability to prioritize traffic. The VLAN tag information included in the IEEE 802.11ac frame defines the VLAN to which the frame belongs, and also specifies a priority code based on the IEEE 802.1p standard. As you will recall in Chapter 3, the internetwork layers can use RSVP quality of service (QoS), which enables them to prioritize traffic using different classes of service. RSVP is most effective when combined with QoS capabilities at the hardware layers (without QoS at the hardware layers, the devices that operate at the hardware layers (e.g., layer-2 switches) would ignore QoS information). With the new 802.11ac Ethernet frame and its ability to carry VLAN information that includes priorities, we now have QoS capabilities in both the internetwork and hardware layers.

The biggest drawbacks to VLANs are their cost and management complexity. VLAN switches are also much newer technologies that have only recently been standardized. Such "bleeding-edge" technologies sometimes introduce other problems that disappear only after the specific products have matured.

MANAGEMENT FOCUS 5-2

VLAN NETWORK AT IONA

IONA Technologies Inc., a 600-person software developer of enterprise middleware, took advantage of its relocation to Waltham, Massachusetts to redesign its network infrastructure. The new network, designed to support 230 users in one office complex, uses a multiswitch VLAN architecture.

IONA has 27 access layer VLAN switches located close to its users—built into their cubicle walls, to be exact. Up to 24 users are connected to each access layer switch, using a mixture of 10/100 Ethernet and 1000Base-T over copper cables (e.g., cat 5e). See Figure 5-10. Each of the first-level

switches are connected via gigabit Ethernet over fiber to a central set of 5 VLAN switches that form the core of the network. IEEE 802.1q is used to communicate among the access layer switches and the distribution layer switches.

Because both the access layer switches and distribution layer switches are modular, it is easy for IONA to upgrade when technologies change.

SOURCE: "Middleware Maker Future Proofs LAN Infrastructure," *Packet,* Cisco Systems Inc., second quarter, 2000.

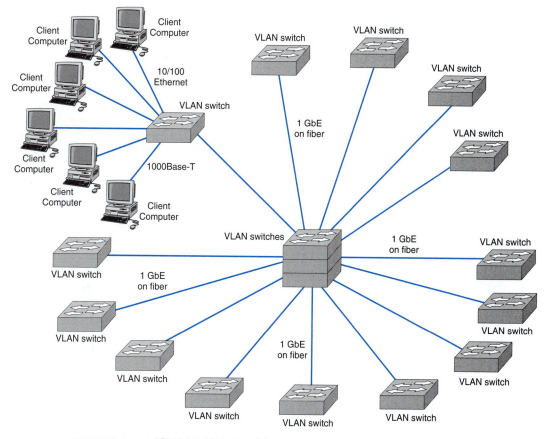

FIGURE 5-10 IONA VLAN (virtual local area network).

FIBER DISTRIBUTED DATA INTERFACE

The *fiber distributed data interface (FDDI)* is a set of standards originally designed in the late 1980s for use in MANs (ANSI X3T9.5). FDDI has since made its way into backbone networks. FDDI was once seen as the logical replacement for Ethernet, but its future is probably limited to specialized applications as gigabit Ethernet and ATM become more popular.

Topology

FDDI uses a shared ring logical topology with a star physical topology. FDDI operates at 100 Mbps, usually over a shared fiber-optic cable. The FDDI standard assumes a maximum of 1,000 stations (i.e., computers, devices) and a 200-kilometer (120 miles) path that requires a repeater or hub every 2 kilometers. FDDI uses two counter-rotating rings called the *primary ring* and the *secondary ring*. Data traffic normally travels on the primary ring. The secondary ring mainly serves as a backup circuit.

All computers on an FDDI network are connected to the primary ring. Some computers are also connected to the secondary ring. Thus there are two types of FDDI computers: the *dual-attachment station (DAS)* on both rings and the *single-attachment station (SAS)* on just the primary ring (see Figure 5-11).

If the cable in the FDDI ring is broken, the ring can still operate in a limited fashion. The DAS nearest to the break reroutes traffic from the primary ring onto the secondary ring. Since the secondary ring is running in the opposite direction, the data travels back around the ring. The DAS nearest the break on the opposite side of the break receives the data on the secondary ring and reroutes it back onto the primary ring. In Figure 5-12, for example, there is a break in the ring between computers F and G. Since both are DAS, G can reroute traffic from H on the primary ring back to A on the secondary ring. The data will travel along the secondary ring from A to B to E to F. F will then reroute the traffic back to E on the primary ring, from where it will flow back on the primary ring to G (F to E to D to C to B to A to H to G).

Media Access Control

Because the single cable is shared by all computers, they must take turns transmitting. The FDDI media access control scheme uses a controlled-access token-passing system. No computer on the network can transmit until it receives the token, a prespecified bit pattern. The token flows through the network from computer to computer. If a computer has a frame to transmit, it waits until it receives the token, attaches the message(s) it wishes to transmit to the token and retransmits the token with the frame. When a computer receives the token, it looks to see if it contains any frames addressed to it, processes them if necessary, and sends the token to the next computer in the ring, unless it has a frame to transmit. The token can contain several frames, each addressed to different computers.

Error Control

FDDI uses a similar ARQ technique to that used by Ethernet, except that it does not stop and wait after each frame. Instead it uses continuous ARQ, in which numerous frames may be in transit simultaneously. If an error is detected only the frames with errors are retransmitted.

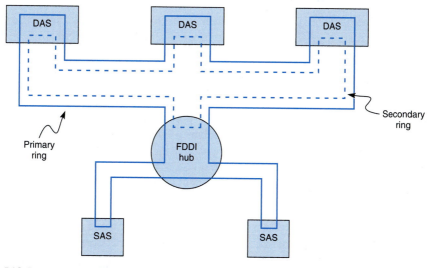

DAS: Dual-attachment station
SAS: Single-attachment station

FIGURE 5-11   Optical cable topology for an FDDI (fiber distributed data interface) local area network. The FDDI has two rings. Data traffic normally travels on the primary ring.

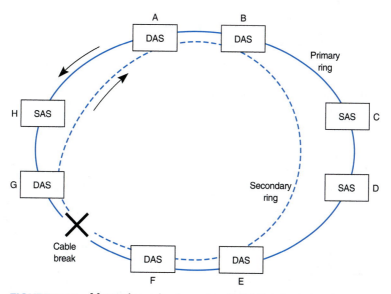

FIGURE 5-12   Managing a broken circuit. DAS = dual-attachment station; SAS = single-attachment station.

Message Delineation

The frame layout of a FDDI frame is shown in Figure 5-13. FDDI uses the same approach to mark the start of the frame as does Ethernet: A start-of-frame sequence with an 8-byte preamble and a 1-byte start delimiter marks the start of the frame. The main body of the frame (called frame check sequence coverage because it is the part of the frame used for the FCS error check calculations) has a 1-byte frame control field (used for the token), a 2-byte or 6-byte destination address (6 is most common), 2-byte or 6-byte source address (6 is most common), a data field of 0–4,500 bytes containing the packets from the higher layers (e.g., TCP/IP and HTTP), and the 4-byte CRC-32 frame check sequence used for error control. Because FDDI does not have a length field as Ethernet has, it must use a special bit pattern to mark the end of the frame. The end-of-frame sequence has a 1-byte end delimiter and a 2 or more byte frame status used to indicate the status of frame as it is passed from computer to computer around the ring.

Data Transmission in the Physical Layer

There are two basic types of FDDI that use different physical media. The most common type uses fiber-optic cable, the other, *copper distributed data interface (CDDI),* uses category 5 twisted-pair cable instead of fiber-optic cable. Both operate in the same way except for the design of the physical media.

FDDI and CDDI use almost exactly the same 4B5B approach to transmission as 100Base-F and 100Base-T Ethernet, for the simple reason that the designers of fast Ethernet copied most of the design of its physical layer from the then well-tested and proven FDDI/CDDI.

ASYNCHRONOUS TRANSFER MODE (ATM)

Simply put, *Asynchronous Transfer Mode (ATM)* is a very unusual technology compared to those we have discussed previously. ATM was originally designed for use in wide area networks intended to carry both voice and data traffic. Many of the differences in its design

Start-of-Frame Sequence		Frame Check Sequence Coverage				End-of-Frame Sequence		
Preamble	Start Delimiter	Frame Control	Destination Address	Source Address	Data	Frame Check Sequence	End Delimiter	Frame Status
8 bytes	1 byte	1 byte	6 bytes	6 bytes	0-4500 bytes	4 bytes	1 byte	2 bytes

FIGURE 5-13   FDDI frame layout.

are due to the original design objective of carrying telephone calls. ATM is sometimes called Cell Relay, and its data packets are called *cells*.[2]

Most designers of backbone networks see ATM as a competitor to Ethernet and FDDI; as such, they see it as a hardware layer technology (i.e., layers 1 and 2). In contrast, designers of wide area networks see ATM as a competitor to TCP/IP; as such, they see it as internetwork layer technology (i.e., layers 3 and 4). In truth, it is both.

For example, ATM provides several different standards for physical transmission and other hardware layer functions; some of these standards are unique to ATM, while others are widely used hardware layer WAN standards (e.g., SONET, which we will discuss in the next chapter). When implemented in WANs, ATM almost always uses SONET as the hardware layer, so WAN designers use ATM's internetworking functions.

When implemented in backbones, we use SONET or one of the ATM-only standards for physical transmission. Since TCP/IP is the dominant internetwork protocol in backbones, we try to avoid thinking of ATM as an internetwork protocol; nonetheless, in order to connect ATM networks into a TCP/IP world, we must use an ATM gateway that converts the TCP/IP and Ethernet addresses on the outside into ATM addresses on the inside and back again at the other end. When implemented in backbones, ATM almost always *pretends* to use TCP/IP as the internetwork layer and simply moves frames as we would expect Ethernet or FDDI to do, so backbone designers use ATM's hardware layer functions.

As you might expect from its ability to function at both the internetwork and hardware layers, ATM is a very complex technology. In this section, we will focus on its use in backbones, and only cover a few of its major components.

Topology

ATM uses switches arranged in *mesh topology*, which means that devices are connected to each other in whatever pattern makes sense (see Figure 5-14). Each circuit is a point-to-point full-duplex circuit, usually operating at 155 Mbps in each direction (for a total of 310 Mbps). Other speeds are possible, such as 622 Mbps (1.24 Gbps total) from switch to switch. Although originally designed to run on fiber-optic cable, there are versions of ATM that can run on category 5e twisted-pair cables.

Full mesh topologies, in which every ATM switch is connected to *every other* ATM switch, are possible but are seldom used because of the extremely high cost. Partial mesh topologies in which each switch is connected only to one or a few other switches are far more common.

The effects of the loss of computers or circuits in a mesh network depend entirely on the circuits available in the network. If there are many possible routes through the network, the loss of one or even several circuits or switches may have few effects beyond the specific computers involved. However, if there are only a few circuits in the network, the loss of even one circuit or switch may seriously impair the network.

---

[2] For more information on ATM, see the ATM Forum Web site at www.atmforum.com.

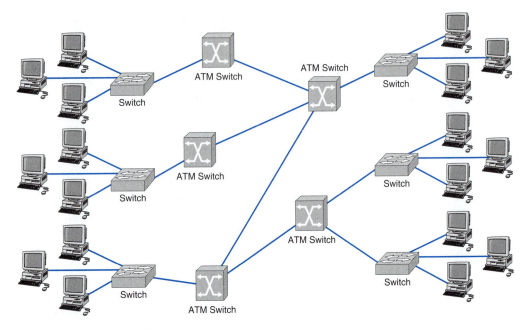

FIGURE 5-14   ATM mesh architecture.

Media Access Control

Because ATM uses full-duplex circuits, media access control is less of an issue. However, compared to the other technologies we have discussed, ATM has a very different way of deciding which packets to transmit when circuits become busy. When non-ATM devices become busy and cannot immediately transmit all the packets they receive, they usually simply transmit packets in the order in which they were received; the first packet received is the first packet transmitted. Because ATM was designed to transmit voice data and voice data cannot tolerate delays in transmission, ATM has several different ways to prioritize the order in which packets or cells are transmitted when the switch becomes busy and cannot immediately transmit all the packets it receives.

ATM prioritizes transmissions based on *quality of service (QoS)*. You may recall that Chapter 3 briefly discussed QoS routing. With QoS routing or QoS switching, different *classes of service* are defined, each with different priorities. Cells move through the network at different priorities based on the QoS in the circuits that they use. ATM defines five service classes (see Technical Focus 5-1) that enable the network to prioritize transmissions. For example, circuits containing voice transmissions receive higher priority than circuits containing e-mail transmissions, because delays in voice transmissions can seriously affect transmission quality, while delays in e-mail transmission are less important. If an ATM switch becomes overloaded and receives traffic on a low-priority circuit, it will store the cell for later transmission or simply refuse the request until it has sufficient capacity.

In order to understand how QoS works, we must first explain how ATM addressing works. ATM uses a very different type of addressing from traditional data link layer protocols (e.g., Ethernet) or network layer protocols (e.g., IP). Ethernet and IP assign addresses

TECHNICAL FOCUS *5 - 1*

ATM CLASSES OF SERVICE

ATM provides five classes of service that each receive different priorities in traveling though the network:

- *Constant bit rate (CBR)* means that the circuit must provide a constant, predefined data rate at all times, much like having a point-to-point physical circuit between the devices. Whenever a CBR circuit is established, ATM guarantees that the switch can provide the circuit; the sum of all CBR circuits at one switch cannot exceed its capacity, even if they are all not active simultaneously. CBR was originally designed to support voice transmissions.

- *Variable bit rate—real time (VBR-RT)* means that the data transmission rate in the circuit will vary, but that all cells received must be switched immediately on arrival because the devices (or people) on the opposite ends of the circuit are waiting for the transmission and expect to receive it in a timely fashion. Each VBR-RT circuit is assigned a standard transmission rate but can exceed it. If the cells in a VBR-RT circuit arrive too

fast to transmit they are lost. Much voice traffic today uses VBR-RT rather than CBR.

- *Variable bit rate–non-real time (VBR–NRT)* means that the data transmission rate in the circuit will vary and that the application is tolerant of delays.

- *Available bit rate (ABR)* means that the circuit can tolerate vide variation in transmission speeds and many delays. AVR circuits have lower priority than VBR-NRT circuits. They receive the lowest amount of guaranteed capacity but can use whatever capacity is available (i.e., not in use by CBR, VBR-RT, and VBR-NRT circuits).

- *Unspecified bit rate (UBR)* means that the circuit has no guaranteed data rate, but cells are transported when capacity is available. When the network is busy, UBR cells are the first to be discarded. UBR is a bit like flying standby on an airline: UBR packets are sent only if there are no other higher-priority packets waiting.

to each computer or device so that all messages sent to the same computer use the same address. While ATM does assign permanent addresses to each ATM NIC, these addresses are not used directly for addressing. Instead, ATM defines a *virtual channel (VC)* (sometimes called a virtual circuit, although this is not the preferred name) between each sender and receiver, and all cells use the virtual circuit identifier as the address. Each VC identifier has two parts, a virtual path identifier and a virtual channel identifier within that path. Each ATM switch contains a VC table that lists all VCs known to that switch (analogous to a routing table in IP). Because there are potentially thousands of VCs and because each switch knows only those VCs in its VC table, a given VC identifier is used only between one switch and the next. Each VC is assigned a specific class of service when it is first established.

When an ATM cell arrives at a switch, the switch looks up the cell's VC identifier in its VC table to determine where to send it and what VC identifier should be used when the cell is transmitted on the outgoing circuit. Figure 5-15, for example, shows two switches each with four ports (or physical circuits). When an incoming cell arrives, the switch looks up the cell's VC identifier in the circuit table, switches the cell to the outgoing port, and changes the VC identifier it had when it arrived to a new VC identifier used by the switch at its destination. For example, a cell arriving at Switch A via port 1 with a VC identifier of 1,10 would be transmitted out on port 4 to Switch B and would be given a new VC identifier of 3,15.

ATM is connection oriented so all cells travel in order through the VC. A VC can be either a *permanent virtual circuit (PVC)* (i.e., defined when the network is established or

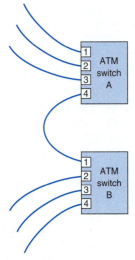

Switch A Circuit Table			
Incoming Port	Incoming Circuit	Outgoing Port	Outgoing Circuit
1	1,10	4	3,15
2	3,18	1	2,10
2	2,11	4	2,11
3	4,10	2	3,26
3	4,11	2	1,18
4	5,10	1	4,21

FIGURE 5-15   Addressing and forwarding with asynchronous transfer mode virtual circuits.

modified) or a *switched virtual circuit (SVC)* (i.e., defined temporarily for one transmission and deleted when the transmission is completed).[3] ATM provides a separate control circuit that is used for nondata communication between devices, such as the setup and takedown of an SVC.

Error Control

ATM uses an error control technique called *throw-it-on-the-floor.* Error checking is done only on the ATM header (not the user data) and if an error is detected, the frame is discarded (i.e., thrown on the floor, so to speak) just like Ethernet. It is up to the source and destination computers to perform error correction and to control for lost messages, whether due to errors or busy circuits causing packets to be discarded, which is usually done in LANs by TCP.

Message Delineation

ATM uses fixed-length frames (or "cells") of 53 bytes. Because the frames have a fixed length, there is no need to mark the end of an ATM frame; once the frame starts, the receiver knows it contains exactly 53 bytes. Fifty-three bytes is very small compared to the 1,500 or 9,000 of Ethernet or the 4,500 of FDDI. It turns out that small frames are ideal for voice traffic, which is why they were chosen for ATM.

---

[3] You will notice a slight change in terminology: VC is virtual *channel* while PVC is permanent virtual *circuit.* The reasons are arbitrary and historical. As you will see in the next chapter, the term *PVC* has the same meaning in X.25 WAN networks, and because X.25 was developed before ATM, ATM has simply adopted the same terminology.

Figure 5-16 shows the cell layout for an ATM cell. The header contains six fields used for control purposes. The 4-bit generic flow control field controls the flow of data across the circuit. The 12-bit virtual path identifier is used to identify the group of channels, while the 12-bit virtual channel identifier gives the specific channel. The 3-bit payload type field indicates the type of data contained in the data field (i.e., control information or user information). The 1-bit cell loss payload field indicates whether or not the cell can be discarded if the circuit gets busy. The 8-bit header error control field uses CRC-8 for error control on just the header portion of the cell. The payload portion of the frame contains 48 bytes of the user data. If less than 48 bytes of data are sent, then the cell is padded with null characters to fill up the remaining bytes.

The ATM cell has no preamble to mark the start of a cell as do Ethernet and FDDI, for example. This is because each ATM cell is inserted into another type of frame for transmission by the physical layer—or more properly, the data link and physical layers.

Data Transmission in the Physical Layer

The initial definition of ATM did not provide specifications for the physical layer. Today, however, the ATM specification has been extended to provide a wide variety of physical layer formats. The most commonly used technology is SONET, a wide area network technology discussed in the next chapter. SONET has its own frame format, as we will discuss in the next chapter. SONET provides a wide range of physical layer data rates, the most common of which for backbones are 155 Mbps (called OC-3), 622 Mbps (called OC-12), and 2.4 Gbps (called OC-48).

ATM and LANs

ATM uses a very different protocol than TCP/IP and Ethernet LANs. ATM has a small 53-byte fixed-length cell sent over virtual channels, while TCP/IP and Ethernet use larger variable-length frames sent using IP addresses. In order to use ATM in a backbone network that connects Ethernet LANs, some translation must be done to enable the LAN packets to flow over the ATM backbone. There are two approaches to this, LANE and MPOA.

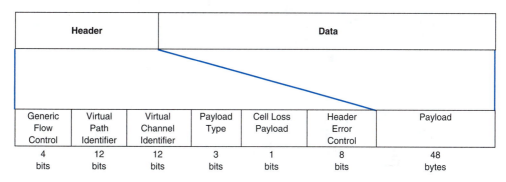

FIGURE 5-16   ATM cell layout.

LANE   With *LAN encapsulation (LANE),* the Ethernet frames from the LAN are left intact; they are broken into 48-byte blocks and surrounded by ATM cells. This process is called *encapsulation* and is done by an *edge switch,* which is in essence, a gateway. The cells flow through the ATM network and are reassembled at an edge switch at the other end before being transmitted into the destination LAN (see Figure 5-17). The use of ATM is transparent to users because LANE leaves the original data link layer frames intact and uses the frame's data link layer address to forward the message through the ATM network.

Translating from Ethernet into ATM (and vice versa) is not simple. First, the Ethernet address must be translated into an ATM VC identifier for the PVC or SVC that leads from the edge switch to the edge switch nearest the destination. This is done through a process similar to that of using an ARP broadcast message on a subnet to locate a data link layer address (see Chapter 3). ATM is a switched point-to-point network, so it lacks a simple built-in ability to issue broadcast messages. LANE enables the transmission of broadcast messages, but so far it has been problematic.

Once the VC address for the destination data link layer address has been found, it can be used to transmit the cell through the ATM backbone. If no PVC is currently defined from the edge switch to the destination edge switch, then the edge switch must establish a new SVC.

Once the VC is ready, the LAN frame is broken into the series of ATM cells and transmitted over the ATM backbone using the ATM VC identifier. The destination edge switch then reassembles the ATM cells into the LAN frame and forwards it to the appropriate device.

This process is not without cost. The resolution of the Ethernet address into an ATM VC identifier, the setup of the SVC (if necessary), and the segmentation and reassembly of

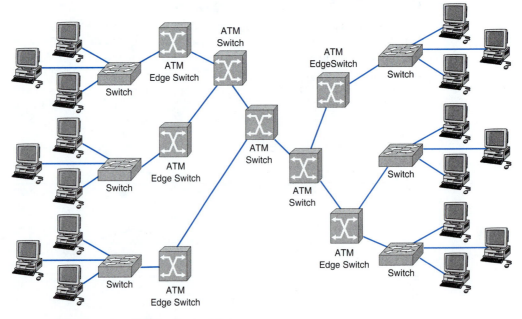

FIGURE 5-17   ATM in the backbone.

the LAN frames to and from ATM cells can impose quite a delay. Recent tests of ATM edge switches suggest that even though they are capable of transmitting at 155 Mbps, the addressing and encapsulation delays can reduce performance significantly.

MPOA *Multiprotocol over ATM (MPOA)* is an extension to LANE. MPOA uses the network layer address (e.g., IP address) in addition to the data link layer address. If the frame destination is in the same subnet, MPOA will use data link layer addresses in the same manner as LANE. If the frame is addressed to a different subnet, MPOA will use the network layer address to forward the frame. In this case, the ATM backbone is operating somewhat similar to both a hierarchical and flat backbone. In an ATM MPOA network, a series of *route servers* (also called MPOA servers or MPS) are provided that perform somewhat the same function as DNS servers in TCP/IP networks (see Chapter 3): route servers translate network layer addresses (e.g., IP addresses) into ATM virtual circuit identifiers.

THE BEST PRACTICE BACKBONE DESIGN

The past few years have seen radical changes in the backbone, both in terms of new technologies (e.g., gigabit Ethernet) and in architectures (e.g., collapsed backbones, VLANs). Ten years ago, the most common backbone architecture was the routed backbone, connected to a series of shared 10Base-T hubs in the LAN. For many years, experts predicted that FDDI or ATM would be the preferred backbone technology and that there was a good chance that ATM would gradually move into the LAN. Today, however, with the arrival of gigabit Ethernet things are different.

Our recommendations for the best practice backbone design depend heavily on data rates and cost, as they did for LANs in the previous chapter. The design of backbone networks raises two new factors: backbone architecture, and the need to translate between protocols. We begin with architectures and then turn our attention to effective data rates, translation, and costs.

Architectures

The most effective architecture in terms of cost and performance is a collapsed backbone (either rack mounted or using a chassis switch) because it provides best performance at the least cost. VLANs come a close second, but as they are less mature at this point, many organizations prefer to stay with tried-and-true technologies. As VLANs mature, more organizations will begin to gain experience with them.

Effective Data Rates

As you will recall, the effective data rate of the hardware layers is the maximum practical speed in bits that the hardware layers can be expected to provide and depends on four basic factors: nominal data rates, error rates, efficiency of the data link layer protocols used, and efficiency of the media access control protocols. We will assume that error rates are similar between different technologies. Our analyses therefore focus on nominal data rates, data link protocol efficiency, media access control protocol efficiency, and the impact of translations. Gigabit Ethernet was examined in the previous chapter, so we focus on FDDI and ATM.

Data Link Protocol Efficiency FDDI adds 29 bytes of overhead to every frame, but permits frames of 4,500 bytes. After considering ACKs/NAKs, this provides efficiency of approximately 99 percent, assuming mostly large frames are transmitted.

ATM adds 5 bytes of overhead to every 53-byte cell. On top of this, we must also include the overhead bits added by the protocols used by the physical layer protocols such as SONET. Without showing all calculations, this gives an efficiency of approximately 87 percent.

Media Access Control Protocol Efficiency FDDI uses a very different media access control protocol from Ethernet's CSMA/CD. Chapter 4 discussed the performance characteristics of CSMA/CD: gradual increases in response time delay to about 50 percent of nominal capacity, more rapid increases in delay to about 80 percent of capacity, and immense increases in delays after 80 percent that rendered the network essentially unusable.

FDDI uses the token-passing controlled-access technique. Token passing, like other controlled-access techniques, imposes more fixed-cost delays initially when traffic is low, because now computers must wait to receive the token before they transmit, rather than just making sure there is no traffic and transmitting at will as with CSMA/CD. However, response time delays increase only slowly up to about 90 to 95 percent of nominal capacity. Once this level is reached, they increase rapidly until the network is 100 percent saturated.

These patterns are shown in Figure 5-18. Remember that lower response time delays are best. The CSMA/CD approach used by Ethernet works best when there is a low amount of traffic relative to the total capacity, while the token-passing approach used by FDDI works best as total traffic approaches the maximum capacity of the network.

This means that FDDI users experience few response time delays as long as the total amount of network traffic remains under 90 percent of the nominal data rate. This means, for example, that an FDDI network with a nominal data rate of 100 Mbps can provide an effective total data rate of about 89 Mbps (99% efficiency × 90% capacity × 100 Mbps). Because FDDI is a shared-circuit technology, this capacity is shared among all active devices or computers.

Because ATM uses full-duplex transmission, its media access control protocol efficiency is almost 100 percent. This means, for example, that an ATM network providing 155-Mbps circuits is capable of providing a total network capacity of about 135 Mbps simultaneously in both directions, or a total of about 270 Mbps (87% efficiency × 100% capacity × 155 Mbps = 135 Mbps). An ATM network providing 622-Mbps circuits is capable of providing a total network capacity of about 540 Mbps simultaneously in both directions, or a total of about 1080 Mbps.

Conversion Between Protocols

FDDI and ATM require Ethernet frames to be converted into FDDI and ATM protocols before they can be sent across backbones using these technologies. FDDI uses *translation,*

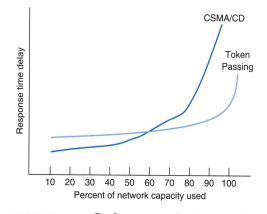

FIGURE 5-18   Performance of token passing compared with CSMA/CD.

which means that the Ethernet frame is removed and replaced with an FDDI frame for transmission through the FDDI ring. Before it leaves the FDDI ring, the FDDI frame is removed and replaced with the new Ethernet frame. Tests suggest that this translation process decreases efficiency anywhere from 10 to 20 percent depending on the specific brand of FDDI equipment in use. This would suggest, then, that the actual effective data rate of 100-Mbps FDDI when used to connect Ethernet LANs is approximately 70 Mbps. This effective data rate is shared among all networks attached to the backbone. In a busy backbone connecting 10 active networks the effective data rate would be close to 7 Mbps, while in a small backbone with only two active networks, the effective data rate would be close to 35 Mbps.

ATM uses *encapsulation* to convert frames, which means that the Ethernet frame is simply surrounded by an ATM cell—or more properly by a series of ATM cells—which are removed when the frame reaches the last ATM switch in the backbone. In general, encapsulation is a faster process than translation. However, FDDI continues to use the TCP/IP packets for routing, while ATM must generate new routing information using its virtual channels. Performing this new routing is very time consuming. Tests suggest this address translation process decreases efficiency anywhere from 30 to 40 percent depending on the specific brand of ATM equipment in use. Thus the actual effective data rate of 155-Mbps ATM when used to connect Ethernet LANs is approximately 80 Mbps in either direction, for a total of 160 Mbps. The actual effective data rate of 622 Mbps is probably closer to 380 Mbps each way or 760 Mbps in total because it suffers from a low percentage of efficiency loss.

As we discussed in the last chapter, the effective data rate of full-duplex gigabit Ethernet is approximately 1.8 Gbps. The results are summarized in Figure 5-19.

Recommendations

Given these trade-offs in costs and effective data rates, there are several best practice recommendations. First, the best practice architecture is a collapsed backbone or VLAN. Second, the best practice recommendation for backbone technology is gigabit

Technology	Effective Data Rate
Full Duplex 1 GbE	1.8 Gbps
Full Duplex 10 GbE	18 Gbps
FDDI	7-70 Mbps depending upon traffic
155 Mbps ATM (Full Duplex)	160 Mbps
622 Mbps ATM (Full Duplex)	760 Mbps
Assumptions: collapsed backbone connecting Ethernet LANs that transmit mostly large frames.	

FIGURE 5-19   Effective data rate estimates for backbone technologies.

Ethernet, which is why shipments of ATM and FDDI have dropped significantly over the past year.

Considering the LAN and backbone environments together, the ideal network design is likely to be a mix of layer-2 and layer-3 Ethernet switches.[4] Figure 5-20 shows one likely design. The access layer (i.e., the LANs) uses 10/100 layer-2 Ethernet switches running on cat 5e or cat 6 twisted-pair cables to provide flexibility for today's common 10Base-T and tomorrow's 100Base-T, with cat 6 enabling a move to 1000Base-T. The distribution layer uses layer-3 Ethernet switches that use 100Base-T or more likely 1000Base-T/F (over fiber or cat 6 or 7) to connect to the access layer. To provide good reliability, some organizations may provide redundant switches, so if one fails, the backbone continues to operate. The core layer uses layer-3 Ethernet switches running 10 GbE or 40 GbE over fiber.

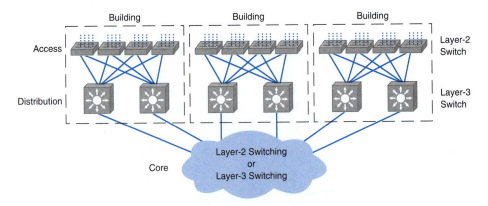

FIGURE 5-20   The best practice network design.

4 We thank our friends at Cisco Systems Inc. for helping us think about this.

SUMMARY

Backbone Architectures   Network designers often think about three distinct technology layers when designing backbones. The access layer is the LAN, the distribution layer connects the LANs together, while the core layer connects the distribution layer backbones together. The distribution layer is usually a backbone within a building, while the core layer often connects buildings and is sometimes called the campus network. A hierarchical backbone uses a set of routers or layer-3 switches to connect LANs together and moves messages using layer-3 addresses. A flat backbone uses a set of bridges or layer-2 switches to connect LANs together and moves messages using layer-2 addresses. A collapsed backbone uses one device, usually a layer-2 or layer-3 switch to connect the LANs. A VLAN uses layer-2 or layer-3 switches to build logical or virtual LANs that enable the network manager to assign capacity separate from physical location.

FDDI   FDDI is a token-passing ring network that operates at 100 Mbps over a fiber-optic cable arranged in two rings that can continue to operate if they are cut. FDDI uses token passing as its media access control protocol and continuous ARQ as its error control protocol. FDDI marks the start of its frame with a preamble similar to the Ethernet, but uses the specific bit pattern called an *end delimiter* to mark the end of the frame.

ATM   ATM (asynchronous transfer mode) is a packet-switched technology originally designed for use in wide area networks. ATM used 53-byte fixed-length cells with no error control of full-duplex 155 Mbps or 622 Mbps point-to-point circuits. ATM enables QoS, and uses virtual circuits rather than permanently assigning addresses to devices. In order to use ATM in a backbone network that connects LANs, some conversion must be done on the LAN frames to enable them to flow over the ATM backbone. With LANE, an ATM edge switch encapsulates the Ethernet frame, leaving the existing data link layer frame intact, and transmits it based on data link layer addresses. MPOA is an alternative that can use network layer addresses for transmission.

Best Practice Backbone Design   The best practice backbone design depends on cost, effective data rates, and the need to convert protocols. While ATM and FDDI provide reasonably fast transmission, the need to convert from the Ethernet frames used in the LAN to ATM cells or FDDI frames in the backbone imposes significant time delays. Given the trade-offs in costs and effective data rates, the best backbone architecture for most organizations is a collapsed backbone (using a rack or a chassis switch). The recommended technology is gigabit Ethernet.

KEY TERMS

access layer
application-based VLAN
Asynchronous Transfer
    Mode (ATM)
backbone architecture
backbone network
bridge
cell
chassis-based collapsed
    backbone
chassis switch
classes of service
collapsed backbone

copper-distributed data
    interface (CDDI)
core layer
distribution layer
dual attachment station
    (DAS)
edge switch
encapsulation
enterprise network
fiber distributed data
    interface (FDDI)
flat backbone
gateway

hierarchical backbone
IEEE 802.1p
IEEE 802.1q
IP-based VLAN
LAN encapsulation
    (LANE)
layer-1 VLAN
layer-2 switch
layer-2 VLAN
layer-3 switch
layer-3 VLAN
layer-4 VLAN
MAC-based VLAN

main distribution facility
    (MDF)
mesh topology
module
multiprotocol over ATM
    (MPOA)
multiprotocol router
multiprotocol switch
multiswitch VLAN
patch cables
permanent virtual circuit
    (PVC)
policy-based VLAN

port-based VLAN	routing switch	symbol	transparent
quality of service (QoS)	single attachment station	throw-it-on-the-floor	virtual channel (VC)
rack	(SAS)	error control	virtual circuit
rack-mounted collapsed	single-switch VLAN	token	virtual LAN (VLAN)
backbone	switched virtual circuit	token passing	wire speed
router	(SVC)	translation	

QUESTIONS

1. Compare and contrast bridges, routers, and gateways.

2. How does a bridge differ from a layer-2 switch?

3. How does a router differ from a routing switch?

4. How does a layer-2 switch differ from a routing switch?

5. Under what circumstances would you want to use a multiprotocol router?

6. What is an enterprise network?

7. What are the three technology layers important in backbone design?

8. Explain how hierarchical backbones work.

9. Explain how flat backbones work.

10. Explain how collapsed backbones work.

11. What are the key advantages and disadvantages among hierarchical, flat, and collapsed backbones?

12. Compare and contrast rack-mounted and chassis-switch-based collapsed backbones.

13. What is a module and why is it important?

14. Explain how single-switch VLANs work.

15. Explain how multiswitch VLANs work.

16. Explain the differences among layer-1, -2, -3, and -4 VLANs.

17. What is IEEE 802.1q?

18. Which backbone architecture is the most flexible? Why?

19. How does FDDI operate in terms of topology, media access control, and error control?

20. What is the layout for an FDDI frame?

21. What is the difference between a DAS and a SAS?

22. What is CDDI?

23. How do FDDI and CDDI transmit at the physical layer?

24. How does ATM operate in terms of topology, media access control, and error control?

25. How does ATM perform addressing?

26. How can ATM be used to link Ethernet LANs?

27. What is encapsulation and how does it differ from translation?

28. Why are broadcast messages important?

29. Which has greater throughput: FDDI, ATM or 1 GbE?

30. How does FDDI LAN carry an Ethernet frame?

31. How does ATM LANE carry an Ethernet frame?

32. What are the preferred technologies used in the three technology layers in backbone design?

33. What are the preferred architectures used in the three technology layers in backbone design?

34. What do you think is the future of ATM and FDDI in the backbone?

35. Several years ago, the ATM Forum, a group of companies that build ATM equipment, announced a version of ATM designed for use in LANs in which the same technology could be used in the LAN as in backbone. It ran at 25 Mbps over fiber-optic cable. Why do you think it did not catch on?

36. Some experts are predicting that Ethernet will move into the WAN. What do you think?

37. Some companies continue to use FDDI in their backbones and to install new FDDI backbones, even though they are aware of the best practice recommendations now favoring gigabit Ethernet. Why do you think they choose FDDI over gigabit Ethernet?

EXERCISES

5-1. Survey the backbone networks used in your organization. Do they use Ethernet, FDDI, ATM, or some other technology? Why?

5-2. Document one backbone network in detail. What devices are attached, what cabling is used, and what is the topology? What networks does the backbone connect?

5-3. You have been hired by a small company to install a backbone to connect four 10Base-T Ethernet LANs (each using one 24-port hub) and to provide a connec-tion to the Internet. Develop a simple backbone and determine the total cost; that is, select the backbone technology and price it, select the cabling and price it, select the devices and price them, and so on. Prices are available at www.datacommwarehouse.com, but use any source that is convenient. For simplicity, assume that cat 5, cat 5e, cat 6, and fiber-optic cable have a fixed cost per circuit to buy and install, regardless of distance, of $80, $100, $250 and $400.

MINI-CASES

I. Pat's Engineering Works

Pat's Engineering Works is a small company that specializes in complex engineering consulting projects. The projects typically involve a team of 4 or 5 engineers who do complex data-intensive analyses for companies. Because so much data is needed, it is stored on their high-capacity server but moved to the engineers' workstations for analysis. The company is moving into new offices and they want you to design their network. They have a staff of 25 engineers (which is expected to grow to 75 over the next five years), plus another 12 management and clerical employees who also need network connections, but whose needs are less intense. Design the network. Be sure to include a diagram.

II. Hospitality Hotel

Hospitality Hotel is a luxury hotel whose guests are mostly business travelers. To improve its quality of service, it has decided to install network connections in each of its 600 guest rooms and 12 conference meeting rooms. Last year the hotel upgraded its own internal networks to switched 10Base-T, but it wants to keep the "public" network (i.e., the guest and meeting rooms) separate from its "private" network (i.e., its own computer systems). Your task is to design the public network; do not worry about how to connect the two networks together (that's the job of another consultant). Be sure to include a diagram.

III. Robin's Web Works

Robin's Web Works is a small company that specializes in Web-development projects. The projects typically involve one or two staff who develop Web systems for a variety of small companies. They have four Web servers, three application servers, and three database servers that are used in the development process. The also have a set of five Web servers, two application servers, and one database server that are production machines used to host the systems they develop. They have a staff of 20 programmers (which is expected to grow to 40 over the next three years), plus another 5 management and clerical employees who also need network connections, but whose needs are less intense. Design the network. Be sure to include a diagram.

CHAPTER 6

HARDWARE LAYERS: METROPOLITAN AND WIDE AREA NETWORKS

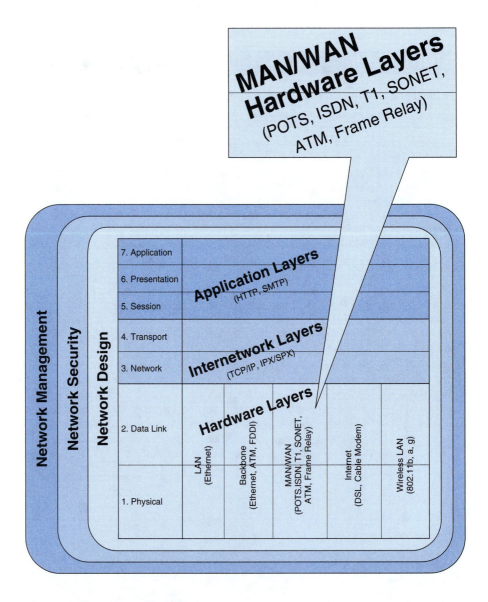

MOST ORGANIZATIONS do not build their own metropolitan or long distance communication circuits, preferring instead to lease them from common carriers, or to use the Internet. Therefore, this chapter focuses on the MAN/WAN topologies and telecommunications *services* offered by common carriers for use in MANs and WANs, not the underlying technology that the carriers use to provide them. We discuss the four principal types of MAN and WAN services that are available: circuit-switched services, dedicated-circuit services, packet-switched services, and virtual private network services. We conclude by discussing our best practice recommendations for WAN design.

OBJECTIVES

- Understand circuit-switched services and topologies
- Understand dedicated-circuit services and topologies
- Understand packet-switched services and topologies
- Be familiar with virtual private network services and topologies
- Understand the best practice recommendations for MAN/WAN design

CHAPTER OUTLINE

INTRODUCTION

THE PUBLIC SWITCHED TELEPHONE NETWORK

  PSTN Architecture

  Analog Transmission

  Digital Transmission of Analog Voice Data

  Multiplexing

CIRCUIT-SWITCHED NETWORKS

  Topology

  Plain Old Telephone Service

  Integrated Services Digital Network

DEDICATED-CIRCUIT NETWORKS

  Topology

  T-Carrier Services

  Synchronous Optical Network

PACKET-SWITCHED NETWORKS

  Topology

INTRODUCTION

Metropolitan area networks (MANs) typically span from 3 to 30 miles and connect backbone networks and LANs. MANs also provide dial-in and dial-out capability to LANs, backbones, and mainframes and access to the Internet. Wide area networks (WANs) connect backbones and MANs across longer distances, often hundreds or thousands of miles.

Although some organizations build their own MANs and WANs, most organizations cannot afford to lay long stretches of cable, build microwave towers, or lease satellites. Instead, most organizations rent or lease services from *common carriers* such as AT&T, Bell Canada, Ameritech, or BellSouth, which operate over the *public switched telephone network (PSTN)*. As a customer, you do not lease physical cables per se; you simply lease services that provide certain transmission characteristics. The carrier decides whether it will use twisted pair, fiber optics, and so on for your circuits.

In this chapter, we first examine the PSTN and then the MAN and WAN services from the viewpoint of a network manager, rather than that of a common carrier. We focus less on internal operations and how the specific technologies work, and more on how these services are offered to network managers and how they can be used to build networks, because most network managers are less concerned with how the services work, and are most concerned with how they can use them effectively. This chapter focuses on corporate data networks, so some of the most common MAN services used by individuals for personal Internet access (e.g., DSL, cable modem) are discussed in the next chapter.

THE PUBLIC SWITCHED TELEPHONE NETWORK

In this chapter we focus on MAN and WAN services in North America. Although there are many similarities in the way data communications networks and services have evolved in different countries, there also are many differences. Most countries have a federal government agency that regulates data and voice communications. In the United States, this agency is the *Federal Communications Commission (FCC);* in Canada it is the *Canadian*

Radio-Television and Telecommunications Commission (CRTC). Each state or province also has its own *public utilities commission (PUC)* to regulate communications within its borders.

A *common carrier* is a private company that sells or leases communication services and facilities to the public. Common carriers are profit oriented, and their primary products are services for voice and data transmissions, over both traditional wired circuits and cellular services. Common carriers often supply a broad range of computer-based services, such as the manufacturing and marketing of specialized communication hardware and software. A common carrier that provides local telephone services (e.g., BellSouth) is commonly called a *local exchange carrier (LEC),* while one that provides long distance services (e.g., Sprint) is commonly called an *interexchange carrier (IXC).* As the LECs move into the long distance market and IXCs move into the local telephone market, this distinction may disappear.

PSTN Architecture

The PSTN differs in two important ways from the previous types of networks we have examined this book: It is *circuit switched* and uses *analog transmission.* Circuit switched means that every time messages need to be transmitted, a physical or logical circuit is established through the network from the sender to the receiver. All the data flow through the physical or logical circuit. Once the messages have been transmitted, the circuit is disconnected. This is what happens when you make a phone call. You pick up the telephone and dial someone's number; a physical circuit is established from your telephone to the receiver's telephone. Once you finish talking, you hang up the phone and the circuit is disconnected.

While the circuit is in operation, all data that is transmitted from your telephone must flow to the receiver's telephone. Neither you nor the receiver can exchange data with any other telephone until the call is complete—unless of course you use conference calling (a multipoint circuit) or are interrupted by call waiting (which is a separate story). This is in sharp contrast to Ethernet networks, in which the same computer can send or receive packets to or from different computers almost simultaneously (i.e., packets from one message from one computer can be interspersed with packets from another message from another computer).

As we discussed in Chapter 4, there are two fundamentally different types of data that can flow through the physical circuit (digital and analog) and two fundamentally different types of data transmission (digital and analog). Computers produce digital data and Ethernet uses digital transmission (different voltages of electricity or different brightnesses of light) to move the data through the cables.

The PSTN was built to transmit analog voice phone call data, and thus it used analog transmission. As digital transmission became more cost effective than analog transmission, much of the PSTN was converted to use digital transmission. Figure 6-1 shows the design of today's PSTN with its combination of both digital and analog transmission. The *local loop*—the part that provides network access to just about every home and business in North America—remains analog. But the part from the switch office that provides your telephone access through the core and distribution layers of the PSTN to the switch office closest to the person you are calling uses digital transmission. Digital transmission is

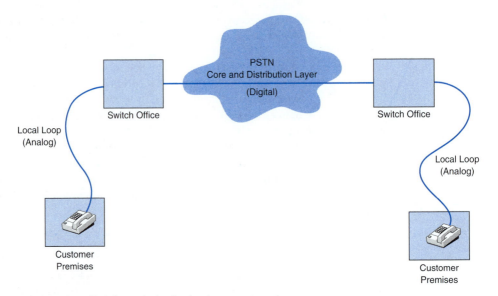

FIGURE 6-1 Public switched telephone network.

cheaper and less susceptible to error than is analog transmission. While we would prefer an all-digital PSTN, the costs of converting the local loop to use digital transmission are prohibitive; estimates range into the hundreds of billions of dollars.

When you make a telephone call, your telephone converts your voice into an analog transmission over the local loop. This analog transmission flows until it hits the first switch office. A device at the switch office converts this incoming analog data into digital data which is transmitted using digital transmission through most of the PSTN until it reaches the last switch office closest to its destination. This switch office then converts the digital transmission into an analog transmission that flows through the local loop to the receiver's telephone.

This architecture means that when you use your telephone to dial up an ISP, your digital computer data must be converted into analog data and transmitted using analog transmission. This is done by a modem. The sending modem translates the digital binary data produced by computers into the analog signals required for transmission and the receiving modem translates the analog signal back into digital data for use at the destination.

In order to understand how the PSTN can be used to provide services for data transmission in MANs and WANs, we must first examine how analog transmission can be used to send digital computer data and how analog voice data can be converted into digital data for transmission over the digital portion of the PSTN.

Analog Transmission

Sound Waves The sound waves transmitted through the analog local loop have three important characteristics (see Figure 6-2). The first is the height of the wave, called *amplitude,* measured in decibels (dB). Every wave has two parts, half above the zero amplitude

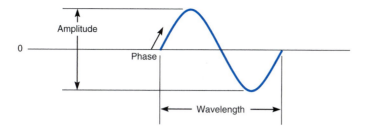

FIGURE 6-2   Sound wave.

point (i.e., positive) and half below (i.e., negative), and both halves are always the same height. The second characteristic is the length of the wave, usually expressed as the number of waves per second or *frequency,* measured in hertz (Hz).[1] A high frequency means that there are many short waves in a one-second interval, while a low frequency means that there are fewer (but longer) waves in one second. The third characteristic is the *phase,* which refers to the direction in which the wave begins and is measured in the number of degrees (°). The wave in Figure 6-2 starts up and to the right, which is defined as a 0° phase wave. Waves can also start down and to the right (which is a 180° phase wave because it is 180° off from the 0° wave shown in Figure 6-2), and in virtually any other part of the wave.

Modulation   When we transmit data, we use the shape of the sound waves (in terms of amplitude, frequency, and phase) to represent different data values. We do this by transmitting a simple wave through the circuit (called the *carrier wave*) and then we *modulate* or change its amplitude, frequency, or phase in different ways to represent binary 1s and 0s. There are three fundamental modulation techniques: amplitude modulation, frequency modulation, and phase modulation.

   With *amplitude modulation (AM),* the sender and receiver agree on how many waves to send per second (or, in other words, the time interval for each *symbol*). Basic amplitude modulation sends one bit per wave (i.e., symbol) by defining two different amplitudes, one for a binary 1 and one for a binary 0. In Figure 6-3a, the highest amplitude (tallest wave) represents a binary 1 and the lowest amplitude represents a binary 0. In this case, when the sending device wants to transmit a 1, it would send a high-amplitude wave.

   It is possible to send 2 bits on one wave (symbol) by defining four different amplitudes in the same way that 1000Base-T sent 2 bits on each electrical pulse. Figure 6-3b shows the case where the highest-amplitude wave is defined to be 2 bits, both 1s. The next-highest amplitude is defined to mean first a 1 and then a 0, and so on. This technique could be further refined to send 3 bits at the same time by defining 8 different amplitude levels or 4 bits by defining 16 amplitude levels, and so on. At some point, however, it becomes very difficult to differentiate between the different amplitudes. The differences are so small that even a small amount of noise could destroy the signal.

   Frequency shift keying (FSK) (also called *frequency modulation*) represents each binary 0 or 1 by the number of waves per second (i.e., a different frequency). In this case,

---

[1] Hertz is the same as "cycles per second"; therefore, 20,000 hertz is equal to 20,000 cycles per second. One hertz (Hz) is the same as 1 cycle per second. One kilohertz (KHz) is 1,000 cycles per second (kilocycles); 1 megahertz (MHz) is 1 million cycles per second (megacycles); and 1 gigahertz (GHz) is 1 billion cycles per second.

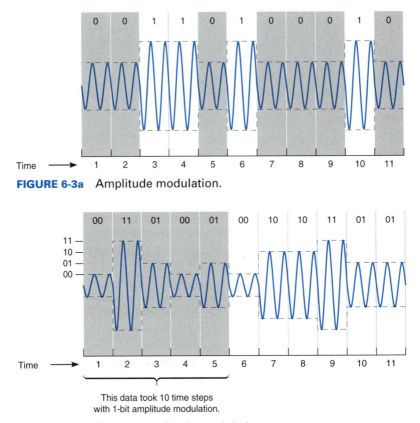

FIGURE 6-3a Amplitude modulation.

FIGURE 6-3b Two-bit amplitude modulation.

the amplitude stays constant. One frequency (i.e., a certain number of waves per second) in a time interval is defined to be 0, and a different frequency (a different number of waves per second) is defined to be 1. In Figure 6-4, the higher-frequency wave (more waves per time period) equals a binary 1, and the lower-frequency wave equals a binary 0. As with AM, it is possible to send more than 1 bit. Two bits could be sent on the same symbol by defining 4 different frequencies, 3 bits by defining 8 frequencies, and so on.

Phase shift keying (PSK) (also called *phase modulation*) is done by changing the direction in which the wave begins. One phase is defined to be a binary 0 and the other phase is defined to be a binary 1. Figure 6-5 shows the case where a phase of 180° is defined to be a binary 0 and a phase of 0° is defined to be a binary 1. PSK is less susceptible to noise than AM or FSK because it takes a much larger amount of interference to change the phase of a wave than to change its amplitude or frequency. Two bits could be sent on the same symbol by defining 4 different phases (0°, 90°, 180°, and 270°), 3 bits by defining 8 phases, and so on.

It is possible to transmit even more bits on each symbol (i.e., sound wave) by combining two different techniques. *Quadrature amplitude modulation (QAM)* combines AM and PSK; it defines 16 different combinations of amplitude and phase so that 4 data bits

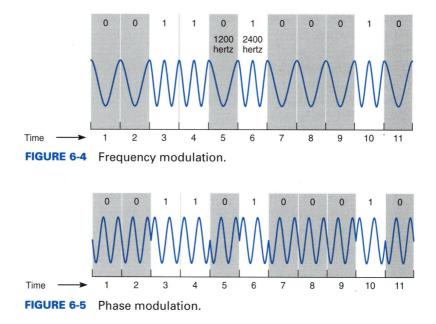

FIGURE 6-4 Frequency modulation.

FIGURE 6-5 Phase modulation.

can be sent on each signal. The combinations are chosen to make the amplitude and phase as different as possible, so that if a slight amount of noise changes the phase or amplitude, there is a very good chance that the correct data can still be recognized. For example, one 4-bit combination (e.g., 1011) might be sent using a 45° phase shift and the highest possible amplitude, while another bit pattern (e.g., 1010) might be sent using a 60° phase shift and a low amplitude, so even if there is some noise that slightly distorts the phase or the amplitude, the correct signal can still be recognized.

Trellis coded modulation (TCM) is an enhancement of QAM that combines AM and PSK into an even greater number of combinations. TCM takes the incoming bit stream and adds additional bit(s) based on the last symbol sent to minimize errors due to noise. Like QAM, TCM chooses the amplitude and phase combinations to minimize the chance that slight distortions can cause one symbol to be mistaken for another. This, combined with the added bit(s), greatly reduces problems due to noise.

Data Transmission   In order to transmit data, both the sender and receiver have to agree on what type of signaling technique they are going to use (e.g., PSK, QAM, TCM) and what frequency ranges they will use. The size of this frequency range, called the *bandwidth,* directly affects the maximum speed at which we can transmit data. The greater the bandwidth, the faster we can transmit. A typical voice circuit in the North American PSTN has a bandwidth of 4,000 Hz in the range from 0 to 4000 Hz because this is the most commonly used range for the human voice.

The data capacity of a circuit is the fastest rate at which you can send data over the circuit in terms of the number of bits per second. The data rate is calculated by multiplying the number of bits sent on each symbol (e.g., PSK with four levels sends 2 bits per symbol) by the *symbol rate* (the number of symbols or waves sent per second). The maximum symbol rate that can be used in analog transmission depends on the bandwidth available and the signal-to-noise ratio (the strength of the signal compared to the amount of noise in the circuit). The maximum symbol rate is usually the same as the bandwidth as measured in hertz *under perfect conditions*. If the circuit is noisy, the maximum symbol rate may fall to 50 percent or less of the bandwidth. Since the bandwidth of today's PSTN is 4,000 Hz, this means that under perfect conditions the PSTN can transmit at a maximum symbol rate of 4,000 Hz (i.e., 4000 symbols per second).

For example, if we were to transmit data using QAM (which has 4 bits per symbol) at a symbol rate of 3,000 Hz (i.e., 3,000 symbols per second), this would provide a data rate of 12 Kbps (4 bits per symbol × 3,000 symbols per second = 12,000 bits per second). If we were to transmit data using the version of TCM that has an average of 9.8 bits per symbol at a symbol rate of 3,200 Hz, this would provide a data rate of 31.36 Kbps (9.8 bits per symbol × 3,200 symbols per second = 31,360 bits per second).

Digital Transmission of Analog Voice Data

In the same way that digital computer data can be sent over analog telephone networks using analog transmission, analog voice data can be sent over digital networks using digital transmission. This process is somewhat similar to the analog transmission of digital data. A pair of special devices called *codecs (code/decode)* is used in the same way that a pair of modems is used to translate the digital data into analog data for transmission in analog telephone networks. One codec is located in the switch office and translates the incoming analog voice signal into a digital signal for transmission across the digital circuit. A second codec at the receiver's switch office translates the digital data back into analog data.

Translating from Analog Data to Digital Data   Analog voice data must first be translated into a series of binary digits before they can be transmitted over a digital circuit. This is done by sampling the amplitude of the sound wave at regular intervals, and translating it into a binary number. Figure 6-6 shows an example where eight different amplitude levels are used (i.e., each amplitude level is represented by 3 bits).

The sender's telephone samples the sender's voice and creates an analog signal of the sound waves. This analog signal is sampled by the codec and the amplitude of the sound wave in each time interval converted into a series of 3-bit digital signals. Sometimes the analog signal does not perfectly match the levels the codec can use, so the codec must "round-off" to the closest level. For example, in the third time period in the figure, the original analog sound wave is between 110 and 111. Ideally, the codec should code this as a "110.7" but it can't; it must choose either 110 or 111. Since the height is closer to 111, it converts it to 111.

This digital signal is then sent through the PSTN's digital circuits until it reaches the codec at the other end. This codec then converts the digital signal back into an analog representation of the sound waves, which are sent to the receiver's telephone.

A careful examination of the original sound wave and the reproduced sound wave will show differences. In time period three, for example, the reproduced sound wave is a perfect 111, while the original was not. The same is true of the other time periods in which the original sound wave was not a perfect match for the codec's levels.

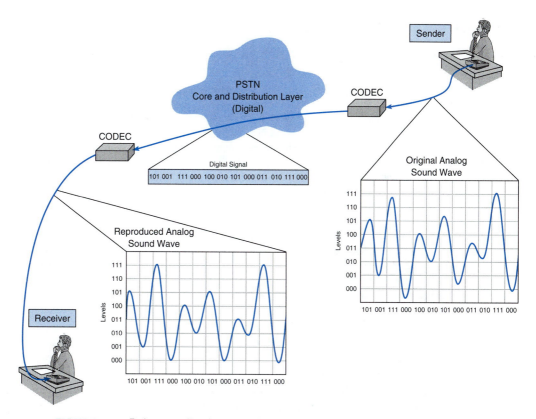

FIGURE 6-6 Pulse amplitude modulation (PAM).

The difference between the two signals is called *quantizing error*. Voice transmissions using digitized signals that have a great deal of quantizing error sound metallic or machine-like to the ear. There are two ways to reduce quantizing error and improve the quality of the digitized signal, but neither is without cost.

The first method is to increase the number of amplitude levels. This minimizes the difference between the levels (the "height" of the "steps") and results in a smoother signal. In Figure 6-6, we could define 16 amplitude levels instead of 8 levels. This would require 4 bits (rather than the current 3 bits) to represent the amplitude, thus increasing the amount of data needed to transmit the digitized signal. No amount of levels or bits will ever result in perfect-quality sound reproduction, but in general, 7 bits ($2^7 = 128$ levels) reproduces human speech adequately. Music, on the other hand, requires at least 16 bits ($2^{16} = 65,536$ levels).

The second method is to sample more frequently. This will reduce the "length" of each "step," also resulting in a smoother signal. To obtain a reasonable-quality voice signal, one must sample at least twice the highest possible frequency in the analog signal. You will recall that the highest frequency transmitted in telephone circuits is 4,000 hertz. Thus the methods used to digitize telephone voice transmissions must sample the input voice signal at a minimum of 8,000 times per second.

TECHNICAL FOCUS *6-1*

HOW INSTANT MESSENGER TRANSMITS VOICE DATA

A 64-Kbps digital circuit works very well for transmitting voice data because it provides very good quality. The problem is that it requires a lot of capacity. Internet users that connect using modems do not have circuits that run as fast as 64 Kbps; 33.6 or 56 Kbps is more common. Therefore, they can't use PCM.

Adaptive differential pulse code modulation (ADPCM) is the alternative used by Instant Messenger and many other applications that want to provide voice services over lower-speed digital circuits. ADPCM works in much the same way as PCM. It samples an incoming voice signal 8,000 times per second and calculates the same 8-bit amplitude value as PCM. However, instead of transmitting the 8-bit value, it instead transmits the *difference* between the 8-bit value in the last time interval and the current 8-bit

value (i.e., how the amplitude has *changed* from one time period to another). Because analog voice signals change slowly, these changes can be adequately represented by using only 4 bits. This means that ADPCM can be used on digital circuits that provide only 32 Kbps (4 bits per sample × 8,000 samples per second = 32,000 bps).

Several versions of ADPCM have been developed and standardized by the ITU-T. There are versions designed for 8-Kbps circuits (which send 1 bit 8,000 times per second) and 16-Kbps circuits (which send 2 bits 8,000 times per second), as well as the original 32-Kbps version. However, there is a trade-off here. While the 32-Kbps version usually provides almost as good sound quality as traditional voice telephone circuits, the 8-Kbps and 16-Kbps versions provide poorer sound quality.

There are many different combinations of sampling frequencies and numbers of bits per sample that could be used. For example, one could sample 4,000 times per second using 128 amplitude levels (i.e., 7 bits), or sample at 16,000 times per second using 256 levels (i.e., 8 bits). Sampling more frequently than this (called *oversampling*) will improve signal quality. RealNetworks.com, which produces Real Audio and other Web-based tools, sets its products to sample at 48,000 times per second to provide higher quality.

The North American telephone network uses *pulse code modulation (PCM)*. With PCM, the input voice signal is sampled 8,000 times per second. Each time the input voice signal is sampled, 8 bits are generated, 7 are data bits and 1 is used for control purposes. Therefore, the transmission speed on the digital circuit must be 64,000 bits per second (8 bits per sample × 8,000 samples per second) in order to transmit a voice signal when it is in digital form. Thus, the North American telephone network is built using millions of 64-Kbps digital circuits that connect via codecs to the millions of miles of analog local loop circuits into users' homes and businesses.

Multiplexing

Multiplexing means to break one high-speed physical communication circuit into several lower-speed logical circuits so that many different devices can use it simultaneously, but still think that they have their own separate circuits (the multiplexer is "*transparent*"). It is multiplexing (specifically wavelength division multiplexing discussed at the end of this section) that has enabled the almost unbelievable growth in network capacity discussed in Chapter 1; without wavelength division multiplexing, the Internet would have collapsed in the 1990s.

Multiplexing often is done in multiples of 4 (e.g., 8, 16). Figure 6-7a shows a four-level multiplexed circuit. Note that two multiplexers are needed for each circuit; one to

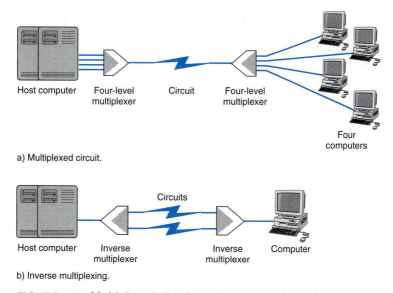

a) Multiplexed circuit.

b) Inverse multiplexing.

FIGURE 6-7   Multiplexed circuit and inverse multiplexing.

combine the four original circuits into the one multiplexed circuit and one to separate them back into the four separate circuits. The primary benefit of multiplexing is to save money by reducing the amount of cable or the number of network circuits that must be installed. For example, if we did not use multiplexers in Figure 6-7a, we would need to run four separate circuits from the clients to the server. If the clients were located close to the server, this would be inexpensive. However, if they were located several miles away, the extra costs could be substantial.

Inverse multiplexing is the opposite of multiplexing: it combines several low-speed circuits to make them appear as one high-speed circuit to the user (see Figure 6-7). Inverse multiplexing is typically used when we have several low-speed circuits but would want to combine them so they appear to be one high-speed circuit.

There are four types of multiplexing: *frequency division multiplexing* (FDM), *wavelength division multiplexing* (WDM), *time division multiplexing* (TDM), and *statistical time division multiplexing* (STDM).

Frequency Division Multiplexing. FDM is used on analog circuits. With FDM, the circuit is divided into a series of separate channels, each transmitting on a different frequency, much like series of different radio or cable TV stations. All signals exist in the media at the same time, but because they are on different frequencies, they do not interfere with each other. In the same way that radio stations must be assigned separate frequencies to prevent interference, so must the signals in a FDM circuit. *Guardbands* are the unused portions of the circuit that separate these frequencies from each other.

With FDM, the total capacity of the physical circuit is simply divided among the multiplexed devices or circuits. For example, suppose we had a physical circuit that had a data rate of 64 Kbps that we wanted to divide into four circuits. We would simply divide the 64 Kbps among the four circuits and assign each circuit 16 Kbps each. However, because FDM needs guardbands, we also have to allocate some of the capacity to the guardbands, so we might actually end up with four circuits each providing 15 Kbps, and the remaining 4 Kbps allocated to the guardbands. There is no requirement that all circuits be the same size, as you will see in the next chapter when we discuss DSL.

Time Division Multiplexing. TDM shares a communication circuit among two or more circuits or devices by having them take turns transmitting. One character is taken from each circuit in turn, transmitted down the circuit, and delivered to the appropriate device at the far end. Time on the circuit is allocated even when data are not be transmitted, so that some capacity is wasted when circuits are idle. Time division multiplexing generally is more efficient than frequency division multiplexing, because it does not need guardbands. Guardbands use "space" on the circuit that otherwise could be used to transmit data. Therefore, if one divides a 64 Kbps circuit into four circuits, the result would be four 16-Kbps circuits.

Statistical Time Division Multiplexing. STDM is the exception to the rule that the capacity of the multiplexed circuit must equal the sum of the circuits it combines. STDM allows more circuits to be connected than FDM or TDM. If you have four computers connected to a TDM multiplexer and each can transmit at 64 Kbps, then you should have a circuit capable of transmitting 256 Kbps (4 × 64 Kbps). However, not all devices will be transmitting continuously at their maximum transmission speed. Users typically pause to read their screens or spend time typing at lower speeds. Therefore, you do not need to provide a total speed of 256 Kbps on this multiplexed circuit. If you assume that only two devices will ever transmit at the same time, 128 Kbps would be enough. STDM is called *statistical* because selecting the transmission speed for the multiplexed circuit is based on a statistical analysis of the usage requirements of the circuits to be multiplexed.

The key benefit of STDM is that it provides more efficient use of the circuit and saves money. You can buy a lower speed, less expensive circuit than you could using FDM or TDM.

STDM introduces two additional complexities. First, STDM can cause time delays. If *all* circuits start transmitting or receiving at the same time (or just more than the statistical assumptions), the multiplexed circuit cannot transmit all the data it receives because it does not have sufficient capacity. Therefore, STDM must have internal memory to store the incoming data that it cannot immediately transmit. When traffic is particularly heavy, you may have a 1 to 30-second delay.

The second problem is that because the logical circuits are not permanently assigned to specific devices as they are in FDM and TDM, the data from the devices is interspersed with each other. The first message might be from the third computer, the second from the first computer, and so on. Therefore, we need to add some address information to each packet to make sure we can identify the logical circuit to which it belongs. This is not a major problem, but does increase the complexity of the multiplexer and also slightly decreases efficiency, because now we must "waste" some of the circuit's capacity in transmitting the extra address we have added to each packet.

Wavelength Division Multiplexing. WDM is a version of FDM used in fiber optic cables. When fiber optic cables were first developed, the devices attached to them were designed to use only one color of light generated by a laser or LED. With one commonly used type of fiber cable, the data rate is 622 Mbps (622 million bits per second). Until recently, the 622 Mbps data rate seemed wonderful. Then the amount of data transferred over the Internet began doubling at fairly regular intervals, and several companies began investigating how we could increase the amount of data sent over the existing fiber optic cables that had already been built.

The answer, in hindsight, was obvious. Light has different frequencies (i.e., colors), so rather than building devices to transmit using only one color, why not send multiple signals, each in a different frequency, through the same fiber cable? By simply attaching different devices that could transmit in the full spectrum of light rather than just one frequency, the capacity of the existing fiber optic cables could be dramatically increased, with no change to the physical cables themselves.

WDM works by using lasers to transmit different frequencies of light (i.e., colors) through the same fiber optic cable. As with FDM, each logical circuit is assigned a different frequency, and none of the devices attached to the circuit know they are multiplexed over the same physical circuit.

Dense WDM (DWDM) is a variant of WDM that further increases the capacity of WDM by adding TDM to WDM. Today, DWDM permits up to 40 simultaneous circuits each transmitting up to 10 Gbps, giving a total network capacity in *one* fiber optic cable of 400 Gbps (i.e., 400 billion bits per second). Remember, this is the same physical cable that until recently produced only 622 Mbps; all we've changed is the devices connected to it.

DWDM is a relatively new technique, so it will continue to improve over the next few years. As we write this, DWDM systems have been announced that provide 128 circuits each at 10 Gbps (1.28 terabits per second [128 Tbps]) in one fiber cable. Experts predict that DWDM transmission speeds should reach 25 terabits per second (i.e., 25 trillion bits) within a few years (and possibly 1 petabit [1 million-billion bits per second]) — all on that same single fiber optic cable that today typically provides 622 Mbps. Once we reach these speeds, the most time-consuming part of the process is converting from the light used in the fiber cables into the electricity used in the computer devices used to route the messages through the Internet. Therefore, many companies are now developing computer devices that run on light, not electricity.

CIRCUIT-SWITCHED NETWORKS

Circuit-switched networks are the oldest and simplest approach to MAN and WAN circuits. These services operate over the *public switched telephone network (PSTN);* that is, the telephone networks operated by the common carriers such as AT&T, Ameritech, Bell-South, and so on. When you telephone someone, you are using the PSTN. The first service we will discuss is the standard dial-up service you use when you call an Internet service provider with a modem—but first we need to discuss the basic topology shared by all circuit-switched services.

Topology

Circuit-switched services use a *cloud topology* with a series of point-to-point circuits. The users lease connection points (e.g., telephone lines) into the common carrier's network,

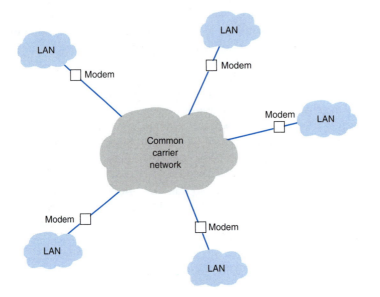

FIGURE 6-8 Circuit-switched service. LAN = local area network.

which is called the *cloud*[2] (see Figure 6-8). A modem takes the place of a NIC in an Ethernet LAN. A person (or computer) dials the telephone number of the destination computer and establishes a temporary circuit between the two computers. The computers exchange data, and when the task is complete the circuit is disconnected (e.g., by hanging up the phone).

This topology is very flexible. Circuits can be established as needed between any computers attached to the cloud at any point. However, data can be transmitted only while a circuit is established, and only to the one location it connects to. If a computer needs to send data to a number of other locations, a series of temporary circuits must be established to and disconnected from each location one after another. In general, only a limited number of circuits can be established from or to any one location at a time (e.g., each location has only so many telephone lines).

Cloud-based designs are simple for the organization because they move the burden of network design and management inside the cloud from the organization to the common carrier. Network managers do not need to worry about the amount of traffic sent between each computer; they just need to specify the amount of traffic entering and leaving each computer and buy the appropriate size and number of connections into the PSTN. However, this comes at a price. Cloud-based designs can be more expensive because users must pay for each connection into the network and pay based on the amount of time each circuit is used. Cloud-based designs are often used when network managers are uncertain of network demand, particularly in a new or rapidly growing network.

---

[2] It is called a cloud because what happens inside the common carrier's network is hidden from view. Network managers really don't care how the common carrier switches the circuit inside their network, just as long as it is fast, accurate, and reliable.

Charges for circuit-switched services usually have a fixed cost per month for network access (i.e., your telephone bill), plus in some cases a usage charge. There are two basic types of switched-circuit services in use today: POTS and ISDN.

Plain Old Telephone Service

Plain old telephone service (POTS) is the name for the common dial-up services you've probably used at one time or another. To use POTS, you need to lease a circuit into the network (i.e., a telephone line) and install special equipment to enable your computer to talk to the PSTN (i.e., a modem). To transfer data with another computer on the network, you instruct your modem to dial the other computer's telephone. Once the modem in your computer connects to the modem at the other end, you can transfer data back and forth. When you are done, you hang up and can then call another computer if you wish. Today, POTS is most commonly used to connect to the Internet, but you can also use it to communicate directly with a private non-Internet server.

POTS may use different circuit paths between the two computers each time a number is dialed. Some circuits have more noise and distortion than others, so the quality and maximum data transmission rate can vary.

Because POTS is just a physical layer specification, there are many different data link layer protocols that can be used to connect two computers over a POTS line. The most commonly used protocol is *Point-to-Point Protocol (PPP),* which was developed in the early 1990s. PPP is designed to transfer data over a point-to-point POTS line, but provides an address so that it can be used on multipoint circuits.

Media Access Control   PPP uses a half-duplex media access control protocol in which the modem waits for the other modem to stop transmitting before it attempts to transmit.

Error Control   PPP uses a continuous ARQ error control technique.

Message Delineation   Figure 6-9 shows a PPP frame. The frame begins and ends with a *flag* (01111110) that marks the start and end of a frame. The next two fields (*address* and *control*) are generally fixed for the duration of any one connection (i.e., telephone call). The *protocol* field specifies the network layer protocol (e.g., IP, IPX). The *message* may be up to 1,500 bytes in length. PPP uses CRC-16 for error control. PPP has an efficiency of approximately 99 percent.

Flag   Address Control Protocol   Message   CRC-16   Flag
(1 byte) (1 byte) (1 byte) (2 bytes)   (variable)   (2 bytes) (1 byte)

FIGURE 6-9   Point-to-Point Protocol (PPP). CRC = cyclical redundancy check.

Data Transmission in the Physical Layer   As we discussed at the start of this chapter, PSTN local loop uses analog transmission. Therefore, the physical layer (i.e., the modem) must convert digital computer data into analog data for transmission over the analog local loop. The modem uses a certain signaling technique (e.g., QAM) at a certain symbol rate. There are several modem standards that define specific combinations of signaling technique and symbol rate, as shown in Figure 6-10. V34+, for example, uses TCM with an average of 9.8 bits per symbol at a maximum symbol rate of 3429 Hz. However, V34+ can only use this combination when the telephone circuit in use has very little noise or interference. When noise is present, V34+ will attempt to lower the symbol rate and lower the average number of bits per symbol so that transmissions are less affected by noise.

Because there are a variety of modems, whenever a modem first connects to another modem, the two modems perform *handshaking*. Handshaking is a process by which two modems trade information to understand what standards each understands and to learn the quality of the telephone circuit that connects them so they can select the fastest possible symbol rate and use the signaling technique with the greatest possible number of bits per symbol.

While there are a variety of modems in use today, the most common are the V.90 and V.92 (the "56-K" modems). As you can see from Figure 6-10, the V.90 and V.92 modems use two different techniques, one for *upstream* transmissions from the client computer to the *Internet service provider (ISP)*, and one for *downstream* transmissions from the ISP to the client computer. V.90 modems are strikingly different from the modems that preceded them because they use digital transmission. The basic idea behind V.90 modems is to take the concepts of PCM (used to convert analog to digital transmissions) and turn them backward (to convert digital transmissions into an analog transmission that is digital). If PCM needs to sample 7 bits 8,000 times per second to accurately digitize human voice on a local loop, it makes sense that the same local loop can accurately transmit 7 bits 8,000 times per second. Thus V.90 and V.92 transmit downstream a 7-bit digital symbol (one of 128 possible amplitudes) 8,000 times per second. This gives a theoretical transmission speed of 56 Kbps (8,000 symbols × 7 bits per symbol).

Modem Standard	Modulation Technique	Bits per Symbol	Maximum Symbol Rate	Maximum Data Rate
V.22	FSK	1	2400 Hz	2.4 Kbps
V.32	QAM	4	2400 Hz	9.6 Kbps
V.34+	TCM	9.8	3429 Hz	33.6 Kbps
V.90				
Upstream	TCM	9.8	3429 Hz	33.6 Kbps
Downstream	PAM	7	8000 Hz	56 Kbps
V.92				
Upstream	PAM	6	8000 Hz	48 Kbps
Downstream	PAM	7	8000 Hz	56 Kbps

FIGURE 6-10   Modem standards.

Noise is a critical issue. Distinguishing among 128 different possible amplitudes is difficult unless the telephone line is very clear. In noisy conditions, the modem can accurately recognize fewer bits per symbol, so the number of bits per symbol must be reduced, thus reducing the data rate. It is estimated that about 20 percent of the telephone lines in North America (mostly the older rural exchanges) are too noisy to use 56 K modems.

For technical reasons beyond the scope of this book, it is easier to control noise in the channel transmitting from the server to the client than in the opposite direction. The older V.90 standard uses digital transmission only in the downstream channel from ISP to client. Upstream communication from client to ISP uses traditional analog transmission with the V.34+ standard, which means a maximum of 33.6 Kbps. The newer V.92 standard uses PAM digital transmission both downstream and upstream.

Data Compression   You will recall that the effective data rate depends upon nominal data rate, error rate, data link layer protocol efficiency, and media access control efficiency. To this we must also add the data compression built into the physical layer, as is done by the modem itself. *Data compression* can increase throughput of data over a communication link literally by compressing the data. *V.42bis* and *V.44,* two ISO standards for data compression that are usually built into the modem hardware, use *Lempel-Ziv* encoding. As a message is being transmitted, Lempel-Ziv encoding builds a dictionary of two-, three-, and four-character combinations that occur in the message. Any time the same character pattern reoccurs in the message, the index to the dictionary entry is transmitted rather than sending the actual data. The reduction provided by V.42bis and V.44 compression depends on the actual data sent, but usually averages between 4:1 and 6:1 (i.e., almost six times as much data can be sent per second using data compression than without it).

Because data compression rates and error rates are unpredictable, it is difficult to compute a reliable average effective data rate for POTS. PPP has a data link protocol efficiency of 99 percent and the point-to-point nature means that the media access control protocol is around 95 percent efficient as well. If we assume modest errors and reasonably effective data compression, then a V.90 modem providing a data rate of 56 Kbps might provide an effective data rate of about 200 to 300 Kbps using V.42 or V.44.

Integrated Services Digital Network

The first generation of *integrated services digital network (ISDN)* combines voice, video, and data over the same digital circuit. Because there is a newer version of ISDN, the original version is occasionally called *narrowband ISDN,* but we will just use the term ISDN. ISDN is widely available from a number of common carriers in North America.

To use ISDN, users first need to lease connection points in the PSTN, which are telephone lines just like POTS. Next, they must have special digital equipment to connect their computers (or networks) into the PSTN. Users need an ISDN *network terminator* (NT1 or NT2) that functions much like a hub, and a network interface card (called a *terminal adapter (TA)* or even an "ISDN modem") in all computers attached to the NT1/NT2. In most cases, the ISDN service appears identical to the regular dialed telephone service, with the exception that usually (but not always) each device attached to the NT1/NT2 needs a unique *service profile identifier (SPID)* to identify it. To connect to another computer using

ISDN, you dial that computer's telephone number(s) using the ISDN NIC in much the same way you would with a modem on a regular telephone line.

ISDN has long been more of a concept than a reliable service in North America. It has been available since the late 1970s, although it has not been widely adopted. Its largest problems are a lack of standards and a lack of interest from common carriers. Acceptance of ISDN has also been slowed because equipment vendors and common carriers have conflicting interpretations of the ISDN standards, and because the data rates it offers are low compared to newer services such as DSL and cable modem discussed in the next chapter. Skeptics claim that ISDN actually stands for "*I Still Don't Know*," "*I Still Don't Need it*," or "*It Still Does Nothing*." ISDN offers two types of "normal" or narrowband service, plus one emerging broadband service.

Basic Rate Interface   *Basic rate interface (BRI)* (sometimes called *basic access service* or *2B+D*) provides a communication circuit with two 64-Kbps digital transmission channels (called B channels) and one 16-Kbps control signaling channel (called a D channel). The two B channels handle digitized voice, data, and image transmissions, providing a total of 128 Kbps. The D channel is used for control messages such as acknowledgments, call setup and termination, and other functions such as automatic number identification. Some common carriers sell just one single 64-Kbps channel to those customers needing less capacity than full BRI. Under some conditions, the D channel can also be used to carry data.

For data transmission in the B channels, ISDN uses either the X.25's LAP-B data link layer protocol (discussed later in this chapter) or the frame relay data link protocol (also discussed later in this chapter). LAP-B uses a half-duplex media access control protocol in which the ISDN modem waits for the other modem to stop transmitting before it attempts to transmit. LAP-B uses a continuous ARQ error control technique. The LAP-B frame adds 8 bytes of overhead to each frame, which is a maximum of 128 bytes in length (for an efficiency of just about 89% with the ACK and NAK). The frame relay protocol uses the same throw-it-on-the-floor approach to error control as does ATM (if an error is discovered, the frame is discarded, and it is up to the other protocols at the source and destination to recognize this). Frame relay adds 6 bytes of overhead to each 1,500-byte frame (99% efficiency).

Assuming LAP-B frames over point-to-point circuits using the D channel for data transmission in addition to the two B channels, ISDN BRI provides an effective data rate of about 122 Kbps (89% efficiency × 95% media access efficiency × 144 Kbps).

One advantage of BRI is that it can be installed in many existing telephone locations without adding any new cable. If the connection from the customer's premises to the common carrier's end office is less than 3.5 miles, the ISDN line can use the existing two pairs of twisted-pair wires. The only changes are the end connections at the customer's location and at the carrier's end office. If the connection is longer than 3.5 miles, then new cable will have to be laid.

Primary Rate Interface   *Primary rate interface (PRI)* (also called *primary access service* or *23B+D*) is typically offered to commercial customers. It consists of 23 64-Kbps B channels plus one 64-Kbps D channel. PRI has almost same capacity as a T1 circuit (1.544 Mbps). ISDN PRI also uses LAP-B or frame relay protocols. Assuming that PRI uses LAP-B frames over point-to-point circuits using the D channel for data transmission in addition to the 23 B channels, ISDN BRI provides an effective data rate of about 1.3 Mbps (89% efficiency $\times$ 95% media access efficiency $\times$ 24 $\times$ 64 Kbps).

In Europe, PRI is defined as 30 B channels plus one D channel, making interconnection between America and Europe more difficult.

Broadband Integrated Services Digital Network   *Broadband ISDN (B-ISDN)* is an emerging type of ISDN that is very different than narrowband ISDN—so different in fact that it really is not ISDN. It requires special wiring and cannot be used over the traditional voice telephone line running into most homes. B-ISDN is backward-compatible with narrowband ISDN, which means it can accept narrowband BRI and PRI transmissions. B-ISDN currently defines three services. The first is a full-duplex channel that operates at 155.52 Mbps; the second provides a full-duplex channel that operates at 622.08 Mbps; and the third is an asymmetrical service with two simplex channels, one from the subscriber at 155.52 Mbps, one from the host to the subscriber at 622.08 Mbps. The first two services are intended for normal bidirectional information exchange. The third, asymmetrical, service, is intended to be used for information distribution services such as digital broadcast television.

B-ISDN often is implemented using SONET as the data link layer (SONET is described in the next section). SONET has an efficiency of about 97 percent.

DEDICATED-CIRCUIT NETWORKS

There are four main drawbacks to POTS and ISDN circuit-switched networks. First, each connection goes through the regular telephone network on a different circuit. These circuits may vary in quality, meaning that while one connection will be fairly clear, the next call may be noisy. Second, the data transmission rates on these circuits are usually low. Generally speaking, transmission rates range from 28.8 Kbps to 56 Kbps for dialed POTS circuits to 128 Kbps to 1.5 Mbps for ISDN circuits. Third, each data transmission requires a new phone call to be placed—there is no *always on* connection as we have in traditional LANs and backbones. Fourth, you usually pay per use for circuit-switched services.

One alternative is to establish a dedicated-circuit network, in which the users lease point-to-point circuits from the common carrier for their exclusive use 24 hours per day, 7 days per week. A series of point-to-point circuits are installed from one room in one building in one city to a different room in a different building in the same city (MAN) or different city (WAN). The circuit is dedicated to the sole use of the organization leasing it, so no other organization can use it. Costs are fixed per month, regardless of how much or how little traffic flows through the circuit.

Topology

With a dedicated circuit network, you lease circuits from common carriers. All connections are point to point, from one building in one city to another building in the same or a different city. The carrier installs the circuit connections at the two end points of the circuit and makes the connection between them. The circuits still run through the common carrier's cloud, but the network behaves as if you have your own physical circuits running from one point to another. See Figure 6-11.

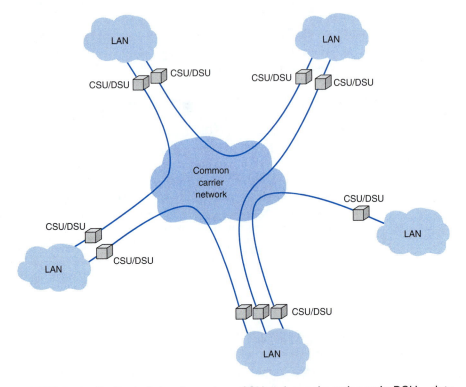

FIGURE 6-11 Dedicated circuit services. CSU = channel service unit; DSU = data service unit.

Once again, the user leases the desired circuit from the common carrier (specifying the physical end points of the circuit) and installs the equipment needed to connect computers and devices (e.g., routers or switches) to the circuit. This equipment is a *channel service unit (CSU)* and/or a *data service unit (DSU)*; a CSU/DSU is the WAN equivalent of a network interface card (NIC) in a LAN.

Unlike circuit-switched services that typically use a pay-per-use model, dedicated circuits are billed at a flat fee per month and the user has unlimited use of the circuit. Once you sign a contract, making changes can be expensive because it means rewiring the buildings and signing a new contract with the carrier. Therefore, dedicated circuits require more care in network design than switched circuits both in terms of locations and the amount of capacity you purchase.

There are three basic topologies used in dedicated-circuit networks: star, ring, and mesh. In practice, most networks use a combination of topologies. For example, a *distributed star topology* has a series of star networks that are connected by a mesh or ring topology.

Ring Topology A *ring topology* connects all computers in a closed loop, with each computer linked to the next (see Figure 6-12). The circuits are full-duplex, meaning that messages flow in both directions around the ring. Computers in the ring may send data in one direction or the other depending upon which direction is the shortest to the destination.

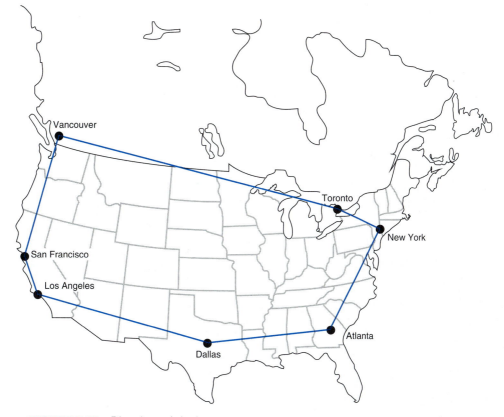

FIGURE 6-12 Ring-based design.

One disadvantage of the ring topology is that messages can take a long time to travel from the sender to the receiver. Messages usually travel through several computers and circuits before they reach their destination, so traffic delays can build up very quickly if one circuit or computer becomes overloaded. A long delay in any one circuit or computer can have significant impacts on the entire network.

In general, in spite of the failure of any one circuit or computer in a ring network the network can continue to function. Messages are simply routed away from the failed circuit or computer in the opposite direction around the ring. However, if the network is operating close to its capacity, this will dramatically increase transmission times because the traffic on the remaining part of the network may come close to doubling (because all traffic originally routed in the direction of the failed link will now be routed in the opposite direction through the longest way around the ring).

Star Topology A *star topology* connects all computers to one central computer that routes messages to the appropriate computer (see Figure 6-13). The star topology is easy to manage because the central computer receives and routes all messages in the network. It can also be faster than the ring network because any message needs to travel through at

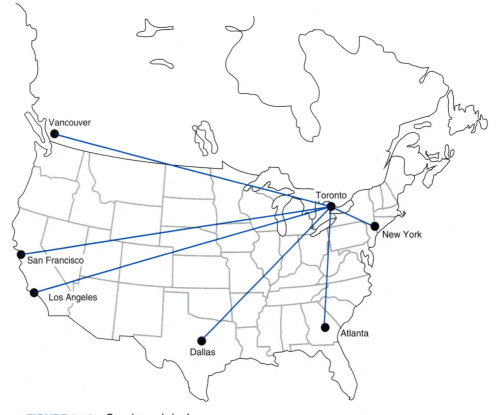

FIGURE 6-13 Star-based design.

most two circuits to reach its destination (whereas messages may have to travel through far more circuits in the ring network). However, the star topology is the most susceptible to traffic problems because the central computer must process all messages on the network. The central computer must have sufficient capacity to handle traffic peaks or it may become overloaded and network performance will suffer.

In general, the failure of any one circuit or computer affects only the one computer on that circuit. However, if the central computer fails, the entire network fails because all traffic must flow through it. It is critical that the central computer be extremely reliable.

Mesh Topology   In a *full mesh topology,* every computer is connected to every other computer (see Figure 6-14a). Full mesh networks are seldom used because of the extremely high cost. *Partial mesh topology,* in which many (but not all) computers are connected, is far more common (see Figure 6-14b). Most WAN networks use partial mesh topologies. Partial mesh topologies are usually just called *mesh topologies* for short.

The effects of the loss of computers or circuits in a mesh network depend entirely on the circuits available in the network. If there are many possible routes through the network, the loss of one or even several circuits or computers may have few effects beyond the spe-

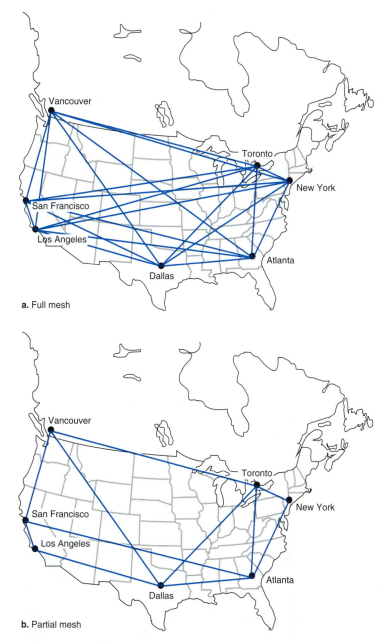

a. Full mesh

b. Partial mesh

FIGURE 6-14 Mesh designs.

cific computers involved. However, if there are only a few circuits in the network, the loss of even one circuit or computer may seriously impair the network.

In general, mesh networks combine the performance benefits of both ring networks and star networks. Mesh networks usually provide relatively short routes through the network (compared to ring networks) and provide many possible routes through the network to prevent any one circuit or computer from becoming overloaded when there is a lot of traffic (compared to star networks in which all traffic goes through one computer).

The drawback is that mesh networks use decentralized routing so that each computer in the network performs its own routing. This requires more processing by each computer in the network than in star or ring networks. Also, the transmission of network status information (e.g., how busy each computer is) wastes network capacity.

There are two types of dedicated-circuit services in common use today: T-carrier services, and SONET services.

T-Carrier Services

T-carrier circuits are the most commonly used form of dedicated-circuit services in North America today. T-carrier services are all digital. As with all dedicated-circuit services, you lease a dedicated circuit from one building in one city to another building in the same or a different city.

The T-carrier services were originally designed to provide the digital transmission circuits needed for the PSTN. Because the PSTN digital circuits use PCM, these digital circuits were built to transmit digital data for PCM's 64-Kbps circuits. These circuits, called *DS-0 circuits,* have a nominal data rate of 64 Kbps, of which 56 Kbps is available to transport user data, the other 8 Kbps being used for control purposes (as we discussed above, PCM produces 7 bits of data plus 1 control bit in each time interval).

The basic building block of the T-carrier services is the *T1* circuit (also called the DS-1 circuit), which is designed to carry 24 DS-0 circuits. The T1 circuit combines these 24 DS-0 circuits using *time division multiplexing (TDM)*; each bit in the multiplexed circuit is sent one after the other (serial transmission) over time. A T1 *multiplexer* (often just called *mux*) samples 8 bits (7 data, 1 control) from each of the 24 incoming DS-0 circuits in each time interval (i.e., 8,000 times per second) and combines them into one frame that is transmitted over the T1 circuit (see Figure 6-15). Each T1 frame contains 193 bits, 168 for data (24 circuits × 7 bits per circuit) plus 25 for control and synchronization. T1 frames

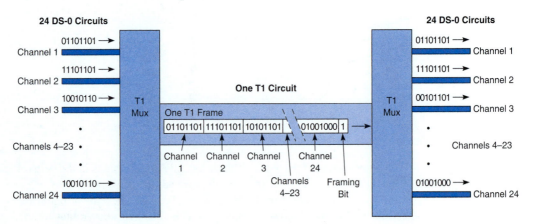

FIGURE 6-15   T1 data transfer with multiplexing.

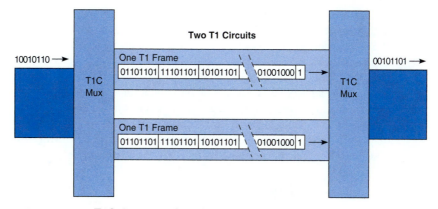

FIGURE 6-16   T1C data transfer with inverse multiplexing.

are transmitted at a rate of 8,000 frames per second, giving a nominal data rate of 1.544 Mbps (193 bits per frame × 8,000 frames per second). The receiving T1 mux receives this frame and then splits it back out into 24 separate DS-0 circuits. T1 provides an efficiency of 87 percent (168/193) over point-to-point circuits, thus giving an effective data rate of 1.3 Mbps (87% × 95% × 1.544 Mbps)

The T1 circuit is used to create a variety of other T-carrier circuits. A T1C circuit, for example, is an inverse multiplexed bundle of two T1 circuits—two T1 circuits are used to transmit data but are bundled together by a T1C mux to provide a total nominal data rate of 3.152 Mbps (2.6 effective rate), in a manner that is the inverse of the way in which T1 mux provides 24 DS-0 circuits The sending T1C mux accepts data at the nominal 3.2 Mbps rate and then splits it across two T1 circuits for transmission (see Figure 6-16). The receiving mux combines the data from these two circuits into the original nominal data stream at 3.5 Mbps.

There are several types of T-carrier services available in North America as shown in Figure 6-17. A *T2* circuit, which transmits data at a rate of 6.312 Mbps, is a multiplexed bundle of four T1 circuits—four T1 circuits are bundled together to provide a total of a nominal 6 Mbps of capacity. A *T3* circuit provides a nominal rate of 45 Mbps, and *T4* provides a nominal rate of 274 Mbps.

Digital Signal Name	T-Carrier Name	Number of DS-1 Channels	Nominal Data Rate	Effective Data Rate
DS-0			64 Kbps	53 Kbps
DS-1	T1	1	1.544 Mbps	1.3 Mbps
DS-1C	T1C	2	3.152 Mbps	2.6 Mbps
DS-2	T2	4	6.312 Mbps	5.2 Mbps
DS-3	T3	28	44.736 Mbps	36 Mbps
DS-4	T4	168	274.176 Mbps	218 Mbps

FIGURE 6-17   Types of T-carrier services.

Fractional T1, sometimes called *FT1,* offers portions of a 1.544 Mbps T1 circuit for a fraction of its full cost. Many (but not all) common carriers offer to lease sets of 64-Kbps DS-0 channels on T1 circuits. The most common FT1 services provide 128 Kbps, 256 Kbps, 384 Kbps, 512 Kbps, and 768 Kbps. In practice, most common carriers provide a full T1 circuit but only charge the users for the number of DS-0 channels they connect.

T-carrier services are available only in North America. *E-carrier* services are equivalent services offered in Europe, South America, Africa, and parts of Asia. Different parts of Mexico use either T-carrier or E-carrier services. E-carrier services use ISDN as their data link layer protocol, so an E-1 is the European version of PRI (30B channels plus one D Channel). Figure 6-18 shows the common E-carrier services.

Synchronous Optical Network

The *synchronous optical network (SONET)* is the American standard (ANSI) for high-speed dedicated-circuit services running over fiber-optic cables. The international telecommunications standards agency (ITU-T) has recently standardized an almost identical service that easily interconnects with SONET under the name of *synchronous digital hierarchy (SDH).*

As with all dedicated-circuit services, you lease a dedicated circuit from one building in one city to another building in the same or a different city. Costs are fixed per month, regardless of how much or how little traffic flows through the circuit.

Figure 6-19 presents the major SONET and SDH services. The slowest-speed version of SONET (called *OC-1* for optical carrier 1) has a nominal rate of 51.84 Mbps.

E-Carrier Name	Number of E-1 Channels	Nominal Data Rate	Effective Data Rate
E-1	1	2.048 Mbps	1.7 Mbps
E-2	4	8.448 Mbps	6.8 Mbps
E-3	16	34.368 Mbps	27 Mbps
E-4	64	139.264 Mbps	109 Mbps
E-5	256	565.148 Mbps	438 Mbps

FIGURE 6-18   Types of E-carrier services

OC Name	Number of OC-1 Channels	Nominal Data Rate	Effective Data Rate
OC-1	1	51.84 Mbps	48 Mbps
OC-3	3	155.52 Mbps	143 Mbps
OC-12	12	622.08 Mbps	571 Mbps
OC-48	48	2.488 Gbps	2.3 Gbps
OC-192	192	9.953 Gbps	9.1 Gbps
OC-768	798	39.812 Gbps	36.4 Gbps

FIGURE 6-19   Types of SONET services.

MANAGEMENT FOCUS *6-1*

CAREGROUP'S DEDICATED-CIRCUIT NETWORK

CareGroup Healthcare System operates six hospitals in the Boston area and uses a MAN and WAN to connect them together to share clinical data (see Figure 6-20). The three major hospitals have high data needs and therefore are connected to each other and the main data center via a MAN that uses a set of OC-1 SONET circuits in a ring topology. They are planning to upgrade to OC-3.

The other three hospitals, with lower data needs, are connected to the data center via a set of T3 circuits in a star topology. The data center also has a T3 connection into the Internet to enable its 3,000 doctors to access clinical data on the hospital network from their private practice offices or from home over the Internet.

SOURCE: "Using the Web to Extend Patient Care," *Network World,* May 29, 2000.

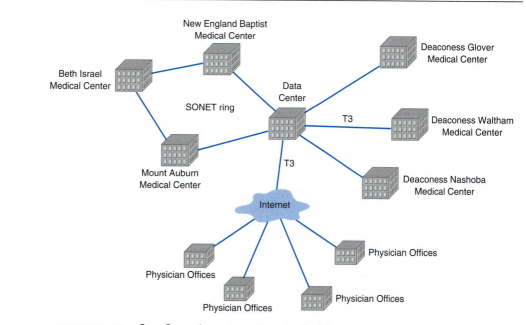

FIGURE 6-20   CareGroup's metropolitan and wide area networks. SONET = synchronous optical network.

SONET frames are 810 bytes in length, transmitted at 8,000 Hz (810 bytes per frame × 8 bits per byte × 8,000 frames per second gives 51.84 Mbps). Each 810-byte SONET frame has 27 bytes of overhead and 783 of data (97% efficiency) over point-to-point circuits (95% efficiency), thus giving an effective data rate of about 50 Mbps.

Each succeeding level in the SONET hierarchy is provided by inverse multiplexing OC-1 circuits. SONET data rates are defined as high as OC-768 or about 40 Gbps. Notice that the slowest SONET transmission rate (OC-1) of 51.84 Mbps is slightly faster than the T3 rate of 45 Mbps. As you will notice, the OC-3 and OC-12 rates match the data rates of ATM, for the simple reason that SONET is typically used as the physical and data link layer for ATM.

PACKET-SWITCHED NETWORKS

Packet-switched networks are quite different from the two types of networks previously discussed. For both circuit-switched and dedicated-circuit networks, a circuit was established between the two communicating computers. This circuit provided a guaranteed data transmission capability that was available for use by only those two computers. For example, if a computer wanted to transmit data to a second computer using an ISDN BRI connection, the connection at both computers must be available. Once in use for this transmission, it is assigned solely to that transmission. No other transmission is possible until the circuit is closed. So, for example, if a third computer attempted to reach either of the first two, it would have to wait until the circuit was closed.

In contrast, packet-switched services enable multiple connections to exist simultaneously between computers over the same physical circuit. Packet-switched circuits function much like Ethernet LANs and backbones, but they also have some very important differences.

Topology

With packet-switched services, the user again buys a connection into the common carrier cloud (see Figure 6-21). The user pays a fixed fee for the connection into the network (depending on the type and capacity of the service) and is charged for the number of packets transmitted.

The user's connection into the network is a *packet assembly/disassembly device (PAD)*, which can be owned and operated by the customer or by the common carrier. The PAD converts the sender's data into the network layer and data link layer packets used by

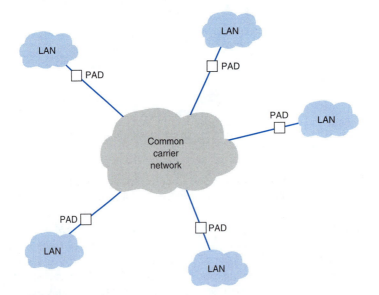

FIGURE 6-21 Packet-switched services. LAN = local area network; PAD = packet assembly/disassembly device.

the packet network and sends them through the packet-switched network. At the other end, another PAD reassembles the packets back into the network layer and data link layer protocols expected by the destination and delivers them to the appropriate computer. The PAD also compensates for differences in transmission speed between sender and receiver; for example, the circuit at the sender might be 1.5 Mbps while the receiver only has a 64-Kbps circuit.

Packet-switched networks work exactly like Ethernet LANs and backbones in that they enable packets from separate messages with different destinations to be *interleaved* for transmission, unlike switched circuits and dedicated circuits. Packet switching is popular because most data communications consist of short bursts of data with intervening spaces that usually last longer than the actual burst of data. Packet switching takes advantage of this characteristic by interleaving bursts of data from many users to maximize use of the shared communication network.

Packet-switched networks provide two different types of service. The first, called *datagram,* is a connectionless service. It adds a destination address and sequence number to each packet, in addition to information about the data stream to which the packet belongs. In this case, a route is chosen for each packet as it is accepted into the packet network. Each packet may follow a different route through the network. At the destination address the sequence number tells the network how to reassemble the packets into a continuous message. The sequence number is necessary because different routes may deliver packets at different speeds, so data packets often arrive out of sequence. Few networks today use datagrams for data transfer.

The second and more common service is a connection-oriented approach called a *virtual circuit.* This is the approach used by ATM, discussed in the previous chapter. In this case, the packet-switched network establishes what *appears* to be one end-to-end circuit between the sender and receiver. All packets for that transmission take the same route over the virtual circuit that has been set up for that particular transmission. The two computers *believe* they have a dedicated point-to-point circuit (but in fact they do not).

Virtual circuits are usually *permanent virtual circuits (PVC),* which means that they are defined for frequent and consistent use by the network. They do not change unless the network manager changes the network. Some common carriers also permit the use of *switched virtual circuits (SVC),* although this is not common. Changing PVCs is done by software, but common carriers usually charge each time a PVC is established or removed. It often takes days or weeks to create or take down PVCs, although this is due mostly to poor management by common carriers, rather than technology issues, so hopefully this will change.

Because most network managers build packet-switched networks using PVCs, *most packet-switched networks behave like dedicated-circuit networks.* At first glance, the basic topology in Figure 6-21 looks very similar to the cloud mesh of circuit-switched services, and in fact they are very similar, because data can move from any computer attached to the cloud to any other on the cloud. However, because virtually all data-intensive networks use PVCs, this means that the network is actually built using virtual circuits that are the software equivalent of the hardware-based dedicated circuits.

Most common carriers permit users to specify two different types of data rates that are negotiated per connection and for each PVC as it is established. The *committed information rate (CIR)* is the data rate the PVC guarantees to transmit. If the network accepts the connection, it guarantees to provide that level of service. Most connections also specify a *maximum allowable rate (MAR),* which is the maximum rate that the network will attempt to provide, over and above the CIR. The circuit will attempt to transmit all packets up to the MAR, but all packets that exceed the CIR are marked as *discard eligible (DE).* If the network becomes overloaded, DE packets are discarded. So while one can transmit faster than the CIR, it is at a risk of lost packets and the need to retransmit them. The CIR can be separately specified for upstream and downstream data rates.

Packet-switched services are often provided by common carriers different from those from which organizations get their usual telephone and data services. Therefore, organizations often lease a dedicated circuit (e.g., T1) from their offices to the packet-switched network *point of presence (POP).* The POP is the location at which the packet-switched network (or any common carrier network, for that matter) connects into the local telephone exchange.

There are five types of packet-switched services: X.25, ATM, frame relay, SMDS and Ethernet/IP packet networks.

X.25

The oldest packet-switched service is *X.25,* a standard developed by ITU-T. X.25 offers datagram, switched virtual circuit, and permanent virtual circuit services. X.25 uses its own internetwork layers and as a result the PADs that connect X.25 networks into traditional TCP/IP networks serve as gateways; they must convert TCP/IP protocols used in LANs and backbones into the X.25 protocols for transmission through the X.25 network. X.25 uses the LAP-B data link layer protocol and the PLP network layer protocol. When packets arrive at the PAD connecting the user's network to the packet-switched network, their data link frames (e.g., Ethernet) and network layer packets (e.g., IP) are removed and PLP packets and LAP-B frames substituted.

Packets are moved through the X.25 network in much the same way as in TCP/IP networks, with the LAP-B frame error checked and replaced at each hop in the network. When they arrive at the edge of the X.25 network, new destination protocol packets (e.g., Ethernet, IP) are created and the message sent on its way. X.25 is sometimes called a *reliable packet service* because it provides complete error control and guaranteed delivery on all packets transmitted at each hop as the packets move through the network. Figure 6-22 illustrates the difference in error control between X.25 networks and the TCP/IP and Ethernet networks we have discussed previously. The left side shows that when a X.25 frame leaves its Source A and moves through Node B, to Node C, to Node D, and finally to its Destination E, each intermediate node checks for errors and sends an acknowledgment as the frame as passes through it. The right side of the figure shows how TCP/IP and Ethernet networks send frames through Node B, Node C, Node D, and on to Destination E. TCP does not perform error control with ACKs as the frame passes through the intermediate nodes. Instead, when Destination E receives the TCP segment, it performs an error check and sends a single acknowledgment back through the ATM nodes to Source A, as shown by the numbers 5, 6, 7, and 8.

Although widely used in Europe, X.25 is not widespread in North America because of its low transmission speed. For many years, the maximum speed into North American X.25 networks was 64 Kbps, but this has increased to 2.048 Mbps, which is the European standard for ISDN. However, for many users, 2.048 Mbps is still not fast enough.

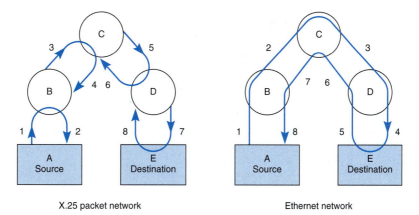

X.25 packet network

Ethernet network

FIGURE 6-22 Ethernet compared with X.25 packet switching. With X.25, each node sends an acknowledgment immediately on receiving a packet. With Ethernet, the final destination sends an acknowledgment, making this technique faster than the X.25 technique.

LAP-B provides a data link efficiency of 94 percent. While packet-switched services are shared, they guarantee to provide the CIR, so there is no reduction in effective data rate. However, the need to convert internetwork protocols from TCP/IP into PLP drops the effective data rate substantially, often by another 20 percent. Thus effective data rates for X.25 services range from about 50 Kbps to 1.5 Mbps.

Asynchronous Transfer Mode

Asynchronous transfer mode (ATM), also standardized, is a newer technology than X.25. ATM for backbone networks was discussed in the previous chapter and ATM for the MAN and WAN is essentially the same.

ATM is similar to X.25 in that it provides packet-switched services, but it has four distinct operating characteristics that differ from X.25. First, ATM performs encapsulation of packets, so packets are delivered unchanged through the network.

Second, ATM provides no error control in the network; error control is the responsibility of the source and destination. Since the user's TCP segment remains intact, it is simple for the devices at the edge of the ATM network to check the error control information in the segment to ensure that no errors have occurred and to request transmission of damaged or lost frames.

Because ATM networks do not perform error control at each device in the network, they are called *unreliable packet services.* Some common carriers have started using the term *fast packet services* instead to refer to these services that do not provide error control because it sounds better for marketing!

Third, ATM provides extensive quality of service information that enables the setting of very precise priorities among different types of transmissions when the network becomes busy: high priority for voice and video, lower priority for e-mail.

MANAGEMENT FOCUS *6-2*

DIGITAL ISLAND'S GLOBAL NETWORK

Digital Island was formed in 1995 to provide network services for global e-business applications. Its clients include many large global corporations, such as Master-Card, Sega, AOL, MTV, ZDNet, and Cisco.

Digital Island's network is organized as a distributed star network (see Figure 6-23). Its six major data centers (Silicon Valley, New York, London, Hong Kong, Tokyo, and Honolulu) are connected via a global ATM network using a mesh topology of OC-3 and higher PVCs. Each of the data centers in turn is connected to a variety of other sites and networks, both client sites and Digital Island offices, over a mix of dedicated lines, including FT1, T1, and T3.

SOURCE: "Digital Island," Cisco Systems, Inc. www.cisco.com.

Finally, ATM is scalable; it is easy to multiplex basic ATM circuits into much faster ATM circuits. Most common carriers offer ATM circuits that provide the same data transmission rates as SONET, because SONET is used in the hardware layers. ATM provides the same effective data rates as SONET, with some additional degradation due to the conversion from TCP/IP protocols into ATM protocols. In the WAN, effective data rates of 500 Mbps full-duplex are not uncommon over OC-3 circuits of 622 Mbps.

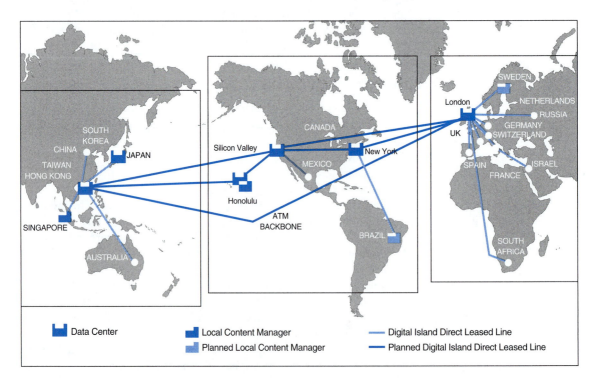

FIGURE 6-23   Digital Island's wide area network. ATM = asynchronous transfer mode.

Frame Relay

Frame relay, just recently standardized, transmits data faster than X.25, but slower than ATM; it has sometimes been called a "poor-man's ATM." Like ATM, frame relay performs encapsulation of packets or frames, so they are delivered unchanged through the network. Like ATM, it is an unreliable packet service because it does not perform error control.[3] It is up to the software at the source and destination to perform error correction and to control for lost messages.

The frame relay data link protocol adds 6 bytes of overhead (used for addressing and marking the start and end of the frame). The standard does not specify a specific maximum length for frames, but most common carriers use maximum frame sizes from 1,600 to 4,096 bytes, chosen so they can be easily used to move Ethernet frames. Thus frame relay is very efficient (99% efficiency).

Frame relay does not yet provide quality of service capabilities, but this is under development. Different common carriers offer frame relay networks with different transmission speeds. Most offer a range of CIR speeds that include 56 Kbps, 128 Kbps, 256 Kbps, 384 Kbps, 1.544 Mbps, 2.048 Mbps, and 45 Mbps.

Switched Multimegabit Data Service

Switched multimegabit data service (SMDS) is an unreliable packet service like ATM and frame relay. Like ATM and frame relay, SMDS does not perform error checking; the user is responsible for error checking. SMDS was originally aimed at the MANs, particularly the interconnection of local area networks, but it has also made its way into the WAN environment. SMDS was not standardized, which meant interconnecting SMDS, MANs and WANs from different common carriers was problematic.

As with ATM and frame relay, SMDS encapsulates incoming packets or frames and delivers them unchanged. But unlike them, it operates a connectionless, datagram-only service that is in many ways better matched to Ethernet LAN traffic. SMDS encapsulates the incoming data with layer-3 packets that in turn are broken into 53-byte data link layer frames for transmission. SMDS adds between 40 and 47 bytes of overhead to each packet at layer 3 (depending on the common carrier) and an additional 9 bytes of overhead on each 53-byte data link layer frame. This converts to about an 81 percent efficiency.

SMDS is available at a variety of nominal data rates, ranging from 56 Kbps (45 Mbps effective data rate) up to 44.736 Mbps (36 Mbps effective data rate). SMDS is popular in Europe, but did not catch on in North America. Frame relay beat it to the punch, and the common carriers providing frame relay offered lower prices than those providing SMDS. Once frame relay become widespread, both customers and common carriers lost interest in SMDS. The future of SMDS is uncertain because it is overshadowed by frame relay.

---

[3] Frame relay does have a CRC-16 field in the frame layout to permit error detection, but as we write this, few common carriers have implemented error control. Frame relay networks do perform error checking, but simply discard frames with errors.

MANAGEMENT FOCUS *6-3*

YIPES AND THE LAW

As a preeminent high-tech law firm, Fenwick & West LLP understands the importance of the Internet. For many years, Fenwick & West LLP relied on T1 circuits and a frame relay cloud to connect its offices. However, the network was saturated; staff often resorted to express mailing floppies, rather than using e-mail or FTP.

Staff at Fenwick & West guessed that they needed to raise their WAN capacity to match their 10Base-T LAN (i.e., 10 Mbps). They began by looking to add more T1 lines, but at $1,500 to $2,500 per circuit (depending on office location), adding multiple T1s into each office was

very expensive. They also considered T3 circuits, but they ranged from $18,000 to $30,000 per month.

Then they contacted YIPES to learn more about Ethernet/IP services. The price, a flat $6,000 per month for 10 Mbps, was noticeably less. The simplicity of connecting into their existing Ethernet and IP backbone was also attractive, as was the flexibility of being able to increase or decrease capacity in 1-Mbps increments.

SOURCE: "Look Beyond T1 and DS-3 to Managed Optical IP Network," *Communications News,* September 2000.

Ethernet/IP Packet Networks

While we have seen rapid increases in capacities and sharp decreases in costs in LAN and backbone technologies, changes in MAN and WAN services offered by common carriers have seen only modest changes over the past decade. That changed in 2000 with the introduction of several Internet startups offering *Ethernet/IP packet networks* (e.g., YIPES.com).

Most organizations today use Ethernet and IP in the LAN and backbone environment. Yet, the four preceding MAN/WAN packet network services (X.25, ATM, frame relay, and SMDS) use different layer-2 protocols. Any LAN or backbone traffic therefore must be translated or encapsulated into a new protocol and destination addresses generated for the new protocol. This takes time, slowing network throughput. It also adds complexity, meaning that companies must add staff knowledgeable in the different MAN/WAN protocols, software, and hardware these technologies require.

Each of the four preceding packet services uses the traditional PSTN and thus they are provided by the common carriers such as AT&T and BellSouth. In contrast, Ethernet/IP packet networks bypass the PSTN; companies offering Ethernet/IP packet networks have laid their own gigabit Ethernet fiber-optic networks in large cities. When an organization signs up for service, the packet network company installs new fiber-optic cables from their citywide MAN backbone into the organization's office complex and connects it to an Ethernet switch. The organization simply plugs its network into the Ethernet switch and begins using the service. All traffic entering the packet network must be Ethernet using IP.

Currently, Ethernet/IP packet network services offer CIR speeds of 1 Mbps up to 1 Gbps in 1-Mbps increments at about one-quarter the cost of traditional packet-switched networks. Because this is an emerging technology, we should see many changes in the next few years.

VIRTUAL PRIVATE NETWORKS

A new type of network topology has emerged with the rise of the Internet. A *virtual private network (VPN)* provides the equivalent of a private packet-switched network over the public Internet[4]. You establish a series of PVCs that run over the Internet (rather than over a common carrier's private network), so that the network acts like a set of dedicated circuits over a private packet network.

Topology

With a VPN, you first lease an Internet connection at whatever access rate and access technology you choose for each location you want to connect. For example, you might lease a T1 circuit from a common carrier that runs from your office to your *Internet service provider (ISP)*. You pay the common carrier for the circuit and the ISP for Internet access. Then you connect a VPN device (a specially designed router or switch) to each Internet access circuit to provide access from your networks to the VPN. The VPN devices enable you to create PVCs through the Internet that are called *tunnels*. See Figure 6-24.

The VPN device at the sender takes the outgoing packet or frame and encapsulates it with a protocol that is used to move it through the tunnel to the VPN device on the other

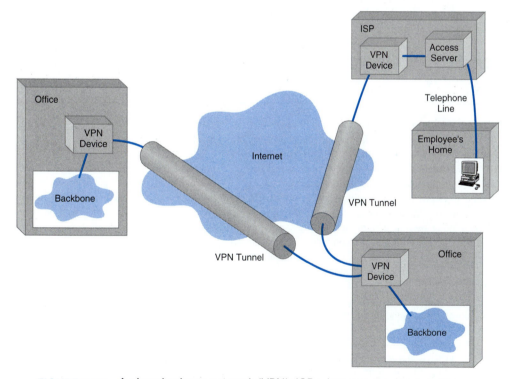

FIGURE 6-24 A virtual private network (VPN). ISP = Internet service provider.

---

[4] Some common carriers and third-party vendors are now providing VPN services that use their own networks rather than the Internet, but by far the majority of VPN services are Internet based. In the interest of simplicity, we will focus on Internet-based VPN services.

side (Technical Focus 6-2 describes this process in more detail). The VPN device at the receiver strips off the VPN frame and delivers the frame to the destination network. The VPN is transparent to the users; it appears as though a traditional packet-switched network PVC is being used. The VPN is also transparent to the ISP and the Internet as a whole; there is simply a stream of Internet packets moving across the Internet.

VPNs operate either at layer 2 or layer 3. A *layer-2 VPN* uses the layer-2 frame (e.g., Ethernet) to select the VPN tunnel and encapsulates the entire frame starting with the layer-2 frame. A *layer-3 VPN* uses the layer-3 packet (e.g., IP) to select the VPN tunnel and encapsulates the entire packet starting with the layer-3 packet; that is, it discards the incoming layer-2 frame and generates an entirely new layer-2 frame at the destination.

The primary advantages of the VPNs are low cost and flexibility. Because they use the Internet to carry messages, the major cost is Internet access, which is inexpensive compared to the cost of circuit-switched services, dedicated-circuit services, or packet-switched services from a common carrier. Likewise, anywhere you can establish Internet service, you can quickly put a VPN.

There are two important disadvantages. First, traffic on the Internet is unpredictable. Sometimes packets travel quickly, while at other times they take a long time to reach their destination. While some VPN vendors advertise quality of service capabilities, these apply

TECHNICAL FOCUS *6-2*

VPN ENCAPSULATION

When a VPN device sends packets or frames through an Internet tunnel, it must first encapsulate (i.e., surround) the existing packet or frame with a VPN frame that provides information to the receiving VPN, so that it knows how to process the frame. This encapsulation is conceptually simple and works in much the same way as ATM or frame relay. However, because the frames must travel over the Internet, things become a bit more complex.

At present, there are several competing approaches to managing VPNs, so there are several incompatible VPN protocols used by different vendors. Layer-2 tunneling protocol (L2TP) is an emerging standard for use by layer-2 access VPNs.

Suppose a user is sending an e-mail message through an access VPN into the corporate network. The user connects to a VPN device at an ISP via a modem over a dial-up circuit (i.e., POTS). The e-mail client software on the user's computer generates an SMTP message at the application layer. The transport and network layers in the client computer add TCP segments and IP packets, respectively. PPP is the most commonly used dial-up data link layer protocol, so the frame that arrives at the VPN device is a PPP frame, containing an IP packet, containing a TCP segment, containing an SMTP message with the e-mail message. See Figure 6-25.

The VPN device encrypts the incoming frame and encapsulates it with the VPN protocol, L2TP. Now the frame is ready for transmission on the Internet. The protocol on the Internet is TCP/IP, so the VPN device now encapsulates the VPN frame with an IP packet that specifies the IP address of the destination VPN device. Each circuit on the Internet is simply a T1, T3, SONET OC-48, or some other circuit. Each of these circuits has its own data link protocol. So the VPN device then surrounds the IP packet with the appropriate frame for the specific Internet circuit the message will use (e.g., SONET). See Figure 6-25.

The message travels through the Internet and arrives at the destination VPN device at the corporate network, perhaps arriving with a different data link layer frame, depending on the type of connection the corporation has with the Internet (e.g., T3). The VPN device strips off the data link layer frame and the IP packet and processes the L2TP frame. It then decrypts the PPP frame and sends it to the corporate access server for processing. As far as the access server is concerned, the frame arrived from a directly connected dial-up circuit. See Figure 6-25.

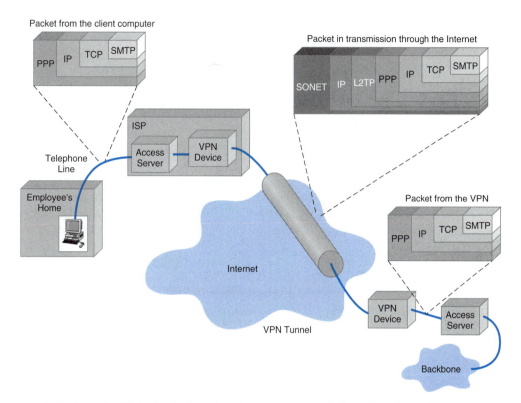

FIGURE 6-25 Virtual private network (VPN) encapsulation of packets. ATM = asynchronous transfer mode; IP = Internet Protocol; L2TP = layer-2 tunneling protocol; PPP = Point-to-Point Protocol; SMTP = Simple Mail Transfer Protocol; TCP = Transmission Control Protocol.

only in the VPN devices themselves; on the Internet a packet is a packet (at least until Internet 2 becomes more common—see the next chapter). Second, because the data travels on the Internet, security is always a concern. Most VPN networks encrypt the packet at the source VPN device before it enters the Internet and decrypt the packet at the destination VPN device (see Chapter 10 for more on encryption).

At present, there are several different approaches to providing VPN services, each supported by different sets of companies, and each moving down the path to standardization. As we write this in early 2002, it appears as though the Multiprotocol Label Switching (MPLS) approach may be emerging as the winner. MPLS is a layer-3 protocol, but work is underway on enlarging it to also cover layer 2. For the moment, it is important to build VPNs using equipment and services from one set of vendors.

VPN Types

Three types of VPN are in common use: intranet VPN, extranet VPN, and access VPN. An *intranet VPN* provides virtual circuits between organization offices over the Internet. The center section of Figure 6-24 illustrates an intranet VPN. Each location has a VPN device that connects that location to another location through the Internet.

An *extranet VPN* is the same as an intranet VPN except that the VPN connects several different organizations, often customers and suppliers, over the Internet.

An *access VPN* enables employees to access an organization's networks from a remote location. Employees have access to the network and all the resources on it in the same way as employees physically located on network. The upper-right part of Figure 6-24 shows an access VPN. The user connects to a local ISP that supports the VPN service via POTS, ISDN, or other connection. The VPN device at the ISP accepts the user's login, establishes the tunnel to the VPN device at the organization's office, and begins forwarding packets over the Internet. An access VPN provides a less expensive connection than having a national toll-free 800 number that connects directly into large sets of modems at the organization's office. Compared to a typical ISP-based remote connection, the access VPN is a more secure connection than simply sending packets over the Internet.

THE BEST PRACTICE MAN/WAN DESIGN

Developing best practice recommendations for MAN and WAN design is more difficult than that for LANs and backbones because the network designer is buying services from different companies, rather than buying products. The relatively stable environment enjoyed by the MAN/WAN common carriers is facing sharp challenges by VPNs at the low end and Ethernet/IP packet networks at the high end. As larger IT and equipment firms begin to enter the VPN and Ethernet/IP packet network markets we should see some major changes in the industry and in the available services and costs.

We also need to point out that the technologies in this chapter are primarily used to connect different corporate locations. Technologies primarily used for Internet access (e.g., DSL, cable modem) are discussed in the next chapter.

We use the same two factors as we have previously for LANs and backbones (effective data rates and cost), plus add two additional factors: reliability and network integration. Reliability refers to the ability to predictably send messages as expected. Network integration refers to the ease with which the MAN/WAN service can be used to connect LANs and backbones.

Figure 6-26 summarizes the major services available today for the MAN and WAN, grouped by the type of service. A few patterns should emerge from the table. For small MANs and WANs with low data transmission needs, POTS dial-up services are a reasonable alternative. POTS can be more difficult to integrate with LANs and backbones, so this a good option only if one is willing to use dial-up connections. Since most of this type of network is used for Internet access, we really need to wait until the next chapter (The Internet) before drawing conclusions.

For networks with moderate data transmission needs (64 Kbps–2 Mbps) there are several distinct choices. If cost is more important than reliability then a VPN is probably a good choice. If you need flexibility in the location of your network connections and you are not completely sure of the volume of traffic you will have between locations, frame relay is probably a good choice. If you have a mature network with predictable demands, then T-carrier services is probably a good choice. See Figure 6-27.

Type of Service	Nominal Data Rates	Effective Data Rates	Relative Cost	Reliability	Network Integration
Circuit Switched Services					
POTS	33.6 Kbps to 56 Kbps	33 to 300 Kbps[1]	Low	High	Difficult
ISDN	128 Kbps to 1.5 Mbps	122 Kbps to 1.3 Mbps	Moderate	Moderate	Difficult
B-ISDN	155 Mbps to 622 Mbps	300 Mbps to 1200 Mbps[2]	High	Low	Difficult
Dedicated Circuit Services					
T Carrier	64 Kbps to 274 Mbps	53 Kbps to 218 Mbps	Moderate	High	Moderate
SONET	50 Mbps to 10 Gbps	48 Mbps to 9.1 Gbps	High	High	Moderate
Packet Switched Services					
X.25	56 Kbps to 2 Mbps	50 Kbps to 1.5 Mbps	Moderate	High	Difficult
ATM	52 Mbps to 10 Gbps	84 Mbps to 16 Gbps[3]	High	Moderate	Moderate
Frame Relay	56 Kbps to 45 Mbps	56 Kbps to 44 Mbps	Moderate	Moderate	Moderate
SMDS	56 Kbps to 45 Mbps	45 Kbps to 36 Mbps	Moderate	Low	Difficult
Ethernet/IP	1 Mbps to 1 Gbps	900 Kbps to 900 Mbps	Low	High	Simple
VPN Services					
VPN	56 Kbps to 2 Mbps	50 Kbps to 1.5 Mbps	Very Low	Low	Moderate

Notes:
1. Assuming data compression and no noise
2. B-ISDN is full duplex
3. ATM is full duplex

FIGURE 6-26   MAN/WAN services.

Network Needs	Recommendation
Low Traffic Needs (64 Kbps or less)	POTS if dial-up is acceptable VPN if reliability is not important Frame relay otherwise
Moderate Traffic Needs (64 Kbps to 2 Mbps)	VPN if reliability is not important T1 if network volume is stable and predictable Frame relay otherwise
High Traffic Needs (2 Mbps to 45 Mbps)	Ethernet/IP if available T3 if network volume is stable and predictable Frame relay otherwise
Very High Traffic Needs (45 Mbps to 10 Gbps)	Ethernet/IP if available SONET if network volume is stable and predictable ATM otherwise

FIGURE 6-27   Best practice MAN/WAN recommendations.

For high-traffic networks (2 Mbps–45 Mbps), the new Ethernet/IP packet networks are a dominant choice. Some organizations may prefer the more mature—and therefore proven—T3 or frame relay services, depending on whether the greater flexibility of packet services provides value or a dedicated circuit makes more sense.

For very-high-traffic networks (45 Mbps–10 Gbps), Ethernet/IP packet networks again are a dominant choice. And again some organizations may prefer the more mature ATM or SONET services, depending on whether the greater flexibility of packet services provides value or a dedicated circuit makes more sense.

Unless their data needs are stable, network managers often start with more flexible packet-switched services and move to the usually cheaper dedicated-circuit services once their needs have become clear and an investment in dedicated services is safer. Some packet-switched services even permit organizations to establish circuits with a zero-CIR (and rely entirely on the availability of the MAR) so network managers can track their needs and lease only what they need.

Network managers often add a packet network service as an overlay network on top of a network built with dedicated circuits to handle peak data needs; data usually travels over the dedicated-circuit network, but when it becomes overloaded with traffic, the extra traffic is routed to the packet network.

SUMMARY

PSTN Architecture   The PSTN uses a combination of analog and digital transmission. We use analog transmission to send digital computer data by modulating a carrier wave—that is, by changing the amplitude, frequency, and/or phase of the wave to indicate binary 1s and 0s. Under perfect conditions, we can send as many signals (i.e., waves) as the size of the bandwidth. To translate from analog voice data into digital data, we sample the amplitude of the incoming sound waves using PCM.

Circuit-Switched Networks   Circuit-switched services enable you to define the end points of the WAN, without specifying all the interconnecting circuits through the carrier's cloud. The user dials the number of the destination computer to establish a temporary circuit, which is disconnected when the data transfer is complete. POTS is the traditional dial-up service. Basic rate interface ISDN provides a communication circuit with two 64-Kbps digital transmission channels and one 16-Kbps control channel. Primary rate interface ISDN consists of 23 64-Kbps data channels and one 64-Kbps control channel. Broadband ISDN, not yet widely available, offers much faster data speeds ranging up to 622 Mbps.

Dedicated-Circuit Networks   A dedicated circuit is leased from the common carrier for exclusive use 24 hours per day, 7 days per week. Faster and more noise-free transmissions are possible, but you must carefully plan the circuits you need because changes can be expensive. The three common topologies are ring, star, and mesh. T-carrier circuits have a set of digital services ranging from FT1 (64 Kbps) to T1 (1.544 Mbps) to T4 (274 Mbps). The Synchronous Optical Network (SONET) uses fiber optics to provide services ranging from OC-1 (51 Mbps) to OC-12 (622 Mbps).

Packet-Switched Networks   Packet switching is a technique in which messages are split into small segments. The user buys a connection into the common carrier cloud and pays a fixed fee for the connection into the network and for the number of packets transmitted. X.25 is an older, traditional service that provides slower service (up to 2 Mbps) but guarantees error-free delivery. ATM does not perform error control and offers data rates up to 622 Mbps. Frame relay is a newer packet-switching service with higher data rates (up to 45 Mbps) but does not perform error control. Switched multi-megabit data service (SMDS) is a nonstandarized service that offers data rates up to 45 Mbps. Ethernet/IP packet networks use Ethernet and IP to transmit packets at speeds from 1 Mbps to 1 Gbps.

VPN Networks   A VPN provides a packet service network over the Internet. The sender and receiver have VPN devices that enable them to send data over the Internet in encrypted form through a VPN tunnel. While VPNs are inexpensive, traffic delays on the Internet can be unpredictable.

The Best Practice MAN/WAN Design   For small, MANs and WANs with low data transmission needs, POTS dial-up services are a reasonable alternative. For networks with moderate data transmission needs (64 Kbps–2 Mbps), a VPN is a good choice if cost is more important than reliability; otherwise, frame relay or T-carrier services are good choices. For high-traffic networks (2 Mbps–45 Mbps), the new Ethernet/IP packet networks are a dominant choice, but some organizations may prefer the more mature—and therefore proven—T3 or frame relay services. For very-high-traffic networks (45 Mbps–10 Gbps), Ethernet/IP packet networks again are a dominant choice but again some organizations may prefer the more mature ATM or SONET services. Unless their data needs are stable, network managers often start with more flexible packet-switched services and move to the usually cheaper dedicated-circuit services once their needs have become clear and an investment in dedicated services is safer.

KEY TERMS

2B+D

23B+D

access VPN

adaptive differential pulse code modulation (ADPCM)

amplitude

amplitude modulation

analog transmission

available bit rate (ABR)

asynchronous transfer mode (ATM)

bandwidth

basic rate interface (BRI)

broadband ISDN (B-ISDN)

Canadian Radio-Television and Telecommunications Commission

carrier wave

channel service unit/data service unit (CSU/DSU)

circuit-switched services

cloud

cloud topology

codec

committed information rate (CIR)

common carrier

datagram

dedicated-circuit services

dense wavelength division multiplexing (DWDM)

digital transmission

discard eligible (DE)

distributed star topology

E-carrier circuit

Ethernet/IP packet network

extranet VPN

fast packet services

Federal Communications Commission (FCC)

fractional T1 (FT-T)

frame relay

frame relay access device (FRAD)

frequency

frequency division multiplexing (FDM)

frequency shift keying (FSK)

Integrated Services Digital Network (ISDN)

Internet service provider (ISP)

interexchange carrier (IXC)

intranet VPN

inverse multiplexing

latency

layer-2 VPN

layer-3 VPN

local exchange carrier (LEC)

maximum allowable rate (MAR)

mesh

mesh topology

modem

multiplexer (mux)

multiplexing

Multiprotocol Lable Switching (MPLS)

narrowband ISDN

network terminator (NT1, NT2)

packet assembly/disassembly (PAD)

packet-switched services

permanent virtual circuit (PVC)

phase

phase shift keying (PSK)

plain old telephone service (POTS)

point of presence (POP)

primary rate interface (PRI)

public switched telephone network (PSTN)

public utilities commission (PUC)

pulse code modulation (PCM)

quadrature amplitude modulation (QAM)

regional Bell operating company (RBOC)

reliable packet services

ring topology

service profile identifier (SPID)

star topology

statistical time division multiplexing (STDM)

switched multimegabit data service (SMDS)

switched virtual circuit (SVC)

symbol

symbol rate

synchronous digital hierarchy (SDH)

Synchronous Optical Network (SONET)	T3	trellis-coded modulation (TCM)	virtual private network (VPN)
T-carrier circuit	T4	unreliable packet serv-	wavelength division
T1	terminal adapter	ices	multiplexing (WDM)
T2	time division multiplex-ing (TDM)	virtual circuit	X.25

QUESTIONS

1. What is a common carrier, a local exchange carrier, and an interexchange carrier?

2. Who regulates common carriers and how is it done?

3. How does analog data differ from digital data?

4. Clearly explain the differences between analog data, analog transmission, digital data, and digital transmission.

5. Explain why most telephone company circuits are now digital.

6. What are three important characteristics of a sound wave?

7. What is bandwidth? What is the bandwidth in a traditional North American telephone circuit?

8. Describe how data could be transmitted using amplitude modulation.

9. Describe how data could be transmitted using frequency shift keying.

10. Describe how data could be transmitted using phase shift keying.

11. Describe how data could be transmitted using a combination of modulation techniques.

12. Is the bit rate the same as the symbol rate? Explain.

13. What is a modem?

14. What is QAM?

15. Explain the importance of trellis-coded modulation.

16. Explain how V.90 and V.92 modems work.

17. What is multiplexing?

18. How does TDM differ from FDM and STDM?

19. How does WDM differ from FDM?

20. Explain how circuit-switched networks work.

21. What is POTS?

22. How does ISDN work?

23. Compare and contrast BRI, PRI, and B-ISDN.

24. What is a 2B+D? Define it.

25. How does broadband ISDN differ from narrowband ISDN?

26. Compare and contrast circuit-switched services, dedicated-circuit services, and packet-switched services.

27. Is a WAN that uses dedicated circuits easier or harder to design than one that uses dialed circuits? Explain.

28. Compare and contrast ring topology, star topology, and mesh topology.

29. What are the most commonly used T-carrier services? What data rates do they provide?

30. Distinguish between T1, T2, T3, and T4 circuits.

31. Describe SONET. How does it differ from SDH?

32. How do packet-switching services differ from other wide area network services?

33. How is a virtual circuit distinguished from other circuits?

34. What does a "packet" in a packet-switched network contain?

35. How does a reliable packet service differ from an unreliable packet service?

36. How do datagram services differ from virtual circuit services?

37. How does a switched virtual circuit differ from a permanent virtual circuit?

38. Compare and contrast X.25, frame relay, ATM, SMDS, and Ethernet/IP packet networks.

39. Which is likely to be the longer-term winner, X.25, frame relay, ATM, SMDS, or Ethernet/IP packet networks?

40. Explain the differences between CIR and MAR.

41. How do VPN services differ from common carrier services?

42. Explain how VPN services work.

43. Compare the three types of VPN.

44. How can you improve WAN performance?

45. Describe four important factors in selecting WAN services.

46. Is the YIPES service a major change in the future of networking or a fly-by-night service?

47. Are there any MAN/WAN services that you would avoid if you were building a network today? Explain.

48. Suppose you joined a company that had a WAN composed of SONET, T-carrier services, ATM, and frame relay, each selected to match a specific network need for a certain set of circuits. Would you say this was a well-designed network? Explain.

49. It is said that packet-switched services and dedicated-circuit services are somewhat similar from the perspective of the network designer. Why?

EXERCISES

6-1. Find out the data rates and costs of T-carrier and ISDN services in your area.

6-2. Find out the data rates and costs of packet- and circuit-switched services in your area.

6-3. Examine Figure 6-20. What other options did Care-Group likely consider? Explain the trade-offs among the different services available. What services would you have selected?

6-4. Examine Figure 6-23. What other options did Digital Island likely consider? Explain the trade-offs among the different services available. What services would you have selected?

6-5. Fenwick & West LLP chose to use YIPES. Explain the trade-offs among the different services available. What services would you have selected?

MINI-CASES

I. Cookies Are Us

Cookies Are Us runs a series of 100 cookie stores across the midwestern United States and central Canada. At the end of each day, the stores express mail a diskette or two of sales and inventory data to headquarters, which uses the data to ship new inventory and plan marketing campaigns. They have decided to move to a WAN. What type of a WAN topology and WAN service would you recommend?

II. MegaCorp

MegaCorp is a large manufacturing firm that operates five factories in Dallas, four factories in Los Angeles, and five factories in Albany, New York. It operates a tightly connected order management system that coordinates orders, raw materials, and inventory across all 14 factories. What type of a WAN topology and WAN service would you recommend?

III. Sunrise Consultancy

Sunrise Consultancy is medium-size consulting firm that operates 17 offices around the world (Dallas, Chicago, New York, Atlanta, Miami, Seattle, Los Angeles, San Jose, Toronto, Montreal, London, Paris, Sao Paulo, Singapore, Hong Kong, Sydney, and Bombay). They have been using Internet connections to exchange e-mail and files, but the volume of traffic has increased to the point that they now want to connect the offices via a WAN. Volume is low but expected to grow quickly once they implement a new knowledge management system. What type of a WAN topology and WAN service would you recommend?

CHAPTER 7

THE INTERNET

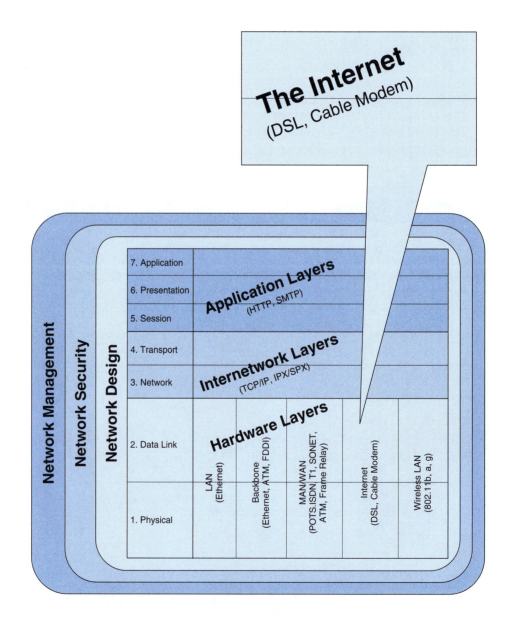

THIS CHAPTER examines the Internet in more detail to explain how it works, and why it is a network of networks. This chapter also examines Internet access technologies, such as DSL and cable modem, as well as the possible future of the Internet in the form of Internet 2.

OBJECTIVES

- Understand the overall design of the Internet
- Understand DSL and cable modem
- Be familiar with wireless services
- Be familiar with Internet 2

CHAPTER OUTLINE

INTRODUCTION

HOW THE INTERNET WORKS

    Basic Architecture

    Connecting to an ISP

    The Internet Today

INTERNET ACCESS TECHNOLOGIES

    Digital Subscriber Line

    Cable Modems

    Fixed Wireless

    Mobile Wireless

    Future Technologies

INTERNET GOVERNANCE

INTERNET 2

THE BEST PRACTICE INTERNET ACCESS DESIGN

SUMMARY

INTRODUCTION

The Internet is the most-used network in the world, but is also one of the least understood. There is no one network that is *the* Internet. Instead, the Internet is a network of networks—a set of separate and distinct networks operated by various national and state government agencies, nonprofit organizations, and for-profit corporations. The Internet exists only to the extent that these thousands of separate networks agree to use Internet protocols (TCP/IP) and to exchange data packets among one another.

The Internet is simultaneously a strict, rigidly controlled club in which deviance from the rules is not tolerated, and a free-wheeling open marketplace of ideas. All networks that connect to the Internet must rigidly conform to a set of standards for the transport and network layers that are unyielding; without these standards, data communication would not be possible. At the same time, content and new application protocols are developed freely and without restriction, and quite literally anyone in the world is able to comment on proposed changes to the Internet protocols.

In this chapter, we first explain how the Internet really works and look inside one of the busiest intersections on the Internet, the Chicago Network Access Point, at which more than 100 separate Internet networks meet to exchange data. We then turn our attention to how you as an individual can access the Internet using DSL and cable modems. We also discuss in less detail several new wireless Internet access technologies and what the Internet may look like in the future.

HOW THE INTERNET WORKS

Basic Architecture

The Internet is hierarchical in structure. At the top are the very large national *Internet service providers (ISPs),* such as Genuity and Sprint, that are responsible for large Internet networks. These *national ISPs* connect together and exchange data at *network access points (NAPs).* See Figure 7-1.

In the early 1990s, when the U.S. portion of the Internet was still primarily run by the U.S. National Science Foundation (NSF), the NSF established four main NAPs in the United States to connect the major national ISPs. When the NSF stopped funding the Internet, the companies running these NAPs began charging the national ISPs for connections, so today the NAPs in the United States are commercial enterprises run by various common carriers such as Ameritech and Sprint (or nonprofit cooperatives). As the Internet has grown, so too has the number of NAPs; today there are about a dozen NAPs in the United States with many more spread around the world.

NAPs were originally designed to connect only national ISPs. These national ISPs in turn provide services for their customers and also to regional ISPs such as BellSouth and Earthlink. These regional ISPs rely on the national ISPs to transmit their messages to national ISPs in other countries. Regional ISPs in turn provide services to their customers and to local ISPs, who sell Internet access to individuals. As the number of ISPs grew, a new form of network access point called a metropolitan area exchange (MAE) had emerged. MAEs are smaller versions of NAPs and typically link a set of regional ISPs whose networks come together in major cities (see Figure 7-1). Today there are about 50 MAEs in the United States.

Because most NAPs, MAEs, and ISPs now are run by commercial firms, many of the early restrictions on who could connect to whom have been lifted. Indiana University, for example, which might be considered a local ISP because it provides Internet access

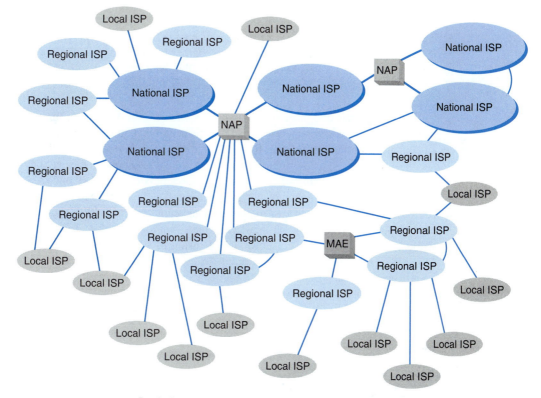

FIGURE 7-1   Basic Internet architecture. ISP = Internet service provider; MAE = metropolitan area exchange; NAP = network access point.

for about 40,000 individuals, has a direct connection into the Chicago NAP, as do several other universities and large corporations. Regional and local ISPs often will have several connections into other national, regional, and local ISPs to provide backup connections in case one Internet connection fails. In this way, they are not dependent on just one higher-level ISP.

In general, ISPs at the same level do not charge each other for transferring the messages they exchange across a NAP or MAE. That is, a national ISP does not charge another national ISP to transmit its messages and a regional ISP does not charge another regional ISP. This is called *peering*. It is peering that makes the Internet work and has led to the belief that the Internet is "free." This is true to some extent, but higher-level ISPs normally charge lower-level ISPs to transmit their data (e.g., a national will charge a regional and a regional will charge a local). And of course, a local ISP will charge individuals like us for access!

In Figure 7-1, each of the ISPs is an *autonomous system,* as defined in Chapter 3. Each ISP is responsible for running its own interior routing protocols and for exchanging routing information via the BGP exterior routing protocol at NAPs and MAEs and any other connection points between individual ISPs.

Connecting to an ISP

Each of the ISPs is responsible for running its own network that forms part of the Internet. ISPs make money by charging customers to connect to their part of the Internet. Local ISPs charge individuals for access (e.g., dial-up, ISDN), while national and regional ISPs (and sometimes local ISPs) charge larger organizations for higher-speed access (e.g., ISDN, frame relay, T1).

Each ISP has one or more *points-of-presence (POP)*. A POP is simply the place at which the ISP provides services to its customers. In order to connect into the Internet, a customer must establish a circuit from his or her location into the ISP POP. For individuals, this is often done using a modem over a traditional telephone line using the PPP protocol (see Figure 7-2). This call connects to the modem pool at the ISP and from there to a *remote access server (RAS),* which checks the userid and password to make sure the caller is a valid customer. Once logged in, the user can begin sending TCP/IP packets from his or her computer over the phone to the RAS, which then forwards them to the backbone network at the POP. Figure 7-2 shows a POP using a collapsed backbone with a layer-2 switch. The POP backbone can take many forms, as we discussed in Chapter 5.

There are many other types of Internet access that ISPs can provide. In the next section, we will discuss newer Internet access technologies such as DSL, cable modem, and

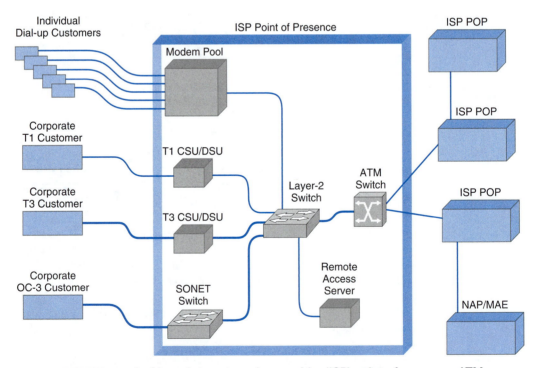

FIGURE 7-2 Inside an Internet service provider (ISP) point-of-presence. ATM = asynchronous transfer mode; CSU = channel service unit; DSU = data service unit; ISP = Internet service provider; MAE = metropolitan area exchange; NAP = network access point.

MANAGEMENT FOCUS 7-1

INSIDE THE CHICAGO NAP

The Chicago NAP is one of the busiest NAPs in the world. As we write this in early 2002, it processes an average of about 4 gigabits of data per second. You can check its URL (see below) to see the current average.

More than 100 different ISPs, including national ISPs (e.g., Genuity and Sprint), regional ISPs (e.g., Michigan's Merit network) and local ISPs (e.g., Indiana University), as well as ISPs in other countries (e.g., Germany's Tiscali network, and the Singapore Advanced Research and Education Network), exchange traffic at the Chicago NAP. At present, roughly half the connections are OC-3, a few are OC-12, and the rest are T3. Pricing starts at about $4,000 per month for T3 (remember, this is only for Internet access; the ISPs must also lease a T3 circuit from their closest POP to the NAP).

The NAP is currently a large Cisco ATM switch that connects the more than 100 separate ISP networks. See Figure 7-3. The ISP networks exchange IP packets through the NAP. They also exchange routing information through

the BGP exterior routing protocol. Normally, the border router at each ISP simply generates BGP packets and sends them to the border routers at the other ISPs connected to the NAP. The Chicago NAP has so many ISPs that this is impossible. Because there are about 100 ISPs, each ISP would send messages to about 100 other ISPs, meaning a total of about 1 million BGP packets moving through the NAP every few minutes.

Instead, the Chicago NAP uses a route server in much the same way large OSPF-based networks used designated routers (see "Routing on the Internet," Technical Focus 3-2). The border router in each ISP sends BGP packets just to the NAP route server. The route server consolidates the routing information and then sends BGP packets back to each border router. This results in more efficient processing and only about 200 messages every few minutes.

SOURCE: nap.aads.net/main.html.

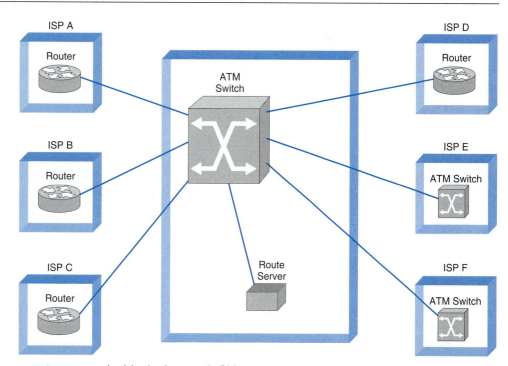

FIGURE 7-3 Inside the Internet's Chicago network access point. ATM = asynchronous transfer mode; ISP = Internet service provider.

WAP. Customers that need more network capacity simply lease a higher-capacity circuit. Figure 7-2 shows customers with T1, T3, and OC-3 connections into the ISP POP. It is important to note that customers must pay for both Internet access (paid to the ISP) and for the circuit connecting from their location to the ISP (usually paid to the local exchange carrier, (e.g., BellSouth, Ameritech), but sometimes the ISP also can provide circuits). For a T1 connection, for example, a company might pay the local exchange carrier $300 per month to provide the T1 circuit from its offices to the ISP POP and also pay the ISP $600 per month to provide the Internet access.

As Figure 7-2 shows, the ISP POP is connected in turn to the other POPs in the ISP's network. Any messages destined for other customers of the same ISP would flow within the ISP's own network. In most cases, the majority of messages are destined outside of the ISP's network and thus must flow through it to the nearest NAP/MAE and from there into some other ISP's network.

This can be less efficient than one might expect. For example, suppose you are connected to the Internet via a local ISP in Minneapolis and request a Web page from another organization in Minneapolis. A short distance, right? Maybe not, if the other organization uses a different local ISP, which in turn uses a different regional ISP, the message may have to travel all the way to the Chicago NAP before it can move between the two separate parts of the Internet.

The Internet Today

Figure 7-4 shows the Internet networks of three ISPs in North America. CAIS and CompuServe are regional ISPs in the United States, while iSTAR Internet is a national ISP in

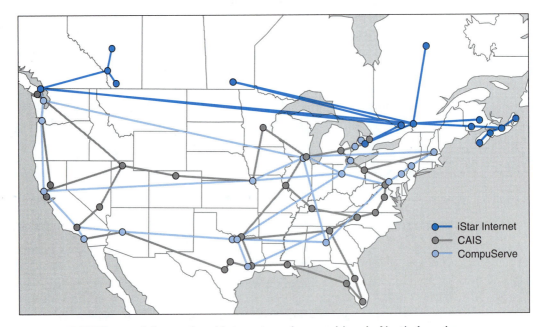

FIGURE 7-4   A few national Internet service providers in North America.

Canada. This figure shows that iSTAR and CAIS meet and peer in London, Ontario, while CAIS and CompuServe meet and peer at the Chicago NAP. Each ISP runs its own set of circuits. Compuserve, for example, runs mostly T3 circuits (45 Mbps) in its network, while CAIS uses a mix of T3 and OC-12 circuits (622 Mbps). In contrast, iSTAR uses mostly T1 circuits (1.5 Mbps).

Today, the backbone circuits of the major national ISPs operate at OC-12 (622 Mbps). Most of the largest national ISPs (e.g., Sprint, Cable & Wireless) plan to convert their principal backbones to OC-192 (10 Gbps) by the end of 2002. A few are now experimenting with OC-768 (40 Gbps), and several are in the planning stages with OC-3072 (160 Gbps). This is good, because the amount of Internet traffic has been growing rapidly. The total amount of traffic on the Internet hit a peak of 2.5 terabits per second (Tbps) in 2001 and is expected to grow to a peak of 35 Tbps by 2005.

As traffic increases, ISPs can add more and faster circuits relatively easily, but where these circuits come together at NAPs and MAEs, bottlenecks are becoming more common. Network vendors such as Cisco and Juniper are making larger and larger switches capable of handling these high-capacity circuits, but it is a daunting task. When circuit capacities increase by 100 percent, switch manufacturers must also increase their capacities by 100 percent, which is far more difficult.

The Internet is constantly changing, so by the time you read this, CAIS, Compuserve, and iSTAR will likely have added extra circuits. An up-to-date map of the major ISPs whose networks make up large portions of the Internet is available at www.caida.org/tools/visualization/mapnet (just click on "run mapnet").

INTERNET ACCESS TECHNOLOGIES

There are many ways in which individuals and organizations can connect to an ISP. Many people today use 56-Kbps dial-up modems over telephone lines. As we discussed in the preceding section, many organizations lease T1 or T3 lines into their ISPs. There are several newer technologies such as DSL and cable modem that are designed to provide faster access from an individual or organization to the ISP. These technologies are commonly called *broadband technologies* because they provide higher-speed communications than traditional modems.[1]

It is important to understand that Internet access technologies are used only to connect from one location to an ISP. Unlike the MAN and WAN technologies in the previous chapter, Internet access technologies cannot be used for general-purpose networking from any point to any point. In this section, we discuss four principal Internet access technologies (DSL, cable modem, fixed wireless, and mobile wireless) and also discuss some future technologies that may become common.

---

[1] *Broadband* is a technical term that means analog transmission (see Chapter 6). The new broadband technologies often use analog transmission, so they are called broadband. However, the term "broadband" has been corrupted in common usage so that for most people it usually means "high speed."

Digital Subscriber Line

Digital subscriber line (DSL) is a family of point-to-point technologies designed to provide high-speed data transmission over traditional telephone lines.[2] The reason for the limited capacity on traditional telephone circuits lies with the telephone and the switching equipment at the end offices. The actual cable in the *local loop* from a home or office to the telephone company end office is capable of providing much higher data transmission rates. So, to convert from traditional telephone service (POTS) to DSL usually just requires changing the telephone equipment, not rewiring the local loop, which is what has made it so attractive.

Topology DSL simultaneously provides a voice circuit and a point-to-point full-duplex data circuit. It uses the existing local loop cable but places different equipment on the customer premises (i.e., the home or office) and in the telephone company end office. The equipment that is installed at the customer location is called the *customer premises equipment (CPE).* Figure 7-5 shows one common type of DSL installation (there are other forms). The CPE in this case includes a *line splitter* that is used to separate the traditional

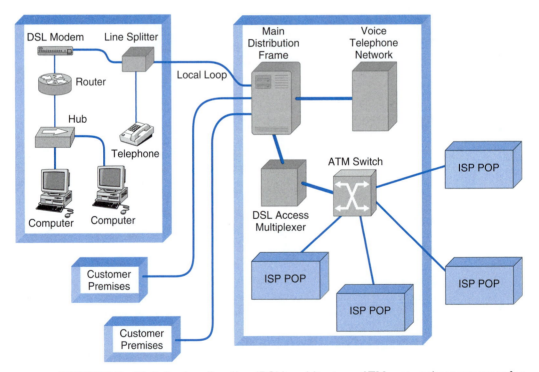

FIGURE 7-5 Digital subscriber line (DSL) architecture. ATM = asynchronous transfer mode; ISP = Internet service provider; POP = point-of-presence.

[2] DSL is rapidly changing because it is so new. More information can be found from the DSL forum (www.adsl.com, www.dsllife.com) and the ITU-T under standard G.992.

voice telephone transmission from the data transmissions. The line splitter directs the telephone signals into the normal telephone system, so that if the DSL equipment fails, voice communications are unaffected.

The line splitter also directs the data transmissions into a *DSL modem,*which is sometimes also called a DSL router. This is both a modem and a multiplexer. The DSL modem produces Ethernet 10Base-T packets, so it can be connected directly into a computer or to a hub so that it can serve the needs of a small network.

Figure 7-5 also shows the architecture within the local carrier's end office (i.e., the telephone company office closest to the customer premises). The local loops from many customers enter and are connected to the main distribution frame (MDF). The MDF works like the CPE line splitter; it splits the voice traffic from the data traffic and directs the voice traffic to the voice telephone network and the data traffic to the *DSL access multiplexer (DSLAM).* The DSLAM demultiplexes the data streams and converts them into ATM data, which are then distributed to the ISPs. Some ISPs are collocated, in that they have their POPs physically in the telephone company end offices. Other ISPs have their POPs located elsewhere.

Media Access Control   DSL provides full-duplex point-to-point transmission, so the effects of media access control are minor.

Error Control   DSL uses continuous ARQ with CRC-16.

Message Delineation   DSL uses the same PPP protocol commonly used for POTS access to ISPs but embeds the PPP frame in a frame similar to the LAP-B frame used by X.25. This results in 16 bytes of overhead per 1,500 bytes of data. Counting ACKs and NAKs, this gives an efficiency of about 98 percent.

Physical Transmission   There are several ways in which DSL can transmit data. One of these is to use a *frequency division multiplexer (FDM)* that splits the physical circuit into three logical channels. Each of the three channels is transmitted on a separate frequency, in much the same way that different radio or TV stations broadcast on different frequencies.

Figure 7-6 illustrates how one version of DSL uses FDM to divide the one circuit into three *channels.* Each channel is a separate logical circuit, and the devices connected to them are unaware that their circuit is multiplexed. A standard voice circuit is used for telephone calls (in the 0–4 KHz bandwidth); an *upstream* data channel moves data from the customer to the telephone switch (in the 300–700 KHz bandwidth); and a *downstream* data channel moves data from the switch to the customer (in the 1,000–10,000 KHz bandwidth). Time division multiplexing is then used within the two data channels to provide a set of one or more individual channels that can be used to carry different data. Because the local loop is analog, data are often transmitted using carrierless amplitude modulation (CAM), which is a form of QAM that transmits 5 bits on each wave using a combination of AM and PSK.[3] The exact combination depends on which flavor of DSL is used. G.Lite ASDL provides one voice circuit, a 1.5-Mbps downstream circuit and a 384-Kbps upstream data channel.

---

[3] Other approaches are echo cancellation instead of FDM and discrete multitone instead of CAM.

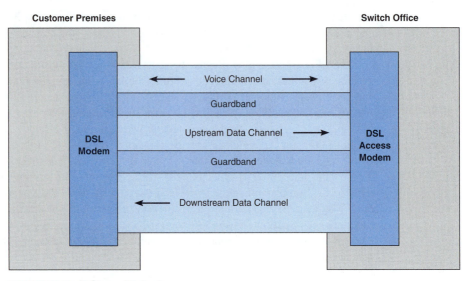

FIGURE 7-6   DSL multiplexing.

In the same way that radio stations must be assigned frequencies somewhat distant from each other to prevent interference, so must the signals in a FDM circuit. The *guardbands* in Figure 7-6 are the unused portions of the circuit (i.e. frequencies) that separate the channels from each other.

Types of DSL   DSL services are relatively new, and they are not available in all locations. In general, DSL services have advanced more quickly in Canada (and Europe, Australia, and Asia) than in the United States due to their newer telephone networks from the end offices to the customer.

There are many different types of DSL. The most common type of DSL in use today is *asymmetric DSL (ADSL),* which has three channels: voice, upstream data,[4] and downstream data. ADSL is called asymmetric because its two data channels have different speeds. Each of the two data channels are further multiplexed using time division multiplexing so they can be further subdivided. The size of the two digital channels depends on the distance from the CPE to the end office. The shorter the distance, the higher the speed, because with a shorter distance, the circuit suffers less attenuation and higher-frequency signals can be used, providing a greater bandwidth for modulation. Figure 7-7 lists the common types of ADSL.

ADSL providers face a challenge in selecting what type of ADSL to offer in a given market. On one hand, customers want the highest-speed access possible. However, because there is a trade-off between speed and distances, if an ADSL provider chooses a high-speed version, they have just limited the number of customers they can serve because a significant proportion of households in the United States are far from the nearest end office. Most

---

[4] Because the second data channel is intended primarily for upstream data communication, many authors imply that this is a simplex channel, but it is actually a set of half-duplex channels.

Type	Maximum Length of Local Loop	Maximum Downstream Rate	Maximum Upstream Rate
T1	18,000 feet	1.5 Mbps	384 Kbps
E1*	16,000 feet	2.0 Mbps	384 Kbps
T2	12,000 feet	6.1 Mbps	384 Kbps
E2*	9,000 feet	8.4 Mbps	640 Kbps

* E1 and E2 are the European standard services similar to T1 and T2 services in North America.

FIGURE 7-7   Asymmetric digital subscriber line data rates.

ADSL providers have therefore chosen the T1 level of ADSL and offer it under the trade-marked name of G.Lite ADSL. Because of the efficient full-duplex protocols used, effective data rates of T1 ADSL are very close to the nominal rates (1.45 Mbps and 376 Kbps).

A second common type of DSL is *very-high-data-rate digital subscriber line (VDSL)*. VDSL is an asymmetric DSL service designed for use over very short local loops of at most 4,500 feet, with 1,000 feet being more typical. It also uses FDM to provide three channels: the normal analog voice channel, an upstream digital channel, and a downstream digital channel. Figure 7-8 lists the types of VDSL we anticipate will become common.

VDSL has not yet been standardized, and five separate standards groups are working on different standards. Therefore, the exact data speeds and channels are likely to change as manufacturers, telephone companies, and ITU-T gain more experience and as the standards groups attempt to merge competing standards. Several companies are also developing symmetric versions of VDSL in which upstream and downstream channels have the same capacity. We expect major changes to VDSL.

Cable Modems

One alternative to DSL is the *cable modem,* a digital service offered by cable television companies. As with DSL, cable modem technology is relatively new and is still evolving. There are several competing standards, but the *Data Over Cable System Interface Specification (DOCSIS)* standard is the dominant one in North America. DOCSIS is not a formal

Type	Maximum Length of Local Loop	Maximum Downstream Rate	Maximum Upstream Rate
1/4 OC-1	4,500 feet	12.96 Mbps	1.6 Mbps
1/2 OC-1	3,000 feet	25.92 Mbps	2.3 Mbps
OC-1	1,000 feet	51.84 Mbps	2.3 Mbps

FIGURE 7-8   Data rates for very-high-data-rate digital subscriber line. OC = optical carrier.

standard, but is the one used by most vendors of *hybrid fiber coax (HFC)* networks (i.e., cable networks that use both fiber-optic and coaxial cable). As with DSL, these technologies are changing rapidly.[5]

Topology   Cable modem architecture is very similar to DSL—with one very important difference. DSL is a point-to-point technology, while cable modems use *shared multipoint* circuits. With cable modems, each user must compete with other users for the available capacity. Furthermore, since the cable circuit is a multipoint circuit, all messages on the circuit go to all computers on the circuit. If your neighbors were hackers they could modify their software to read all messages that travel over the cable, including yours.

Figure 7-9 shows the most common topology for cable modems. The cable TV circuit enters the customer premises through a cable splitter that separates the data transmissions from the TV transmissions and sends the TV signals to the TV network and the data signals to the cable modem. The cable modem (both a modem and frequency division multiplexer) translates from the cable data into 10Base-T Ethernet frames, which then can be directed into a computer or into a hub for distribution in a small network.

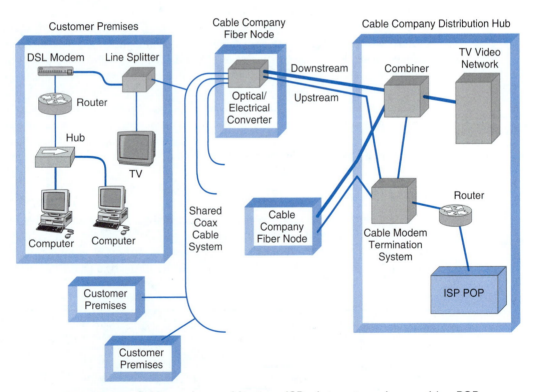

FIGURE 7-9   Cable modem architecture. ISP = Internet service provider; POP = point-of-presence.

---

[5] More information can be found at cablemodem.com and cable-modems.org.

The TV cable entering the customer premises is a standard coxial cable that is shared by anywhere from 300 to 1,000 customers, depending upon the cable company that operates the cable. These 300 to 1,000 customers share the available data capacity, but of course, not all customers who have cable TV will choose to install cable modems. This coax cable runs to a *fiber node,* which has an *optical/electrical (OE)* converter to convert between the coax cable on the customer side and fiber-optic cable on the cable TV company side. Each fiber node serves as many as half a dozen separate coax cable runs.

The fiber nodes are in turn connected to the cable company *distribution hub* (sometimes called a *headend*) through two separate circuits, an upstream circuit and a downstream circuit. The upstream circuit, containing data traffic from the customer, is connected into a *cable modem termination system (CMTS).* The CMTS contains a series of cable modems/multiplexers and converts the data from cable modem protocols into protocols needed for Internet traffic, before passing them to a router connected to an ISP POP. Often, the cable company is an Internet regional ISP, but sometimes it just provides Internet access to a third-party ISP.

The downstream circuit to the customer contains both ordinary video transmissions from the cable TV video network and data transmissions from the Internet. Downstream data traffic enters the distribution hub from the ISP POP and is routed through the CMTS, which produces the cable modem signals. This traffic is then sent to a *combiner,* which combines the Internet data traffic with the ordinary TV video traffic and sends it back to the fiber node for distribution.

Media Access Control   Cable modems use a combination of contention media access control protocols (like Ethernet's CSMA/CD) and controlled access (like FDDI's token passing). The downstream is pure contention, but since there is usually only one device transmitting (the headend), collisions do not occur. We can use the entire nominal data rate. The upstream channel uses a mix of contention and controlled access. Most time slots in the upstream channel are designated as controlled slots. Client computers can transmit only when the headend gives them permission to transmit and tells them which time slots they can use. The contention slots are available using much the same protocol as Ethernet's CSMA/CD approach but are used only by the clients to request permission to use the controlled slots. Thus the media access control efficiency is very similar to that of FDDI: good performance up to about 90 percent of the circuit capacity.

Error Control   Cable modems use a continuous ARQ approach with CRC-16.

Message Delineation   Cable modems use different frame formats for upstream transmission (often short Web requests) and downstream transmission. Upstream formats—and there are several different formats that are in use—tend to be small frames. One version, for example, uses ATM cells in a 16-bit data link layer frame. Downstream formats—and there are several different versions in use—tend to be larger frames. One version adds 16 bytes of overhead to 188 bytes of data for an efficiency of 85 percent (counting ACKs and NAKs). Some cable modem ISPs permit maximum packet sizes of 1,500 bytes, thus giving an efficiency of 98 percent.

Physical Transmission As we have mentioned several times, there are many different types of cable modems. Unlike the telephone common carriers, cable TV operators do not need to ensure their cable TV systems can interconnect with other cable TV systems, because the only connections are outside the cable TV portion of the network. While there are some standards for cable modems, each cable TV operator is free to operate its cable network as it chooses.

One physical layer standard is to run the upstream channel in the 5- to 65-MHz range with a total bandwidth of 2 MHz, using either 1-bit PSK or 4-bit QAM as the modulation technique for a total upstream data rate of 3 Mbps. The downstream channel runs in the 65- to 850-MHz range with a total bandwidth of 6 to 7 MHz and uses either 64-QAM (a version of QAM with 64 levels or 6 bits per signal) or 256-QAM (a version of QAM with 256 levels or 8 bits per signal) for a total data rate of up to 56 Mbps.

Types of Cable Modems There are few widely used standards in the cable modem industry, because unlike the telephone system, each cable TV company was able to build very different HFC cable plants because each cable company was a separate entity with no need to connect to other cable TV networks. In theory, cable modems can provide downstream speeds of 27 to 56 Mbps and upstream speeds of 2 to 10 Mbps, depending on the exact nature and quality of the HFC cable plant. In practice, most cable systems do not offer speeds at this rate, because this capacity is shared among many users. Today, typical downstream speeds range between 1.5 and 2 Mbps and typical upstream speeds range between 200 Kbps and 2 Mbps. However, as cable modems become more common and as certain standards emerge as dominant standards, we should see a consolidation in the types of cable modem services offered.

Fixed Wireless

The most popular type of *fixed wireless* is *wireless DSL,* which requires a line of sight between the communicating transmitters. For this reason it has limited application, because it requires tall buildings or towers to be effective. Its most common use today is to provide Internet access to multitenant buildings such as remote office buildings, apartment buildings, and hotels where wired DSL and cable modem services are not available. Transmitters are used to connect the building to the ISP, and DSL is used inside the building to connect to the wireless transceiver. See Figure 7-10.

Fixed wireless comes in both point-to-point and multipoint versions. The point-to-point version is designed to connect only two locations and is often used as backbone between buildings owned by the same organization. The multipoint version is sometimes called point-to-multipoint because there is one central receiver and all other locations communicate only with it. The multipoint version is designed as an alternative to DSL and cable modems and is intended for use by an ISP supporting a small number of customers. Like cable modems, the circuit is a shared circuit, so users must compete for the shared capacity, but most installations are limited to a few dozen users. Nominal data rates for both versions range from 1.5 Mbps to 11 Mbps depending on the vendor; the effective data rates will be much lower due to error rates, media access protocols, and data link protocols.

A second type of fixed wireless Internet service that is becoming more popular is *satellite Internet access.* With satellite Internet access, you install a small (2 foot by 3 foot)

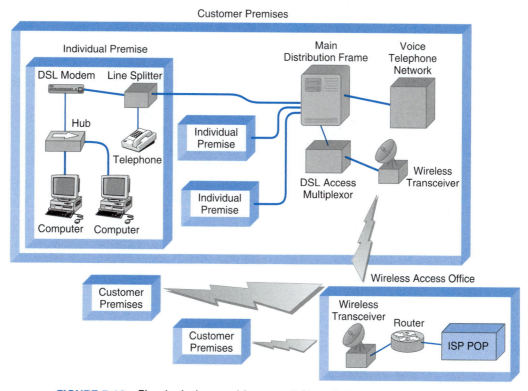

FIGURE 7-10   Fixed wireless architecture. DSL = digital subscriber line; POP = point-of-presence.

satellite dish outside your home or office. The satellite dish sends to and receives from a satellite that is orbiting approximately 22,300 miles above the Earth in a geosynchronous orbit, which means that the satellite remains stationary over one point on the Earth. Satellite Internet services usually provide effective data rates of about 500 Kbps downstream and 128 Kbps upstream. A less expensive version provides just 500 Kbps downstream and requires you to use a regular dial-up modem for upstream communications.

One disadvantage of satellite Internet access is the *propagation delay* that occurs because the signal has to travel out into space and back to Earth. The propagation delay is approximately 0.25 seconds from the sending ground station to the satellite and back to the receiving ground station. This covers two links of 22,300 miles each, and two times 22,300 divided by 186,000 equals 0.24 seconds (satellite transmissions travel at about 186,000 miles per second.). If you factor in the delay on an initial HTTP or SMTP request, then the total round trip propagation delay is about half a second. So while satellite data rates can be fast compared to dial-up circuits, the propagation delay can be annoying.

The solution to this propagation delay is to use low Earth orbit (LEO) satellites that are only 500 miles above the Earth. At present, no such satellites are available for Internet access, but several companies, including Microsoft, have made significant investments in building LEO satellites for Internet access.

Mobile Wireless

Mobile wireless technologies enable users to access the Internet from any location where there is mobile wireless service. Widespread mobile wireless Internet access is probably the next major change in networking. Mobile wireless Internet access technologies exist today (e.g., cell phone connections), but most are slow compared to wired access, whether DSL, cable modem, or simply a dial-up modem.

Providing access to small mobile devices such as handheld personal digital assistants (PDAs) presents both a hardware layer and an application layer challenge. The hardware layer challenge is simply to provide some sort of relatively fast physical and data link connection via wireless. The application layer challenge is to provide a way to deliver Web content intended for large-screen devices such as computers to very-small-screen devices such as PDAs and cell phones. We consider each in turn.

Hardware Layers: 2G, 3G, and 4G Wireless

The current technology used to provide mobile wireless access is the digital cell phone network, which is sometimes called *2G wireless* because it is the second-generation mobile phone service (old analog cell phones were the first generation). These phones enable limited data transfer, often only 14.4 Kbps, because the cell phone network was designed primarily for phone calls, not data transmission.

One of the newest forms of mobile wireless is *3G wireless,* so called because it is the third generation of public wireless networks, although the official name is *Universal Mobile Telecommunications Systems (UMTS).*[6] 3G will be a subscription-based public access service, in the same way as current cell phones. Service providers will install wireless towers in cities and urban areas and provide access in the same way that cell phone companies currently provide cell phone coverage. Anyone with a 3G wireless device (telephone, PDA, or computer) will then be able to access the Internet in the same way as one would use a cell phone today.

Although 3G wireless is still under development with no clear standards at this point, some vendors are pushing *Enhanced Data GSM Environment (EDGE)* as the 3G standard. As the name suggests, EDGE is an enhancement of the current Global System for Mobile Communication (GSM) telephone standard that is widely used outside of the United States for cell phones. EDGE provides a data rate of 384 Kbps, so it is sometimes called GSM384. Other vendors are arguing for a higher-speed version that will provide up to 2 Mbps.

Meanwhile, other vendors are beginning to talk about *4G wireless* services—the next generation after 3G—because 384 Kbps or 2 Mbps data rates are not as powerful as current wireless LAN technologies such as 802.11b, which are discussed in the next chapter. Some vendors have begun to call for universal public 802.11b access as a 4G option. In the next chapter, we will see that many businesses (e.g., restaurants, coffee houses, airports) are already installing these 802.11b wireless LANs with Internet access. Some experts are even predicting that the increasingly rapid deployment of 802.11b in public areas, as a 4G technology, will kill widespread use of the not-yet-ready 3G technology. Stay tuned, because this battle is just starting.

---

[6] More information on 3G can be found at www.umts-forum.org.

Application Layers: WAP   *Wireless Application Protocol (WAP)* provides a set of application and network protocols called the *Wireless Application Environment (WAE)* to support mobile wireless Internet applications. WAP is designed to enable the use of normal Web applications on computers and devices with small display screens operating over low-speed wireless connections. Figure 7-11 shows the basic WAP architecture.

The WAP client (a mobile phone, palm computer, or larger computer) runs special WAP software called a WAE user agent. This software generates WAE requests that are similar in many ways to HTTP requests and transmits them wirelessly to a WAP gateway. A transceiver at the WAP gateway passes the requests to a *wireless telephony application (WTA)* server. This server responds to the requests and, if the client has requested a Web page on the Internet, sends a WAE request to a *WAP proxy*. The WAP proxy translates the WAE request in HTTP and sends it over the Internet to the desired Web server.

This Web server responds to the request and sends back to the WAP proxy an HTTP response that contains HTML, jpeg, and other Internet application protocols. The WAP proxy in turn translates these into their WAE equivalents and sends them to the WTA server, which sends them to the client.

Future Technologies

Internet access technologies are one of the fastest growth areas in networking, so there are several new technologies that have the potential to become important alternatives to DSL,

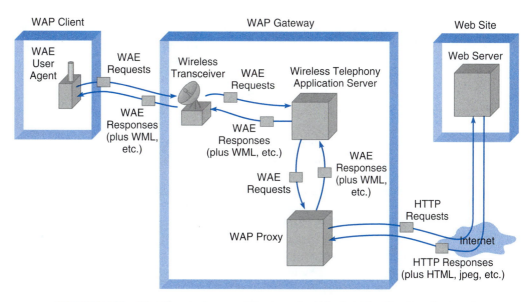

FIGURE 7-11   Mobile wireless architecture for Wireless Application Protocol (WAP) applications. HTML = Hypertext Markup Language; HTTP = Hypertext Transfer Protocol; WAE = Wireless Application Environment; WML = Wireless Markup Language.

MANAGEMENT FOCUS *7-2*

BANKING ON WAP

SkandiaBanken, a leading Swedish Internet bank, provides retail banking services to over 350,000 clients. The bank operates entirely via the Internet, having no traditional branches. Customers communicate with the bank through the Web, e-mail, telephones, and now WAP technology.

SkandiaBanken chose to implement WAP to provide customers with safe and easy access to their financial data from anywhere in the world. Customers can securely view their deposit and credit card accounts, execute their credit card payments, make balance inquiries, as well as pay their bills. Users of the mobile service may also check the foreign exchange, gold, and Treasury bill rates, as well as access information on the bank's range of financial products. There is even location-based information available, such as city guides, restaurant reviews, movies, theatres, museums, art galleries, libraries and other important facilities.

SOURCE: "Financial Institutions Worldwide Use Infinite WAP Server to Offer Mobile Banking," Infinite.com, January 21, 2001.

---

cable modems, and wireless technologies. In this section, we focus on two up-and-coming technologies: Ethernet and passive optical networking.

Passive Optical Networking *Passive optical networking (PON),* sometimes called *fiber-to-the-home (FTTH),* is exactly what it sounds like: running fiber-optic cable into the home. The traditional set of hundreds of copper telephone lines that run from the telephone company switch office is replaced by one fiber-optic cable that is run past each house or office in the neighborhood. Data is transmitted down the signal fiber cable using WDM, providing hundreds or thousands of separate channels. At each subscriber location, a fiber splitter separates the channels belonging to that location and runs them into an optical-electrical converter, which then connects to a 10Base-T hub.

This approach is called passive optical because the splitters require no electrical current and thus are quicker and easier to install than traditional electrical-based hubs and repeaters. However, because they are passive, the optical signal fades more quickly, giving a maximum length of about 10 miles.

Each single fiber has a capacity of about 155 Mbps, which must be allocated among the subscribers. This means about 1.5 Mbps if there are 100 subscribers per fiber, or 15 Mbps if there are only 10 subscribers. At present there are no standards for PON and FTTH, but several vendors have joined together to develop standards. The larger problem, of course, is the cost of laying miles and miles of fiber-optic cable.

Ethernet to the Home Perhaps the most exciting possibility is Ethernet to the home. If we were to start over and design an entirely new network for Internet access from home, we would probably start with Ethernet, due to its low cost and popularity in organizational LANs. Using common protocols would make the whole task of networking much simpler for everyone involved.

Pioneered by YIPES.com, that is exactly what is happening in several major U.S. cities. With this approach, the common carrier installs a TCP/IP router with 10Base-T or 100Base-T connections into the customer's network. The IP/Ethernet traffic moves from the router into the carrier's all-fiber Ethernet MAN and then onto the Internet.

While this approach is also limited due to the cost to provide Ethernet fiber to the customer, we believe this has great potential. Because conversions between protocols are not required at the customer site, connecting to the network is much simpler than with other Internet access technologies.

INTERNET GOVERNANCE

Because the Internet is a network of networks, no one organization operates the Internet. The closest the Internet has to an "owning" organization is the *Internet Society (ISOC)* (www.isoc.org). ISOC is an open-membership professional society with more than 175 organizational and 8,000 individual members in over 100 countries including corporations, government agencies, and foundations that have created the Internet and its technologies. Because membership in ISOC is open, anyone, including students, is welcome to join and vote on key issues facing the Internet.

The ISOC mission is "To assure the open development, evolution and use of the Internet for the benefit of all people throughout the world."[7] ISOC works in three general areas: public policy, education, and standards. In terms of public policy, ISOC participates in the national and international debates on important issues such as censorship, copyright, privacy, and universal access. ISOC delivers training and education programs targeted at improving the Internet infrastructure in developing nations. The most important ISOC activity lies in the development and maintenance of Internet standards. ISOC works through four interrelated standards bodies: IETF, IESG, IAB, and IRTF.

The *Internet Engineering Task Force (IETF)* (www.ietf.org) is a large, open international community of network designers, operators, vendors, and researchers concerned with the evolution of the Internet architecture and the smooth operation of the Internet. IETF works through a series of working groups, which are organized by topic (e.g., routing, transport, security). The requests for comment (RFC) that form the basis for Internet standards are developed by the IETF and its working groups.

Closely related to the IETF is the *Internet Engineering Steering Group (IESG)*. The IESG is responsible for technical management of IETF activities and the Internet standards process. It administers the process according to the rules and procedures that have been ratified by the ISOC trustees. The IESG is directly responsible for the actions associated with entry into and movement along the Internet "standards track," including final approval of specifications as Internet Standards. Each IETF working group is chaired by a member of the IESG.

While the IETF develops standards and the IESG provides the operational leadership for the IETF working groups, the *Internet Architecture Board (IAB)* provides strategic architectural oversight.

The IAB attempts to develop conclusions on strategic issues (e.g., top-level domain names, use of international character sets) that can be passed on as guidance to the IESG, or turned into published statements, or simply passed directly to the relevant IETF working group. In general, the IAB does not produce polished technical proposals but rather tries to stimulate action by the IESG or the IETF that will lead to proposals that meet general con-

[7] See www.isoc.org/isoc/mission.

sensus. The IAB appoints the IETF chair and all IESG members from a list provided by the IETF nominating committee. The IAB also adjudicates appeals when someone complains that the IESG has failed.

The *Internet Research Task Force (IRTF)* operates much like the IETF, through small research groups focused on specific issues. While IETF working groups focus on current issues, IRTF research groups work on long-term issues related to Internet protocols, applications, architecture, and technology. The IRTF chair is appointed by the IAB.

INTERNET 2

The Internet is changing. New applications and access technologies are being developed at a lightning pace. But these innovations do not change the fundamental structure of the Internet; it has evolved more slowly because the core technologies (TCP/IP) are harder to change gradually; it is difficult to change one part of the Internet without changing the parts attached to it.

Many organizations in many different countries are working on dozens of different projects in an attempt to design new technologies for the next version of the Internet.[8] The two primary American projects working on the future Internet got started at about the same time in 1996. The U.S. National Science Foundation provided $100 million to start the *Next Generation Internet (NGI)* program, which developed the *very-high-performance Backbone Network Service (vBNS)* now run by MCI Worldcom, and 34 universities got together to start what turned into the *University Corporation for Advanced Internet Development (UCAID)*, which developed the *Abilene network,* commonly called *Internet 2.* In 1997, the Canadian government established the *Advanced Research and Development Network Operations Center (ARDNOC),* which developed *CA*Net 3,* the Canadian project on the future Internet.[9]

Figure 7-12 shows the major high-speed circuits in the Internet 2's Abilene network, NGI's vBNS network, and ARDNOC's CA*Net 3 network. This figure is a shapshot of these networks as of 2001; these networks will have changed by the time you read this. These circuits, mostly SONET OC-48 circuits running at 2.4 Gbps, plus a few SONET OC-12 (622 Mbps), are the major high-speed circuits in these networks.

Each of the networks has a set of access points called *gigapops,* so named because they provide a point-of-presence at gigabit speeds. While traditional Internet NAPs provide connections between networks at T1, T3, OC-1, OC-3, and occasionally OC-12 speeds, gigapops are designed to provide access at much higher speeds so that different networks can exchange data at much higher rates of speed. Gigapops also usually provide a wider range of services than traditional NAPs, which are primarily just layer-2 data exchange points.

Besides providing very-high-speed Internet connections, these networks are intended to experiment with new protocols that one day may end up as part of the future Internet. For example, most of these networks run IPv6 as the primary network layer protocol, rather than IPv4. Most are also working on new ways to provide quality of service (QoS) and multicasting. Some, such as Internet 2, are also working on developing new applications for a high-speed Internet, such as teleimmersion and videoconferencing.

---

[8] For a listing of several major international projects, see www.startap.net.

[9] For more information on these projects, see www.internet2.org, www.vbns.org, www.ucaid.edu/abilene, and www.canet3.org.

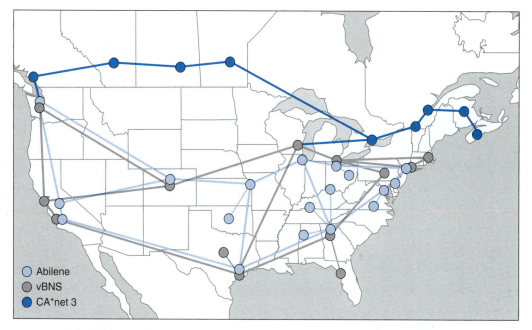

FIGURE 7-12 Gigapops and high-speed backbones of Internet 2/Abilene, very-high-performance Backbone Network Service (vBNS), and CA*net 3.

THE BEST PRACTICE INTERNET ACCESS DESIGN

Our recommendations for the best practice Internet access again rely on effective data rates and cost, but add in the need for mobility. If mobility is important, then the decision is simple: WAP plus 3G or other mobile wireless technologies.

In considering options for Internet access, we also need to revisit the technologies discussed in Chapter 6. All of those technologies (e.g., ISDN, T1, SONET, frame relay) can be used for Internet access, but for most small companies and personal use, the only reasonable low-cost alternatives from Chapter 6 are POTS and ISDN.

Figure 7-14 summarizes the most common options for low-cost Internet access: POTS, ISDN BRI, ADSL, cable modem, wireless DSL, and satellite. The effective data rates before compression for POTS and ISDN BRI were discussed in Chapter 6.

The effective data rates of DSL depend on which service is in use. Assuming we are using ADSL with nominal data rates of 1.5 Mbps downstream and 384 Kbps upstream, the effective data rates are very close to these (full-duplex media access control with 98% efficiency in data link layer protocols).

Estimating the effective data rates for cable modem services is much more difficult because of the wide variety of possible types and the need to share the cable among all subscribers on the same segment. Assuming we have a service with a nominal data rate of 1.5 Mbps downstream and 384 Kbps upstream (with a 90 percent efficient media access control and a 98 percent efficiency in data link layer protocols) we get 1.3 Mbps downstream

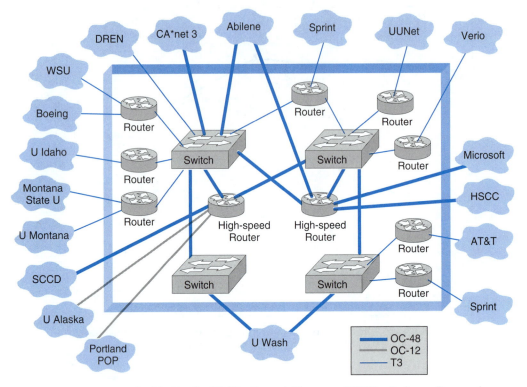

FIGURE 7-13 Inside the Pacific/Northwest Gigapop. DREN = Defense Research Engineering; HSCC = High Speed Connectivity Consortium; OC = optical carrier.

and 340 Kbps upstream. But these data rates are shared among all the active users on the same segment. If we assume that there 500 subscribers on the same segment (a fairly common number) and that 10 percent of customers subscribe to cable modem data service, we

MANAGEMENT FOCUS *7-3*

INSIDE THE PACIFIC/NORTHWEST GIGAPOP

The Pacific/Northwest Gigapop is located in Seattle, Washington and is run by the University of Washington and UCAID (i.e., Internet 2). It provides OC-48 (2.4 Gbps) connections to several high-speed networks such as Abilene, CA*Net 3, Microsoft, and the High Speed Connectivity Consortium (HSCC), which is funded by the U.S. Department of Defense. It also provides a connection point (i.e., a NAP) for these high-speed networks to connect to lower-speed networks of the traditional Internet, such as those run by Sprint, AT&T,

and UUnet, as well as a number of universities in the Pacific Northwest.

The basic structure of the gigapop is a set of four high-speed switches, connected to two high-speed routers (see Figure 7-13). High-speed networks such as Abilene connect directly into this set of six core devices, while lower-speed networks connect into the core via a set of routers.

SOURCE: www.pnw-gigapop.net.

		Low Traffic Environment		Medium Traffic Environment		High Traffic Environment	
Technology	Cost per Month	Upstream	Downstream	Upstream	Downstream	Upstream	Downstream
POTS	$20	40 Kbps	50 Kbps	40 Kbps	50 Kbps	40 Kbps	50 Kbps
ISDN BRI	$60	122 Kbps	122 Kbps	122 Kbps	122 Kbps	122 Kbps	122 Kbps
ADSL	$60	375 Kbps	1.4 Mbps	375 Kbps	1.4 Mbps	375 Kbps	1.4 Mbps
Cable Modem	$40	340 Kbps	1.3 Mbps	50 Kbps	260 Kbps	15 Kbps	50 Kbps
Wireless DSL	$70	375 Kbps	1.4 Mbps	375 Kbps	1.4 Mbps	375 Kbps	400 Kbps
Satellite*	$70	128 Kbps	500 Kbps	128 Kbps	500 Kbps	64 Kbps	150 Kbps

* It is important to remember that satellite systems add about 1/2 second delay to all requests (1/4 second on the upstream request and 1/4 second on the upstream response), so for small files the effective data rates as experienced by the user are much lower than these numbers would suggest.

FIGURE 7-14 Effective data rate estimates for low-cost Internet access technology.

have 50 users who can possibly be active at the same time. If we assume that 10 to 50 percent of those are active at peak times, this gives us 5 to 25 active users sharing in these capacities (by comparison, in our shared Ethernet calculations, we assumed an average of 2 to 10 active users out of 20 per Ethernet segment). This provides effective data rates of about 50 Kbps downstream and 15 Kbps upstream for 25 active users. If only 5 users are active (i.e., 1% of the total number of subscribers on a given segment), we have effective data rates of 260 Kbps downstream and 68 Kbps upstream.

Thus the primary driving factor in the effective data rates for cable modems is not really the technology itself, but the number of active users on your cable TV segment. This can vary dramatically from one city to another—or even from one neighborhood to another within the same city. This is why some users have been very satisfied with their cable modem services and why others have been very dissatisfied.

The same is true to some extent for wireless DSL and satellite because both have a shared element. Wireless DSL shares one wireless circuit into the building that is often 11 Mbps, which is large enough to support a medium number of simultaneous users, but can significantly impact performance in high-traffic environments. Satellite systems usually are designed to support up to about 5000 simultaneous users. Once there are more than that number, then performance degrades as users must share the available 5000 circuits.

The other important factor that impacts the performance of different services is the capacity of the service provider from their POP to their Internet connection; that is, once you reach the DSL switch office or the cable TV office, what circuits the ISP has leased into the Internet? If the ISP does not have enough capacity from its POP into the Internet, then the capacity of DSL or cable modem services in the local loop will not matter; users will experience poor performance because messages cannot move between the ISP and the Internet fast enough. Thus a cable modem service could outperform a DSL service if the DSL ISP has insufficient capacity into the MAE or NAP at which it exchanges traffic with other ISPs.

These two factors—number of users on the shared segments, and the capacity from the ISP's POP into the Internet—make comparisons between services difficult in general.

If we make some reasonable assumptions about the number of users and assume all ISPs provide an appropriate capacity into the Internet for the number of users they have (not always a valid assumption), then the best practice is DSL services, unless the relative costs are outrageously different.

SUMMARY

How the Internet Works   The Internet is a set of separate networks, ranging from large national ISPs to midsize regional ISPs to small local ISPs who connect with each other at network access points (NAPs) and metropolitan area exchanges (MAEs). NAPs and MAEs charge the ISPs to connect, but similar-sized ISPs usually do not charge each other to exchange data. Each ISP has a set of points-of-presence (POPs) through which it charges its users (individuals, businesses, and smaller ISPs) to connect to the Internet. Users connect to a POP to get access to the Internet. This connection may be via a dial-up modem over a telephone line, or via a higher-speed circuit such as a T1.

DSL   Digital subscriber line (DSL) enables users to connect to an ISP POP over a standard telephone line. The customer installs a DSL modem that connects via Ethernet to his or her computer system. The modem communicates with a DSLAM at the telephone company office, which sends the data to the ISP POP. ADSL is the most common type of DSL and often provides 1.5 Mbps downstream and 384 Kbps upstream. VDSL is a faster version that runs over short distances with speeds up to 51.8 Mbps.

Cable Modem   Cable modems use a shared multipoint circuit that runs through the TV cable. They also provide the customer with a modem that connects via Ethernet to his or her computer system. The modem communicates with a CMTS at the cable company office, which sends the data to the ISP POP. The DOCSIS standard is the dominant one, but there are no standard data rates today. Typical downstream speeds range between 1.5 and 2 Mbps and typical upstream speeds range between 200 Kbps and 2 Mbps.

Wireless   Fixed wireless systems provide DSL-like speeds over a single line-of-sight wireless circuit to a multitenant building. Inside the building, DSL is used to provide service to a large number of users over the existing phone lines. Satellite Internet access enables users to surf the Internet over their satellite disk, but does impose delays. Mobile wireless uses cellular telephone technologies to provide access to small handheld devices using WAP. WAP translates traditional Internet protocols such as HTTP and HTML into their WAE equivalents for use in the small devices.

Internet Governance   The closest the Internet has to an "owning" organization is the *Internet Society (ISOC)*, which works on public policy, education, and Internet standards. Standards are developed through four related organizations governed by ISOC. The IETF develops the actual standards through a series of working groups. The IESG manages IETF activities. The IAB sets long-term strategic directions, while the IRTF works on future issues through working groups in much the same way as the IETF.

Internet 2   There are many different organizations currently working on the next generation of the Internet, including the Abilene network, vBNS, and CA*Net 3. While each is working in a slightly different fashion, they join together with each other and parts of the regular Internet at gigapops (gigabit points of presence).

Best Practice Internet Access Design   DSL services provide a range of data rates, with 1.5 Mbps downstream and 384 Kbps upstream being common. Effective data rates are very close to the nominal rates because of the full-duplex point-to-point circuits and very efficient data link protocol. Cable modem services vary widely and are less efficient. Because cable modem services share their capacity with 500 or more users on the same segment, performance can be unpredictable. DSL is usually the best practice.

KEY TERMS

Abilene network
Advanced Research and
    Development
    Network Operations
    Center (ARDNOC)
asymmetric DSL
    (ADSL)
autonomous systems
broadband technologies
cable modem
cable modem termina-
    tion system (CMTS)
carrierless amplitude
    modulation (CAM)
CA*Net 3
channel
combiner
customer premises
    equipment (CPE)
Data Over Cable System
    Interface Specification
    (DOCSIS)
digital subscriber line
    (DSL)
distribution hub
downstream
DSL access multiplexer
    (DSLAM)

DSL modem
Enhanced Data GSM
    Environment
    (EDGE)
fiber node
fiber-to-the-home
    (FTTH)
fixed wireless
frequency division mul-
    tiplexer (FDM)
G.Lite ASDL
guardband
hybrid fiber coax (HFC)
Internet Architecture
    Board (IAB)
Internet Assigned Num-
    bers Authority
    (IANA)
Internet Engineering
    Steering Group
    (IESG)
Internet Engineering
    Task Force (IETF)
Internet Research Task
    Force (IRTF)
Internet service provider
    (ISP)
Internet Society (ISOC)

Internet 2
line splitter
local ISP
local loop
main distribution frame
    (MDF)
mobile wireless
national ISP
network access point
    (NAP)
next generation Internet
    (NGI)
optical-electrical
    converter
passive optical network-
    ing (PON)
peering
point-of-presence
    (POP)
regional ISP
remote access server
    (RAS)
request for comment
    (RFC)
satellite Internet access
time division
    multiplexing
    (TDM)

Universal Mobile
    Telecommunications
    Systems (UMTS)
University Corporation
    for Advanced Internet
    Development
    (UCAID)
upstream
very-high-data-rate
    digital subscriber line
    (VDSL)
very-high-performance
    backbone network
    service (vBNS)
WAP proxy
Wireless application
    environment (WAE)
wireless application
    protocol (WAP)
wireless telephony
    application (WTA)
    server
wireless DSL
YIPES.com
2G wireless
3G wireless
4G wireless

QUESTIONS

1. What is the basic structure of the Internet?

2. Explain how the Internet is a network of networks.

3. Compare and contrast NAP and MAE.

4. What is a POP?

5. Explain one reason why you might experience long response times in getting a page from a server in your own city.

6. What type of circuits are commonly used to build the Internet today? What type of circuits are commonly used to build Internet 2?

7. Compare and contrast cable modem and DSL.

8. Explain how DSL works in terms of topology, media access control, and error control.

9. How does a DSL modem differ from a DSLAM?

10. Explain how ADSL works.

11. Explain how VDSL works.

12. Compare and contrast ADSL and VDSL.

13. How efficient is DSL? Why?

14. Explain how a cable modem works in terms of topology, media access control, and error control.

15. What is an O/E converter? A CMTS?

16. Which is better, cable modem or DSL? Explain.

17. Explain how one type of fixed wireless called wireless DSL works.

18. Explain how satellite Internet access works.

19. Compare and contrast mobile wireless and fixed wireless.

20. Explain how WAP works.

21. What are some future technologies that might change how we access the Internet?

22. What is PON and how does it work?

23. Explain how YIPES.com works.

24. What are the principal organizations responsible for Internet governance and what do they do?

25. How is the IETF related to the IRTF?

26. What are two principal American organizations working on the future of the Internet?

27. What is Internet 2?

28. What is a gigapop?

29. There are many different organizations working on their vision of a high-speed Internet. Is this good or bad? Would we be better off just having one organization working on this and coordinating the work?

30. Today, there is no clear winner in the competition for higher-speed Internet access. What technology (or technologies) do you think will dominate in two years' time? Why?

31. Some experts believe that in five years the modem will have disappeared. What do you think?

32. Many experts predicted that small local ISPs would disappear as regional and national ISPs began offering local access. This hasn't happened. Why?

EXERCISES

7-1. Describe the current network structure of the Abilene network, the vBNS network, and the CA*Net 3 network.

7-2. Provide the service details (e.g., pricing) for at least two high-speed Internet access service providers in your area.

7-3. Many people are wiring their homes for 10Base-T or 100Base-T. Suppose a friend who is building a house asks you what—if any—network to put inside the house and what Internet access technology to use. What would you recommend?

MINI-CASES

I. Cathy's Collectibles

Your cousin Cathy runs a part-time business out of her apartment. She buys and sells collectibles such as antique prints, baseball cards, and cartoon cells, and has recently discovered the Web with its many auction sites. She has begun buying and selling on the Web by bidding on collectibles at lesser-known sites and selling them at a profit at more well known sites. She downloads and uploads lots of graphics (pictures of the items she's buying and selling). She is getting frustrated with the slow Internet access she has with her 56-Kbps dial-up modem and asks you for advice.

DSL is available at a cost of $60 per month for 1.5 Mbps down and 384 Kbps up. Cable modem service is available for a cost of $50 per month for 1.5 Mbps down and 640 Kbps up. Wireless DSL is available in her apartment building for $45 per month for 1.5 Mbps down and 256 Kbps up. Satellite Internet access is available for $70 per month for 500 Kbps down and 256 Kbps up. Explain the differences in these services and make a recommendation.

II. Surfing Sam

Sam likes to surf the Web for fun, to buy things, and to research for his classes. Suppose the same Internet access technologies are available as in part I above. Explain the differences in these services and make a recommendation.

III. Cookies Are US

Cookies Are Us runs a series of 100 cookie stores across the midwestern U.S. and central Canada. At the end of each day, the stores express mail a diskette or two of sales and inventory data to headquarters, which uses the data to ship new inventory and plan marketing campaigns. They have decided to move data over a WAN or the Internet. What type of a WAN topology and service (see Chapter 6) or Internet connection would you recommend?

CHAPTER 8

HARDWARE LAYERS: WIRELESS LOCAL AREA NETWORKS

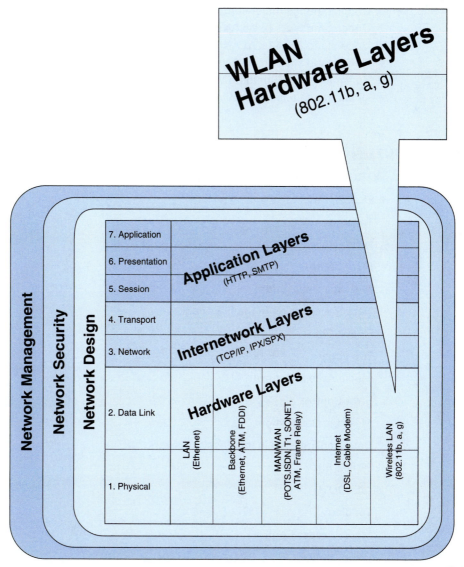

ALTHOUGH TRADITIONAL wired Ethernet LANs dominate today's network environment, wireless LANs (WLANs) are becoming increasingly common. This chapter examines three common WLAN technologies (802.11b wireless, 802.11a wireless and Bluetooth) and one emerging technology (802.11g). The chapter ends with a discussion of best practice recommendations for WLAN design.

OBJECTIVES

- Understand the major components of WLANs
- Understand 802.11b WLANs
- Understand 802.11a WLANs
- Understand 802.11g WLANs
- Be familiar with Bluetooth WLANs
- Understand the best practice recommendations for WLAN design

CHAPTER OUTLINE

INTRODUCTION

IEEE 802.11b

    Topology

    Media Access Control

    Error Control

    Message Delineation

    Data Transmission in the Physical Layer

IEEE 802.11a

    Topology

    Media Access Control

    Error Control

    Message Delineation

    Data Transmission in the Physical Layer

IEEE 802.11g

BLUETOOTH

    Topology

    Media Access Control

    Error Control

INTRODUCTION

Wireless LANs (WLANs) form only a small percentage of LANs in operation today, but their use is growing rapidly; a recent survey of network managers indicated that 75 percent of companies expect to be using wireless LANs by 2004. Wireless LANs transmit data through the air using radio transmission rather than through twisted-pair cable or fiber-optic cable. Until recently, there were few widely accepted standards for wireless LANs, and as a result equipment from different vendors could not be used in the same network. Over the past few years, however, several standards for wireless LANs have emerged and the market has taken off.

WLANs serve the same purpose as LANs: They are used to connect a series of computers in the same small local area to each other and to a backbone network. WLANs are usually not totally wireless in that they are most commonly used to connect a set of wireless computers into a wired network. However, WLANs enable you to use the network in places where it is impractical to put a wired network (either because of cost or access). WLANs can enable staff to pull up a chair and work on the network from a lunchroom, a corridor, or an outdoor patio. WLANs also enable mobile staff to work at different locations in the office building or to easily move their computers from one location to another. WLANs are becoming very popular in hospitals, for example, because they enable doctors and nurses to use laptop computers to access patient records. WLANs are also becoming popular in airports because they enable business travelers to connect to the Internet from any waiting area.

This chapter examines the data link layers and physical layers of three principal WLAN technologies (802.11b wireless, 802.11a wireless, and Bluetooth) as well as some emerging technologies (802.11g). The chapter ends with a discussion of best practice recommendations for WLAN design.

You may be wondering why we discuss 802.11b before 802.11a, because common sense would suggest that a should come before b. Discussions on 802.11a started before 802.11b (so it is labeled a), but 802.11b proved easier to develop because it is a slower-speed WLAN. The standard was set fairly easily and products reached the market first.

IEEE 802.11b

The IEEE *802.11b* standard is the dominant standard for WLANs. It reuses many of the Ethernet LLC components and is designed to easily connect into Ethernet LANs. For these reason, IEEE 802.11b is usually called *wireless Ethernet,* although its official name is *wireless LAN.*[1] A group of vendors selling 802.11b equipment have trademarked the name *Wi-Fi* to refer to 802.11b, because they believe that consumers are more likely to buy equipment with a catchier name than 802.11b; Wi-Fi is intended to evoke memories of Hi-Fi, as the original stereo music systems were called.

There are two different versions of 802.11b. *Frequency-hopping spread-spectrum (FHSS)* systems run at 1 Mbps and 2 Mbps. *Direct-sequence spread-spectrum (DSSS)* systems run at 1 Mbps, 2 Mbps, 5.5 Mbps, and 11 Mbps. DSSS systems dominate the marketplace because they are faster, so we will examine only DSSS systems in this chapter.[2] In general, 802.11b systems run at the highest data rate of 11 Mbps. Only when there is significant interference or the signal begins to weaken because the user is moving far from the WLAN do they drop to a slower data rate in an attempt to improve signal quality. Thus for those users close to the center of the WLAN, 5–11 Mbps is the norm.

Topology

The logical and physical topologies of wireless Ethernet are the same as those of shared Ethernet. They are a physical star and a logical bus (see Figure 8-1). Each computer has a wireless *network interface card (NIC)* that is used to connect the computer into the WLAN. The NIC is a radio transceiver, in that it sends and receives radio signals through a short range, usually only about 100 to 150 meters or 300 to 500 feet. WLAN NICs are available for laptops as PCMCIA cards and as standard cards for desktop computers, but laptop NICs are most common. See Figure 8-2b.

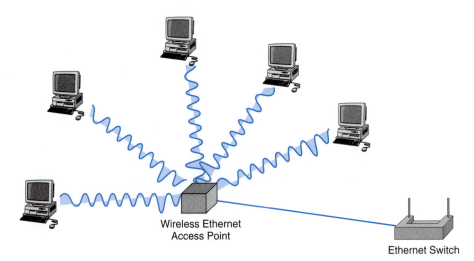

Wireless Ethernet
Access Point

Ethernet Switch

FIGURE 8-1   A wireless Ethernet access point connected into an Ethernet switch.

---

[1] For more information, see the IEEE standards site at grouper.ieee.org/groups/802/11 and the Wireless Ethernet Compatibility Alliance at www.wirelessethernet.org.

[2] For information on FHSS see grouper.ieee.org/groups/802/11/.

a

b

FIGURE 8-2 (a) Wireless access point; (b) Wireless card for laptop.

A central wireless *access point (AP)* is a radio transceiver that plays the same role as a hub in wired Ethernet LANs (see Figure 8-2a) and also connects the WLAN into wired LANs using 10BaseT or 100Base-T. The AP acts as a repeater to ensure that all computers within range of the AP can hear the signals of all other computers in the WLANs. All NICs in the WLAN transmit their frames to the AP and then the AP retransmits the frame over the wireless network to its destination—or retransmits the frame over the wired network to its destination. Wireless NICs never communicate with each other directly; they always transmit through the AP. Therefore, if a message has to be transmitted from one wireless computer to another, it is transmitted twice, once from the sender to the AP and then from the AP to the destination. At first glance this may seem a bit strange because it doubles the number of transmissions in the WLAN. However, very few messages are ever sent from client computer to client computer in a WLAN. Most messages are exchanged between client computers and a server of some kind. For this reason, servers should never be placed on a WLAN; even if they are intended to serve clients on a WLAN, they should always be placed on the wired portion of the LAN.

802.11b provides three separate radio frequency channels that can be used. All devices using one AP use the same channel, so the WLAN functions as a shared-media LAN in the same manner as shared Ethernet: Computers must take turns using the one shared circuit. Usually a set of APs are installed, so that there is complete wireless coverage in some area, enabling users to roam from AP to AP. Each AP is set to send and receive data on a different radio channel, so that transmissions from one AP and the computers it communicates with do not interfere with another AP and its computers. When a NIC is first turned on, it listens to and may attempt to transmit using all of the available channels. Based on these tests, it selects the channel with the strongest signal strength and the fewest number of errors and associates itself with the AP using that channel.

As the user *roams* through a building, the NIC continues to use its original channel until the signal strength starts to drop. When this happens, the NIC again listens to and may attempt to transmit using all of the available channels to find a new channel that has the strongest signal. Some—but not all—NICs also periodically check for better channels when the channel they are using becomes busy. Thus for these WLANs, it is possible to set up several APs in the same area to provide several different channels so computers have more network capacity available (much like installing three Ethernet hubs in the same general area).

One potential problem with WLANs is security. Because anyone within range of a WLAN can receive transmissions, eavesdropping is a serious threat. Most WLANs encrypt transmissions so that only authorized computers can decode and read the messages (encryption is discussed in Chapter 10).

Media Access Control

Media access control in wireless Ethernet is Carrier Sense Multiple Access with Collision Avoidance (CSMA/CA), which is similar to the CSMA/CD used by traditional Ethernet. With CSMA/CA, computers listen before they transmit and if no one else is transmitting, they transmit. Detecting collisions is more difficult in radio transmission than in transmission over wired networks, so wireless Ethernet attempts to avoid collisions to a greater extent than traditional Ethernet. CSMA/CA uses two media access control approaches simultaneously.

Distributed Coordination Function   The first media access control method is the *distributed coordination function (DCF)* (also called *physical carrier sense method* because it relies on the ability of computers to physically listen before they transmit). With DCF, each frame in CSMA/CA is sent using stop-and-wait ARQ. After the sender transmits one frame, it immediately stops and waits for an ACK from the receiver before attempting to send another frame. When the receiver of a frame detects the end of the frame in a transmission, it waits a fraction of a second to make sure the sender has really stopped transmitting, and then immediately transmits an ACK (or a NAK). The original sender can then send another frame, stop and wait for an ACK, and so on.

While the sender and receiver are exchanging frames and ACKs, other computers may also want to transmit. So when the sender ends its transmission, why doesn't some other computer begin transmitting before the receiver can transmit an ACK? The answer is that the physical carrier sense method is designed so that the time the receiver waits after the transmission ends before sending an ACK is significantly less than the time a computer must listen to determine no one else is transmitting before initiating a new transmission. Thus the time interval between a transmission and the matching ACK is so short that no other computer has the opportunity to begin transmitting.

Point Coordination Function The second media access control technique is called the *point coordination function (PCF)* (also called the *virtual carrier sense method*). The PCF works well in traditional Ethernet, because every computer on the shared circuit receives every transmission on the shared circuit. However, in a wireless environment, this is not always true. A computer at the extreme edge of the range limit from the AP on one side may not receive transmissions from a computer on the extreme opposite edge of the AP's range limit. In Figure 8-1, all computers may be within range of the AP, but not be within range of each other. In this case, if one computer transmits, the other computer on the opposite edge may not sense the other transmission and transmit at the same time, causing a collision at the AP. This is called the *hidden node problem,* because the computers at the opposite edges of the WLAN are hidden from each other.

When the hidden node problem exists, the AP is the only device guaranteed to be able to communicate with all computers on the WLAN. Therefore, the AP must manage the shared circuit using a *controlled-access* technique, not the contention-based approach of traditional Ethernet. With this approach, any computer wishing to transmit first sends a request to transmit (RTS) to the AP, which may or may not be heard by all computers. The RTS requests permission to transmit and to reserve the circuit for the sole use of the requesting computer for a specified time period. If no other computer is transmitting, the AP responds with a clear to transmit (CTS) specifying the amount of time for which the circuit is reserved for the requesting computer. All computers hear the CTS and remain silent for the specified time period.

MANAGEMENT FOCUS *8-1*

T.G.I. WIRELESS

Employees at T.G.I. Friday's restaurants must juggle plenty of constantly changing information, such as table availability, waiting lists, and orders. When guests arrive at the door, the host or hostess enters their name and the number of guests in the waiting list system at the kiosk at the front door, which is networked with the main server. When a table of the appropriate size becomes available, the system highlights the guests' name and the host/hostess seats them.

When the restaurant becomes busy, the kiosk becomes a bottleneck and sometimes tables sit empty while the waiting list gets longer. New restaurants have added a pen-based system that communicates with the waiting-list system via a wireless LAN in addition to the standard wired kiosk. The pen-based system provides a second access point to the system but also enables the host/hostess to walk around the restaurant and enter data directly from tables, rather than having to walk to the front door to enter the data. The wireless system not only reduces the wait time, but was actually cheaper than installing a second wired kiosk.

SOURCE: "Wireless LAN Makes for Better Service at Restaurant Chain," Wireless-nets.com, November 2000.

The virtual carrier sense method is optional. It can be used always, never, or just for frames exceeding a certain size, as set by the LAN manager. Controlled-access methods provide poorer performance in low-traffic networks and better performance in high-traffic networks because computers must wait for permission before transmitting, rather than just waiting for an unused time period. However, controlled-access techniques work better in high-traffic LANs because without controlled access there are many collisions. Think of a large class discussion in which the instructor selects who will speak (controlled access) versus one in which any student can shout out a comment at any time.

Error Control

802.11b uses the same stop-and-wait error control as 802.3 Ethernet.

Message Delineation

802.11b uses a frame layout that is similar to that of 802.3ac. The AP converts the 802.11b frames into standard 802.3ac frames before transmitting them into the wired network to which it is connected. Figure 8-3 shows the frame layout for the DSSS version of 802.11b, which has five parts: preamble, PLCP header, payload header, LLC PDU, and payload trailer.

Preamble The purpose of the *preamble* is to mark the start of the frame. As with Ethernet, the receiver is constantly monitoring the wireless circuit for possible incoming data. When the receiver recognizes the bit patterns of the preamble, it understands that the WLAN frame is about to follow, and begins to process the incoming data. The preamble is always transmitted at 1 Mbps, regardless of the speed used in the rest of the transmission.

The preamble has two parts. The first is a set of 16 sync bytes (in the case of a *long preamble*) that have alternating 1s and 0s (i.e., 10101010). The second is a 1-byte start-of-frame delimiter (10101011). When the receiver recognizes the start-of-frame delimiter, it knows that the PLCP header immediately follows. There is also a *short preamble* that may be used instead of the long preamble that has 7 sync bytes followed by the start-of-frame delimiter (in which case, the 1s and 0s in both the sync bytes and start-of-frame delimiter are reversed).

PLCP Header The purpose of the *Physical Layer Convergence Protocol (PLCP)* header is to enable the NICs and AP to determine what data rate is being used and how long the frame is. The PLCP is transmitted at 1 Mbps if a long preamble is used and at 2 Mbps if a short preamble is used, regardless of whether higher speeds can be used or not. If higher speeds can be used, they are used to transmit the remaining three parts of the frame.

The first field in the PLCP header is the 1-byte signal rate, which indicates which of the four speeds will be used for the rest of the transmission (1 Mbps, 2 Mbps, 5.5 Mbps, or 11 Mbps). The *service* field is reserved for future use. An Ethernet frame can vary in length depending on the length of the message it contains, so the 2-byte *length* field indicates the length in 8-bit bytes of the payload portion of the frame; this length field is required, because without it the receiver would have no way of knowing when the message ended.

Preamble	PLCP Header	Payload Header	LLC Protocol Data Unit	Payload Trailer

Preamble

Sync Bytes	Start of Frame
7 or 16 bytes	2 bytes

PLCP Header:

Signal Rate	Service	Length	Header Error Check
1 byte	1 byte	2 bytes	2 bytes

Payload Header:

Frame Control	Duration ID	Destination Address	Source Address	Address 3	Sequence Control	Address 4
2 bytes	2 bytes	6 bytes	6 bytes	6 bytes	2 bytes	6 bytes

LLC PDU:

DSAP	SSAP	Control	Data
1 byte	1 byte	1-2 bytes	43-1497 bytes

Payload Trailer:

FCS
4 bytes

FIGURE 8-3 Ethernet 802.11b DSSS frame layout.

The final field is the *header error check,* which is a 2-byte CRC-16 used to see if there are any errors in the header. If errors are discovered the frame is discarded.

Payload Header The purpose of the *payload header* is to provide the source and destination addresses and control information. The first field in the payload header is the 2-byte frame control field that indicates which version of the 802.11b standard is being used and contains any ACK/NAK signals and the RTS/CTS signals. The 6-byte *destination address* field specifies the destination Ethernet address of the receiving wireless NIC, if the frame is sent by the AP. If the frame is sent by a wireless computer's NIC to the AP for retransmission to some other computer, the destination address field contains the Ethernet address of the AP, and the *address 3* field contains the Ethernet address of the actual destination. The 6-byte *source address* field specifies the Ethernet address of sender. If the sender is the AP retransmitting the frame on behalf of another wireless NIC, then the *address 3* field contains the Ethernet address of the original sender. The 2-byte *sequence control* field contains the frame number for error control. The 6-byte *address 4* field contains the Ethernet address of the original sending wireless NIC only in the case where a wireless computer is transmitting directly to another wireless computer across the same access point; otherwise it is not used.

LLC PDU   The LLC PDU is the same as the LLC PDU used in 802.3, described in Chapter 4.

Payload Trailer   The payload trailer is the same 4-byte frame check sequence (CRC-32) used by 802.3 Ethernet, described in Chapter 4.

Data Transmission in the Physical Layer

802.11b transmits data via radio waves in much the same way as modems transmit data through the telephone line using sound waves. As we discussed in Chapter 7, there are two fundamentally different types of data that can flow through the physical circuit (digital and analog) and two fundamentally different types of data transmission (digital and analog). Ethernet WLANs use radio waves, not cables, and radio is an analog medium. This means that the digital computer data must be transmitted using *analog transmission.* The sending AP or NIC translates the digital binary data produced by computers into the analog signals required by radio waves for transmission and the receiving AP or NIC translates the analog signal back into digital data for use at the destination.

Frequencies and Bandwidth   In order to transmit data, both the sender and receiver have to agree on what type of signaling technique to use (e.g., AM) and what frequency ranges to use. The size of this range of frequencies, called the *bandwidth,* directly affects the maximum speed at which we can transmit data. The greater the bandwidth, the faster we can transmit.

While there are a wide range of frequencies available for radio transmission, most frequency ranges are currently in use. In creating new radio-based wireless LANs, one of the most challenging parts was simply agreeing on what range of frequencies to use because this would mean changing the current assignment of frequencies. In North America, 802.11b operates in the 2.4000 to 2.4835 GHz range and gives a bandwidth of 83.5 MHz (2.400 GHz – 2.4835 GHz = 83.5 MHz).[3]

Transmission   DSSS 803.11b takes this bandwidth and divides it into three separate channels of 22 MHz each.[4] Because there is a potential for interference between these channels, the frequency ranges are assigned with a 3-MHz *guardband* of "empty" frequencies between each channel to prevent interference. In case you're wondering, the three channels are the 22 MHz centered on 2.412 GHz, on 2.437 GHz, and on 2.462 GHz.

The data capacity of a circuit is the fastest rate at which you can send your data over the circuit in terms of the number of bits per second, which is calculated by multiplying the number of bits sent on each symbol (e.g., AM with four levels sends 2 bits per symbol) by

[3] In Japan the range is 2.471–2.497 GHz, while in France it is 2.4465–2.4835 GHz.

[4] The original proposal was for 11 overlapping channels, but most vendors have implemented three nonoverlapping channels.

the symbol rate. The maximum symbol rate depends on the bandwidth available and the signal-to-noise ratio (the strength of the signal compared to the amount of noise in the circuit). This means that a bandwidth of 22 MHz provides a maximum symbol rate of 22 million symbols per second *under perfect conditions.* The actual symbol rate—and resulting data rate—is often less than the maximum would suggest.

DSSS assumes that there will be interference present in the real environments in which 802.11b will be used, so it goes to great lengths to try to minimize the effects of this expected noise. Before each bit is transmitted it is converted into a special 8-bit or 11-bit code that is designed to reduce the effects of interference. These codes are such that in many cases, even if several bits of the code are lost in transmission due to the noise, the receiver can still understand the bit that the transmitter intended to send. So, DSSS does not send each bit one at a time, but instead converts each bit into a set of bits, thus "spreading" into many bits across the frequency spectrum, which gives DSSS its name.

The 1-Mbps version of DSSS converts each bit into an 11-bit *Barker sequence.* A sequence of 10111101000 is used for a binary 0 and the inverse (0100010111) is used for a binary 1. By choosing the inverse pattern of bits for sequences for 0 and 1, this increases the chance that the receiver can determine whether a binary 0 or 1 was transmitted, even if some bits in the Barker sequence are corrupted by noise during transmission. This 11-bit Barker sequence is then transmitted using *differential binary phase shift keying (DBPSK).* DBPSK is a two-level transmission technique similar to PSK, in which one bit is sent in every time interval. A binary 1 is represented by a 180° *change* in the phase from the preceding wave and a binary 0 is represented as a 0° wave change (i.e., no change). A signaling rate of 11 Mbps is used, which gives a data rate of 1 Mbps (1 bit is converted into an 11-bit sequence, which is sent using 1 bit/symbol at a rate of 11 million symbols per second = 1 Mbps).[5] Figure 8-4 shows how this works.

The 2-Mbps version of DSSS also converts each bit into an 11-bit Barker sequence, but this time uses *differential quadrature phase shift keying (DQPSK).* DQPSK works exactly like BPSK, but uses four different levels of phase changes (0°, 90°, 180°, and 270°) so that 2 bits are transmitted in each time interval. In this case we have 1 bit converted into an 11-bit sequence, which is sent using 2 bits per symbol at a rate of 11 million symbols per second = 2 Mbps.

The 5.5 Mbps version of DSSS uses a different coding scheme called *complementary code keying (CCK).* In this case, DSSS groups the data that needs to be transmitted into sets of 4 data bits. CCK converts the last 2 of the 4 data bits into 8-bit sequences called CCK code words. Just like the Barker sequences, the CCK code words are chosen to be as different as possible from each other so that even if some of the bits are corrupted, the receiver can often still determine which of the four possible CCK code words was transmitted. The 8-bit code word is then sent using DQPSK, using four different phases, but this time, DQPSK is used to modulate the entire word, not each bit individually. That is, all the bits in the entire CCK word as represented by a specific wave pattern of phase shifts are again modulated using one of four possible phases (see Figure 8-5). The first 2 data bits of the 4 data bits are used to select which one of the four possible phases will be used. In summary, we process 4 incoming

---

[5] You will read that 1-Mbps DSSS uses a symbol rate of 1 million symbols per second. This means that one Barker sequence symbol is transmitted per second, not that 1 bit is sent per second. For more details on how DSSS works, see standards.ieee.org/getieee802/802.11.html.

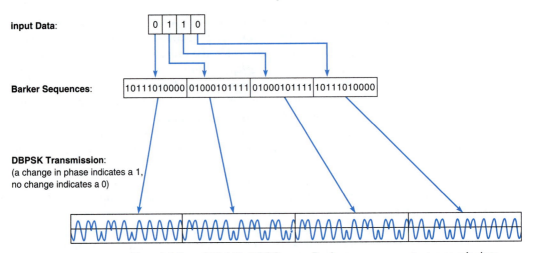

FIGURE 8-4 How 1 Mbps 802.11b DSSS uses Barker sequences to transmit data.

bits at a time; we use the last 2 data bits to select the 8-bit CCK word that will be used and the first 2 data bits to select the DQPSK phase that will be used to transmit the word. Thus each 8-bit CCK word transmits 4 bits of data. Each bit in the CCK word is sent at the usual rate of 11 million symbols per second; thus we get a data rate of 5.5 Mbps.

The 11-Mbps version of DSSS works on groups of 8 data bits. The last 6 bits are used to choose which 8-bit CCK code word will be used and the first 2 bits are again used to select which DQPSK phase will be used. In this case, each 8-bit CCK word transmits 8 bits of data. Each bit in the CCK word is sent at the usual rate of 11 million symbols per second; thus we get a data rate of 11 Mbps.

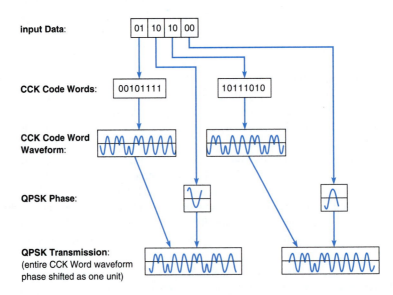

FIGURE 8-5 How 5.5-Mbps 802.11b DSSS uses CCK code words to transmit data.

IEEE 802.11a

The IEEE *802.11a* standard for wireless LANs is relatively new. In North America, it operates in a 5-GHz frequency range. The total bandwidth is 300 MHz, substantially more than the 22 MHz of 802.11b. This means that it can transmit data faster than 802.11b; the possible data rates are: 6 Mbps, 9 Mbps, 12 Mbps, 18 Mbps, 24 Mbps, 36 Mbps, 48 Mbps, and 54 Mbps.

Topology

802.11a uses the same topology as 802.11b: A set of NICs communicate with one AP. Because higher frequencies are used, the range is reduced to only 50 meters or 150 feet between the NICs and the AP. As with 802.11b, the data speeds drop off the farther you move from the AP, so users at the extreme edge of the range or those facing interference will not be able to communicate at the 54 Mbps. Initial analyses suggest a 54-Mbps data rate is reliable and consistent only at 15 meters (just under 50 feet) or less from the AP.

802.11a provides 12 channels, compared to the 802.11b's three channels, which is important because the range of 802.11a is so much smaller than that of 802.11b. An area that requires only one 802.11b AP to provide 5.5-11 Mbps would require four 802.11a APs to provide a 12- to 24-Mbps data rate (see Figure 8-6). To get a 30- to 54-Mbps data rate, more than 30 802.11a APs would be required.

The provision of 12 channels also means that it is possible to collocate several APs in the same room, each operating on a different channel. The NICs in the room could then be assigned to different channels to provide greater network capacity. For example, by putting four APs in the same room, each operating on different channels, we could provide a total capacity of 4 × 54 Mbps = 216 Mbps to be shared among the computers in one room. While this moves closer to the ideal of switched Ethernet—which dedicates one cable

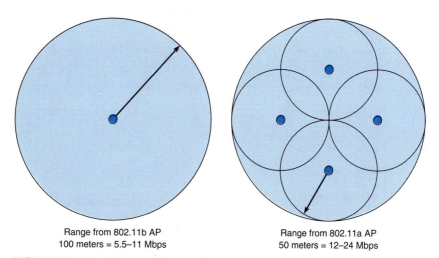

Range from 802.11b AP
100 meters = 5.5–11 Mbps

Range from 802.11a AP
50 meters = 12–24 Mbps

FIGURE 8-6 It takes more 802.11a access points to provide the same coverage as one 802.11b access point.

(equivalent to one channel) to each computer—it is still shared Ethernet, albeit with fewer computers sharing each AP.

Media Access Control

802.11a uses the same media access control protocols as 802.11b.

Error Control

802.11a uses the same stop-and-wait error control as 802.11b.

Message Delineation

802.11a uses a frame layout that is similar to that of 802.11b. Figure 8-7 shows the frame layout for 802.11a, which has the same five parts as 802.11b: preamble, PLCP header, payload header, LLC PDU, and payload trailer.

Preamble	PLCP Header	Payload Header	LLC Protocol Data Unit	Payload Trailer

Preamble

Sync Bytes	Start of Frame
8 bytes	2 bytes

PLCP Header:

Rate	Reserved	Length	Parity	Tail
4 bits	1 bit	12 bits	1 bit	6 bits

Payload Header:

Service	Frame Control	Duration ID	Destination Address	Source Address	Address 3	Sequence Control	Address 4
2 bytes	2 bytes	2 bytes	6 bytes	6 bytes	6 bytes	2 bytes	6 bytes

LLC PDU:

DSAP	SSAP	Control	Data
1 byte	1 byte	1-2 bytes	43-1497 bytes

Payload Trailer:

FCS	Tail
4 bytes	6 bits

FIGURE 8-7   Ethernet 802.11a frame layout.

Preamble   The purpose of the *preamble* is to mark the start of the frame. As with 803.11b, the receiver is constantly monitoring the wireless circuit for possible incoming data. When the receiver recognizes the bit patterns of the preamble, it understands that the WLAN frame is about to follow and begins to process the incoming data. The preamble is always transmitted at 6 Mbps, regardless of the speed used in the rest of the transmission. The 802.11a preamble is a series of sync bits formed in a manner slightly different from that of 802.11b.

PLCP Header   The purpose of the *Physical Layer Convergence Protocol (PLCP)* header is to enable the NICs and AP to determine what data is being used and how long the frame is. The PLCP is transmitted at 6 Mbps, regardless of whether higher speeds can be used or not. If higher speeds can be used, they are used to transmit the remaining three parts of the frame.

The first field in the PLCP header is the 4-bit *rate,* which indicates which of the eight speeds will be used for the rest of the transmission. The *reserved* field is reserved for future use. An Ethernet frame can vary in length depending on the length of the message it contains, so the 12-bit *length* field indicates the length in 8-bit bytes of the payload portion of the frame; this length field is required because without it, the receiver would have no way of knowing when the message ended. The next field is a 1-bit even-parity bit used to see if there are any errors in the header. The sender counts the number of binary 1 bits in the rate, reserved, and length fields and sets the parity bit to a binary 1 or 0 so that there are an even number of binary 1s in these fields (e.g., suppose that the bit pattern in the three fields was 0101-0-000000101010; in this case we have five binary 1s—an odd number—so the parity bit would be set to a 1 to make a total of six 1s, because 6 is an even number). The receiver counts the number of 1s in these four fields (rate, reserved, length, and parity) and, if there is not an even number of 1s, realizes that an error has occurred and discards the frame. The final field is used to pad the header to an even number of 8-bit bytes.

Payload Header   The payload header is identical to the 802.11b payload header, with the exception of the addition of the *service* field. The service field is used to synchronize the electronics in the receiver with those in the transmitter.

LLC PDU   The LLC PDU is identical to that of 802.11b.

Payload Trailer   The payload trailer starts with the same 4-byte frame check sequence (CRC-32) used by 802.11b but includes a new 6-*bit* tail field. This is a set of 6 binary 0s, used to reset the electronics in the receiver.

Data Transmission in the Physical Layer

802.11a transmits data using radio waves using many of the same assumptions and techniques as 802.11b. 802.11a also assumes there will be interference and spreads its transmission over a wider range of frequencies. Each of the 12 channels has a bandwidth of 20 MHz, which is broken into 52 separate subchannels of 312.5 KHz, plus guardbands. Only 48 of these subchannels are used to transmit data; the other four are used for control purposes. Data is sent across all 48 subchannels in parallel using a process called *orthogonal frequency division multiplexing (OFDM).*

The 6-Mbps version of 802.11a groups the data that needs to be transmitted into sets of 24 data bits. Each group of 24 data bits is converted into one OFDM symbol of 48 bits. The pattern of bits in the OFDM symbol is chosen so that even if some of the bits are corrupted in transmission, the receiver often still can determine which of the ODFM symbols was transmitted. Each bit in the OFDM symbol is transmitted in one of the 48 separate subchannels using the same BPSK as in 802.11b but this time sending at 250 KHz. See Figure 8-8. So we get 24 bits of data transmitted on each symbol at 250 KHz = 6 Mbps.

The 9-Mbps version works in exactly the same manner, but instead groups the data into sets of 36 bits. Each set of 36 bits is converted into one OFDM symbol and sent using BPSK at 250 KHz, for a total of 9 Mbps.

The 12-Mbps version groups the data into sets of 48 bits. Each set of 48 bits is converted into two OFDM symbols and sent using QPSK at 250KHz. Because QPSK has four levels of phases, it sends 2 bits on one signal, so the receiver gets two OFDM symbols 250,000 times per second for a total of 12 Mbps. The 18-Mbps version selects groups of 72 bits and converts them into two OFDM symbols, again sent using QPSK at 250 KHz, for a total of 18 Mbps.

The 24-Mbps version groups the data into sets of 96 bits, which are converted into four OFDM symbols, which are sent using *quadrature amplitude modulation (QAM)* at 250 KHz. QAM combines PSK and amplitude modulation to provide a set of 16 different possible values—or 4 bits on every signal. The 36-Mbps version groups the data into 128-bit groups and converts them into four OFDM symbols sent using QAM. See Figure 8-9.

The 48-Mbps version groups data into 192-bit groups, which are converted into six OFDM symbols. These symbols are sent using 64-QAM, a 64-level, 6-bit-per-signal version of QAM, at the same 250 KHz. The 54-Mbps version uses 216-bit groups converted to six OFDM symbols sent by 64-QAM.

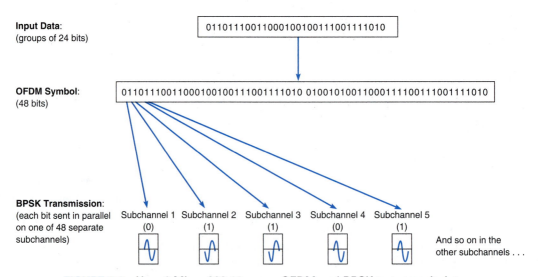

FIGURE 8-8   How 6 Mbps 802.11a uses OFDM and BPSK to transmit data.

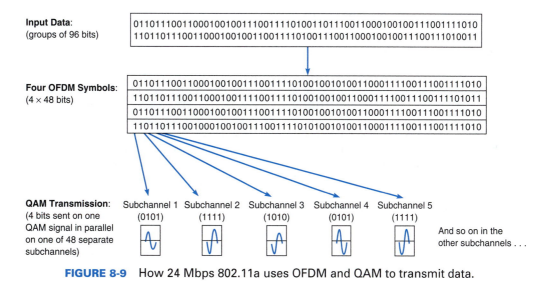

Input Data:
(groups of 96 bits)

011011100110001001001110011110100110111001100010010011100111010
110110111001100010010011001111010011001100010010011100111010011

Four OFDM Symbols:
(4 × 48 bits)

011011100110001001001110011110100100101001100011110011100111010
110110111001100010010011100111101001001001100011110011100111101011
011011100110001001001110011110100100101001100011110011100111010
110110111001000100100111001111010100101001100011110011100111010

QAM Transmission:
(4 bits sent on one
QAM signal in parallel
on one of 48 separate
subchannels)

Subchannel 1   Subchannel 2   Subchannel 3   Subchannel 4   Subchannel 5
(0101)   (1111)   (1010)   (0101)   (1111)

And so on in the
other subchannels . . .

FIGURE 8-9   How 24 Mbps 802.11a uses OFDM and QAM to transmit data.

IEEE 802.11g

IEEE 802.11g is the newest technology in the IEEE 802.11 family. 802.11g is designed to combine many of the advantages of 802.11b and 802.11a, but as we write this in early 2002, the standard has not been finalized and no products have reached the market. 802.11b provides a good range (100–150 meters) but at low speed (5.5–11 Mbps). 802.11a offers higher speed (54 Mbps) but only for very short distances (15 meters), and as distance from the AP increases, speeds drop close to those of 802.11b (12–24 Mbps). The goal of 802.11g is to offer higher data rates in the same 2.4 GHz band as 802.11b so that the signal can travel farther than the higher-frequency signal of 802.11a. 802.11g will also be compatible with 802.11b so that access points can communicate with both, much like autosensing 10/100 wired Ethernet.

Initial work has focused on a 22-Mbps data rate that can reach 100–150 meters. A 54-Mbps data rate is also possible, but over much shorter distances. To do this, designers have taken the OFDM transmission approach used by 802.11a and redesigned it into the 2.4-GHz frequency range of 802.11. The exact details are likely to change as 802.11g moves through the standard process and into products.[6]

Because the standard is not defined and products are not yet shipping, experts are divided on the value of 802.11g. Some see 802.11g as technology that is destined to fail once 802.11a becomes widely available because once 802.11a is available, why do we need another standard? Others see 802.11g as a technology that will kill both 802.11b (because it is faster) and 802.11a (because it will provide almost as fast data rates over a much longer range). Only the future will tell.

[6] For more details, see grouper.ieee.org/groups/802/11 and www.palowireless.com/ofdm.

MANAGEMENT FOCUS *8-2*

LIKE HAVING A PAY PHONE

In 2001, Starbucks announced plans to install 802.11b access points in 70 percent of its stores in North America. These access points would connect into DSL or other Internet access technologies so that customers could surf the Web or read e-mail as they slurp their coffee.

Many other restaurants, coffee houses, and bars are installing 802.11b as an amenity for customers. Few if any are charging customers for access, because the cost to install the equipment is relatively low—less than the cost of wiring traditional Ethernet—and is often subsidized by the ISP providing Internet access.

For most restaurateurs, wireless Internet access is still a sideshow. According to Quinn McKenna, vice president of operations for Lark Creek Restaurant Group in San Francisco, wireless Internet is "kind of like having a pay phone." It's a service that may draw in more customers or encourage them to stay longer, thereby increasing the restaurant's core business.

In the battle for public wireless Internet access, 3G is the one getting the most press, but today, 802.11b has the greater installed customer base and offers faster access.

SOURCE: "Gimme a Cappuccino and Wi-Fi, Please," *Mbusiness*, August 2001.

BLUETOOTH

Bluetooth is standardized as IEEE 802.15, which calls it *Wireless Personal Area Network (WPAN)*. Bluetooth is a strikingly different type of wireless LAN from the others discussed in this chapter. Its goal is to provide seamless networking of data and/or voice devices in a very small area (up to 10 meters or 30 feet, possibly to increase to about 100 meters or 300 feet with the next generation of technology). Bluetooth devices are small (about 1/3 of an inch square) and cheap and are designed to replace short-distance cabling between devices such as keyboards, mice, and a telephone handset and base or to link your PDA with your car so that your door unlocks and automatically opens as you approach. Bluetooth provides a basic data rate of 1 Mbps that can be divided into several separate voice and data channels.

Because Bluetooth is not intended as a general-purpose network in competition with 802.11a/b/g wireless LANs or 802.3 wired LANs, we will discuss it briefly—not in the same depth as the other WLAN technologies.[7] In case you're wondering, Bluetooth's Scandinavian inventor decided to name it after Danish King Harold Bluetooth.

Topology

A Bluetooth network is called a *piconet* and consists of no more than 8 devices, but can be linked to other piconets to form a larger network. One device is considered the piconet *master,* and all other devices are *slaves*. The master controls the piconet, selecting frequencies and access control used by the master and the slaves. All messages are sent from a slave to the master and from the master to a slave. The slaves do not communicate directly. All devices share the same frequency ranges so the network behaves in the same manner as a shared bus topology.

---

[7] For more details, see www.bluetooth.com.

Media Access Control

The master controls access to the media in much the same manner as the AP controls access in 802.11b WLANs when the PCF media access control approach is in use. Bluetooth uses *frequency-hopping spread-spectrum (FHSS),* in which the available frequency range (2.400–2.4385 GHz) is divided into 79 separate 1-MHz channels. Each channel is used in turn to transmit signals; a short burst of data is sent on one frequency and then the sender changes to another frequency channel and broadcasts another burst of data before changing to another channel, and so on. There are usually 1,600 channel changes (called *hops*) per second. The master controls which channels will be used, so the master and the slave with which it is communicating are synchronized so that they both know which frequencies will be used at which point. This approach also minimizes interference because if one frequency channel suffers from interference, it will soon be avoided.

Because Bluetooth operates in the same 2.4-GHz range as 802.11b, it has the potential to cause problems for 802.11b LANs. However, because Bluetooth uses FHSS, in which it rapidly hops between frequencies, and because 802.11b uses DSSS, in which it spreads the signal over a wide frequency and can easily cope with the loss of some bits of each Barker sequence or CCK code word, tests suggest that good management can prevent problems. As long as no Bluetooth piconets are located within 2 meters of an 802.11b NIC or AP and as long as only a moderate number of Bluetooth piconets are operating in the same area as an 802.11b LAN, neither the Bluetooth piconets nor the 802.11b LAN appear to suffer any problems.

Error Control

Bluetooth uses a stop-and-wait ARQ error control technique similar to that of 802.11b.

Message Delineation

Because Bluetooth can be used to connect different types of devices, such as both computer devices (e.g., keyboards) and voice devices (e.g., headsets to phones), there are several different types of frame formats. A typical layout for a Bluetooth data frame is shown in Figure 8-10. A Bluetooth frame has three parts: access code, header, payload header, payload, and payload trailer.

The access code contains three fields and is intended to synchronize the sender and receiver. The 4-bit preamble is an alternating series of binary 1s and 0s. The sync bytes are bit patterns based on the address of the master or slave, depending upon the type of frame being transmitted. The trailer is an alternating series of binary 1s and 0s.

The header has four fields used to address the frame and provide error control information. The 3-bit address field is the address of the slave that is sending or receiving. The 4-bit type specifies which type of payload is being transmitted (e.g., data, control, media access request). Flow control is used to ensure that the receiver is never overwhelmed by data from the sender. If it is set to 1 then the sender can continue to transmit; if the receiver requests a temporary pause, it sets this field to a 0 during an acknowledgment. The ARQ ACK/NAK field is used to send ACKs (1) and NAKs (0) for error control. The sequence number is used to indicate frame numbers for the ACKs and NAKs. The header error check

Access Code	Header	Payload Header	Payload Data	Payload Trailer

Access Code:

Preamble	Sync Bytes	Trailer
4 bits	64 bits	4 bits

Header:

Address	Type	Flow Control	ARQ ACK/NAK	Sequence Number	Header Error Check
3 bits	4 bits	1 bit	1 bit	1 bit	8 bits

Payload Header:

Logical Channel	Flow Control	Length	Future Use
2 bits	1 bit	9 bits	4 bits

Payload Data:

Data
0-2729 bits

Payload Trailer:

FCS
16 bits

FIGURE 8-10   Bluetooth data frame layout.

(CRC-8) is used to detect errors in the header during transmission; if an error is detected, the frame is discarded.

The payload header has four fields. The 2-bit logical channel field indicates whether the payload frame is a data frame or a control frame. The 1-bit flow control field performs the same function as the flow control field in the header (but for a different part of the Bluetooth software). The 9-bit length is the length of the payload data field in bytes. The last field is reserved for future use.

The payload data can take on a variety of different formats depending on the type of data transmitted.

The payload trailer is a CRC-16 error check code.

Data Transmission in the Physical Layer

Bluetooth uses frequency shift keying (FSK) to transmit data. As you will recall, from Chapter 6, FSK defines two levels of frequencies: one frequency for a binary 0, and a different frequency for a binary 1. Bluetooth uses a lower frequency to send a binary 1 and a higher frequency to send a binary 0. Each FSK symbol is sent at 1 MHz, so this gives a maximum data rate of 1 Mbps.

THE BEST PRACTICE WLAN DESIGN

As with the best practice LAN design, our recommendations for the best practice WLAN design are based primarily on the trade-off between effective data rates and costs. Bluetooth is not intended to be used for general networking, so we do not include it in our discussions here. Likewise, 802.1g is an emerging technology, so we do not include it either. Because WLANs are competitors for traditional wired LANs, we also consider the issue of LAN versus WLAN, which is perhaps the more interesting question.

Effective Data Rates

As you will recall, the effective data rates of the hardware layers are the maximum practical speeds in bits that the hardware layers can be expected to provide and depend on four basic factors: nominal data rates, error rates, efficiency of the data link layer protocols used, and efficiency of the media access control protocols. Error plays a greater role in WLANs than it does in wired LANs because interference can significantly affect performance by increasing the number of retransmissions and by forcing the WLAN to drop to a slower data rate. In this analysis, we will make the *major* assumption that the APs have been well placed so that all users attempting to work on the WLAN have good signal quality and are able to operate at the maximum nominal data rate provided by the WLAN: 11 Mbps for 802.11b and 54 Mbps for 802.11a.

Data Link Protocol Efficiency   802.11a and 802.11b both use data link layer protocols similar to those used by their wired Ethernet cousins, 10Base-T, 100Base-T, and so on. Wireless Ethernet frames have a typical overhead of 51 bytes (if a short preamble is used) on 1,500-byte frames, plus the ACK/NAK. However, this calculation is complicated by the fact that many of the overhead bits are transmitted at the slowest data rate, not at the maximum data rate. Assuming we have the same mix of short and full-length frames and without going into all the calculations, the efficiency for 802.11b is about 85 percent and the efficiency of 802.11a is about 75 percent.

Media Access Control Protocol Efficiency   The next factor is the efficiency of the media access control protocols. Wireless Ethernet uses a very different media access control protocol from wired Ethernet's CSMA/CD. Chapter 4 discussed the performance characteristics of CSMA/CD: gradual increases in response time delay to about 50 percent of nominal capacity, more rapid increases in delay to about 80 percent of capacity, and immense increases in delays after 80 percent that rendered the network essentially unusable.

Wireless Ethernet uses the PCF controlled-access technique. PCF, like the controlled-access technique used by FDDI, imposes more fixed cost delays initially when traffic is low, because now computers must request permission before they transmit, rather than just making sure there is no traffic and transmitting at will as with CSMA/CD. However, response time delays increase only slowly up to about 85 to 90 percent of nominal capacity. Once this level is reached, they increase rapidly until the network is 100 percent saturated.

These patterns are shown in Figure 8-11. Remember that lower response time delays are best. The CSMA/CD approach used by wired Ethernet works best when there is a low amount of traffic relative to the total capacity, while the PCF approach used by wireless Ethernet works best as total traffic approaches the maximum capacity of the network.

Wireless Ethernet users experience few response time delays as long as the total amount of network traffic remains under 85 to 90 percent of the nominal data rate. This means, for example, that a 802.11b WLAN with a nominal data rate of 11 Mbps can provide an effective total data rate of about 9.6 Mbps, assuming that there is no substantial interference (85% efficiency × 85% capacity × 11 Mbps = 9.6 Mbps). This capacity is shared by all computers on the WLAN, so if we had a low-traffic network with only two active computers on the one 802.11b AP this would mean that, on average, each computer could realistically use about 4.8 Mbps—under perfect operating conditions. As the number of active computers increases, the average capacity drops; see Figure 8-12. Under more normal operating conditions (5.5-Mbps nominal data rate) effective data rates are also lower.

802.11a, with its nominal data of 54 Mbps, has an effective rate of about 34 Mbps under perfect operating conditions within a range of 15 meters from the hub (75% efficiency × 85% capacity × 54 Mbps = 34.4 Mbps). This capacity is shared by all computers on the WLAN, so in a low-traffic network with two active computers on one 802.11a AP this would mean that, on average, each computer could realistically use about 17.2 Mbps. As traffic increases (say 10 active users), the capacity available to each user drops to about 3.4 Mbps on average; see Figure 8-12.

However, if the computers are operating at more than 15 meters from the AP, the effective data rate may be closer to 12Mbps, which dramatically lowers performance; see Figure 8-12.

We could boost the effective data rate by placing four APs in the same area, for example, thus providing four separate channels and assigning the different NICs into dif-

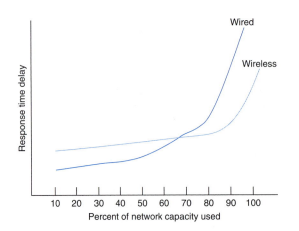

FIGURE 8-11 Performance of wireless versus wired Ethernet LANs.

Technology	Effective Data Rate per User		
	Low Traffic	Moderate Traffic	High Traffic
802.11b under perfect conditions (11 Mbps)	4.8 Mbps	1.9 Mbps	960 Kbps
802.11b under normal conditions (5.5 Mbps)	2.4 Mbps	1 Mbps	480 Kbps
802.11a under perfect conditions (54 Mbps)	17.2 Mbps	6.9 Mbps	3.4 Mbps
802.11a at long range (12 Mbps)	3.8 Mbps	1.5 Mbps	760 Kbps
802.11a under perfect conditions with four APs (54 Mbps)	34.4 Mbps	27.5 Mbps	13.7 Mbps

Assumptions:
1. Most frames are 1500 bytes or larger.
2. No transmission errors occur.
3. Low traffic means 2 active users, moderate traffic means 5 active users, high traffic means 10 active users.

FIGURE 8-12   Effective data rate estimates for wireless Ethernet.

ferent channels. Four APs at a nominal rate of 54 Mbps would then provide an effective data rate of 13.6 Mbps in a high-traffic network.

Costs

802.11b WLAN NICs and APs are modest in cost and prices are dropping quickly. As 802.11a products are just being introduced, the costs are high, but should drop over the next year or two. The cost of a 802.11b NIC is about $100 more than a 10/100Base-T NIC. The cost of an 802.11b AP is only $400 more than the cost of a 10/100Base-T switch. However, the largest cost associated with wired Ethernet LANs using twisted-pair cabling is not the cost of the NICs, hubs, or switches; it is the cost of installing the cables. Installing a cable can cost anywhere from $50 to $400 per cable, depending upon the condition of building in which the cable is to be installed. It is cheapest to install cable during the construction of a new building, and much more expensive to install cable after the fact in an old building.

Thus for new construction, wired LANs are cheaper than their wireless counterparts, but only by a modest amount. For installation in an existing building that lacks cabling, wireless 802.11b LANs may be cheaper than wired LANs.

Recommendations

There is, of course, on other major factor: mobility. Wireless LANs provide the ability for computers and employees to move seamlessly throughout an indoor or outdoor area and to work in locations that wires cannot reach.

Given these trade-offs in costs and effective data rates, and the importance of mobility, there are several best practice recommendations (see Figure 8-13). The differences between 802.11a and 802.11b are not as great as they might at first seem, unless we can assume perfect operating conditions for 802.11a. Given the price differences, and the fact

| Most WLAN networks | 802.11b |
| WLANs with high capacity needs | 802.11a |

FIGURE 8-13 Best practice WLAN recommedations.

that 802.11b technology has a longer track record than 802.11a, our recommendations favor 802.11b, unless there is a critical need for high capacity. However, we do encourage organizations to experiment with 802.11a to see how well it operates in the less-than-perfect environments in the field.

In either case, these data rates are similar to the effective data rates for shared 10Base-T and compare favorably to the 9 Mbps of switched 100Base-T (see Figure 4-17 in Chapter 4). For most networks, the wired switched 10Base-T previously recommended still provides the best trade-off between cost and performance. But 802.11b networks are a very close competitor. In cases where mobility is important or wiring is expensive, 802.11b is the best practice.

Most interesting, perhaps is the relationship between 802.11a and 802.11b. Under perfect operating conditions, 802.11a is clearly better. However, as one moves more than 15 meters away from the AP, the performance of 802.11a falls so that it is very close to that of 802.11b. As 802.11a drops in price and our experience with it grows, it may become more popular and reduce the advantages of wired Ethernet.

Because of this, many organizations today are using WLANs as *overlay networks.* They build the usual switched Ethernet networks as the primary LAN, but install WLANs in addition, so that employees can easily move their laptops in and out of the offices, and to provide connectivity in places not normally wired, such as hallways and lunchrooms so employees can work as they choose.

MANAGEMENT FOCUS *8-3*

WIRELESS MANUFACTURING

Corrugated Supplies Corporation is a small Midwest manufacturer of specialty paper products that has two production facilities in suburban Chicago. Service is critical in the custom paper business, so Corrugated Supplies added a wireless overlay network to improve its manufacturing operations. The backbone network in each building is a collapsed backbone with a gigabit Ethernet routing switch at its heart (see Figure 8-14). Most offices use traditional wired 10/100 switched Ethernet. Each building has three 802.11b access points that are used to provide access in training facilities and on the production lines themselves (to make reconfigurations easy). The access points also enable forklift drivers to access the network from the computers mounted in their cabs so they can more efficiently find and retrieve the materials needed by the production lines.

The two buildings are about 2 blocks apart, which makes traditional backbone wiring impossible. Corrugated investigated leasing traditional MAN circuits such multiple T1 lines to connect to the two buildings, but the costs were about $100,000 for installation and a three-year contract. Instead, they purchased two point-to-point fixed wireless bridges that each provide 11 Mbps for up to 25 miles; they only needed one, but wanted two to provide redundancy in event of problems.

SOURCE: "Thinking outside the Box," *Network Magazine,* June 2001; and "Putting Dreams on Paper," *Cisco Packet Magazine,* Second Quarter, 2001.

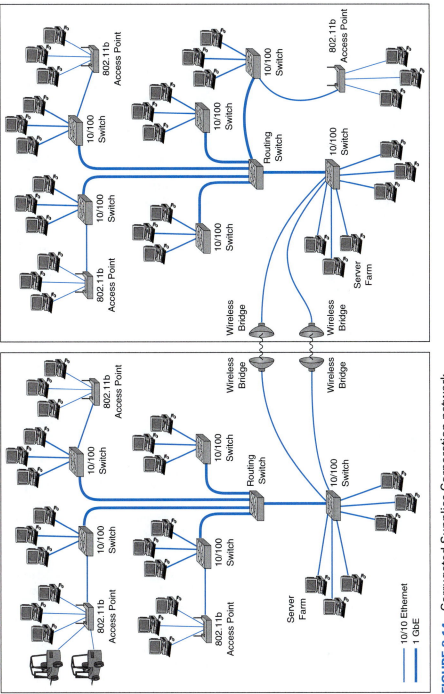

FIGURE 8-14 Corrugated Supplies Corporation network.

SUMMARY

IEEE 802.11b   Wireless Ethernet is a small but growing form of Ethernet that provides data speeds of 1 Mbps to 11 Mbps via radio transmission in the 2.4-GHz frequency range. Wireless Ethernet has a radio transmitter access point that acts like a hub, so it provides a bus-oriented shared multipoint circuit like traditional Ethernet. It uses a similar contention-based media access control approach as traditional Ethernet, but also has the ability to provide more controlled access by permitting stations to reserve time to transmit to prevent collisions.

IEEE 802.11a   Although work on IEEE 802.11a started before work on 802.11b, it has proved more difficult to develop a standard, in part because it operates in the 5-GHz frequency range. The possible data rates are 6 Mbps, 9 Mbps, 12 Mbps, 18 Mbps, 24 Mbps, 36 Mbps, 48 Mbps, and 54 Mbps, although the range is much shorter—50 meters for 6 to 12 Mbps and only 15 meters for 36 to 54 Mbps. 802.11a works in much the same way as 802.11b, except at the physical layer. It uses frequency division multiplexing to create 48 separate channels through the frequency range that when combined provide the total data rates.

Bluetooth   *Bluetooth* is strikingly different from the other WLANs because its goal is to provide networking of data and/or voice devices in a very small area (up to 10 meters). It is designed to replace short-distance cabling between devices such as keyboards, mice, and a telephone handset. Bluetooth provides a basic data rate of 1 Mbps, which can be divided into several separate channels (e.g., three separate voice channels) that operate in the same 2.4-GHz bandwidth as 802.11b, but initial tests suggest that there is little interference between Bluetooth and 802.11b LANs, provided they are not within 2 meters of each other.

Best Practice WLAN Design   If mobility is important, 802.11b appears to be the best choice. Given the trade-offs in costs and effective data rates, the best LAN for most networks is still the switched 10Base-T with category 5/5e cables from Chapter 4. However, 802.11b comes close and as 802.11a and 802.11g become more mature, they will provide serious competition.

KEY TERMS

access point (AP)
analog transmission
bandwidth
Barker sequence
Bluetooth
bus topology
collision
collision avoidance (CA)
Complementary Code
    Keying (CCK)
contention
CSMA/CA
data rate
differential binary phase
    shift keying (DBPSK)
differential quadrature
    phase shift keying
    (DQPSK)
direct-sequence spread-
    spectrum (DSSS)

distributed coordination
    function (DCF)
frequency
frequency-hopping
    spread-spectrum
    (FHSS)
frequency modulation
    (FM)
frequency shift keying
    (FSK)
guardband
half duplex
hertz (Hz)
hidden node problem
IEEE 802.11a
IEEE 802.11b
logical carrier sense
    method
logical topology
long preamble

modulate
multipoint circuit
orthogonal frequency
    division
    multiplexing
    (OFDM)
overlay network
PCMCIA slot
physical carrier sense
    method
Physical Layer
    Convergence
    Protocol (PLCP)
physical topology
piconet
point coordination func-
    tion (PCF)
preamble
quadrature amplitude
    modulation (QAM)

roaming
shared circuit
shared Ethernet
short preamble
symbol rate
virtual carrier sense
    method
Wi-Fi
wireless Ethernet
wireless LAN
    (WLAN)
Wireless Personal
    Area Network
    (WPAN)
802.11a
802.11b
802.11g

QUESTIONS

1. Explain how the 802.11b differs from 802.11a.
2. What data rates are provided by 802.11b?
3. How do direct-sequence spread-spectrum (DSSS) WLANs differ from frequency-hopping spread-spectrum (FHSS) WLANs?
4. How does 802.11b differ from 802.3 in terms of topology, media access control, and error control?
5. How do the NIC and AP work together to transmit messages in an 802.11b WLAN?
6. How does roaming work?
7. Explain how CSMA/CA DCF works.
8. Explain how CSMA/CA PCF works.
9. Explain the different parts of an 802.11b message.
10. In what ways is an 802.11b message similar to that of 802.3ac?
11. In what ways is an 802.11a message similar to that of 802.3ac?
12. How does DBPSK differ from PSK?
13. How does DBPSK differ from DQPSK?
14. What is a guardband and why does 802.11b need it?
15. How does 802.11b transmit messages through the physical layer at 1 Mbps? 2 Mbps?
16. How does 802.11b transmit messages through the physical layer at 5.5 Mbps? 11 Mbps?
17. How does 802.11a transmit messages through the physical layer?
18. How does 802.11g differ from 802.11b and 802.11a?
19. How does a WPAN differ from a WLAN?
20. Explain the topology, media access control, and error control of Bluetooth.
21. Explain the different parts of a Bluetooth frame.
22. How does Bluetooth transmit data in the physical layer?
23. What are the best practice recommendations for WLAN design?
24. Some people believe Bluetooth is a revolution, while others see it as a simple replacement for cables among devices. What do you think? Is Bluetooth a revolution?
25. Given the dramatic changes ahead in WLANs (e.g., IEEE 802.11a/b/g), would you install a WLAN today? Explain.
26. If IEEE 802.11a is widely available in the next few years, what are the implications for networks of the future? Will 10Base-T still be around, or will we eliminate wired offices?
27. Many of the wired and wireless LANs share the same or almost similar components (e.g., error control). Why?
28. What do you think are the future prospects for 802.11b, 802.11a, and 802.11g? Why?

EXERCISES

8-1. Survey the WLANs used in your organization. Are they 802.11b, 802.11a, Bluetooth, or other technology?
8-2. You have been hired by a small company to install a simple WLAN for their 18 Windows computers. Develop a simple WLAN and determine the total cost; i.e., select AP, and NICs and price them.
8-3. Investigate the current state of wireless technologies moving through the IEEE standards process.

MINI-CASES

I. General Hospital

General Hospital has five floors, each about 30,000 square feet in size, for a total of about 150,000 square feet. They want to provide a wireless overlay network in addition to their switched 10Base-T. They have a bid for 802.11b access points at a cost of $600 each and a bid for 802.11a access points at a cost of $1,000 each. They

MINI-CASES

expect to need 200 NICs. 802.11b NICs cost about $100 each, and 802.11a NICs cost about $150 each. What would you recommend?

II. Central University

Central University wants to add a wireless overlay network to one 20,000-square-foot floor in its business school. They have a bid for 802.11b access points at a cost of $600 each and a bid for 802.11a access points at a cost of $1,000 each. Students will buy their own NICs, so they expect to need only about 50 NICs. 802.11b NICs cost about $100 each, and 802.11a NICs cost about $150 each. What would you recommend?

CHAPTER 9

NETWORK DESIGN

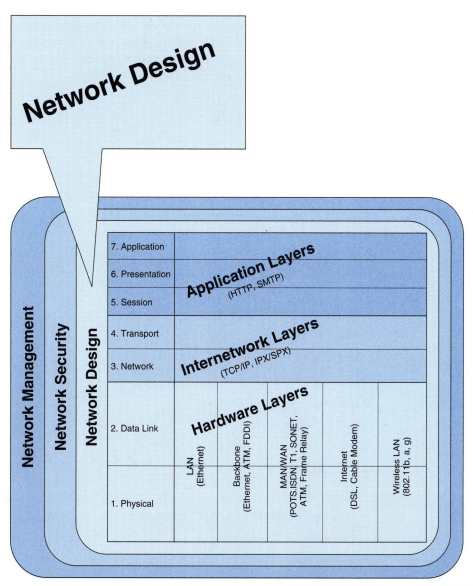

NETWORK MANAGERS perform two key tasks: (1) designing new networks and network upgrades and (2) managing the day-to-day operation of existing networks. This chapter examines network design. Network design is an interactive process in which the designer examines users' needs, develops an initial set of technology designs, assesses their cost, and then revisits the needs analysis until the final network design emerges.

OBJECTIVES

- Be familiar with the overall process of designing and implementing a network
- Be familiar with techniques for developing a logical network design
- Be familiar with techniques for developing a physical network design
- Be familiar with network design principles

CHAPTER OUTLINE

INTRODUCTION

The Traditional Network Design Process

The Building-Block Network Design Process

NEEDS ANALYSIS

Geographic Scope

Application Systems

Network Users

Categorizing Network Needs

Deliverables

TECHNOLOGY DESIGN

Designing Clients and Servers

Designing Circuits and Devices

Network Design Tools

Deliverables

COST ASSESSMENT

Request for Proposal

Selling the Proposal to Management

Deliverables

DESIGNING FOR NETWORK PERFORMANCE

Managed Networks

INTRODUCTION

Most organizations today have networks, which means that most network design projects are the design of upgrades or extensions to existing networks, rather than the construction of entirely new networks. Even the network for an entirely new building is likely to be integrated with the organization's existing backbone network (BN) or WAN, so even new projects can be seen as extensions of existing networks. Nonetheless, network design is very challenging.

The Traditional Network Design Process

The *traditional network design process* follows a very structured systems analysis and design process similar to that used to build application systems. First, the network analyst meets with users to identify user needs and the application systems planned for the network. Second, the analyst develops a precise estimate of the amount of data that each user will send and receive and uses this to estimate the total amount of traffic on each part of the network. Third, the circuits needed to support this traffic plus a modest increase in traffic are designed and cost estimates are obtained from vendors. Finally, 1 or 2 years later, the network is built and implemented.

This traditional process, although expensive and time consuming, works well for static or slowly evolving networks. Unfortunately, networking today is significantly different from what it was when the traditional process was developed. Three forces are making the traditional design process less appropriate for many of today's networks.

First, the underlying technology of the client and server computers, networking devices, and the circuits themselves is changing very rapidly. In the early 1990s, mainframes dominated networks, the typical client computer was an 8-MHz 386 with 1 megabyte (MB) of random access memory (RAM) and 40 MB of hard disk space, and a typical circuit was a 9,600-bps mainframe connection or an amazingly fast 1-Mbps LAN. Today, client computers and servers are significantly more powerful, and circuit speeds of 100 Mbps and 1 Gbps are common. We now have more processing capability and network capacity than ever before; both are no longer scarce commodities that we need to manage carefully.

Second, the growth in network traffic is immense. The challenge is not in estimating today's user demand but in estimating its rate of growth. In the early 1990s, e-mail and the Web were novelties primarily used by university professors and scientists. In the past, network demand essentially was driven by predictable business systems such as order processing. Today, much network demand is driven by less predictable user behavior, such as e-mail and Web searches. Many experts expect the rapid increase in network demand to continue, especially as video, voice, and multimedia applications become commonplace on networks. At a 10 percent growth rate, user demand on a given network will increase by one third in 3

MANAGEMENT FOCUS *9 - 1*

THE END OF ARCHITECTURE

All good things must end. After a century of predictability, the telephone network as we know it is fading into oblivion. Lulled to sleep by relatively predictable voice and data traffic forecasts, interexchange carriers (IXCs) set a timetable for a gradual replacement of existing networks with faster all-ATM, (asynchronous transfer mode) network architectures. Their leisurely replacement timetable ran smack into a brick wall.

Huge increases in data traffic, primarily due to the booming growth of the Internet, have caused IXCs to throw out the nicely planned replacements of their core telephone networks. Rather than investing in all-ATM architectures whose main benefit is the ability to handle voice, data, and video on the same circuits, IXCs are building "overlay networks." Overlay networks coexist with the primary core voice networks and support separate services

in an attempt to keep up with the demand. One set of overlay networks, for example, is designed to support Internet traffic, another carries frame relay wide area network traffic, another carries switched multimegabit data services, and so on.

The core telephone network is gradually changing from a centrally designed and managed hierarchical network to a decentralized set of networks, much the same changes that have been seen in the office environment as decentralized client–server local area networks have replaced the centralized host-based mainframe systems. The key challenges now facing IXCs are how to manage this huge—and rapidly growing—collection of distinct networks and how to route traffic from one network to another.

SOURCE: "The End of Architecture," *tele.com,* September 1996.

---

years. At 20 percent, it will increase by about 75 percent in 3 years. At 30 percent, it will double in less than 3 years. A minor mistake in estimating the growth rate can lead to major problems. With such rapid growth, it is no longer possible to accurately predict network needs for most networks. In the past, it was not uncommon for networks to be designed to last for 5 to 10 years. Today, most network designers use a 3-year planning horizon.

Finally, the balance of costs have changed dramatically over the past 10 years. In the early 1990s, the most expensive item in any network was the hardware (circuits, devices, and servers). Today, the most expensive part of the network is the staff members who design, operate, and maintain it. As the costs have shifted, the emphasis in network design in no longer on minimizing hardware cost (although it is important); the emphasis today is on designing networks to reduce the staff time needed to operate them.

The traditional process minimizes the equipment cost by tailoring the equipment to a careful assessment of needs but often results in a mismash of different devices with different capabilities. Two resulting problems are that staff members need to learn to operate and maintain many different devices and that it often takes longer to perform network management activities because each device may use slightly different software.

Today, the cost of staff time is far more expensive than the cost of equipment. Thus, the traditional process can lead to a false economy—save money now in equipment costs but pay much more over the long term in staff costs.

The Building-Block Network Design Process

Some organizations still use the traditional process to network design, particularly for those applications for which hardware or network circuits are unusually expensive (e.g.,

WANs that cover long distances through many different countries). However, many other organizations now use a simpler approach to network design that we call the *building-block process.* The key concept in the building-block process is that networks that use a few standard components throughout the network are cheaper in the long run than networks that use a variety of different components on different parts of the network.

Rather than attempting to accurately predict user traffic on the network and build networks to meet those demands, the building-block process instead starts with a few standard components and uses them over and over again, even if they provide more capacity than is needed. The goal is simplicity of design. This strategy is sometimes called "narrow and deep" because a very narrow range of technologies and devices are used over and over again (very deeply throughout the organization). The result is a simpler design process and a more easily managed network built with a smaller range of components.

In this chapter, we focus on the building-block process to network design. The basic design process involves three steps that are performed repeatedly: needs analysis, technology design, and cost assessment (Figure 9-1). This process begins with *needs analysis,* during which the designer attempts to understand the fundamental current and future network needs of the various users, departments, and applications. This is likely to be an educated guess at best. Users and applications are classified as typical or high volume. Specific technology needs are identified (e.g., the ability to dial in with current modem technologies).

The next step, *technology design,* examines the available technologies and assesses which options will meet users' needs. The designer makes some estimates about the network needs of each category of user and circuit in terms of current technology (e.g., 10Base-T, 100Base-T, 1000Base-T) and matches needs to technologies. Because the basic

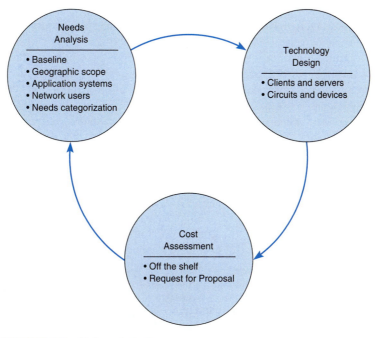

FIGURE 9-1 Network design.

MANAGEMENT FOCUS *9-2*

WHY NETWORK PROJECTS FAIL

CIMI Corporation surveyed almost 300 organizations about the key success factors in network design. These 300 organizations reported on 1,370 network design projects. Of these, 475 (35%) were considered complete successes and 125 (9%) were considered complete failures. The rest (56%) were only partial successes.

Network managers reported that the key problems leading to failure in the 125 failed projects were as follows (multiple answers were permitted):

- Needs analysis problems
  - Had requirements that were incomplete or inaccurate: 64 percent
  - Encountered a significant change in business requirements as the network was installed: 30 percent

- Technology design problems
  - Bought the wrong equipment or services—often the right technology but the wrong products or features: 99 percent
  - Encountered vendor misrepresentation—the products and/or services did not work as promised: 38 percent
- Overall problems with the design process
  - Lacked network design skills internally and did not use external consultants or systems integrators: 34 percent
  - Used external network consultants or systems integrators who bungled the project: 32 Percent

SOURCE: "Why Projects Fail," *Network World,* July 7, 1997.

network design is general, it can easily be changed as needs and technologies change. The difficulty, of course, lies in predicting user demand so one can define the technologies needed. Most organizations solve this by building more capacity than they expect to need and by designing networks that can easily grow and then closely monitoring growth so they expand the network ahead of the growth pattern.

In the third step, cost assessment, the relative costs of the technologies are considered. The process then cycles back to the needs analysis, which is refined using the technology and cost information to produce a new assessment of users' needs. This in turn triggers changes in the technology design and cost assessment and so on. By cycling through these three processes, the network design settles on the final network design (Figure 9-2).

NEEDS ANALYSIS

The goal of the needs analysis is to understand why the network is being built and what users and applications it will support. In many cases, the network is being designed to improve poor performance or enable new applications to be used. In other cases, the network is upgraded to replace unreliable or aging equipment or to standardize equipment so that only one type of equipment, one protocol (e.g., TCP/IP, Ethernet), or one vendor's equipment is used everywhere in the network.

Often, the goals in network design are slightly different between LANs and BNs on the one hand and MANs and WANs on the other. In the LAN and BN environment, the organization owns and operates the equipment and the circuits. Once they are paid for,

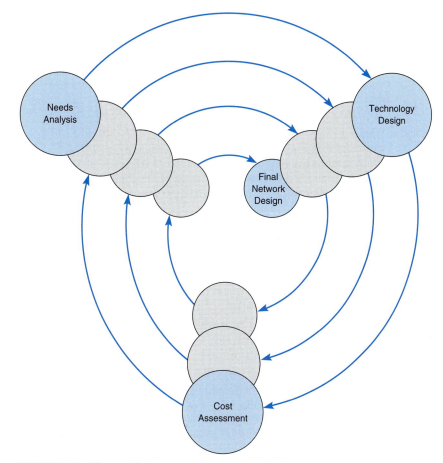

FIGURE 9-2 The cyclical nature of network design.

there are no additional charges for usage. However, if major changes must be made, the organization will need to spend additional funds. In this case, most network designers tend to err on the side of building too big a network—that is, building in more capacity than they expect to need.

In contrast, in most MANs and WANs, the organization leases circuits from a common carrier and pays for them on monthly or per-use basis. Understanding capacity becomes more important in this situation because additional capacity comes at a noticeable cost. In this case, most network designers tend to err on the side of building too small a network, because they can lease additional capacity if they need it—but it is much more difficult to cancel a long-term contract for capacity they are not using.

Much of the needs analysis may already have been done, because most network design projects today are network upgrades rather than the design of entirely new networks. In this case, there is already a fairly good understanding of the existing traffic in the network and, most important, of the rate of growth of network traffic. It is important to gain an understanding of the current operations (application systems and messages). This step provides a *baseline* against which future design requirements can be gauged. It should provide a clear picture of the present sequence of operations, processing times, work volumes, current communication network (if one exists), existing costs, and user/management needs. Whether the network is a new network or a network upgrade, the primary objective of this stage is to define (1) the geographic scope of the network and (2) the users and applications that will use it.

The goal of the needs analysis step is to produce a *logical network design,* which is a statement of the network elements needed to meet the needs of the organization. The logical design does not specify technologies or products to be used (although any specific requirements are noted). Instead, it focuses on the fundamental functionality needed, such as a high-speed access network, which in the technology design stage will be translated into specific technologies (e.g., switched 100Base-T).

Geographic Scope

The first step in needs analysis is to break the network into three conceptual parts on the basis of their geographic and logical scope: the access layer, the distribution layer, and the core layer, as first discussed in Chapter 3.[1] The *access layer* is the technology that is closest to the user—the user's first contact with the network—and is often a LAN or a dial-up connection over a MAN. The *distribution layer* is the next part of the network that connects the access layer to the rest of the network, such as the BN(s) in a specific building. The *core layer* is the innermost part of the network, the part that connects the different distribution-layer networks to each other, such as the primary BN on a campus or a set of MAN or WAN circuits connecting different offices together. As the name suggests, the core layer is usually the busiest, most important part of the network. Not all layers are present in all networks; small networks, for example, may not have a distribution layer, because their core may the BN that directly connects the parts of the access layer together.

Within each of these parts of the network, the network designer must identify some basic technical constraints. For example, if the access layer is a MAN, in that the users need to connect to the network over the public telephone network, this provides some constraints on the technologies to be used; one could not use 100Base-T Ethernet, for example. Likewise, if the access layer is a LAN, it would be silly to consider using T1 circuits.

Sometimes, the current network infrastructure also imposes constraints. For example, if we are adding a new building to an existing office complex that used 100Base-T in the access-layer LANs, then we will probably choose to use 100Base-T for the access layer in the new building. Likewise, if we are running a dial-up ISP, we will probably need to support the V.90 and V.92 modems of our customers. All such constraints are noted.

It is easiest to start with the highest level, so most designers begin by drawing a network diagram for any WANs with international or countrywide locations that must be connected. A diagram that shows the logical network going between the locations is sufficient. Details such as the type of circuit and other considerations will be added later. Next, the individual locations connected to the WAN are drawn, usually in a series of separate diagrams, but for a simple network, one diagram may be sufficient.

---

[1] It is important to understand that these three layers refer to geographic parts of the network, not the five conceptal layers in the network model, such as application layer, transport layer, and so on.

At this point, the designers gather general information and characteristics of the environment in which the network must operate. For example, they determine whether there are any legal requirements, such as local, state/provincial, federal, or international laws, regulations, or building codes, that might affect the network.

Figure 9-3 shows an the initial drawing of a network design for an organization with offices in four areas connected to the core network, which is a WAN. The Toronto location, for example has a distribution layer (a BN) connecting three distinct access-layer LANs, which could be three distinct LANs in the same office building. Chicago has a similar structure, with the addition of a fourth access part that connects to the Internet; that is, the organization has only one Internet connection, so all Internet traffic must be routed through the core network to the Chicago location. The Atlantic Canada network section has two distinct access layer parts: one is a LAN and one access layer is a MAN (e.g., dial-up). The New York network section is more complex, having its own core network component (a BN connected into the core WAN), which in turn supports three distribution layer BNs. Each of these support several access-layer LANs.

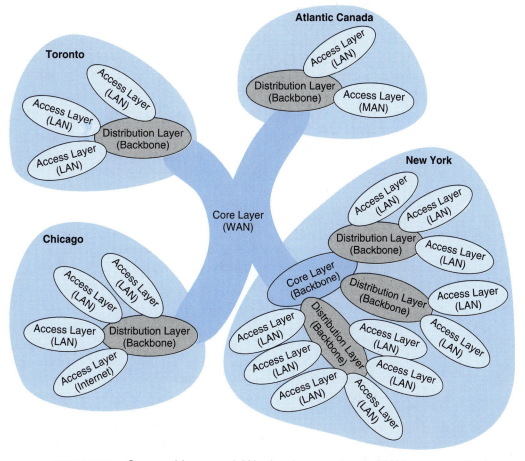

FIGURE 9-3   Geographic scope. LAN = local area network; MAN = metropolitan area network; WAN = wide area network.

Application Systems

Once the basic geographic scope is identified, the designers must review the list of applications that will use the network and identify the location of each. This information should be added to the emerging network diagrams. This process is called baselining. Next, those applications that are expected to use the network in the future are added.

In many cases, the applications will be relatively well defined. Specific internal applications (e.g., payroll) and external applications (e.g., Web servers) may already be part of the "old" network. However, it is important to review the organization's long-range and short-range plans concerning changes in company goals, strategic plans, development plans for new products or services, projections of sales, research and development projects, major capital expenditures, possible changes in product mix, new offices that must be served by the communications network, security issues, and future commitments to technology. For example, a major expansion in the number of offices or a major electronic commerce initiative will have a significant impact on network requirements.

It also is helpful to identify the hardware and software requirements of each application that will use the network and, if possible, the protocol each application uses (e.g., HTTP over TCP/IP, Windows file access to a Novell file server over SPX/IPX). This knowledge helps now and will be particularly useful later when developing technological solutions. For example, if the main financial application payroll runs on an IBM maniframe, the network may need to support SNA traffic and provide a gateway to translate it into more standard TCP/IP protocols.

Network Users

In the past, application systems accounted for the majority of network traffic. Today, much network traffic is produced by the discretionary use of the Internet. Applications such as e-mail and the Web are generating significant traffic, so the network manager is no longer in total control of the network traffic generated on his or her networks. This is likely to continue in the future as network-hungry applications such as desktop videoconferencing become more common. Therefore, in addition to understanding the applications, you must also assess the number and type of users that will generate and receive network traffic and identify their location on the emerging network diagram.

Categorizing Network Needs

At this point, the network has been designed in terms of geographic scope, application systems, and users. The next step is to assess the relative amount of traffic generated in each part of the network. With the traditional design approach, this involves considerable detailed analysis. With the building-block approach, the goal is provide some rough assessment of the relative magnitude of network needs. Each application system is assessed in general terms to determine the amount of network traffic it can be expected to generate today and in the future, compared with other applications. Likewise, each user is categorized as either a typical user or a high-traffic user. These assessments will be refined in the next stage of the design process.

This assessment can be problematic, but the goal is some relative understanding of the network needs. Some simple rules of thumb can help. For example, applications that require large amounts of multimedia data or those that load executables over the network are likely to be high-traffic applications. Applications that are time sensitive or need constant updates (e.g., financial information systems, order processing) are likely to be high-traffic applications.

Once the network requirements have been identified, they also should be organized into *mandatory requirements, desirable requirements,* and *wish-list requirements.* This information enables the development of a minimum level of mandatory requirements and a negotiable list of desirable requirements that are dependent on cost and availability. For example, desktop videoconferencing may be a wish-list item, but it will be omitted if it increases the cost of the network beyond what is desired.

At this point, the local facility network diagrams are prepared. For really large network, there may be several levels. For example, the designer of the network in Figure 9-3 might choose to draw another set of diagrams, one each for Toronto, Chicago, Atlantic Canada, and New York. Conversely, the designer might just add more detail to Figure 9-3 and develop separate, more detailed, diagrams for New York. The choice is up to the designer, provided the diagrams and supporting text clearly explain the network's needs.

Deliverables

The key deliverable for the needs assessments stage are a set of logical network diagrams, showing the applications, circuits, clients, and servers in the proposed network, each categorized as either typical or high traffic. The logical diagram is the conceptual plan for the network and does not consider the specific physical elements (e.g., routers, switches, circuits) that will be used to implement the network.

Figure 9-4 shows the results of a needs assessment for one of the New York parts of the network from Figure 9-3. This figure shows the distribution and access parts in the building with the series of six access LANs connected by one distribution BN, which is in turn connected to a campus-area core BN. One of the six LANs is highlighted as a high-traffic LAN, whereas the others are typical. Three mandatory applications are identified that will be used by all network users: e-mail, Web, and file sharing. One wish-list requirement (desktop video conferencing) is also identified for a portion of the network.

TECHNOLOGY DESIGN

Once the needs have been defined in the logical network design, the next step is to develop a *physical network design* (or set of possible designs). The physical network design starts with the client and server computers needed to support the users and applications. If the network is a new network, new computers will need to be purchased. If the network is an existing network, the servers may needed to be upgraded to the newest technology. Once these are designed, then the circuits and devices connecting them are designed.

Designing Clients and Servers

The idea behind the building-block approach is to specify the computers needed in terms of some standard units. Typical users are allocated the base-level client computers, as are

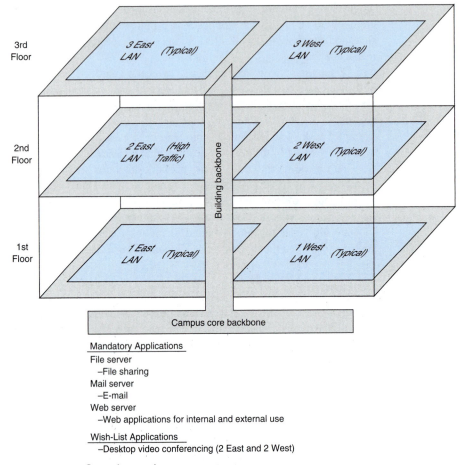

Mandatory Applications
File server
 –File sharing
Mail server
 –E-mail
Web server
 –Web applications for internal and external use

Wish-List Applications
 –Desktop video conferencing (2 East and 2 West)

FIGURE 9-4 Sample needs assessment.

servers supporting typical applications. Users and servers for applications needing more powerful computers are assigned some advanced computer. As the specifications for computers rapidly improve and costs drop (usually every 4 months), today's typical user may receive the type of computer originally intended for the advanced user when the network is actually implemented, and the advanced users may end up with a computer not available when the network was designed.

Designing Circuits and Devices

The same is true for network circuits and devices (e.g., hubs, routers, switches). There are two interrelated decisions in designing network circuits and devices: the fundamental technology and protocols (e.g., Ethernet, ATM, TCP/IP), and the capacity of each circuit (e.g., 10 Mbps, 100 Mbps, 1,000 Mbps). These are interrelated, because each technology offers different circuit capacities.

Designing the circuit capacity means *capacity planning,* estimating the size and type of the standard and advanced network circuits for each type of network (LAN, BN, WAN). For example, should the standard LAN circuit be 10Base-T, or 10/100 switched Ethernet? Likewise, should the standard BN circuit be 100Base-T, 1000Base-T, or ATM OC-3?

This requires some assessment of the current and future *circuit loading* (the amount of data transmitted on a circuit). This analysis can focus on either the *average* circuit traffic or the *peak* circuit traffic. For example, in an online banking network, traffic volume peaks usually are in the midmorning (bank opening) and just prior to closing. Airline and rental car reservations network designers look for peak message volumes before and during holidays or other vacation periods, whereas telephone companies normally have their highest peak volumes on Mother's Day. Designing for peak circuit traffic is the ideal.

The designer usually starts with the total characters transmitted per day on each circuit or, if possible, the maximum number of characters transmitted per 2-second interval if peaks must be met. You can calculate message volumes by counting messages in a current network and applying some estimated growth rate. If an existing network is in place, network monitors/analyzers (see Chapter 11) may be able to provide an actual circuit character count of the volume transmitted per minute or per day.

A good rule of thumb is that 80 percent of this circuit-loading information is easy to gather. The last 20 percent needed for very precise estimates is extremely difficult and expensive to find. However, precision usually is not a major concern because of the stairstep nature of communication circuits and the need to project future needs. For example, the difference between 10Base-T and 100Base-T is quite large, and assessing which level is needed for typical traffic does not require a lot of precision. Forecasts are inherently less precise than understanding current network traffic. The *turnpike effect* results when the network is used to a greater extent than was anticipated because it is available, is very efficient, and provides new services. The annual growth factor for network use may vary from 5 to 50 percent and, in some cases, may exceed 100 percent for high-growth organizations.

Although no organization wants to overbuild its network and pay for more capacity than it needs, in most cases, upgrading a network costs 50 to 80 percent more than building it right the first time. Few organizations complain about having too much network capacity, but being under capacity can cause significant problems. Given the rapid growth in network demand and the difficulty of accurately predicting it, most organizations intentionally overbuild (build more capacity into their network than they plan to use), and most end up using this supposedly unneeded capacity within 3 years.

Network Design Tools

Network modeling and design tools can perform a number of functions to help in the technology design process. With most tools, the first step is to enter a diagram or model of the existing network or proposed network design. Some modeling tools require the user to create the network diagram from scratch. That is, the user must enter all of the network components by hand, placing each server, client computer, and circuit on the diagram and defining what each is (e.g., 10Base-T, frame relay circuit with a 1-Mbps committed information rate).

Other tools can "discover" the existing network; that is, once installed on the network, they will explore the network to draw a network diagram. In this case, the user provides some starting point, and the modeling software explores the network and automatically draws the diagram itself. Once the diagram is complete, the user can then change it to reflect the new network design. Obviously, a tool that can perform network discovery by itself is most helpful when the network being designed is an upgrade to an existing network and when the network is very complex.

Once the diagram is complete, the next step is to add information about the expected network traffic and see if the network can support the level of traffic that is expected. *Simulation* is used to model the behavior of the communication network. Simulation is a mathematical technique in which the network comes to life and behaves as it would under real conditions: Applications and users generate and respond to messages, the simulator tracks the number of packets in the network and the delays encountered at each point in the network.

Simulation models may be tailored to the user's needs by entering parameter values specific to the network at hand (e.g., this computer will generate an average of three 100-byte packets per minute). Alternatively, the user may prefer to rely primarily on the set of average values provided by the network.

Once the simulation is complete, the user can examine the results to see the estimated response times and throughput. It is important to note that these network design tools provide only estimates, which may vary from the actual results. At this point, the user can change the network design, in an attempt to eliminate bottlenecks, and rerun the simulation. Good modeling tools not only produce simulation results but also highlight potential trouble spots (e.g., servers, circuits, or devices that experienced long response times). The very best tools offer suggestions on how to overcome the problems that the simulation identified (e.g., network segmentation, increasing from T1 to T3).

Deliverables

The key deliverable is a set of one or more physical network designs. Most designers like to prepare several physical designs so they can trade off technical benefits (e.g.,

MANAGEMENT FOCUS *9-3*

MAKING PREDICTIONS AT MTV

MTV Networks (MTVN) creates innovative programming for MTV, VH1, Nickelodeon, Nick at Night, and TV Land, as well as other networks. MTVN operates more than 80 offices worldwide, in the United States, Canada, Latin America, Australia, Europe, and Asia. Because of its reliance on an extensive wide area network (WAN), predicting network performance and designing the WAN to support peak data flows was very important.

MTVN first used CACI's Predictor to model its current WAN. It then captured network usage data from a set of test users for several new network-intensive applications

soon to be used throughout MTVN's network. It added this information into the model developed by Predictor and performed a series of what-if analyses to see the effect of widespread use of these applications on overall network performance. In this way, MTV can anticipate the effects of new applications and upgrade its networks, before users begin using the new application systems and encountering problems.

SOURCE: "What's My Line," *Communications News*, September 1999.

performance) against cost. In most cases, the critical part is the design of the network circuits and devices. In the case of a new network designed from scratch, it is also important to define the client computers with care, because these will form a large portion of the total cost of the network. Usually, however, the network will replace an existing network, and only a few of the client computers in the existing network will be upgraded.

Figure 9-5 shows a physical network design for the simple network in Figure 9-4. In this case, a switched 10/100Base-T collapsed backbone is used in the distribution layer, and switched 10Base-T Ethernet has been chosen as the standard network for typical users in the access layer. High-traffic users (2 East) will used switched 10/100Base-T. All LAN cabling will be category 5 cable so that all users can easily move to 100 Mbps in the future. The building backbone will be connected directly into the campus backbone using a router. The building backbone will use fiber-optic cable to enable the possible future addition of desktop videoconferencing.

COST ASSESSMENT

The purpose of this step is to assess the costs of various physical network design alternatives produced in the previous step. The main items are the costs of software, hardware, and circuits. These three factors are all interconnected and must be considered

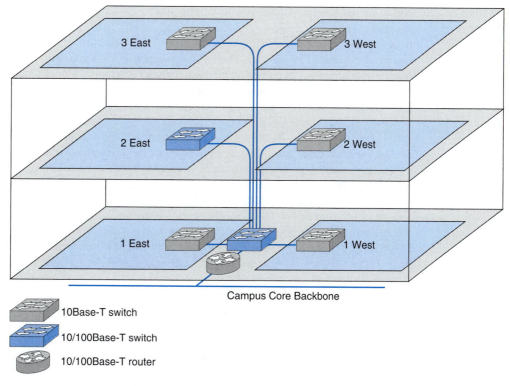

FIGURE 9-5   Physical network design.

along with the performance and reliability required. All factors are interrelated with regard to cost.

Estimating the cost of a network is quite complex because many factors are not immediately obvious. Some of the costs that must be considered are

- Circuit costs, including costs of circuits provided by common carriers or the cost of purchasing and installing your own cable
- Internetworking devices such as switches and routers
- Hardware costs, including server computers, NICs, hubs, memory, printers, uninterruptible power supplies, and backup tape drives
- Software costs for network operating system, application software, and middleware
- Network management costs, including special hardware, software, and training needed to develop a network management system for ongoing redesign, monitoring, and diagnosing of problems
- Test and maintenance costs for special monitoring equipment and software, plus the cost of onsite spare parts
- Costs to operate the network

Request for Proposal

Although some network components can be purchased off the shelf, most organizations develop a *request for proposal (RFP)* before making large network purchases. RFPs specify what equipment, software, and services are desired and ask vendors to provide their best prices. Some RFPs are very specific about what items are to be provided in what time frame. In other cases, items are defined as mandatory, important, or desirable, or several scenarios are provided and the vendor is asked to propose the best solution. In a few cases, RFPs specify generally what is required and the vendors are asked to propose their own network designs. Figure 9-6 provides a summary of the key parts of an RFP.

Once the vendors have submitted their proposals, the organization evaluates them against specified criteria and selects the winner(s). Depending on the scope and complexity of the network, it is sometimes necessary to redesign the network on the basis of the information in the vendors' proposals.

One of the key decisions in the RFP process is the scope of the RFP. Will you use one vendor or several vendors for all hardware, software, and services? Multivendor environments tend to provide better performance because it is unlikely that one vendor makes the best hardware, software, and services in all categories. Multivendor networks also tend to be less expensive because it is unlikely that one vendor will always have the cheapest hardware, software, and services in all product categories.

Multivendor environments can be more difficult to manage, however. If equipment is not working properly and it is provided by two different vendors, each can blame the other for the problem. In contrast, a single vendor is solely responsible for everything.

Selling the Proposal to Management

One of the main problems in network design is obtaining the support of senior management. To management, the network is simply a cost center, something on which the organization

Information in a Typical Request for Proposal
- Background information
  - Organizational profile
  - Overview of current network
  - Overview of new network
  - Goals of new network
- Network requirements
  - Choice sets of possible network designs (hardware, software, circuits)
  - Mandatory, desirable, and wish-list items
  - Security and control requirements
  - Response-time requirements
  - Guidelines for proposing new network designs
- Service requirements
  - Implementation time plan
  - Training courses and materials
  - Support services (e.g., spare parts on site)
  - Reliability and performance guarantees
- Bidding process
  - Time schedule for the bidding process
  - Ground rules
  - Bid evaluation criteria
  - Availability of additional information
- Information required from vendor
  - Vendor corporate profile
  - Experience with similar networks
  - Hardware and software benchmarks
  - Reference list

FIGURE 9-6 Request for proposal.

is spending a lot of money with little apparent change. The network keeps on running just as it did the year before.

The key to gaining the acceptance of senior management lies in speaking management's language. It is pointless to talk about upgrades from 10 Mbps to 100 Mbps on the backbone, because this terminology is meaningless from a business perspective. A more compelling argument is to discuss the growth in network use. For example, a simple graph that shows network usage growing at 25 percent per year, compared with network budget growing at 10 percent per year, presents a powerful illustration that the network costs are well managed, not out of control.

Likewise, a focus on network reliability is an easily understandable issue. For example, if the network supports a mission-critical system such as order processing or moving point-of-sale data from retail stores to corporate offices, it is clear from a business perspective that the network must be available and performing properly, or the organization will lose revenue.

Deliverables

There are three key deliverables for this step. The first is an RFP that goes to potential vendors. The second deliverable, after the vendor has been selected, is the revised physical network diagram (e.g., Figure 9-5) with the technology design complete. Exact products and costs are specified at this point (e.g., a layer-3 switch with four 16-port 10Base-T modules). The third deliverable is the business case that provides support for the network design, expressed in business objectives.

DESIGNING FOR NETWORK PERFORMANCE

At the end of the previous chapters we have discussed the best practice design for LANs, backbones, MANs, WANs, and WLANs and examined how different technologies and services offered different effective data rates at different costs. In the backbone and MAN/WAN chapters we also examined different topologies and contrasted the advantages and disadvantages of each. So at this point, you should have a good understanding of the best choices for technologies and services and how to put them together into a good network design. In this section, we examine several higher-level concepts used to design the network for the best performance.

Managed Networks

The single most important element that contributes to the performance of a network is a *managed network* that uses *managed devices*. Managed devices are standard devices, such as switches and routers, that have small onboard computers to monitor traffic flows through the device as well as the status of the device and other devices connected to it. Managed devices perform their functions (e.g., routing, switching) and also record data on the messages they process. These data can be sent to the network manager's computer when the device receives a special control message requesting the data, or it can send an *alarm* message to the network manager's computer if the device detects a critical situation such as a failing device or a huge increase in traffic.

In this way, network problems can be detected and reported by the devices themselves before problems become serious. In the case of the failing network card, a managed device could record the increased number of retransmissions required to successfully transmit messages and inform the network management software of the problem. A managed hub or switch might even be able to detect the faulty transmissions from a failing network card, disable the incoming circuit so that the card could not send any more messages, and issue an alarm to the network manager. In either case, finding and fixing problems is much simpler, requiring minutes not hours.

Network Management Software
A managed network requires both hardware and software: hardware to monitor, collect, and transmit traffic reports and problem alerts, and network management software to store, organize, and analyze these reports and alerts. There are three fundamentally different types of network management software.

Device management software (sometimes called point management software) is designed to provide information about the specific devices on a network. It enables the net-

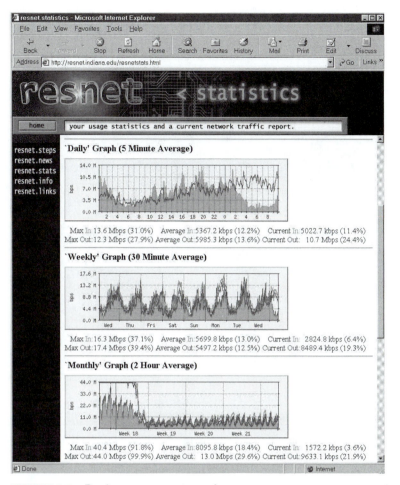

FIGURE 9-7   Device management software.

work manager to monitor important devices such as servers, routers, and gateways, and typically report configuration information, traffic volumes, and error conditions for each device. Figure 9-7 shows some sample displays from a device management package running at Indiana University. This figure shows the amount of traffic in terms of inbound traffic (light gray area) and outbound traffic (dark gray line) over several network segments. The monthly graph shows, for example, that inbound traffic maxed out the resnet T3 circuit in week 18. This tool is available on the Web at resnet.Indiana.edu/resnetstats.html, so you can investigate the network structure and performance.

System management software (sometimes called enterprise management software or a network management framework) provides the same configuration, traffic, and error information as device management systems, but can analyze the device information to diagnose patterns, not just display individual device problems. This is important when a critical device fails (e.g., a router into a high-traffic building). With device management software, all of the devices that depend on the failed device will attempt to send warning

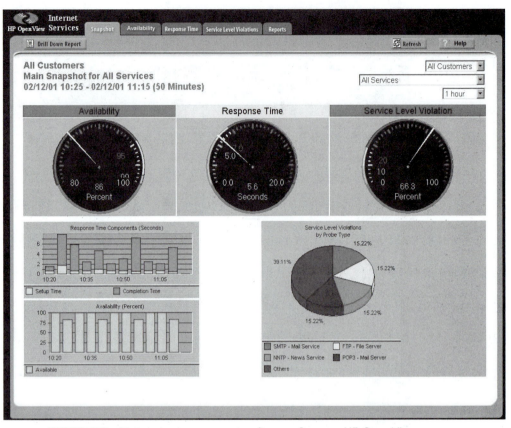

FIGURE 9-8   Network management software. SOURCE: HP OpenView.

messages to the network administrator. One failure often generates several dozen problem reports, called an *alarm storm,* making it difficult to quickly pinpoint the true source of the problem. The dozens of error messages are symptoms that mask the root cause. System management software tools correlate the individual error messages into a pattern to find the true cause, which is called *root cause analysis,* and then report the pattern to the network manager. Rather than first seeing pages and pages of error messages, the network manager instead is informed of the root cause of the problem. Figure 9-8 shows a sample from HP OpenView. This too is available on the Web at www.openview.hp.com/products/vpis/seetrybuy/Product_HTML-265.asp.

Application management software also builds on the device management software, but instead of monitoring systems, it monitors applications. In many organizations, there are mission-critical applications that should get priority over other network traffic. For example, real-time order-entry systems used by telephone operators need priority over e-mail. Application management systems track delays and problems with application layer packets and inform the network manager if problems occur and these packets for priority applications experience important delays.

Network Management Standards One important problem is ensuring that hardware devices from different vendors can understand and respond to the messages sent by the network management software of other vendors. By this point in this book, the solution should be obvious: standards. A number of formal and de facto standards have been developed for network management. These standards are application layer protocols that define the type of information collected by network devices and the format of control messages that the devices understand.

The two most commonly used network management protocols are *Simple Network Management Protocol (SNMP)* and *Common Management Interface Protocol (CMIP)*. Both perform the same basic functions, but are incompatible. SNMP is the Internet network management standard, while CMIP is a newer protocol for OSI-type networks developed by the ISO. SNMP is the most commonly used today, although most of the major network management software tools understand both SNMP and CMIP and can operate with hardware that uses either standard.

SNMP was developed originally to control and monitor the status of network devices on TCP/IP networks, but it is now available for other network protocols (e.g., IPX/SPX). Each SNMP device (e.g., router, gateway, server) has an *agent* that collects information about itself and the messages it processes and stores that information in a central database called the *management information base (MIB)*. The network manager's management station that runs the *network management software* has access to the MIB. Using this software, the network manager can send control messages to individual devices or groups of devices asking them to report the information stored in their MIB.

Most SNMP devices have the ability for *remote monitoring (RMON)*. Most first-generation SNMP tools reported all network monitoring information to one central network management database. Each device would transmit updates to its MIB to the server every few minutes, greatly increasing network traffic. RMON SNMP software enables MIB information to be stored on the device itself or on distributed *RMON probes* that store MIB information closer to the devices that generate it. The data is not transmitted to the central server until the network manager requests the data, thus reducing network traffic. See Figure 9-9.

Network information is recorded based on the data link layer protocols, network layer protocols, and application layer protocols, so that network managers can get a very clear picture of the exact types of network traffic in the network. Statistics are also collected based on network addresses so the network manager can see how much network traffic any particular computer is sending and receiving. A wide variety of *alarms* can be defined, such as instructing a device to send a warning message if certain items in the MIB exceed certain values (e.g., if circuit utilization exceeds 50%).

As the name suggests, SNMP is a simple protocol with a limited number of functions. One problem with SNMP is that many vendors have defined their own extensions to it. So the network devices sold by a vendor may be SNMP compliant, but the MIBs they produce contain additional information that can be used only by network management software produced by the same vendor. Therefore, while SNMP was designed to make it easier to manage devices from different vendors, in practice this is not always the case.

Policy-Based Management A new approach to managing performance is policy-based management. With *policy-based management,* the network manager uses special software to set priority policies for network traffic that take effect when the network

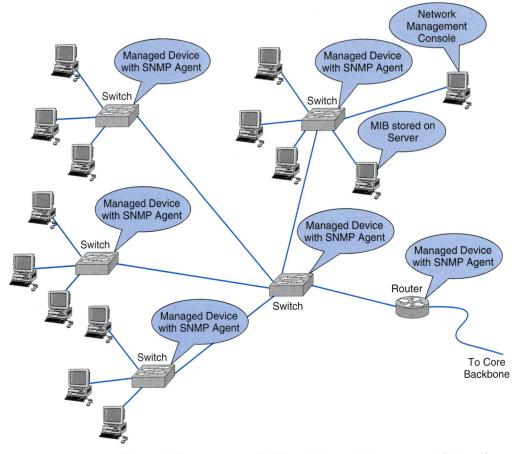

FIGURE 9-9 Network Management with Simple Network Management Protocol (SNMP). MIB = management information base.

becomes busy. For example, the network manager might say that order processing and videoconferencing get the highest priority (order processing because it is the lifeblood of the company and videoconferencing because poor response time will have the greatest impact on it). The policy management software would then configure the network devices using the quality of service (QoS) capabilities in TCP/IP and/or ATM and/or its VLANs to give these applications the highest priority when the devices become busy. Policy-based management is not widely deployed today but will become more important.

Network Circuits

In designing a network for maximum performance, it is obvious that the network circuits play a critical role, whether they are under the direct control of the organization itself (in the case of LANs, backbones, and WLANs) or leased as services from common carriers (in the case of MANs and WANs). Sizing the circuits and placing them to match traffic patterns is important. We discussed circuit loading and capacity planning in the earlier sections. In this section we add two considerations, primarily for MANs and WANs, because circuits are most important in these networks in which you pay for network capacity: traffic analysis, and service level agreements.

Traffic Analysis   In managing a network and planning for network upgrades, it is important to know the amount of traffic on each network circuit to find which circuits are approaching capacity. These circuits then can be upgraded to provide more capacity and less-used circuits can be downgraded to save costs. A more sophisticated approach involves a *traffic analysis* to pinpoint *why* some circuits are heavily used.

For example, Figure 9-10 shows the same partial mesh WAN we showed in Chapter 6. Suppose we discover that the circuit from Toronto to Dallas is heavily used. The immediate reaction might be to upgrade this circuit from a T1 to a T3. However, much traffic on this circuit may not originate in Toronto or be destined for Dallas. It may, for example, be going from New York to Los Angeles, in which case the best solution is a new circuit that directly connects them, rather than upgrading an existing circuit. The only way to be sure is to perform a traffic analysis to see the source and destination of the traffic.

Service Level Agreements   Most organizations establish a *service level agreement (SLA)* with their common carrier and Internet service provider. An SLA specifies the exact type of performance that the common carrier will provide and the penalties if this performance is not provided. For example, the SLA might state that circuits must be available 99 percent or 99.9 percent of the time. A 99 percent availability means, for example, that the circuit can be down 3.65 days per year with no penalty, while 99.9 percent means

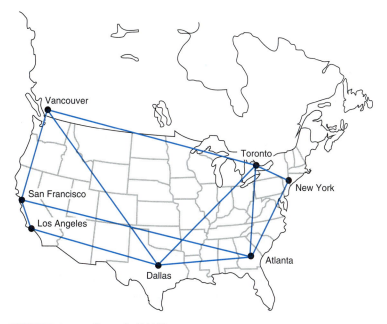

FIGURE 9-10   Sample WAN.

8.76 hours per year. In many cases, SLA includes maximum allowable response times. Some organizations are also starting to use an SLA internally to clearly define relationships between the networking group and its organizational "customers."

Network Devices

In previous chapters, we have treated the devices used to build the network as commodities. We have talked about 10/100Base-T switches and routers as though all were the same. This not true; in the same way that computers from different manufacturers provide different capabilities, so too do network devices. Some devices are simply faster or more reliable than similar devices from other manufacturers. In this section we examine three factors important in network performance: device latency, device memory, and load balancing.

Device Latency   *Latency* is the delay imposed by the device in processing messages. A high-latency device is a one that takes a long time to process a message, while a low-latency device is fast. The type of computer processor installed in the device affects latency. The fastest devices run at *wire speed,* which means they operate as fast as the circuits they connect and add virtually no delays.

For networks with heavy traffic, latency is a critical issue, because any delay affects all packets that move through the device. If the device does not operate at wire speed, then packets arrive faster than the device can process them and transmit them on the outgoing circuits. If the incoming circuit is operating at close to capacity, then this will result in long traffic backups in the same way that long lines of traffic form at tollbooths on major highways during rush hour.

Latency is less important in low-traffic networks because packets arrive less frequently and long lines seldom build up even if the device cannot process all packets that the circuits can deliver. The actual delay itself—usually a few microseconds—is not noticeable by users.

Device Memory   Memory and latency go hand-in-hand. If network devices do not operate at wire speed, this means that packets can arrive faster than they can be processed. In this case, the device must have sufficient memory to store the packets. If there is not enough memory, then packets are simply lost and must be retransmitted—thus increasing traffic even more so. The amount of memory needed is directly proportional to the latency (slower devices with higher latencies need more memory).

Memory is also important for servers, whether they are Web servers or file servers. Memory is many times faster than hard disks so Web servers and file servers usually store the most frequently requested files in memory to decrease the time they require to process a request. The larger the memory that a server has, the more files it can store in memory and the more likely it is to be able to process a request quickly. In general, it is always worthwhile to have the greatest amount of memory practical in Web and file servers.

Load Balancing   In all large-scale networks today, servers are clustered together in *server farms.* These server farms sometimes have hundreds of servers that perform the same task. Yahoo.com, for example, has hundreds of Web servers that do nothing but respond to Web search requests. In this case, it is important to ensure that when a request

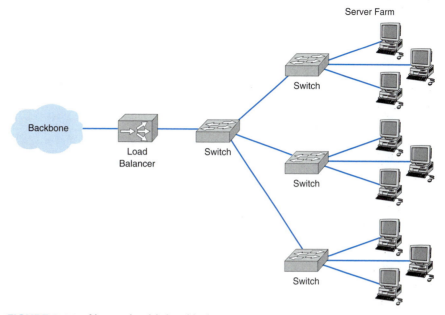

FIGURE 9-11   Network with load balancer.

arrives at the server farm, it is immediately forwarded to a server that is not busy—or is the least busy.

A special device called a *load balancing server* or *virtual server* acts as a router at the front of the server farm (see Figure 9-11). All requests are directed to the load balancer at its IP address. When a request hits the load balancer it forwards it to one specific server using its IP address. Sometimes a simple round-robin formula is used (requests go to each server one after the other in turn), while in other cases, more complex formulas track how busy each server actually is. If a server crashes, the load balancer stops sending requests to it and the network continues to operate without the failed server.

Minimizing Network Traffic

Most approaches to improving network performance attempt to maximize the speed at which the network can move the traffic it receives. The opposite—and equally effective approach—is to minimize the amount of traffic the network receives. This may seem quite difficult at first glance—after all, how can we reduce the number of Web pages people request? We can't reduce all types of network traffic, but if we move the most commonly used data closer to the users who need it, we can reduce traffic enough to have an impact. We do this by providing servers with duplicate copies of commonly used information at points closer to the users than the original source of the data. Two approaches are emerging: content caching and content delivery.

Content Caching   The basic idea behind *content caching* is to store other people's Web data closer to your users. With content caching, you install a *cache engine* close to

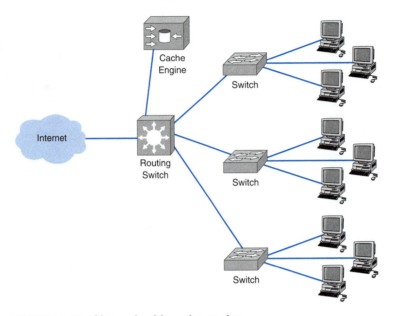

FIGURE 9-12 Network with cache engine.

your Internet connection and install special content management software on the router or routing switch (see Figure 9-12). The router or routing switch directs all outgoing Web requests and the files that come back in response to those requests to the cache engine. The cache engine stores the request and the static files that are returned in response (e.g., graphics files, banners). The cache engine also examines each outgoing Web request to see if it is requesting static content that the cache engine has already stored. If the request is for content already in the cache engine, it intercepts the request and responds directly itself with the stored file, but makes it appear as though the request came from the URL specified by the user. The user receives a response almost instantaneously and is unaware that the cache engine responded. The cache engine is *transparent.*

While not all Web content will be in the cache engine's memory, content from many of the most commonly accessed sites on the Internet will be (e.g., Yahoo.com, google.com, Amazon.com). The contents of the cache engine reflect the most common requests for each individual organization that uses it, and changes over time as the pattern of pages and files changes. Each page or file also has a limited life in the cache before a new copy is retrieved from the original source so that pages that occasionally change will be accurate.

For content caching to work properly, the cache engine must operate at almost wire speeds, or else it imposes additional delays on outgoing messages that result in worse performance, not better. By reducing outgoing traffic (and incoming traffic in response to requests), the cache engine enables the organization to purchase a smaller WAN or MAN circuit into the Internet. So not only does content caching improve performance, but it can also reduce network costs if the organization produces a large volume of network requests.

Content Delivery   *Content delivery,* pioneered by Akamai,[2] is a special type of Internet service that works in the opposite direction. Rather than storing other people's Web files closer to their own internal users, a *content delivery provider* stores Web files for its clients closer to their potential users. Akamai, for example, operates almost 10,000 Web servers located near the busiest Internet NAPs, MAPs, and other exchanges. These servers contain the most commonly requested Web information for some of the busiest sites on the Internet (e.g., yahoo.com, monster.com, ticketmaster.com).

When someone accesses a Web page of one of Akamai's client organizations, special software on the client's Web server determines if there is an Akamai server containing any static parts of the requested information (e.g., graphics, advertisements, banners) closer to the user. If so, the client's Web server redirects portions of the request to the Akamai server nearest the user. The user interacts with the client's Web site for dynamic content or HTML pages with the Akamai server providing static content. In Figure 9-13, for example, when a user in Singapore requests a Web page from yahoo.com, the main yahoo.com server farm responds with the dynamic HTML page. This page contains several static graphic files. Rather than provide an address on the yahoo.com site, the Web page is dynamically changed by the Akamai software on the yahoo.com site to pull the static content from the Akamai server in Singapore. If you use Netscape and watch the bottom action bar closely while some of your favorite sites are loading, you'll see references to Akamai's servers.

Akamai servers benefit both the user and the organization that are Akamai's client, as well as many ISPs and all Internet users not directly involved with the Web request. Because more Web content is now processed by the Akamai server and not the client organization's

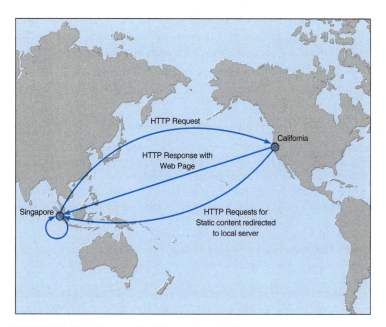

FIGURE 9-13   Network with content delivery.

---

[2] Akamai (pronounced *AH-kuh-my*) is Hawaiian for intelligent, clever, and "cool." See www.akamai.com.

MANAGEMENT FOCUS *9-4*

AKAMAI SPEEDS UP TICKETMASTER

Ticketmaster is one largest online sellers of tickets in the world, and one of the busiest sites on the Internet when tickets for certain events go on sale. On peak days, Ticketmaster serves 10 million page views, with most of that occurring in within a 45-minute period. Ticketmaster's Online-Citysearch is a related portal that provides in-depth content for more than 30 metropolitan areas around the United States. San Francisco, for example, has 40,000 pages of information.

Both parts of Ticketmaster use the Akamai content delivery service. Since implementing the service, Ticketmaster has seen a 50-percent reduction in download times and a 40-percent reduction in the load on Ticketmaster's own servers and switches. Ticketmaster was able to prevent a $1 million addition to its own Web site.

Users have noticed the difference too. The number of page views and average duration of a visit has increased by 70 percent. This means that the number of advertisements displayed to users has increased 70 percent as well, thus providing a noticeable increase in advertising revenue.

SOURCE: "Ticketmaster Online-Citysearch: A Tale of Two Sites," Akamai.com.

more distant Web server, the user benefits from a much faster response time; in Figure 9-13, for example, more requests never have to leave Singapore. The client organization benefits because it serves its users with less traffic reaching its Web server; Yahoo! for example, need not spend as much on its server farm or the Internet connection into its server farm. In our example, the ISPs providing the circuits across the Pacific benefit because now less traffic flows through their network—traffic which is not paid for because of Internet peering agreements. Likewise, all other Internet users in Singapore (as well as users in the United States accessing Web sites in Singapore) benefit because there is now less traffic across the Pacific and response times are faster.

SUMMARY

Traditional Network Design The traditional network design approach follows a very structured systems analysis and design process similar to that used to build application systems. It attempts to develop precise estimates of network traffic for each network user and network segment. Although this is expensive and time consuming, it works well for static or slowly evolving networks. Unfortunately, computer and networking technology is changing very rapidly, the growth in network traffic is immense, and hardware and circuit costs are relatively less expensive than they used to be. Therefore, use of the traditional network design approach is decreasing.

Building-Block Approach to Network Design The building-block approach attempts to build the network using a series of simple building predefined components, resulting in a simpler design process and a more easily managed network built with a smaller range of components. The basic process involves three steps that are performed repeatedly. Needs analysis involves developing a logical network design that includes the geographic scope of the network and a categorization of current and future network needs of the various network segments, users, and applications as either typical or high traffic. The next step, technology design, results in a set of one or more physical network designs. Network design and simulation tools can play an important role in selecting the technology that typical and high-volume users, applications, and network segments will use. The final step, cost assessment, gathers cost information for the network, usually through an RFP that specifies what equipment, software, and services are desired and asks vendors to provide their best prices. One of the keys to gaining acceptance by senior management of the network design lies in speaking management's language (cost, network growth, and reliability), not the language of the technology (Ethernet, ATM, and DSL).

KEY TERMS

access layer
Akamai
agent
alarm
alarm storm
application management
    software
baseline
building-block process
cache engine
capacity planning
circuit loading
Common Management
    Interface Protocol
    (CMIP)
content caching

content delivery
content delivery provider
core layer
cost assessment
desirable requirements
device management
    software
distribution layer
geographic scope
latency
load balancing server
logical network design
managed device
managed network
management informa-
    tion base (MIB)

mandatory requirements
needs analysis
needs categorization
network management
    software
physical network
    design
policy-based
    management
remote monitoring
    (RMON)
request for proposal
    (RFP)
RMON probe
root cause analysis
server farm

service level agreement
    (SLA)
simulation
Simple Network
    Management
    Protocol (SNMP)
system management
    software
technology design
traditional network
    design process
traffic analysis
turnpike effect
virtual server
wire speed
wish-list requirements

QUESTIONS

1. What are the keys to designing a successful data communications network?

2. How does the traditional approach to network design differ from the building-block approach?

3. Describe the three major steps in current network design.

4. What is the most important principle in designing networks?

5. Why is it important to analyze needs in terms of both application systems and users?

6. Describe the key parts of the technology design step.

7. How can a network design tool help in network design?

8. On what should the design plan be based?

9. What is an RFP, and why do companies use them?

10. What are the key parts of an RFP?

11. What are some major problems that can cause network designs to fail?

12. What is a network baseline, and when is it established?

13. What issues are important to consider in explaining a network design to senior management?

14. What is the turnpike effect and why is it important in network design?

15. How can you design networks to improve performance?

16. How does a managed network differ from an unmanaged network?

17. Compare and contrast device management software, system management software, and application management software.

18. What are SNMP and RMON?

19. What is a traffic analysis and when is it useful?

20. What is a service level agreement?

21. How do device latency and memory affect performance?

22. How does load balancing software work?

23. How does content caching differ from content delivery?

24. Why do you think some organizations were slow to adopt a building-block approach to network design?

25. For what types of networks are network design tools most important? Why?

EXERCISES

9-1. What factors might cause peak loads in a network? How can a network designer determine if they are important, and how are they taken into account when designing a data communications network?

9-2. Collect information about two network design tools and compare and contrast what they can and cannot do.

9-3. Investigate the latest versions of SNMP and RMON and describe the functions that have been added in the latest version of the standard.

9-4. Investigate and report on the purpose, relative advantages, and relative disadvantages of two network management software tools (e.g., Open View, Tivoli TME).

MINI-CASES

I. Computer Dynamics

Computer Dynamics is a microcomputer software development company that has a 300-computer network. The company is located in three adjacent five-story buildings in an office park, with about 100 computers in each building. The current network is a poorly designed mix of Ethernet and token ring (Ethernet in two buildings and token ring in the other). The networks in all three buildings are heavily overloaded, and the company anticipates significant growth in network traffic. There is currently no network connection among the buildings, but this is one objective in building the new network. Describe the network you would recommend and how it would be configured with the goal of building a new network that will support the company's needs for the next 3 years with few additional investments. Be sure to include the devices and type of network circuits you would use. You will need to make some assumptions, so be sure to document your assumptions and explain why you have designed the network in this way.

II. Drop and Forge

Drop and Forge is a small manufacturing firm with a 60-computer network. The company has one very large manufacturing plant with an adjacent office building. The office building houses 50 computers, with an additional 10 computers in the plant. The current network is an old 1-Mbps Ethernet that will need to be completely replaced. Describe the network you would recommend and how it would be configured. The goal is to build a new network that will support the company's needs for the next 3 years with few additional investments. Be sure to include the devices and type of network circuits you would use. You will need to make some assumptions, so be sure to document your assumptions and explain why you have designed the network in this way.

III. Mary's Manufacturing

Mary's Manufacturing is a small manufacturing company that has a network with eight LANs (each with about 20 computers on them using switched 10Base-T) connected via 100Base-T over fiber-optic cable into a core switch (i.e., a collapsed BN). The switch is connected to the company's ISP over a fractional T1 circuit. Most computers are used for order processing and standard office applications, but some are used to control the manufacturing equipment in the plant. The current network is working fine and there have been no major problems, but Mary is wondering whether she should invest in network management software. It will cost about $5,000 to replace the current hardware with SNMP-capable hardware. Mary can buy SNMP device management software for $2,000 or spend $7,000 to buy SNMP system management software. Should Mary install SNMP, and if so, which software should she buy? Why?

IV. Network Simulator

The Web site for this book has a network simulator that shows what a network management system for a small company might look like. The simulator shows a series of network alerts that indicate problems in network. Identify the problems and state how would you fix them.

CHAPTER 10

NETWORK SECURITY

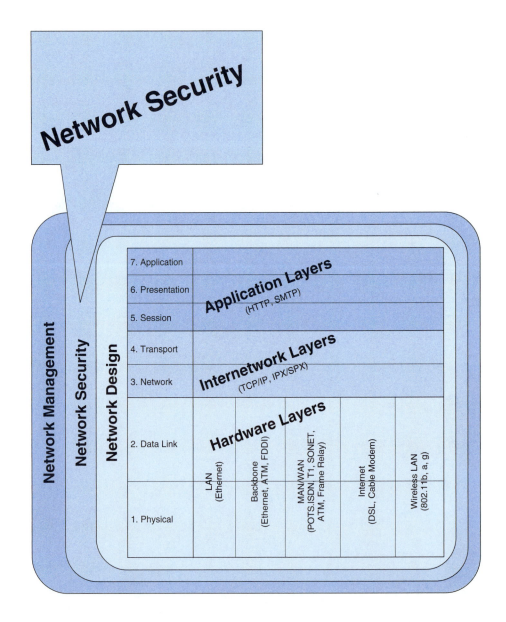

THIS CHAPTER describes why networks need security and how to provide it. The first step in any security plan is risk assessment: understanding the key assets that need protection and assessing the threats to each. There are a variety of steps that can be taken to prevent, detect, and correct security problems due to disruptions, destruction, and disaster, and unauthorized access.

OBJECTIVES

- Be familiar the major threats to network security
- Be familiar with how to conduct a risk assessment
- Understand how to prevent, detect, and correct disruptions, destruction, and disaster
- Understand how to prevent, detect, and correct unauthorized access

CHAPTER OUTLINE

INTRODUCTION

  Why Networks Need Security

  Types of Security Threats

  Network Controls

RISK ASSESSMENT

  Develop a Control Spreadsheet

  Identify and Document the Controls

  Evaluate the Network's Security

CONTROLLING DISRUPTION, DESTRUCTION, AND DISASTER

  Preventing Disruption, Destruction, and Disaster

  Detecting Disruption, Destruction, and Disaster

  Correcting Disruption, Destruction, and Disaster

CONTROLLING UNAUTHORIZED ACCESS

  Preventing Unauthorized Access

  Detecting Unauthorized Access

  Correcting Unauthorized Access

SUMMARY

INTRODUCTION

Both business and government were concerned with security long before the need for computer-related security was recognized. They always have been interested in the physical protection of assets through means such as locks, barriers, and guards, but the introduction of computer processing, large databases, and the Internet has increased the need for security.[1] Approximately 90 percent of the respondents to the 2000 Computer Security Institute/FBI Computer Crime and Security Survey reported that they had detected security breaches in the last 12 months. Almost 75 percent reported they suffered a measurable financial loss because of the security problem, with the average loss being just under $1 million. *Information Week* estimates that worldwide annual losses due to security problems exceeds $1.6 trillion.

For many people, security means preventing unauthorized access, such as preventing hackers from breaking into their computers. Security is more than that, however. It also includes being able to recover from temporary service problems (e.g., a circuit breaks) or from disasters (e.g., fire, earthquake). Figure 10-1 shows some threats to a computer center, the data communication circuits, and the attached computers.

Why Networks Need Security

In recent years, organizations have become increasingly dependent on data communication networks for their daily business communications, database information retrieval, distributed data processing, and the internetworking of LANs. The rise of the Internet with opportunities to connect computers anywhere in the world has significantly increased the potential vulnerability of the organization's assets. Emphasis on network security also has increased as result of well-publicized security break-ins and as government regulatory agencies have issued security-related pronouncements.

The losses associated with the security failures can be huge. The average loss of about $1 million sounds large enough, but this is just the tip of the iceberg. The potential loss of consumer confidence from a well-publicized security break-in can cost much more in lost business. More important than these losses, however, are the potential losses from the disruption of application systems that run on computer networks. As organizations have come to depend on computer systems, computer networks have become "mission critical." Bank of America, one of the largest banks in the United States, estimates that it would cost the bank $50 million if its computer networks were unavailable for 24 hours. Other large organizations have produced similar estimates. The value of the data stored on most organizations' networks and the value provided by the application systems in use far exceeds the cost of the network themselves. For this reason, the primary goal of network security is to protect the organization's data and application software.

Types of Security Threats

In general, network security threats can be classified into one of two categories: (1) disruption, destruction, and disaster; and (2) unauthorized access.

---

[1] There are many good security sites, including www.cert.org and www.infosyssec.net.

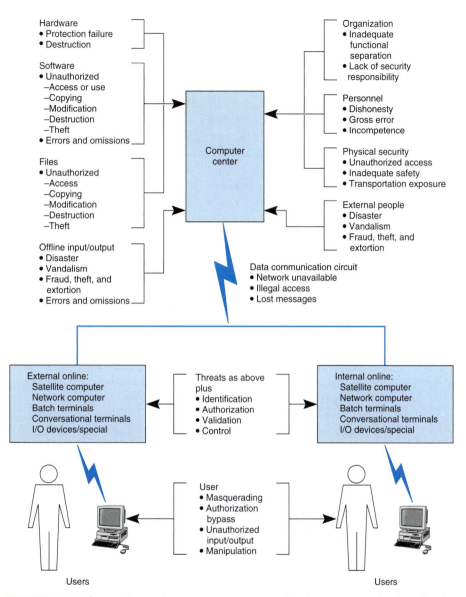

Hardware
- Protection failure
- Destruction

Software
- Unauthorized
  - Access or use
  - Copying
  - Modification
  - Destruction
  - Theft
- Errors and omissions

Files
- Unauthorized
  - Access
  - Copying
  - Modification
  - Destruction
  - Theft

Offline input/output
- Disaster
- Vandalism
- Fraud, theft, and extortion
- Errors and omissions

Computer center

Organization
- Inadequate functional separation
- Lack of security responsibility

Personnel
- Dishonesty
- Gross error
- Incompetence

Physical security
- Unauthorized access
- Inadequate safety
- Transportation exposure

External people
- Disaster
- Vandalism
- Fraud, theft, and extortion

Data communication circuit
- Network unavailable
- Illegal access
- Lost messages

External online:
Satellite computer
Network computer
Batch terminals
Conversational terminals
I/O devices/special

Threats as above plus
- Identification
- Authorization
- Validation
- Control

Internal online:
Satellite computer
Network computer
Batch terminals
Conversational terminals
I/O devices/special

User
- Masquerading
- Authorization bypass
- Unauthorized input/output
- Manipulation

Users   Users

FIGURE 10-1   Some threats to a computer center, the data communication circuits, and the client computers.

Disruptions are the loss of or reduction in network service. Disruptions may be minor and temporary. For example, a network switch might fail or a circuit may be cut, causing part of the network to cease functioning until the failed component can be replaced. Some users may be affected, but others are not. Some disruptions may also be caused by or result in the *destruction* of data. For example a virus may destroy files, or the "crash" of a hard disk may cause files to be destroyed. Other disruptions may be catastrophic.

Natural (or human-made) *disasters* may occur that destroy host computers or large sections of the network. For example, fires, floods, earthquakes, mudslides, tornadoes, and terrorist attacks can destroy large parts of the buildings and networks in their path.

Unauthorized access is often viewed as hackers' gaining access to organizational data files and resources from across the Internet. However, most unauthorized access incidents involve employees. Unauthorized access may have only minor effects. A curious intruder may simply explore the system, gaining knowledge that has little value. A more serious intruder may be a competitor bent on industrial espionage who could attempt to gain access to information on products under development or the details and price of a bid on a large contract. Worse still, the intruder could change files to commit fraud or theft or could destroy information to injure the organization.

Although computer security is improving, so, too, are the number and frequency of problems. The *Computer Emergency Response Team (CERT)* at Carnegie Mellon University (whose mission is to work with the Internet community to respond to computer security problems, raise awareness of computer security issues, and prevent security breaches) was established by the U.S. Department of Defense in 1988 after a virus (called the Internet Worm) shut down almost 10 percent of the computers on the Internet. In 1989, its first full year of operation, the CERT responded to 137 incidents. In 2000, CERT responded to 21,756 incidents. The number of Internet security incidents reported to CERT has doubled every year for the last few years (Figure 10-2).

Part of the reason for the increase is the increasing availability of sophisticated tools for breaking into networks. Just a few years ago, a hacker wanting to break into a network needed to have some expertise. Today, even inexperienced hackers can obtain hacking tools from a Web site and immediately begin trying to break into networks. Fortunately, laws have begun to catch up with the rapidly changing Internet. Breaking into a computer in the United States—even without causing damage—is a federal crime punishable by a fine and/or imprisonment.

MANAGEMENT FOCUS *10-1*

BREAKING INTO WESTERN UNION.COM

On September 9, 2000, a hacker broke into the Web site of Western Union, a money transfer company that enables customers to send money over the Internet, and stole credit card numbers for 15,700 customers. Western Union quickly reported the theft to its customers and to the National Bankcard Association so that the card numbers could not be used. No attempts to use the stolen card numbers were made.

The security problem was caused by human error. The Web site was revised earlier in the week, and staff members mistakenly left a file unprotected, creating a security breach that enabled the hacker to enter the site. A routine performance audit found the break-in and staff members immediately shut down the site. It took 5 days before the site was repaired and security tightened. Not counting the actual cost to fix the problem or the loss in reputation, experts estimated that the 5-day outage had cost Western Union more than $1 million in lost business.

SOURCE: "Western.Union.com Back Online after Theft of Credit-Card Data," *ComputerWorld,* September 14, 2000.

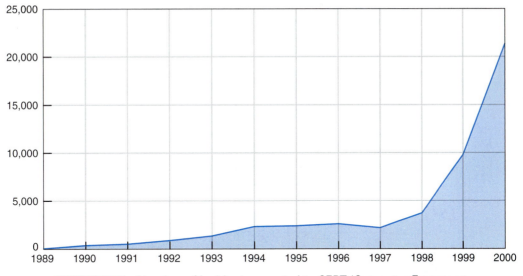

FIGURE 10-2 Number of incidents reported to CERT (Computer Emergency Response Team). SOURCE: CERT Statistics, www.cert.org/stats/cert_stats.html.

Network Controls

Developing a secure network means developing *controls.* Controls are mechanisms that reduce or eliminate the threats to network security. There are three types of controls that *prevent, detect,* and *correct* whatever might happen to the organization through the threats faced by its computer-based systems.

Preventive controls mitigate or stop a person from acting or an event from occurring. For example, a password can prevent illegal entry into the system or a second set of circuits can prevent a network from crashing. Preventive controls also act as a deterrent by discouraging or restraining someone from acting or proceeding because of fear or doubt. For example, a guard or a security lock on a door may deter an attempt to gain illegal entry.

Detective controls reveal or discover unwanted events. For example, software that looks for illegal network entry or a virus can detect these problems. They also document an event, a situation, or a trespass, providing evidence for subsequent action against the individuals or organizations involved or to enable corrective action to be taken. For example, the same software that detects the problem must report it immediately so that someone or some automated process can take corrective action.

Corrective controls remedy an unwanted event or a trespass. Either computer programs or humans verify and check data to correct errors or fix a security breach so it will not recur in the future. Controls also can aid recovery from network errors or disasters. For example, software can recover and restart the communication circuits automatically when there is a data communication failure.

The remainder of this chapter discusses the various controls that might be used to prevent, detect, and correct threats. We also present a control spreadsheet and risk analysis methodology for identifying the threats and their associated controls. The control spreadsheet provides a data communications network manager with a good view of the current threats and any controls that are in place to mitigate the occurrence of threats.

Nonetheless, it is important to remember that it is not enough to just establish a series of controls; someone or some department must be accountable for the control and security of the network. This includes being responsible for the developing controls, ensuring they are operating effectively, and determining when they need to be updated or replaced.

Controls must be reviewed periodically to be sure that they are still useful. They also should be verified and tested. Verifying ensures that the controls are present, and testing determines whether the controls are working as originally specified.

It is also important to recognize that there may be occasions in which a person must override a control. This may be when the network or one of its software or hardware subsystems is not operating properly and controls must be suspended temporarily. Such overrides should be tightly controlled, and there should be a formal procedure to document this occurrence should it happen.

RISK ASSESSMENT

One key step in developing a secure network is to conduct a *risk assessment.* This assigns levels of risk to various threats to the network security by comparing the nature of the threats to the controls designed to reduce them. It is done by developing a control spreadsheet and then rating the importance of each risk. This section provides a brief summary of this process.[2]

Develop a Control Spreadsheet

To be sure that the data communications network and microcomputer workstations have the necessary controls and that these controls offer adequate protection, it is best to build a *control spreadsheet* (Figure 10-3). Threats to the network are listed across the top, and the network assets are listed down the side. The center of the spreadsheet incorporates all the controls that *currently* are in the network. This will become the benchmark on which to base future security reviews.

Assets   The first step is to identify the assets on the network. An *asset* is something of value and can be either hardware or software. Probably the most important asset on a network is the organization's data. For example, suppose someone destroyed a mainframe worth $10 million. The mainframe could be replaced, simply by buying a new one. It would be expensive, but the problem would be solved in a few weeks. Now suppose someone destroyed all the student records at your university so that no one knew what courses anyone had taken or what grades anyone had received. The cost would far exceed the cost of replacing a $10 million computer. The lawsuits alone would easily exceed $10 million, the cost of hiring a staff to find and reenter paper records would be enormous, and the reentry certainly would take more than a few weeks. Even temporary disruptions in service that

---

[2] For a detailed risk-assessment procedure, see the OCTAVE method developed by CERT at www.cert.org/octave.

Threats \ Assets (with Priority)	Disruption, Destruction, Disaster				Unauthorized Access			
	Fire	Flood	Power Loss	Circuit Failure	Virus	External Intruder	Internal Intruder	Eaves-drop
(92) Mail server								
(90) Web server								
(90) DNS server								
(50) Computers on sixth floor								
(50) Sixth-floor LAN circuits								
(80) Building A backbone								
(70) Router in building A								
(30) Network software								
(100) Client database								
(100) Financial database								
(70) Network technical staff								

FIGURE 10-3 Sample control spreadsheet with some assets and threats. The relative importance of the asset is shown by the number in parentheses. DNS = Domain Name Service; LAN = local area network.

cause no data loss can have significant costs. The cost of disruptions to a company's primary Web site or the LANs and backbones that support telephone sales operations are often measured in the millions. Amazon.com, for example, has revenues of more $10 million per hour, so if their Web site were unavailable for an hour or even part of an hour it would cost them millions of dollars in lost revenue. Companies that do less e-business or telephone sales have lower costs, but recent surveys suggest losses of $100,000–$200,000 per hour are not uncommon. Even the disruption of a single LAN has cost implications; surveys suggest that most businesses estimate the cost of lost work at $1,000–5,000 per hour. Figure 10-4 summarizes some typical assets.

An important type of asset is the *mission-critical application*. A mission-critical application is an information system that is literally critical to the survival of the organization. It is an application that cannot be permitted to fail, and if it does fail the network staff drops everything else to fix it. For example, for an Internet bank that has no brick and mortar branches, the Web site is a mission-critical application. If the Web site crashes, the bank cannot conduct business with its customers. Mission-critical applications are usually clearly identified so their importance is not overlooked.

Once you have a list of assets, they should be evaluated on the basis of their importance. There will rarely be enough time and money to protect all assets perfectly, so it is important to focus the organization's attention on the most important ones.

Threats A *threat* to the data communications network is any potential adverse occurrence that can do harm, interrupt the systems using the network, or cause a monetary loss to the organization. Although threats may be listed in generic terms (e.g., theft of data, destruc-

Hardware	• Servers, such as mail servers, web servers, DNS servers, DHCP servers, and LAN file servers • Client computers • Devices such as hubs, switches, and routers
Circuits	• Locally operated circuits such LANs and backbones • Contracted circuits such as MAN and WAN circuits • Internet access circuits
Network software	• Server operating systems and system settings • Applications software such as mail server and Web server software
Client software	• Operating systems and system settings • Application software such as word processors
Organizational data	• Databases with organizational records
Mission-critical applications	• For example, for an Internet bank, its Web site is mission critical

FIGURE 10-4   Types of assets. DNS = Domain Name Service; DHCP = Dynamic Host Control Protocol; LAN = local area network; MAN = metropolitan area network; WAN = wide area network.

tion of data), it is better to be specific and use actual data from the organization being assessed (e.g., theft of customer credit card numbers, destruction of the inventory database).

Once the threats are identified, they can be prioritized on their probability of occurrence and possible cost. Figure 10-5, based on several different surveys, summarizes the most common threats and their likelihood of occurring. The actual probability of a threat to your organization depends on your business. An Internet bank, for example, is more likely to be a target of fraud than is a restaurant with a simple Web site. Likewise, the costs are rough approximations as well. Nonetheless, Figure 10-5 provides some general guidance.

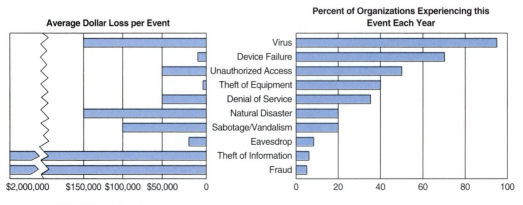

FIGURE 10-5   Common threats.

From Figure 10-5 you can see that the most likely event is a virus infection, suffered by almost 95 percent of organizations each year. The average cost to clean up a virus that slips through the security system and infects an average number of computers is about $150,000 per virus. Depending upon your background, this was probably not the first security threat that came to mind; most people first think about hackers breaking into a network across the Internet. This does happen, too; unauthorized access is experienced by about 50 percent of all organizations each year, with 20 percent experiencing an act of sabotage or vandalism. The average cost to recover after these attacks is $50,000 for unauthorized access and $100,000 for sabotage/vandalism. Denial of service attacks, in which a hacker blocks access to your networks, are also becoming more common (35%) and costly ($50,000 per event).

You will also see that device failure and computer equipment theft are common problems but usually result in low dollar losses compared to intentional security violations. Natural disasters (e.g., fire, flood) are also fairly common, experienced by 20% of organizations each year, and result in high dollar losses (about $150,000 per event).

Finally, two low probability events (fraud and theft of proprietary information) can be quite expensive. While few organizations experience these, the cost to recover afterwards can be very high, both in dollar cost and bad publicity. Several major companies have had their networks broken into and have had proprietary information such as customer credit card numbers stolen. Winning back customers whose credit card information was stolen can be an even greater challenge than fixing the security breach.

For many years, the greatest threat to networks has come from inside the organization itself. Ever since the early 1980s when the FBI first began keeping computer crime statistics and security firms began conducting surveys of computer crime, organizational employees have perpetrated the vast majority of computer crimes. For years, 80 percent of unauthorized access incidents, thefts and sabotage have been committed by insiders, leaving only 20 percent to hackers external to the organizations.

In 2001, that changed. Depending on what survey you read, the percent of incidents attributed to external hackers in 2001 has increased to 50–70 percent of all incidents, meaning that the greatest risk facing organizations is now from the outside. While some of this shift may be due to better internal security and better communications with employees to prevent security problems, much of it is simply due to an increase in activity by external hackers.

Identify and Document the Controls

Once the specific assets and threats have been identified, you can begin working on the network *controls*. A control is something that mitigates or stops a threat or protects an asset. During this step, you identify the current in-place controls and list them in the cell for each asset and threat. Begin by considering the asset and the specific threat and then describe each control that prevents, detects, or corrects that threat. The description of the control (and its role) is placed in a numeric list, and the control's number is placed in the cell. For example, assume 24 controls have been identified as being in use. Each one is described, named, and numbered consecutively. The numbered list of controls has no ranking attached to it: The first control is number 1 just because it is the first control identified.

Figure 10-6 shows a partially completed spreadsheet. The assets and their priorities are listed as rows, with threats as columns. Each cell lists one or more controls that protects one asset against one threat. For example, in the first row, the mail server is currently protected from a fire threat by a halon fire suppression system, and there is a disaster recovery plan in place. The placement of the mail server above ground level protects against flood, and the disaster recovery plan helps here, too.

Threats / Assets (with Priority)	Distribution, Destruction, Disaster					Unauthorized Access		
	Fire	Flood	Power Loss	Circuit Failure	Virus	External Intruder	Internal Intruder	Eavesdrop
(92) Mail server	1, 2	1, 3	4	5, 6	7, 8	9, 10, 11	9, 10	
(90) Web server	1, 2	1, 3	4	5, 6	7, 8	9, 10, 11	9, 10	
(90) DNS server	1, 2	1, 3	4	5, 6	7, 8	9, 10, 11	9, 10	
(50) Computers on sixth floor	1, 2	1, 3			7, 8	10, 11	10	
(50) Sixth-floor LAN circuits	1, 2	1, 3						
(80) Building A backbone	1, 2	1, 3		6				
(70) Router in building A	1, 2	1, 3				9	9	
(30) Network software					7, 8	9, 10, 11	9, 10	
(100) Client database					7, 8	9, 10, 11	9, 10	
(100) Financial database					7, 8	9, 10, 11	9, 10	
(70) Network technical staff	1	1						

Controls

1. Disaster recovery plan
2. Halon fire system in server room; sprinklers in rest of building
3. Not on or below ground level
4. Uninterruptable power supply (UPS) on all major network servers
5. Contract guarantees from interexchange carriers
6. Extra backbone fiber cable laid in different conduits
7. Virus checking software present on the network
8. Extensive user training about viruses and reminders in monthly newsletter
9. Strong password software
10. Extensive user training about password security and reminders in monthly newsletter
11. Application-layer firewall

FIGURE 10-6   Sample control spreadsheet with some assets, threats, and controls. DNS = Domain Name Service; LAN = local area network.

Evaluate the Network's Security

The last step in using a control spreadsheet is to evaluate the adequacy of the existing controls and the resulting degree of risk associated with each threat. On the basis of this assessment, priorities can be established to determine which threats must be addressed immediately. Assessment is done by reviewing each set of controls as it relates to each threat and network component. The objective of this step is to answer the specific question "Are the controls adequate to effectively prevent, detect, and correct this specific threat?"

The assessment can be done by the network manager, but it is better done by a team of experts chosen for their in-depth knowledge about the network and environment being reviewed. This team, known as the *Delphi team,* is composed of three to nine key people. Key managers should be team members because they deal with both the long-term and day-to-day operational aspects of the network. More important, their participation means the final results can be implemented quickly, without further justification, because they make the final decisions affecting the network.

CONTROLLING DISRUPTION, DESTRUCTION, AND DISASTER

Disruption, destruction, and disaster are interruptions in network service or loss of data due to network failure. In this section, we discuss controls that attempt to prevent, detect, and correct for these threats.

Preventing Disruption, Destruction, and Disaster

The key principle in preventing disruption, destruction, and disaster—or at least reducing their impact—is *redundancy.* Redundant hardware that automatically recognizes failure and intervenes to replace the failed component can mask a failure that would otherwise result in a service disruption. Redundancy can be built into any network component.

Using Redundant Hardware   The most common example of redundancy is an *uninterruptable power supply (UPS).* A UPS is a separate battery-operated power supply unit that can supply power for minutes (or even hours) in the event of a power loss. The UPS is installed on the network server so that in the event of a power failure, the server continues to operate until power is restored or until the UPS battery becomes low. When the UPS battery begins to weaken, many UPSs can send a special message to the server, enabling it to start a normal shutdown.

You can also buy a special-purpose *fault tolerant server* that contains many redundant components to prevent failure. One common strategy, *disk mirroring,* uses a second redundant disk for every disk on the server. Every data item written to the primary disk is automatically duplicated on the mirrored disk. If the primary disk fails, the mirrored disk automatically takes over, with no observable effects on any network applications. This concept can be extended to include disk controllers (called *disk duplexing*), so that even if the disk controller fails, the server continues to operate.

Redundancy can be applied to other network components as well. For example, additional client computers, circuits, or devices (e.g., routers, bridges, multiplexers) can be

MANAGEMENT FOCUS *10-2*

MICROSOFT DISRUPTION, PART 1

Microsoft's Web sites and the Web sites of affiliated companies such as MSN.com, MSNBC.com, Expedia.com, Carpoint.com, and Hotmail.com together form the third most visited Internet domain. All were down for about 22 hours in January 2001 owing to a technician's mistake.

Although the problem was caused by one individual's mistake, a poor network design is really to blame. Microsoft had placed all four of its Domain Name Service (DNS) servers on the same network segment, meaning they were connected to the Internet via the same set of routers. The technician loaded incorrect routing table information into the routers on the network, and thus, no messages could reach any of the DNS servers. Without

DNS servers, no one could locate IP addresses for the entire Microsoft family of sites. If Microsoft had just placed some of the DNS servers on different network segments, the problem could have been avoided.

The routing information was eventually corrected and the DNS were servers back up, but experts estimate that Microsoft lost more than $4 million in advertising revenue during the 22-hour outage. Much more was lost through sales at Expedia.com and other sales-oriented sites.

SOURCE: "Microsoft's 'Incredibly Embarrassing' Week," Yahoo.com, January 26, 2001.

---

installed to ensure that the network remains operational should any of these components fail. The last control point is the network personnel and equipment in the network control center, which oversees network management and operation, the test equipment, reports, documentation, and the like.

Preventing Natural Disaster   Natural disasters can be huge: An entire site can be destroyed. Even if redundant components are present, often the scope of the loss is such that returning the network to operation is extremely difficult. The best solution is to have a completely redundant network that duplicates every network component but is in a separate location.

Generally speaking, preventing natural disasters is difficult. How do you prevent an earthquake? There are, however, some practical commonsense steps that can be taken to prevent the full impact of disasters. The most fundamental principle is to decentralize the network resources. Don't store all critical data on the same server or even multiple servers in the same building (or even in the same part of the country). By decentralizing critical data, you can eliminate the chance that a huge natural disaster can destroy all your data resources.

Other steps depend on the type of disaster to be prevented. For example, to reduce the risks due to flooding, do not locate key network components in basement rooms near rivers or oceans. To reduce risks from fire, install halon fire suppression systems in rooms containing important network equipment. To reduce the risks from terrorist attacks, keep secret the location of key network components and protect them with security guards.

Preventing Theft   In some cases, the disruption is intentional. One often overlooked security risk is theft. Computers and network devices are commonly stolen. There is a good secondhand market for such equipment, making these items valuable to steal. Several industry sources estimate that about $1 billion is lost each year through theft of computers and related equipment. Any security plan should include an evaluation of ways to prevent people from stealing equipment, such as the use of security cables to connect computers to desks and private security guards.

Preventing Viruses Special attention also must be paid to preventing computer *viruses.* Viruses cause unwanted events—some are harmless (such as nuisance messages); others are serious (such as the destruction of data). In most cases, disruptions or the destruction of data are local and affect only a small number of components (although the failure of one WAN or BN circuit may affect many computers). Such disruptions are usually fairly easy to deal with; the failed component is replaced or the virus is removed and the network continues to operate.

Most viruses attach themselves to other programs or to special parts on disks. As those files execute or are accessed, the virus spreads. *Macroviruses,* viruses that are contained in documents or spreadsheet files, can spread when an infected file simply is opened. Macroviruses are the fastest growing type of virus, accounting for more than 75 percent of all virus problems. Some viruses change their appearances as they spread, making detection more difficult.

The best way to prevent the spread of viruses is to not copy or download files of unknown origin, or at least to check every file you do copy or download. Many antivirus software packages are available to check disks and files to ensure that they are virus free. Always check all diskettes and files for viruses before using them—even those from friends! Researchers estimate that six new viruses are developed every day, so it is important to frequently update the virus information files that are provided by antivirus software.

A *worm* is special type of virus that spreads itself without human intervention. Most viruses attach themselves to a file and require a person to copy the file, but a worm copies itself from computer to computer. Worms spread when they install themselves on a computer and then send copies of themselves to other computers, sometimes by e-mail, sometimes via security holes in server software (security holes are described later in this chapter).

Preventing Denial-of-Service Attacks Another special case is the *denial-of-service (DoS) attack.* With a DoS attack, a hacker attempts to disrupt the network by flooding the network with messages so that the network cannot process messages from normal users. The simplest approach is to flood a Web server, mail server, and so on, with incoming messages. The server attempts to respond to these, but there are so many messages that it cannot.

One might expect that it would be possible to filter messages from one source IP so that if one user floods the network, the messages from this person can be filtered out before they reach the Web server being targeted. This could work, but most hackers use tools that enable them to put false source IP addresses on the incoming messages so that it is impossible to quickly recognize a message as a real message or a DoS message.

A *distributed denial-of-service attack (DDoS)* is even more disruptive. With a DDoS attack, the hacker breaks into and takes control of many computers on the Internet (often several hundred to several thousand) and plants software on them called a *DDoS agent.* The hacker then uses software called a *DDoS handler* to control the agents. The handler issues instructions to the computers under the hacker's control, which simultaneously begin sending messages to the target site. In this way, the target is deluged with messages from

MANAGEMENT FOCUS *10-3*

SECURITY MEANS NEVER HAVING TO SAY, "I LOVE YOU"

On May 4, 2000, the "I Love You" e-mail virus swept the world. Frank Wood, chief operations officer of the New Mexico State Highway Department (NMSHD), was in a meeting when he received an emergency call from his Santa Fe office informing him that the NMSHD network was decimated.

The "I Love You" virus spread through the e-mail system, deleting files and then e-mailing itself to others in the infected user's address book. Wood estimates that NMSHD's engineering group alone had more than 50,000 files infected.

The first step was to shut down the entire network—for 2 days. Wood's team first removed the virus from the cen-

tral e-mail servers and then installed special antivirus software to prevent the virus from reinfecting the servers. Then the remaining 100 servers were scanned and cleaned. Once the network was turned on, the 1,750 client computers were scanned and cleaned. After one week, NMSHD was back at 90 percent.

Computer Economics, a research firm, puts the worldwide cost of the "I Love You" virus at $6.7 billion for the first 5 days.

SOURCE: "Security Means Never Having to Say, 'I Love You'" *InfoWorld,* July 10, 2000.

TECHNICAL FOCUS *10-1*

INSIDE A DENIAL-OF-SERVICE ATTACK

A denial-of-service (DoS) attack typically involves the misuse of standard TCP/IP protocols or connection processes so that the target for the DoS attack responds in a way designed to create maximum trouble. Five common types of attacks include:

- **Smurf attacks:** The network is flooded with Internet Control Message Protocol (ICMP) echo requests (i.e., pings) that have a broadcast destination address and a faked source address of the intended target. Because it is a broadcast message, every computer on the network responds to the faked source address, so that the target is overwhelmed by responses. Because there are often dozens of computers in the same broadcast domain, each smurf message generates dozens of messages at the target.

- **Fraggle attacks:** A fraggle attack is similar to a smurf attack, except that it uses User Datagram Protocol (UDP) echo requests instead of ICMP echo requests.

- **TCP SYN floods:** The target is swamped with repeated SYN requests to establish a TCP connection, but when the target responds (usually to a faked source address), there is no response. The target continues to allocate TCP control blocks, expecting each of the requests to be completed, and gradually runs out of memory.

- **UNIX process table attacks:** These are similar to a TCP SYN flood, but instead of being flooded with TCP SYN packets, the target is swamped by UNIX open connection requests that are never completed. The target opens connections and gradually runs out of memory.

- **Finger of death attacks:** These are similar to the TCP SYN flood, but instead the target is swamped by finger requests that are never disconnected.

SOURCE: "Web Site Security and Denial of Service Protection," www.nwfusion.com, February 2, 2001.

many different sources, making it harder to identify the DoS messages and greatly increasing the number of messages hitting the target.

At present, there is little an individual firm can do to prevent DoS and DDoS attacks. One possibility is to set up many different servers around the world as some companies have done (see Management Focus 10-4). Other companies are experimenting with new intrusion detection systems that monitor for DoS attacks; these systems are discussed later in this chapter. Another possibility under discussion by the Internet community as a whole is to require ISPs to verify that all incoming messages they receive from their customers have valid source IP addresses. This would prevent the use of faked IP addresses and enable users to easily filter out DoS messages from a given address. It would make virtually impossible for a DoS attack to succeed and much harder for a DDoS attack to succeed. Many ISPs are beginning to impose security restrictions on the small-to-medium sized businesses that are often the unwitting accomplices in DDoS attacks because of their poor security, such as requiring firewalls to prevent unauthorized access. (Firewalls are discussed later in this chapter.)

Detecting Disruption, Destruction, and Disaster

Major problems need to be quickly recognized. As we discussed in Chapter 9, one function of network management software is to alert network managers to problems so these can be

MANAGEMENT FOCUS *10-4*

MICROSOFT DISRUPTION, PART 2

Microsoft has come under a number of distributed denial-of-service (DDoS) attacks over the years, but the one in January 2001 was the one that provoked Microsoft to redesign its network.

The attack was a clever one. The hackers gained control of a large number of computers and planted DDoS software that they launched on cue. The DDoS targeted not Microsoft's Web servers or mail servers but something more important that had been overlooked: Microsoft's Domain Name Service (DNS) servers. Microsoft runs four DNS servers responsible for providing IP addresses for its vast array of Web sites such as Microsoft.com, MSN.com, MSNBC.com, and Hotmail.com. By poor design, Microsoft had placed all four DNS servers on the same network segment, meaning that the DDoS attack could be concentrated on one network segment. The DDoS attack focused on the routers for the DNS network segment and brought them to a crawl on several occasions before Microsoft was able to redesign the network to put the DNS servers on separate segments.

Microsoft also contracted with Akamai.com to reduce the chance of this happening again. Akamai.com has approximately 10,000 Web servers spread around the world, most located at major ISPs. These Web servers contain the pages most commonly used by its many customers, such as Microsoft, Barnes & Noble, and Lands' End. When a user requests a page from one of Akamai.com's customers, the page is provided from the Akamai.com server closest to the customer, rather than from the customer's own server. If the Akamai.com server does not have the page, then the HTTP request continues on its way to the customer's site. In this way, many of the most popular pages on the Web are provided from servers closer to the user, thus reducing the response time—and reducing traffic on the Web—which helps everyone.

SOURCE: "Under Attack, Microsoft Outsources Web Security," Yahoo.com, January 29, 2001.

corrected. Some intelligent network servers even can be programmed to send an alarm to a pager if necessary. The organization's disaster procedures should include notifying the network managers as soon as possible.

Detecting minor disruptions and destruction can be more difficult. A network drive may develop bad spots that remain unnoticed unless the drive is routinely checked. Likewise, a network cable may be partially damaged by hungry squirrels, resulting in intermittent problems. These types of problems require ongoing monitoring. The network should routinely log fault information to enable network managers to recognize minor service problems before they become major ones. In addition, there should be a clear procedure by which network users can report problems.

Correcting Disruption, Destruction, and Disaster

Disaster Recovery Plan   A critical element in correcting problems is the *disaster recovery plan,* which should address various levels of response to a number of possible disasters and should provide for partial or complete recovery of all data, application software, network components, and physical facilities. A complete disaster recovery plan covering all these areas is beyond the scope of this text. Figure 10-7 provides a summary of many key issues. The plan itself should be stored in many places, including the laptop computers of all IS managers.

Elements of a Disaster Recovery Plan

A good disaster recovery plan should include

- The name of the decision-making manager who is in charge of the disaster recovery operation. A second manager should be indicated in case the first manager is unavailable.
- Staff assignments and responsibilities during the disaster
- A pre-established list of priorities that states what is to be fixed first
- Location of alternative facilities operated by the company or a professional disaster recovery firm and procedures for switching operations to those facilities using backups of data and software
- Recovery procedures for the data communication facilities (backbone network, metropolitan area network, wide area network, and local area network), servers, and application systems. This includes information on the location of circuits and devices, whom to contact for information, and the support that can be expected from vendors, along with the name and telephone number of the person at each vendor to contact.
- Action to be taken in case of partial damage or threats such as bomb threats, fire, water or electrical damage, sabotage, civil disorders, and vendor failures
- Manual processes to be used until the network is functional
- Procedures to ensure adequate updating and testing of the disaster recovery plan
- Storage of the data, software, and the disaster recovery plan itself in a safe area where they cannot be destroyed by a catastrophe. This area must be accessible, however, to those who need to use the plan.

FIGURE 10-7   Elements of a disaster recovery plan.

The most important elements of the disaster recovery plan are *backup and recovery controls* that enable the organization to recover its data and restart its application software should some portion of the network fail. The simplest approach is to routinely make backup copies of all organizational data and software and to store these backup copies off-site at a different location. Most organizations make daily backups of all critical information, with less important information (e.g., e-mail files) backed up weekly.

Backups ensure that important data are safe. However, it does not guarantee the data can be used. The disaster recovery plan should include a documented and tested approach to recovery, going from the backups to an operating application software system. The recovery plan should have specific goals for different types of disasters. For example, if the main database server was destroyed, how long should it take the organization to have the software and data back in operation by using the backups? Conversely, if the main data center was completely destroyed, how long should it take? The answers to these questions have very different implications for costs. Having a spare network server or a server with extra capacity that can be used in the event of the loss of the primary server is one thing. Having a spare data center ready to operate within 12 hours (for example) is an entirely different proposition.

Although many organizations have a disaster recovery plan, only a few test their plans. A *disaster recovery drill* is much like a fire drill in that it tests the disaster recovery plan and provides staff members the opportunity to practice little-used skills to see what works and what doesn't work before a disaster happens and the staff members must use the plan for real. Without regular disaster recovery drills, the only time a plan is tested is when it must be used.

MANAGEMENT FOCUS *10-5*

RECOVERING FROM THE WORLD TRADE CENTER DISASTER

TradeWeb is the market leader in electronic bond trading, linking 16 major dealers that conduct approximately $30 billion of trades per day. Prior to September 11, 2001, its headquarters was on the 51st floor of One World Trade Center. All 82 employees escaped after the terrorist attacks, but its data center and offices were destroyed.

TradeWeb immediately changed its DNS entries to redirect all Internet traffic to the backup data center at its London offices and was quickly back on the Web, but rebuilding its data network took longer. A temporary office facility with Internet connectivity was established in 7 days, but reestablishing dedicated circuits for the 13 U.S. dealers that had been connected to TradeWeb's World Trade Center office to its London office took 3 weeks.

Allstate Insurance lost a small office in Two World Trade Center with no employee casualties, but its primary New York City data network, located in a building beside the World Trade Center, was destroyed by fire. All 100 of its New York City offices were without network communications at the very moment they were preparing for an onslaught of claims.

Allstate's disaster recovery plan had anticipated this type of problem. It had a stockpile of LAN-in-a-box dialup network kits that could provide temporary network communications from an office LAN over telephone lines to the corporate network until the regular network was reestablished. The problem was that Allstate only had 25 kits; it had not anticipated a disaster that would knock out 100 offices. IS staff quickly cannibalized a stockpile of returned equipment to create another 24 kits and within 3 days, 50 offices were back on the network. UUNet Technologies responded to Allstate's emergency and managed to supply enough kits so that the remaining offices were back up within 4 days.

SOURCE: "Bounce Back," *Information Week*, October 22, 2001.

MANAGEMENT FOCUS *10-6*

DISASTER RECOVERY HITS HOME

"The building is on fire" were the first words she said as I answered the phone. It was just before noon, and one of my students had called me from her office on the top floor of the business school at the University of Georgia. The roofing contractor had just started what would turn out to be the worst fire in more than 20 years, although we didn't know it then. I had enough time to gather up the really important things from my office on the ground floor (memorabilia, awards, and pictures from 10 years in academia) when the fire alarm went off. I didn't bother with the computer; all the files were backed up off-site.

Ten hours, 100 firefighters, and 1.5 million gallons of water later, the fire was out. Then our work began. The fire had completely destroyed the top floor of the building, including my 20-computer networking lab. Water had severely damaged the rest of the main part of the building, including my office, which, I learned later, had been flooded by almost 2 feet of water at the height of the fire. My computer, and virtually all the computers in the building, were so damaged by the water that they were unusable.

My personal files were unaffected by the loss of the computer in my office; I simply used the backups and continued working—after making new backups and giving them to a friend to store at his house. The Web server I managed had been backed up to another server on the opposite side of campus 2 days before (on its usual weekly backup cycle), so we had lost only 2 day's worth of changes. In less than 24 hours, our Web site was operational; I had our server's files mounted on the university library's Web server and redirected the university's DNS server to route traffic from our old server address to our new temporary home.

Unfortunately, the rest of our network did not fare as well. Our primary Web server had been backed up to tape the night before, and although the tapes were stored off-site, the tape drive was not; the tape drive was destroyed and no one else on campus had one that could read our tapes. It took 5 days to get a replacement and re-establish the Web site. Within 30 days, we were operating from temporary offices with a new network, and 90 percent of the office computers and their data had been successfully recovered.

Living through a fire changes a person. I'm more careful now about backing up my files, and I move ever so much more quickly when a fire alarm sounds.

Alan Dennis

Disaster Recovery Outsourcing   Most large organizations have a two-level disaster recovery plan. When they build networks, they build enough capacity and have enough spare equipment to recover from a minor disaster such as loss of a major server or portion of the network (if any such disaster can truly be called minor). This is the first level. Building a network that has sufficient capacity to quickly recover from a major disaster such as the loss of an entire data center is beyond the resources of most firms. Therefore, most large organizations rely on professional disaster recovery firms to provide this second level support for major disasters.

Many large firms outsource their disaster recovery efforts by hiring *disaster recovery firms* that provide a wide range of services. At the simplest, disaster recovery firms provide secure storage for backups. Full services include a complete networked data center, that clients can use when they experience a disaster. Once a company declares a disaster, the disaster recovery firm immediately begins recovery operations using the backups stored on-site and can have the organization's entire data network back in operation on the disaster recovery firm's computer systems within hours. Full services are not cheap, but compared with the potential millions of dollars that can be lost per day from the inability to access critical data and application systems, these systems quickly pay for themselves in time of disaster.

CONTROLLING UNAUTHORIZED ACCESS

Unauthorized access is the second main type of security problem, and the one that tends to receive the most attention. No one wants an intruder breaking into his or her network.

There are four types of intruders who attempt to gain unauthorized access to computer networks. The first are casual hackers who have only a limited knowledge of computer security. They simply cruise along the Internet trying to access any computer they come across. Their unsophisticated techniques are the equivalent of trying doorknobs, and, until recently, only those networks that left their front doors unlocked were at risk. Unfortunately, there are now a variety of hacking tools available on the Internet that enable even novices to launch sophisticated intrusion attempts. Novice hackers who use such tools are sometimes called *script kiddies.*

The second type of intruders are experts in security but are motivated by the thrill of the hunt. They break into computer networks because they enjoy the challenge and enjoy showing off for friends or embarrassing the network owners. These intruders often have a strong philosophy against ownership of data and software. Most cause little damage and make little attempt to profit from their exploits, but those who do, sometimes called *crackers,* can cause major problems.

The third type of intruder is the most dangerous—the professional hacker who breaks into corporate or government computers for specific purposes, such as espionage, fraud, or intentional destruction. The U.S. Department of Defense (DOD), which routinely monitors attacks against U.S. military targets, has until recently concluded that most attacks are individuals or small groups of hackers in the first two categories. Although some of their attacks have been embarrassing (e.g., defacement of some military and intelligence Web sites), there have been no serious security risks. However, in the late 1990s, the DOD noticed a small but growing set of intentional attacks that it classifies as exercises, exploratory attacks designed to test the effectiveness of certain weapons. Therefore, the DOD established an *information warfare* program and a new organization responsible for coordinating the defense of military networks under the U.S. Space Command.

The fourth type of intruder is also very dangerous. These are organization employees who have legitimate access to the network but who gain access to information they are not authorized to use. This information could be used for their own personal gain, sold to competitors, or fraudulently changed to give the employee extra income. Most security breaches are caused by this type of intruder.

Preventing Unauthorized Access

The key principle in preventing unauthorized access is to be *proactive.* This means routinely testing your security systems before an intruder does. Many steps can be taken to prevent unauthorized access to organizational data and networks, but no network is completely safe. There are three basic access points into most organizational networks: the Internet, dial-up access through a modem, and internal LANs inside the organization. Recent surveys suggest that the most common access point used by hackers is the Internet (about 50%), followed by internal LANs (30%) and dial-up (20%). The best rule for high security is to do what the military does: Do not keep extremely sensitive data online. Data

MANAGEMENT FOCUS *10-7*

CYBERWAR IN THE MIDDLE EAST

While Israelis and Palestinians have been slugging it out on the ground with guns and stones, others have gone into battle with mouse and modem. Although cyberattacks are not new, this is the first conflict in which two sides have fought each other in such an organized way over the Internet. The most common attacks are of two types, both fairly primitive.

The first is the equivalent of scrawling graffiti on a poster: Someone breaks into an "enemy" Web site and defaces it. Israeli supporters, for example, broke into several Hezbollah-related Web sites, planting Israeli flags and other material on their pages. Palestinian supporters retaliated by defacing the Israel Institute of Technology Web site.

The second is the denial-of-service attack. Israeli supporters, for example, crashed Albawaba.com, a Jordanian-based portal site, by deluging its chat room with large image files. In return, Palestinian supporters attacked Netvision, the Israeli Internet service provider (ISP) that hosts Web sites for the Knesset, the foreign ministry, and the defense forces. Netvision service became extremely slow for a couple of weeks and ordinary subscribers had difficulty logging on.

In reality, there is no evidence that these crude attacks have caused lasting damage, but a more sophisticated attack hit the American–Israel Public Affairs Committee (AIPAC), a pro-Israel lobbying group. The attacker not only defaced the site but also downloaded the credit card details for 700 people—including a Republican senator—who had subscribed to AIPAC via the Internet.

In the crude form that it takes in the Middle East conflict, there is no sign that cyberwar is doing much to advance the cause of either side. However, we have yet to see the full weight of a government's resources deployed in a cyberattack.

Source: "Cyber-Attacks," *The Guardian,* November 30, 2000.

---

that needs special security are stored in computers isolated from other networks. There are eight general security areas related to preventing unauthorized access: a security policy, user profiles, physical security, dial-in security, firewalls, network address translation, security holes, and encryption.

Security Policy   In the same way that a disaster recovery plan is critical to controlling risks due to disruption, destruction, and disaster, a *security policy* is critical to controlling risk due to unauthorized access. The security policy should clearly define the important assets to be safeguarded and the important controls needed to do that. It should contain a section devoted to what employees should and should not do. It should contain a clear plan for routinely training employees—particularly end users with little computer expertise—on key security rules and a clear plan for routinely testing and improving the security controls in place (Figure 10-8).

One of the most common ways for hackers to break into a system, even master hackers, is through *social engineering*—breaking security simply by asking. For example, hackers routinely phone unsuspecting users and, imitating someone such as a technician or senior manager, ask for a password. Unfortunately, too many users simply provide the requested information. Most security experts no longer test for social-engineering attacks; they know from experience that social engineering will eventually succeed in any organization and therefore assume that hackers can gain access at will to normal user accounts. Training end users not to divulge passwords may not eliminate social-engineering attacks, but it may reduce its effectiveness so that hackers give up and move on to easier targets.

Elements of a Security Policy

A good security policy should include

- The name of the decision-making manager who is in charge of security
- An incident-reporting system and a rapid-response team to respond to security breaches in progress
- A risk assessment with priorities as to which assets are most important
- Effective controls placed at all major access points into the network to prevent or deter access by external agents
- Effective controls placed within the network to ensure that internal users cannot exceed their authorized access
- Use of minimum number of controls possible to reduce management time and to provide the least inconvenience to users
- An acceptable use policy that explains to users what they can and cannot do, including guidelines for accessing others' accounts, password security, e-mail rules, and so on
- A procedure for monitoring changes to important network components (e.g., routers, DNS servers)
- A plan to routinely train users regarding security policies and build awareness of security risks
- A plan to routinely test and update all security controls that includes monitoring of popular press and vendor reports of security holes
- An annual audit and review of the security practices

FIGURE 10-8   Elements of a security policy.

User Profiles   The basis of network access is the *user profile* for each user's *account* that is assigned by the network manager. Each user's profile specifies what data and network resources he or she can access and the type of access (read only, write, create, delete). Gaining access to an account can be based on what you know, what you have, or what you are. The most common approach is what you know, usually a password. Before users can log in, they need to enter a password. Unfortunately, passwords are often poorly chosen, enabling intruders to guess them and gain access.

More and more systems are requiring users to enter a password in conjunction with something they have, such as a *smart card*. A smart card is a card about the size of a credit card that contains a small processing chip and a memory chip. This card can be read by a smart card reader; to gain access to the network, the user inserts the card and types a password. Intruders must have access to both before they can break in. A good example of this is the automated teller machine (ATM) network operated by your bank. Before you can gain access to you account, you must have both your ATM card and the access number.

In high-security applications, users may be required to present something they are, such as a finger, hand, or the retina of one eye for scanning by the system. These *biometric systems* scan the user to ensure that the user is the sole individual authorized to access the network account. Although most biometric systems are developed for high-security users, several low-cost biometric systems are now on the market. The most popular biometric system is the fingerprint scanner. Several vendors sell devices the size of a mouse that can scan a user's fingerprint for less than $100. Other technologies include facial scans via

MANAGEMENT FOCUS *10-8*

SELECTING PASSWORDS

The keys to users' accounts are passwords; each account has a unique password chosen by the user. The problem is that passwords are often chosen poorly and not changed regularly. Many network managers require users to change passwords periodically (e.g., every 90 days), but this does not ensure that users choose good passwords.

A good password is one that the user finds easy to remember but is difficult for potential intruders to guess. Several studies have found that about three quarters of passwords fall into one of four categories:

- Names of family members or pets
- Important numbers in the user's life (e.g., Social Security number, birthday)
- Words in a dictionary, whether an English or other language dictionary (e.g., *cat, hunter, supercilious, gracias, ici*)
- Keyboard patterns (e.g., *QWERTY, ASDF*)

The best advice is to avoid these categories because such passwords can be guessed easily. Better choices are passwords that

- Are meaningful to the user but to no one else
- Are at least seven characters long
- Are made of two or more words that have several letters omitted (e.g., *pplepi [apple pie]*) or are the first letters of the words in a phrase that is not in common usage (e.g., no song lyrics), such as *hapwicac (hot apple pie with ice cream and cheese)*
- Include characters such as numbers or punctuation marks in the middle of the password (e.g., *1hapwic,&c* for *one hot apple pie with ice cream, and cheese*)
- Include some uppercase and lowercase letters (e.g., *1HAPwic,&c*)

For more information, see www.securitystats.com/tools/password.asp.

small desktop videoconferencing cameras and retina scans by more sophisticated devices. Although some banks have begun using fingerprint devices for customer access to their accounts over the Internet, such devices have not become widespread, which we find a bit puzzling. The fingerprint method is unobtrusive and means users no longer have to remember arcane passwords.

User profiles can limit the allowable log-in days, time of day, physical locations, and the allowable number of incorrect log-in attempts. Some will also automatically log off a user if that person has not performed any network activity for a certain length of time (e.g., the user has gone to lunch and has forgotten to log off the network). Regular security checks throughout the day when the user is logged in can determine whether a user is still permitted access to the network. For example, the network manager might have disabled the user's profile while the user is logged in, or the user's account may have run out of funds.

Creating accounts and profiles is simple. When a new staff member joins an organization, that person is assigned a user account and profile. One security problem is the removal of user accounts when someone leaves an organization. Often, network managers are not informed of the departure and accounts remain in the system. For example, a recent examination of the user accounts at the University of Georgia found 30 percent belonged to staff members no longer employed by the university. If the staff member's departure was not friendly, there is a risk that he or she may attempt to access data and resources and use them for personal gain or destroy them to get back at the organization. Many systems permit the network manager to assign expiration dates to user accounts to ensure that unused profiles are automatically deleted or deactivated, but these actions do not negate the need to notify network managers about an employee's departure.

It is important to screen and classify both users and data. Some organizations, especially in government, assign different security clearance levels to users as well as to data, thus permitting users to see only what they need to know.

The impact of any security software packages that restrict or control access to files, records, or data items should be reviewed. Independent of the data communications software, these packages may offer a unique password and identification for each user and allow access only to the specific functions assigned to that user. Some packages also offer additional features, such as file security and layers of passwords to the record or field level, terminal security, transaction security, batch reports on all activity, automatic sign-off of unattended terminals, and immediate online notification of security violations.

Adequate user training on network security should be provided through self-teaching manuals, newsletters, policy statements, and short courses. A well-publicized security campaign may deter potential intruders.

Physical Security   One important element of security is *physical security,* preventing outside intruders from gaining access to the organization's offices or network equipment facilities. Both main and remote physical facilities should be secured adequately and have the proper controls. Good security requires implementing the proper access controls so that only authorized personnel can enter closed areas where network equipment is located or access the network. The network components themselves also have a level of physical security. Computers can have locks on their power switches or passwords that disable the screen and keyboard. Network circuits can be locked by having the network manager disable them after hours.

Proper security education, background checks, and the implementation of error and fraud controls are important. In many cases, the simplest means for gaining access is to become employed as a janitor and access the network at night. In some ways, this is easier than the previous methods because the intruder only has to insert a listening device or computer into the organization's network to record messages. Two areas are vulnerable to this type of unauthorized access: network cabling and network devices.

Network cables are the easiest target for eavesdropping because they often run long distances and usually are not regularly checked for tampering. The cables owned by the organization and installed within its facility are usually the first choice for eavesdropping. It is 100 times easier to tap a local cable than it is to tap an interexchange channel, because it is extremely difficult to identify the specific circuits belonging to any one organization in a highly multiplexed switched interexchange circuit operated by a common carrier. Local cables should be secured behind walls and above ceilings, and telephone equipment and switching rooms (wiring closets) should be locked and their doors equipped with alarms. The primary goal is to control physical access by employees or vendors to the connector cables and modems. This includes restricting their access to the wiring closets in which all the communication wires and cables are connected.

Certain types of cable can impair or increase security by making eavesdropping easier or more difficult. Obviously, any wireless network is at extreme risk for eavesdropping because anyone in the area of the transmission can easily install devices to monitor the radio or infrared signals. Conversely, fiber-optic cables are harder to tap, thus increasing security. Some companies offer armored cable that is virtually impossible to cut without special tools. Other cables have built-in alarm systems. The U.S. Air Force, for example, uses pressurized cables that are filled with gas. If the cable is cut, the gas escapes, pressure drops, and an alarm sounds.

Physical protection of the network's local loop and interexchange telephone circuits is the responsibility of the common carrier. You cannot do much about it, except to audit the telephone company's physical security procedures and possibly encrypt the data before it leaves your building to go out onto the public network. All local loops leaving the building should be physically secured and out of harm's way to prevent physical damage or an easy telephone tap. Formal procedures should exist to help identify breaches of security or illegal entries to the network.

Network devices such as controllers, hubs, and bridges should be secured in a locked wiring closet. As discussed in Chapter 4, all messages within a given LAN are actually received by all computers on the LAN, although they process only those messages addressed to them. It is rather simple to install a *sniffer program* that records all messages received for later (unauthorized) analysis. A computer with a sniffer program could then be plugged into an unattended hub or bridge to eavesdrop on all message traffic. A *secure hub* makes this type of eavesdropping more difficult by requiring a special authorization code to be entered before new computers can be added.

Dial-In Security Any organization that permits staff members to access its network via dial-in modems opens itself to a broader range of intruders. Some dial-up modem controls include changing the modem telephone numbers periodically, keeping telephone numbers confidential, and requiring the use of computers that have an electronic identification chip for all dial-up ports.

Another common strategy is to use a *call-back modem.* In this case, the user dials the organization's modem's telephone number and logs in to his or her account. Once the user enters the correct password, the modem automatically hangs ups and dials the user's modem's telephone number. In this way, unauthorized intruders cannot access others' accounts because the host computer or communications server will permit access only via modems calling from prespecified numbers. The drawback to this is that only one remote telephone number can be defined for each account. If users have several locations from which they wish to have access (e.g., the user's home and remote office), call-back modems won't work. In recent years, this technique been extended to use automatic number identification (ANI). The network manager can specify several telephone numbers authorized to access each account. When a user successfully logs on to an account, the source of incoming phone call is identified using ANI, and if it is one of the authorized numbers, the log-in is accepted; otherwise, the host computer or communications server disconnects the call.

Neither call-back modems nor ANI permits users who frequently travel (e.g., sales representatives) to have secure dial-in access. Such users often call from hotel rooms and have no knowledge of telephone numbers in advance. One solution is to use *one-time passwords.* The user connects into the network as usual, and after the user's password is accepted, the system generates a one-time password. The user must enter this password to gain access; otherwise, the connection is terminated. The user can receive this one-time password in a number of ways. Some systems send the password to the user's pager. Other systems provide the user with a unique number that must be entered into a separate hand-held device (called a *token* system), which in turn displays the password for the user to enter. To gain access, an intruder must know the user's account name and password and have access to the user's pager or password device.

Firewalls With the increasing use of the Internet, it becomes important to prevent unauthorized access to the network from intruders on other networks. The obvious solution is to disconnect any computer or network containing confidential information from the Internet, which is often not a practical solution. In many cases, organizations are disconnecting unneeded applications to improve security. For example, a Web server often does not need e-mail, so network managers often remove e-mail software to reduce the number of entry points that a hacker has into the network. A firewall is another solution.

A *firewall* is a router or special-purpose computer that examines packets flowing into and out of a network and restricts access to the organization's network. The network is designed so that a firewall is placed on every network connection between the organization and the Internet (Figure 10-9). No access is permitted except through the firewall. Some firewalls have the ability to detect and prevent DoS attacks, as well as unauthorized access attempts. Two commonly used types of firewalls are packet-level firewalls and application-level firewalls.

A *packet-level firewall* examines the source and destination address of every network packet that passes through it. It allows into or out of the organization's networks only those packets that have acceptable source and destination addresses. In general, the addresses are examined only at the transport layer (TCP port ID) and network layer (IP address). Each packet is examined individually, so the firewall has no knowledge of what the user is attempting to do. It simply chooses to permit entry or exit on the basis of the contents of the packet itself. This type of firewall is the simplest and least secure because it does not monitor the contents of the packets or why they are being transmitted and typically does not log the packets for later analysis.

Some packet-level firewalls are vulnerable to *IP spoofing*. The goal of an intruder using IP spoofing is to send packets to a target computer requesting certain privileges be granted to some user (e.g., setting up a new account for the intruder or changing access permission or password for an existing account). Such a message would not be accepted by the target computer unless it can be fooled into believing that the request is genuine.

IP spoofing is done by changing the source address on incoming packets from their real IP address to an IP address inside the organization's network. Seeing a valid internal address, the firewall lets the packets through to their destination. The destination computer believes the packets are from a valid internal user and processes them. Typically, IP spoofing is more complex than this, because such changes often require a dialogue between the

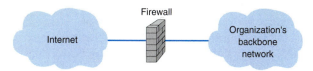

FIGURE 10-9 Using a firewall to protect networks.

MANAGEMENT FOCUS *10-9*

BASIC CONTROL PRINCIPLES OF A SECURE NETWORK

- The less complex a control, the better.
- A control's cost should be equivalent to the identified risk. It often is not possible to ascertain the expected loss, so this is a subjective judgment in many cases.
- Preventing a security incident is always preferable to detecting and correcting it after it occurs.
- An adequate system of internal controls is one that provides "just enough" control to protect the network, taking into account both the risks and costs of the controls.
- Automated controls (computer driven) always are more reliable than manual controls that depend on human interaction.
- Controls should apply to everyone, not just a few select individuals.
- When a control has an override mechanism, make sure that it is documented and that the override procedure has its own controls to avoid misuse.
- Institute the various security levels in an organization on the basis of need to know. If you do not need to know, you do not need to access the network.
- The control documentation should be confidential.
- Names, uses, and locations of network components should not be publicly available.
- Controls must be sufficient to ensure that the network can be audited. This means there should be transaction trails and historical records.
- When designing controls, assume that you are operating in a hostile environment.

- Always convey an image of high security by providing education and training.
- Make sure the controls provide the proper separation of duties. This applies especially to those who design and install the controls and those who are responsible for everyday use and monitoring.
- It is desirable to implement entrapment controls in networks to identify hackers who gain illegal access.
- When a control fails, the network should default to a condition in which everyone is denied access. A period of failure is when the network is most vulnerable.
- Controls should still work even when only one part of a network fails. For example, if a backbone network fails, all local area networks (LANs) connected to it should still be operational, with their own independent controls providing protection.
- Don't forget the LAN. Security and disaster recovery planning has traditionally focused on host mainframe computers and wide area networks. However, LANs now play an increasingly important role in most organizations but are often overlooked by central site network managers.
- Always have insurance as the last resort should all controls fail.
- Always assume your opponent (a hacker) is smarter than you.

---

computers. Because the target computer believes it is talking to an internal computer, it directs its messages to it, not to the intruders' computer. Intruders therefore have to guess at the nature and timing of these messages, so that they can generate more spoofed messages that appear to be responses to the target computer's messages. In practice, expert intruders have enough knowledge to have a reasonable chance of getting this right.

Many firewalls have had their security strengthened since the first documented case of IP spoofing occurred in December 1994. For example, some firewalls automatically delete any packets arriving from the Internet that have internal source addresses. However, IP spoofing still remains a problem, because not all packet-level firewalls prevent it.

An *application-level firewall* acts as an intermediate host computer between the Internet and the rest of the organization's networks. This kind of firewall is generally more

TECHNICAL FOCUS *10-2*

HOW PACKET-LEVEL FIREWALLS WORK

Remember from Chapter 3 that TCP/IP networks such as the Internet use TCP packets and IP packets. IP packets provide the source and destination IP addresses. TCP packets provide application-layer port numbers that indicate the application-layer software to which the packet should be sent. For example, the Web uses port 80, Telnet uses port 23, and File Transfer Protocol (FTP) uses port 21.

Packet-level firewalls enable the network administrator to establish a series of rules that define what packets should be allowed to pass through and what packets should be deleted. Suppose, for example, that the organization had a Web server with an IP address of 128.192.55.55 that was for internal use only. The administrator could define a rule on the firewall that instructed the firewall to delete any

packet from the Internet that listed 128.192.55.55 as a destination. In this case, the firewall simply needs to examine the destination address.

Suppose, however, that the organization had a Web server (128.192.44.44) that was intended to be available to Internet users. However, to prevent anyone on the Internet from making changes to the server, the organization wants to prevent any Telnet, FTP, or other similar packets from reaching the server. In this case, the administrator could define a rule that instructed the firewall to permit TCP packets with a destination port address of 80 and a destination IP address of 128.192.44.44 to pass through. A second rule would instruct the firewall to delete any packets with any other port number and that destination IP address.

---

complicated to install and manage than is a packet-level one. Anyone wishing to access the organization's networks from the Internet must log in to this firewall and can access only the information he or she is authorized for, based on the firewall account profile he or she accesses. This places an additional burden on users who must now remember an additional set of passwords. With application-level firewalls, any access that has not been explicitly authorized is prohibited. In contrast, with a packet-level firewall, any access that has not been disabled is permitted.

In many cases, special programming codes must be written to permit the use of application software unique to the organization (as opposed to commercial off-the-shelf software such as that for e-mail, which is built into the firewall). Many application-level firewalls prohibit external users from uploading executable files. In this way, intruders (or authorized users) cannot modify any software unless they have physical access to the firewall. Some firewalls refuse changes to their software unless the changes are made by the vendor. Other firewalls also actively monitor their own software and automatically disable outside connections if they detect any changes.

Network Address Translation   *Network address translation (NAT)* is the process of translating between one set of private addresses inside a network and a set of public addresses outside the network. NAT is transparent, in that no computer notices that it is being done. Although NAT can be done for several reasons, the primary reason today is security. The *NAT proxy server* is usually considered to be a firewall.

The *NAT proxy server* uses an address table to translate the private IP addresses used inside the organization into proxy IP addresses used on the Internet. When a computer inside the organization accesses a computer on the Internet, the proxy server changes the source IP address in the outgoing IP packet to its own address. It also sets the source port number in the TCP packet to a unique number that it uses as an index into its address table to find the IP address of the actual sending computer in the organization's internal network. When the external computer responds to the request, it addresses the message to the proxy server's IP address. The proxy server receives the incoming message and, after ensuring the packet should be permitted inside, changes the destination IP address to the private IP address of the internal computer and changes the TCP port ID to the correct port ID before transmitting it on the internal network.

This way, systems outside the organization never see the actual internal IP addresses and thus they think there is only one computer on the internal network. Some organizations also increase security by using illegal internal addresses. For example, if the organization has been assigned the Internet 128.192.55.X address domain, the NAT proxy server would be assigned an address such as 128.192.55.1. Internal computers, however, would *not* be assigned addresses in the 128.192.55.X subnet. Instead, they would be assigned unauthorized Internet addresses such as 10.3.3.55. (Addresses in the 10.X.X.X domain are not assigned to organizations but instead are reserved for special purposes.) Because these internal addresses are never used on the Internet but are always converted by the proxy server, this poses no problems for the users. However, even if intruders discovered the actual internal IP address, it would be impossible for them to reach the internal address from the Internet because the addresses could not be used to reach the organization's computers.

NAT proxy servers work very well and are replacing traditional firewalls. They do, however, slow message transfer between internal networks and the Internet. They also require a separate DNS server for use by external users on the Internet and a separate internal DNS server for use on the internal networks. Because an organization's own employees are the greatest risk for unauthorized access, many organizations use internal firewalls to prevent employees in one part of an organization from accessing resources in a different part.

Many organizations use a combination of NAT proxy servers and packet-level and application-level firewalls (Figure 10-10). Packet-level firewalls are used as an initial screen from the Internet into a network devoted solely to servers intended to provide public access (e.g., Web servers, public DNS servers). This network is sometimes called the DMZ (demilitarized zone) because it contains the organization's servers but does not provide complete security for them. This packet-level firewall will permit Web requests and similar access to the DMZ network servers, but will deny FTP access to these servers from the Internet because no one except internal users should have the right to modify the servers. This DMZ network contains a proxy server that provides access to the organization's internal networks. Each major portion of the organization's internal networks has its own proxy server to grant (or deny) access on the basis of rules established by that part of the organization.

While firewalls and NAT proxy servers were originally designed for large corporations who are most often the targets of hackers, they are becoming increasingly important for individuals as well. With the arrival of broadband Internet access technologies, such as cable modem and DSL, residential computers are more vulnerable to attack because they are always on the Internet whenever they are powered on. Thus it is easier for hackers to attack them now than when they were only occasionally connected to the Internet over dial-up services. As DDoS attacks become more common, hackers are more frequently trying to break-in to less heavily protected residential computers to install DDoS agents to aid

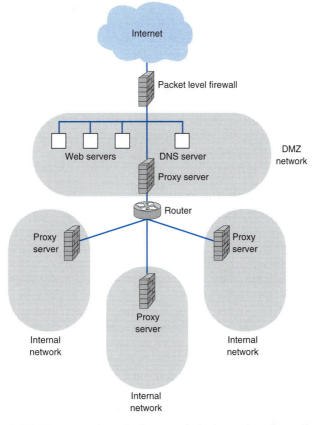

FIGURE 10-10 A typical network design using firewalls.

in their attacks. Many inexpensive routers intended for home use with cable modem and DSL services now provide NAT.

Security Holes Even with physical security, dial-in security, firewalls, and NAT, a network may not be safe because of *security holes*. A security hole is simply a bug that permits unauthorized access. Many commonly used operating systems have major security holes well known to potential intruders. Many security holes have been documented, and patches are available from vendors to fix them, but network managers may be unaware of all the holes or simply forget to regularly update their systems with new patches.

A complete discussion of security holes is beyond the scope of the book. Many security holes are highly technical—for example, sending a message designed to overflow a network buffer, thereby placing a short command into a very specific memory area that unlocks a user profile. Others are rather simple but not obvious. For example, the hacker sends a message that lists the server's address as both the sender and the destination, so the server repeatedly sends messages to itself until it crashes.

Once a security hole is discovered, it is quickly circulated through the Internet. The race begins between hackers and security teams; hackers share their discovery with other hackers and security teams share the discovery with other security teams. CERT is the central clearinghouse for major Internet-related security holes, so the CERT team quickly responds to reports of new security problems and posts alerts and advisories on the Web and e-mails them to those who subscribe to its service. The developer of the software with the security hole usually works quickly to fix the security hole and produces a *patch* that corrects the hole. This patch is then shared with customers so they can download it and apply it to their systems to prevent hackers from exploiting the hole to break in. The problem is that many network managers do not routinely respond to such security threats by immediately downloading and installing the patch. Often, it takes many months for patches to be distributed to most sites.[3]

Other security holes are not really holes but simply policies adopted by computer vendors that open the door for security problems, such as computer systems that come with a variety of preinstalled user accounts. These accounts and their initial passwords are well documented and known to all potential intruders. This wouldn't be a problem if network managers didn't sometimes forget to change the passwords on these well-known accounts, thus enabling a hacker to slip in.

The U.S. government requires certain levels of security in the operating systems and network operating systems it uses for certain applications. The minimum level of security is C2. Most major operating systems (e.g., Windows) provide at least C2. Most widely used systems are striving to meet the requirements of much higher security levels, such as B2. Very few systems meet the highest levels of security (A1 and A2).

Symmetric Encryption   One of the best ways to prevent unauthorized access is *encryption,* which is a means of disguising information by the use of mathematical rules known as *algorithms.*[4] Actually, *cryptography* is the more general and proper term. *Encryption* is the process of disguising information, whereas *decryption* is the process of restoring it to readable form. When information is in readable form, it is called *plaintext;* when in encrypted form, it is called *ciphertext.*

There are two fundamentally different types of encryption: symmetric and asymmetric. A *symmetric algorithm* is one in which the key used to encrypt a message is the *same* as the one used to decrypt it. An *asymmetric algorithm* is one in which the key used to decrypt is *different* from the one used to encrypt it. In this section, we discuss symmetric encryption; the next section is devoted to asymmetric encryption.

A symmetric encryption system (also call single-key encryption) has two parts: the algorithm itself and the *key,* which personalizes the algorithm by making the transformation of data unique. Two pieces of identical information encrypted with the same algorithm but with different keys produce completely different ciphertexts. When using most encryption systems, communicating parties must share this key. If the algorithm is adequate and the key is kept secret, acquisition of the ciphertext by unauthorized personnel is of no consequence to the communicating parties.

---

[3] For an example of one CERT advisory posted about problems with the most common DNS server software used on the Internet, see www.cert.org/advisories/CA-2001-02.html. The history in this advisory shows that it took about 8 months for the patch for the previous advisory in this family (issued in November 1999) to be installed on most DNS servers around the world.

[4] For more information on cryptography, see www.rsasecurity.com/rsalabs/faq.

TECHNICAL FOCUS *10-3*

EXPLOITING A SECURITY HOLE

To exploit a security hole, the hacker has to know it's there. So how does a hacker find out? It's simple in the era of automated tools.

First, the hacker has to find the servers on a network. The hacker could start by using network-scanning software to systematically probe every IP address on a network to find all the servers on the network. At this point, the hacker has narrowed the potential targets to a few servers.

Second, the hacker needs to learn what services are available on each server. To do this, he or she could use port-scanning software to systematically probe every port on a given server. This would reveal which ports are in use and thus what services the server offers. For example, if the server has software that responds to port 80, it is a Web server, whereas if it responds to port 25, it is a mail server.

Third, the hacker would begin to seek out the exact software and version number of the server software providing each service. For example, suppose the hacker decides to target mail servers. There is a variety of tools that can probe the mail server software and, on the basis of how the server software responds to certain messages, determine which manufacturer and version number of software is being used.

Finally, once the hacker knows which package and version number the server is using, the hacker uses tools designed to exploit the known security holes in the software. For example, some older mail server software packages do not require users to authenticate themselves (e.g., by a user ID and password) before accepting Simple Mail Transfer Protocol (SMTP) packets for the mail server to forward. In this case, a hacker could create SMTP packets with fake source addresses and use the server to flood the Internet with spam (i.e., junk mail). In another case, a certain version of a well-known e-commerce package enabled users to pass operating system commands to the server simply by including a UNIX pipe symbol (|) and the command in the name of a file name to be uploaded; when the system opened the uploaded file, it also executed the command attached to it.

Good encryption systems do not depend on keeping the algorithm secret. Only the keys need to be kept secret. The key is a relatively small numeric value (in terms of the number of bits). The larger the key, the more secure the encryption, because large "key space" protects the ciphertext against those who try to break it by *brute-force attacks*—which are simply trying every possible key. There should be a large enough number of possible keys that an exhaustive brute-force attack would take inordinately long or would cost more than the value of the encrypted information.

Because the same key is used to encrypt and decrypt, symmetric algorithms can cause problems with *key management;* keys must be shared among the senders and receivers very carefully. Before two computers in a network to can communicate using encryption, both must have the same key. This means that both computers can then send and read any messages that use that key. Companies often do not want one company to be able to read messages they send to another company, so this means that there must be a separate key used for communication with each company. These keys must be recorded but kept secure so that they cannot be stolen. Because the algorithm is known publicly, the disclosure of the key means the total compromise of encrypted messages. Managing this system of keys can be challenging.

One commonly used symmetric encryption algorithm is the *Data Encryption Standard (DES),* which was developed in the mid-1970s by the U.S. government in conjunction with IBM. DES is maintained by the National Institute of Standards and Technology (NIST). The most common form of DES uses a 56-bit key but can be broken by brute-force attacks. In a recent test using a special decryption supercomputer, 56-bit DES was broken in 56 hours. In another attempt, this same computer, working with the help of 10,000 microcomputers distributed over the Internet, broke a 56-bit DES in 22 hours. DES is no longer recommended for government use, although the commercial sector continues to use it for less important messages.

Another commonly used symmetric encryption algorithm is *RC4,* developed by Ron Rivest of RSA Data Security. Inc. RC4 can use a key up to 256 bits long but most commonly uses a 40-bit key. It is faster to use than DES but suffers from the same problems from brute-force attacks: It can be broken by a determined attacker.

Triple DES (3DES) is a newer standard that is harder to break. As the name suggest, it involves using DES three times, usually with three different keys to produce the encrypted text,[5] which produces a stronger level of security, because it has a total of 168 bits as the key (i.e., 3×56 bits).

The NIST's new *Advanced Encryption Standard (AES)* is designed to replace DES and 3DES with the *Rijndael* (pronounced "rain doll") *algorithm,* developed by two Flemish researchers.[6] AES will have key sizes of 128, 192, and 256 bits. NIST estimates that using the most advanced computers and techniques available today, cracking AES by brute force would require about 150 trillion years. As computers and techniques improve, the time requirement will drop, but AES seems secure for the foreseeable future; the original DES lasted 20 years, so AES may have a similar life span.

Today, the U.S. government considers encryption to be a weapon and regulates its export in the same way it regulates the export of machine guns or bombs. Present rules prohibit the export of encryption techniques with keys longer than 56 bits (for some algorithms, 64 bits and 168 bits are permitted), although exports to Canada and the European Union are permitted, and American banks and Fortune 100 companies are now permitted to use more powerful encryption techniques in their foreign offices. This policy made sense when only U.S. companies had the expertise to develop powerful encryption software. Today, however, many companies outside the United States are developing encryption software that is more powerful than U.S. software that is limited by these rules. Therefore, the U.S. software industry is lobbying the government to change the rules so that it can successfully compete overseas.[7]

Public Key Encryption   The most popular form of *public key encryption* (also called asymmetric encryption) is *RSA,* which was invented at Massachusetts Institute of Technology in 1977 by Ron Rivest, Adi Shamir, and Leonard Adleman. The inventors of the initial algorithm founded RSA Data Security in 1982, and many companies have licensed the RSA patented technique. The patent expired in 2000, so many new companies have entered the market and public key software has dropped in price. The RSA technique forms the basis for today's *public key infrastructure (PKI).*

[5] There are several versions of 3DES. One version (called 3DES-EEE) simply encrypts the message three times with different keys, as one would expect. Another version (3DES-EDE) encrypts with one key, decrypts with a second key (i.e., reverse encrypts), and then encrypts with a third key. There are other variants, as you can imagine.

[6] It was developed by Joan Daemen and Vincent Rijmen. It was Rijmen's doctoral dissertation. For more information on Rijndael, see csrc.nist.gov/encryption/aes/rijndael.

[7] The rules have been changed several times in recent years, so for more recent information, see www.bxa.doc.gov/Encryption.

Public key encryption is inherently different from symmetric single-key systems like DES. Because public key encryption is asymmetric, there are two keys. One key (called the *public key*) is used to encrypt the message and a second, very different *private key* is used to decrypt the message. Keys are often 512 or 1,024 bits in length.

Public key systems are based on one-way functions. Even though you originally know both the contents of your message and the public encryption key, once it is encrypted by the one-way function, the message cannot be decrypted without the private key. One-way functions, which are relatively easy to calculate in one direction, are impossible to "uncalculate" in the reverse direction. Public key encryption is one of the most secure encryption techniques available, excluding special encryption techniques developed by national security agencies.

Public key encryption greatly reduces the key management problem. Each user has its public key that is used to encrypt messages sent to it. These public keys are widely publicized (e.g., listed in a telephone book-style directory)—that's why they're called *public* keys. In addition, each user has a private key that decrypts only the messages that were encrypted by its public key. This private key is kept secret. The net result is that if two parties wish to communicate with one another, there is no need to exchange keys beforehand. Each knows the other's public key from the listing in a public directory and can communicate encrypted information immediately. The key management problem is reduced to the on-site protection of the private key.

Figure 10-11 illustrates how this process works. All public keys are published in a directory. When organization A wants to send an encrypted message to organization B, it looks through the directory to find its public key. It then encrypts the message using B's public key. This encrypted message is then sent through the network to organization B, which decrypts the message using its private key.

Public key encryption also permits *authentication* (or *digital signatures*). When one user sends a message to another, it is difficult to legally prove who actually sent the message. Legal proof is important in many communications, such as bank transfers and buy/sell orders in currency and stock trading, which normally require legal signatures. Public key encryption algorithms are invertable, meaning that text encrypted with either key can be decrypted by the other. Normally, we encrypt with the public key and decrypt with the private key. However, it is possible to do the inverse: Encrypt with the private key and decrypt with the public key. Because the private key is secret, only the real user could use it to encrypt a message. Thus, a digital signature or authentication sequence is used as a legal signature on many financial transactions. This signature is usually the name of the signing party plus other *key contents* such as unique information from the message (e.g., date, time, or dollar amount). This signature and the other key contents are encrypted by the sender using the private key. The receiver uses the sender's public key to decrypt the signature block and compares the result to the name and other key contents in the rest of the message to ensure a match.

Figure 10-12 illustrates how authentication can be combined with public encryption to provide a secure and authenticated transmission. The plaintext message is first encrypted using organization A's private key and then encrypted using organization's B public key. It is then transmitted to B. Organization B first decrypts the message using its private key. It sees that part of the message (the key contents) is still in ciphertext, indicating it is an authenticated message. B then decrypts the key contents part of the message

Organization A

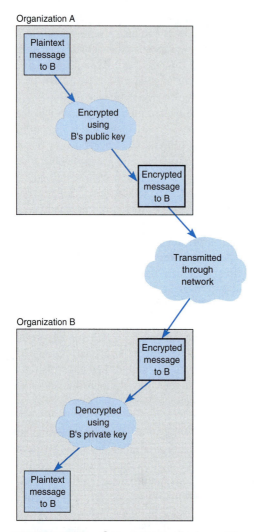

Organization B

FIGURE 10-11 Secure transmission with public key encryption.

using A's public key to produce the plaintext message. Because only A has the private key that matches A's public key, B can safely assume that A sent the message.

The only problem with this approach lies in ensuring that the person or organization who sent the document with the correct private key is actually the person or organization claimed. Anyone can post a public key on the Internet, so there is no way of knowing for sure who that person actually is. For example, it would be possible for someone other than organization A in this example to claim to be organization A when in fact that someone is an imposter.

This is where the Internet's PKI becomes important.[8] The PKI is a set of hardware, software, organizations, and policies designed to make public key encryption work on the

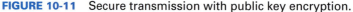

[8] For more on the PKI, see www.ietf.org/internet-drafts/draft-ietf-pkix-roadmap-06.txt.

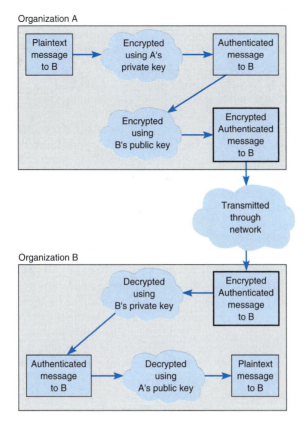

FIGURE 10-12   Authenticated and secure transmission with public key encryption.

Internet. PKI begins with a *certificate authority (CA),* which is a trusted organization that can vouch for the authenticity of the person or organization using authentication (e.g., VeriSign). A person wanting to use a CA registers with the CA and must provide some proof of identify. There are several levels of certification, ranging from a simple confirmation from a valid e-mail address to a complete police-style background check with an in-person interview. The CA issues a digital *certificate* that is the requestor's public key encrypted using the CA's private key as proof of identify. This certificate is then attached to the user's e-mail or Web transactions in addition to the authentication information. The receiver then verifies the certificate by decrypting it with the CA's public key—and must also contact the CA to ensure that the user's certificate has not been revoked by the CA.

For higher-security certifications, the CA requires that a unique "fingerprint" be issued by the CA for each message sent by the user. The user submits the message to the CA, who creates the unique fingerprint by combining the CA's private key with the message's authentication key contents. Because the user must obtain a unique fingerprint for each message, this ensures that the CA has not revoked the certificate between the time it was issued and the time the message was sent by the user.

Pretty Good Privacy (PGP) is a freeware public key encryption package developed by Philip Zimmermann that is often used to encrypt e-mail. Users post their public key on Web pages, for example, and anyone wishing to send them an encrypted message simply cuts and pastes the key off the Web page into the PGP software, which encrypts and sends the message.[9] There are also a variety of PGP key servers around the Internet that enable you to search for and extract someone's public key using their e-mail address (e.g., pgp5.ai.mit.edu)

Secure Sockets Layer (SSL) is an encryption protocol widely used on the Web. SSL operates between the application-layer software and the transport layer (in what the OSI model calls the presentation layer). SSL encrypts outbound packets coming out of the application layer before they reach the transport layer and decrypts inbound packets coming out of the transport layer before they reach the application layer. With SSL, the client and the server start with a handshake for PKI authentication and for the server to provide its public key and preferred encryption technique to the client (usually RC4, DES, or 3DES). The client then generates a key for this encryption technique, which is sent to the server encrypted with the server's public key. The rest of the communication then uses this encryption technique and key.

IP Security Protocol (IPSec) is another widely used encryption protocol. IPSec differs from SSL in that SSL is focused on Web applications, whereas IPSec can be used with a much wider variety of application-layer protocols. IPSec sits between IP at the network layer and TCP/UDP at the transport layer. IPSec can use a wide variety of encryption techniques, so the first step is to the sender and receiver to establish the technique and key to be used. This is done using *Internet Key Exchange (IKE)*. Both parties generate a random key and send to the other using an encrypted authenticated PKI process then put these two numbers together to produce the key.[10] The encryption technique is also negotiated between the two, often being DES or 3DES. Once the keys and technique have been established, IPSec can begin transmitting data.

IPSec can operate in either transport mode or tunnel mode. In *transport mode,* IPSec encrypts just the IP payload, leaving the IP packet header unchanged so it can be easily routed through the Internet. In this case, IPSec adds an additional packet (either an authentication header [AH] or an encapsulating security payload [ESP]) at the start of the IP packet that provides encryption information for the receiver.

In *tunnel mode,* IPSec encrypts the entire IP packet and must therefore add an entirely new IP packet that contains the encrypted packet, as well as the IPSec AH or ESP packets. In tunnel mode, the newly added IP packet just identifies the IPSec encryption agent at the destination, not the final destination; once the IPSec packet arrives at the encryption agent, the encrypted packet is decrypted and sent on its way. In tunnel mode, attackers can learn only the end points of the tunnel, not the ultimate source and destination of the packets.

Detecting Unauthorized Access

The previous section focused on preventing unauthorized access. Although one hopes that these techniques are successful, the possibility of a security break-in still remains. Therefore, networks sometimes need an *intrusion detection system (IDS)*.

---

[9] For example, Cisco posts the public keys it uses for security incident reporting on its Web site. You will find a link to the Cisco PGP Public keys near the bottom of the page at: www.cisco.com/warp/public/707/sec_incident_response.shtml. For more information on PGP, see www.pgpi.org and www.pgp.com.

[10] This is done using the Diffie–Hellman process; see www.rsasecurity.com/rsalabs/faq/3–6–1.html.

MANAGEMENT FOCUS *10-10*

ANATOMY OF A FRIENDLY HACK

If you've seen the movie *Sneakers,* you know that there are professional security firms that organizations can hire to break in to their own networks to test security. BABank was about to launch a new online banking service, so it hired such a firm to test its security before the launch. The bank's system failed the security test.

The security team began by mapping the bank's network. It used DNS searches, sniffer software, network security analysis software (e.g., SATAN), and dialing software to test for dial-in ports. The mapping process found a computer running an old mail program with a known security hole and a bunch of maintenance accounts with unchanged passwords. The team then used social engineering to gain passwords to several high-privilege accounts. Once into these computers, the team used password-cracking software to find passwords on these computers and ultimately gain the administrator passwords on several servers and routers.

At this point, the team transferred $1,000 into their test account. They could have transferred more, but the security point was made. Finally, the team launched a successful denial-of-service attack that crashed the online banking system.

SOURCE: *Network World,* February 2, 1998.

There are three general types of IDS, and many network managers choose to install all three. The first type is a *network-based IDS.* With a network-based IDS, *IDS sensors* are placed on key network circuits. An IDS sensor is simply a device running a special operating system that monitors all network packets on that circuit and reports intrusions to an *IDS management console.*

The second type of IDS is the *host-based IDS,* which, as the name suggests, is a software package installed on a host or server. The host-based IDS monitors activity on the server and the incoming circuits and reports intrusions to the IDS management console. The third type, *application-based IDS,* is a specialized form of host-based IDS that just monitors one application on the server, often a Web server.

There are two fundamental techniques that these three types of IDS can use to determine that an intrusion is in progress; most IDSs use both techniques. The first technique is *misuse detection,* which compares monitored activities with signatures of known attacks. Whenever an attack signature is recognized, the IDS issues an alert and discards the suspicious packets. The problem, of course, is keeping the database of attack signatures up-to-date as new attacks are invented.

The second fundamental technique is *anomaly detection,* which works well in stable networks by comparing monitored activities with the "normal" set of activities. When a major deviation is detected (e.g., a sudden flood of ICMP ping packets, an unusual number of failed logins to the network manager's account), the IDS issues an alert and discards the suspicious packets. The problem, of course, is false alarms when situations arise that produce valid network traffic that is different from normal (e.g., on a heavy trading day on Wall Street, E-trade receives a larger-than-normal volume of messages).

IDSs are often used in conjunction with other security tools such as firewalls (Figure 10-13). In fact, some firewalls now include IDS functions. One problem is that the IDS and its sensors and management console are a prime target for hackers. The IDS must be very secure against attack. Some organizations deploy redundant IDS from different vendors

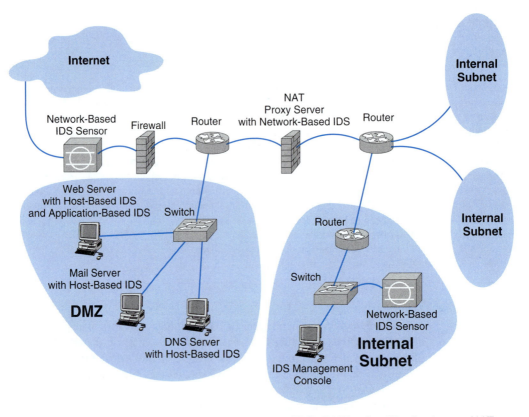

FIGURE 10-13 Intrusion detection system (IDS). DMZ = demilitarized zone. NAT = network address translation.

(e.g., a network-based IDS from one vendor and a host-based IDS from another) to decrease the chance that the IDS can be hacked.

Correcting Unauthorized Access

Although IDS monitoring is important, it has little value unless there is a clear plan for responding to a security breach in progress. Every organization should have a clear response planned if a break-in is discovered. Many large organizations have emergency response "SWAT" teams ready to be called into action if a problem is discovered. The best example is CERT, the Internet's emergency response team. CERT has helped many organizations establish such teams.

Responding to an intrusion can be more complicated than it at first seems. For example, suppose the IDS detects a DoS attack from a certain IP address. The immediate reaction could be to discard all packets from that IP address; however, in the age of IP spoofing, the attacker could fake the address of your best customer and trick you into discarding packets from it.

Once an intrusion has been detected, the first step is to identify how the intruder gained unauthorized access and prevent others from breaking in the same way. Some organizations will simply choose to close the door on the hacker and fix the security problem

TECHNICAL FOCUS *10-4*

INTRUSION DETECTION GETS ACTIVE

Worms have been responsible for some of the most costly virus infections because they spread much more quickly than traditional viruses. The "Code Red" worm for example, spread by using a security hole in Microsoft's IIS Web server software. By sending an HTTP request that is too large for the server's incoming message buffer, the server can be tricked into running operating system commands contained in the HTTP request. The commands imbedded in the request install the worm, which then attempt to infect other computers by sending the same HTTP request to more computers.

A new IDS freely available on the Internet has developed a way to trap worms that minimizes or prevents their spread. Called LaBrea for the LaBrea tarpits in California that trapped hundreds of dinosaurs, the tool traps the connection requests that many worms use when they spread. LaBrea is the first of a new breed of IDS that detect and attempt to disable the intrusion.

When Code Red and similar worms attempt to spread, they send HTTP requests containing the worm addressed to all IP addresses they can think of (e.g., if they have infected a company with an IP range of 128.196.x.x, they first try 128.196.1.1, then 128.196.1.2, then 128.196.1.3 and so on). In most cases, there are no Web servers on most of these addresses, so the worm ends up trying to reach computers that do not exist. When the worm sends an HTTP request, the TCP software on the infected computer first sends a TCP open connection request to selected IP address before the HTTP request is sent (see the TCP/IP example in Chapter 3). The TCP request eventually reaches the router that is the gateway into the TCP/IP subnet that would have a Web server with the IP address if the computer existed. If there is no server with the requested IP address, the router doesn't have an Ethernet address that matches the IP address in its memory, and thus the router broadcasts an ARP, requesting that the computer with that IP address send its Ethernet address to the router. Of course, no computer will respond because there is no computer with that IP address. ARP is a tenacious protocol. Because it expects that there really is a computer with that IP address, the router will issue the ARP many times without getting an answer before it gives up and returns the message to the sender as undeliverable.

This is where LaBrea steps in. After hearing several ARP requests for the same IP address go unanswered, LaBrea will issue an ARP response to the router, giving its computer's Ethernet address as the one that matches the phantom IP address. From this point forward, all messages targeted at the phantom IP address will be delivered to the LaBrea software. When LaBrea receives the TCP open connection request that precedes HTTP request containing the worm, LaBrea will accept the open connection but not acknowledge the TCP segment in the normal way. TCP is also a tenacious protocol, which means that the TCP software at the infected machine will keep trying to send data, but will never quite succeed because LaBrea never responds properly. LaBrea will also try to trick the sending computer's TCP software into accepting a "persistent connection" which means that the connection will not be closed until the receiver (i.e., the LaBrea software) closes it – which, of course, it will never do.

By holding the connection open, the LaBrea software prevents the worm from moving onto the next IP address in its sequence or at least significantly delays its movement to the next IP address. And of course, the next false IP address that the worm tries will be again met by the LaBrea software.

Because LaBrea holds connections open indefinitely, it becomes much easier to contact the owners of the infected computer and enable them to identify and fix the problem. LaBrea will respond to all requests, not just HTTP requests, so it is able to capture and hold open connections from port scanning software often used by hackers—which again makes it possible to trace them more easily.

Other organizations may take a more aggressive response by logging the intruder's activities and working with police to catch the individuals involved. Once identified, the hacker will be charged with criminal activities, and/or sued in civil court.

A whole new area called *computer forensics* has recently opened up. Computer forensics is the use of computer analysis techniques to gather evidence for criminal and/or

MANAGEMENT FOCUS *10-11*

SNAPPING A HONEY TRAP

After a 6-month investigation, British police arrested three men with links to organized crime who attempted to rob an online bank, London's Egg PLC. The men exploited a security hole in the bank's application software that enabled them to open multiple accounts and apply for multiple credit cards and loans.

After discovering the security hole, the bank choose to pursue and prosecute the intruders. First, however, the bank closed the hole to other would-be thieves but permit-

ted the three men to continue with their activities. Working with police, the bank installed special software to monitor and track the thieves. Once enough evidence had been collected, Britain's National Crime Squad swooped in and arrested them.

SOURCE: "U.K. Police Catch E-bank Robbers," *Computer World*, August 23, 2000.

---

civil trials. The basic steps of computer forensics are similar to those of traditional forensics, but the techniques are different. First, identify potential evidence. Second, preserve evidence by making backup copies and use those copies for all analysis. Third, analyze the evidence. Finally, prepare a detailed legal report for use in prosecutions.

Although criminal law has been slow to keep up with the Internet, most industrialized countries now have criminal laws under which hackers can be prosecuted. Companies are sometimes tempted to launch counterattacks (or counterhacks) against intruders, but this can be illegal.

Many organizations have taken their own steps to snare intruders by using *entrapment* techniques. The objective is to divert the hackers' attention from the real network to an attractive server that contains only fake information. This server is often called a *honey pot*. The honey pot server contains highly interesting fake information, available only through illegal intrusion, to bait the intruder. The honey pot server has sophisticated tracking software to monitor access to this information that allows the organization and law enforcement officials to trace and legally document the intruder's actions. Possession of this information then becomes final legal proof of the intrusion.

SUMMARY

Types of Security Threats   In general, network security threats can be classified into one of two categories: (1) disruption, destruction, and disaster; and (2) unauthorized access. Disruptions are usually minor and temporary. Some disruptions may also be caused by or result in the destruction of data. Natural (or human-made) disasters may occur that destroy host computers or large sections of the network. Unauthorized access refers to intruder's (external hackers or organizational employees) gaining unauthorized access to files. Intruders may gain knowledge, change files to commit fraud or theft, or destroy information to injure the organization.

Risk Assessment   Developing a secure network means developing controls that reduce or eliminate threats to the network. Controls prevent, detect, and correct whatever might happen to the organization when its computer-based systems are threatened. The first step in developing a secure network is to conduct a risk assessment. This is done by identifying the key assets and threats and comparing the nature of the threats to the controls designed to protect the assets. A control spreadsheet lists the assets, threats, and controls, which a network manager uses to assess the level of risk.

Controlling Disruption, Destruction, and Disaster The key principle in controlling these threats—or at least reducing their impact—is redundancy. Redundant hardware that automatically recognizes failure and intervenes to replace the failed component can mask a failure that would otherwise result in a service disruption. Special attention needs to be given to preventing computer viruses and DoS attacks. Generally speaking, preventing disasters is difficult, so the best option is a well-designed disaster recovery plan that includes backups and sometimes a professional disaster recovery firm.

Controlling Unauthorized Access The key principle in controlling unauthorized access is to be proactive in routinely testing and upgrading security controls. Contrary to popular belief, unauthorized intruders are usually organization employees, not external hackers. There are eight general areas to preventing unauthorized access: a security policy, user profiles, physical security, dial-in security, firewalls, network address translation, security holes, and encryption. The basic principle in detecting unauthorized access is using an intrusion detection system to monitor for known attacks and/or to look for anything out of the ordinary. The intrusion system should trigger a rapid-response team once an intrusion is detected.

KEY TERMS

account
Advanced Encryption Standard (AES)
anomaly detection
application-based IDS
application-level firewall
asset
asymmetric algorithm
authentication
backup controls
biometric system
block cipher
brute-force attack
call-back modem
certificate
certificate authority (CA)
ciphertext
Computer Emergency Response Team (CERT)
computer forensics
control principles
control spreadsheet
controls
cracker
Data Encryption Standard (DES)

decryption
Delphi team
denial-of-service (DoS) attack
digital signature
disaster recovery drill
disaster recovery firm
disaster recovery plan
disk mirroring
distributed denial-of-service (DDoS) attack
DDoS agent
DDoS handler
eavesdropping
encryption
entrapment
fault-tolerant server
firewall
hacker
honey pot
host-based IDS
IDS management console
IDS sensor
information warfare
Internet Key Exchange (IKE)

intrusion detection system (IDS)
IP Security Protocol (IPSec)
IPSec transport mode
IPSec tunnel mode
IP spoofing
key
key escrow
key management
macrovirus
mission-critical application
misuse detection
NAT proxy server
network address translation (NAT)
network-based IDS
one-time password
packet-level firewall
password
patch
physical security
plaintext
Pretty Good Privacy (PGP)
private key
public key

public key encryption
public key infrastructure (PKI)
RC4
recovery controls
redundancy
Rijndael algorithm
risk assessment
RSA
script kiddies
secure hub
Secure Sockets Layer (SSL)
security hole
security policy
smart card
sniffer program
social engineering
symmetric algorithm
triple DES (3DES)
uninterruptable power supply (UPS)
user profile
threat
token
virus
worm

QUESTIONS

1. What factors have brought about increased emphasis on network security?
2. Briefly outline the steps required to complete a risk assessment.
3. Name at least six assets that should have controls in a data communications network.
4. What are some of the criteria that can be used to rank security risks?
5. What is the primary principle of controlling disruption, destruction, and disaster?
6. What is the primary principle of controlling unauthorized access?
7. What is the purpose of a disaster recovery plan? What are five major elements of a typical disaster recovery plan?
8. What are the most common security threats? What are the most critical?
9. What is a computer virus?
10. How can one reduce the risk of natural disaster?
11. Explain how a DoS attack works.
12. How does a DoS attack differ from a DDoS attack?
13. What is a disaster recovery firm? When and why would you establish a contract with them?
14. Reread Management Focus 10-2 and 10-4, which discussed the security problems experienced by Microsoft. Which disruption had the greatest impact? What are the implications for security?
15. People who attempt unauthorized access can be classified into four different categories. Describe them.
16. What are five major elements of a security policy?
17. What is social engineering?
18. What is a token (in the security meaning of the word, not the medium access control meaning of the word)? A smart card?
19. Explain how a biometric system can improve security.
20. What is a security hole, and how do you fix it?
21. What is a sniffer?
22. Describe the purpose of a call-back modem.
23. Describe the three general ways of restricting access to a network.
24. What do you think are the three most important security controls that can be placed on a network? Why?
25. What is a firewall?
26. What are the differences between the different types of firewalls?
27. What is IP spoofing?
28. What is a NAT proxy server, and how does it work?
29. Compare and contrast symmetric and asymmetric encryption.
30. Is it possible first to encrypt with a public key and then to decrypt with a private (secret) key, as well as first to encrypt with the private key and then to decrypt that message with the public key?
31. Describe how symmetric encryption and decryption work.
32. Describe how asymmetric encryption and decryption work.
33. What is key management?
34. How does DES differ from 3DES? From RC4? From AES?
35. Compare and contrast DES and public key encryption.
36. Explain how authentication works.
37. What is a certificate authority?
38. How does PGP differ from SSL?
39. How does SSL differ from IPSec?
40. Compare and contrast IPSec tunnel mode and IPSec transfer mode.
41. What is an intrusion detection system?
42. Compare and contrast a network-based IDS, a host-based IDS, and an application-based IDS.
43. How does IDS anomaly detection differ from misuse detection?
44. What is computer forensics?
45. What is a honey pot?
46. A few security consultants have said that broadband and wireless technologies are their best friends. Explain.
47. Some experts argue that CERT's posting of security holes on its Web site causes more security break-ins than it prevents and should be stopped. What are the pros and cons on both sides of this argument? What do you think?
48. If you had the ability to invent a fabulous new security tool, what would it be?
49. Suppose you started working as a network manager at a medium-size firm with an Internet presence and dis-

covered that the previous network manager had done a terrible job of network security. Which four security controls would be your top priority? Why?

50. Although it is important to protect all servers, some servers are more important than others. What server is the most important to protect and why?

EXERCISES

10-1. Conduct a risk assessment of your organization's networks. Some information may be confidential, so report what you can.

10-2. Investigate and report on the activities of CERT.

10-3. Investigate the capabilities and costs of three firewall products.

10-4. Investigate the capabilities and costs of three IDSs.

10-5. Investigate the capabilities and costs of three encryption software packages.

MINI-CASES

I. Belmont State Bank

Belmont State Bank is a large bank with hundreds of branches that are connected to a central computer system. Some branches are connected over dedicated circuits, and others use the dial-up telephone network. Each branch has a variety of client computers and ATMs connected to a server. The server stores the branch's daily transaction data and transmits it several times during the day to the central computer system. Tellers at each branch use a four-digit numeric password, and each teller's computer is transaction-coded to accept only its authorized transactions. Perform a risk assessment.

II. Western Bank

Western Bank is a small family-owned bank with six branches spread over one county. It has decided to move onto the Internet with a Web site that permits customers to access their accounts and pay bills. Design the key security hardware and software the bank should use.

III. Classic Catalog Company

Classic Catalog Company runs a small but rapidly growing catalog sales business. It has outsourced its Web operations to a local ISP for several years but as sales over the Web has become a larger portion of its business, it has decided to move its Web site onto its own internal computer systems. It has also decided to undertake a major upgrade of its own internal networks. The company has two buildings, an office complex and a warehouse. The 2-story office building has 60 computers. The first floor has 40 computers, 30 of which are devoted to telephone sales. The company expects to add another 10 telephone sales computers over the coming year. The warehouse, located 400 feet across the company's parking lot from the office building, has about 100,000 square feet, all on one floor. The warehouse has 15 computers in the shipping department located at one end of the warehouse. The company wants to experiment with using wireless handheld computers to help employees more quickly locate and pick products for customer orders. Based on traffic projections for the coming year, the company plans to use a T1 connection from its office to its ISP, but wants to make sure that the network is designed to be easily expandable should traffic increase more rapidly than expected. It expects to need at least three servers: the main Web server, an e-mail server, and an internal application server for its application systems (e.g., orders, payroll). Design the network.

CHAPTER 11

NETWORK MANAGEMENT

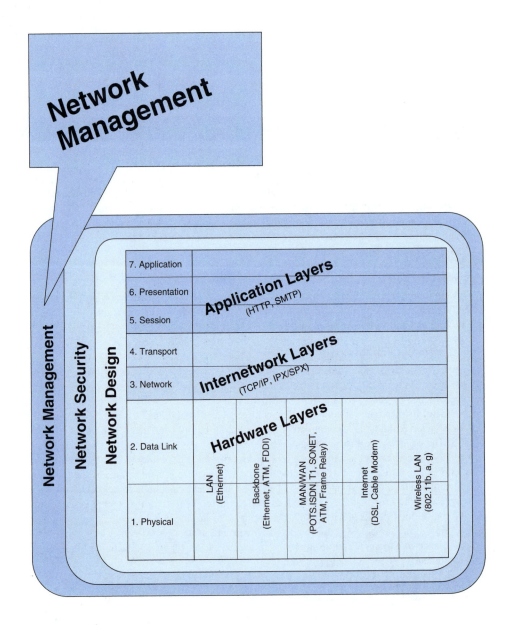

NETWORK MANAGERS spend most of their time managing the day-to-day operation of existing networks. This chapter examines day-to-day network management, discussing the things that must be done to ensure that the network functions properly. We discuss the network management organization and the basic functions that a network manager must perform to operate a successful network.

OBJECTIVES

- Understand what is required to manage the day-to-day operation of networks
- Be familiar with the network management organization
- Understand configuration management
- Understand performance and fault management
- Be familiar with end-user support
- Be familiar with cost management

CHAPTER OUTLINE

INTRODUCTION

ORGANIZING THE NETWORK MANAGEMENT FUNCTION

   The Shift to LANs and the Internet

   Integrating LANs, WANs, and the Internet

   Integrating Voice and Data Communications

CONFIGURATION MANAGEMENT

   Configuring the Network and Client Computers

   Documenting the Configuration

PERFORMANCE AND FAULT MANAGEMENT

   Network Monitoring

   Failure Control Function

   Performance and Failure Statistics

END-USER SUPPORT

   Resolving Problems

   Providing End-User Training

INTRODUCTION

Network management is the process of operating, monitoring, and controlling the network to ensure it works as intended and provides value to its users. The primary objective of the data communications function is to move application-layer data from one location to another in a timely fashion and to provide the resources that allow this transfer to occur. This transfer of information may take place within a single department, between departments in an organization, or with entities outside the organization across private networks or the Internet.

Without a well-planned, well-designed network and without a well-organized network management staff, operating the network becomes extremely difficult. Unfortunately, many network managers spend most of their time *firefighting*—dealing with breakdowns and immediate problems. If managers do not spend enough time on planning and organizing the network and networking staff, which are needed to predict and prevent problems, they are destined to be reactive rather than proactive in solving problems.

In this chapter, we examine the network management function. We begin by examining the job of the network manager and how the network management function can be organized within companies. We then break down the activities that network managers perform into four basic functions: configuration management (knowing what hardware and software are where), performance and fault management (making sure the network operates as desired), end-user support (assisting end users), and cost management (minimizing the cost of providing network services). In practice, it is difficult to separate the network manager's job into these four neat categories, but these are useful ways to help understand what a network manager does.

ORGANIZING THE NETWORK MANAGEMENT FUNCTION

Communication and networking functions present special organizational problems because they are both centralized and decentralized. The developers, gatherers, and users of data are typically decentralized. The need for communications and networking affects every business function, so the management of voice and data communications has traditionally been highly centralized. Networks and mainframe servers were "owned" and operated by centralized IT departments that were used to controlling every aspect of the IT and communication environment.

The Shift to LANs and the Internet

Since the late 1980s, this picture has changed dramatically. There has been an explosion in the use of microcomputer-based networks. In fact, more than 90 percent of most organizations' total computer processing power (measured in millions of instructions per seconds) now resides on microcomputer-based LANs. This trend is continuing; since the early 1990s, the number of computers attached to LANs has grown by almost 40 percent *per year.* Today, the host mainframe computer will provide less than 10 percent of the organization's total computing power, although the number of Internet-based servers (e.g., Web servers, mail servers) has grown dramatically.

Although the management of host-based mainframe networks will always be important, the future of network management lies in the successful management of multiple clients and servers communicating over LANs, BNs, and the Internet. Many LANs and Web servers were initially designed and implemented by individual departments as separate networks and applications, whose goals were to best meet the needs of their individual owners, not to integrate with other networks and applications.

Today, the critical issue is the integration of all organizational networks and applications. Because each LAN was developed by a different department within the organization, not all LANs use the same architecture (e.g., shared 10Base-T versus switched 10Base-T, routed backbone versus collapsed backbone, TCP/IP versus IPX/SPX). Having different protocols and technologies means that routers or gateways must be used to connect the different LANs to organizational backbones and mainframe and that network managers and technicians must be familiar with many types of networks. The more different types of network technology used, the more complex network management becomes.

MANAGEMENT FOCUS *11-1*

WHAT DO NETWORK MANAGERS DO?

If you were to become a network manager, some of your responsibilities and tasks would be to

- Manage the day-to-day operations of the network.
- Provide support to network users.
- Ensure the network is operating reliably.
- Evaluate and acquire network hardware, software, and services.
- Manage the network technical staff.
- Manage the network budget, with emphasis on controlling costs.
- Develop a strategic (long-term) networking and voice communications plan to meet the organization's policies and goals.

- Keep abreast of the latest technological developments in computers, data communications devices, network software, and the Internet.
- Keep abreast of the latest technological developments in telephone technologies and metropolitan area and local area network services.
- Assist senior management in understanding the business implications of network decisions and the role of the network in business operations.

MANAGEMENT FOCUS *11-2*

FIVE KEY MANAGEMENT TASKS

Planning activities require
- Forecasting
- Establishing objectives
- Scheduling
- Budgeting
- Allocating resources
- Developing policies

Organizing activities require
- Developing organizational structure
- Delegating
- Establishing relationships
- Establishing procedures
- Integrating the smaller organization with the larger organization

Directing activities require
- Initiating activities
- Decision making
- Communicating
- Motivating

Controlling activities require
- Establishing performance standards
- Measuring performance
- Evaluating performance
- Correcting performance

Staffing activities require
- Interviewing people
- Selecting people
- Developing people

Integrating LANs, WANs, and the Internet

The key to integrating LANs, WANs, and the Internet into one overall organization network is for both LAN/Web and WAN managers to recognize that they no longer have the power they once had. No longer can network managers make independent decisions without considering their impacts on other parts of the organization's network. There must be a single overall communications and networking goal that best meets the needs of the entire organization. This will require some network managers to compromise on policies that are not in the best interest of their own departments or networks.

The central data communication network organization should have a written charter that defines its purpose, operational philosophy, and long-range goals. These goals must conform to both the parent organization's information processing goals and to its own departmental goals. Along with its long-term policies, the organization must develop individual procedures with which to implement the policies. Individual departments and LAN/Web managers must be free to implement their own policies and procedures that guide the day-to-day tasks of network staff.

Integrating Voice and Data Communications

Another major organizational challenge is the prospect of combining the voice communication function with the data communication function. Traditionally, voice communications were handled by a manager in the facilities department who supervised the telephone switchboard systems and also coordinated the installation and maintenance of the organization's voice telephone networks. By contrast, data communications traditionally were

MANAGEMENT FOCUS *11-3*

KEY NETWORK MANAGEMENT SKILLS

What skills do network managers see as important? A survey of more than 350 network managers identified the following skills:

Very important skills

- Network design
- Project management
- Knowledge of TCP/IP
- Knowledge of routing technologies

Moderately important skills

- Capacity planning
- Knowledge of Web technologies

- Knowledge of Windows NT
- Knowledge of UNIX

Less important skills

- Knowledge of asynchronous transfer mode
- Knowledge of frame relay
- Knowledge of integrated services digital network
- Knowledge of Notes/Domino

SOURCE: "Making the Best of a Difficult Situation," *Communications Week,* July 1, 1996.

---

handled by the IT department because the staff installed their own communication circuits as the need arose, rather than coordinating with the voice communications staff.

This separation of voice and data worked well over the years, but now changing communication technologies are causing enormous pressures to combine these functions. These pressures are magnified by the high cost of maintaining separate facilities, the low efficiency and productivity of the organization's employees because there are two separate network functions, and the potential political problems within an organization when neither manager wants to relinquish his or her functional duties or job position. A key factor in voice–data integration might turn out to be the elimination of one key management position and the merging of two staffs.

There is no perfect solution to this problem because it must be handled in a way unique to each organization. Depending on the business environment and specific communication needs, some organizations may want to combine these functions, whereas others may find it better to keep them separate. We can state unequivocally that an organization that avoids studying this situation might be promoting inefficient communication systems, lower employee productivity, and increased operating costs for its separate voice and data networks.

In communications, we are moving from an era in which the computer system is the dominant IT function to one in which communications networks are the dominant IT function. In some organizations, the total cost of both voice and data communications will equal or exceed the total cost of the computer systems.

CONFIGURATION MANAGEMENT

Configuration management means managing the network's hardware and software configuration and documenting it (and ensuring it is updated as the configuration changes).

Configuring the Network and Client Computers

One of the most common configuration activities is adding and deleting user accounts. When new users are added to the network, they are usually categorized as being a member of some group of users (e.g., faculty, students, accounting department, personnel department). Each user group has its own access privileges, which define what file servers, directories, and files they can access and provide a standard login script. The log-in script specifies what commands are to be run when the user first logs in (e.g., setting default directories, connecting to public disks, running menu programs).

Another common activity is updating the software on the client computers attached the network. Every time a new application system is developed or updated (or, for that matter, when a new version is released), each client computer in the organization must be updated. Traditionally, this has meant that someone from the networking staff has had to go to each client computer and manually install the software, either from diskettes/CDs or by downloading over the network. For a small organization, this is time consuming but not a major problem. For a large organization with hundreds or thousands of client computers (possibly with a mixture of Windows and Apples), this can be a nightmare.

Electronic software distribution (ESD), sometimes called *desktop management,* is one solution to the configuration problem. ESD enables network managers to install software on client computers over the network without physically touching each client computer. Most ESD packages provide application-layer software for the network server and all client computers. The server software communicates directly with the ESD application software on the clients and can be instructed to download and install certain application packages on each client at some predefined time (e.g., at midnight on a Saturday).

ESD software greatly reduces the cost of configuration management over the long term because it eliminates the need to manually update each and every client computer. It also automatically produces and maintains accurate documentation of all software installed on each client computer and enables network managers to produce a variety of useful reports. However, ESD increases costs in the short term because it costs money (typically $50 to $100 per client computer) and requires network staff to manually install it on each client computer. Desktop Management Interface (DMI) is the emerging standard in ESD software.

Documenting the Configuration

Configuration documentation includes information about network hardware, network software, user and application profiles, and network documentation. The most basic information about network hardware is a set of network configuration diagrams that document the number, type, and placement of network circuits (whether organization owned or leased from a common carrier), network servers, network devices (e.g., hubs, routers), and client computers. For most organizations, this is a large set of diagrams: one for each LAN, BN, MAN, and WAN. Figure 11-1 shows a diagram of network devices in one office location.

These diagrams must be supplemented by documentation on each individual network component (e.g., circuit, hub, server). Documentation should include the type of device, serial number, vendor, date of purchase, warranty information, repair history, telephone number for repairs, and any additional information or comments the network man-

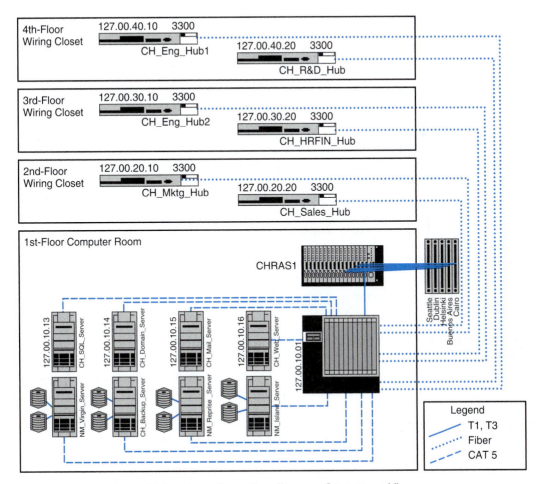

FIGURE 11-1 Network configuration diagram. SOURCE: netViz.

ager wishes to add. For example, it would be useful to include the dial-in numbers for communication servers, contact names and telephone numbers for the individual network managers responsible for each separate LAN within the network, and common carrier circuit control telephone contact index and log. (Whenever possible, establish a national account with the common carrier rather than dealing with individual common carriers in separate states and areas.)

A similar approach can be used for network software. This includes the network operating system and any special-purpose network software. For example, it is important to record which network operating system and which version or release date is installed on each network server. The same is true of application software. As discussed in Chapter 4 on LANs, sharing software on networks can greatly reduce costs, although it is important to ensure that the organization is not violating any software license rules.

Software documentation can also help in negotiating site licenses for software. Many users buy software on a copy-by-copy basis, paying retail price for each copy. It may be cheaper to negotiate the payment of one large fee for an unlimited use license for widely used software packages instead of paying on a per-copy basis.

Another type of documentation is the user and application profiles, which should be automatically provided by the network operating system or additional vendor or third-party software agreements. These should enable the network manager to easily identify the files and directories to which each user has access and each user's access rights (e.g., read-only, edit, delete). Equally important is the ability to access this information in the "opposite" direction; that is, to be able to select a file or directory and obtain a list of all authorized users and their access rights.

In addition, other documentation must be routinely developed and updated pertaining to the network. This includes network hardware and software manuals, application software manuals, standards manuals, operations manuals for network staff, vendor contracts and agreements, and licenses for software. The documentation should include details about performance and fault management (e.g., preventive maintenance guidelines and schedules, disaster recovery plan, and diagnostic techniques), end-user support (e.g., applications software manuals, vendor support telephone numbers), and cost management (e.g., annual budgets, repair costs for each device). The documentation should also include any legal requirements to comply with local or federal laws, control, or regulatory bodies.

PERFORMANCE AND FAULT MANAGEMENT

Performance management means ensuring the network is operating as efficiently as possible, whereas *fault management* means preventing, detecting, and correcting faults in the network circuits, hardware, and software (e.g., a broken hub or improperly installed software). Fault management and performance management are closely related, because any faults in the network reduce performance. Both require *network monitoring,* which means keeping track of the operation of network circuits and devices to ensure they are functioning properly and to determine how heavily they are used.

Network Monitoring

Most large organizations and many smaller ones use *network management software* to monitor and control their networks. One function provided by these systems is to collect operational statistics from the network devices. For small networks, network monitoring is often done by one person, aided by a few simple tools (as discussed in Chapter 9). These tools collect information and send messages to the network manager's computer.

In large networks, network monitoring becomes more important. Large networks that support organizations operating 24 hours a day are often mission critical, which means a network problem can have serious business consequences. For example, consider the impact of a network failure for an IXC such as AT&T or for the air traffic control system. These networks often have a dedicated *network operations center (NOC)* that is responsible for monitoring and fixing problems. Such centers are staffed by a set of skilled network technicians that use sophisticated network management software. When a problem occurs, the software immediately detects the problems and sends an alarm to the NOC. Staff members in the NOC diagnose the problem and can sometimes fix the problem from the NOC

MANAGEMENT FOCUS *11-4*

RIDING THE STORM AT WEATHER.COM

Mark Ryan, chief technology officer of weather.com, the Web counterpart of The Weather Channel, has more to worry about than getting wet when he sees a storm approaching. He has to consider whether a flood of visitors will overwhelm his information technology infrastructure.

Weather.com has unique requirements. The content is dynamic, usage spikes are unpredictable, and visitors demand instant access or will head elsewhere on the Web. Most companies can scale their network infrastructure gradually to well-known peaks (e.g., the Christmas rush for e-commerce sites), but weather.com is not so fortunate. For example, it had to scale from a low of 4 million to 5 million page views per day to a peak of 19 million to 22 million, over a single 2-day period in the face of a major storm.

Weather.com used an initial strategy of "just throw hardware at it" to meet the rapidly growing demands

over its first few years. The result was a hodgepodge of different systems, which produced a network management nightmare. The solution was a narrow and deep strategy: weather.com put in the identical hardware, wherever possible. Rather than use expensive high-performance hardware, custom tailored to different jobs, weather.com has standardized on many more less expensive Linux servers all configured in the same way. Page load times have dropped from a high of 18 to 25 seconds to a fairly consistent 2 seconds—even during hurricane season, when weather.com averages 15 million page views per day.

SOURCE: "Riding the Storm," *Intelligent Enterprise,* February 16, 2001.

(e.g., restarting a failed device). Other times, when a device or circuit fails, they must change routing tables to route traffic away from the device and inform the common carrier or dispatch a technician to fix or replace it.

The parameters monitored by a network management system fall into two distinct categories: physical network statistics and logical network information. Gathering statistics on the *physical network parameters* includes monitoring the operation of the network's modems, multiplexers, circuits linking the various hardware devices, and any other network devices. Monitoring the physical network consists of keeping track of circuits that may be down and tracing malfunctioning devices. *Logical network parameters* include performance measurement systems that keep track of user response times, the volume of traffic on a specific circuit, the destination of data routed across various networks, and any other indicators showing the level of service provided by the network.

Some types of management software operate passively, collecting the information and reporting it back to the central NOC. Others are active, in that they routinely send test messages to the servers or applications being monitored (e.g., an HTTP Web page request) and record the response times.[1]

Performance tracking is important because it enables the network manager to be proactive and respond to performance problems before users begin to complain. Poor network reporting leads to an organization that is overburdened with current problems and lacks time to address future needs. Management requires adequate reports if it is to address future needs.

---

[1] Two examples of performance tracking on the Internet that provide a simple overview are www.InternetTrafficReport.com and www.my.keynote.com/MyKeynote/mykeynote.asp.

MANAGEMENT FOCUS *11-5*

LONG NIGHT ON THE NET WATCH

At an hour when most network personnel are asleep, Walter Snider and Willie Williams are huddled over a network management console in railroad giant CSX Corporation's network operations center (NOC) trying to determine why a circuit between Jacksonville and Baltimore is down. The problem becomes urgent when the dispatcher tells the Snider the outage will delay trains if it is not fixed soon.

A quick check of the circuit shows it is fine. The multiplexer ports on both ends pass tests, too. Williams becomes convinced that the dispatcher has reported the wrong circuit number and begins checking other circuits out of Baltimore. He quickly finds one that does not respond, reboots the multiplexer, and the circuit begins working. He calls the dispatcher who reports that the circuit is working again.

The night shift is the quietest shift at CSX's network control center in Jacksonville, which gives network per-

sonnel the chance to learn new skills and identify network improvements. However, staff members need the greatest range of skills and have more autonomy to solve problems. Unlike their daytime counterparts, they have a harder time reaching managers and other network personnel for help. Although CSX policy requires the NOC to contact network managers and support personnel in the event of a major problem, no one likes to wake up colleagues.

At 4:00 A.M., 5 hours after beginning the shift, Williams notices an alarm go off, indicating the failure of a major circuit in the Washington area. He begins to zero in on the trouble spot when the circuit comes back up. "Probably just line noise or a power surge," he says, and returns to his doughnut and coffee.

SOURCE: "Long Night on the Net Watch," *Network World*, February 9, 1998.

Failure Control Function

Failure control requires developing a central control philosophy for problem reporting, whether the problems are first identified by the NOC or by users calling the NOC or a help desk. Whether problem reporting is done by the NOC or the help desk, the organization should maintain a central telephone number for network users to call when any problem occurs in the network. As a central troubleshooting function, only this group or its designee should have the authority to call hardware or software vendors or common carriers.

Many years ago, before the importance (and cost) of network management was widely recognized, most networks ignored the importance of fault management. Network devices were "dumb" in that they did only what they were designed to do (e.g., routing packets) but did not provide any network management information.

For example, suppose a network interface card fails and begins to randomly transmit garbage messages. Network performance immediately begins to deteriorate because these random messages destroy the messages transmitted by other computers, which need to be retransmitted. Users notice a delay in response time and complain to the network support group, which begins to search for the cause. Even if the network support group suspects a failing network card (which is unlikely unless such an event has occurred before), locating the faulty card is very difficult and time consuming.

Most network managers today are installing *managed devices* that perform their functions (e.g., routing, switching) and also record data on the messages they process. These data can be sent to the network manager's computer when the device receives a special control message requesting the data, or it can send an *alarm* message to the network manager's computer if the device detects a critical situation. In this way, network faults

MANAGEMENT FOCUS *11-6*

TECHNICAL REPORTS

Technical reports that are helpful to network managers are those that provide summary information, as well as details that enable the managers to improve the network. Technical details include

- Circuit use
- Usage rate of critical hardware such as host computers, front-end processors, and servers
- File activity rates for database systems
- Usage by various categories of client computers

- Response time analysis per circuit or per computer
- Voice versus data usage per circuit
- Queue-length descriptions, whether in the host computer, in the front-end processor, or at remote sites
- Distribution of traffic by time of day, location, and type of application software
- Failure rates for circuits, hardware, and software
- Details of any network faults

---

and performance problems can be detected and reported by the devices themselves before they become serious. In the case of the failing network card, a managed device could record the increased number of retransmissions required to successfully transmit messages and inform the network management software of the problem. A managed hub or switch might even be able to detect the faulty transmissions from the failing network card, disable the incoming circuit so that the card could not send any more messages, and issue an alarm to the network manager. In either case, finding and fixing the fault is much simpler, requiring minutes, not hours.

Numerous software packages are available for recording fault information. The reports they produce are known as *trouble tickets*. The software packages assist the help desk personnel so they can type the trouble report immediately into a computerized failure analysis program. They also automatically produce various statistical reports to track how many failures have occurred for each piece of hardware, circuit, or software package. Automated trouble tickets are better than paper because they allow management personnel to gather problem and vendor statistics. There are four main reasons for trouble tickets: problem tracking, problem statistics, problem-solving methodology, and management reports.

Problem tracking allows the network manager to determine who is responsible for correcting any outstanding problems. This is important because some problems often are forgotten in the rush of a very hectic day. In addition, anyone might request information on the status of a problem. The network manager can determine whether the problem-solving mechanism is meeting predetermined schedules. Finally, the manager can be assured that all problems are being addressed. Problem tracking also can assist in problem resolution. Are problems being resolved in a timely manner? Are overdue problems being flagged? Are all resources and information available for problem solving?

Problem statistics are important because they are a control device for the network managers as well as for vendors. With this information, a manager can see how well the network is meeting the needs of end users. These statistics also can be used to determine whether vendors are meeting their contractual maintenance commitments. Finally, they help to determine whether problem-solving objectives are being met.

TECHNICAL FOCUS *11-1*

ELEMENTS OF A TROUBLE REPORT

When a problem is reported, in the trouble log staff members should record the following:
- Time and date of the report
- Name and telephone number of the person who reported the problem
- The time and date of the problem (and the time and date of the call)

- Location of the problem
- The nature of the problem
- When the problem was identified
- Why and how the problem happened

Problem prioritizing helps ensure that critical problems get priority over less important ones. For example, a network support staff member should not work on a problem on one client computer if an entire circuit with dozens of computers is waiting for help. Moreover, a manager must know whether problem-resolution objectives are being met. For example, how long is it taking to resolve critical problems?

Management reports are required to determine network availability, product and vendor reliability (mean time between failures), and vendor responsiveness. Without them, a manager has nothing more than a "best guess" estimate for the effectiveness of either the network's technicians or the vendor's technicians. Regardless of whether this information is typed immediately into an automated trouble ticket package or recorded manually in a bound notebook-style trouble log, the objectives are the same.

The purposes of the trouble log are to record problems that must be corrected and to keep track of statistics associated with these problems. For example, the log might reveal that there were 37 calls for software problems (3 for one package, 4 for another package, and 30 for a third software package), 26 calls for modems evenly distributed among two vendors, 49 calls for client computers, and 2 calls to the common carrier that provides the network circuits. These data are valuable when the design and analysis group begins redesigning the network to meet future requirements.

Performance and Failure Statistics

There are many different types of failure and recovery statistics that can be collected. The most obvious performance statistics are those discussed above: how many packets are being moved on what circuits and what the response time is. Failure statistics also tell an important story.

One important failure statistic is *availability,* the percentage of time the network is available to users. It is calculated as the number of hours per month the network is available divided by the total number of hours per month (i.e., 24 hours per day × 30 days per month = 720 hours). The *downtime* includes times when the network is unavailable because of faults and to routine maintenance and network upgrades. Most network managers strive for 99 to 99.5 percent availability, with downtime scheduled after normal working hours. Unplanned network outages should be minimal with average availability excluding planned outages of 99.95 percent.

The *mean time between failures (MTBF)* is the number of hours or days of continuous operation before the component fails. Obviously, devices with higher MTBF are more reliable.

When faults occur, and devices or circuits go down, the *mean time to repair (MTTR)* is the average number of minutes or hours until the failed device or circuit is operational again. The MTTR is composed of these separate elements:

$$MTTR = MTTDiagnose + MTTRespond + MTTFix$$

The *mean time to diagnose* is the average number of minutes until the root cause of the failure is correctly diagnosed. This is an indicator of the efficiency of problem management personnel in the NOC or help desk who receive the problem report.

The *mean time to respond* is average number of minutes or hours until service personnel arrive at the problem location to begin work on the problem. This is a valuable statistic because it indicates how quickly vendors and internal groups respond to emergencies. Compilation of these figures over time can lead to a change of vendors or internal management policies or, at the minimum, can exert pressure on vendors who do not respond to problems promptly.

Finally, after the vendor or internal support group arrives on the premises, the last statistic is the *mean time to fix*. This figure tells how quickly the staff is able to correct the problem after they arrive. A very long time to fix in comparison with the time of other vendors may indicate faulty equipment design, inadequately trained customer service technicians, or even the fact that inexperienced personnel are repeatedly sent to fix problems.

The MTBF can be influenced by the original selection of vendor-supplied equipment. The mean time to diagnose relates directly to the ability of network personnel to isolate and diagnose failures and can often be improved by training. The mean time to respond can be influenced by showing vendors or internal groups how good or bad their response times have been in the past. The mean time to fix can be affected by the technical expertise of internal or vendor staff and the availability of spare parts on-site.

For MAN and WAN environments, the MTBF and MTTR for circuits are based on the service level agreement you sign with the carrier. Many carriers set MTTR at 2–4 hours; some carriers will agree to a lower MTTR, but will charge more for the circuits. For devices such as switches and routers that you buy and install in your own LANs and backbones, the MTBF depends on the quality of the manufacturer. In general, low cost hardware tends to have a MTBF of 3–5 years and high-cost equipment a MTBF of 10 years or longer (but you probably won't keep devices that long anyway!). These numbers refer to hardware failures, not software crashes, and most network failures are due to software problems, not hardware failures. Several studies suggest that the MTBF for network software embedded in devices or running on servers is about 3–6 months. That is, on average, a server or device will crash with a software failure about 2–4 times per year. The average MTTR for such a software failure is about 2 hours, depending on the quality of your network staff.

Another set of statistics that should be gathered are those collected daily by the network operations group, which uses network management software. These statistics record the normal operation of the network, such as the number of errors (retransmissions) per communication circuit. Statistics also should be collected on the daily volume of transmissions

TECHNICAL FOCUS *11-2*

MANAGEMENT REPORTS

Management-oriented reports that are helpful to network managers and their supervisors provide summary information for overall evaluation and for network planning and design. Details include

- Graphs of daily/weekly/monthly usage, number of errors, or whatever is appropriate to the network
- Network availability (uptime) for yesterday, the last 5 days, the last month, or any other specific period
- Percentage of hours per week the network is unavailable because of network maintenance and repair

- Fault diagnosis
- Whether most response times are less than or equal to 3 seconds for online real-time traffic
- Whether management reports are timely and contain the most up-to-date statistics
- Peak volume statistics as well as average volume statistics per circuit
- Comparison of activity between today and a similar previous period

(characters per hour) for each communication circuit, each computer, or whatever is appropriate for the network. It is important to closely monitor usage rates, the percentage of the theoretical capacity that is being used. These data can identify computers/devices or communication circuits that have higher-than-average error or usage rates, and they may be used for predicting future growth patterns and failures. A device or circuit that is approaching maximum usage obviously needs to be upgraded.

Such predictions can be accomplished by establishing simple *quality-control charts* similar to those used in manufacturing. Programs use an upper control limit and a lower control limit with regard to the number of blocks in error per day or per week. Notice how Figure 11-2 identifies when the common carrier moved a circuit from one microwave channel to another (circuit B), how a deteriorating circuit can be located and fixed before it goes through the upper control limit (circuit A) and causes problems for the users, or how

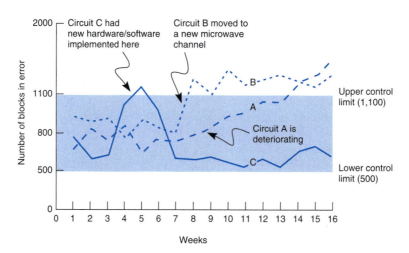

FIGURE 11-2 Quality control chart for circuits.

TECHNICAL FOCUS *11-3*

INSIDE A SERVICE-LEVEL AGREEMENT

There are many elements to a solid service-level agreement (SLA) with a common carrier. Some of the important ones include

- Network availability, measured over a month as the percentage of time the network is available (e.g., [total hours—hours unavailable]/total hours) should be at least 99.5 percent (about 3.5 hours per month).
- Average round trip permanent virtual circuit (PVC) delay, measured over a month as the number of seconds it takes a message to travel over the PVC from sender to receiver, should be less than 110 milliseconds, although some carriers will offer discounted services for SLA guarantees of 300 milliseconds.
- PVC throughput, measured over a month as the number of outbound packets sent over a PVC divided by

the inbound packets received at the destination (not counting packets over the committed information rate, which are discard eligible), should be above 99 percent—ideally, 99.99 percent.

- Mean time to respond, measured as a monthly average of the time from inception of trouble ticket until repair personnel are on-site, should be 4 hours or less.
- Mean time to fix, measured as a monthly average of the time from the arrival of repair personnel on-site until the problem is repaired, should be 4 hours or less.

SOURCE: "Carrier Service-Level Agreements," International Engineering Consortium Tutorial, www.iec.org, February 2001.

---

a temporary high rate of errors (circuit C) can be encountered when installing new hardware and software.

END-USER SUPPORT

Providing end-user support means solving whatever problems users encounter while using the network. There are three main functions within end-user support: resolving network faults, resolving user problems, and training. We have already discussed how to resolve network faults, and now we focus on resolution of user problems and on end-user training.

Resolving Problems

Problems with user equipment (as distinct from network equipment) usually stem from three major sources. The first is a failed hardware device. These are usually the easiest to fix. A network technician simply fixes the device or installs a new part.

The second type of problem is a lack of user knowledge. These problems can usually be solved by discussing the situation with the user and taking that person through the process step-by-step. This is the next easiest type of problem to solve and can often be done by e-mail or over the telephone.

The third type of problem is a one with the software, software settings, or an incompatibility between the software and network software and hardware. In this case, there may be a bug in the software, or the software may not function properly on a certain combination of hardware and software. Solving these problems may be difficult because they require expertise with the specific software package in use and sometimes require software upgrades from the vendor.

Resolving either type of software problem begins with a request for assistance from the help desk. Requests for assistance are usually handled in the same manner as network faults. A trouble log is maintained to document all incoming requests and the manner in which they are resolved. The staff member receiving the request attempts to resolve the problem in the best manner possible. Staff members should be provided with the set of standard procedures or scripts for soliciting information from the user about problems. In large organizations, this process may be supported by special software.

There are often several levels to the problem-resolution process. The first level is the most basic. All staff members working at the help desk should be able to resolve most of the these. Most organizations strive to resolve between 75 and 85 percent of requests at this first level in less than an hour. If the request cannot be resolved, it is escalated to the second level of problem resolution. Staff members who handle second-level support have specialized skills in certain problem areas or with certain types of software and hardware. In most cases, problems are resolved at this level. Some large organizations also have a third level of resolution in which specialists spend many hours developing and testing various solutions to the problem, often in conjunction with staff members from the vendors of network software and hardware.

Providing End-User Training

End-user training is an ongoing responsibility of the network manager. Training is a key part in the implementation of new networks or network components. It is also important to have an ongoing training program because employees may change job functions and new employees require training to use the organization's networks.

Training usually is conducted through in-class or one-on-one instruction and through the documentation and training manuals provided. In-class training should focus on the 20 percent of the network functions that the user will use 80 percent of the time instead of attempting to cover all network functions. By getting in-depth instruction of the fundamentals, users become confident about what they need to do. The training should also explain how to locate additional information from training manuals, documentation, or the help desk.

COST MANAGEMENT

As the demand for network services grows, so do their costs. Effective and efficient management of data communications networks is important because more and more organizational resources are being spent on networks. In this section, we examine the major sources of costs and discuss several ways to reduce them.

Sources of Costs

The *total cost of ownership (TCO)* is a measure of how much it costs per year to keep one computer operating. TCO includes the cost of repair parts, software upgrades, and support staff members to maintain the network, install software, administer the network (e.g., create user IDs, backup user data), provide training and technical support, and upgrade hardware and software. It also includes the cost of time "wasted" by the user when problems occur or when the user is attempting to learn new software.

Several studies over the past few years by Gartner Group, Inc. (a leading industry research firm) suggest that the TCO of a computer is astoundingly high. Most studies suggest that the TCO for typical Windows computers on a network is about $10,000 *per computer per year.* In other words, it costs almost five times as much *each year* to operate a computer than it does to purchase it in the first place. Other studies by firms such as IBM and *InformationWeek* (an industry magazine) have produced TCO estimates of between $8,000 and $12,000 per year, suggesting that the Gartner Group's estimates are reasonable.

Although TCO has been accepted by many organizations, other firms argue against the practice of including "wasted" time in the calculation. For example, using the Gartner Group approach, the TCO of a coffee machine is more than $50,000 per year—not counting the cost of the coffee or supplies. The assumption that getting coffee "wastes" 12 minutes per day times 5 days per week yields 1 hour per week, or about 50 hours per year, of wasted time. If you assume the coffeepot serves 20 employees who have an average cost of $50 per hour (not an unusually high number), you have a loss of $50,000 per year.

Some organizations, therefore, prefer to focus on costing methods that examine only the direct costs of operating the computers, omitting softer costs such as wasted time. Such measures, often called *network cost of ownership (NCO)* or real cost of ownership, have found that network management costs (TCO without "wasted" time) range between $1,500 and $3,500 *per computer per year.* The typical network management group for a 100-user network would therefore have an annual budget of about $150,000 to $350,000. The most expensive item is personnel (network managers and technicians), which typically accounts for 50 to 70 percent of total costs. The second most expensive cost item is WAN circuits, followed by hardware upgrades and replacement parts.

There is one very important message from this pattern of costs. Because the largest cost item is personnel time, the primary focus of cost management lies in designing networks and developing policies to reduce personnel time, not to reduce hardware cost. Over the long term, it makes more sense to buy more expensive equipment if it can reduce the cost of network management.

Figure 11-3 shows the average breakdown of personnel costs by function. The largest time cost (where staff members spend most of their time) is systems management, which includes configuration, fault, and performance management tasks that focus on the network as a whole. The second largest item is end-user support.

Network managers often find it difficult to manage their budgets because networks grow so rapidly. They often find themselves having to defend ever-increasing requests for more equipment and staff. To counter these escalating costs, many large organizations have adopted *chargeback policies* for users of WANs and mainframe-based networks. (A chargeback policy attempts to allocate the costs associated with the network to specific users.) These users must "pay" for their network usage by transferring part of their budget allocations to the network group. Such policies are seldom used in LANs, making one more potential cultural difference between network management styles.

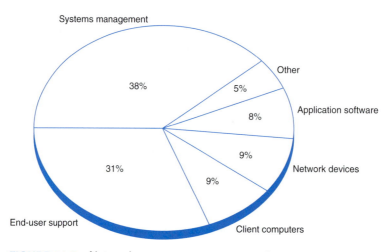

FIGURE 11-3 Network management personnel costs.

Reducing Costs

Given the huge amounts in TCO or even the substantial amounts spent in NCO, there is considerable pressure on network managers to reduce costs. Figure 11-4 summarizes five steps to reduce network costs.

The first and most important step is to develop standards for client computers, servers, and network devices (i.e., switches, routers). These standards define one configuration (or a small set of configurations) that are permitted for all computers and devices. Standardizing hardware and software makes it easier to diagnose and fix problems. Also, there are fewer software packages for the network support staff members to learn. The downside, of course, is that rigid adherence to standards reduces innovation.

The second most important step is to automate as much of the network management process as possible. ESD can significantly reduce the cost to upgrade when new software is released. It also enables faster installation of new computers and faster recovery when software needs to be reinstalled and helps enforce the standards policies. Dynamic address assignment (e.g., DHCP; see Chapter 3) can reduce time spent on managing TCP/IP addresses. The use of network management software to identify and diagnose problems

---

Five Steps to Reduce Network Costs
- Develop standard hardware and software configurations for client computers and servers.
- Automate as much of the network management function as possible by deploying a solid set of network management tools.
- Reduce the costs of installing new hardware and software by working with vendors.
- Centralize help desks.
- Move to thin-client architectures.

FIGURE 11-4 Reducing network costs.

can significantly reduce time spent in performance and fault management. Likewise, help desk software can cut the cost of the end-support function.

A third step is to do everything possible to reduce the time spent installing new hardware and software. The cost of a network technician's spending half a day to install and configure new computers is often $300 to $500. ESD is an important step to reducing costs, but careful purchasing can also go a long way. The installation of standard hardware and software (e.g., Microsoft Office) by the hardware vendor can significantly reduce costs. Likewise, careful monitoring of hardware failures can quickly identify vendors of less reliable equipment who can be avoided in the next purchasing cycle.

Traditionally, help desks have been decentralized into user departments. The result is a proliferation of help desks and support staff members, many of whom tend to be generalists rather than specialists in one area. Many organizations have found that centralizing help desks enables them to reduce the number of generalists and provide more specialists in key technology areas. This results in faster resolution of difficult problems. Centralization also makes it easier to identify common problems occurring in different parts of the organization and take actions to reduce them.

Finally, many network experts argue that moving to thin-client architectures, particularly those using network computers or just Web browsers on the client (see Chapter 2), can significantly reduce costs. Although network computers cost slightly less than traditional computers, the real saving lies in the support costs. Because they are restricted to a narrow set of functions and generally do not permit software installations, they become much easier to manage. TCO and NCO drop by 20 to 40 percent. However, there is not a lot of software available for network computers today, although this may change. Most organizations anticipate using network computers selectively, in areas where application software is well defined and can easily be restricted (e.g., receptionists' telephone sales), if at all.

MANAGEMENT FOCUS *11-7*

OUTSOURCING NETWORK MANAGEMENT AT NASA

After a 1998 survey of 11 NASA installations found a network cost of ownership (NCO) of just under $3,000 per desktop per year, NASA decided to outsource the network support for its desktops to focus on its core competency: space flight. So far, NASA has outsourced the management of 27,000 desktops to third parties. Reducing NCO was not the only driving force behind the decision, but it was the most important one.

Because of its mission priorities, NASA has a real mix of desktop technologies, including seven very different types of Windows, Apple, and UNIX computers. After a tough competition, NASA approved seven firms to provide network management service, such as Computer Sciences Corporation, Wang, and Federal Data Corp. Local NASA managers can select which of the seven vendors to use. Prices range from $1,800 to $2,200 per computer per year, depending on the level of service desired. This has resulted in a clear drop in operating expenses, as well as better service. NASA now has a well-documented network configuration, one phone number to call for service, and total certainty of the cost of operating its desktops.

Source: "Every Last Dime," *CIO Magazine,* November 15, 2000.

SUMMARY

Integrating LANs, WANs, and the Internet   Today, the critical issue is the integration of all organizational networks. The keys to integrating LANs, WANs, and the Web into one overall organization network are for WAN managers to recognize that LAN/Web managers can make independent decisions and for LAN/Web managers to realize that they need to work within organizational standards.

Integrating Voice and Data Communications   Another major challenge is combining voice communications with data and image communications. This separation of voice and data worked well for years, but changing communication technologies are generating enormous pressures to combine them. A key factor in voice–data integration might turn out to be the elimination of one key management position and the merging of two staffs into one.

Configuration Management   Configuration management means managing the network's hardware and software configuration and documenting it (and ensuring the documentation is updated as the configuration changes). The most common configuration management activity is adding and deleting user accounts. The most basic documentation about network hardware is a set of network configuration diagrams, supplemented by documentation on each individual network component. A similar approach can be used for network software. ESD plays a key role in simplifying configuration management by automating and documenting the network configurations. User and application profiles should be automatically provided by the network and ESD software. There are variety of other documentation that must be routinely developed and updated, including users' manuals and organizational policies.

Performance and Fault Management   Performance management means ensuring the network is operating as efficiently as possible. Fault management means preventing, detecting, and correcting any faults in the network circuits, hardware, and software. The two are closely related because any faults in the network reduce performance and because both require network monitoring. Today, most networks use a combination of smart devices to monitor the network and issue alarms and a help desk to respond to user problems. Problem tracking allows the network manager to determine problem ownership or who is responsible for correcting any outstanding problems. Problem statistics are important because they are a control device for the network operators as well as for vendors.

Providing End-User Support   Providing end-user support means solving whatever network problems users encounter. Support consists of resolving network faults, resolving software problems, and training. Software problems often stem from lack of user knowledge and fundamental problems with the software or an incompatibility between the software and the network's software and hardware. There are often several levels to problem resolution. End-user training is an ongoing responsibility of the network manager. Training usually has two parts: (1) in-class instruction and (2) the documentation and training manuals that the user keeps for reference.

Cost Management   As the demand for network services grows, so does its cost. The TCO for typical networked computers is about $10,000 per year per computer, far more than the initial purchase price. The network management cost (omitting "wasted" time) is between $1,500 and $3,500 per year per computer. The largest single cost item is staff salaries. The best way to control rapidly increasing network costs is to reduce the amount of time taken to perform network management functions, often by automating as many routine ones as possible.

KEY TERMS

charge-back policy	electronic software	error-free seconds	help desk
desktop management	distribution	(EFS)	logical network
downtime	(ESD)	firefighting	parameters

mean time between failures (MTBF)
mean time to diagnose
mean time to fix
mean time to repair (MTTR)
mean time to respond

monitor
network cost of ownership (NCO)
network documentation
network management
network operations center (NOC)

passive analyzer/monitor
patch panel
physical network parameters
problem statistics
problem tracking
quality-control chart

total cost of ownership (TCO)
trouble ticket
uptime

QUESTIONS

1. What are some differences between LAN and WAN management?

2. What is firefighting?

3. Why is combining voice and data a major organizational challenge?

4. Describe what configuration management encompasses.

5. People tend to think of software when documentation is mentioned. What is documentation in a network situation?

6. What is electronic software delivery, and why is it important?

7. What is performance and fault management?

8. What does a help desk do?

9. What do trouble tickets report?

10. Several important statistics related to network uptime and downtime are discussed in this chapter. What are they, and why are they important?

11. How is network availability calculated?

12. What is problem escalation?

13. What are the primary functions of end-user support?

14. What is TCO?

15. Why is the TCO so high?

16. How can network costs be reduced?

17. How does network cost of ownership differ from total cost of ownership? Which is the most useful measure of network costs from the point of view of the network manager? Why?

18. Many organizations do not have a formal trouble reporting system. Why do you think this is the case?

19. Reread Management Focus 11-3. Compare and contrast the skills labeled "very important" with those labeled "moderately important" and "less important." What patterns do you notice? Why do you think there are such patterns?

EXERCISES

11-1. What factors might cause peak loads in a network? How can a network manager determine if they are important and how are they taken into account when designing a data communications network?

11-2. Today's network managers face a number of demanding problems. Investigate and discuss three major issues.

11-3. Research the networking budget in your organization and discuss the major cost areas. Discuss several ways of reducing costs over the long term.

MINI-CASES

I. Mary's Manufacturing

Mary's Manufacturing is a small manufacturing company that has a network with eight LANs (each with about 20 computers on them using switched 10Base-T) connected via 100Base-T over fiber-optic cable into a core switch (i.e., a collapsed BN). The switch is connected to the company's ISP over a fractional T1 circuit. Most computers are used for order processing and standard office applications, but some are used to control the manufacturing equipment in the plant. The current network is working fine and there have been no major problems, but Mary is wondering whether she should invest in network management software. It will cost about $5,000 to replace the current hardware with SNMP-capable hardware. Mary can buy SNMP device management software for $2,000 or spend $7,000 to buy SNMP system management software. Should Mary install SNMP, and if so, which software should she buy? Why?

II. Network Simulator

The Web site for this book has a network simulator that shows what a network management system for a small company might look like. The simulator shows a series of network alerts that indicate problems in network. Identify the problems and state how would you fix them.

TCP/IP GAME (VERSION 3)

Introduction

The purpose of this game is to help you better understand how messages are transmitted in TCP/IP-based computer networks. Players are organized into five-person teams that represent different computers in the network. Each person in the team assumes the role of one layer of software or hardware on that computer (e.g., data link layer) and works with the others to send messages through the network.

General Rules

1. This is a team game. The class will be broken into a set of five-member teams, with each team being one computer in the communications network. Each person in the team will role-play one layer in the computer, either the application layer, the transport layer, the network layer, the data link layer, or the physical layer.

2. Messages will be created by the application layer and passed to the transport layer. The transport layer will break the message into several smaller messages if necessary and pass them to the network layer. The network layer will address and route the message and pass the message to the data link layer. The data link layer will format the message and pass the message to the physical layer for transmission. The physical layer will transmit the message to the physical layer of the destination computer. Messages are sent using the forms in Figure A-1. Be sure to make lots of copies of the forms before the game starts.

3. Each layer will have a set of instructions to follow to ensure the messages are sent and received properly. Follow them carefully. These instructions explain what you are to write on the message forms. Never write anything on the message form in an area used by another layer.

4. At some point, someone will make a mistake. If you receive a message that contains an error, hand it back to the person who gave it to you and explain the error to that person.

5. And remember, the game is meant to be fun, too!

SMTP	From	To	Message	

TCP	Sequence Number	Ack	User Data	
	of			

IP	Final Destination	Next Node	User Data	

Ethernet	Source	Destination	Error	User Data	

FIGURE A-1 Forms for the TCP/IP game.

Application Layer

Activities

1. Send messages to other computers. We have simplified this by not having DNS requests.
2. Respond to messages from other computers.

Tools Needed

- Several blank SMTP forms
- List of messages

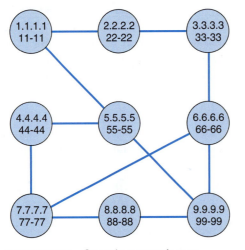

FIGURE A-2 Sample network map.

- Network map (Figure A-2 shows an example; the instructor will draw one for your class.)
- A blank piece of paper

Sending Outgoing Messages   To send a message, you must

1. Find a blank SMTP form.

2. Write the *IP address* of your computer in the **From** box.

3. Use the network map to select a computer as the destination for this message. Write the *IP address* of the destination computer in the **To** box. Don't send all your messages to one computer; we want to even out the messages. Try to send a few messages to computers close to you and a few to computers far away.

4. Write the message you wish to send in the **Message** box. To make the message simple to understand, please use a hyphen (-) to indicate spaces between words. Select a message from the list of messages (see below). Try to have at least one hyphen in the message (this is to help the data link layer do error control) or add one at the end or at the start if you must.

5. Write the message and the name of the computer to which you send the message on the blank piece of paper. This will help you understand the responses you get to your messages.

6. Pass the SMTP form to the transport layer for transmission.

Responding to Incoming Messages   Eventually, you will receive an incoming message from the transport layer that was sent to you by some other computer asking you a question. To respond to the message, you will send a message that answers the question. Follow the same steps above to send a message, but in step 4, write your answer in the **Message** box. For example, if the message you received asked what your favorite color was, you might write *red* or *blue* in the **Message** box.

List of Messages   Here are a list of messages you can send. Remember to use a hyphen instead of a space to separate the words. Rather than writing the entire message, you can omit the words *What is your.*

- What is your favorite color?
- What is your birthday?
- What is your phone number?
- What are your favorite holidays?
- What is your favorite car?

Transport Layer

Activities

1. Accept outgoing SMTP messages from the application layer, segment them, and pass them to the network layer. We have simplified this by not having TCP open a connection.

2. Accept incoming messages from the network layer and, if they are made up of several segments, assemble the entire SMTP message before passing it to the application layer. We have simplified this by not having TCP do a check-sum calculation.

Tools Needed

- TCP forms
- Tape
- A log sheet which is a piece of paper with the following column headings:
    Time, Sequence Number, From, To, Message

Accepting Outgoing Messages from the Application Layer   Every few
minutes, the application layer will hand you an outgoing message to transmit. To transmit them, you must

1. Break the SMTP message into smaller packets. Tear the SMTP form into two parts at the dotted line. If there is writing on both parts, then you must send each part as a separate message. If the second half of the SMTP form has no writing on it, throw it away and ignore it.

2. Find one or two blank TCP forms.

3. Fill in the **Sequence Number** box. If there is only one part of the SMTP form, write "1 of 1" in the **Sequence Number** box. If there are two parts of the SMTP form, write "1 of 2" on the first TCP form and "2 of 2" on the second TCP form.

4. Tape the SMTP form(s) to the TCP form(s) over the **User Data** space. (The packet[s] will be too big to fit, but don't worry about it.)

5. Write an asterisk (*) in the **ACK** box.

6. Make a copy of the one or two TCP + SMTP packets by writing the current time and the information on the forms in the correct columns on the log sheet (don't bother with the **ACK** box).

7. Pass the TCP + SMTP forms(s) to the network layer for transmission.

Accepting Incoming Messages from the Network Layer   Every few
minutes, the network layer will hand you an incoming message. To process it, you must

- **If the message is complete (that is, if the** Sequence Number **box says "1 of 1"** and the ACK box contains an asterisk):
    1. You first send an acknowledgment to the sender telling them that the message was received. Find a *blank* TCP form and write "1 of 1" in the **Sequence Number box.** Write the work "ACK" in the **ACK** box. Write the from and to IP addresses on the incoming message in the **User Data** box. Pass this TCP form to the network layer for transmission.
    2. Take the TCP form off of the incoming SMTP form and throw away the TCP form.
    3. Pass the SMTP form to the application layer.

- **If the message is not complete (that is, if the** Sequence Number **box says "1 of 2"):**

   1. You first send an acknowledgment to the sender telling them that the message was received. Find a *blank* TCP form and write "1 of 1" in the **Sequence Number box.** Write the work "ACK" in the **ACK** box. Write the from and to IP addresses on the incoming message in the **User Data** box. Pass this TCP form to the network layer for transmission.
   2. Wait for the second part of the message to arrive.
   3. Take the TCP forms off of both SMTP forms and throw away the TCP forms.
   4. Tape the two parts of the SMTP form back together.
   5. Pass the SMTP form to the application layer.

- **If the ACK box contains the word ACK:**

   1. Cross out the message on the log sheet that matches the message in the acknowledgment.
   2. Throw away the acknowledgement.

Every 10 minutes, you must look for messages that have timed out.

TCP is responsible for providing reliable delivery, so if it has not received an acknowledgment on a message after a reasonable length of time, it times out and resends the message. The network in the game is *very* slow, so we will allow a 10 minute timeout period.

   If a message on your log sheet has not been crossed out 10-minutes or more after it was sent, you must resend it.

1. Find a *blank* TCP form and a *blank* SMTP form. Copy the information on the log sheet into the proper boxes on these forms. Tape the SMTP form to the TCP form. Pass the TCP + SMTP forms to the network layer for transmission.

Network Layer

Activities

1. Accept messages from the transport layer, route them, and pass them to the data link layer.
2. Accept messages from the data link layer and, if they are addressed to you, pass them to the transport layer; if they are not addressed to you, route them and pass them back to the data link layer

Tools Needed

- IP forms
- Tape
- Network map

Accepting Outgoing Messages from the Transport Layer   Every few minutes, the transport layer will hand you an outgoing message to transmit. To transmit them, you must

1. Find a blank IP form.
2. Address the message by writing the IP address in the **To** box of the SMTP form into the **Final Destination** box of the IP form.
3. Route the message by finding the next computer in the network map to which the message should be sent and writing its Ethernet address in the **Next Node** box. If your computer is directly connected to the final destination computer, the next node is the same as the final destination. If your computer is not directly connected to the destination, you must use the network map to select the best route that the message should follow and specify one of the computers to which you are connected.
4. Tape the TCP + SMTP forms to the IP form over the **User Data** space. (It will be too big to fit, but don't worry about it.)
5. Pass the IP + TCP + SMTP forms to the data link layer for transmission.

Accepting Incoming Messages from the Data Link Layer   Every few minutes, the data link layer will hand you a message to process. You must

- **If the message is addressed to you (that is, if the** Final Destination **box in the IP packet lists your IP address):**
  1. Remove the IP form from the SMTP + TCP forms and throw the IP form away.
  2. Pass the SMTP + TCP forms to the transport layer.

- **If the message is not addressed to you (that is, if the** Final Destination **box in the IP packet lists someone else's IP address):**
  1. Scratch out or erase the address in the **Next Node** box.
  2. Route the message by finding the next computer in the network map to which the message should be sent in and writing its data link layer address in the **Next Node** box. If your computer is directly connected to the destination computer, the next node is the same as the destination. If your computer is not directly connected to the destination, you must select the best route that the message should follow and specify one of the computers to which you are connected.
  3. Pass the SMTP + TCP + IP forms to the data link layer for transmission.

Data Link Layer

Activities

1. Accept outgoing messages from the network layer, format them, add error-control information, and pass them to the physical layer.
2. Accept incoming messages from the physical layer. If they contain no errors, pass them to the network layer. If they contain an error, destroy the message.

Tools Needed

- Ethernet forms
- Tape
- Network map

Accepting Outgoing Messages from the Network Layer   Every few minutes, the network layer will hand you a message to transmit. For each message, you must

1. Find a blank Ethernet form.
2. Format the message for the physical layer by writing your Ethernet address in the **Source** box. Copy the Ethernet address in the **Next Node** box in the IP form into the **Destination** box.
3. Add error-control information. Most error control is very sophisticated, but in this game, we'll use something very simple. Count the number of hyphens in the user data (the SMTP form, the TCP form and the IP form [but not the Ethernet form]) and write this number in the **Error** box on the Ethernet packet.
4. Tape the SMTP + TCP + IP forms to the Ethernet form over the **User Data** space. (It will be too big to fit, but don't worry about it.)
5. Pass the message to the physical layer for transmission.

Accepting Incoming Messages from the Physical Layer   Every few minutes, the physical layer will hand you a message to process. For each message, you must

1. Perform error checking. Count the number of hyphens in the user data (the SMTP form, the TCP form, and the IP form [but not the Ethernet form]). If this number is the same as the number in the **Error** box, no errors have occurred. If they are different, an error has occurred.
2. If no errors have occurred:
   a. Remove the Ethernet form from the incoming message and throw the Ethernet form away.
   b. Pass the incoming SMTP + TCP + IP forms to the network layer.
3. If an error has occurred, throw away the message.

Physical Layer

Activities

1. Accept messages from the data link layer and pass them to the physical layer of the computer to which they are to go, possibly introducing a transmission error.
2. Accept messages from the physical layer of other computers and pass them to the data link layer.

Tools Needed

- Network map
- Two coins

Accepting Messages from the Data Link Layer

Every few minutes, the data link layer will hand you a message to transmit. To transmit, you must

1. Determine if there will be an error in transmission by tossing two coins; if they are both heads, you error by erasing (or stroking out) all the data in the SMTP **Message** box.

2. Pass the SMTP + TCP + IP + Ethernet forms to the physical layer of the computer whose address is listed in the **Destination** box.

Accepting Messages from the Physical Layer of Another Computer

Every few minutes, the physical layer of another computer will hand you a message. Simply hand the message to the data link layer.

Note to Instructors

Background

This game helps students *really* understand what the various layers actually do and how they must work together to send a message. Reading about it is one thing; having to perform a simple version of the function is something else altogether. Experiential learning can be an extremely powerful tool. I have noticed a distinct improvement in students' understanding of this material since I have begun using the game.

The game is an extremely simplified version of what happens in a real TCP/IP/Ethernet network. Nonetheless, it can be complicated. Students have to work together and sometimes make mistakes. Ideally, students will recognize mistakes themselves and will help one another learn. Participation is key to the learning objectives. It's also key to making a somewhat dry conceptual set of issues, more real—and more fun.

When I teach the course, I usually use this game after I complete Chapter 4. At this point students will have learned everything they need to know to run the game, and it will reinforce the material.

Preparing to Teach the Game

This game contains all the materials you will need to run the game, except a set of coins and paper (which you can rely on students to have), enough tape for each group (bring many rolls), and a network map (which you draw on the board just before the game starts). You will also have to make copies of the four types of packets. You will need a lot of forms. I usually plan on the class sending about 10–20 messages per team; for a 40-person class, this means you will need about 200 SMTP, TCP, IP, and Ethernet forms.

I have found from experience that it takes the students a little while to catch onto the game. Be sure to tell the students to read the game before they come to class.

Running the Game

It usually takes 20 minutes before the game gets going. The first step is to organize the class into five-person teams. Each team represents one computer in the network.

Draw the network map on the board. The map will have a circle to represent each team (i.e., computer). Try to draw the circles to represent the actual physical placement of the teams within the classroom. Inside each circle, write

- The IP address (e.g., 1.1.1.1). Arbitrarily choose a number for each team but keep it short and easy to remember.
- The Ethernet address (e.g., 11-11). Arbitrarily choose a number for each team but keep it short and easy to remember. It helps if it matches the IP address in some way. Be sure to have at least one hyphen in the address to help reinforce the error-control concepts.

Next, connect the computers (i.e., teams) by drawing lines (i.e., circuits) between the circles. Don't draw in all possible circuits, because you want some teams to have to route messages through other teams to reach their final destination. Likewise, don't put too few circuits, or else all messages will take a long time to send.

Do a simple example. Walk through the sending of one message on the board and have the students follow by replicating each step you do for one of their own messages. Once the message has reached the physical layer on the next computer, I turn the students loose and let them play. I usually walk around the classroom answering questions and listening in on discussions as the game progresses.

Because each layer performs a unique function, it is useful to have each student play each layer if time permits. I try to have students rotate layers after 15 minutes. I keep the game going so that the students playing one layer need to explain to the person taking over their layer what is going on and how to play. The easiest way to rotate is downward; that is, the person playing the application layer moves to the transport layer, and so on.

Discussion Questions   After each person has had the opportunity to play several layers, it is useful to ask what the students have learned. This gives you the opportunity to reinforce the concepts the game was designed to teach. Some possible discussion questions are

1. Why are standards important?
2. How could you improve network performance by changing the topology?
3. How do errors affect the network?

GLOSSARY

A

Abilene network: The Abilene network is the part of Internet 2 that is run by Indiana University.

access layer: The access layer is the part of a network that connects clients or servers to the rest of the network. It is often a LAN.

access point (AP): The part of the wireless LAN that connects the LAN to other networks.

ACK: *See* **acknowledgment (ACK).**

acknowledgment (ACK): A character indicating a positive acknowledgment that a message has been received correctly.

ACM: Association for Computing Machinery. The ACM is an association of computer professionals.

acronym: A word formed from the initial letters or groups of letters of words in a phrase. An example is the word *laser,* which means *l*ight *a*mplification by *s*timulated *e*mission of *r*adiation.

address: A coded representation of the destination of data or of its originating source. For example, multiple computers on one communication circuit must each have a unique data link layer address.

address resolution: The process of determining the lower-layer address from a higher-layer address. For example, IP address resolution means determining the IP address from the application layer address, whereas data link layer address resolution means determining the data link layer address from an IP address.

Address Resolution Protocol (ARP): The network-layer protocol standard for data link layer address resolution requests.

ADSL: *See* **asymmetric DSL (ADSL).**

Advanced Encryption Standard (AES): A new single-key encryption standard authorized by NIST that replaces DES. It uses the Rijndael (pronounced "rain doll") algorithm and has key sizes of 128, 192 and 256 bits. NIST estimates that using the most advanced computers and techniques available today, it will require about 150 trillion years to crack AES by brute force.

Advanced Research and Development Network Operations Center (ARDNOC): The agency funded by the Canadian government to develop new Internet 2 technologies and protocols.

AES: *See* **Advanced Encryption Standard (AES).**

American National Standards Institute (ANSI): The principal standards-setting body in the United States. ANSI is a nonprofit, nongovernmental organization supported by more than 1,000 trade organizations, professional societies, and companies. It belongs to the ITU-T CCITT and the ISO.

American Standard Code for Information Interchange: *See* **ASCII.**

amplifier: A device used to boost the strength of a signal. Amplifiers are spaced at intervals throughout the length of a communication circuit to increase the distance a signal can travel. *See also* **repeater.**

amplitude modulation: *See* **modulation, amplitude.**

analog: Pertaining to representation by means of continuously variable quantity, such as varying frequencies. Physical quantities such as temperature are continuous variables and therefore are "analog."

analog signal: A signal in the form of a continuously varying quantity such as amplitude, which reflects variations in the loudness of the human voice.

analog transmission: Transmission of a continuously variable signal as opposed to a discrete on/off signal. The traditional way of transmitting a telephone or voice signal is analog.

ANI: *See* **automatic number identification (ANI).**

anonymous FTP: *See* **File Transfer Protocol (FTP).**

ANSI: *See* **American National Standards Institute (ANSI).**

AP: *See* **access point (AP).**

API: Application Program Interface. API is the way IBM links incompatible equipment for microcomputer-to-mainframe links. API allows applications on micro-computers and mainframes to speak directly to each other at the application software level, even though the equipment is from different vendors.

Apple Talk: A set of communication protocols that defines networking for Apple computers. Rarely used today.

application service provider (ASP): An application service develops an application system (e.g., an airline reservation system, a payroll system) and companies purchase the service, without ever installing the software on their own computers. They simply use the service, the same way you might use a Web hosting service to publish your own Web pages rather than attempting to purchase and operate your own Web server.

ARCnet: Attached Resource Computing network. A proprietary token-bus LAN developed by the Datapoint Corporation.

ARDNOC: *See* **Advanced Research and Development Network Operations Center (ARDNOC).**

ARPANET: One of the early packet-switching networks. ARPANET was developed by the U.S. Department of Defense Advanced Research Projects Agency. It was the predecessor of the Internet.

ARP: *See* **Address Resolution Protocol (ARP).**

ARQ: Automatic Repeat reQuest. A system employing an error-detecting code so conceived that any error initiates a repetition of the transmission of the incorrectly received message.

ASCII: American Standard Code for Information Interchange. Pronounced "ask-e." An eight-level code for data transfer adopted by the ANSI to achieve compatibility among data devices.

asymmetric DSL (ADSL): A data link layer technology that provides high-speed ("broadband") communication over traditional telephone lines. A DSL modem is used to provide three channels: a traditional voice channel, an upstream channel for communicating from the client to the ISP (often at speeds of 64 to 640 Kbps), and a downstream channel for communicating from the ISP to the client (often at speeds of 640 Kbps to 6 Mbps).

asynchronous transfer mode (ATM): A communication switch that handles interface speeds ranging from 25 million to 622 million bps. It multiplexes data streams onto the same backbone by using cell relay techniques. ATM switches can handle multimedia traffic, such as data, graphics, voice, and video.

asynchronous transmission: Transmission in which each information character is individually synchronized, usually by start-and-stop bits. The gap between each character is not a fixed length. *Compare with* **synchronous transmission.**

ATM: *See* **asynchronous tranfer mode (ATM).** In banking, an **automated teller machine.**

attenuation: As a signal travels through a circuit, it gradually attenuates, or loses power. Expressed in decibels, attenuation is the difference between the transmitted and received power caused by loss of signal strength through the equipment, communication circuits, or other devices.

authentication: A security method of guaranteeing that a message is genuine, that it has arrived unaltered, and that it comes from the source indicated.

automatic number identification (ANI): The process whereby a long-distance common carrier provides its customers with a visual display of an incoming caller's telephone number.

Automatic Repeat reQuest: *See* **ARQ.**

B

backbone network (BN): A large network to which many networks within an organization are connected. It usually is a network that interconnects all networks on a single site, but it can be larger if it connects all the organization's terminals, microcomputers, mainframes, LANs, and other communication equipment.

BALUN: balanced/unbalanced. An impedance-matching device to connect balanced twisted-pair cabling with unbalanced coaxial cable.

bandwidth: The difference between the highest and lowest frequencies in a band. For example, a voice-grade circuit has a 4,000-Hz bandwidth. In common usage, *bandwidth* refers to circuit capacity; when people say they need more bandwidth, they need a higher transmission speed.

basic rate interface (BRI): In ISDN, two 64,000-bps B circuits for data transmission and one 16,000-bps D circuit for signaling (2 B+D). Also called basic rate access. *See also* **primary rate interface (PRI).**

baud: Unit of signaling speed. Now obsolete and replaced by the term *symbol rate.* The speed in baud is the number of signal elements per second. If each signal represents only 1 bit, *baud* is the same as *bits per second (bps).* When each signal contains more than 1 bit, *baud* does not equal *bps.*

BCC: *See* **block check character (BCC).**

BER: bit-error rate. The number of bits received in error divided by the total number of bits received. An indicator of circuit quality.

BERT: bit-error rate testing. Testing a data line with a pattern of bits that are compared before and after the transmission to detect errors.

BGP: *See* **Border Gateway Protocol (BGP).**

binary: A number system using only the two symbols 0 and 1 that is especially well adapted to computer usage because 0 and 1 can be represented as "on" and "off," respectively or as negative charges and positive charges, respectively. The binary digits appear in strings of 0's and 1's.

bipolar transmission: A method of digital transmission in which binary 0 is sent as a negative pulse and binary 1 is sent as a positive pulse.

Bit: 1. An abbreviation of the term *binary digit.* 2. A single pulse in a group of pulses. 3. A unit of information capacity.

bit-error rate (BER): *See* **BER.**

bit-error rate testing (BERT): *See* **BERT.**

bit rate: The rate at which bits are transmitted over a communication path, normally expressed in bits per second (bps). The bit rate should not be confused with the data signaling rate *(baud),* which measures the rate of signal changes being transmitted. *See also* **bps.**

bit stream: A continuous series of bits being transmitted on a transmission line.

bits per second (bps): *See* **bps.**

BKER: Block-error rate. The number of blocks received in error divided by the total number of blocks received.

BKERT: Block-error rate testing. Testing a data link with groups of information arranged into transmission blocks for error checking.

block: Sets of contiguous bits or bytes that make up a message, frame, or packet.

block check character (BCC): The character(s) at the end of a binary synchronous communications (BSC) message used to check for errors.

block-error rate (BKER): *See* **BKER.**

block-error rate testing (BKERT): *See* **BKERT.**

Bluetooth: A standard for short-distance wireless communication.

BN: *See* **backbone network (BN).**

BOC: *See* **RBOC.**

BONDING: (Bandwidth on Demand Interoperatibility Networking Group) is an inverse multiplexing proposal for combining several 56-Kbps or 64-Kbps circuits into one higher-speed circuit.

Border Gateway Protocol (BGP): A network layer standard protocol used to exchange route information between routers using dynamic decentralized routing.

Used only between different TCP/IP autonomous systems (i.e., major sections of the Internet).

bps: Bits per second. The basic unit of data communication rate measurement. Usually refers to rate of information bits transmitted. *Contrast with* **baud** and **bit rate.**

BRI: *See* **basic rate interface (BRI).**

bridge: A device that connects two similar networks using the same data link and network protocols. *Compare with* **gateway, router,** and **brouter.**

broadband circuit: An analog communication circuit.

broadband communications: Originally, the term referred to analog communications, but it has become corrupted in common usage so that it now usually means high-speed communications networks, typically Internet access technologies with access speeds of 1 Mbp or higher.

broadband Ethernet: The 10Broad36 version of Ethernet IEEE 802.3, meaning that it transmits at 10 million bps in broadband with a maximum distance of 3,600 meters.

broadcast routing: *See* **decentralized routing.**

brouter: A piece of hardware that combines the functions of a bridge and a router. *See also* **bridge** and **router.**

brute-force attack: A way of breaking an encrypted message by trying all possible values of the key.

buffer: A device used for the temporary storage of data, primarily to compensate for differences in data flow rates (for example, between a terminal and its transmission circuit) but also as a security measure to allow retransmission of data if an error is detected during transmission.

burst error: A series of consecutive errors in data transmission. Refers to the phenomenon on communication circuits in which errors are highly prone to occurring in groups or clusters.

bus: A transmission path or circuit. Typically an electrical connection with one or more conductors in which all attached devices receive all transmissions at the same time.

byte: A small group of data bits that is handled as a unit. In most cases, it is an 8-bit byte and it is known as a *character.*

C

cache engine: A server that regularly stores incoming static content such as banners and graphics files so that future requests for those items can be processed internally without using capacity on the organization's Internet connection.

call-back modem: When a user calls a host computer, the modem disconnects the call after receiving the password and calls back to the caller's predefined telephone number to establish a connection.

CA*net 3: CA*net 3 is the Canadian network that forms part of Internet 2.

carrier: An analog signal at some fixed amplitude and frequency that then is combined with an information-bearing signal to produce an intelligent output signal suitable for transmission of meaningful information. *Also called carrier wave* or **carrier frequency.**

carrier frequency: The basic frequency or pulse repetition rate of a signal bearing no intelligence until it is modulated by another signal that does impart intelligence.

Carrier Sense Multiple Access: *See* **CSMA/CA** and **CSMA/CD.**

CCITT: *See* **Consultative Committee on International Telegraph and Telephone (CCITT).** Now obsolete and renamed **International Telecommunications Union—Telecommunications (ITU-T).**

CD: 1. Collision detection in the CSMA (Carrier Sense Multiple Access) protocol for LANs. 2. Carrier detect occurs when a modem detects a carrier signal to be received.

central office: The switching and control facility set up by the local telephone company (common carrier) where the subscriber's local loop terminates. Central offices handle calls within a specified geographic area, which is identified by the first three digits of the telephone number. *Also called* an **end office** or **exchange office.**

central processing unit (CPU): *See* **CPU.**

CENTREX: A widespread telephone company switching service that uses dedicated central office switching equipment. CENTREX CPE is where the user site also has customer premises equipment (CPE).

CERT: *See* **Computer Emergency Response Team (CERT).**

certificate authority (CA): A CA is a trusted organization that can vouch for the authenticity of the person or organization using authentication (e.g., VeriSign). A person wanting to use a CA registers with the CA and must provide some proof of identify. CA issues a digital certificate that is the requestor's public key encrypted using the CA's private key as proof of identify that can be attached to the user's e-mail or Web transactions.

channel: 1. A path for transmission of electromagnetic signals. *Synonym for* **line** or **link.** *Compare with* **circuit.** 2. A data communications path. Circuits may be divided into subcircuits.

character: A member of a set of elements used for the organization, control, or representation of data. Characters may be letters, digits, punctuation marks, or other symbols. *Also called* a **byte.**

cheapnet: *See* **thin Ethernet.**

checking, echo: A method of checking the accuracy of transmitted data in which the received data are returned to the sending end for comparison with the original data.

checking, parity: *See* **parity check.**

checking, polynomial: *See* **polynomial checking.**

circuit: The path over which the voice, data, or image transmission travels. Circuits can be twisted-wire pairs, coaxial cables, fiber-optic cables, microwave transmissions, and so forth. *Compare with* **channel, line,** and **link.**

circuit switching: A method of communications whereby an electrical connection between calling and called stations is established on demand for exclusive use of the circuit until the connection is terminated.

cladding: A layer of material (usually glass) that surrounds the glass core of an optical fiber. Prevents loss of signal by reflecting light back into the core.

client: The input–output hardware device at the user's end of a communication circuit. There are three major categories of clients: microcomputers, terminals, and special-purpose terminals.

cluster controller: A device that controls the input–output operations of the cluster of devices (microcomputers, terminals, printers, and so forth) attached to it. *Also called* a *terminal controller.* For example, the 3274 Control Unit is a cluster controller that directs all communications between the host computer and remote devices attached to it.

CMIP: *See* **Common Management Interface Protocol (CMIP).**

coaxial cable: An insulated wire that runs through the middle of a cable. A second braided wire surrounds the insulation of the inner wire like a sheath. Used on LANs for transmitting messages between devices.

code: A transformation or representation of information in a different form according to some set of preestablished conventions. *See also* **ASCII** and **EBCDIC.**

codec: A codec translates analog voice data into digital data for transmission over computer networks. Two codecs are needed—one at the sender's end and one at the receiver's end.

code conversion: A hardware box or software that converts from one code to another, such as from ASCII to EBCDIC.

collapsed backbone network: In a collapsed backbone, the set of routers in a typical backbone is replaced by one switch and a set of circuits to each LAN. The collapsed backbone has more cable but fewer devices. There is no backbone cable. The "backbone" exists only in the switch.

collision: When two computers or devices transmit at the same time on a shared multipoint circuit, their signals collide and destroy each other.

common carrier: An organization in the business of providing regulated telephone, telegraph, telex, and data communications services, such as AT&T, MCI, Bell-South, and NYNEX. This term is applied most often to U.S. and Canadian commercial organizations, but sometimes it is used to refer to telecommunication entities, such as government-operated suppliers of communication services in other countries. *See also* **PTT.**

Common Management Interface Protocol (CMIP): CMIP is a network management system that monitors and tracks network usage and other parameters for user workstations and other nodes. It is similar to SNMP, but it is more complete and is better in many ways.

communication services: A group of transmission facilities that is available for lease or purchase.

comparison risk ranking: The process by which the members of a Delphi team reach a consensus on which network threats have the highest risk. It produces a ranked list from high risk to low risk.

component: One of the specific pieces of a network, system, or application. When these components are assembled, they become the network, system, or application. Components are the individual parts of the network that we want to safeguard or restrict by using controls.

compression: *See* **data compression.**

Computer Emergency Response Team (CERT): The job of CERT, located at Carnegie Mellon University, is to respond to computer security problems on the Internet, raise awareness of computer security issues, and prevent security breaches. It was established by the U.S. Department of Defense in 1988 after a virus shut down almost 10 percent of the computers on the Internet. Many organizations are starting their own computer emergency response teams, so the term is beginning to refer to any response team, not just the one at Carnegie Mellon University.

concentrator: A device that multiplexes several low-speed communication circuits onto a single high-speed trunk. A remote data concentrator (RDC) is similar in function to a multiplexer but differs because the host computer software usually must be rewritten to accommodate the RDC. RDCs differ from statistical multiplexes because the total capacity of the high-speed outgoing circuit, in characters per second, is equal to the total capacity of the incoming low-speed circuits. On the other hand, output capacity of a statistical multiplexer (stat mux) is less than the total capacity of the incoming circuits.

conditioning: A technique of applying electronic filtering elements to a communication line to improve the capability of that line so it can support higher data transmission rates. *See also* **equalization.**

configuration: The actual or practical layout of a network that takes into account its software, hardware, and cabling. Configurations may be multidrop, point-to-point, LANs, and the like. By contrast, a topology is the geometric layout (ring, bus, star) of the configuration. Topologies are the building blocks of configurations. *Compare with* **topology.**

connectionless routing: Connectionless routing means each packet is treated separately and makes its own way through the network. It is possible that different packets will take different routes through the network depending on the type of routing used and the amount of traffic.

connection-oriented routing: Connection-oriented routing sets up a virtual circuit (one that appears to use point-to-point circuit switching) between the sender and receiver. The network layer makes one routing decision when the connection is established, and all packets follow the same route. All packets in the same message arrive at the destination in the same order in which they were sent.

Consultative Committee on International Telegraph and Telephone (CCITT): An international organization that sets worldwide communication standards. Its new name is **International Telecommunications Union—Telecommunications (ITU-T).**

content caching: Storing content from other Web sites on your network to reduce traffic on your Internet connection. A cache engine regularly stores incoming static content such as banners and graphics files so that future requests for those items can be processed internally.

content delivery: Storing content for your Web sites on the content delivery provider's servers spread around the Internet to reduce traffic on your Internet connection. The content delivery provider's servers contain the static content on your pages such as banners and graphics files. Software on your Web server locates the nearest content delivery server to the user (based on his or her IP address) and changes the references on your Web pages to draw the static content from that server. Content delivery was pioneered by Akamai, which is one of the leading content delivery services on the Internet.

contention: A method by which devices on the same shared multipoint circuit compete for time on the circuit.

control: A mechanism to ensure that the threats to a network are mitigated. There are two levels of controls: system-level controls and application-level controls.

control character: A character whose occurrence in a particular context specifies some network operation or function.

control spreadsheet: A two-dimensional matrix showing the relationship between the controls in a network, the threats that are being mitigated, and the components that are being protected. The controls listed in each cell represent the specific control enacted to reduce or eliminate the exposure.

core layer: The core layer is the central part of a network that provides access to the distribution layer. It is often a very fast backbone that runs through the center of a campus or office complex.

COS: Corporation for Open Systems. An organization of computer and communications equipment vendors and users formed to accelerate the introduction of products based on the seven-layer OSI model. Its primary interest is the application layer (layer 7) of the OSI model and the X.400 e-mail standard.

CPE: *See* **customer premises equipment (CPE).**

CPU: central processing unit.

CRC: Cyclical redundancy check. An error-checking control technique using a specific binary prime divisor that results in a unique remainder. It usually is a 16- to 32-bit character.

CSMA/CA: Carrier Sense Multiple Access (CSMA) with Collision Avoidance (CA). This protocol is similar to the Carrier Sense Multiple Access (CSMA) with Collision Detection (CD) protocol. Whereas CSMA/CD sends a data packet and then reports back if it collides with another packet, CSMA/CA sends a small preliminary packet to determine whether the network is busy. If there is a collision, it is with the small packet rather than with the entire message. CA is thought to be more efficient because it reduces the time required to recover from collisions.

CSMA/CD: Carrier Sense Multiple Access (CSMA) with Collision Detection (CD). A system used in contention networks. The network interface unit listens for the presence of a carrier before attempting to send and detects the presence of a collision by monitoring for a distorted pulse.

customer premises equipment (CPE): Equipment that provides the interface between the customer's CENTREX system and the telephone network. It physically resides at the customer's site rather than the telephone company's end office. *CPE* generally refers to voice telephone equipment instead of data transmission equipment.

cyclical redundancy check (CRC): *See* **CRC.**

D

data: 1. Specific individual facts or a list of such items. 2. Facts from which conclusions can be drawn.

data circuit terminating equipment (DCE): *See* **DCE.**

data compression: The technique that provides for the transmission of fewer data bits without the loss of information. The receiving location expands the received data bits into the original bit sequence.

Data Encryption Standard (DES): *See* **DES.**

Data over Cable System Interface Specification (DOCSIS): A de facto data link layer standard for transmitting data via a cable modem using Ethernet-like protocols.

Data-over-Voice (DOV): When data and voice share the same transmission medium. Data transmissions are superimposed over the voice transmission.

data terminal equipment (DTE): *See* **DTE.**

datagram: A datagram is a connectionless service in packet-switched networks. Each packet has a destination and sequence number and may follow a different route through the network. Different routes may deliver packets at different speeds, so data packets often arrive out of sequence. The sequence number tells the network how to reassemble the packets into a continuous message.

dB: *See* **decibel (dB).**

DCE: Data circuit terminating equipment. The equipment (usually the modem) installed at the user's site that provides all the functions required to establish, maintain, and terminate a connection, including the signal conversion and coding between the data terminal equipment (DTE) and the common carrier's line.

DDoS attack: *See* **distributed denial-of-service (DDoS) attack.**

decentralized routing: With decentralized routing, all computers in the network make their own routing decisions. There are three major types of decentralized routing. With static routing, the routing table is developed by the network manager and remains unchanged until the network manager updates it. With dynamic routing, the goal is to improve network performance by routing messages over the fastest possible route; an initial routing table is developed by the network manager but is continuously updated to reflect changing network conditions, such as message traffic. With broadcast routing, the message is sent to all computers, but it is processed only by the computer to which it is addressed.

decibel (dB): A tenth of a bel. A unit for measuring relative strength of a signal parameter such as power and voltage. The number of decibels is ten times the logarithm (base 10) of the ratio of the power of two signals, or ratio of the power of one signal to a reference level. The reference level always must be indicated, such as 1 milliwatt for power ratio.

dedicated circuit: A leased communication circuit that goes from your site to some other location. It is a clear, unbroken communication path that is yours to use 24 hours per day, 7 days per week. *Also called a private circuit* or **leased circuit.**

delay distortion: A distortion on communication lines that is caused because some frequencies travel more slowly than others in a given transmission medium and therefore arrive at the destination at slightly different times. Delay distortion is measured in microseconds of delay relative to the delay at 1,700 Hz. This type of distortion does not affect voice, but it can have a serious effect on data transmissions.

delay equalizer: A corrective device for making the phase delay or envelope delay of a circuit substantially constant over a desired frequency range. *See also* **equalizer.**

Delphi group: A small group of experts (three to nine people) who meet to develop a consensus when it may be impossible or too expensive to collect more accurate data. For example, a Delphi group of communication experts might assemble to reach a consensus on the various threats to a communication network, the potential dollar losses for each occurrence of each threat, and the estimated frequency of occurrence for each threat.

denial of service (DoS) attack: A DoS attempts to disrupt the network by flooding the network with messages so that the network cannot process messages from normal users.

DES: Data Encryption Standard. Developed by IBM and the U.S. National Institute of Standards, this widely used single-key encryption algorithm uses a 64-bit key.

desktop videoconferencing: With desktop videoconferencing, small cameras are installed on top of each user's computer so that participants can hold meetings from their offices.

DHCP: *See* **Dynamic Host Control Protocol (DHCP).**

digital signal: A discrete or discontinuous signal whose various states are discrete intervals apart, such as +15 volts and −15 volts.

digital subscriber line (DSL): A data link layer technology that provides high-speed ("broadband") communication over traditional telephone lines. A DSL modem is used to provide three channels: a traditional voice channel, an upstream channel for communicating from the client to the ISP (often at speeds of 64 to 640 Kbps), and a downstream channel for communicating from the ISP to the client (often at speeds of 640 Kbps to 6 Mbps).

distortion: The unwanted modification or change of signals from their true form by some characteristic of the communication line or equipment being used for transmission—for example, delay distortion and amplitude distortion.

distortion types: 1. *Bias:* A type of distortion resulting when the intervals of modulation do not all have exactly their normal durations. 2. *Characteristic:* Distortion caused by transient disturbances that are present in the transmission circuit because of modulation. 3. *Delay:* Distortion occurring when the envelope delay of a circuit is not consistent over the frequency range required for transmission. 4. *End:* Distortion of start–stop signals. The shifting of the end of all marking pulses from their proper positions in relation to the beginning of the start pulse. 5. *Jitter:* A type of distortion that results in the intermittent shortening or lengthening of the signals. This distortion is entirely random in nature and can be caused by hits on the line. 6. *Harmonic:* The resultant process of harmonic frequencies (due to nonlinear characteristics of a transmission circuit) in the response when a sinusoidal stimulus is applied.

distributed denial of service (DDoS) attack: With a DDoS attack, a hacker breaks into and takes control of many computers on the Internet (often several hundred to several thousand) and uses them to launch the DoS attack from thousands of computers at the same time.

distribution layer: The distribution layer is the part of a network that connects the access layer to other access layers and to the core layer. It is often a BN in a building.

DNS: *See* **Domain Name Service (DNS).**

DOCSIS: *See* **Data Over Cable System Interface Specification (DOCSIS).**

Domain Name Service (DNS): A server that provides a directory used to supply IP addresses for application layer addresses—that is, a server that performs IP address resolution.

DoS attack: *See* **denial of service (DoS) attack.**

download: The process of loading software and data into the nodes of a network from the central node. Downloading usually refers to the movement of data from a host mainframe computer to a remote terminal or microcomputer.

DPSK: Differential phase shift keying. *See* **modulation, phase.**

DSL: *See* **digital subscriber line (DSL).**

DTE: Data terminal equipment. Any piece of equipment at which a communication path begins or ends, such as a terminal.

duplexing: An alternative to the process of mirroring, which occurs when a database server mirrors or backs up the database with each transaction. In mirroring, the server writes on two different hard disks through two different disk controllers. Duplexing is more redundant and therefore even safer than mirroring, because the database is written to two different hard disks on two different disk circuits. *Compare with* **mirroring.**

Dynamic Host Control Protocol (DHCP): A network-layer protocol standard used to supply TCP/IP address information using dynamic address assignment.

dynamic routing: *See* **decentralized routing.**

E

e-mail: *See* **electronic mail (e-mail).**

EBCDIC: Extended Binary Coded Decimal Interchange Code. A standard code consisting of a set of 8-bit characters used for information representation and interchange among data processing and communication systems. Very common in IBM equipment.

echo cancellation: Used in higher-speed modems to isolate and filter out (cancel) echoes when half-duplex transmissions use stop-and-wait ARQ (Automatic Repeat reQuest) protocols. Needed especially for satellite links.

echo checking: *See* **checking, echo.**

echo suppressor: A device for use in a two-way telephone circuit (especially circuits over 900 miles long) to attenuate echo currents in one direction caused by telephone currents in the other direction. This is done by sending an appropriate disabling tone to the circuit.

ECMA: *See* **European Computer Manufacturers Association (ECMA).**

EDI: *See* **Electronic Data Interchange (EDI).**

EIA: *See* **Electronic Industries Association (EIA).**

Electronic Data Interchange (EDI): Electronic Data Interchange for Administration, Commerce, and Transport. Standardizes the electronic interchange of business documents for both ASCII and graphics. Endorsed by the ISO. Defines major components of the ANSI X.12 EDI standard.

Electronic Industries Association (EIA): Composed of electronic manufacturers in the United States. Recommends standards for electrical and functional characteristics of interface equipment. Belongs to the ANSI. Known for the RS232 interface connector cable standard.

electronic mail (e-mail): A networking application that allows users to send and receive mail electronically.

electronic software distribution (ESD): ESD enables network managers to install software on client computers over the network without physically touching each client computer. ESD client software is installed on each client and enables an ESD server to download and install certain application packages on each client at some predefined time (e.g., at midnight on a Saturday).

emulate: Computer vendors provide software and hardware emulators that accept hardware and software from other vendors and enable them to run on their hardware or software.

encapsulation: A technique in which a frame from one network is placed within the data field of the frame in another network for transmission on the second network. For example, it enables a message initiated on a coaxial cable-based Ethernet LAN to be transmitted over an ATM fiber optic–based network and then placed onto another Ethernet LAN at the other end.

encryption: The technique of modifying a known bit stream on a transmission circuit so that to an unauthorized observer, it appears to be a random sequence of bits.

end office: The telephone company switching office for the interconnection of calls. *See also* **central office.**

envelope delay distortion: A derivative of the circuit phase shift with respect to the frequency. This distortion affects the time it takes for different frequencies to propagate the length of a communication circuit so that two signals arrive at different times.

equalization: The process of reducing frequency and phase distortion of a circuit by introducing time differences to compensate for the difference in attenuation or time delay at the various frequencies in the transmission band.

equalizer: Any combination (usually adjustable) of coils, capacitors, or resistors inserted in the transmission circuit or amplifier to improve its frequency response.

error control: An arrangement that detects the presence of errors. In some networks, refinements are added that correct the detected errors, either by operations on the received data or by retransmission from the source.

ESD: *See* **electronic software distribution (ESD).**

Ethernet: A LAN developed by the Xerox Corporation. It uses coaxial cable or twisted-pair wires to connect the stations. It was standardized as **IEEE 802.3.**

European Computer Manufacturers Association (ECMA): Recommends standards for computer components manufactured or used in Europe. Belongs to the International Organization for Standardization (ISO).

exchange office: *See* **central office.**

exposure: The calculated or estimated loss resulting from the occurrence of a threat, as in "The exposure from theft could be $42,000 this year." It can be either tangible and therefore measurable in dollars or intangible and therefore not directly measurable in dollars. *See also* **comparison risk ranking.**

Extended Binary Coded Decimal Interchange Code (EBCDIC): *See* **EBCDIC.**

extranet: Using the Internet to provide access to information intended for a selected set of users, not the public at large. Usually done by requiring a password to access a selected set of Web sites.

F

FCC: *See* **Federal Communications Commission (FCC).**

FCS: *See* **frame check sequence (FCC).**

FDDI: *See* **fiber distributed data interface (FDDI).**

FDM: Frequency division multiplexing. *See* **multiplexer.**

feasibility study: A study undertaken to determine the possibility or probability of improving the existing system within a reasonable cost. Determines what the problem is and what its causes are and makes recommendations for solving the problem.

FEC: *See* **forward error correction (FEC).**

Federal Communications Commission (FCC): A board of seven commissioners appointed by the U.S. president under the Communication Act of 1934, having the power to regulate all interstate and foreign electrical communication systems originating in the United States.

FEP: *See* **front-end processor (FEP).**

fiber distributed data interface (FDDI): A token ring-like LAN technology that permits transmission speeds of 100 million bps using fiber-optic cables (ANSI standard X3T9.5).

fiber-optic cable: A transmission medium that uses glass or plastic cable instead of copper wires.

fiber optics: A transmission technology in which modulated visible lightwave signals containing information are sent down hair-thin plastic or glass fibers and demodulated back into electrical signals at the other end by a special light-sensitive receiver.

File Transfer Protocol (FTP): FTP enables users to send and receive files over the Internet. There are two types of FTP sites: closed (which require users to have an account and a password) and anonymous (which permit anyone to use them).

firewall: A firewall is a router, gateway, or special-purpose computer that filters packets flowing into and out of a network. No access to the organization's networks is permitted except through the firewall. Two commonly used types of firewalls are packet level and application level.

firmware: A set of software instructions set permanently or semipermanently into a read-only memory (ROM).

flow control: The capability of the network nodes to manage buffering schemes that allow devices of different data transmission speeds to communicate with each other.

forward error correction (FEC): A technique that identifies errors at the received station and automatically corrects those errors without retransmitting the message.

fractional T1 (FT1): A portion of a T1 circuit. A full T1 allows transmission at 1,544,000 bps. A fractional T1 circuit allows transmission at lower speeds of 384,000, 512,000, or 768,000 bps. *See also* **T carrier.**

frame: Generally, a group of data bits having bits at each end to indicate the beginning and end of the frame. Frames also contain source addresses, destination addresses, frame type identifiers, and a data message.

frame check sequence (FCS): Used for error checking. FCS uses a 16-bit field with cyclical redundancy checking for error detection with retransmission.

frame relay: Frame relay is a type of packet-switching technology that transmits data faster than X.25 standard. The key difference is that unlike X.25 networks, frame relay does not perform error correction at each computer in the network. Instead, it simply discards any messages with errors. It is up to the application software at the source and destination to perform error correction and to control for lost messages.

frequency: The rate at which a current alternates, measured in Hertz, kilohertz, megahertz, and so forth. Other units of measure are cycles, kilocycles, or megacycles; *hertz* and *cycles per second* are synonymous.

frequency division multiplexing (FDM): *See* **multiplexer.**

frequency modulation: *See* **modulation, frequency.**

frequency shift keying (FSK): *See* **FSK.**

front-end processor (FEP): An auxiliary processor that is placed between a computer's CPU and the transmission facilities. This device normally handles housekeeping functions like circuit management and code translation, which otherwise would interfere with efficient operation of the CPU.

FSK: Frequency shift keying. A modulation technique whereby 0 and 1 are represented by a different frequency and the amplitude does not vary.

FTP: *See* **File Transfer Protocol (FTP).**

full-duplex: The capability of transmission in both directions at one time. *Contrast with* **half-duplex** and **simplex.**

G

gateway: A device that connects two dissimilar networks. Allows networks of different vendors to communicate by translating one vendor's protocol into another. *See also* **bridge, router,** and **brouter.**

Gaussian noise: *See* **noise, Gaussian.**

Gbps: Gigabit per second; 1 Gbps is equal to 1 billion bps.

GHz: Gigahertz; 1 GHz is equal to 1 billion cycles per second in a frequency.

gigabyte: One billion bytes.

G.Lite: One de facto standard form of ADSL.

guardband: A small bandwidth of frequency that separates two voice-grade circuits. Also, the frequencies between subcircuits in FDM systems that guard against subcircuit interference.

H

hacker: A person who sleuths for passwords to gain illegal access to important computer files. Hackers may rummage through corporate trash cans looking for carelessly discarded printouts.

half-duplex: A circuit that permits transmission of a signal in two directions but not at the same time. *Contrast*

with **full-duplex** and **simplex.**

Hamming code: A forward error correction (FEC) technique named for its inventor.

handshaking: Exchange of predetermined signals when a connection is established between two data set devices. This is used to establish the circuit and message path.

HDLC: *See* **high-level data link control (HDLC).**

hertz (Hz): Same as cycles per second; for example, 3,000 Hz is 3,000 cycles per second.

high-level data link control (HDLC): A bit-oriented protocol in which control of data links is specified by series of bits rather than by control characters (bytes).

home page: A home page is the main starting point or page for a World Wide Web entry.

host computer: The computer that lies at the center of the network. It generally performs the basic centralized data processing functions for which the network was designed. The host used to be where the network communication control functions took place, but today these functions tend to take place in the front-end processor or further out in the network. *Also called* a *central computer.*

hotline: A service that provides direct connection between customers in various cities using a dedicated circuit.

HTML: Web text files or pages use a structural language called HTML (Hypertext Markup Language) to store their information. HTML enables the author to define different type styles and sizes for the text, titles, and headings, and a variety of other formatting information. HTML also permits the author to define links to other pages that may be stored on the same Web server or on any Web server anywhere on the Internet.

hub: Network hubs act as junction boxes, permitting new computers to be connected to the network as easily as plugging a power cord into an electrical socket, and provide an easy way to connect network cables. Hubs also act as repeaters or amplifiers. Hubs are sometimes also called concentrators, multistation access units, or transceivers.

Hypertext Markup Language (HTML): *See* **HTML.**

Hz: *See* **hertz (Hz).**

I

IAB: *See* **Internet Architecture Board (IAB).**

IANA: *See* **Internet Assigned Numbers Authority (IANA).**

ICMP: *See* **Internet Control Message Protocol (ICMP).**

idle character: A transmitted character indicating "no information" that does not manifest itself as part of a message at the destination point.

IDS: *See* **intrusion detection system (IDS).**

IEEE: *See* **Institute of Electrical and Electronics Engineers (IEEE).** IEEE has defined numerous standards for LANs and BNs; see Chapters 4, 5, and 8.

IESG: Internet Engineering Steering Group.

IETF: Internet Engineering Task Force.

IMAP: *See* **Internet Mail Access Protocol (IMAP).**

impulse noise: *See* **noise, impulse.**

in-band signaling: The transmission signaling information at some frequency or frequencies that lie within a carrier circuit normally used for information transmission.

Institute of Electrical and Electronics Engineers (IEEE): A professional organization for engineers in the United States. Issues standards and belongs to the ANSI and the ISO.

integrated services digital network (ISDN): *See* **ISDN.**

interexchange circuit (IXC): A circuit or circuits between end offices (central offices).

interLATA: Circuits that cross from one LATA (local access and transport area) into another.

intermodulation distortion: An analog line impairment whereby two frequencies create a third erroneous frequency, which in turn distorts the data signal representation.

International Organization for Standardization (ISO): *See* **ISO.**

International Telecommunications Union—Telecommunications (ITU-T): An International organization that sets worldwide communication standards. Its old name was **Consultative Committee on International Telegraph and Telephone (CCITT).**

Internet: The information superhighway. The network of networks that spans the world, linking more than 20 million users.

Internet Architecture Board (IAB): IAB provides strategic architectural oversight (e.g., top-level domain names, use of international character sets) that can be passed on as guidance to the IESG or turned into published statements or simply passed directly to the relevant IETF working group. The IAB does not produce polished technical proposals but rather tries to stimulate action by the IESG or the IETF that will lead to proposals that meet general consensus. The IAB appoints the IETF chair and all IESG members.

Internet Assigned Numbers Authority (IANA): IANA governs the assignment of IP numbers.

Internet Control Message Protocol (ICMP): A simple network layer protocol standard intended to exchange limited routing information between routers. Most commonly known as a ping, after the DOS and UNIX command.

Internet Engineering Steering Group (IESG): The IESG is responsible for technical management of IETF activities and the Internet standards process. It administers the process according to the rules and procedures and is directly responsible for the actions associated with entry into and movement along the Internet "standards track," including final approval of specifications as Internet standards. Each IETF working group is chaired by a member of the IESG.

Internet Engineering Task Force (IETF): IETF is a large, open international community of network designers, operators, vendors, and researchers concerned with the evolution of the Internet architecture and the smooth operation of the Internet. IETF operates through a series of working groups, which are organized by topic (e.g., routing, transport, security). The requests for comment (RFCs) that form the basis for Internet standards are developed by the IETF and its working groups.

Internet Mail Access Protocol (IMAP): An application layer protocol standard that covers communication between an e-mail client and an e-mail server.

Internet Research Task Force (IRTF): IRTF operates much like the IETF, through small research groups focused on specific issues. Although IETF working groups focus on current issues, IRTF research groups work on long-term issues related to Internet protocols, applications, architecture, and technology. The IRTF chair is appointed by the IAB.

Internet service provider (ISP): ISPs offer connections to the Internet. Some access providers charge a flat monthly fee for unlimited access (much like the telephone company), whereas others charge per hour of use (much like a long-distance telephone call).

Internet Society (ISOC): ISOC is the closet the Internet has to an owner. ISOC is an open-membership professional society with more than 175 organizational and 8,000 individual members in over 100 countries and includes corporations, government agencies, and foundations that have created the Internet and its technologies.

internetworking: Connecting several networks together so workstations can address messages to the workstations on each of the other networks.

Internet 2: There are many different organizations currently working on the next generation of the Internet, including the Abilene network, vBNS, and CA*net 3. Although each is working in a slightly different fashion, they join together with each other and parts of the regular Internet at gigapops (gigabit points of presence).

interoperability: The interconnection of dissimilar networks in a manner that allows them to operate as though they were similar.

intraLATA: Circuits that are totally within one LATA (local access transport area).

intranet: Using Internet protocols on an network internal to an organization so that information is accessible using a browser, for example, but only by employees, not the public at large. Usually done by requiring a password to access a selected set of Web sites and protecting the site by a firewall so no outsiders can access it.

intrusion detection system (IDS): An IDS monitors a network segment, a server, or an application on the server for signs of unauthorized access and issues an alarm when an intrusion is detected. A misuse detection IDS compares monitored activities with signatures of known attacks, whereas an anomaly detection IDS compares monitored activities with the "normal" set of activities.

inverse multiplexer: Hardware that takes one high-speed transmission and divides it among several transmission circuits.

IPX/SPX: Internetwork packet exchange/sequenced packet exchange (IPX/SPX), based on a routing protocol developed by Xerox in the 1970s, is the primary network protocol used by Novell NetWare. About 40 percent of all installed LANs use it.

IRTF: *See* **Internet Research Task Force (IRTF).**

ISDN: Integrated services digital network. A hierarchy of digital switching and transmission systems. The ISDN provides voice, data, and image in a unified manner. It is synchronized so all digital elements speak the same "language" at the same speed. *See also* **basic rate interface (BRI)** and **primary rate interface (PRI).**

ISO: International Organization for Standardization, Geneva, Switzerland. The initials *ISO* stand for its French name. This international standards-making body is best known in data communications for developing the internationally recognized seven-layer network model called the Open Systems Interconnection (OSI) Reference model. *See also* **OSI model.**

ISOC: *See* **Internet Society (ISOC).**

ISP: *See* **Internet service provider (ISP).**

ITU-T: *See* **International Telecommunications Union—Telecommunications (ITU-T).**

IXC: *See* **interexchange circuit (IXC).**

J

jack: The physical connecting device at the interface that mates with a compatible receptacle—a plug.

jitter: Type of analog communication line distortion caused by the variation of a signal from its reference timing positions, which can cause data transmission errors, particularly at high speeds. This variation can be in amplitude, time, frequency, or phase.

jumper: 1. A small connector that fits over a set of pins on a microcomputer circuit card. 2. A patch cable or wire used to establish a circuit for testing or diagnostics.

K

K: A standard quantity measurement of computer storage. A K is defined loosely as 1,000 bytes. In fact, it is 1,024 bytes, which is the equivalent of 2^{10}.

Kbps: Kilobits per second. A data rate equal to 10^3 bps (1,000 bps).

Kermit: Kermit is a very popular asynchronous file transfer protocol named after Kermit the Frog. Kermit protocol was developed by Columbia University, which released it as a free software communications package. Various versions of Kermit can be found on public bulletin board systems for downloading to a microcomputer.

key management: The process of controlling the secret keys used in encryption.

KHz: Kilohertz; 1 KHz is equal to 1,000 cycles per second in a frequency.

kilobits per second (Kbps): *See* **Kbps.**

kilometer: A metric measurement equal to 0.621 mile or 3,280.8 feet.

L

LAN: *See* **local area network (LAN).**

laser: *L*ight *a*mplification by *s*timulated *e*mission of *r*adiation. A device that transmits an extremely narrow and coherent beam of electromagnetic energy in the visible light spectrum. (*Coherent* means that the separate waves are in phase with one another rather than jumbled as in normal light.)

LATA: Local access transport area. One of approximately 200 local telephone service areas in the United States roughly paralleling major metropolitan areas. The LATA subdivisions were established as a result of the AT&T/Bell divestiture to distinguish local from long-distance service. Circuits with both end points within the LATA (intraLATAs) generally are the sole responsibility of the local telephone company. Circuits that cross outside the LATA (interLATAs) are passed on to an interexchange carrier like AT&T, MCI, or Sprint.

leased circuit: A leased communication circuit that goes from your site to some other location. It is a clear, unbroken communication path that is yours to use 24 hours per day, 7 days per week. *Also called private circuit* or **dedicated circuit.**

line: A circuit, channel, or link. It carries the data communication signals. An early telephone technology term that may imply a physical connection, such as with a copper wire. *Compare with* **channel, circuit,** *and* **link.**

link: An unbroken circuit path between two points. *Sometimes called a* **line, channel,** *or* **circuit.**

Listserv: A listserver (or Listserv) is a mailing list. One part, the Listserv processor, processes commands such as requests to subscribe, unsubscribe, or to provide more information about the Listserv. The second part is the Listserv mailer. Any message send to the Listserv mailer is re-sent to everyone on the mailing list.

LLC: The logical link control, or LLC, sublayer is just an interface between the MAC sublayer and software in layer 3 (the network layer) that enables the software and hardware in the MAC sublayer to be separated from the logical functions in the LLC sublayer. By separating the LLC sublayer from the MAC sublayer, it is simpler to change the MAC hardware and software without affecting the software in layer 3. The most commonly used LLC protocol is IEEE 802.2.

load balancing server: A load balancing server is placed in front of a server farm to balance the number of requests sent to each server. All IP packets for the server farm are addressed to the load balancing server, which then changes the destination IP address to the selected server before retransmitting the packet to the server. Several routers and routing switches now include load balancing capabilities.

local access transport area (LATA): *See* **LATA.**

local area network (LAN): A network that is located in a small geographic area, such as an office, a building, a complex of buildings, or a campus, and whose communication technology provides a high-bandwidth, low-cost medium to which many nodes can be connected. These networks typically do not use common carrier circuits, and their circuits do not cross public thoroughfares or property owned by others. LANs are not regulated by the FCC or state public utilities commissions.

local exchange carrier: The local telephone company, such as one of the seven regional Bell operating companies (RBOCs).

local loop: The part of a communication circuit between the subscriber's equipment and the equipment in the local central office.

log: 1. A record of everything pertinent to a system function. 2. A collection of messages that provides a history of message traffic.

logical link control (LLC): *See* **LLC.**

longitudinal redundancy check (LRC): A system of error control based on the formation of a block check following preset rules. The check formation rule is applied in the same manner to each character. In a simple case, the LRC is created by forming a parity check on each bit position of all characters in the block. (That is, the first bit of the LRC character creates odd parity among the 1-bit positions of the characters in the block.)

LRC: *See* **longitudinal redundancy check (LRC).**

M

M: Mega. The designation for 1 million, as in 3 megabits per second (3 Mbit/s).

MAC: *See* **media access control (MAC).**

MAN: *See* **metropolitan area network (MAN).**

Manchester encoding: The digital transmission technique used in the physical layer of Ethernet LANs. *See* Chapter 4.

management information base (MIB): The extent of information that can be retrieved from a user microcomputer when using the Simple Network Management Protocol (SNMP) for network management. MIBs are sets of attributes and definitions that pertain to specific network devices.

Mbps: A data rate equal to 10^6 bps. Sometimes called megabits per second (1,000,000 bps).

mean times: *See* **MTBF, MTTD, MTTF,** and **MTTR.**

media access control (MAC): A data link layer protocol that defines how packets are transmitted on a local area network. *See also* **CSMA/CD, token bus,** and **token ring.**

medium: The matter or substance that carries the voice or data transmission. For example, the medium can be copper (wires), glass (fiber-optic cables), or air (microwave or satellite).

megabit: One million bits.

megabyte: One million bytes.

mesh network: A network topology in which there are direct point-to-point connections among the computers.

message: A communication of information from a source to one or more destinations. A message usually is composed of three parts: (1) a heading, containing a suitable indicator of the beginning of the message together with some of the following information: source, destination, date, time, routing; (2) a body containing the information to be communicated; (3) an ending containing a suitable indicator of the end of the message.

message switching: An operation in which the entire message being transmitted is switched to the other location without regard to whether the circuits actually are interconnected at the time of your call. This usually involves a message store-and-forward facility.

meter: A metric measurement equal to 39.37 inches.

metropolitan area network (MAN): A network that usually covers a citywide area. Because MANs use LAN and fiber-optic technologies, transmission speeds can vary between 2 million and 100 million bps.

MHz: megahertz; 1 MHz is equal to 1 million cycles per second in a frequency.

MIB: *See* **management information base (MIB).**

MIME: *See* **Multipurpose Internet Mail Extension (MIME).**

MIPS: One million instructions per second. Used to describe a computer's processing power.

mirroring: A process in which the database server automatically backs up the disk during each database transaction. During this process, the computer writes on two different hard disks on the same disk circuit every time the hard disk is updated. This creates two mirror images of the database data. Disk mirroring can be accomplished only when the database server contains two physical disk drives, because the records or data structures are written to both disks simultaneously. Should a problem develop with one disk, the second disk is available instantly with identical information on it. *Compare with* **duplexing.**

mnemonic: A group of characters used to assist the human memory. A mnemonic frequently is an acronym.

modem: A contraction of the words *mo*dulator-*dem*odulator. A modem is a device for performing necessary signal transformation between terminal devices and communication circuits. Modems are used in pairs, one at either end of the communication circuit.

modulation, amplitude: The form of modulation in which the amplitude of the carrier is varied in accordance with the instantaneous value of the modulating signal.

modulation, frequency: A form of modulation in which the frequency of the carrier is varied in accordance with the instantaneous value of the modulating signal.

modulation, phase: A form of modulation in which the phase of the carrier is varied in accordance with the instantaneous value of the modulating signal. Phase modulation has two related techniques. Phase shift keying (PSK) uses a 180° change in phase to indicate a change in the binary value (0 or 1), differential phase shift keying (DPSK) uses a 180° change in phase every time a 1 bit is transmitted; otherwise, the phase remains the same.

modulation, pulse code: *See* **pulse code modulation (PCM).**

MTBF: mean time between failures. The statistic developed by vendors to show the reliability of their equipment. It can be an actual calculated figure that generally is more accurate, or it can be a practical (theoretical) figure.

MTTD: Mean time to diagnose. The time it takes the network testing and problem management staff to diagnose a network problem.

MTTF: Mean time to fix. The time it takes vendors to remedy a network problem once they arrive on the premises.

MTTR: 1. Mean time to repair—the combination of mean time to diagnose, mean time to respond, and mean time to fix, indicating the entire length of time it takes to fix a fault in equipment. 2. Mean time to respond—the time it takes the vendor to respond when a network problem is reported.

multidrop (multipoint): A line or circuit interconnecting several stations/nodes in a sequential fashion.

multiplexer: A device that combines data traffic from several low-speed communication circuits onto a single high-speed circuit. The two popular types of multiplexing are FDM (frequency division multiplexing) and TDM (time division multiplexing). In FDM, the voice-grade link is divided into subcircuits, each covering a different frequency range in such a manner that each subcircuit can be employed as though it were an individual circuit. In TDM, separate time segments are assigned to each terminal. During these time segments, data may be sent without conflicting with data sent from another terminal.

multiplexing (mux): The subdivision of a transmission circuit into two or more separate circuits. This can be achieved by splitting the frequency range of the circuit into narrow frequency bands (**frequency division multiplexing**) or by assigning a given circuit successively to several different users at different times (**time division multiplexing**).

Multipurpose Internet Mail Extension (MIME): An application-layer standard protocol that enables SMTP mail messages to transfer nontext characters such as graphics and software. The sending e-mail client translates the nontext characters into something that resembles text using MIME codes and attaches it to the message. The receiving e-mail client translates the MIME codes back into the original graphic or software file.

mux: *See* **multiplexing (mux).**

N

NAK: *See* **negative acknowledgment (ACK).**

nanosecond: One billionth ($1/_{1,000,000,000}$) of a second or 10^{-9}.

NAP: *See* **network access point (NAP).**

NAT: *See* **network address translation (NAT).**

National Institute of Standards and Technology (NIST): Formerly the National Bureau of Standards. The agency of the U.S. government responsible for developing information processing standards for the federal government.

NCO: *See* **network cost of ownership (NCO).**

negative acknowledgment (NAK): The return signal that reports an error in the message received. The opposite of **acknowledgment (ACK).**

network: 1. A series of points connected by communication circuits. 2. The switched telephone network is the network of telephone lines normally used for dialed telephone calls. 3. A private network is a network of communication circuits confined to the use of one customer.

network access point (NAP): An "intersection" on the Internet where many national and regional ISPs connect to exchange data.

network address translation (NAT): NAT is the process of translating between one set of private IP addresses inside a network and a set of public IP addresses outside the network for use on the Internet. NAT is transparent in that no computer notices that it is being done.

network cost of ownership (NCO): NCO is a measure of how much it costs per year to keep one computer operating. NCO includes the cost of support staff to attach it to the network, install software, administer the network (e.g., create user IDs, back up user data), provide training and technical support, and upgrade hardware and software. NCO is often $1,500 to $3,500 per com-

puter per year. *Compare with* **total cost of ownership (TCO).**

network interface card (NIC): An NIC allows the computer to be physically connected to the network cable; the NIC provides the physical layer connection from the computer to the network.

network operating system (NOS): The NOS is the software that controls the network. The NOS provides the data link and the network layers and must interact with the application software and the computer's own operating system. Every NOS provides two sets of software: one that runs on the network server(s) and one that runs on the network client(s).

network operations center (NOC): Any centralized network management control site.

network profile: Every LAN microcomputer has a profile that outlines what resources it has available to other microcomputers in the network and what resources it can use elsewhere in the network.

network service: An application available on a network—for example, file storage.

NIC: *See* **network interface card (NIC).**

NIST: *See* **National Institute of Standards and Technology (NIST).**

NOC: *See* **network operations center (NOC).**

node: In a description of a network, the point at which the links join input–output devices. It could be a computer or a special-purpose device such as a router.

noise: The unwanted change in waveform that occurs between two points in a transmission circuit.

noise, amplitude: A sudden change in the level of power with differing effects, depending on the type of modulation used by the modem.

noise, cross-talk: Noise resulting from the interchange of signals on two adjacent circuits; manifests itself when it is possible to hear other people's telephone conversations.

noise, echo: The "hollow" or echoing characteristic that is heard on voice-grade lines with improper echo suppression.

noise, Gaussian: Noise that is characterized statistically by a Gaussian, or random, distribution.

noise, impulse: Noise caused by individual impulses on the circuit.

noise, intermodulation: Noise that occurs when signals from two independent lines intermodulate. A new signal forms and falls into a frequency band differing from those of both inputs. The new signal may fall into a frequency band reserved for another signal.

NOS: *See* **network operating system (NOS).**

NRZ: Nonreturn to zero. A binary encoding and transmission scheme in which 1's and 0's are represented by opposite and alternating high and low voltages, and in which there is no return to a reference (zero) voltage between encoded bits.

NRZI: Nonreturn to zero inverted. A binary encoding scheme that inverts the signal on a 1 and leaves the signal unchanged for a 0, and in which a change in the voltage state signals a 1-bit value and the absence of a change denotes a 0-bit value.

null character: A control character that can be inserted into or withdrawn from a sequence of characters without altering the message.

null modem cable: A 6- to 8-foot RS232 cable that makes the two microcomputers connected at each end of the cable think they are talking through modems.

O

office, central or end: The common carrier's switching office closest to the subscriber.

Open Shortest Path First (OSPF): A network layer standard protocol used to exchange route information between routers using dynamic decentralized routing.

Open Systems Interconnection (OSI) Reference model: *See* **OSI model.**

optical fibers: Hair-thin strands of very pure glass (sometimes plastic) over which light waves travel. They are used as a medium over which information is transmitted.

OSI model: The seven-layer Open Systems Interconnection (OSI) Reference model developed by the ISO subcommittee. The OSI model serves as a logical framework of protocols for computer-to-computer communications. Its purpose is to facilitate the interconnection of networks.

OSPF: *See* **Open Shortest Path First (OSPF).**

out-of-band signaling: A method of signaling that uses a frequency that is within the passband of the transmission facility but outside of a carrier circuit normally used for data transmission.

overhead: Computer time used to keep track of or run the system, as compared with computer time used to process data.

P

packet: A group of binary digits, including data and control signals, that is switched as a composite whole. The data, control signals, and error-control information are arranged in a specific format. A packet often is a 128-character block of data.

packet assembly/disassembly (PAD): *See* **PAD.**

Packet Layer Protocol (PLP): *See* **PLP.**

packet switching: Process whereby messages are broken into finite-size packets that always are accepted by the network. The message packets are forwarded to the other party over a multitude of different circuit paths. At the other end of the circuit, the packets are reassembled into the message, which is then passed on to the receiving terminal.

packet-switching network (PSN): A network designed to carry data in the form of packets. The packet and its format are internal to that network. The external interfaces may handle data in different formats, and format conversion may be done by the user's computer.

PAD: Packet assembly/disassembly. Equipment providing packet assembly and disassembly between asynchronous transmission and the packet-switching network.

PAM: *See* **pulse amplitude modulation (PAM).**

parallel: Describes the way the internal transfer of binary data takes place within a computer. It may be transmitted as a parallel word, but it is converted to a serial or bit-by-bit data stream for transmission.

parity bit: A binary bit appended to an array of bits to make the number of 1 bits always be odd or even for an individual character. For example, odd parity may require three 1 bits and even parity may require four 1 bits.

parity check: Addition of noninformation bits to a message to detect any changes in the original bit structure from the time it leaves the sending device to the time it is received.

parity checking: *See* **checking, parity.**

PBX: private branch exchange. Telephone switch located at a customer's site that primarily establishes voice communications over tie lines or circuits as well as between individual users and the switched telephone network. Typically also provides switching within a customer site and usually offers numerous other enhanced features, such as least-cost routing and call detail recording.

PCM: *See* **pulse code modulation (PCM).**

PDN: *See* **public data network (PDN).**

Pbps: Petabits per second. A data rate equal to 1 quadrillion bits per second (1,000,000,000,000,000).

peer: A dictionary definition of *peer* is "A person who is equal to another in abilities." A peer-to-peer network, therefore, is one in which each microcomputer node has equal abilities. In communications, a peer is a node or station that is on the same protocol layer as another.

peer-to-peer communications: 1. Communication between two or more processes or programs by which both ends of the session exchange data with equal privilege. 2. Communication between two or more network nodes in which either side can initiate sessions because no primary–secondary relationship exists.

peer-to-peer LAN: A network in which a microcomputer can serve as both a server and a user. Every microcomputer has access to all the network's resources on an equal basis.

permanent virtual circuit (PVC): A virtual circuit that resembles a leased line because it can be dedicated to a single user. Its connections are controlled by software.

phase modulation: *See* **modulation, phase.**

pirate: A person who obtains the latest software programs without paying for them. A skilled software pirate is able to break the protection scheme that is designed to prevent copying.

plain old telephone network (POTS): The nickname for the public switched telephone network. Often used when referring to dial-up Internet access using a modem.

PKI: *See* **public key infrastructure (PKI).**

PLP: Packet Layer Protocol (PLP) is the routing protocol that performs the network layer functions (e.g., routing and addressing) in X.25 networks.

point of presence (POP): The physical access location of an ISP or voice or data communications carrier.

point-to-point: Denoting a circuit, circuit, or line that has only two terminals. A link. An example is a single microcomputer connected to a mainframe.

polling: Any procedure that sequentially queries several terminals in a network.

polling, hub: A type of sequential polling in which the polling device contacts a terminal, that terminal contacts the next terminal, and so on, until all the terminals have been contacted.

polling, roll call: Polling accomplished from a prespecified list in a fixed sequence, with polling restarted when the list is completed.

polynomial checking: A checking method using polynomial functions to test for errors in data in transmission. Also called **cyclical redundancy check (CRC).**

POP: 1. *See* **Post Office Protocol (POP).** 2. *See* **point-of-presence (POP).**

port: One of the circuit connection points on a front-end processor or local intelligent controller.

Post Office Protocol (POP): An application-layer standard used to communicate between the client and the e-mail server.

POTS: *See* **plain old telephone network (POTS).**

PPP: PPP (multilink Point-to-Point Protocol) is an inverse multiplexing protocol for combining circuits of different speeds (e.g., a 64,000-bps circuit with a 14,400-bps circuit), with data allocated to each circuit is based on speed and need. PPP enables the user to change the circuits allocated to the PPP multiplexed circuit in mid-transmission so that the PPP circuit can increase or decrease the capacity. PPP is the successor to SLIP.

primary rate interface In ISDN, twenty-three 64,000 bits per second D circuits for data and one 64,000 bits per second B circuit for signaling (23 B+D). See also **basic rate interface.**

private branch exchange (PBX): *See* **PBX.**

propagation delay: The time necessary for a signal to travel from one point on the circuit to another, such as from a satellite dish up to a satellite or from Los Angeles to New York.

protocol: A formal set of conventions governing the format and control of inputs and outputs between two communicating devices. This includes the rules by which these two devices communicate as well as handshaking and line discipline.

protocol stack: The set of software required to process a set of protocols.

PSK: Phase shift keying; *see* **modulation, phase.**

PSN: *See* **packet-switching network (PSN).**

PTT: Postal, telephone and telegraph. These are the common carriers owned by governments; the government is the sole or monopoly supplier of communication facilities.

public data network (PDN): A network established and operated for the specific purpose of providing data transmission services to the public. It can be a public packet-switched network or a circuit-switched network. Public data networks normally offer value-added services for resource sharing at reduced costs and with high reliability. These time-sharing networks are available to anyone with a modem.

public key encryption: Public key encryption uses two keys. The public key is used to encrypt the message, and a second, very different private key is used to decrypt the message. Even though the sender knows both the contents of the outgoing message and the public encryption key, once it is encrypted, the message cannot be decrypted without the private key. Public key encryption is one of the most secure encryption techniques available.

public key infrastructure (PKI): The PKI is the process of using public key encryption on the Internet. PKI begins with a certificate authority (CA), which is a trusted organization that can vouch for the authenticity of the person or organization using authentication (e.g., VeriSign). The CA issues a digital certificate that is the requestor's public key encrypted using the CA's private key as proof of identify. This certificate is then attached to the user's e-mail or Web transactions. The receiver then verifies the certificate by decrypting it with the CA's public key—and must also contact the CA to ensure that the user's certificate has not been revoked by the CA.

pulse amplitude modulation (PAM): Amplitude modulation of a pulse carrier. PAM is used to translate analog voice data into a series of binary digits before they are transmitted.

pulse code modulation (PCM): Representation of a speech signal by sampling at a regular rate and converting each sample to a binary number. In PCM, the information signals are sampled at regular intervals, and a series of pulses in coded form are transmitted, representing the amplitude of the information signal at that time.

Q

QAM: Quadrature amplitude modulation. A sophisticated modulation technique that uses variations in signal amplitude, which allows data-encoded symbols to be represented as any of 16 states to send 4 bits on each signal.

Quality of Service (QoS): The ability of devices to give different priorities to different types of messages so that some messages (e.g., voice telephone data) are transmitted faster than other messages (e.g., e-mail).

quantizing error: The difference between the PAM signal and the original voice signal. The original signal has a smooth flow, but the PAM signal has jagged "steps."

R

RBOC: Regional Bell operating company. One of the seven companies created after divestiture of the old Bell system to provide local communications. Includes Ameritech, Bell Atlantic, BellSouth, NYNEX, Pacific Telesis, Southwestern Bell, and US West.

reclocking time: *See* **turnaround time.**

redundancy: The portion of the total information contained in a message that can be eliminated without loss of essential information.

Regional Bell operating company (RBOC): *See* **RBOC.**

reliability: A characteristic of the equipment, software, or network that relates to the integrity of the system against failure. Reliability usually is measured in terms of mean time between failures (MTBF), the statistical measure of the interval between successive failures of the hardware or software under consideration.

request for comment (RFC): A proposed standard for the Internet on which anyone in the world is invited to comment.

request for proposal (RFP): A request for proposal is used to solicit bids from vendors for new network hardware, software, and services. RFPs specify what equipment, software, and services are desired and ask vendors to provide their best prices.

repeater: A device used to boost the strength of a signal. Repeaters are spaced at intervals throughout the length of a communication circuit.

response time: The time the system takes to react to a given input; the time interval from when the user presses the last key to the terminal's typing the first letter of the reply. Response time includes (1) transmission time to the computer; (2) processing time at the computer, including access time to obtain any file records needed to answer the inquiry; and (3) transmission time back to the terminal.

retrain time: *See* **turnaround time.**

RFC: *See* **request for comment (RFC).**

RFP: *See* **request for proposal (RFP).**

ring: 1. The hot wire in a telephone circuit. 2. An audible sound used for signaling the recipient of an incoming telephone call. 3. A LAN topology having a logical geometric arrangement in the shape of a ring.

RIP: *See* **Routing Information Protocol (RIP).**

risk: The level or amount of exposure to an item when compared with other items. It is a hazard or chance of loss. Risk is the degree of difference, as in, "What level of risk does one threat have when compared to the other threats?"

risk assessment: The process by which one identifies threats, uses a methodology to determine the tangible or intangible exposures, and develops a sequenced list of the threats from the one having the highest risk to the one having the lowest risk. The list may be in a sequence based on tangible dollar losses or on intangible criteria such as public embarrassment, likelihood of occurrence, most dangerous, most critical to the organization, and greatest delay. *Also called risk ranking* or *risk analysis.*

RMON: Remote monitoring. The definitions of what is stored and therefore retrievable from a remote user microcomputer when using the Simple Network Management Protocol (SNMP). It is referred to as the RMON MIB (management information base). *See also* **management information base (MIB)** and **Simple Network Management Protocol (SNMP).**

router: A device that connects two similar networks having the same network protocol. It also chooses the best route between two networks when there are multiple paths between them. *Compare with* **bridge, brouter,** and **gateway.**

Routing Information Protocol (RIP): A network layer standard protocol used to exchange route information between routers using dynamic decentralized routing.

RS232: A technical specification published by the Electronic Industries Association that specifies the mechanical and electrical characteristics of the interface for connecting data terminal equipment (DTE) and data circuit terminating equipment (DCE). It defines interface circuit functions and their corresponding connector pin assignments.

RS449: An Electronic Industries Association standard for data terminal equipment (DTE) and data circuit terminating equipment (DCE) connection that specifies interface requirements for expanded transmission speeds (up to 2 million bps), longer cable lengths, and 10 additional functions.

S

SDLC: *See* **synchronous data link control (SDLC).**

serial: 1. Transmitting bits one at a time and in sequence. 2. The sequential or consecutive occurrence of two or more related activities in a single device or circuit.

server: A computer that provides a particular service to the client computers on the network. In larger LANs, the server is dedicated to being a server. In a peer-to-peer LAN, the server may be both a server and a client computer. There may be file, database, network, access, modem, facsimile, printer, and gateway servers.

server farm: A group of servers located in the same area.

service-level agreement (SLA): An SLA specifies the exact type of performance and fault conditions that the organization will accept and what compensation the service provider must provide if it fails to meet the SLA. For example, the SLA might state that network availability must be 99 percent or higher and that the MTBF for T1 circuits must be 120 days or more.

session: A logical connection between two terminals. This is the part of the message transmission when the two parties are exchanging messages. It takes place

after the communication circuit has been set up and is functioning.

signal: A signal is something that is sent over a communication circuit. It might be a control signal used by the network to control itself.

signal-to-noise ratio: The ratio, expressed in dB, of the usable signal to the noise signal present.

Simple Network Management Protocol (SNMP): An application layer protocol standard used in network management for monitoring and configuring network devices. *See also* **management information base (MIB)** and **RMON.**

Simple Mail Transfer Protocol (SMTP): An application-layer protocol standard used to transfer e-mail messages across the Internet.

simplex: A circuit capable of transmission in one direction only. *Contrast with* **full-duplex** and **half-duplex.**

single cable: A one-cable system in broadband LANs in which a portion of the bandwidth is allocated for "send" signals and a portion for "receive" signals, with a guardband in between to provide isolation from interference.

sliding window: A reliable delivery technique used by TCP to ensure that all packets are received and that the sender is not overwhelmed by receiving more segments than it can process. The sender and receiver agree on the maximum number of segments that can be sent (the "window") before the sender stops and waits for the receiver to acknowledge that the packets have been received and the sender can transmit more.

SLIP: Serial Line Internet Protocol (SLIP) is a proposed standard for inverse multiplexing. It has been surpassed by PPP.

SMDS: Switched multimegabit data service.

SMTP: *See* **Simple Mail Transfer Protocol (SMTP).**

SNA: *See* **systems network architecture (SNA).**

SNMP: *See* **Simple Network Management Protocol (SNMP).**

SONET: *See* **synchronous optical network (SONET).**

spike: A sudden increase of electrical power on a communication circuit. *Spike* is a term used in the communication industry. *Contrast with* **surge.**

spread spectrum: The U.S. military developed spread spectrum through-the-air radio transmission technology primarily to overcome the problem of intentional interference by hostile jamming and secondarily for security. A spread spectrum signal is created by modulating the original transmitted radio frequency (RF) signal with a spreading code that causes "hopping" of the frequency from one frequency to another. By contrast, conventional AM and FM radio uses only one frequency to transmit its signal.

start bit: A bit that precedes the group of bits representing a character. Used to signal the arrival of the character in asynchronous transmission.

static routing: *See* **decentralized routing.**

statistical multiplexer: Stat mux or STDM. A time division multiplexer (TDM) that dynamically allocates communication circuit time to each of the various attached terminals, according to whether a terminal is active or inactive at a particular moment. Buffering and queuing functions also are included. *See also* **concentrator.**

stop-and-wait: A reliable delivery technique in which the sender stops and waits for the receiver to send an acknowledgment that the packet was received before sending the next packet.

stop bit: A bit that follows the group of bits representing a character. Used to signal the end of a character in asynchronous transmission.

store-and-forward: A data communications technique that accepts messages or transactions, stores them, and then forwards them to the next location or person as addressed in the message header.

STX: A control character used in ASCII and EBCDIC data communications to mean start of text.

surge: A sudden increase in voltage on a 120-volt electrical power line. A term used in the electric utilities industry. *Contrast with* **spike.**

switch: Switches connect more than two LAN segments that use the same data link and network protocol. They may connect the same or different types of cable. Switches typically provide ports for 4, 8, 16, or 32 separate LAN segments, and most enable all ports to be in use simultaneously, so they are faster than bridges.

switched circuit: A dial-up circuit in which the communication path is established by dialing. If the entire circuit path is unavailable, there is a busy signal, which prevents completion of the circuit connection.

Switched Multimegabit Data Service (SMDS): *See* **SMDS.**

switched network: Any network that has switches used for directing messages from the sender to the ultimate recipient.

switched network, circuit switched: A switched network in which switching is accomplished by disconnecting and reconnecting lines in different configurations to set up a continuous pathway between the sender and the recipient. *See also* **circuit switching.**

switched network, store-and-forward: A switched network in which the store-and-forward principle is used to handle transmission between senders and recipients. *See also* **store-and-forward.**

switching: Identifying and connecting independent transmission links to form a continuous path from one location to another.

symbol rate: The speed in baud is the number of symbols per second. If each signal represents only one bit, *symbol rate* is the same as *bits per second.* When each signal contains more than one bit, *symbol rate* does not equal *bits per second.*

synchronization character (SYN): An 8-bit control character that is sent at the beginning of a message block to establish synchronization (timing) between the sender and the receiver. Term used for the characters preceding an Ethernet packet. Term used for a TCP open connection request.

synchronous data link control (SDLC): A protocol for managing synchronous, code-transparent, serial bit-by-bit information transfer over a link connection. Transmission exchanges may be full-duplex or half duplex and over switched or nonswitched links. The configurations of the link connection may be point-to-point, multipoint, or loop. SDLC is the protocol used in IBM's systems network architecture.

synchronous optical network (SONET): The National Exchange Carriers Association standard for optical transmission at gigabits-per-second speeds. For example, digital signals transmit on T1 circuits at 1,544,000 bps and on T3 circuits at 44,376,000 bps. The slowest SONET OC-1 optical transmission rate of 51,840,000 bps is slightly faster than the T3 rate.

synchronous transmission: Form of transmission in which data is sent as a fixed-length block or frame. *Compare with* **asynchonous transmission.**

systems network architecture (SNA): The name of IBM's conceptual framework that defines the data communication interaction between computer systems or terminals.

T

T carrier: A hierarchy of digital circuits designed to carry speech and other signals in digital form. Designated T1 (1.544 Mbps), T2 (6.313 Mbps), T3 (44.736 Mbps), and T4 (274.176 Mbps).

tariff: The formal schedule of rates and regulations pertaining to the communication services, equipment, and facilities that constitute the contract between the user and the common carrier. Tariffs are filed with the appropriate regulatory agency (FCC or state public utilities commission) for approval and published when approved.

TASI: Time-assisted speech interpolation. The process of interleaving two or more voice calls on the same telephone circuit simultaneously.

Tbps: Terabits per second. A data rate equal to 1 trillion bits per second (1,000,000,000,000).

TCM: Trellis-coded modulation (TCM) is a modulation technique related to QAM that combines phase modulation and amplitude modulation. There are several different forms of TCM that transmit 5, 6, 7, or 8 bits per signal, respectively.

TCP/IP: Transmission Control Protocol/Internet Protocol is probably the oldest networking standard, developed for ARPANET, and now used on the Internet. One of the most commonly used network protocols.

TDM: *See* **multiplexer.**

telecommunications: A term encompassing voice, data, and image transmissions that are sent over some medium in the form of coded signals.

telecommuting: Telecommuting employees perform some or all of their work at home instead of going to the office each day.

teleconferencing: With teleconferencing, people from diverse geographic locations can "attend" a business meeting in both voice and picture format. In fact, even documents can be shown and copied at any of the remote locations.

telephony: A generic term to describe voice communications. Pronounced "tel-*ef*-on-e," not "tel-e-*fon*-e."

Telnet: Telnet enables users on one computer to log in to other computers on the Internet.

10Base-T: An Ethernet LAN standard (IEEE 802.3) that runs at 10 million bps and uses unshielded twisted-pair wires.

10Base2: An Ethernet LAN standard that runs at 10 million bps, uses baseband transmission techniques, and allows 200 meters maximum cable length.

10Base5: An Ethernet LAN standard that runs at 10 million bps, uses baseband transmission techniques, and allows 500 meters maximum cable length.

10Broad36: An Ethernet LAN standard that runs at 10 million bps, uses broadband transmission techniques, and allows 3,600 meters maximum cable length.

100Base-T: An Ethernet LAN standard that runs at 100 million bps and uses unshielded twisted-pair wires.

1000Base-T: An Ethernet LAN standard the runs at 1 billion bps and uses unshielded twisted-pair wires.

thick Ethernet: Refers to the original Ethernet specifica-

tion that uses thick coaxial cable that is both grounded and shielded. The many layers of shielding are of polyvinyl and aluminum, which make the cable wider in diameter than other Ethernet cables. The heavy shielding also makes the cable more expensive and less flexible; therefore, it is impractical for many installations.

thin Ethernet: Refers to the 10Base2 baseband Ethernet, meaning the version that transmits at 10 million bps in baseband at 200 meters maximum. It uses thin coaxial cable. *Also called* **cheapnet.**

threat: A potentially adverse occurrence or unwanted event that could be injurious to the network, the computing environment, the organization, or a business application. Threats are acts or events the organization wants to prevent from taking place, such as lost data, theft, disasters, virus infections, errors, illegal access, and unauthorized disclosure. In other words, threats are events no one wants to occur.

3DES: *See* **triple DES (3DES).**

throughput: The total amount of useful information that is processed or communicated during a specific time period.

time-assisted speech interpolation (TASI): *See* **TASI.**

Time division multiplexing (TDM): *See* **multiplexer.**

timeout: The sender waits for some time longer than it expects to receive an acknowledgment that a packet has been sent and if no acknowledgment is received, it "times out" and resends the message (presuming that the message was lost or damaged by an error).

token: The special sequence of characters used to gain access to a token ring or token-bus network to transmit a packet.

token bus: A LAN with a bus topology that uses a token-passing approach to network access. In a token-bus LAN, the next logical node or station is not necessarily the next physical node because it uses preassigned priority algorithms. Message requests are not handled in consecutive order by stations. *Contrast with* **token ring.**

token passing: A method of allocating network access wherein a terminal can send a message only after it has acquired the network's electronic token.

token ring: A LAN with a ring topology that uses a token-passing approach to network access. In a token ring LAN, the next logical station also is the next physical station because the token passes from node to node. *Contrast with* **token bus.**

topology: The basic physical or geometric arrangement of the network—for example, a ring, star, or bus layout.

The topology is the network's logical arrangement, but it is influenced by the physical connections of its links and nodes. This is in contrast to its configuration, which is the actual or practical layout, including software and hardware constraints. Topologies are the building blocks of a network configuration. *Compare with* **configuration.**

total cost of ownership (TCO): TCO is a measure of how much it costs per year to keep one computer operating. TCO includes the cost of support staff to attach it to the network, install software, administer the network (e.g., create user IDs, back up user data), provide training and technical support, and upgrade hardware and software, along with the cost of "wasted time" when the network is down. TCO is often $10,000 per computer per year. *Compare to* **network cost of ownership (NCO).**

transceiver: A device that transmits and/or receives data to or from computers on an Ethernet LAN. Also a hub.

transmission rate of information bits (TRIB): *See* **TRIB.**

tree: A network arrangement in which the stations hang off a common "branch," or data bus, like leaves on the branch of a tree.

TRIB: Transmission rate of information bits. A TRIB is the network's throughput. It is the effective rate of data transfer over a communication circuit per unit of time. Usually expressed in bits per second.

triple DES (3DES): 3DES is a symmetric encryption technique that involves using DES three times, usually with three different keys, to produce the encrypted text, which produces a stronger level of security than DES, because it has a total of 168 bits as the key (i.e., 3×56 bits).

trunk: A voice communication circuit between switching devices or end offices.

turnaround time: The time required to reverse the direction of transmission from send to receive or vice versa on a half-duplex circuit.

twisted pair: A pair of wires used in standard telephone wiring. They are twisted to reduce interference caused by the other twisted pairs in the same cable bundle. Twisted-pair wires go from homes and offices to the telephone company end office.

U

UDP: *See* **User Datagram Protocol (UDP).**

uninterruptible power supply (UPS): Provides backup electrical power if the normal electrical power fails or if the voltage drops to unacceptably low levels.

unipolar transmission: A form of digital transmission in which the voltage changes between 0 volts to represent a binary 0 and some positive value (e.g., +15 volts) to represent a binary 1. *See also* **bipolar transmission.**

uniform resource locator (URL): *See* **URL.**

unshielded twisted-pair (UTP) wires: The type of wiring used in 10Base-T Ethernet networks. Same as **twisted pair.**

upload: The process of loading software and data from the nodes of a network (terminals or microcomputers), over the network media, and to the host mainframe computer.

UPS: *See* **uninterruptible power supply (UPS).**

URL: Uniform Resource Locator. To use a browser to access a Web server, you must enter the server's addresses or URL (uniform resource locator). All Web addresses begin with seven characters: http://.

USASCII: *See* **ASCII.**

User Datagram Protocol (UDP): A connectionless transport layer protocol standard used by TCP to send short messages such as DNS requests.

user profile: The user profile specifies what data and network resources a user can access, and the type of access (read-only, write, create, delete, etc.).

UTP: *See* **unshielded twisted-pair (UTP) wires.**

V

V.*nn*: The V.*nn* series of ITU-T standards relating to the connection of digital equipment to the analog telephone network. Primarily concerned with the modem interface. See Chapter 6 for definitions.

value-added network (VAN): A corporation that sells services of a value-added network. Such a network is built using the communication offerings of traditional common carriers, connected to computers that permit new types of telecommunication tariffs to be offered. The network may be a packet-switching or message-switching network.

VBNS: *See* **very-high-performance backbone network service (vBNS).**

VDSL: *See* **very-high-data-rate digital subscriber line (VDSL).**

VDT: Video display terminal.

vertical redundancy check (VRC): *See* **parity check.**

very-high-data-rate digital subscriber line (VDSL): A form of DSL that provides very high speed transmission (e.g., up to 51 Mbps) over traditional telephone lines for very short distances.

very-high-performance backbone network service (vBNS): One part of Internet 2 run by MCI Worldcom.

video teleconferencing: Video teleconferencing provides real-time transmission of video and audio signals to enable people in two or more locations to have a meeting.

virtual: Conceptual or appearing to be, rather than actually being.

virtual circuit: A temporary transmission circuit in which sequential data packets are routed between two points. It is created by the software in such a way that users think they have a dedicated point-to-point leased circuit.

virtual server: A load balancing server placed in front of a server farm that balances the number of requests sent to each server. All IP packets for the server farm are addressed to the virtual server, which then changes the destination IP address to the selected server before retransmitting the packet to the server. A virtual server gets its name because the client computer believes that it is a server, but it is not. Several routers and routing switches now include virtual server capabilities.

virtual private network (VPN): A hybrid network that includes both public and private facilities. The user leases a bundle of circuits and configures the VPN on an as-needed basis so that some traffic travels on the private leased network and some travels on the common carrier's public network.

virus: Viruses are executable programs that copy themselves onto other computers. Most viruses attach themselves to other programs or to special parts on disks, and as those files execute or are accessed, the virus spreads. Viruses cause unwanted events—some are harmless (such as nuisance messages) and others are serious (such as the destruction of data). Some viruses change their appearances as they spread, making detection more difficult.

voice-grade circuit: A term that applies to circuits suitable for transmission of speech, digital or analog data, or facsimile, generally with a frequency range of about 300 to 3,300 Hz contained within a 4,000-Hz circuit.

VPN: *See* **virtual private network (VPN).**

VRC: Vertical redundancy check. Same as **parity check.**

W

WAN: *See* **wide area network (WAN).**

WAP: *See* **Wireless Application Protocol (WAP).**

Web: *See* **World Wide Web.**

Web browser: A software package on the client computer that enables a user to access a Web server.

Web crawler: A Web crawler searches through all the Web servers it knows to find information about a particular topic.

Web server: A Web server stores information in a series of text files called pages. These text files or pages use a structured language called HTML (Hypertext Markup Language) to store their information.

wide area network (WAN): A network spanning a large geographical area. Its nodes can span city, state, or national boundaries. WANs typically use circuits provided by common carriers. *Contrast with* **backbone network, local area network (LAN),** and **metropolitan area network (MAN).**

Wireless Application Protocol (WAP): A de facto standard set of protocols for connecting wireless devices to the Web. WAP provides a variety of protocols at the application, transport, and network layers to enable devices with very small display screen to display standard Web information.

wire speed: The data rate of the incoming and outgoing circuits. A device that operates at wire speeds introduces no delay in processing frames.

wiring closet: A central point at which all the circuits in a system begin or end, to allow cross-connection.

World Wide Web: The Web provides a graphical user interface and enables the display of rich graphical images, pictures, full-motion video, and sound clips.

worm: A virus capable of spreading itself, usually by way of e-mail or Web requests (HTTP).

X

X.*nn*: The X.*nn* series of ITU-T standards relating to transmission over public data networks.

X.400: An OSI standard that defines how messages are to be encoded for the transmission of e-mail and graphics between dissimilar computers and terminals. X.400 defines what is in an electronic address and what the electronic envelope should look like. Approved by the CCITT.

X.500: An OSI standard that defines where to find the address to put on the electronic envelope of a X.400 transmission. X.500 is the directory of names and addresses similar to the yellow pages of a telephone directory.

Xmodem: Xmodem is an asynchronous file transmission protocol that takes the data being transmitted and divides it into blocks. Each block has a start of header (SOH) character, a 1-byte block number, 128 bytes of data, and a 1-byte checksum for error checking.

Y

Ymodem: Ymodem is an asynchronous file transmission protocol. The primary benefit of the Ymodem protocol is CRC-16 error checking.

Z

Zmodem: Zmodem is a newer asynchronous file transmission protocol written to overcome some of the problems in older protocols. It uses CRC-32 with continuous ARQ and dynamically adjusts its packet size according to communication circuit conditions to increase efficiency. It usually is the preferred protocol of most bulletin board systems.

INDEX

403